PREVENTING TORTURE

Preventing Torture

*A Study of the European Convention
for the Prevention of Torture and Inhuman
or Degrading Treatment or Punishment*

MALCOLM D. EVANS

and

ROD MORGAN

OXFORD
UNIVERSITY PRESS

Oxford University Press, Great Clarendon Street, Oxford OX2 6DP
Oxford New York
Athens Auckland Bangkok Bogota Bombay Buenos Aires
Calcutta Cape Town Dar es Salaam Delhi Florence Hong Kong Istanbul
Karachi Kuala Lumpur Madras Madrid Melbourne Mexico City
Nairobi Paris Singapore Taipei Tokyo Toronto Warsaw
and associated companies in
Berlin Ibadan

Oxford is a registered trade mark of Oxford University Press

Published in the United States
by Oxford University Press Inc., New York

British Library Cataloguing in Publication Data
Data available

Library of Congress Cataloging-in-Publication Data
Evans, Malcolm.
Preventing torture : a study of the European Convention for the
Prevention of Torture and Inhuman or Degrading Treatment or
Punishment / Malcolm D. Evans and Rod Morgan.
p. cm.
Includes bibliographical references and index.
1. European Convention for the Prevention of Torture and Inhuman
or Degrading Treatment or Punishment (1987) 2. European Committee
for the Prevention of Torture and Inhuman or Degrading Treatment or
Punishment. 3. Torture (International law) 4. Torture—Europe—
Prevention. I. Morgan, Rodney. II. Title.
KJC9400.5.T67E95 1998
341.4'81—dc21 98–24190
ISBN 0–19–826257–4

1 3 5 7 9 10 8 6 4 2

Typeset by Graphicraft Limited, Hong Kong
Printed in Great Britain
on acid-free paper by
Bookcraft Ltd., Midsomer Norton, Somerset

Preface

During the winter of 1989–90 one of us, Rod Morgan, was invited by the European Committee for the Prevention of Torture (the CPT) to lead a workshop in Strasbourg on the business of inspecting police stations. The workshop was one of a series of events organised by and for the newly formed Committee as part of their preparation for undertaking their first visits of inspection in 1990.[1] Precisely what triggered the invitation is unknown, but it must have arisen from our long-standing research interest in custodial conditions, processes, and organization,[2] an interest clearly made known to the CPT Secretariat. The outcome was that at the beginning of 1990 the Secretary to the CPT, Trevor Stevens, invited one of us to accompany the CPT on the Committee's first visit of inspection, to Austria in May 1990, as an *ad hoc* expert.[3] This was a fascinating experience which subsequently stimulated a good deal of conversation with the other of us, Malcolm Evans, who, as an international lawyer, was interested in the emergence of the European Convention for the Prevention of Torture and Inhuman or Degrading Treatment or Punishment (ECPT) as an innovation in international human-rights law. The conjunction led to the long-term collaboration of which this study is the latest and, to date, the most ambitious product.[4] Several aspects of this collaboration need to be highlighted.

[1] See Gen Rep 1, paras 10 and 37.

[2] See, for example: King, R and Morgan, R (1980) *The Future of the Prison System* (Farnborough: Gower); Maguire, M, Vagg, J and Morgan, R (1985) *Accountability and Prisons: Opening Up a Closed World* (London: Tavistock); Morgan, R and Smith, D (1989) *Coming To Terms With Policing* (Basingstoke: Macmillan).

[3] See Austria 1 (see p. xxi below, Note on the Citation of CPT Documents).

[4] We have jointly published a number of articles and chapters in books on the CPT, in particular: Evans, MD and Morgan, R (1992) 'The European Convention for the Prevention of Torture: Operational Practice', 41 ICLQ 590; Morgan, R and Evans, MD (1994) 'Inspecting Prisons: the View from Strasbourg', *BJC*, Spring, 145 (also published in King, R and Maguire, M (eds) *Prisons in Context* (Oxford: Clarendon Press)); Evans, MD and Morgan, R (1994) 'The European Torture Committee: Membership Issues', 5 EJIL 249; Morgan, R and Evans, MD (1996) 'A European Committee for the Prevention of Torture' in *The Challenges of a Greater Europe* (*Les Enjeux De La Grande Europe*), (Strasbourg: Council of Europe), 85; Morgan, R (1996) 'Tortures et Traitements Degradants ou Inhumains en Europe: Quelques Données, Quelques Questions' in Faugeron, C, Chauvenet, P and Combessie, P (eds) *Approches de la Prison* (Paris: DeBoeck Université, et Les Presses de L'Université de Montréal et d'Ottawa), 323; Evans, MD and Morgan, R (1997a) 'The European Convention for the Prevention of Torture: 1992–1997', 46 ICLQ 663; Evans, MD and Morgan, R (1997b) 'The Origins and Drafting of the ECPT: A Salutary Lesson?', in *20 Ans Consacrés à la Réalisation d'une Idée: Receueil d'articles en l'honneur de Jean-Jacques Gautier* (Geneva: Association for the Prevention of Torture), 85; Evans, MD (1997) 'The Impact of the CPT: Lessons From Southern Europe', 1(3) *MJHR* 227; Morgan, R (forthcoming) 'The CPT and the Academy' and Evans, MD (forthcoming) 'The CPT: Future Challenges' in Association for the Prevention of Torture/British Institute of Human Rights, *The European Convention for the Prevention of Torture: Issues and Mechanisms for Preventing Torture and Ill-Treatment*.

First, one of us is an *insider* and the other an *outsider* to the work of the CPT. That is, one of us has from its earliest days been repeatedly involved with the Committee as an *ad hoc* expert accompanying visiting delegations.[5] This has been a privilege and an opportunity, but an opportunity attended by a certain amount of practical sensitivity and requiring great circumspection. The work of the CPT is highly confidential, particularly until, and if, the state party being visited authorizes publication of the report arising out of the visit. Moreover, even if the state authorizes publication, there is much that takes place during the preparation for a visit, the visit itself, and discussion of the draft report in the aftermath of a visit, which is not committed to paper and which must remain confidential. Without a high level of trust between Committee members, their Secretariat, and the *ad hoc* experts who assist them, the CPT could not function effectively. If follows that *ad hoc* experts assisting the Committee (or indeed CPT members or Secretariat colleagues) who, because of their broader research or policy interests, speak publicly or write about the work of the CPT, are bound to be viewed with some suspicion by those within the CPT who must be assured that confidences have not been breached and will in future be preserved. There is also a question of courtesy and good faith. The legitimacy of the Committee in the eyes of state parties depends partly on its members being seen as expert, professional, and impartial assessors: were anything written which indicated that that was not entirely the case, it might undermine the standing of the Committee, quite apart from alienating members and making future working relationships untenable.

For these reasons we have always taken care to explain the nature of our research—the methods being pursued, the data being collected, the publication plans nurtured—to the CPT Bureau[6] and Secretariat. We did not seek permission to undertake the study, because no permission was required. Nor did we seek approval: to give it would have compromised the CPT. Nor did we seek privileged access to CPT material—that is, information judged confidential—because we knew that no privileged access could or would be granted. But we judged it important to make our plans transparent, in order that the *insider* among us continue to be eligible for further work with the Committee. That is, we undertook, without being asked, to act in a manner not unlike a juryman who, having heard inadmissible evidence in court, is told by the judge to disregard it when reaching a verdict. This self-imposed schizophrenic stance is not

---

[5] On visits to Austria (1990), Sweden (1991), Finland (1992), Turkey (1992), Norway (1993), Turkey (1994), Portugal (1995), Denmark (1996), Portugal (1996), Norway (1997), Estonia (1997), and Sweden (1998).

[6] The CPT Bureau comprises the elected President and First and Second Vice Presidents of the Committee.

easy. But we hope and believe that this study, like all our previous writings on the CPT, has preserved the confidentiality upon which the work of the Committee depends: that is, this book is based almost entirely on evidence which lies in the public domain and is therefore admissible.

We should nevertheless like to record our thanks to the CPT Bureau and Secretariat for their unstinting helpfulness. The Secretariat has answered many practical queries and thereby saved us much time trawling through voluminous documents. One important instance of assistance should be recorded. In September 1996 we met in Strasbourg with the Bureau and Trevor Stephens in order to put questions to them about aspects of the Committee's *modus operandi* about which, on the basis of the written record, we were uncertain. We wished to clarify our understanding. At various places in this text we note where this formal conversation informs the conclusions to which we have come. We wish also to thank Hanno Hartig, Head of the Human Rights Directorate within the Council of Europe, who allowed us to see the *traveaux préparatoires* of the ECPT. This was a privilege for which we are grateful. Although we had already seen many of the documents making up the *traveaux* (copies of which are held by individuals and organisations party to the discussions in Strasbourg) the chance to view these materials as an organic whole, rather than in isolation, greatly assisted our understanding of the process.

Secondly, there is the question of chronology: why and when did we judge it sensible to embark on aspects of our project, and how was it made possible? There is never a perfect time to write a book about a developing institution like the CPT. In the early years, 1990–2, the CPT was finding its feet, working out how to do things, deciding what standards to apply. There then followed a period, roughly 1992–4, of uncertain reaction. It was unclear how many state parties would authorize publication of the CPT's reports and, thus, whether external commentators would learn much about what the CPT had found or recommended. Then, during the period 1994 to the present, there arose questions as to: how the CPT would carry out second and subsequent visits?; how the new state parties in Eastern Europe would be covered?; whether the custodial conditions now being encountered in Eastern Europe would affect the methodology and standards of the Committee?; and how the domestic policies of long-standing state parties might be influenced by the work of the CPT? From 1990 onwards we absorbed every CPT document published by the Council of Europe—annual general reports, country visit reports as and when they were published, occasional documents on the interpretation of the Convention—and we collected whatever press or other comments on the work of the CPT emerged. Not until 1992, however, did we think there was sufficient material to start interpreting and commenting in print on the

Committee's *modus operandi*,[7] and in subsequent years, as more material entered the public domain on which we could draw, we broadened our appraisal in a series of articles. By 1993/4, however, we were persuaded that the time was ripe for a more thorough and searching inquiry than could be derived from documentary analysis alone. We wished to talk to people—civil servants, non-governmental organization (NGO) representatives, politicians, and the like—whose work might be influenced by the reports from the CPT. And, naturally, we wanted to talk to such people throughout Europe, a relatively expensive undertaking. In 1994, therefore, we sought financial assistance for our efforts and successfully secured a grant from the Airey Neave Trust. This proved a turning point and we are profoundly grateful to the Airey Neave Trustees for their support. During 1994–7 their grant made it possible for us to visit the majority of the original state parties and one or two new ones.[8]

Our application to the Airey Neave Trust represented an ambitious —almost certainly over-ambitious—proposal. The rationale for our country visits went beyond gathering opinions about the CPT. We hoped to assess the influence of the CPT on the domestic policy of member states. That is, we wished to appraise the effectiveness of the Committee not just according to *procedural* and *substantive* criteria—the operationalization of the Convention with reference to the aims and methods envisaged by the framers of the Convention, and the fact-finding and jurisprudential record of the Committee—but acccording to *impact* criteria. Was the Committee's work widely known and was it being cited in and influencing official government reports, parliamentary debates, domestic court judgments, NGO submissions to governments, and so on? Had the nature of what was regarded as torture or inhuman and degrading treatment or punishment been altered as a result? Had the shape and direction of domestic policy been affected? Was there any discernible decline in the incidence of ill-treatment as a result?[9] These were the difficult, but ultimately the most important, questions we wished to explore.

In the text that follows we fully discuss in detail what we have termed the *procedural* and *substantive* aspects of effectiveness and we have tentatively explored some aspects of the *impact* criteria. But policy impact assessments are notoriously difficult methodologically. Seldom can a policy

---

[7] Evans and Morgan (1992).

[8] We visited Austria, Belgium, Bulgaria, Cyprus, the Czech Republic, Denmark, France, Germany, Greece, Hungary, Ireland, Malta, the Netherlands, Poland, Slovakia, Spain, Sweden, Switzerland. We also talked to officials and NGO representatives in the UK. It should be recalled, moreover, that one of us (Rod Morgan) took part in CPT visits to a further five countries—Estonia, Finland, Norway, Portugal, and Turkey—not visited under our own steam.

[9] See Morgan, R (1995) 'The European Convention for the Prevention of Torture: Evaluating its Effectiveness', *4th British Society of Criminology Conference*, University of Loughborough, July.

initiative be attributed to a single precipitating cause: policy formation is more akin to a stream of consciousness in which many bodies, factors, and events play a mutually reinforcing part. Moreover, CPT reports are particularly unlikely candidates for stimulating revolutionary change. They arise very intermittently from the Council of Europe in Strasbourg, a distant institution about which there remains a good deal of ignorance and not a little suspicion or doubt. They emerge and typically are published long after visits of inspection have taken place. They are usually concerned with issues long debated domestically both within official circles and by NGOs. They cover matters great and small, relatively simple and structurally complex—everything from the size of a single punishment cell or waiting cubicle to the provision of legal services in police stations and the organization of prison health services. They deal with questions of great sensitivity—ill-treatment at the hands of state officials—about which there is naturally great defensiveness and a deep-seated unwillingness to concede culpability. Thus any assessment of *impact* effectiveness was bound to arrive at a judgment not unlike that of the curate regarding his egg: good (or effective) in parts. Moreover, as we better appreciate now, though we think eight years of operation is a suitable lapse of time on which to base a detailed study of the CPT, eight years is nevertheless too brief a span to gauge significant shifts in policy. In most jurisdictions, a major criminal justice scandal—a death in custody, a gross miscarriage of justice, a serious catalogue of child abuse in a residential home for juvenile offenders, or a large-scale prison riot—even when followed by an official judicial or committee of inquiry, often takes years to result in a significant reallocation of resources, procedural or organisational change, or the introduction of new legislation, if it leads to change at all. It is highly unlikely, therefore, that a report from a relatively obscure body based in Strasbourg will make much impact, certainly in the short term, on domestic policy-makers.

This text therefore represents research in progress on a body which is still developing and the extent of whose influence remains uncertain. In early 1998, as we hand over our manuscript, the CPT faces new challenges and is adjusting its working methods accordingly. We anticipate continuing to ask the questions which inform this text about the *modus operandi* and impact of the Committee in future essays.

Thirdly, no study of this nature can be conducted without the assistance and collaborative support of many organizations and individuals all over Europe too numerous to mention. Four organizations have been particularly important. The Geneva-based Swiss Committee Against Torture, now the Association for the Prevention of Torture (APT), has played, as we recount in Chapters 4 and 5, a particularly important role in the genesis and implementation of the ECPT, and we owe a particular debt of gratitude to François de Vargas, Carol Mottet and Claudine Heanni and all their APT colleagues for their assistance. We wish also to thank the many colleagues within the International Committee of the Red Cross (ICRC) in Geneva, and at Amnesty International's International Secretariat in London, for their constant willingness to compare notes and track down references which have been vital in charting the patchwork quilt of preventive effort within which any agency concerned with torture and other forms of ill-treatment must collegially operate. We are particularly indebted to Jacques Stroun and Pascal Daudin at the ICRC, and Eric Prokosch at Amnesty International. Finally, we are grateful to several officers of the United Nations who have kept us supplied with documents and assisted us during our visits to Geneva. By these means we hope we have gained a reasonable understanding of the work of the UN Special Rapporteur for the Prevention of Torture, Nigel Rodley, and the UN Committee Against Torture. It goes without saying that to the extent that we have misunderstood the work of any of these organisations, the fault is entirely ours.

The layout of what follows is simple. We have never been convinced by the argument that torture is morally, philosophically, and legally a straightforward matter, the absolute prevention of which is difficult because of essentially political and administrative considerations. This view implicitly underpins the suggestion that torture is almost universally proscribed and deprecated and is engaged in only by aberrant individuals or regimes, mostly in far-away places: that is, a phenomenon that need not much concern us in Europe. We think, on the contrary, that in the same way that all criminal justice systems provide for the detention of suspects and the punishment of offenders, and justify to a greater or lesser extent the coercion of the culpable or allegedly culpable in order to protect the interests of the allegedly innocent, so the justification for, and certainly the temptation to use, forms of coercion that might be judged to constitute torture lies at best only just below the surface of everyday police and custodial practice. Moreover, prisoners are among the most marginal of social groups, legally condemned, morally cast out, and politically of no account, held in places surrounded by secrecy justified in the name of security and accessed only with difficulty. They are in any society peculiarly vulnerable to relative neglect and abuse. For all these reasons we think it wise to assume that no state can afford to be complacent about the likelihood of torture or inhuman or degrading treatment occurring.

We have therefore judged it important to begin this study with a review of the historical use and eventual prohibition of judicial torture (Chapter 1) and to follow it (Chapter 2) with some consideration of three well-documented post-War case studies of the extensive use of torture by democratic regimes faced, as the governments argued, with grave threats to the integrity of the state. There then follows (Chapter 3) an account of the prohibition of torture in international law and an examination of the key terms—'torture' and 'inhuman' or 'degrading' treatment—employed by the various judicial and other international organs charged with deciding whether such ill-treatment has occurred or with preventing the phenomenon, with particular emphasis on the European Commission and Court of Human Rights. This provides the lead-in to the drafting and content of the ECPT (Chapter 4) and our examination of the constitution and working methods of the Committee, the CPT, brought into being by the ECPT (Chapter 5). The following three chapters (6, 7 and 8) comprise detailed examinations of the CPT's use of the key terms incorporated in the title of the Convention, and the Committee's preventive safeguards and standards regarding police and prison custody respectively. In each of these three chapters the usages and standards of the CPT have been compared to those of other relevant bodies. Readers should note that these chapters do not provide exhaustive coverage of the usages and standards of the CPT, however. We have not examined in any detail, for example, the CPT's pronouncements regarding medical and mental health matters or the arrangements appropriate for persons detained under immigration legislation, both of which questions have received a good deal of CPT attention. The core CPT pronouncements on these matters are reproduced in Appendix 7, but we decided that to go into the degree of detail we judged appropriate on *every* issue would make this too unwieldy a study. Finally, Chapter 9 provides an overview of the whole. It considers contemporary developments in Europe which have a bearing on the work of the Committee, summarizes how effectively we think the CPT is working, and ponders how the Committee might tackle the challenges facing it in the near future. Those readers who do not have the patience to read the whole work may find Chapter 9 a useful synthesis of the study and a summary of most of our conclusions.

In spite of the size of this study—much larger than we originally envisaged—there are several aspects of the CPT which receive little or no attention. For example, we do not explore the merits and demerits of a body like the CPT developing detailed standards. Further, we give only marginal attention (in Chapter 9) to the question of whether the CPT should adopt a more a relativistic approach to the application of its jurisprudence in countries with very different cultural traditions and economic resources. These are issues that will be considered, or considered more fully, in a collection of essays on the impact of the CPT relative to other international bodies and individual member states shortly to be published by Oxford University Press under the title *Protecting Prisoners.*[10]

---

[10] Provisional title.

The present text will, we hope, serve as the historical reference work which will provide a foundation for subsequent more applied studies. It endeavours to present a picture of the Committee and its work as at 31 December 1997, although some materials published shortly before completion could not be fully taken into account.

Finally, we should like to thank research colleagues who assisted us with parts of the fieldwork—Roland Bank (formerly of the *Max-Planck-Institut für ausländisches und internationales Strafrecht*, Freiburg, Germany and now a research fellow at the European University Institute, Florence) with respect to Germany, and Jenny Monahan (researcher and journalist) with respect to France. Last but not least, our thanks to administrative colleagues in the Department of Law at the University of Bristol—and in particular, Rachel Nee—who greatly assisted us in the preparation of successive drafts. Their unfailing good humour and careful attention to detail saved us from many an error and delay.

Malcolm D. Evans   Faculty of Law
Rod Morgan   University of Bristol
23 January 1998

ADDENDUM

A number of developments have occured since the text was finalized.

A. Ratifications

1. Latvia ratified the ECPT and its protocols on 10.02.98 and the Convention entered into force for Latvia on 01.06.98.
2. Russia ratified the ECPT and its Protocols on 05.05.98 and the Convention will enter into force for Russia on 01.09.98.
   (In consequence, Lithunania is now the only member state of the Council of Europe which is yet to ratify the ECPT).
3. Portugal ratified Protocol No. 1 on 20.03.98.

B. Reports

The publication of the following Reports has been authorized in the course of 1998:

1. Portugal: Report and Response arising from the CPT's *follow-up* visit in October 1996
2. Norway: Response arising from the CPT's *ad hoc* visit in March 1997

3. Switzerland: Follow-up Report arising from the CPT's *periodic* visit in February 1996
4. Romania: Report and Responses arising from the CPT's *periodic* visit in Sept./October 1995
5. Denmark: Follow-Up Report arising from the CPT *periodic* visit in Sept./October 1996
6. France: Report and Responses arising from the CPT's *periodic* visit in October 1996
7. Spain: Report and Response arising out of the CPT's *ad hoc* visit in April 1997.

The publication of the Romania Report means that Turkey remains the only state of which can be identified as a 'persistent non-publisher'— although Poland may soon enter that category if publication of the Report arising out the CPT's periodic visit in June/July 1996 is not authorized soon.

2 June 1998

Contents

Table of Cases

Table of Principal Treaties, Declarations, Codes of Conduct, and other International Instruments (Principal Instruments)

A Note on the Citation of CPT Documents

Reports of visits undertaken by the CPT, the responses of states, and other documentation relevant to the functioning of the Committee is published —when authorized—in a numbered series carrying the prefix 'CPT/Inf', followed by the year of publication and the document number. In this book a simplified system of citation has been adopted. The name of the country concerned will be given, followed by a number indicating whether the document in question relates to a first, second, third, etc visit to the country in question. Where reference is being made to a state response, this will be indicated following the visit number. Interim reports will be called 'R 1' and Follow-up reports 'R 2'. Where only one response was requested (or, in one case, known to have been given) this will appear simply as 'R'. Thus 'UK 1' refers to the CPT report on the first visit to the UK and 'UK 1 R 2' refers to the 2nd UK response to that report. Likewise, the Annual Reports of the CPT are referred to as 'Gen Rep 1', 'Gen Rep 2', etc. A table setting out the full CPT/Inf reference number of all reports cited is set out in Appendix 8.

All published CPT documents are available from the Council of Europe and many are now accessible on the Committee's web-site: www.cpt.coe.fr. The first volume of a 'Yearbook on the European Convention for the Prevention of Torture' published by the University of Nottingham Human Rights Law Centre will also carry these materials.

List of Tables

Abbreviations

ACAT	*Action des Chrétiens pour l'Abolition de la Torture*
AJIL	American Journal of International Law
APT	Association for the Prevention of Torture
BJC	*British Journal of Criminology*
CAT	Committee Against Torture
CDDH	Steering Committee for Human Rights (Council of Europe)
CETP	Collected Edition of the *Travaux Préparatoires* of the ECHR
CHR	United Nations Commission on Human Rights
CLAHR	Committee on Legal Affairs and Human Rights
CLJ	Cambridge Law Journal
CPT	Committee for the Prevention of Torture and Inhuman or Degrading Treatment or Punishment
Comm Dec	Decision of the European Commission of Human Rights
Comm Rep	Report of the European Commission of Human Rights
CSCE	Conference on Security and Co-operation in Europe
DH-EX	Committee of Experts of the CDDH
DR	*Decisions and Reports* (of the European Commission of Human Rights)
ECHR	European Convention on Human Rights and Fundamental Freedoms
ECHRYb	*Yearbook of the European Convention on Human Rights*
ECOSOC	UN Economic and Social Council
ECPT	European Convention for the Prevention of Torture and Inhuman or Degrading Treatment or Punishment
EHRR	*European Human Rights Reports*
EHRLR	European Human Rights Law Review
EJIL	European Journal of International Law
ELRev	European Law Review
EPR	European Prison Rules
ESA	*Elliniki Stratiotiki Astynomia*
ETA	*Euskadi ta Askatasuna*
FLN	*Fronte Libération Nationale* (Algeria)
FIACAT	*Fédération Internationale de l'Action des Chrétiens pour l'Abolition de la Torture*

GSS	Israeli General Security Service
Gen Com	General Comment of the UN Human Rights Committee
HRC	Human Rights Committee
HRLJ	Human Rights Law Journal
ICCPR	International Covenant on Civil and Political Rights
ICJ	International Committee of Jurists
ICLQ	International and Comparative Law Quarterly
ICRC	International Committee of the Red Cross
IHRR	*International Human Rights Reports*
ILC	International Law Commission
ILCYb	*Yearbook of the International Law Commission*
ILR	International Law Reports
ILM	International Legal Materials
IRA	Irish Republican Army
IsLR	Israeli Law Review
MJHR	*Mediterranean Journal of Human Rights*
MLR	Modern Law Review
Neth Quart HR	*Netherlands Quarterly on Human Rights*
NGO	Non-Governmental Organization
NIS	National Investigation Service (Bulgaria)
OAS	Organization of American States
PLO	Palestinian Liberation Organization
PRI	Prison Reform International
RJD	*Reports of Judgments and Decisions* (of the European Court and Commission of Human Rights)
SCAT	Swiss Committee Against Torture
SD	*Selected Decisions* (of the HRC)
SMR	UN Standard Minimum Rules for the Treatment of Prisoners
SRT	UN Special Rapporteur on Torture
TAT	*Torturaten Aurkako Taldea*
'TFYRO Macedonia'	'The Former Yugoslav Republic of Macedonia'
UDHR	Universal Declaration of Human Rights
UK	United Kingdom of Great Britain and Northern Ireland
UN	United Nations
UNCAT	United Nations Convention Against Torture
UNGA Res	United Nations General Assembly Resolution
UNTS	*United Nations Treaty Series*
WHO	World Health Organization
WMA	World Medical Associaition
YEL	*Yearbook of European Law*

1

The Decline and Re-emergence of Torture

1 TORTURE IN ANCIENT TIMES

Torture has recently been the subject of extensive historical scholarship and in the context of this study we need do no more than sketch the main contours of what that scholarship has revealed.[1]

Torture appears to have been used in all societies in the ancient world, with the possible exception of the Hebrew people. In the Judaic tradition the practice was regarded as contrary to the 'law of God', and this view was perpetuated by leaders of the early Christian church.[2] Elsewhere, however, prisoners of war were either slaughtered or taken into slavery, and slavery implied, almost by definition, being subject to torture. This was true of ancient Egypt, Greece, and Rome.

In ancient Greece, and during the Roman empire, torture—what the Greeks termed *basanos* and the Romans *quaestio*—was used to elicit the truth in cases of serious crimes. The terminology is itself of interest. *Basanos* was the touchstone used to test gold for purity. And gold, the metal least liable to corruption, became emblematic of integrity in human character. Thus *basanos* became a metaphor to connote a test for purity or baseness and eventually came to have a second concrete meaning, the physical test of truth through torture.[3] Examples of the methods of torture employed are to be found in Aristophanes' satire *Frogs*. Xanthus, servant of Bacchus, accompanies his master to the underworld. Xanthus goes in the guise of Heracles and Bacchus is disguised as his slave. On arriving in Hades the pair are challenged by Aecus and Xanthus offers his slave for torture:

Aecus: 'How am I to torture him?'
Xanthus: 'In every way, by tying him to a ladder, by suspending him, by scourging him with a whip, by cudgeling him, by racking him and further, by pouring vinegar into his nostrils, by heaping bricks on him and every other way . . .'

Basanos was grounded on the assumption that slaves will always tell the truth if tortured. However, it is clear that some commentators had

---

[1] For an excellent bibliographical introduction to the topic, see Peters, E (1996) *Torture* (Pennsylvania: University of Pennsylvania), 2nd edn, 188–288.
[2] Ruthven, M (1978) *Torture: The Grand Conspiracy* (London: Weidenfeld and Nicolson), 23 and 43.
[3] duBois, P (1991) *Torture and Truth* (London: Routledge), ch 2.

doubts as to whether truth resulted from the procedure. The Romans, for example, recognized that the evidence obtained through torture was *res fragilis et periculosa*, a difficult and dangerous business:

It was declared by the Imperial Constitutions that while confidence should not always be reposed in torture, it ought not to be rejected as absolutely unworthy of it, as the evidence is weak and dangerous, and inimical to the truth; for most persons, either through their power of endurance, or through the severity of the torment, so despise suffering that the truth can in no way be extorted from them. Others are so little able to suffer that they prefer to lie rather than to endure the question, and hence it happens that they make confessions of different kinds, and they implicate not only themselves, but others as well.[4]

Likewise Quintilian, echoing Aristotle's earlier scepticism about the conclusive value of evidence obtained by torture,[5] maintained that attitudes towards torture depended on the side favoured:

... one party will style it an infallible method of discovering the truth, while the other will allege that it often results in false confessions ... What more needs to be said on the subject? Ancient and Modern writers have said everything. If the question of the application of torture arises, everything will depend on who demands it, who offers it, who is subjected to it, against whom the evidence sought will tell, and what is the motive behind the demand ... Such questions are as varied as the number of individual cases.[6]

It was possibly for these reasons that torture enjoyed a low status. In both ancient Greece and during the Roman empire only citizens or freemen could provide evidence in criminal proceedings without having been subjected to torture, from which they were exempt: the word of non-citizens, slaves, and foreigners was acceptable only if coerced. Why were slaves to be tortured? It is suggested that:

a slave who knew anything material would frequently belong to one of the litigants, and so would be afraid to say anything contrary to his owner's interests, unless the pressure put on him to reveal the truth was even greater than the punishment for revealing it which he could expect from his master.[7]

The problem with this doctrine was, as Aristotle saw it, that there is legal slavery and natural slavery. Some men are slaves by nature in that they apprehend but do not possess reason. By contrast noble men could be captured in war and legally enslaved. It followed that the distinction between slave and free, citizen and non-citizen, Greek or Roman and foreigner, was an unstable one, relative not absolute. The consequence, for the sceptics, was that truth was not the certain product of torture:

---

[4] The *Digest* of Ulpian's *Treatises*: quoted in Peters (1996), 34.
[5] Aristotle, *Rhetoric*, I, xv, 26.
[6] Quintilian, *De Institutione Oratoria*, V, 4, quoted in Ruthven (1978), 31.
[7] MacDowell, DM (1978) *The Law in Classical Athens* (London: Thames and Hudson), 8.

... for those under compulsion are as likely to give false evidence as true, some being ready to endure everything rather than tell the truth, while others are equally ready to make false charges against others, in the hope of being sooner released from torture ... It may also be said that evidence given under torture is not true; for the thick-witted and thick-skinned persons, and those who are stout-hearted heroically hold out under sufferings, while the cowardly and cautious, before they see the sufferings before them, are bold enough; wherefore evidence from torture may be considered utterly untrustworthy.[8]

The ideal of a citizen's exemption from torture was eroded with time. By the late Roman empire anyone, free or unfree, could be tortured if suspected of a crime sufficiently serious, such as treason, and lower classes of freemen could be tortured alongside slaves if suspected of relatively mundane offences. The application of torture was even extended to witnesses in cases judged sufficiently serious.[9]

The early Germanic and Visigothic codes echoed these hierarchical Roman traditions. Torture, in so far as it was used at all, was reserved for slaves. Criminal proceedings were private and a freeman's oath was normally deemed sufficient to establish the truth. However, if a charge was serious, or if the accused was ill-reputed, the truth might be established by combat or by ordeal, the idea being that justice was immanent: divine intervention would determine survival or victory, and thus where truth lay. Trial by ordeal, condemned from the twelfth century onwards as irrational and barbarous, bore all the appearance of torture and from the ninth century onwards was frequently presided over by the clergy.

2 TORTURE IN THE ROMAN-CANONICAL TRADITION

During the twelfth century there occurred what most historians describe as a legal revolution which shaped criminal proceedings until the eighteenth century. The degree to which this revolution was the product of the rediscovery and subsequent influence of Roman law is disputed.[10] Developments in government, procedural changes in the secular law, and the campaign of the Christian Church against heresy under canonical law, were important. Moreover, the use of torture during the Middle Ages went well beyond anything that Roman law would have sanctioned.[11] The

[8] Aristotle, *Rhetoric*, 1376b–1377a, quoted in duBois (1991), 67.

[9] Peters, E (1995) 'Prison before the Prison' in Morris, N and Rothman, DJ (eds) *The Oxford History of the Prison: The Practice of Punishment in Western Society* (New York: Oxford University Press), 16.

[10] Ruthven (1978), 50–1, for example, takes issue with Mellor, A (1966) *La Torture* (Paris), 77.

[11] Mellor (1966), 66–7.

secular and canonical legal systems became fused and, as one commentator has concluded, the worst of both was retained.[12] In the canonical tradition a confession was required—indeed heresy was almost unprovable
without it—but torture was forbidden. In the secular tradition torture could
be used, but only if lack of proof required it. Now confessions were almost
demanded and torture, or the threat of torture, became the means of obtaining them. Torture became a key element in a statutory system of proofs
the objectivity of which, in contrast with the non-rational Germanic tradition of ordeals, is said to have given the system legitimacy.

Private law gave way to public law and inquisitorial procedure largely
replaced accusatorial procedure. The concept of immanent justice was sup-
planted by that of human judicial competence and authority, decisions
being placed in the hands of judges and juries. A hierarchy of evidence or
'proofs' was established. Pre-eminent among proofs was the confession,
the so-called 'queen of proofs'. There could be *indicia*, or circumstantial
evidence, of guilt, but *indicia* were not sufficient to secure conviction. In
the absence of eye-witness testimony from two witnesses, confessions
became vital. It was in this context that torture, in its classical form, was
resurrected, initially as a police procedure, later as a legal procedure, in
both secular and ecclesiastical law. Heresy was aligned with treason and
both offences required the same proofs.

From the thirteenth to the eighteenth centuries torture was part of
the ordinary criminal procedure of the Latin Church and of most states
in Europe, though there was a wide divergence between theory and practice. There developed an elaborate jurisprudence of judicial torture. The
extraordinarily elaborate codification of this jurisprudence was interpreted by eighteenth-century reformers as evidence of the inhumanity
of judges during the Middle Ages. But the reverse is arguably the case.[13]
Codification represented an attempt by lawyers and legislators—an
attempt which all the evidence suggests failed—to control the reckless use
of torture and torture methods. That the codification was not pursued
further—with even more detailed description of how suspects were to
be tortured thereby to regularize the procedure—was hindered only by
what it was considered decent to incorporate in a statute.[14] It is doubtful
that it was to the suspect's advantage that the codes of practice were not
followed.

Once a judge had established that a crime had taken place and an accused
had been identified, the judge could embark on a particular inquiry, and
by the fourteenth century a public prosecutor had emerged to manage the
case against the accused. Accused persons had to be told of the *indicia*

[12] Ruthven (1978), 50–1.   [13] ibid, 66.
[14] See Langbein, JH (1977) *Torture and the Law of Proof* (Chicago: Chicago University Press),
15.

against them and could cross-examine witnesses.[15] They could also appeal against the use of torture on the grounds that the *indicia* were insufficient. Judges were advised that leading or suggestive questions were to be avoided and that information or confessions elicited under torture were to be investigated and verified wherever feasible. Not everyone could be tortured—children under, and adults over, a certain age, pregnant women, and persons of high status were exempt (though as in Roman times, status exemptions were gradually eroded)—and there were protocols about the nature of torture itself.

It could not be savage or cause death or permanent injury; it should be of the ordinary kind, with new tortures frowned upon; a medical expert had to be present, and a notary had to make an official record of the procedure.[16]

Furthermore, confessions elicited under torture were not valid as evidence. The confession had to be repeated away from the place of torture, though if the accused subsequently recanted, his confession under torture was an *indicium*.

In 1584 Grillandus, a Florentine lawyer, provided a detailed account of the proper use of one method, the *strappado*, a traditional and widely approved torture in which the victim's wrists were tied behind his back and used as the point by which he was hoist from a pulley or beam. Five degrees of severity, proportionate to the *indicia* and gravamen of the alleged offence, were described. First, the victim was to be stripped and tied: this was said to be sufficient to elicit a confession in many cases. Second, the victim was hoist for a short time, so-called light torture for grave offences for which there were insufficient *indicia*. Third, the victim was hoist for a long time where the *indicia* were adequate. Fourth, the victim was hoist and jerked in cases of serious crimes such as sacrilege and murder. Fifth, the victim was hoist and jerked while weights were attached to the legs. This fifth degree, designated for the most serious crimes of heresy and treason, wrought terrible effects: bones could be shattered and limbs torn 'often wrenching them completely from the body'.[17]

In theory the Romano-canonical law of evidence eliminated judicial discretion in that it insisted on objective criteria of proof and thereby made the judgment of men palatable. But this was true only where there were witnesses to the offence or when offenders were repentant. In difficult cases, where these proofs were lacking, the system was unworkable. Torture filled the gap: 'the two-eyewitness rule left the Roman-canon system dependent upon the use of torture'.[18] And the use of torture involved considerable judicial discretion which all the contemporary evidence

---

[15] For a detailed summary of the written rules see Langbein (1977), ch 1, note 1, 12–17.
[16] Peters (1996), 57.   [17] Quoted in Ruthven (1978), 58–9.   [18] Langbein (1977), 8.

indicates was widely abused. It was repeatedly said that judges rarely stuck to the strict written guidance. When judges or prosecutors engaged in suggestive questioning it could seldom be detected or prevented. Verifiable evidence, particularly in cases such as heresy, was often lacking. A wide variety of torture methods was resorted to. And in any case, the written rules were full of contradictions, contradictions which were inherent in the practice. How, for example, could judges be compassionate, as they were advised to be, yet 'take no notice of the screams, cries, sighs, tremblings or pain of the accused'? How could they ensure that no permanent injury was caused when even approved methods of torture might involve limbs being torn apart?[19]

It was no doubt for these reasons that the reservations expressed in ancient Greece and Rome about the value and wisdom of using torture were repeated throughout the Middle Ages. The jurisprudence of torture survived in spite of the doubts, which were widely appreciated, because the law of statutory proofs depended on it.

The Romano-Canonical tradition was not pursued everywhere in Europe and there were wide variations in practice. It is no coincidence that in the English system—where juries were able to convict offenders on the basis of circumstantial evidence which, if the rules were followed, was insufficient to justify further investigation under torture on the Continent—that judicial torture had no place in criminal proceedings from the twelfth century onwards. It follows that in England there was no need to place the same premium on confessions. Torture *was* employed in England, particularly in the sixteenth and seventeenth centuries, but its function was to gain information and its use was strictly controlled by the Privy Council. By contrast torture had never ceased to be part of procedure in Spain, whereas in Scandinavia, like England, torture was not part of legal procedure though it was used from the sixteenth century onwards on executive authority.

Outside Europe the status and use of torture varied greatly. It was used and recognised by the Ottoman Imperial authorities despite the fact that Islamic Law did not recognize the validity of confessions obtained under duress. It was also used in Japan during the Tokugawa period and in Russia until the end of the eighteenth century. Furthermore, evidence from a number of colonial territories—India under the British, for example—suggests that the use of torture by the police represented a continuation of traditions and methods well entrenched in the service of local landlords and potentates from pre-colonial times.[20] As more than one historian of the subject has observed, the practice of coercing evidence from suspects did not need to be invented by Greek, Roman, or medieval lawyers: it is a

[19] See Ruthven (1978), 63–4; Langbein (1977), 9.   [20] See Ruthven (1978), ch 8.

method so obvious that it is difficult to imagine an age or place where it would not have been known or done.[21] If nothing else, confessions elicited through torture represent a seemingly direct indication of human intentions and actions and information derived from torture is always likely to be attractive to the lazy, simple, or ill-equipped investigator. As Sir James Fitzjames Stephens famously recorded, with the revelations of a Commission investigating the use of torture under the British in Madras fresh in his mind,[22] and the testimony of an Indian civil servant to recall: 'It is far pleasanter to sit comfortably in the shade rubbing red pepper into a poor devil's eyes than to go about in the sun hunting up evidence.'[23]

What is clear is that jurists throughout the period that torture was an integral part of most European criminal justice proceedings were well aware of its shortcomings. But it appears that the importance attached to gaining confessions led to their doubts being over-ridden, though the extent to which torture was actually employed is little known and many forms of torture were much milder than those indicated by the theatres of horror so lovingly reproduced in late twentieth-century museums.[24]

3 THE ENLIGHTENMENT AND THE EMERGENCE OF THE MODERN STATE

Not until the eighteenth century did torture become excoriated and its abolition regarded as a landmark of the Enlightenment, marking the passage from superstition to reason. All the leading thinkers of the age —Montesquieu, Voltaire, and Beccaria—railed against the use of torture and their objections were moral as well as practical and legal. Beccaria, for example, dubbed torture 'a cruelty accepted by most nations'[25] and combined his appeal to humanity with an appeal to reason. It was, he maintained, an absurd practice. Pain could not be the test of truth:

in such a way that physical suffering comes to be the crucible in which truth is assayed, as if such a test could be carried out in the sufferer's muscles and sinews. This is a sure route for the acquittal of robust ruffians and the conviction of weak innocents.[26]

---

[21] See, for example, Fiorelli quoted in Langbein (1977), 8.

[22] *Report of the Commission for investigating the alleged cases of torture in Madras with correspondence relating thereto* (1855) Fort St George. See Ruthven (1978), ch 8.

[23] Fitzjames Stephen, Sir James (1883) *A History of the Criminal Law in England* (London: MacMillan), Vol 1, 442, n 1.

[24] Spierenburg, P (1995) 'The body and the state' in Morris and Rothman.

[25] All quotations are from Davies' translation of Cesare Beccaria's essay *On Crimes and Punishments* (Livorno, 1764) as contained in Bellamy, R (ed) (1995) *Beccaria: On Crimes and Punishments and Other Writings* (Cambridge: Cambridge University Press), 39.

[26] ibid, 39.

Harsh torturous punishments were equally ridiculous, for:

The harsher the punishment and the worse the evil he faces, the more anxious
the criminal is to avoid it, and it makes him commit other crimes to escape the
punishment of the first. The times and places in which the punishments have been
the fiercest have been those of the bloodiest and most inhuman actions. Because
the same brutal spirit which guided the hand of the lawgiver, also moved the
parricide's and the assassin's. He decreed iron laws for the savage souls of
slaves, who duly obeyed them; and in secluded darkness he urged men to murder tyrants only to create new ones.[27]

Such views appeared politically to prevail and most accounts of the
nineteenth-century demise of torture have given them causal primacy.
Following his summary of the influence of the writings of Montesquieu,
Voltaire, and Beccaria, one nineteenth-century writer concluded his history of torture thus:

in the general enlightenment which caused and accompanied the Reformation,
there passed away gradually the passions which had created the rigid institutions
of the Middle Ages. Those institutions had fulfilled their mission, and the savage
tribes that had broken down the worn-out civilization of Rome were at last becoming fitted for a higher civilization than the world had yet seen . . . In the slow evolution of the centuries, it is only by comparing distant periods that we can mark our
progress; but progress nevertheless exists, and future generations, perhaps, may
be able to emancipate themselves wholly from the cruel and arbitrary domination
of superstition and force.[28]

However, in the same way that contemporary historians of penal
policy have called into question the notion that the general displacement
of capital and corporal punishments by the use of imprisonment in the
late eighteenth and early nineteenth centuries represented simply the
triumph of moral progress and civilized sensibility, so recent historians
of torture have dismissed as a fairy tale the humanitarian-progressivist
account of its legislated abolition.[29] Revisionist historians have attributed
the abolition of torture to changes in the law of evidence and the emergence of new criminal sanctions, new sanctions which other historians have
linked to economic change, the development of the state, and legitimating
theories of the state.[30] The revisionist interpretation is worth considering

---

[27] Beccaria, in Bellamy (1995), 63.
[28] Lea, HC (1866) *Superstition and Force* (Philadelphia: University of Pennsylvania Press),
524.
[29] Langbein (1977), ch 3.
[30] See Foucault, M (1977) *Discipline and Punish: The Birth of the Prison* (London: Allen Lane);
Ignatieff, M (1978) *A Just Measure of Pain: the Penitentiary in the Industrial Revolution
1750–1850* (London: MacMillan); Melossi, D and Pavarini, M (1981) *The Prison and the Factory*
(Basingstoke: Macmillan); Morris and Rothman (1995).

in a little detail, not least because it arguably points to important lessons for the prevention of torture at the end of the twentieth century.

The traditional account of the abolition of torture has been that the practice persisted unabated until the seventeenth century. Then the progressive-humanitarian cause was taken up by several able publicists, notably Voltaire and Beccaria. Their influence aroused the public conscience and led the leading Enlightenment monarchs to proscribe torture. This coincided with the demise of capital and corporal punishments and in turn led to changes in the Roman-canonical law of proof in the nineteenth century.

This account is said to be unsatisfactory on two principal grounds. First, nothing that Voltaire and Beccaria said had not been said many times before. Thus 'to say that abolition was an idea whose time had come is to beg the question, why had it come?'[31] Secondly, if the abolition of torture *preceded* reform of the Roman-canonical law of proof by at least a century, how did a system which was said logically to be *dependent* on torture survive?

The revisionist interpretation is that through a process of subtle, previously unrecognized or misinterpreted developments in the law of evidence, a process about which Voltaire and Beccaria ironically had no knowledge or understanding—ironic because had they known or understood they could have made out their abolitionist case *even* more effectively—the system gradually weaned itself from its dependence on torture *before* abolition was enacted.

The argument is as follows. The system of *indicia* or proofs was fundamental to a system that made little distinction between examination and punishment. The accused was not considered innocent while under investigation. Suspicion was itself graded according to the *indicia* and was considered a crime and punishable. 'The objection that the innocent might suffer torture therefore did not arise . . . since so long as the rules were observed no one could be tortured unless there was a degree of proof equivalent to the severity of the torture.'[32] If the accused failed to confess under torture, he was not considered to have suffered wrongfully: he had purged the *indicia* against him. Thus, by contrast with modern reasoning:

Guilt did not begin when all the evidence was gathered together, piece by piece, it was constituted by each of the elements that made it possible to recognise a guilty person. Thus a semi-proof did not leave the suspect innocent until such time as it was completed; it made him semi-guity; slight evidence of a serious crime marked someone as slightly criminal. In short, penal demonstration did not obey a dualistic system: true or false; but a principle of continuous gradation; a degree reached in the demonstration already formed a degree of guilt and consequently involved a degree of punishment.[33]

[31] Langbein (1977), 11. [32] Ruthven (1978), 56–7. [33] Foucault (1977), 42.

In the sixteenth and seventeenth centuries this doctrine was developed to bridge the disjunction arising out of the growth of judicial discretion regarding sentencing and the relative inflexibility of the law of proof. New penalties emerged and began to supplant capital and corporal penalties— the Continental equivalents of the English bridewell and workhouse, and galley slavery, the analogue of transportation in Britain. Discretionary sentencing—fitting the punishment to the crime—was well established by the end of the sixteenth century. Discretionary sentencing paved the way for the more discretionary use of circumstantial evidence which professional judges, now generally well established, were considered capable of evaluating.

The new non-mandatory *poena extraordinaria* were by the seventeenth century being used in two situations where full proof was lacking. First, in cases where the *indicia* were sufficient to torture but a confession was not forthcoming. Secondly, where there were persuasive *indicia* which the rules held were insufficient to justify examination under torture. In these circumstances 'in order to achieve a verbal or formal harmony between the *poena extraordinaria* and the Roman-canon law of proof, it was said that the accused was being punished on account of the suspicion amassed against him, rather than condemned for the crime itself'.[34] *Verdachtesstrafe*, technically punishment for what was suspected, was not, as was generally thought, *really* punishment for what was merely suspected. It was in reality a punishment imposed when the court was persuaded that the accused *was* guilty, but when that guilt could not be established under the formal rules of the Roman-canonical law of proof. *Verdactesstrafe* reflected a more flexible judicial evaluation of circumstantial evidence. 'It was an alterative and subsidiary system of proof subsisting alongside the Roman-canon law of proof.'[35]

The consequence of this subsidiary but widely acknowledged system was that the Roman-canonical standards of full proof were no longer critical in criminal proceedings. Thus the seeds were sown for the redundancy and abolition of torture. Torture had never been available for petty non-capital crimes. In the sixteenth and seventeenth centuries the courts extended by analogy the new sanctions of imprisonment and forced labour to the established procedure for petty crime. They no longer needed to torture persons suspected of even serious offences because they could impose relatively serious penalties on the basis of circumstantial evidence without it. The Continental judges had in effect provided themselves with the room for manoeuvre that English judges, able to frame the indictment and direct the jury, had always had. And so, by the middle of the sixteenth century, some French commentators were already describing

---

[34] Langbein (1977), 47.   [35] ibid, 48.

torture as *'un usage ancien'*, of little contemporary relevance and utility. Prosecutors no longer needed to torture to get their man.[36]

This, according to the revisionist version of abolition, explains why the use of torture declined significantly well before its abolition and why, when it was abolished in countries like Prussia and Austria, the new codes fully recognized the doctrine that severity of punishment should be in proportion to the degree of proof of guilt as well as the heinousness of the crime:

If no proof of the crime can be established against the accused other than the correlation of circumstances against him, the punishment must always be reduced in length one degree what the statute prescribes for the crime when it is proven by another means.[37]

To conclude, revisionist historians do not argue that eloquent publicists like Voltaire and Beccaria were unimportant. The abolition of torture was both a legal and a political process: it is one thing for the use of a legal practice to decline and quite another for it to be prohibited. But they maintain that the well-known assaults by the eighteenth century publicists represented a philosophical nail in a coffin that was legally all but shut already. Judicial torture did not survive into the eighteenth century because its shortcomings were unrecognized. Rather it survived in spite of those defects, because the system was held to depend on it. It became possible fully to acknowledge those defects and move towards abolition, when the legal system, through a creative development in the law of evidence, found other means of managing its business—convicting and punishing those offenders on which its efforts were concentrated. And even then, it should be noted, several European jurisdictions made abolition a secret communication to the courts. Other jurisdictions abolished the practice provisionally or in a qualified manner.[38] There was initially no great confidence that the system could do without both the pressure and deterrent of torture.

The emergent view of contemporary historians is then that the decline and abolition of torture was intimately bound up with the growth of the state, the establishment of a more professional judiciary, the emergence of incarceration and forced labour as punishments, and subtle changes in the law of evidence. This view does not rule out the part played by humanitarian motives. Most of the recent research has focused on statutes and treatises setting out the rules governing the use of torture. Remarkably little is known about the degree to which torture was actually used and what inspired judges to exercise their discretion in the way that they did.

---

[36] Quoted in ibid, 55.
[37] The Austrian Code under Joseph II, 1789, quoted in Langbein (1977), 63.
[38] ibid, 67.

Humanitarianism may well have been an important factor in this process. There is no doubt that the reformist Enlightenment publicists, and the legislators they influenced, were inspired by humanitarian motives. Also beyond doubt is the fact that the legal abolition of torture was celebrated as a landmark achievement of progressive civilizing reform. It was celebrated alongside the decline and abolition, at least in public, of corporal and capital punishments. The new prisons, ostensibly reforming as well as punishing their charges, were said to be for the protection of citizens, proclaiming and safeguarding their pre-existing rights. It became particularly appropriate that those citizens who, through increasingly complex due process of criminal law, were proved to have abused their liberty, should be punished by losing it. It was no longer deemed sensible to visit punishment on the body, any more than it was deemed sensible to establish truth by testing the body. Whereas the body of the accused had previously been viewed almost as an imprint of the offence, and was thus the appropriate object for vengeance, evidence and punishment were now matters of the mind, calculated, refined, and, allegedly, rational.

The movement for the abolition of torture and for the establishment of penal reform swept Europe and by 1850 every jurisdiction had introduced legislation to outlaw torture and governments had produced funds for the erection of the new model prisons. If it was not a triumph of morality, it was widely regarded as such.

Today, with the hindsight of the late twentieth century, these nineteenth-century moral claims and assertions of humanitarian progress are viewed with a good deal of scepticism. The reformed processes of criminal justice scarcely reduced the likelihood that the most disadvantaged sections of society would be caught up in a system of punishments that continued to be harsh. The new model prisons proved to be as productive of human misery as many of the corporal punishments and less orderly gaols that they replaced. And there was a good deal of hypocrisy about the condemnations heaped on the Austrians and Italians for the repressive methods—which included torture—employed following the failure of the 1848 revolutions, or the Ottoman Turks during their conflicts in Greece, Bulgaria, and Bosnia.[39] The British, for example, displayed a high moral tone about the use of force and torture in Europe, but were willing, as were other European colonial powers, to rely on those same methods in their new-found possessions in Africa, Australasia, and Asia.[40] Outside Europe the white man's burden was almost everywhere eased with a rather free resort to force and brutality of every kind.

[39] See Ruthven (1978), ch 7; and Wheatcroft, A (1995) *The Ottomans: Dissolving Images* (Harmondsworth: Penguin).
[40] See, for example, Ruthven (1978), ch 8; and Pakenham, T (1991) *The Scramble for Africa* (London: Weidenfeld and Nicolson).

Nevertheless the fact that, after the end of the eighteenth century, torture invited such condemnation and acquired such universal pejorative associations, represented a change which cannot be overestimated. Torture came, at least in Europe, 'to be considered the institutional antithesis of human rights, the supreme enemy of humanitarian jurisprudence and of liberalism, and the greatest threat to law and reason that the nineteenth century could imagine'.[41] Even in a country like France, which underwent a series of cataclysmic political changes, and which was foremost in the establishment of modernizing techniques of police surveillance in defence of the state, the evidence suggests that torture was remarkably little used.[42] By the closing decades of the nineteenth century it was widely thought that torture was a barbaric practice that belonged to history. It was not to be.

4 TORTURE IN THE TWENTIETH CENTURY: RE-EMERGENCE AND EXPLANATION

It is clear to us now that torture was never truly eliminated in the nineteenth century. In Russia, for example, abolition of the practice had repeatedly to be emphasized by decree and the evidence suggests that torture continued to be used, not least by the Okhrana, the Czars' secret police. Opponents of the Czarist regime suffered torture right up to the 1917 Revolution.[43] The Russian experience was not unique. In Italy and Austria revolutionary opponents of the authorities suffered the same fate after 1848.[44] Moreover, as we have noted above, accusations of torture were periodically levelled at colonial administrations, and whatever their truth or extent these tendencies were certainly exacerbated during the final stages of colonial rule in numerous countries. In Palestine, for example, during the Arab revolt of 1936–9, the 'emergence of black and tan tendencies' among the British section of the Palestinian police was noted (the original 1922 British *gendarmerie* in Palestine was largely recruited from the disbanded ranks of the Royal Irish Constabulary and their auxiliary division, the notorious 'Black and Tans').[45] In 1938:

Suspects arrested for interrogation and held in police stations were now tortured as a matter of course; bastinado, suspending suspects upside down and urinating in their nostrils, extracting fingernails and pumping water into a suspect before stamping on him, became commonplace.[46]

[41] Peters (1996), 75.   [42] Ruthven (1978), 176–7.   [43] ibid, 266–7.   [44] ibid.
[45] Smith, C (1992) 'Communal conflict and insurrection in Palestine 1936–48' in Anderson, DM and Killingray, D (eds) *Policing and Decolonisation: Politics, Nationalism and the Police 1917–65* (Manchester: Manchester University Press), 71.
[46] ibid.

All the evidence suggests that when civil order broke down in Palestine
the British Palestinian police plied a trade that had been learnt by
their senior officers in Ireland prior to the signing of the 1921 Anglo-Irish
Treaty.[47] In other colonies where the independence movement mounted
a campaign of terrorism, as in Cyprus from 1954 to 1960, similar allegations of torture arose, though the extent to which allegations were
simply the propagandist product of the independence movement is
inevitably disputed.[48]

Nor are there grounds for confidence that torture had been eliminated
in at least some countries that were democratic, politically stable, eco-
nomically advanced, and adamant about the legal rights of the accused.
An interesting case in point are the findings of a 1931 national commission of inquiry into law enforcement—the Wickersham Commission, so
named after its chairman—appointed by the President of the United
States,[49] the findings of which were made more accessible by a number
of journalistic exposés.[50]

Among the studies undertaken for and published by the Commission was one on lawlessness in law enforcement, in particular the 'third
degree'.[51] The authors were senior establishment lawyers whose pains-
taking methodology included an analysis of cases between 1920 and 1930
in which appellate courts were satisfied that 'third degree' methods had
been used by the police. Searching inquiries were also made into police
practices in fifteen major cities ranging from New York, Chicago, and San
Francisco to Dallas and El Paso. The authors defined the 'third degree'—
a term the etymology of which is confused, but which bears an uncomfortable resemblance to the degrees of severity of torture which could
be applied in the middle ages—as a 'secret and illegal practice' whereby
the police use 'methods which inflict suffering, physical or mental, upon
a person in order to obtain information about a crime'.[52] The inquiry
unequivocally concluded that use of the 'third degree ... is widespread
throughout the country', that 'physical brutality [by the police] is extens-

[47] Smith (1992), 78–9.

[48] See, for example, Anderson, DM (1992) 'Policing and Communal Conflict: the Cyprus
Emergency, 1954–60' in Anderson and Killingray.

[49] Wickersham Report (1931) *Report of the National Commission on Law Observance and
Enforcement* Vols I-VI. Washington.

[50] See, for example, Hopkins, EJ (1931) *Our Lawless Police: A Study of the Unlawful
Enforcement of the Law* (New York): Lavine, EH (1933) *The Third Degree: American Police Methods*
(New York). See also Leo, RA (1992) 'From coercion to deception: the changing nature of
police interrogation in America', in *Crime, Law and Social Change*, 18, 35.

[51] Chaffee, Z, Pollak, WH and Stern, CS (1931) *The Third Degree: Report on Lawlessness
in Law Enforcement* (National Commission on Law Observance and Enforcement, Vol IV,
No 11, Washington).

[52] ibid, 19.

ively practised . . .' and that 'the methods are various . . . [and] range from beating to harsher forms of torture'.[53]

The report documented a large number of cases, only a small number of which had successfully been brought to the attention of the courts, where suspects had been whipped, beaten with rubber hoses—a widely-favoured method of physical assault it appeared—and repeatedly hit in the stomach by officers wearing boxing gloves, or struck on the head with heavy telephone directories. Most common, however, were psychological methods of pressure and intimidation—keeping prisoners incommun-icado—in flagrant violation of *habeus corpus* provisions—sometimes for periods of days or weeks, in some states and cities in specially designated 'cold storage' or 'incommunicado cells', depriving prisoners of food or sleep, making them stand in stress positions for long periods, and inten-sive, prolonged, and aggressive interviewing, sometimes under bright lights and invariably accompanied by threats of violence.[54] Neither the courts, where cases were exposed, nor the authors of the report, had any hesita-tion in describing a good deal of what they found as torture, the purpose of which was to extort a confession or extract information. The extent and nature of 'third degree' methods varied greatly from city to city, depend-ing, it appeared, on the attitudes of senior police officers and public prosecutors, the vigilance of the local judiciary and the organized inter-vention of the local bar. But in some cities the practice was commonplace. In Cleveland, for example, it was found to be 'prevalent', with a former prosecutor reporting: 'You can't overstate it'.[55] In Chicago the 'third degree' was found to be 'thoroughly at home',[56] in Dallas it was the 'pre-vailing' practice,[57] and in Seattle 'severe beating' was said to be 'the usual practice'.[58] Particularly telling in the Wickersham Report are the number of colloquial terms employed by the police to describe locally-favoured routines. In Detroit prisoners were taken for a trip 'around the loop', mean-ing that they were transferred, generally in a patrol wagon at midnight, from outlying station to outlying station, thereby enabling the police to hold them in custody for long periods without their attorneys knowing where they were.[59] In Mississippi the 'water cure', pouring water into the nose of a suspect while officers stood on his neck and chest, was dis-covered,[60] while in Dallas there was reference to the 'electric monkey', a device said formerly to have been in use, principally 'against Negroes'.[61] More commonplace were district attorney's references to police officer inter-rogators 'doing their work' with a suspect in the station gymnasium, while the district attorney waited in another room to take a statement when it was forthcoming.[62]

---

[53] ibid, 153. [54] ibid, 52–152. [55] ibid, 118. [56] ibid, 125. [57] ibid, 138.
[58] ibid, 149. [59] ibid, 121. [60] ibid, 67–8. [61] ibid, 139. [62] ibid, 59.

If torture was found by an official inquiry to be so prevalent in the United States in the 1930s, it seems very likely that it was employed, particularly against black Americans, even more in earlier decades when a brutalizing environment of lawlessness characterized by extremes of summary street justice were more widespread. This was especially true in the southern states. Particularly striking in the Wickersham Report are the cases of black prisoners being shown a mob standing outside the police station and told that if they failed to confess and were released then the police would not be answerable for their safety.[63] It is estimated that some 2,000 black Americans were lynched in the United States during the two decades 1890–1909, a good many while local law-enforcement eyes were averted.[64] The number of recorded cases of lynching gradually declined during the early decades of the twentieth century, but 146 were recorded for a period as late as 1930–47.

It was the use of torture on a grand scale by the emergent totalitarian regimes, however, that marked what is generally taken to be the principal change in the twentieth century. In Nazi Germany and Fascist Italy the state was said to be the embodiment of the people, and the individual—particularly those individuals accused of challenging the state—became of little worth. Individuals were malleable and, ultimately, expendable. Torture was extensively resorted to and, as these regimes faced the real prospect of defeat during the Second World War years, interrogation methods euphemistically termed 'the third degree', and which included flogging to get information, were officially sanctioned. The Nuremberg trials revealed that in 1942 Hitler ordered that:

The troops have the rights and duty to use in this struggle any and unlimited means, even against women and children, if only conducive to success. Scruples of any sort whatsoever are a crime against the German people and against the front-line soldier who bears the consequences of attacks by guerrillas and their associates.[65]

This was only the official culmination of a brutal process that had been unofficially approved over the previous decade. And the Gestapo, it is generally agreed, modelled their methods on those of the Bolsheviks in the early days of the Russian, or more accurately the Bolshevik, Revolution.

War weariness and an almost complete absence of effective government precipitated the abdication of the Czar and the establishment of a provisional government in Russia in February 1917. But the provisional

---

[63] For example, Chaffee, Pollak and Stern (1931), 63, 70, and 78.
[64] Ploski, H and Williams, J (1983) *The Negro Almanac: A Reference Work on the Afro-American* (New York) 4th edn.
[65] Quoted in Ruthven (1978), 289.

government lacked legitimacy and its decrees were not obeyed. Russian soldiers began returning to their villages from the First World War front in droves. The Bolsheviks found that they were the strongest among the multiple political parties vying for power and, when the moment came in October 1917, they picked up the baton of power rather than seized it. There was a power vacuum. The Russian economy lay in ruins and the situation in the country was anarchic. It therefore required no ideological flights of Communist rhetoric to breed paranoid fears of counter-revolution: there was a substantial threat to the revolution from all sides. Until 1920 the country was plunged into a ferocious civil war in which the counter-revolutionary White Russian forces were assisted militarily by foreign powers, notably Britain, France, the United States, Japan, Poland, Serbia, Greece, and Romania. The leading Bolsheviks acknowledged that, according to Communist theory, Russia was not ripe for a proletarian revolution—the economy was insufficiently developed—and that, even if the White Russian armies were beaten off, there would be massive resistance to a communist system from within the country—notably from the peasants. These were years of crisis and during them the seeds were sown within which the use of torture flourished.

The Bolsheviks took up Marx's concept of 'the dictatorship of the proletariat'. Lenin defined it as a period of 'rule won and maintained by the use of violence by the proletariat against the bourgeoisie, rule that is unrestricted by any laws'.[66] Central to the defence of the revolution from the beginning was the formation of an All-Russian Extraordinary Commission, what became known as the Cheka, a secret police whose task it was to identify, investigate, and extinguish counter-revolution wherever it found it:

The need for this organ [the secret police] was felt more acutely because the Soviet government had no apparatus for the spiritual education of the people ... The masses of the people were still imbued with the old spirit ... and not infrequently joined with their class enemies against the Soviets. Hence the acute necessity for an apparatus of coercion and purification.[67]

During the Civil War the opposition of those Party members who insisted that offenders be dealt with through semi-judicial processes by means of the revolutionary and people's courts were overruled. The Cheka was given a substantial degree of autonomy, and Cheka personnel were not answerable to the courts or Commissars of Justice. Cheka members could on their own initiative arrest a suspected enemy of Soviet power at any

[66] Lenin, VI (1960–70) *Collected Works*, Vol 28, 236, quoted in Gerson, LD (1976) *The Secret Police in Lenin's Russia* (Philadelphia: Temple University Press), 5.
[67] Martyn Latsis, Chair of the All-Ukrainian Cheka, quoted in ibid, 7.

place or time. It was the investigator's task to determine the guilt or innocence of arrested suspects and if jurisdiction was not transferred to the
courts—and in the majority of cases during the Civil War period jurisdiction was not transferred—the Cheka was given administrative power
to exile, commit to forced labour or execute detainees. It became normal
procedure for investigators to resort to beatings and torture to further
their investigations and it was officially acknowledged that thousands of
executions were carried out by the Cheka during and immediately following the Civil War.[68] Following the unsuccessful assassination attempt on
Lenin's life in August 1918 the Cheka was charged with prosecuting the
'Red terror'. Not surprisingly critics within the Party could see little difference between the methods and unaccountable powers being exercised
by the Cheka, and the Czar's Okhrana. The leadership disagreed:

Many did not understand that the October days did not solve the question of the
class struggle, that this struggle had only begun, that the enemy was not asleep,
but only in hiding, gaining strength; that therefore there was no time for senti-
mental dreaming—the enemy had to be finished off.[69]

Yet whatever the depth of the political crisis and the justification for their
methods, it is clear that the Cheka was as much feared and hated as its
secret police predecessor.

The successful conclusion, from the revolutionary standpoint, of the
Civil War led the Cheka to redirect their counter-revolutionary efforts.
They focused now on peasant resistance, the bandit gangs that controlled
much of the countryside and those socialists within the Communist Party
opposed to Bolshevik policies. Their extraordinary powers and use of torture continued. Though the Cheka was formally abolished in February
1922, a new secret police force, the GPU (later the OGPU, later part of
the NKVD, later the NKGB, later the MVD, later the MGB), was created.
But most of the personnel remained, and though the GPU was initially denied the ability to determine guilt and inflict punishment (issues
now to be determined by the courts), some of their former powers were
restored in October 1922. The GPU was administratively enabled to exile
persons guilty of counter-revolutionary activity for up to three years and
could punish bandits or robbers caught red-handed. Its punitive powers
included the power to execute.[70] Given the broad definition of counter-
revolutionary crimes:

An act designed to overthrow, undermine or weaken the authority of the
workers' and peasants' soviets and the workers' and peasants' government of

[68] Martyn Latsis, Chair of the All-Ukrainian Cheka, quoted in Gerson (1976), 53.
[69] Yakov Peters, senior Cheka official, 1924, quoted in ibid, 58.
[70] ibid, 226.

the [USSR, etc] . . . and of the basic economic, political and national achievements of the proletarian revolution (Criminal Code, Article 58),

the substantial autonomy of the NKVD, and its extraordinary powers, it is scarcely surprising that there was continuing use made of torture.[71] One does not have to take a view about the different estimates which have been advanced about the numbers of Soviet citizens put to death during the Civil War, the period of agricultural collectivization, or the great purges of the Communist Party during the 1930s. Nor need one take sides in the controversy over the causes of, and responsibility for, those pogroms.[72] What every serious commentator is agreed on is that the Communist Party and its agents made widespread use of repressive violence and that torture was an integral part of the terror which prevailed throughout the Stalinist period. In 1956 Khrushchev, reflecting on the great so-called 'show trials' of the 1930s, remarked:

How is it possible that a person confesses to crimes which he has not committed? Only in one way—because of application of physical methods of pressuring him, tortures, bringing him to a state of unconsciousness, depriving him of his judgement, taking away his human dignity. In this manner were 'confessions' acquired.[73]

And confessions and denunciations were required because, as in the case of heresy in the Middle Ages, there was generally little other evidence to support counter-revolutionary charges.

The Soviet secret police made use of a number of traditional torture techniques—beating with fists and implements, *strappado* (apparently known as the 'swallow' in Russia and misleadingly described by Conquest as an 'improvised' method),[74] the removal of nails with pincers, being hit in the pit of the stomach with a sandbag, and so on. More typical, however, were what we shall refer to as modern techniques, techniques designed to wear down the resistance of victims, but leave no obvious physical marks other than the looks of vacant exhaustion which it is said many of those who repeated their confessions wore when it came to their trial. Prisoners were made to stand for long periods in stress positions (the *stoika*), were deprived of natural light, food, and sleep, and were questioned almost continuously by relays of investigators while facing bright lights—the so-called 'conveyor' method.[75] Victims were also told that if they failed to confess, their loved ones would be arrested.

---

[71] Conquest, R (1990) *The Great Terror: A Reassessment* (London: Hutchinson).

[72] For example, Ruthven (1978), ch 9, takes the view that a mixture of peasant lack of education and superstition combined with genuine revolutionary fervour was a more significant factor than the dictatorial machinations of Stalin and his acolytes, as argued by Conquest (1990), ch 15.

[73] Quoted in Conquest (1990), 121.   [74] ibid, 121.   [75] ibid, 121–7.

There is no evidence that, following the period of the Civil War—when, as we have seen, the Cheka were given licence to do more or less whatever they considered necessary—torture as such was authorized. But this changed during the party purges and show trials in the late 1930s. Secret permission to use 'any method' was issued in July 1936 and this permission was eventually acknowledged more widely. In 1939 a telegram was sent to Party Secretaries explaining that the:

application of methods of physical pressure in NKVD practice is permissible from 1937 on, in accordance with permission of the Party Central Committee . . . It is known that all bourgeois intelligence services use methods of physical influence against the representatives of the socialist proletariat and that they use them in their most scandalous forms. The question arises as to why the socialist intelligence service should be more humanitarian against the mad agents of the bourgeoisie . . . The Party Central Committee considers that physical pressure should be used obligatorily, as an exception and applicable to known and obstinate enemies of the people, as a method both justifiable and appropriate.[76]

In the decades since the end of the Second World War the torture and other gross brutalities perpetrated in the name of Nazism, Fascism, and Bolshevik Communism during the 1920s, 1930s, and 1940s have been matched by numerous totalitarian or authoritarian regimes throughout the globe. The examples are legion. In China and elsewhere in Asia violence has been used against the citizenry in the name of Communism. In South America it has been done in the name of anti-Communism. In South Africa it was done in the name of Apartheid. In the Middle East it has been done in the name of Islam, and elsewhere in the name of secularism or moderation against alleged Islamic extremism or so-called fundamentalism. In many parts of the world it has been done in the name of national unity or identity. The degree to which terrorism has been the cause or the result of these excesses is a matter for debate.

Yet, after 1945, it was the overwhelming evidence of what had been done in the name of the Revolution in Russia, and Nazism and Fascism in Germany and Italy, that prompted the demand that the legacy of the Enlightenment in Western Europe be sealed by international agreement: that human rights be proclaimed and, *inter alia*, torture denounced by the international community. We shall recall and review those international initiatives in Chapter 3, but before we reach that stage a question needs to be addressed. It is generally agreed that even though torture had been far from eliminated by the end of the nineteenth century, the first half of the twentieth century nevertheless saw a massive resurgence of the practice. How is that resurgence to be explained?

[76] Quoted in ibid, 122.

5 EXPLAINING CONTEMPORARY TORTURE

Edward Peters, in his authoritative and widely acclaimed review of the history and historiography of torture, has identified various theories, implicit and explicit, to account for its twentieth-century resurgence.[77]

In what Peters refers to as the humanitarian-progressivist model the abolition of torture in the eighteenth and nineteenth century represented the ascendancy of civilization over barbarianism, rationality over superstition. It also 'joined moral outrage to judicial reforms'.[78] In this account, as we have seen, the passionate prose of writers like Voltaire and Beccaria played a major role. According to the logic of this approach it follows that the return of torture in the twentieth century must somehow have been underpinned by a return to values—or possibly a continuity of values if we accept that torture was never fully eliminated—hitherto considered outmoded. The world, or parts of the world, must have become less humanitarian, or certain groups of perpetrators and supporters less progressive, less rational, and more superstitious. Or, as Ruthven in his discussion of torture in Russia after the Revolution stresses, those groups politically empowered were predominantly ill-educated peasants who were vulnerable to accusations of evil intent. Such accusations, which certainly Stalin and other leaders did everything to encourage, were less deliberately invented or consciously manufactured. They represented a *continuity* of superstitious beliefs which would earlier have been expressed in terms of religion-based evil:

It is more than probable that the essential elements of popular belief in maleficium or harmful magic conducted through the agency of evil spirits or demons were present in early 20th century Russia, just as they were in mediaeval Europe.[79]

Thus, according to Ruthven, the purges of the 1920s and 1930s were generated as much from the bottom as from the top of the Communist Party by a powerful combination of belief, commitment, and fear.

The problem with this explanatory approach is that the values central to the progressivist-humanitarian model—summarized in words like progressive, rational, superstition—have not been precisely defined independently of torture. Thus such explanations have a tautological tendency. As Peters puts it:

Reason and humanitarianism are . . . difficult to quantify, and a model of history which sees them increasing and decreasing in intensity is a difficult model to grasp and use and, even more difficult, one it is impossible to agree upon.[80]

---

[77] Peters (1996), chs 3 and 4.   [78] ibid, 75.
[79] Ruthven (1978), 260.   [80] Peters (1996), 77.

A variation on the humanitarian-progressivist approach is the view that the new totalitarian ideologies represented secular religions requiring of their adherents a devotion to the 'cause' and a subjection of the individual to the collectivity which could be equated with primitive religious beliefs. Within this framework anti-revolutionary sentiments, or insults to the *Führer* or the *volk*, became secular heresies and were visited with the same brutal responses. According to this view the twentieth-century totalitarian ideologies promoted faith in an abstract good which effectively represented a return to superstition.

But one does not have to adopt this critical stance regarding twentieth-century absolutist ideologies to recognize that in the hands of grand theory ideologues the idea of the watchdog state with all its nineteenth-century liberal safeguards—constitutional government, periodic elections, the separation of powers, and so on—was dramatically superseded by the new totalitarian regimes. The ideal or goal of a state with certain prescribed characteristics held little sway with the political elites of Marxism or National Socialism. It was a means to power which once attained enabled the political elites to employ all the branches of a greatly expanded state, all the powers of the new mass media, and all the new technologies of information, communication, and surveillance, to consolidate power and quell opposition. The minimal state gave way to the all-encompassing state whose tentacles reached into the interstices of all political, economic, and social life, gathering intelligence and deploying it for the consolidation of power. Torture became one of the means of gathering intelligence. It also sent a terrifying message to the populace at large. It became the ultimate expression of the police state. Against this onslaught the safeguards of the minimal liberal state erected by the nineteenth-century reformers proved fragile and were relatively easily swept aside.

We may term this the state-terrorism model.[81] In it the state represents a perversion of the Enlightenment ideal. Beccaria, like his mentor Verri and his successor John Stuart Mill, employed a modified empiricist epistemology in which the operations of the senses were married to a capacity to reason, utilitarianism allied to the idea of a social contract. Following Hobbes, Beccaria argued that:

Laws are the terms under which independent and isolated men come together in society. Wearied by living in an unending state of war and by a freedom rendered useless by the uncertainty of retaining it, they sacrifice a part of that freedom in order to enjoy what remains in security and calm.[82]

---

[81] See Rejali, DM (1994) *Torture and Modernity: Self, Society, and State in Modern Iran* (Boulder, Colo: Westview), 167–8.

[82] Beccaria, in Bellamy (1995), 9.

According to this ideal individuals sacrifice only a *part* of their freedom, and punishment—the necessary '*tangible motive*' for obeying the law—'not derived from absolute necessity is tyrannous'.[83] The welfare of the individual is secured through the protection provided by a minimalist impartial state of certain basic interests, most particularly the security of individual citizens and their possessions. In France after 1789, as Peters notes, the concept of *lèse-majesté* gave way to *lèse-nation*, injury to the abstract nation representing the people—the sovereign state—rather than the ruler personally embodying the nation.[84] It was this abstraction, glimpsed embryonically in post-revolutionary France, which was to be perverted in the all-powerful police states of the twentieth century.

It follows that the re-emergence of torture in the twentieth century can be seen both from idealist and structural standpoints, as a practice paradoxically serving new ideals *and* shaped by new technologies of power. What the re-emergence of torture does call into question is the Foucauldian thesis that contemporary technologies of power rely on the control of the mind rather than the body; that there is no longer any need for the state to use torture when resort can be had to labour discipline, police surveillance, panoptic prisons, and judges employing probabilistic reasoning.[85] For the essence of torture, as Elaine Scarry has powerfully argued, is the reduction of the person to being literally no more than a body.[86] Yet there is not necessarily any incompatibility here. The torture of the few, acting on the body, may be employed as a method to weaken, through terror, the minds of the many. And general terror achieved through police-state practices, including torture, are, as Kate Millet has argued, deeply subversive of democratic processes and the development of civil society.[87]

Yet the employment of torture for these purposes contradicts Foucault's implicit assumption that torture (though Foucault deals less with torture than corporeal punishment) is the antithesis of the 'disciplinary technology' which is the hallmark of the socialized citizen in the modern world. There is a parallel assumption in the developmental models of political science which assumes that:

as individuals are introduced to civic and labor discipline, they learn to regulate themselves according to their consciences. External sanctions, at least barbaric ones, are no longer necessary to maintain order.[88]

---

[83] ibid, 9–10.　　[84] Peters (1996), 104.　　[85] Foucault (1977).
[86] Scarry, E (1984) *The Body in Pain* (New York: Oxford University Press), ch 1.
[87] Millet, K (1994) *The Politics of Cruelty: an essay on the literature of political imprisonment* (London: Viking).
[88] Rejali (1994), 165.

According to both Foucault and the developmental theorists—thus we may call this the developmental model—torture is wasteful and inefficient. There are more potent and effective technologies of power available. There may be developmental phases when economic development outstrips political development and the emergence of civic institutions, and in these conditions instability involving violence may be the short-term consequence. But eventually, through a process of training and institution building, so the developmental argument goes, political and economic development is brought into equilibrium. Discipline and development are two sides of the same coin.[89]

The difficulty with this approach, as with the values implicit in the progressivist-humanitarian model, is that waste or efficiency is extraordinarily difficult to measure in relation to all the activities of the nation state. And in any case efficiency and effectiveness, particularly in the context of the ideological, religious, and nationalistic currents that have charged political decision-making in the twentieth century, are not value-free terms. Utility is a matter of normative interpretation. It depends on political and economic objectives. Moreover, as is increasingly recognized, decision making within states is more and more the product of non-territorial or global forces. Polities or economies of violence, in which torture becomes a 'mode of governance' may, as Chomsky and Herman argue, develop in response to pressures exerted by multi-national corporations, with or without the assistance of imperialist powers.[90] Much torture may now be said to have been exported, used on behalf of, or in the interests of, developed states, or the interests incorporated in developed states. Yet that torture will at home unequivocally be condemned and disavowed by those same states.

However, economies of violence may equally develop in response to movements for independence from colonial rule, or ethnic or religious nationhood, or the threat of terrorism or international organized crime, such as that allegedly represented by drug trafficking. It is doubtful whether the pervasiveness of torture in the late twentieth century can be attributed to a single cause, nor does the object of torture typically serve grand purposes. The factors are many and various and, as we shall see, the daily reality is often confused and mundane.

The immediate post-war period brought with it both a sense of relief and a determination to put in place stronger safeguards against the likely employment of torture. The retreat from grand theory was only partial, however, and the late-modern world brought with it a host of new

---

[89] See, for example, Huntington, SP (1968) *Political Order in Changing Societies* (New Haven: Yale University Press).

[90] See, for example, Chomsky, N and Herman, ES (1979) *The Political Economy of Human Rights Vol I* (Montreal: The Washington Connection).

threats to the idea of the liberal state such that torture has persisted, albeit in modified, more subtle, secretive, and disquietingly mundane guises. Most of the torture identified by the leading organizations concerned to monitor the practice is currently to be found outside Europe. However, because this book is concerned with the European Convention Against Torture we shall illustrate the contemporary use of torture by focusing our attention in Chapter 2 on the practice of torture, or what some observers have wished to call torture, in three countries in Europe or close to European preoccupations. All three examples are taken from the period since 1945 and one remains disturbingly with us.

2

Torture and the Liberal Democratic State: Three Modern Case Studies

In the period after 1945 the opening of the Cold War belied the hopes which attended the end of the Second World War. Grand political theory shored up by monolithic state apparatuses that showed little sign of withering persisted in the Soviet Union, in China, and in South East Asia. Not until Khrushchev's landmark speeches of 1961 were there tangible signs of a critical breakthrough in the Soviet Union, and it was to be another twenty-five years before the Soviet Empire, and its justifying ideology, began to be dismantled. In China grand theory and the strong state continue to be proclaimed. Elsewhere—in Cambodia during the rule of the *Khmer Rouge* from 1975–9, and in Albania until 1991, for example—monolithic ideological regimes held terrifying sway and went their own isolationist ways. In Africa and elsewhere the post-colonialist period brought with it the political instability, economic insecurity, and debt dependency which generally plagues the third world. In South America—in Argentina (1976–1983), Chile (1974–1990), and Uruguay (1972–1985), for example—authoritarian military dictatorships wrested power from civilian governments ostensibly to save collapsing states from anarchy. In Europe, the old corporate dictatorships in Portugal and Spain survived until 1974 and 1975 respectively and there were coups leading to periods of military rule in Greece in 1967 and Turkey in 1960 and 1980. In all four countries democracy was restored, but the periods of authoritarian rule bequeathed conflicts and an impoverishment of civil society which made adaptation to democracy in many ways almost as difficult as that confronting the former Communist satellite states of Eastern Europe after the the dismantling of the Berlin wall in 1989. In Africa, despite initial post-independence multi-party aspirations, colonial rule gave way to one-party-rule, or undisguised dictatorship, ostensibly to bring stability in the face of severe class, regional, or tribal conflict. But in several countries —Ethiopia, Somalia, Afghanistan, Gambia, Zaire, and so on—the state has literally collapsed and an anarchy of competing fiefdoms controlled by warlords or ideological factions compete for territory, support, and power, deploying all the force at their command. In many of these countries characterized by unstable or fragile government, torture and other human rights abuses were and are the order of the day.

Torture may be widely employed in the second half of the twentieth century, its horror may be all too intimately familiar to countless victims, but the possible justifications for torture, and its character and impact, are most widely known to non-victims as a result of what have come to be regarded as certain landmark events and public debates, events on which the developed world has focused its attention.

Because this text is concerned with a European-based initiative for the prevention of torture we shall look closely at three examples of the use of torture which have occurred in Europe or in countries within the immediate European sphere of influence since 1945. There is a further reason for the choice we have made. In order that our examples not be distanced from the systems of democracy which, fortunately, now characterize all the state parties to the European Convention with which we are concerned, we have selected examples of torture which remain disturbingly with us, either because they continue literally or because their consequences remain our preoccupation. Our thesis, to which we shall return, is that torture cannot be regarded as a medieval or Third World practice separated in time and space from states that regard themselves as modern and civilized. Rather, torture is a practice that lies all too uncomfortably just below the surface of the largely peaceful and for the most part democratic order which the citizens of most developed countries now take for granted.

1 ALGERIA 1954–62

The War for Algerian Independence, a war fought with unremitting brutality on both sides, brought with it revelations that the French security forces were making extensive use of torture when interrogating suspected members of the armed independence movement—the FLN (*Fronte Libération Nationale*). The revelations first appeared in a newspaper article by François Mauriac in 1955[1] and stimulated a debate not just in France, but world-wide. The question was simply posed. How could France, a country which prided itself on the advanced state of its culture and civilization, a country whose rich traditions included the 1789 Revolution and '*les droits de l'homme*', have reached the point that it eventually acknowledged, condoned, rationalized, justified, and systematically perpetrated the use of torture?

The background to the events can be briefly stated as follows. Algeria was colonized by France in the 1840s and was proclaimed an integral part of France in 1848. The country had been extensively settled by Europeans, the so-called *pieds noirs*, so that by the 1950s they and their descendants

---

[1] The article was entitled '*La Question*' and appeared in the newspaper *L'Express*.

numbered over one million compared to a rapidly expanding and increasingly impoverished indigenous Muslim population of almost nine millions.
Political power, economic wealth, and access to public services lay disproportionately with the minority European settlers, while the majority
Muslim population was relatively neglected.[2] Factions in the Muslim community favouring armed struggle to gain independence saw the humiliation of the French army at Dien Bien Phu, the defeat that brought about
the end of the Indo-China War, as a signal that the French would have
little stomach for a fight in Algeria. A co-ordinated but largely ineffective revolt, including attacks on police stations, was staged in October 1954.
However, the massive deployment and repressive tactics of the French
military forces in response to these attacks—'L'*Algérie c'est la France*' being
the dominant political alarm in France—proved to be a most effective
recruiting sergeant for the FLN which managed, through what are now
recognized as classical terrorist tactics, to transform Algerian political
life into a military situation thereby alienating the previously quiescent
Muslim population against the French state. That the FLN committed
appalling atrocities against soft targets—the massacre and frightful mutilation of *pieds noirs* women and children at Phillippeville in 1955, and
thereafter—to achieve this end, is not disputed.[3] The FLN also employed
terror—including the assassination and display of mutilated 'loyalists'
or 'collaborators'—against the Muslim community, thereby polarizing the
country. Thereafter, armed insurgency gathered pace, as did the repressive tactics of the French police and military forces, particularly after 1956
when the FLN carried their fight into the urban areas, the Battle of Algiers.
As the war dragged on, and the FLN were substantially subdued within
large parts of Algeria by more than half a million French troops, behind-
the-scenes negotiations began to take place. The settler community and
sections of the armed forces, increasingly suspicious that their interests
were to be sold out, embarked on their own campaign. In 1961, with the
formation of the *Organisation Armée Secrète*, they also turned to systematic
terrorism. When a cease-fire was declared, and agreement finally reached
in 1962, the vast majority of the settler community made a panic exit,
destroying as they fled as many of Algeria's resources as they were able.
In the final days of the war Algeria had been reduced to bloody anarchy.

The principal events regarding the use of and the debate about torture by the French were as follows.[4] Following Mauriac's 1955 article the
French Government ordered an inquiry into the allegations that torture was

[2] See Horne, A (1987) *A Savage War of Peace: Algeria 1954–62* (London: MacMillan), 2nd
edn, ch 2.
[3] See, for example, ibid, 115–24.
[4] The following account draws heavily on Maran, R (1989) *Torture: the Role of Ideology in
the French Algerian War* (New York: Praeger).

being used. The enquiry was conducted by Roger Wuillaume, Inspector General in Algiers, a man of complete integrity, as the then Minister of the Interior, François Mitterand, described him. The Wuillaume Report[5] had three components. First, it described the forms of violence employed by the security forces (*les services*). Secondly, it described the authority under which the maltreatment occurred (*les responsibilités*). And, thirdly, it discussed the efficacy of the methods employed (*l'utilité, dans certaines conditions, des services*). Wuillaume did not define torture and the word 'torture' was never included in his terms of reference. But he employed the word and he used it in a manner indicating excessive maltreatment. He concluded that the allegations of torture were true—'maltreatments have been committed, certain ones are truly serious and have the character of true tortures'. He described the forms of violence used by the police. He asserted that these forms represented 'well-established practice'. And he reported that magistrates were typically undemanding about the methods employed to bring people and evidence before them. The methods included beatings, submersion in water, electric shocks, filling the stomach with water through a pipe, and prolonged imprisonment. Wuillaume discussed which of these methods left sequelae and which did not. He also concluded that it was difficult to determine who was responsible for the acts of torture.

Wuillaume reported that he was not in a position to say which methods were most effective. He relied on the experts. He proposed that some methods, the most brutal, be abandoned, though he qualified this by writing that the 'reports of the results are magnificent' and he would not 'cast aspersions on a body of civil servants who can, in their defence, point to so many acts of devotion to duty, even of heroism'. Indeed, he proposed that 'rewards or letters of congratulation' be sent to relieve any sense of wrong-doing that the Algerian colonial administration might be suffering. He thought that other 'less brutal' methods should be retained, because he saw that there was a need for 'various forms of violence . . . if the police are to do their job satisfactorily'. These less brutal methods should be used under controlled conditions. He considered that the Government should not be hypocritical. Now that the truth had come to light and had been acknowledged, the sensible course was 'to recognise and cover with authority certain procedures'. Thus:

The procedures of the water-pipe and electricity, when used with caution, would produce a shock with a much more psychological effect than physical, and therefore that excludes all excessive cruelty.[6]

---

[5] The text of the Wuillaume Report is contained in Vidal-Naquet, P (1962) *La Raison d'état* (Paris: Textes publiés par le Comité Maurice Audin).

[6] Quoted in Maran (1989), 47.

Wuillaume's report was presented in March 1955 to the Governor General of Algeria, who passed it to the French Prime Minister and the President. The report was buried. Though torture was absolutely prohibited by international and French domestic law, nothing was done by the French authorities to stop its use in Algeria. It is now clear that General Jacques Massu, the paratroop commander charged with countering the 1956 FLN terrorist campaign in Algiers, encouraged the extensive use of torture to gather intelligence. He and other senior officers under his command even went so far as to try out the effect of electric shocks on themselves.[7] Under Massu's command the Battle of Algiers was won for the French by the end of 1957. There were mass arrests and interrogations, the bomb factories were discovered, and those responsible for making and placing the bombs, many of them women, identified and eliminated. The leading French military participants justified and subsequently claimed success for that which they had done.[8]

That torture was a major factor in the gathering of the intelligence that made the short-run French victory in Algiers possible is not disputed by commentators who have examined the evidence.[9] There was another, long-term, side to the story, however. It is estimated that during 1956–7 up to three thousand victims of the clamp-down died in custody: they either died under torture or were extra-judicially executed.[10] The Battle of Algiers may have been won, but most analysts are agreed that the manner of its winning ensured that the struggle to retain Algeria was thereafter hopelessly lost.[11]

After General De Gaulle became President in 1958, Henry Alleg, a European Jew whose family had settled in Algeria during the Second World War and was the communist editor of a republican Algerian newspaper, published a vivid account of his own torture by the French security forces.[12] The book received wide publicity and caused an uproar in France. Two senior French figures—Andre Malraux, then Minister of Information, and Michel Debré, then a Member of the Senate—both made statements indicating that they knew about the continuing use of torture in Algeria. But President De Gaulle never spoke of the matter and still no action was taken.

The aftermath to the Algerian War brought further information about what exactly had been done, evidence of the impact of the torture on both perpetrators and victims and what those who had commanded the situation felt they had been justified in doing. For example, a study undertaken

---

[7] Horne (1987), 199.

[8] Trinquier, R (1961) *La Guerre Moderne* (Paris): and (1968) *Guerre, Subversion, Révolution* (Paris): Massu, J (1971) *La Vrai Bataille d'Alger* (Paris).

[9] Maran (1989), ch 9; Ruedy, J (1992) *Modern Algeria: The Origins and Development of a Nation* (Bloomington, Ind: Indiana Univeristy Press), 167–8.

[10] Horne (1987), 202.   [11] ibid, 204–7; Ruedy (1992), 168–70.

[12] Alleg, H (1958) *La Question* (Paris: Editions de Minuit).

and published by a Catholic magazine investigated the Algerian War experiences of French soldiers, commissioned and non-commissioned. Among the worst experiences that the former combatants recalled were acts of torture that were so varied and routine that they were considered normal. The survey revealed that many of the soldiers had been socialized to think of Algerian Arabs as an inferior race against whom such brutality was justified.[13] General Massu, for example, defended the French tactics. Seeking to legitimate his own orders, he quoted an address by an army chaplain, Père Delarue, to his parachutist forces:

in fighting revolutionary warfare, Père Delarue said 'talk sessions and appeals to good sense were a waste of time.' When dealing with recalcitrant prisoners from whom information was urgently needed, it was imperative to find 'effective methods, without hesitating, even if they are unaccustomed methods, and apply them without weakness'.[14]

Massu reported his chaplain as arguing that it was right to submit a criminal to 'harsh interrogation'. It was to be 'an interrogation without sadism, but efficacious', to be conducted 'without joy, but also without shame, done only because of concern with duty, this crude need so contrary to our habits as soldiers and civilised men'.[15]

The methods employed during the Algerian War of Independence were also justified on another, in the long-term, more important basis: the changing nature of warfare basis. This was the message of a senior French officer, Colonel Trinquier, who used his Algerian experience as the basis for a general study on the nature of modern warfare. This was no longer a struggle between two traditional opposing armies on a designated field of battle, one emerging as the clear victor. Modern warfare, as in Algiers, was a 'war in the crowd, a war in the social milieu'. It involved an interlocking system of actions—political, economic, psychological, and military. In these circumstances 'torture . . . the particular bane of the terrorist was to be another instrumentality of the French army because, whatever the cost, the FLN had to be defeated and Algeria kept French'. If the French army refused to employ all the weapons of modern warfare 'it could no longer fulfil its mission . . . Our national independence, the civilisation we hold dear, our very freedom would probably perish'.[16] In this Trinquier was invoking the advice of Clausewitz:

---

[13] Quoted in Maran (1989), 76.   [14] Quoted in Maran (1989), 98.
[15] From which Maran (1989), 98 concludes: 'The civilising mission thus came to the foot soldier from the sources of the highest authority in his life, the military commander and the religious counsellor, both of whom invoked it affirmatively through two powerful arguments. Torturing a terrorist who holds critical information was justified on utilitarian grounds when the welfare of a large number of people were at stake . . . the welfare of the single individual was to be treated as secondary. Also the ultimate cause served in Algeria was preservation of the values of Christians and of the civilised men that we are . . .'.
[16] Trinquier (1961), quoted in Maran (1989), 99.

War . . . is an act of violence . . . Self-imposed restrictions, almost imperceptible and hardly worth mentioning, termed usages of *international law*, accompany it without essentially impairing its power . . . Now, philanthropists may easily imagine there is a skilful method of disarming and overcoming an enemy without causing great bloodshed . . . However plausible this may appear, still it is an error which must be extirpated; for in such dangerous things as war, the errors which proceed from a spirit of benevolence are the worst.[17]

The French use and justification of torture has, as we shall see, found an echo in debates in other professed liberal democracies, and no doubt many more debates on these points have taken place elsewhere behind closed doors. But the immediate result of the French policy in Algeria, a policy pursued in defence of a colonial empire for which there was little sympathy elsewhere, was denunciation both domestically[18] and internationally.[19] In the end the revelations of torture and extra-judicial executions in Algeria, quite apart from driving the Arab population into the arms of the FLN, horrified French public opinion and eventually brought about general disillusionment with a policy which apparently required such methods. Moreover, the events in Algeria were among a series of incidents leading to the foundation of Amnesty International in 1961.

2 NORTHERN IRELAND AND THE 'TROUBLES' 1963–94

On 9 August 1971 the Prime Minister of Northern Ireland, Mr Brian Faulkner, announced that he was exercising special powers, introduced in 1922,[20] by arresting, detaining, and interning persons suspected of involvement in terrorist activities. His justification was the deteriorating security situation in the province and an increased number of killings, bombings, and arms finds.[21] Large numbers of arrests followed and soon thereafter allegations of ill-treatment and torture emerged which, following domestic and international investigation, were substantially upheld. The background to these events is well-known and need be summarized only briefly here.

The six counties of Northern Ireland remained part of the United Kingdom following the partition of Ireland and the formation of the Irish Free State (subsequently the Irish Republic) in 1922. This settlement,

[17] von Clausewitz, C (1982) *On War* (Harmondsworth: Penguin), 101–2.
[18] The French bishops collectively denounced French policy in Algeria in 1961 and 1962. See Peters (1996), 156.
[19] In December 1960 the UN General Assembly overwhelmingly supported a resolution recognizing the right of the Algerian people to self-determination; see Horne (1987), 464–5.
[20] Civil Authorities (Special Powers) Act (Northern Ireland) 1922.
[21] Compton Report (1971) *Report of the enquiry into allegations against the security forces of physical brutality in Northern Ireland arising out of events on the 9th August, 1971*, (Chairman, Sir Edward Compton), Cmnd 4823 (London: HMSO), iii.

which was devised to placate the Protestant majority in Northern Ireland, a community traditionally opposed to the formation of a united Ireland independent of the United Kingdom, was largely objected to by that section of the Northern Ireland population which is Catholic. Moreover the settlement did not become more acceptable with time. Political party activity in Northern Ireland tended to exacerbate the divide which was reflected in a permanent parliamentary majority for the Protestant Unionists right up to the imposition of direct rule from London following the breakdown of law and order in 1972. In 1963 the Catholic community, feeling itself discriminated against in all the principal areas of social and economic life—a complaint substantially upheld by a government inquiry report in 1969[22]—embarked on a civil rights campaign. This campaign was met with some violence from a Protestant para-military group but it was not until 1967–8 that civil rights marches led to clashes with the Protestant community and large-scale rioting. There was also evidence of increased para-military activity on the Protestant side and in 1970 this appears to have led to the Irish Republican Army (IRA)—a proscribed group whose origins pre-dated partition—embarking on a substantial bombing campaign in 1970. Though para-military groups on both sides of the communal divide were responsible for the bombings that occurred in 1970–1, it is generally agreed that the vast majority were carried out by the IRA. This was the chain reaction which led to the use of the Special Powers Act.

The ordinary law, Mr Faulkner claimed, could not 'deal comprehensively or quickly enough with such ruthless viciousness'.[23] Mass arrests followed and, though the majority of those arrested were released, several hundred persons were detained or interned.[24] There soon emerged allegations of physical brutality which received widespread publicity. The Home Secretary appointed a committee, chaired by Sir Edmund Compton, to inquire into the allegations.

The Compton Report was the product of a skewed investigation because, with one exception, none of the persons arrested (copies of some of whose complaints were sent by newspapers to the Commission) was prepared to co-operate with the investigating committee. Most detainees said they had complaints, but were not willing to submit their testimony to the Committee. The Committee therefore had no alternative but to set hearsay evidence from prisoners against the direct evidence they collected from official sources. The Committee was nevertheless able to come to some significant conclusions.

---

[22] Cameron Report (1969) *Disturbances in Northern Ireland: report of the commission: appointed by the Governor of Northern Ireland*, (Chairman, Lord Cameron), CMD 532 (Belfast: HMSO).
[23] Compton Report (1971), iv.   [24] ibid.

The Committee found that some of those arrested had been subjected to what was described as 'in-depth' interrogation following the making of detention orders against them. The officials interviewed by Compton admitted that in-depth interrogation might involve the use of four techniques: *wall standing*, in which detainees were made to stand with their arms against a wall, but allegedly 'not in a position of stress'; *hooding*, in which a black pillow-slip was placed over the detainee's head; *noise*, in which detainees were subjected to continuous white noise; and *a bread and water diet*. It was said by officials that these techniques inculcated discipline and heightened the suspect's sense of isolation making it possible to obtain information more rapidly. But the techniques were also justified on the grounds that they safeguarded both suspects' and interrogators' security. *Wall standing* was said to reduce the need for physical contact between detainees and guards and *hooding* reduced the likelihood that suspects would be identified by fellow suspects.[25] The government was keen that the Compton Committee should reproduce in their report a 'Note on Interrogation' which showed that the 'techniques of interrogation currently in use have . . . been employed in many previous . . . internal security operations in which H.M.G. [Her Majesty's Government] have been involved since the last war [meaning the Second World War] and that the rules had most recently been revised in 1966 following events in Aden'.[26]

The written allegations that the Committee received bore a close resemblance to the techniques that the military authorities admitted employing, but with certain important additions. First, all the complainants' statements mentioned the four techniques described above, but added a fifth: they said they were deprived of sleep for two or three days. Secondly, they said that the wall-standing technique did involve stress: they were 'forced with batons to maintain posture', they were so kept until they collapsed, and this continued for up to four days. Most of the complainants claimed that they were struck or beaten with fists or batons whenever they relaxed their position. Thirdly, they said that they received less food than the bread and water diet was officially said to involve and no food or drink for the first two or three days.[27]

The officials who had dealt with the complainants denied the beatings or physical assaults to maintain wall standing but 'confirmed that detainees attempting to rest or sleep by propping their heads against the wall were prevented from doing so'. They also agreed that 'if a detainee collapsed on the floor, he was picked up by the armpits and placed against the wall to resume the approved posture'. Further, they confirmed that 'it was the general policy to deprive the men of opportunity to sleep during the early days of the operation'.[28] The detention records showed that:

[25] Compton Report (1971), 12–13.   [26] ibid, 12.   [27] ibid, 15–18.   [28] ibid, 16.

the detainees had been kept standing at the wall for many hours, four out of eleven of them for between 29 and 44 hours; they had all lost weight; and the medical records of several detainees recorded injuries for which no explanation from officials was forthcoming.[29]

The Compton Committee found that despite the paucity of the evidence, and discrepancies in that evidence, all five techniques had been used and all five amounted to physical ill-treatment. However, the Committee did not think that this ill-treatment amounted to 'physical brutality'—the term employed in their terms of reference—because 'brutality is an inhuman or savage form of cruelty, and that cruelty implies a disposition to inflict suffering, coupled with indifference to, or pleasure in, the victim's pain', and 'we do not think that happened here'.[30] No conclusions were reached regarding individual allegations of beating. No recommendations were asked for or given regarding the continued use of the five interrogation techniques.

A few days after Compton reported, Mr Heath, then British Prime Minister, appointed a Committee of three Privy Counsellors, chaired by Lord Parker, to consider whether 'the procedures currently authorised for the interrogation of persons suspected of terrorism and for their custody while subject to interrogation require amendment'.[31] The Parker Committee focused less on what had been done but rather on whether it should be done. In the event, the three Privy Counsellors could not agree on fundamental issues. Lord Gardiner, a senior judge, submitted a minority report which is significantly longer than the main report and proved more influential, at least as far as political decisions in Britain are concerned.

The Parker Report is a brief document but is particularly illuminating on certain key points. First, it reveals that the five interrogation techniques—it appears now to have been officially agreed that there were five and not the four initially described to Compton—had been employed in 'Palestine, Malaya, Kenya and Cyprus and more recently in the British Cameroons (1960–61), Brunei (1963), British Guiana (1964), Aden (1964–67), Borneo/Malaysia (1965–66), [and] the Persian Gulf (1970–71)' prior to their use in Northern Ireland.[32] Secondly, though the techniques were subject to a 'Joint Directive on Military Interrogation in Internal Security Operations Overseas', the directive only set the upper limits within which the techniques should fall.[33] The techniques were not described in the directive. The directive simply provided, in accordance with the provisions of the Geneva Convention, that certain acts—violence to life and

---

[29] ibid, 16–17.   [30] ibid, para 105.
[31] Parker Report (1972) *Report of the Committee of Privy Counsellors appointed to consider authorised procedures for the interrogation of persons suspected of terrorism,* (Chairman, Lord Parker), Cmnd 4981 (London: HMSO), para 1.
[32] ibid, para 10.   [33] ibid, Appendix.

person, in particular mutilation, cruel treatment and torture, and outrages to personal dignity, in particular, humiliating and degrading treatment —were prohibited.[34] Further, though the techniques (and resistance to them) were taught at intelligence centres, there were 'no standing orders or manuals' detailing them: everything, it appeared, was in the heads of those who taught them or had been taught them.[35] Thus, the Committee recognized, use of the techniques might in practice be rather different from whatever was taught at the training schools: the training might be inadequate, there might be a shortage of personnel or appropriate accommodation, and so on. 'In these circumstances, and in the absence of definite guidelines, there is a risk that the techniques will be applied to a greater degree than is justified morally or under the Directive.'[36]

The Committee explored various operational questions with the authorities. Was there any medical risk attached to use of the techniques, for example? They were persuaded that, though there were risks, if the techniques were applied in the limited fashion envisaged by the trainers —and these limits appear, according to the evidence in the Compton Report, to have been exceeded in Northern Ireland (this issue is never fully made clear in the Parker Report)—the risks of physical injury were 'negligible'. Furthermore, providing certain medical safeguards were in place, there was no 'real' risk of injury to mental health.[37]

Were the techniques effective in that confessions or intelligence was gathered, which could not have been gathered by other means? The Committee, presumably forced to rely entirely on the untested assertions of military and police witnesses, had 'no doubt that when used in the past these techniques have produced very valuable results'.[38] As far as the recent operations in Northern Ireland were concerned the Committee reported that 'new information' had been obtained, that 'individual responsibility' for 85 'previously unexplained' incidents had been 'discovered', and the recovery of arms and ammunition following the mass arrests greatly increased.[39] As a result of the absence of intelligence prior to the mass arrests it was said that the security forces were hampered in their searches with the consequence that they 'were liable to harass and antagonize innocent citizens'.[40] However, no reference was made to confessions— or prosecutions pending or completed—and, given the general increase in military intervention and activity, it would have been surprising had arms finds not increased whatever methods were employed. No real assessment of alternative policing methods was made except that the

---

[34] Parker Report (1972), Appendix.
[35] ibid, para 13.   [36] ibid.   [37] ibid, paras 14–17.   [38] ibid, para 18.
[39] ibid, paras 19–21.   [40] ibid, para 19.

Committee was persuaded that 'interrogation as conducted in conditions of war'—and this apparently mean using 'stool pigeons' and the bugging of conversations of prisoners kept in groups—would be unlikely to obtain valuable information quickly.[41]

If the Parker Report is insufficiently probing regarding police methods it claims nevertheless to be realistic regarding the philosophical and legal issues posed. The authors maintain that they 'do not subscribe to the principle that the end justifies the means'. However, they do think that what is 'morally acceptable' depends on 'the conditions prevailing'.[42] Thus what counts as inhuman or degrading depends on the 'light of circumstances'. If there is 'urban guerrilla warfare in which completely innocent lives are at risk . . . there is a degree of urgency . . . [and there are] security and safety . . . considerations'.[43] Thus, those who argue that utilitarian and contextual considerations should not apply are being 'unrealistic'. The context, 'though short of war in its ordinary sense . . . [is] in many ways worse than war'. Friend and foe are not identifiable, the rebels are ruthless, the attacks indiscriminate, 'time must be of the essence' and ' "humanitarian" law as well as domestic law will allow a measure of self-defence'.[44] 'Even under normal conditions it is accepted that a person suspected of ordinary crime . . . can be subjected to some measure of discomfort, hardship and mental anxiety'. Thus the answer to the moral question depends on the 'intensity with which these techniques are applied'.[45] And the Committee concluded:

Viewed in this way we think that the application of these techniques, subject to proper safeguards, limiting the occasion on which and the degree to which they can be applied, would be in conformity with the Directive . . . Subject to these safeguards . . . there is no reason to rule out these techniques on moral grounds . . . it is possible to operate them in a manner consistent with the highest standards of our society.[46]

Given that the majority of the Committee considered that 'use of some if not all the techniques in question would constitute criminal assault and might also give rise to civil proceedings under English law', it is clear that, within limits, they did think that the ends justified the means.[47]

Lord Gardiner, the third member of the Committee, saw things differently. In his minority report he was concerned to go back to the Compton Report and question some of its findings and assumptions. For example, he noted that Compton reported only the aggregate periods for which detainees had been kept standing at the wall and not the periods for which they had been required continuously so to do, which was typically nine hours but in some cases fifteen or sixteen hours. Further, the reported

---

[41] ibid, paras 25–6. [42] ibid, para 27. [43] ibid, para 30. [44] ibid, para 32.
[45] ibid, paras 33–4. [46] ibid, paras 30 and 34. [47] ibid, para 2.

weight losses were based on doctors' estimates of detainees' weights on arrival, but even so there were losses of 'up to 1 stone and 2 lbs in six days'. Finally he found the Compton Committee's definition of brutality 'remarkable' and could not agree with it:

Under this definition . . . if an interrogator believed, to his great regret, that it was necessary for him to cut off the fingers of a detainee one by one to get the required information out of him for the sole purpose of saving life, this would not be cruel and, because not cruel, not brutal.[48]

Lord Gardiner did not disagree with those witnesses who thought that this definition was worthy of the Inquisition.

Nor was Lord Gardiner persuaded that the techniques in question had been authorized or could have been authorized. He is clear that the techniques involved unlawful behaviour and could therefore not lawfully have been authorized, even if there was evidence that they had been, which there was not (no evidence was given that any minister had ever been informed as to what the interrogation techniques comprised). Given that the techniques involved illegal acts under domestic law, he saw no need to offer an opinion as to whether they were contrary to international law.

As far as the possible effects of the techniques were concerned Lord Gardiner considered these under several heads. He was less sanguine than his colleagues about the risk of injury to detainees. He thought it 'unlikely' that there would *not* be 'minor physical injuries' and his review (much more detailed than that contained in the Parker Report) of the likely mental health consequences indicated that some medical witnesses thought the short-term outcome would in some subjects be artificial psychoses or panic attacks, the long-term effects of which were difficult to predict.[49] As far as the harvest of intelligence was concerned he was more sceptical than his colleagues that the information undoubtedly collected following the mass arrests was attributable to the use of in-depth interrogation techniques. Moreover, he was not persuaded that other, equally effective or more effective, techniques could not have been used.[50] Finally, as far as the consequences for relations in Northern Ireland and for Britain's reputation in the world were concerned—an issue about which the Parker Report had nothing to say—Lord Gardiner was severe. In addition to the potentially damaging loss of sympathy for the authorities in the community, he thought that approval of the techniques would

---

[48] Parker Report (1972), *II. The Minority Report*, para 7.
[49] ibid, para 13.   [50] ibid, para 14.

involve a departure 'from world standards which we have helped to create'. This would 'gravely damage our own reputation and deal a severe blow to the whole world movement to improve Human Rights'.[51]

What, he asked, were his colleagues on the Parker Committee proposing?

If it was to be made legal to employ methods not now legal against a man whom the police believe to have, but who may not have, information which the police desire to obtain, I . . . have . . . been unable to find, either in logic or in morals, any limit to the degree of ill-treatment to be legalised. The only logical limit to the degree of ill-treatment to be legalised would appear to be whatever degree of ill-treatment proves to be necessary to get the information out of him, which would include, if necessary, extreme torture.'[52]

Be that as it may, were the Parker Report recommendations to be implemented, Lord Gardiner could envisage only two courses of action. Either Parliament would have to pass legislation enabling the minister, in times of civil emergency, to 'fix the limits of permissible degrees of ill-treatment to be employed when interrogating suspects and that such limits should then be kept secret', or the minister would have to fix secret limits 'without the authority of Parliament, that is to say illegally, and then, if found out, ask Parliament for an Act of Indemnity'.[53] Either course he considered objectionable. Quite apart from the fact that he could see no basis on which limits might be set by either parliament or the minister, the first option would mean, in effect, empowering the minister to make secret laws—because 'citizens would have no right to know what the law was about police powers of interrogation'. The second option would 'be a flagrant breach of the whole basis of the Rule of Law and of the principles of democratic government'.[54] The events giving rise to the Compton and Parker inquiries comprised, in Lord Gardiner's view, a 'sorry story' the blame for which:

must lie with those who, many years ago, decided that in emergency conditions in Colonial-type situations we should abandon our legal, well-tried and highly successful wartime interrogation methods and replace them by procedures which were secret, illegal, not morally justifiable and alien to the traditions of what I still believe to be the greatest democracy in the world.[55]

Use of the five interrogation techniques was officially forbidden from November 1971 and unqualified undertakings given that they would not be allowed in the future. Internment of terrorist suspects without trial was abandoned. Lord Gardiner's opinion, if not all his sentiments, prevailed.

---

[51] ibid, para 20.　　[52] ibid, para 20.　　[53] ibid, para 20(4).
[54] ibid.　　[55] ibid, para 21.

The matter did not end here, however. Following the recommendations of yet another official inquiry[56] the law regarding, *inter alia*, the admissibility of confessions was relaxed so as to allow statements made under interrogation to be admitted as evidence unless it was proved, on a balance of probabilities, that they were obtained by subjecting the accused to torture or to inhuman or degrading treatment.[57] As we shall see in Chapter 3, the Irish Government pursued an important application to Strasbourg for breach of Article 3 of the European Convention for Human Rights (which prohibits torture and inhuman and degrading treatment) in connection with the use of the five techniques. However, though the Court found that there had been a breach of Article 3, it was not alleged that use of the five techniques had continued after 1971 and the Court drew no conclusion about those cases submitted which related to the period after that date. Nevertheless, allegations of ill-treatment, some of them bearing a resemblance to one or another of the five techniques— hooding, deprivation of sleep, and forced adoption of stress positions, for example—continued to emerge from Northern Ireland throughout the 1970s.[58] These allegations, which included brutality amounting to torture, were judged by the British government to be sufficiently serious to institute a second official inquiry into police interrogation procedures in 1979,[59] as a result of which yet further amendments to the law were made and fresh safeguards for terrorist suspects introduced. By 1979 it was not being alleged that use of any of the by now notorious in-depth interrogation techniques was officially authorized—indeed it had officially been said since 1972 that use of the former techniques was considered 'counter-productive'. The techniques were said to hinder 'the creation of rapport between the person questioned and his questioner which makes him feel the need to unburden himself'.[60] Yet there continued to emerge evidence of injuries consistent with some detainees' allegations. All the evidence pointed to a heritage of abuse and mistrust which almost certainly meant that some police officers continued to ill-treat their prisoners and that some prisoners, probably on instructions from the para-military organisations of which they were members, were

[56] Diplock Report (1972) *Report of the Commission to consider legal procedures to deal with terrorist activities in Northern Ireland* (Chairman, Lord Diplock), Cmnd 5185 (London: HMSO), paras 73–92.

[57] Northern Ireland (Emergency Provisions) Act 1973, s 6.

[58] See, for example, Foul, D and Murray, R (1978) *The Castlereagh File: Allegations of RUC Brutality 1976–1977* (No publisher or place of publication stated); Taylor, P (1980) *Beating the Terrorists* (Harmondsworth: Penguin).

[59] Bennet Report (1979) *Report of The Committee of Inquiry into Police Interrogation Procedures In Northern Ireland*, Cmnd 749 (London: HMSO).

[60] Diplock Report (1972), para 84.

able falsely, and with telling propagandist effect, to accuse their captors of continuing brutality.[61]

3 ISRAEL

The whole experience of the British security forces in Northern Ireland played a major part, as we shall see, in the methods and thinking of the Israeli authorities when faced with armed opposition. There is another relevant Irish connection. During the period of the British military administration from 1917 to 1948, Palestine was policed by a body part of which originally comprised a British Palestinian *gendarmerie* of 700 officers and men most of whose members were recruited, following the establishment of the Irish Republic, from the disbanded Royal Irish Constabulary and their notorious auxiliary division, the 'Black and Tans'. It was from the ranks of these men that the senior officers in what became the Palestinian Police Force were drawn and against whom, in the late 1930s, during a period of Arab revolt against the settlement of Jewish refugees in Palestine, accusations of torture were made. We know now that what were described at the time as 'Black and Tan tendencies' included the commonplace use of severe torture.[62]

The birth of the modern state of Israel was of course framed by National Socialism and the holocaust. It was also preceded by the use of terrorism by Zionist groups against the British, a scourge which has in turn been employed against the Israeli people by displaced Palestinians. Ever since their occupation of the West Bank in 1967, the Israeli authorities have repeatedly been accused of systematically employing violence and torture against the Palestinian people, particularly those suspected of terrorism or of belonging to organizations employing terrorism.[63] These accusations have persisted not just since the start of the Palestinian *intifada* (uprising) in 1987,[64] but also since the agreement with the Palestinian Liberation Organisation (PLO) in 1994 for the setting up, under the control of the latter, of a Palestinian Authority for the Gaza Strip and Jericho Areas. Most recently, the Palestinian Authority itself stands accused of employing torture against fellow Palestinians opposed to the agreement

---

[61] See, for example, Bennet Report (1979), paras 158–64.   [62] See Smith (1992), 71.

[63] See Amnesty International (1984), 'Israel and the Occupied Territories' in *Torture in the Eighties* (London: Amnesty International, International Secretariat), 233–6.

[64] See, for example, B'Tselem (1991) *The Interrogation of Palestinians During the Intifada: Ill-Treatment, 'Moderate Physical Pressure' or Torture?* (Jerusalem: B'Tselem); B'Tselem (1992) *The Interrogation of Palestinians during the Intifada: Follow-up to March 1991 B'Tselem Report* (Jerusalem: B'Tselem).

with the Israeli authorities.[65] Israel's history is bathed in blood and provides possibly the best-known twentieth-century example of a state the
very existence of which is fiercely contested. It is not surprising, therefore, that Israel, a constitutional democracy that proudly proclaims its belief
in the rule of law, and which is now signatory to all the principal international instruments prohibiting torture, provides a revealing test bed for
the dilemmas said to confront a state under seige from forces within and
without.

In 1985–7 two political scandals[66] concerning the Israeli security forces
and their treatment of prisoners or suspects, led to the establishment, under
Mr Justice Moshe Landau, a former Supreme Court President, of an official inquiry into the methods of investigation employed by the Israeli
General Security Services (GSS) against alleged terrorists. The Landau Commission *Report*[67] provides a fascinating example of contemporary official
discourse regarding the possible justification of torture or practices that
might be judged to constitute torture.The Landau Commission carefully
built a case on which its controversial conclusions and recommendations
were grounded as follows.

First, Israel is confronted by several organizations dedicated to its
destruction through armed struggle. These organizations perpetrate terrorism, making no distinction between civilian or military targets. Their
membership is highly trained and disciplined and though only a minority of the Arab population in the Occupied Territories is involved 'the
terrorist organizations enjoy the overt or covert sympathy of the majority of the Arab population'.[68] Those Arab citizens who dare to criticize
the terrorist organizations are said to be ruthlessly eliminated. It follows

[65] See, for example, Amnesty International (1995a) *Report 1995* (London: Amnesty
International, International Secretariat), 170–3; Amnesty International (1996a) *Report 1996*
(London: Amnesty International, International Secretariat), 184–8; Amnesty International
(1996b) *Palestinian Authority: Prolonged Political Detention, Torture and Unfair Trials* (London:
Amnesty International, International Secretariat).

[66] The 'No 300 Bus Affair' concerned the rescue of a bus hijacked by Palestinians. The
hijackers were said officially to have been killed by cross-fire during the rescue, but press
photographs revealed that they had been alive when taken into custody. It was later shown
that the hijackers had been executed on the orders of the Israeli General Security Service
(GSS) and that GSS personnel had conspired to hide this fact from subsequent investigations. The Attorney General resigned over the affair and in 1986 the Israeli President par-
doned all the GSS officials involved, including the Head of the GSS, after they had also
resigned from the Service. The second scandal, 'Izzat Nafsu Affair', concerned an Israeli
army officer sentenced in 1982 to 18 years imprisonment for offences of treason and espion-
age. Nafsu maintained that his confession had been coerced. In May 1987 the Supreme Court
accepted his appeal, thereby accepting that the security officers who had testified at his trial
and initial appeal had lied about the methods used to interrogate him, and ordered his release.
The Landau Commission was then set up in response.

[67] Landau Commission (1987) *Report of the Commission of Inquiry into the Methods of Investigation of the General Security Service Regarding Hostile Terrorist Activity, Part One* (Jerusalem).

[68] ibid, para 2.11.

that the threat posed by these organizations is extremely difficult to foil. Evidence is hard to come by, perpetrators are trained to resist questioning, and retaliation awaits them if they fail to resist. It is the duty of GSS personnel to counter this threat.

Secondly, a distinction is drawn between the GSS and the police. Though the GSS, like the police, is keen successfully to convict individual perpetrators of terrorism and ensure that they are duly punished, the collection of intelligence is their primary interest, and how and what intelligence they collect must often remain secret so that the security of methods and sources is preserved. The GSS goal is less the pursuit of individual just deserts and more the protection of 'the very existence of society and the State . . . to collect information about terrorists and their modes of organization and to thwart the perpetration of terrorist acts whilst they are still at a state of incubation'.[69] Whereas the police are generally able to collect evidence from a variety of sources, the GSS is largely reliant on intelligence gathered from interrogating suspects arrested on the basis of 'a well-founded assumption, usually from classified sources'.[70] Further, the evidence collected by GSS cannot always be used to pursue prosecutions 'either because it is inadmissible under the laws of evidence or because the harm liable to be caused by its disclosure outweighs the benefit of bringing it before the court'.[71] The Landau Commission concluded that this consideration lay at the heart of the perjury which it found GSS personnel had routinely engaged in over many years and which prompted the scandals leading to the appointment of the Landau Inquiry. When interrogating suspects GSS personnel used physical and other pressures which in court they denied using: 'They simply lied.'[72] Both their interrogation methods and their subsequent perjury were explicitly approved by their superiors. The policy was the logical extension of the secretive compartmentalization of their work which GSS were trained to regard as essential for their effectiveness.

Thirdly, the Landau Commission accepted GSS contentions both as to the effectiveness and necessity of their methods and, ironically, given their perjury about using physical pressure, the integrity of their personnel. The Landau *Report*: repeatedly praises the GSS for the 'large number of successes to its credit';[73] accepts GSS contentions that 80–90 per cent of terrorist perpetrators were captured as a result of the methods employed;[74] notes, apparently without concern, that 'the overwhelming majority of those tried were convicted on the basis of their confession' alone;[75] accepts the GSS view that 'effective interrogation of terrorist suspects is impossible without the use of means of pressure';[76] presents as an intolerable

---

[69] ibid, para 2.18.   [70] ibid, para 2.18.   [71] ibid, para 2.19.
[72] ibid, para 2.27.   [73] ibid, para 2.16.   [74] ibid, para 2.20.
[75] ibid, paras 2.20, 2.28, and 2.38.   [76] ibid, para 4.6.

moral dilemma (a dilemma which GSS personnel should never have been called on to face) that they were obliged to use methods about which they subsequently felt it necessary to lie;[77] and apparently accepts without reservation that GSS personnel used only those methods of physical pressure of which their superiors, and subsequently the Landau Commission, approved.[78]

This was the utilitarian foundation for the presentation of the choices which the Commission saw before it. The first option was to leave the security services in a ' "twilight zone" which is outside the realm of law'.[79] The second option was 'that of the hypocrites (who) declare that they abide by the rule of law, but turn a blind eye to what goes on beneath the surface'.[80] The third option, which the Commission chose, was 'the truthful road of the rule of law',[81] namely to make legally legitimate the means of pressure which the GSS claimed previously to have employed and which the Service considered necessary to accomplish the 'sacred mission' given it.[82] Precisely what these methods were the Commission said had been kept secret and had to remain secret, on the grounds that the methods would be ineffective if 'known to the adversary':[83] the methods are described in the second (secret and therefore unpublished) part of the Commission's *Report*.

GSS members testified to the Commission that their 'sacred mission' justified 'the means, any means'.[84] The Commission did not go so far (and, given the evidence emerging that the GSS were using methods which by any standard unequivocally comprised torture,[85] somewhat disingenuously accepted the GSS assertion that interrogators had *not gone that far*). However, the Commission accepted that the defences of 'necessity' and 'lesser evil'[86] were important when considering the actions of GSS personnel[87] and subsequently mulled over the much debated, and possibly apocryphal, 'ticking bomb' scenario.[88] A bomb has just been planted in a

---

[77] Landau Commission (1987), paras 2.28 and 2.34.
[78] ibid, para 2.41.   [79] ibid, para 4.3.   [80] ibid, para 4.4.   [81] ibid, para 4.5.
[82] ibid, para 2.40.   [83] ibid, para 2.25.   [84] ibid, para 2.40.
[85] See nn 108 and 111.   [86] See Robinson, P (1984) *Criminal Law Defences*, Vol 2, 45.
[87] Landau Commission (1987), para 3.8.
[88] The ticking bomb scenario may not, contrary to what most commentators have said, be a purely fictional device. In his study of the Algerian War, Horne (1987), 204, recounts that this very dilemma faced Paul Teitgen, Secretary-General at the Prefecture in Algeria in 1957. Teitgen was asked by the chief of police to authorize the torture of Fernand Yveton, a communist caught red-handed placing a bomb in some gasworks. It was alleged that Yveton had placed a second bomb in the gasworks which, if not discovered and defused, might cause a general gas explosion likely to kill thousands of people. Teitgen refused to authorize the torture and, according to his own account, 'trembled the whole afternoon. Finally the bomb did not go off. Thank God I was right. Because if you once get into this torture business, you're lost.' What is not made absolutely clear in this account is whether there was actually a second bomb.

crowded public place and may explode at any moment. What action is an interrogator entitled to take with a suspect who he believes knows the whereabouts of the bomb? The Commission had no doubt about their conclusion.

The deciding factor is not the element of time [the imminence of the danger], but the comparison between the gravity of the two evils—the evil of contravening the law as opposed to the evil which will occur sooner or later . . . [W]eighing these two evils, one against the other, must be performed according to the concept of morality implanted in the heart of every decent and honest person. To put it bluntly, the alternative is: are we to accept the offence of assault entailed in slapping a suspect's face, or threatening him, in order to induce him to talk and reveal a cache of explosive materials meant for use in carrying out an act of mass terror against a civilian population, and thereby prevent the greater evil which is about to occur? The answer is self-evident.[89]

Further, the Commission quote with approval a view that the correct test is not the *actual* evil in prospect, but the evil which the actor reasonably *believes* to be in prospect.[90] There are fundamental problems associated with this reasoning which have long been recognized.[91]

First, Landau justifies the systematic use of physical pressure by the state on the basis of the criminal-law defence of necessity. This, as several commentators have argued, is a highly questionable use of the concept of necessity in criminal law. The defence of necessity in individual cases rests on 'the unique, isolated and extraordinary character of the situation which makes it an exception to the rule . . . [whereas] The granting of power to an authority is an integral part of the legal system, and the exercise of that power in accordance with rules is studied, institutionalized and normal.'[92] Necessity, as the old adage has it, knows no law. It is the most 'lawless of legal doctrines . . . an emergency measure', designed to fill lacunae, 'not suited to situations which recur over long periods of time . . . especially so when the claimant to the benefits of the defense is a state agency (or its members)'.[93] To justify a regular state practice on this basis would mean standardizing allegedly compelling circumstances incapable of standardization. It means granting GSS personnel a general discretion to use physical pressure: where, *in an individual case*, there is no necessary urgency; where no specific harm prevented

---

[89] Landau Commission (1987), para 3.15.   [90] ibid, para 3.16.

[91] Jeremy Bentham, for example, in an unpublished essay, explored them in detail. See Twining, WL and Twining, PE (1973) 'Bentham on Torture', 24 Northern Ireland Legal Quarterly 305.

[92] Kremnitzer, M (1989) 'The Landau Commission Report: Was the Security Service Subordinated to the Law, or the Law to the "Needs" of the Security Service?', 24 Is LR 237.

[93] Dershowitz, A (1989) 'Is it Necessary to apply "physical pressure" to terrorists—and to lie about it?', 24 Is LR, 196–7.

by gathering intelligence from that particular suspect can precisely be identified; where the guilt of the suspect has not been proved; and where the suspect's capacity to provide information about the alleged threat is assumed (possibly reasonably) but not independently tested. It is, in short, a recipe for precisely the abuse of power which Landau found *had* been perpetrated in the Nafsu case which led to the appointment of the Landau Commission.[94]

Secondly, even if a genuine 'ticking bomb' situation were to arise, and force were to be used by the GSS (or any other security force) in order to obtain information to dispel the imminent threat, and even were that conduct by the security forces subsequently to be excused, that would not mean that the evidence derived from the exercise should be capable of being used, as Landau proposes, in criminal proceedings for a past crime. There is a difference between averting a future harm and punishing an old one. To allow evidence collected by force to be used in criminal proceedings would be to create an incentive *routinely* to apply coercive means to *all* suspects resisting interrogation.[95] It would also mean allowing the police to treat suspects in a way which, if done by others, would constitute a criminal offence—the objection which Lord Gardiner had to the interrogation methods in Northern Ireland.[96] It would mean licensing the police to use the very practices which the criminal-law and criminal-justice system is ostensibly designed to prevent. This could only mean bringing the system generally into contempt. For, were the use of force to be allowed to the police against citizens subject to the presumption of innocence wishing to preserve their right to remain silent, it would no longer be clear to citizens that their security was being safeguarded by the system. How would the behaviour of the security forces be distinguishable from that of criminals?

The Landau Commission does not approve giving interrogators *carte blanche* discretion over the level of force they may apply. That would irreparably pervert 'the image of the State as a law-abiding polity which preserves the rights of the citizen'[97] (it is interesting to note that it is the 'image' and not the 'reality' of the law-abiding State which is said to be risked). First, there must not be disproportionate pressure: it 'must never reach the level of physical torture or maltreatment of the suspect or grievous harm to his honour which deprives him of his human dignity'. Secondly, 'the possible use of less serious measures must be weighed against the degree of anticipated danger, according to the information in the possession of the interrogator'. Thirdly, the permitted physical and

---

[94] Landau Commission (1987), para 2.7.

[95] See Zuckerman, A (1989) 'Coercion and Judicial Ascertainment of Truth', 24 Is LR 364.

[96] See above, 37–9.   [97] Landau Commission (1987), para 3.16.

psychological means of pressure must be defined and regulated, and breaches of conduct strictly sanctioned.[98]

Precisely what means of pressure the Landau Commission has approved we do not know, but they:

should principally take the form of non-violent psychological pressure through a vigorous and extensive interrogation, with the use of stratagems, including acts of deception. However, when these do not attain their purpose, the exertion of a moderate measure of physical pressure cannot be avoided.[99]

In that part of their *Report* that has been published the Landau Commission assures their readers: 'That it is certain that the substance of the means of pressure permitted . . . is less severe than the "techniques" which occupied the British Commissions of Inquiry that considered the methods of the war against terrorism in Northern Ireland'.[100] It should also be noted that in one of the scandals which prompted the setting up of the Landau Commission, the Izzat Nafsu case, the appellant alleged his interrogators had committed acts of violence which included:

pulling his hair, shaking him, throwing him to the ground, kicks, slaps and insults. He was ordered to strip and was sent to take a shower with cold water. He was prevented from sleeping for hours at a stretch, during the day but chiefly at night, and was forced to stand in the yard of the prison premises for long hours also when he was not being interrogated'.[101]

Following their investigation Nafsu's GSS interrogators 'admitted the validity of most of Nafsu's claims . . . concerning the means of pressure exerted on him, with the exception of his contentions regarding blows and slaps' and said that in using the means of pressure which they admitted they had not gone beyond the methods approved in GSS directives at the time.[102] The limited discussion in the Landau Report of the admitted GSS methods suggests that Nafsu's interrogators were judged to have overstepped the mark not in using the methods separately but 'in combination': that was, according to the Commission's understanding, what the European Court had found made the five techniques 'inhuman and degrading' in the Northern Ireland case. It was in the words of the original Israel Supreme Court's judgment 'the combined weight of their actions' that rendered the GSS investigators' actions impermissible.[103]

It would seem to follow, therefore, that among the pressure techniques previously employed and approved by the GSS, and now approved by the Landau Commission—methods of interrogation 'which are largely to be defended, both morally and legally',[104] and to be used separately if not in combination—are: sleep deprivation; physical shaking; stripping

---

[98] ibid.   [99] ibid, para 4.7.   [100] ibid, para 4.13.   [101] ibid, para 2.2.
[102] ibid, paras 2.4–2.5.   [103] ibid, para 3.22.   [104] ibid, para 1.8.

naked; exposure to cold water; and prolonged standing (it is not clear whether this involves being made to stand in the sun). Moreover, elsewhere in their report the Landau Commission specifically indicate tolerance, if not approval, of the use of 'blackmail and threats' against suspects[105] and report, this time critically, that prisoners are held by the GSS in 'dark cells without sufficient lighting or ventilation'.[106] Whether such pressure techniques are likely to be employed *without* being accompanied by occasional slaps, kicks, and other blows—what is an interrogator to do if a suspect fails physically to comply with the modes of physical pressure that are approved?—is a question on which it is scarcely necessary to comment.

What is clear is that the use of coercive techniques which it seems probable the Landau Commission approved, but about the precise nature of which the Commission was so coy, are prominent among the techniques regularly documented and complained about by both Israeli and international human rights agencies. B'Tselem, the Israeli Information Centre for Human Rights in the Occupied Territories, has systematically collated allegations and evidence of ill-treatment from a variety of historical sources, as well as interviewing a sample of recently released and detained prisoners about their interrogation and the period leading up to their interrogation.[107] According to the B'Tselem review, complaints about the use of violence by the Israeli authorities, particularly the GSS, began to appear in the late 1960s and were given international prominence by a series of articles in a British newspaper, the *Sunday Times*, in 1977. It was said that 'repeated cold showers, beatings and electric shock' were being used to extract confessions.[108] The allegations and stories increased in the early 1980s, though it is noticeable that Amnesty International, in its 1984 review, did not use the word 'torture' to describe the methods allegedly then being used. Some Palestinians, during or preceding interrogation, were said to:

have been hooded, handcuffed and forced to stand without moving for many hours at a time for several days, and have been exposed while naked to cold showers or cold air ventilators for long periods of time. Detainees have also been deprived of food, sleep and toilet and medical facilities, and have been subjected to abuse, insults and threats against themselves and the female members of their families.[109]

At about the same time, al-Haq, a Palestinian Human Rights organization, reported the use of physical disorientation by hooding and/or extended isolation in dirty and wet cells, beatings, repeated cold showers,

---

[105] Landau Commission (1987), para 4.20.

[106] ibid, para 2.60. The Commission recommended that these cells should be 'outfitted with reasonable lighting and proper ventilation . . . if possible daylight should be made to enter them' (para 4.9).

[107] B'Tselem (1991); B'Tselem (1992).   [108] B'Tselem (1991), 32.

[109] Amnesty International (1984), 234.

being forced to stand for long periods, food and sleep deprivation, and various forms of psychological humiliation.[110] When it became apparent that the *Intifada*, (which began in December 1987) was to be a prolonged protest, reports of more severe methods began to appear. In its 1989 Annual Report al-Haq described the following practices:

'Al-Shabah' (tying the detainee's hands in front or behind his body with plastic or metal cuffs. He is blindfolded or his head is covered to the neck with sacking with only a slit left open to breath. He stands in this position in an open yard, or sometimes with his hands tied to a pole, for several days during which he is interrogated for several hours each day); inadequate food; sleep deprivation (sometimes for up to a week) and restriction of toilet facilities; beating (with clubs, fists or boots, sometimes on the genitals or head, sometimes banging the head on the wall); the 'cupboard' (being placed in a closed dark space, some one meter by one meter for hours or days); partial suffocation (by pressure on the windpipe or by placing sacks on the head and pressing them against the nose and mouth); 'falaqa' (beating the soles of the feet with a stick or plastic hose, usually while the detainee is handcuffed and hooded).[111]

During this period there were also reports of the use of electric shocks and suspension.[112]

B'Tselem's survey of current and released prisoners in 1990–1 revealed that an estimated 20 per cent of Palestinian detainees in the Occupied Territories had undergone 'intensive interrogation' at the hands of the GSS.[113] The authors of the resulting report did not find the distinction between physical and psychological methods helpful: different forms of pressure, including poor conditions of detention, were being employed in combination or in sequence to soften up the suspect. It was more helpful, B'Tselem argued, to talk of 'verbal', 'conditioning', and 'physical' techniques all of which were designed gradually to weaken and demoralize the suspect so as to 'arouse feelings of helplessness (when) facing the omnipotent interrogator'.[114] The survey revealed that the following techniques were being extensively employed:

- insults and abuse;
- threats to the detainee (including use of severe methods of torture such as electric shock) or his family (particularly female members);
- prolonged deprivation of sleep and food;
- prolonged confinement in small closets or cold cells without light;
- tying up for prolonged periods in 'stress' positions—'al-Shabah' (hands behind the back and raised above the head tied to a wall fitting) or the 'banana' (hands and wrists tied to the legs on either side of the stool over which the victim is bent backwards;

[110] Reported in B'Tselem (1991), 33. [111] Quoted in ibid, 35.
[112] ibid, 35–6. [113] ibid, 45. [114] ibid, 54.

- treating victims as if they are collaborators in front of fellow prisoners, or placing prisoners with collaborators between interrogation sessions;
- forced physical exercises;
- water—drenching prisoners or placing them beneath dripping or running gutters or taps;
- hooding or 'sacking' (often with foul-smelling sacks);
- beating with fists or implements.

Many of these methods were employed simultaneously. For example, prisoners would be tied up and hooded, in confined spaces, for prolonged periods without food, when it was also difficult or impossible for them to sleep.[115] A year later B'tselem found that the pattern of ill-treatment was much the same.[116] Three years later an international investigation recorded similar findings, though the evidence pointed to a further shift away from crude physical methods towards more prolonged use of techniques designed to exhaust and wear down the suspect.[117]

The evidence points, therefore, to the Landau Commission having ruled against, and the GSS having to some extent abandoned, harsher physical forms of ill-treatment, methods which would unequivocally be condemned as torture—electric shock, *falaka*, and suspension—and the approval and use of more subtle forms of ill-treatment—threats, abuse, psychological stress, and physical exhaustion—applied over longer periods. The Landau Commission and the Israeli authorities claim these methods to be justified and necessary, to fall short of torture, and to be compatible with Israeli law and Israel's international obligations.

At the time of writing, however, there is evidence that use of these, and more brutal, methods continues, as does the threat to which they are the approved response. In October 1994 twenty-two people were killed in a Tel Aviv bus by a Palestinian suicide bomber who belonged to *Hamas*, the armed group opposed to a settlement with Israel regarding the occupied territories. The Ministerial Committee set up in the wake of the Landau Commission to oversee GSS activities allowed GSS interrogators an 'exceptional dispensation' to use increased physical pressures on suspects.[118] In November 1995 Israeli Prime Minister Yitzhak Rabin was assassinated by an orthodox Jewish extremist opposed to the peace process for which Rabin had largely been responsible. In late February 1996 a spate of suicide bombing attacks killed almost sixty civilians in public places in Jerusalem. Responsibility was claimed by *Hamas*.

---

[115] Reported in B'tselem (1991), 56–74.   [116] B'Tselem (1992).

[117] Human Rights Watch (1994) *Torture and Ill-Treatment: Israel's Interrogation of Palestinians from the Occupied Territories* (New York: Human Rights Watch), ch 3.

[118] Amnesty International (1996c) '*Under constant medical supervision: torture, ill-treatment and the health professions in Israel and the Occupied Territories*' (London: Amnesty International, International Secretariat), 3.

In 1995–6 several attempts were made in the Knesset to legalize 'oppressive questioning' which critics maintain amounts to, or spills over into, torture. In autumn 1995 a committee headed by the Attorney General set up to incorporate the United Nations Convention Against Torture into Israeli Law, for example, proposed that an amendment be made to Article 277 of the Israel Penal Law so as to define torture as 'pain and suffering except for pain or suffering inherent in interrogation procedures or punishment according to law'.[119] In January 1996 a *Proposed Law of the General Security Service 1996* incorporated approval of 'pressure' against suspects in the course of interrogation in circumstances 'to prevent actual danger to the security of the state' when 'no other reasonable way exists to prevent said danger'. The pressure should not cause 'severe pain or suffering' or be 'cruel or inhumane', which of course the methods secretly approved by the Landau Commission are alleged not to be.[120] Domestic and international protests have so far led to this legislation being reconsidered. There is abundant evidence that hooding, sleep deprivation, *shabeh* (being forced to adopt painful prolonged physical-stress positions), and violent shaking continue to be used, however. Indeed, it now seems clear that violent shaking by the suspect's collar was approved by Landau and continues to be approved by the Ministerial Committee, though shaking by holding the shoulders is disapproved.[121] In April 1995, a Palestinian suspected of being a member of *Hamas* died, according to the subsequent autopsy, of a brain haemorrhage as a result of being violently shaken by his interrogators.[122] Yet in August 1995 the Ministerial Committee overseeing the GSS aproved the continued use of shaking, provided it was authorized by the head of the GSS, and in January 1996 the Israel Supreme Court rescinded an injunction preventing further use of physical force, including shaking, on another suspect who had allegedly been tortured and confessed to placing bombs but who, according to GSS might have additional information.[123] Meanwhile the police forces of the Palestinian Authority, presided over by Yasser Arafat and under pressure from Israel and internationally to suppress *Hamas* activity, have since 1994 repeatedly been accused of using the same and more brutal methods of torture including: burning with electric elements and cigarettes; beating while suspended from a hook; beating with electric cables; and dropping molten plastic on the body. There have been several deaths in custody here also.[124]

---

[119] Amnesty International (1996a), 185.
[120] Amnesty International (1996c), 3.   [121] ibid, 12.
[122] Amnesty International (1995b) *Death by shaking: the case of 'Abd al-Samad Harizat* (London: Amnesty International, International Secretariat).
[123] Abd al-Halim Belbaysi, see Amnesty International (1996c), 12.
[124] Amnesty International (1996b), 16–22.

4 CONCLUSIONS: CLASSICAL AND CONTEMPORARY TORTURE

If the practice of torture by the state and its servants can in no circumstances be justified or condoned, how are we to characterize torture in the late twentieth century? How does it differ from the torture of former times? Certain general themes emerge from the historical account presented in Chapter 1 and the three case studies recounted above.

First, torture has been used and is used by the state for a variety of purposes. Though some of the aims that inform torture today are identical to those of the torturers of the ancient world, others are different and the balance of aims appears to have shifted. When torture is used in the service of terror, for example—and this is very much a feature of the modern totalitarian state—the purpose appears to be as much to send out a message to the population generally as to elicit a response from the individual victim.

Secondly, torture is intimately bound up with punishment. It is not merely that some writers discuss torture incidental to the investigatory process in the same breath as they speak of the character of judicial punishment—the corporality of both processes in Western Europe up to the end of the eighteenth century,[125] and the continuation of that tradition in countries like Iran up to the present day[126]—but, as we saw from the Roman-canonical tradition, what it has been thought acceptable to do to a suspect pre-trial is intimately tied up with the gravity of the alleged offence and the likely penalty. That close legal connection has in recent times been largely severed, but it has not disappeared. Many countries, including Britain and Israel, have special statutory provisions governing the detention of persons suspected of what is regarded as the particularly grave offence of terrorism. But even where there is no longer a legal connection, the moral link may still be made by practitioners. Whatever the law books may say, desert is not a concept only reserved for those persons who stand formally convicted. Police investigators claim to 'know' who the guilty are and in some jurisdictions feel they have a mandate—indeed are expected by the people—to dispense summary justice, albeit in the guise of criminal investigation.[127]

Thirdly, and closely connected with the preceding point, the use of torture is generally status-related. In Ancient Greece and Rome the original doctrine was that only slaves or foreigners could be tortured, or persons

---

[125] Foucault (1977).   [126] See Rejali (1994).

[127] In India, for example, it is claimed that: 'Members of the public complained against those police officers who did not torture or beat up suspects, adding that these officers were not making a serious effort to detect crime; giving up these methods would result in deterioration of the law and order situation, and crime would go up; and criminals would escape punishment in a large number of cases'. Misra, S (1986) *Police Brutality: An Analysis of Police Behaviour* (New Delhi), 49.

whose suspected crimes were so heinous that they were of little worth, scarcely human. In the United States, if the evidence placed before the Wickersham Commission is any guide, African-Americans were particularly vulnerable to the worst forms of the 'third degree', especially in the Southern States where racism borne of slavery was a powerful force.[128] In post-Revolutionary Russia, counter-revolutionaries—persons suffering from false consciousness—were vulnerable. Under fascism, in Hitler's Germany from the beginning and in Italy under Mussolini from 1938, those not considered racially pure were vulnerable. In Algeria French soldiers were taught not to think of Arabs as humans.[129] In South Africa the same doctrine prevailed during the *apartheid* years. To torture, as Scarry has argued, is to deny humanity, to reduce a person to being merely a body,[130] a bundle of 'muscles and sinews' in Beccaria's phrase, a person without voice. It follows that when those responsible for certain crimes are casually described as 'animals' or 'beasts', we should beware: for these terms are assigned to those outcasts, or lesser beings, to whom, in the eyes of some, anything may morally be done.

Fourthly, the use and nature of torture is closely related to the changing character of the state and the relationship of citizens to the state. This is not just a question of citizens' rights, but of ideology. It is also a question of power. In the pre-industrial world the body of the accused was literally placed at the disposal of the master, the lord, or the sovereign but when, during the industrial revolution, the modern state emerged with its accompanying doctrines of citizens' rights and the social contract, submission so corporeal and seemingly capricious was deemed inappropriate. The Age of Reason involved the formation of rule-governed discipline the locus of which was the mind rather than the body of the accused. It was now the trial rather than the initial exmination and the punishment which became the ritual focus. In the twentieth century, however, states have accrued powers and technologies of control undreamt of in the eighteenth century. This has opened up vistas of exploitation by the state for which the founders of liberal state-constitutions were unprepared. But those same technologies have enabled weak and liberal states to be challenged in an unprecedented fashion. And, as we have seen from the examples of Algeria, Northern Ireland, and Israel/Palestine, much contemporary torture is integral to the process whereby the authority of the state is contested. States and counter-states vie for power. The overweening state may be used as a mechanism to oppress its citizens, but equally, organised groups—ideological, ethnic, religious, linguistic, tribal, or regionally based—may also employ torture as part of a strategy of terror in their bids for state power.

[128] See Chapter 1, pp. 14–16. [129] Maran (1989). [130] Scarry (1984).

Our purpose in this and the preceding chapter has been implicitly to argue that if torture is to be prevented it must first be understood. And any evaluation of the effectiveness of a preventive mechanism—the purpose of this study—needs to be grounded in a realistic appraisal of the nature of that which is to be prevented. In Chapter 3, as part of an account of the proscription of torture in international law, we shall necessarily pay close attention to the definition in law of torture and the closely related concept of 'inhuman or degrading treatment or punishment'. But before doing so we need to summarize how torture in the post-industrial world differs from that in the ancient and pre-industrial world.

First, torture used to be a legitimate judicial procedure. We shall call this classical torture. Torture was not used everywhere, in all periods, and in all jurisdictions. But until the Enlightenment, despite widespread doubts about its reliability, judicial torture was a generally approved method for eliciting information from persons against whom there were well-founded suspicions that either they or their associates were guilty of crimes of thought or deed, secular or religious. This is no longer the case. Today torture is nowhere regarded, officially at least, as a legitimate judicial procedure for eliciting the truth. Constitutions outlaw the practice. The criminal law generally punishes it. The courts are almost everywhere required to exclude evidence collected by means of pressure generally considered to render that evidence unsafe. Torture is so excoriated that allegations that it has been used are generally denied in the most vigorous terms.

This is generally the official legal position. Just beneath the surface, however, there is clearly a view, prevalent in many jurisdictions among security and police personnel, that torture, or means of physical or psychological pressure that we may term *near-torture*, may have to be resorted to in certain circumstances. These circumstances are held to be abnormal and may involve a degree of desperation on the part of the security forces, as when, for example, the integrity of the state, or public safety, is said to be seriously threatened by offenders who are highly organized and engaged in activities involving grave harm (terrorism and drug trafficking, for example) or when individuals, particularly hardened repeat offenders, are suspected of very serious offences exciting public alarm. In these circumstances the pressure on the security services to get 'results' is great and, in the short term at least, the security services may feel that they are unable to succeed without resort to methods going beyond the 'normal', legal, and officially approved.

In most jurisdictions politicians are from time to time exhorted by security and police personnel to give their services room for manoeuvre such that pressure can more effectively be brought to bear on these classes of allegedly abnormal suspects. The room for manoeuvre sought typically involves additional time to question suspects before the judicial authorities are brought into play. It also involves the exclusion from places of detention—exclusion justified on grounds of security—of other persons and agencies (lawyers, monitors, personal visitors) and the removal of any obligation to divulge information to third persons as to the nature or progress of the investigation.

Whatever rules govern the room for manoeuvre granted to the security services, they are likely to be exceeded whenever the prevailing 'police culture' judges it necessary and morally justified; what one sociologist of the police has termed the 'law of inevitable increment—whatever powers the police have they will exceed by a given margin'.[131] If corners are cut and pressures applied, they will subsequently be denied and in some jurisdictions the authorities, executive and judicial,[132] may turn a Nelsonian blind eye to these 'noble cause' excesses.[133] In jurisdictions where such tolerance by the authorities is generally displayed, or where effective mechanisms for judicial and independent scrutiny of police procedure are lacking, it is probable that short cuts will be taken and pressures applied to suspects generally. A culture of police violence may develop, particularly in environments where police resources are poor, police training is rudimentary, where the police enjoy little public regard, and where their professional culture is largely undeveloped. Moreover, in jurisdictions without serious pretensions to democracy and public acountability the security forces may politically be cultivated as an instrument of the state entirely subservient to the interests of the ruling political elite. In such jurisictions more cynical use is likely to be made of the legal prohibition of torture. The prohibition may be no more than a legal or constitutional fig-leaf.

The second distinction, therefore, between the classical and modern practice of torture is that whereas formerly torture was an avowed and open practice, it is now secret and denied.[134] In ancient times and in the Roman-canonical tradition the practice of torture may have been subject to doubt, but there was no reason to be ashamed of its use. It was a normal and acknowledged aspect of procedure. The torturer may have

---

[131] Reiner, R (1981) 'The politics of police power' in *Politics and Power 4: Law Politics and Justice* (London: Routledge), 38.

[132] Members of the legal and medical professions may also be complicit. See, for example, Raynor, M (1987) *Turning a Blind Eye?: Medical Accountability and the Prevention of Torture in South Africa* (Washington DC: Committee on Scientific Freedom and Responsibility); British Medical Association (1992) *Medicine Betrayed: The Participation of Doctors in Human Rights Abuses* (London: BMA/Zed Books); Physicians for Human Rights (1996) *Torture in Turkey and Its Unwilling Accomplices* (Boston, Mass: Physicians for Human Rights).

[133] For references to so-called 'noble cause' corruption see Morgan, R (1996) 'The process is the rule and the punishment is the process', 59 MLR 306.

[134] See Cohen, S (1993) 'Human Rights and Crimes of the State: The Culture of Denial', 26 *Australian and New Zealand Journal of Criminology*, 87.

plied his trade in the darkest recesses of forbidding dungeons, but where
that was the case, it was an integral part of the torture process, designed,
like the instruments of torture themselves, to be part of the menace. That
a suspect should be 'put to the question' was a public decision and the
answers given following torture were formally recorded in documents
designed to be made public.

This is no longer the case. Torture is not acknowledged. The instruments of torture are hidden and their existence disclaimed. Places of torture are inaccessible, not to increase the terror—though they do of course
serve that purpose, and the physical and social isolation of victims is part
of the design—but because they *may not* be known. What is done may
not be seen or heard. There must be no spectators, no witnesses. Indeed,
the most potent threat in the hands of the contemporary torturer is that:
"No one will hear your cry. No one knows that you are here. No one cares
whether you live or die. No one will ever know."[135]—a threat that the
power of the secretive state can all too often make true. In states employing terror as a systematic instrument of political power, the reputation
that particular police locations may have, and the fate of those who enter
them, may become an integral part of the process of terror. The secrecy
surrounding reputed places of torture in totalitarian states becomes a
manifestation of the invincibility of state control. But, generally speaking,
the reality will be denied. Terror is served by rumour, uncertainty, and
insecurity—the threat of an unknown menace. Torture may be the preamble to extra-judicial execution or disappearance, the torture chamber
the ante-room to a void.[136]

Thirdly, because classical torture was an acknowledged judicial process it was also rule-governed. There was a jurisprudence of torture. The
rules may not always have been followed, but they were there to be
appealed to. The process could legally be challenged. And because the
use of torture was open and rule-governed the wisdom and morality of
employing torture could be and was publicly debated. In ancient Greece
and Rome, and again during the Middle Ages, leading commentators
discussed the rules and wisdom of torture. They questioned the rules
or made recommendations as to their judicial interpretation. This is no
longer the case. The orthodoxy of human rights, combined with political
hypocricy, has made torture and its discussion taboo, except by way of
simple condemnation. The culture of denial and secrecy has driven the
practical rationale for and rationalization of torture underground. It cannot realistically be discussed because it is said that there is nothing to

---

[135] See Millett (1994).
[136] See Amnesty International (1994) *'Disappearances' and Political Killings: Human Rights
Crisis of the 1990s—A Manual for Action* (London: Amnesty International, International
Secretariat).

discuss. Allegations of torture are generally dismissed as propagandist disinformation. Practically no one defends torture. Torture, like sin, is not something to which anyone owns up. Torture is generally held to be an issue only in far-off places, where political regimes conspicuously not members of the civilized club are said to be more or less immune to democratic or human rights reasoning. Or it is said to be a problem in precariously balanced polities where it may not be wise too robustly to pursue a human rights critique on the grounds that greater political instability may be the consequence.[137] Or, as in most developed democracies, torture is said not to be a structural issue, only the product of the occasional rotten apple in an otherwise clean law enforcement barrel. Likewise the relationship between developed and the developing economies is generally judged irrelevant. Responsibility lies elsewhere. There is virtually no debate—only orthodox arms-length condemnation.

This is the most remarkable aspect of the Israeli Landau Commission: that it existed. That the issue of torture or near-torture was discussed and at least part of that discussion published. Yet even in the case of Israel the issue was not fully and openly discussed. The evidence made available to the Landau Commission was not publicly disclosed. There was no independent expert appraisal of the evidence provided to the Commission by the security services. The regulatory code employed by the security services for the conduct of interrogation of terrorist suspects was not revealed, and the practical recommendations of the Landau Commission itself were kept secret. And in any case, as the Commission repeatedly emphasized, that which was being discussed and condoned was not torture, only a process euphemistically termed 'moderate physical pressure', designed to break down the resistance of suspects, but neither inhuman nor degrading.

It is the culture of denial and the absence of debate that makes contemporary as opposed to classical torture the more difficult to combat. Torture in the late twentieth century is a will-o'-the-wisp. In the same way that the abolition of capital punishment was made more difficult to achieve once executions were removed from the public domain—such that civic sensibilities were no longer directly engaged—so torture now is hidden from sight and comment. There is no torture discourse. Torture is the imaginary product of radical dissent. It is the outcome of carefully engineered propaganda designed to discredit the state. It is the child of rumour and disinformation or, more charitably, misinformation. It is the vindictive allegation of those who—morally, politically, and legally—are said not to deserve an audience or to be believed.

---

[137] See, for example, the discussion on preserving democracy in Cohen, S (1995) 'State Crimes of Previous Regimes: Knowledge, Accountability and the Policing of the Past', 20 *Law and Social Inquiry*, 7.

All of which means that torture or near-torture can no longer easily be regulated. Because it cannot be acknowledged torture nowadays lies within the discretionary power of those agents of the state the security-sensitivity of whose work is said to warrant more or less unaccountable and privileged secret space. It is for this reason, paradoxically, that contemporary torture may be unrestrained and may involve any number of methods.[138] Paradoxical because, prompted by the fearsome instruments of torture preserved in our museums, we have come to think of torture in the classical period as unrestrainedly savage. But it was not so. It was undoubtedly cruel. It could involve seemingly unendurable pain. But it was not savage in the sense of being untamedly ferocious: it was a carefully-regulated practice. Today there can be no proper regulation of the practice which may be restrained only by the personal sensibility of the torturers.

It follows also that the use of torture can no longer easily be discovered, let alone monitored. Nor can the justice and reasonableness of its application be gauged, because justice and reasonableness are no longer deemed appropriate terms to use in relation to torture. Thus torture may be applied arbitrarily, indiscriminately, or disproportionately, without cause that any external observer might judge reasonable. For the classical jurisprudential discourse of torture is banned, even if the situations that continue to give rise to the thoughts and the practices are not. And the discourse may not be permitted to re-emerge, because to do so would legitimate that which is officially deemed illegitimate. An exercise like the Landau Commission is unlikely to be repeated.

Fourthly, it follows that the methods of torture have generally changed. The technology of contemporary torture has largely been removed from the medieval museum of horrors. It generally lies more in the psychological manipulation of feelings of powerlessness and despair than the physical tearing of bodies. It leaves few visible marks. Because torture must be and is denied, it must be deniable.

Classical torture, because it was an acknowledged rule-governed judicial process, was a ritualistic procedure. The instruments of torture were explicitly designed for the task: an assault on the body to extract the essence of the truth that lay therein. It was hoped that the mere sight of the instruments, terrifying and functionally unmistakable, and the location where they were to be applied, often a dedicated and planned environment, would suffice. Proportionate bodily pain, swiftly imposed—clamping or searing the flesh, stretching the muscles or sinews—was the avowed purpose of the exercise. Further, though the rules discouraged modes of torture which thereafter rendered the body useless, the fundemental illogicality

---

[138] See Foucault (1977).

of this aspect of the process made practitioners careless of the admonition. But there was no question of hiding the process of torture, of leaving the body unmarked or of considering the more subtle consequences of designedly painful experience.

Nowadays torture remains typically crude and, contrary to some contemporary commentary,[139] the purpose of much torture remains narrowly instrumental—to gain information or force an admission of guilt—the focus being where it always has been: on the body, the nerve pathways, as a way into the head. But because torture is no longer judicially approved, because it must be hidden and denied, torture is no longer conspicuously ritualistic. Specific and unambiguous instruments of torture are generally avoided, unless the torture is to be conducted in environments without risk of instrusion by potentially critical appraisers, a facility seldom availiable in democratic jurisdictions or states fully participating in the burgeoning world of international inspection. Today, therefore, the means of torture are usually mundane and familiar: everyday objects, ambiguous, inconspicuous, unobjectionable. When blows from fists or feet will not suffice, standard handcuffs will secure the victim, a telephone directory may be used to strike the head, a conventional police baton used to beat the soles of the feet, or a supermarket plastic bag employed to cover the face. These methods can be applied anywhere, in cells or corridors, storerooms, conventional police offices, or station washrooms. They may even be used away from designated police sites: arrestees may be taken into the country, hung from a tree, or beaten on a piece of waste ground, their detention unrecorded, their contact with the security forces leaving no paper trace. Many methods, moreover, can be used so as to leave few or no marks on the body, or marks the origins of which are ambiguous, easily disclaimed, or said to have been acquired legitimately —the product of a scuffle when the suspect resisted arrest or injuries self-inflicted by malevolent complainants. Moreover, the cries of victims can be drowned by a portable radio or television, the presence of which is said to be for the detainees' entertainment or comfort.

Even more difficult to discern and prove after the event are those favoured psychological tactics designed to wear suspects down: deprivation of sleep, threats against family or loved ones, incessant interrogative harrassment, petty humiliations, disorienting noise, bright lights, blindfolding or hooding, low or high cell temperatures, prolonged isolation in dark or otherwise sensory deprived circumstances, use of physically stressful constant standing or crouching while handcuffed to a pipe or radiator. These stresses can be made to appear almost incidental to the fact of legal custody itself. If the custody is *incommunicado*, a provision

[139] *Contra* Peters (1996).

often permitted under emergency anti-terrorist or anti-organized-crime legislation, then the incremental piling of one psychological assault upon another can be achieved without resort to cruder more immediate visceral methods leaving their tell-tale somatic traces.

Fifthly, and finally, whereas prior to the development of the modern state torture was a specific, discrete, relatively well-defined process involving the individual suspect and the judicial authority, it is nowadays more likely to comprise merely one tactic in the overarching politics of state control and organized counter-state opposition. In this context it is not so much the individual who is being worked on by the torturer but rather the member of a group, the purpose of the torture being as much to break the ring or send a message to a community, constituency, or cadre. The torture may be part of a seamless web of police surveillance and intelligence gathering, group harrassment and penetration or, in extreme cases, terror—extra-judicial execution and disappearance. Even when no information is elicited, it may be said that it was forthcoming, the purpose being to prise open tight-knit groups and sow seeds of mistrust. Similar tactics may be employed against agents of the state by opposition groups, or they may be deployed among whole communities whose loyalties are divided and whose support base is being sought, if necessary through processes of intimidation. Where these conditions prevail torture is no longer a narrowly instrumental individual process. It is a form of governance, an integral part of government through terror. In these circumstances the potency of torture, wherever it is used widely, lies as much in its anticipation as in its reality. One never knows when the knock on the door may come. In this form torture can be seen in its most insidious form, subversive of democratic participation and political organization *per se*, the most fundamental enemy of civil society.

3

The Prohibition of Torture and Inhuman or Degrading Treatment or Punishment

1 THE WEB OF PROHIBITION: AN OVERVIEW

The prohibition of torture and inhuman or degrading treatment or punishment is probably the most well attested in the entire human rights catalogue. Article 5 of the Universal Declaration of Human Rights (UDHR) proclaims that:

No one shall be subjected to torture or to cruel, inhuman or degrading treatment or punishment.

Although the UDHR is not itself a direct source of legal obligation, the UN Commission on Human Rights used this wording when drafting what became Article 7 of the UN International Covenant on Civil and Political Rights[1] which has now been ratified by 140 states.[2] Article 3 of the European Convention on Human Rights, Article 5(2) of the Inter-American Convention on Human Rights, and Article 5 of the African Charter on Human and Peoples Rights also draw upon the wording of the UDHR and provide further evidence of the universal condemnation of torture and ill treatment.

In 1975 the UN General Assembly adopted, by consensus, Resolution 3542 (XXX), the 'Declaration on the Protection of All Persons from being Subjected to Torture and other Cruel, Inhuman or Degrading Treatment or Punishment'. This was followed in 1984 by the UN Convention Against Torture and other Cruel, Inhuman or Degrading Treatment of Punishment, which has now attracted 104 ratifications.[3] The Organization of American States has adopted the Inter-American Convention to Prevent and Punish Torture, whilst the Council of Europe has adopted the European Convention for the Prevention of Torture and Inhuman or

---

[1] This provoked comparatively little discussion, although the UK pressed for the removal of the word 'cruel', thus harmonizing the text with Article 3 of the ECHR, whilst the Philippines suggested the inclusion of 'unusual', treatment or punishment. See Bossuyt, MJ (1987) *Guide to the 'Travaux Préparatoires' of the International Covenant on Civil and Political Rights* (Dordrecht: Martinus Nijhoff), 151.

[2] As at 31 December 1997.   [3] As at 31 December 1997.

Degrading Treatment or Punishment. Other standard-setting documents promulgated by the UN presuppose the prohibition of torture.[4]

In consequence it is generally accepted that the prohibition of torture has passed into customary international law[5] and, as such, applies to all states irrespective of whether they have become a party to a particular international instrument. This view has been endorsed by decisions in a number of domestic jurisdictions, including the landmark US case of *Filártiga v Peña-Irala*[6] and, more recently, *Kadic v Karadzic*.[7] Other US decisions have gone further and expressed the view that acts of official torture violated norms of *ius cogens*.[8] In England and Wales, the Courts also indicated that the prohibition of torture is a norm of *ius cogens* in *Al Adsani v The Government of Kuwait*.[9] Indeed, torture was included by the International Law Commission (ILC) in the list of matters over which the projected International Criminal Court would be able to exercise jurisdiction if, in a given case, the conduct alleged amounted to 'an exceptionally serious crime of international concern'.[10]

Accepting that the prohibition does indeed have such a status is, however, little more than a gateway into a series of procedural and definitional difficulties which adds further complexity to the intricate

[4] These include the UN Standard Minimum Rules for the Treatment of Prisoners (ECOSOC Res 663 C (XXIV), 31 July 1957 and Res 2076 (LXII), adopted 13 May 1977), the Code of Conduct for Law Enforcement Officials (GA Res 34/169, adopted 19 December 1979), the Principles of Medical Ethics Relevant to the Role of Health Personnel, Particularly Physicians, in the Protection of Prisoners and Detainees Against Torture and Other Cruel, Inhuman or Degrading Treatment or Punishment (GA Res 37/194, 1982) and the Body of Principles for the Protection of All Persons Under Any Form of Detention or Imprisonment (GA Res 43/173, 1988). Finally, the 1993 Vienna Declaration and Programme of Action adopted at the UN Conference on Human Rights further emphasized that 'one of the most atrocious violations against human dignity is the act of torture' (A/CONF 157/23, para 55). The Vienna Declaration devotes 8 of its 100 paragraphs (paras 54–61) to the freedom from torture. It also stated that torture and other cruel, inhuman, or degrading treatment or punishment constituted serious obstacles to the full enjoyment of all human rights (para 30).

[5] Rodley, N (1987) *The Treatment of Prisoners Under International Law* (Oxford: Clarendon Press), 63–70; Meron, T (1989) *Human Rights and Humanitarian Norms as Customary International Law* (Oxford: Clarendon Press), 94–5.

[6] 630 F 2d 876 (2d Cir 1980), 77 ILR 169.

[7] 70 F 3d 232 (2d Cir 1995), 104 ILR 136. For comment see Posner, TR (1996) 'Note: Kadic v. Karadzic', 90 AJIL 658. See also *Tel-Oren v Libyan Arab Republic*, 726 F 2d 744 (DC Cir 1984), 77 ILR 192; *Forti v Suarez-Mason*, 672 F Supp 1531 (ND Cal 1987), 95 ILR 624, *Xuncax v Gramajo*, 866 F Supp 162 (1995), 104 ILR 165.

[8] eg, *Committee of US Citizens Living in Nicaragua v Reagan*, 859 F 2d 929 (DC Cir 1988), 85 ILR 248; *Siderman de Blake v Republic of Argentina* 965 F 2d 699 (1992), 103 ILR 455.

[9] See the judgment of 21 January 1994, 100 ILR 465, in which the Court of Appeal granted leave to serve proceedings outside of the jurisdiction and (unreported) Judgment of 15 March 1995 by Mantell J (QBD), 103 ILR 420, and of 12 March 1996 (*The Times*, 29 March 1996). For comment see Marks, S (1997) 'Torture and the Jurisdictional Immunity of Foreign States', 56 CLJ 8.

[10] ILC Draft Statute for an International Criminal Court, Art 20(e) and Commentary, para (20), [1994] *ILCYB* Vol II, Pt 2, 41. See also Crawford, J (1994) 'The ILC Adopts a Draft Statute for an International Criminal Court', 88 AJIL 404, 412.

web of protective mechanisms that has developed in an incremental fashion over the last fifty years. The following sub-sections will sketch these developments.

(a) Customary international law

The UDHR was intended to be 'a common standard of achievement for all peoples and all nations' rather than a source of legal obligation. Two consequences flowed from this. First, a state would only become subject to an obligation concerning the prohibition of torture and ill-treatment if it subsequently chose to become a party to any legal instrument that might subsequently be drafted.[11] Secondly, since it did not oblige any state to do anything, the UDHR did not attempt to establish any mechanisms through which its standards could be enforced. If a state breaches customary international law in its dealings with another state, the state in breach is liable to the other state under the normal rules of state responsibility. The problem, however, is that if a state breaches customary international law by violating the human rights of its own citizens, there is no one other state that has had its particular interests violated. Either no other state has *locus standi* to bring an international claim against that state or else all other states have such a capacity.

Although international law has tended to eschew the possibility of states bringing an *actio popularis*, the International Court of Justice in the *Barcelona Traction* case identified 'the principles and rules concerning basic rights of the human person' as being obligations owed *erga omnes*, that is to say, 'obligations of a State towards the international community as a whole'.[12] It is widely accepted that Article 5 of the UDHR is an example of an obligation *erga omnes*,[13] and as such any state might seek to enforce it on the international plane. Whether this theoretical possibility is a significant addition to the list of tools at the disposal of the

[11] Strictly speaking, the UN Charter does not oblige member states to respect human rights. Rather, member States pledge to promote respect and observance of human rights and fundamental freedoms (UN Charter, Arts 55 and 56). Nevertheless, the International Court of Justice has expressed the opinion that, taken together, these articles amount to an obligation to observe and respect human rights. See *Legal Consequences for States of the Continued Presence of South Africa in Namibia (South West Africa) notwithstanding Security Council Resolution 276 (1970)*, Advisory Opinion, *ICJ Reports 1971*, p. 16 at paras 128–31.

[12] *Barcelona Traction* case, Judgment, ICJ Reports 1970, p. 3, paras 33–4. See also *East Timor (Portugal v Australia)*, Judgment, ICJ Reports 1995, p. 90, para 29 in which the principle of *erga omnes* obligations was again endorsed by the ICJ.

[13] See, for example, the Third Restatement of US Foreign Relations Law (1987), S 702 (d); Meron (1989), 188–208. Meron would also have included Article 10(1) of the ICCPR in the list. But cf Ragazzi, M (1997), *The Concept of International Obligations 'Erga Omnes'* (Oxford: Clarendon Press), 135–45 where there is a cautious approach to the extention of categories of *erga omnes* obligations beyond those expressly listed by the ICJ.

international community is questionable.[14] Certainly there is no evidence of such claims having been brought and the tendency is for this to take place either through the mechanisms developed by the UN or, when applicable, through the organs created by the various regional and international Conventions.

(b) The United Nations

The UN has two distinct spheres of competence. First, it has developed a number of 'Charter-based' mechanisms which allow the UN to exercise a degree of oversight as regards the human rights record of all member states, premised upon their Charter commitments. The procedure established under ECOSOC (the UN Economic and Social Council) Resolution 1503 (1970) enables a confidential examination to be conducted of communications which appear to reveal a consistent pattern of gross and reliably attested violations of human rights. Further, ECOSOC Resolution 1235 (1967) enables the UN Commission on Human Rights (CHR) to debate situations publicly and investigate them.[15] These procedures are of most use when systematic abuses of human rights are taking place as a matter of state policy. However, the confidential 1503 procedure is extremely cumbersome and has been the object of strong criticism. In contrast, the 1235 procedure continues to provide the CHR with the basis for mandating Working Groups or Special Rapporteurs, or requesting the UN Secretary General, to examine the human rights situation in a considerable number of countries, for debating their reports, and for adopting resolutions which are often extremely condemnatory. However, the decision to examine a situation under this procedure is more a statement of political denunciation by the international community than a means of seeking redress for violation.[16]

Another weapon in the UN armoury is its 'thematic mandates'. These have taken the form of either a working group or of a Special Rapporteur established by a resolution of the Commission to investigate and report back on particular human rights issues. A Special Rapporteur on Torture (SRT) was appointed in 1985. Although his mandate was originally limited to one year, it has subsequently been renewed for periods of three years, most recently in 1995.[17] The techniques used by the SRT include: requesting governments to provide information concerning individual

---

[14] See, for example, the doubts expressed by Higgins, R (1994), *Problems and Process: International Law and How We Use It* (Oxford: Clarendon Press), 57, n 3.

[15] Alston, P (1992b) 'The Commission on Human Rights' in Alston, P (ed) (1992a) *The United Nations and Human Rights* (Oxford: Clarendon Press), 156.

[16] For a measured assessment of the strengths and weaknesses of the 1503 and 1235 procedures, including a review of other commentators' opinions, see Alston (1992b), 145–73.

[17] See CHR Res 1995/37 B.

cases; issuing urgent appeals to governments concerning individuals allegedly being subjected to torture or at risk of torture; and, when invited, visiting countries to have consultations with the authorities and NGOs. Finally, the Annual Report presented by the SRT to the Commission is in itself a source of pressure upon states, since it places a mass of detail concerning individual cases in the public domain. It also makes it easy to see which countries respond to requests for information and appeals for urgent action, and allows the public to make their own judgments upon the matter.[18]

The second aspect of the UN's function concerns its relationship with treaty-based mechanisms, two of which merit particular attention here. The International Covenant on Civil and Political Rights (ICCPR) established the Human Rights Committee (HRC) to oversee the implementation of the obligations assumed by those states which became a party to it. All state parties are obliged to submit reports to the HRC on the measures they have adopted which give effect to the rights contained in the Covenant. The process of examining these Reports provides an opportunity for some rigorous examinations of particular situations[19] and, in common with other UN treaty monitoring bodies, the HRC now makes 'Concluding Observations' highlighting matters of particular concern and making recommendations. The HRC also issued a 'General Comment' on Articles 7 and 10(1)[20] of the ICCPR in 1982, subsequently updated in 1992, which set outs its understanding of what, in the eyes of the HRC, these provisions mean for state parties.

The HRC also has the capacity to consider 'communications' concerning alleged violations of a state's obligations under the Covenant. This procedure is dependant upon a state party to the Covenant declaring that it is willing for the Committee to consider a complaint made against it by another state that has made a similar declaration (under Article 41 of the Covenant) or by an individual (under the provisions of the First Optional Protocol to the Covenant). Although both these procedures are in force, no inter-state complaint has yet been brought. The HRC has,

---

[18] Peter Kooijmans was the first Special Rapporteur on Torture and he gave an insightful presentation of his work in Koojimans, PH (1991) 'The Role and Action of the UN Special Rapportuer on Torture' in Cassese, A (ed), *The International Fight Against Torture* (Baden-Baden: Nomos), 56. The current Rapporteur, Nigel Rodley, has also commented publicly on his work in Boyle, K (1995) 'Interview with Special Rapporteur on Torture Nigel Rodley', 13 *Neth Quart HR*, 43. For a general overview of the mandate see Alston (1992b), 177–9.

[19] See Opsahl, T (1992) 'The Human Rights Committee' in Alston (1992a), 397–419; McGoldrick, D (1991) *The Human Rights Committee* (Oxford: Clarendon Press), 44–104.

[20] Article 10(1) of the Covenant provides that 'All persons deprived of their liberty shall be treated with humanity and with respect for the inherent dignity of the human person'. This is seen as an extension of Article 7 (prohibiting torture, etc) and to form an element in a continuum.

however, received over 800 individual communications, many of which have concerned the application of Articles 7 and 10(1).

Although not an organ of the UN, the HRC is closely woven into its structures, being funded by it and serviced by the UN Secretariat, and it submits an Annual Report to the General Assembly through ECOSOC. The General Assembly also receives the Annual Report of the Committee Against Torture (CAT), the body established by the 1984 UN Convention Against Torture (UNCAT). Like the HRC, the CAT receives and considers reports submitted by state parties and, under optional procedures contained in Articles 21 and 22, communications from either states or from individuals respectively.[21] Unlike the HRC, the CAT can initiate investigations if it considers there to be 'reliable information which appears to it to contain well founded indications that torture is being systematically practised in the territory of a State party'.[22] This procedure is confidential but the CAT has the power to include a summary account of such an investigation in its Annual Report if it wishes.[23] It has done so twice, in relation to Turkey in 1993[24] and Egypt in 1996.[25] States may choose to opt out of this provision when becoming a party to the Convention.[26]

(c) Regional inter-governmental organizations

Regional human rights organizations have, like the UN, also devised systems and structures. The Inter-American Convention on Human Rights utilizes the Inter-American Commission on Human Rights set up by the Organization of American States (OAS) and establishes a Court of Human Rights.[27] Under the Convention the Commission can hear complaints from 'any person, group of persons, or any non-governmental entity legally recognized in one or more member states of the Organization' concerning violations of their rights under the convention.[28] However, it may only consider inter-state complaints if both (or all) states concerned have accepted the competence of the Commission to do so.[29] The Commission also exercises a general supervisory function in relation to the obligations in the Charter of the OAS. The Court of Human Rights established

[21] As at 31 December 1997 39 of the 104 state parties had made declarations under Articles 21 and 22, and the UK and the USA had made a declaration under Article 22 only.
[22] Article 20.   [23] Article 20(4). See also Chapter 4, n 122.
[24] See A/48/44/Add 1. See also (1993) 14 HRLJ 426; (1997) *IHRR* 223.
[25] See A/51/44, paras 180–222; See also (1997) 4 *IHRR* 235.   [26] Article 28.
[27] For an overview of the work of the OAS relative to torture, see Nikken, P (1991) 'L'action contre la torture dans le système interaméricain des droit de l'homme' in Cassese (1991), 73.
[28] Inter-American Convention on Human Rights, Article 44. The requirement that the petition should normally be lodged by the victim of a violation flows from Article 46, setting out the requirements of admissibility.
[29] Article 45.

by the Convention may consider cases referred to it by the Commission or by a state party concerned, but not by an individual, provided that all the states concerned in the case have made a declaration accepting the Court's jurisdiction.

This system closely resembles that established by the European Convention on Human Rights under the auspices of the Council of Europe. As originally conceived, the European Commission on Human Rights had automatic jurisdiction over inter-state complaints but not over individual petitions. Petitions submitted by individuals could be considered by the Commission only if the state whose acts are called into question has made a declaration accepting its jurisdiction. Cases could be referred to the European Court of Human Rights, either by the Commission, by a state party concerned or (for those states party to the 9th Protocol to the ECHR) by the applicant, provided that the states concerned in the case had accepted the Court's jurisdiction by making a declaration. The 11th Protocol to the Convention, adopted in 1994 and which enters into force on 1 November 1998, will replace this current two-tier system with a single Court of Human Rights having compulsory jurisdiction over both inter-state and individual petitions.[30]

Both the OAS and the Council of Europe have drawn up regional Conventions concerning torture. Like the UN Convention, however, the 1985 Inter-American Convention is primarily aimed at acts of torture, as opposed to conditions of detention, and does not establish any new monitoring body. By contrast the European Convention for the Prevention of Torture and Inhuman or Degrading Treatment or Punishment (the ECPT) is of a fundamentally different nature. Although it owes its origin to the obligation contained in Article 3 of the ECHR, the purpose of the Convention is to establish a Committee (the CPT) which 'shall, by means of visits, examine the treatment of persons deprived of their liberty with a view to strengthening, if necessary, the protection of such persons from torture and from inhuman or degrading treatment or punishment'.[31]

The CPT, therefore, is the first body developed within the international body of human rights law-making that uses a visit mechanism as the principal means of securing compliance with human rights obligations.[32]

---

[30] The background, operation and potential impact of the 11th Protocol has received extensive examination. See, for example, Drzemczewski, A and Meyer-Ladevig, J (1994) 'Principal Characteristics of the new ECHR Control Mechanism', 15 HRLJ 81; Bernhart, R (1995) 'Reform of the Control Machinery under the European Convention on Human Rights: Protocol No 11', 89 AJIL 145; Cameron, I (1995) 'Protocol 11 to the ECHR: The Court of Human Rights as a Constitutional Court', 15 YEL 219; Harris, DJ, O'Boyle, M and Warbrick, C (1995), *Law of the European Convention on Human Rights* (London: Butterworths), 706–14.

[31] ECPT, Article 1.

[32] The ICRC does, of course, use visit mechanism to oversee compliance with the obligations imposed by international humanitarian law.

Although the CPT occupies only a small niche within the panoply of international human rights mechanisms, it represents a crucial evolutionary step within that lineage. Moreover, it represents the first fruits of a broader initiative, aimed at the establishment of such a mechanism at the UN level. As will be seen below, the origins of the ECPT lie in the frustrations surrounding the attempt to incorporate a visit mechanism into the UNCAT in the early 1980s.[33] A working group of the UN Commission on Human Rights is currently considering the draft of an Optional Protocol to the 1984 Torture Convention that would establish a body with similar powers.[34]

One of the advantages of the complex maze of mechanisms described above is that all states are touched by it in one or more ways: no state is beyond the reach of international scrutiny. The principal disadvantage is that although each of the various mechanisms may be seeking to advance the prohibition of torture and ill-treatment, each is influenced and bound by its own particular context. In consequence, each mechanism operates in isolation from the others. This is not to say that the mechanisms do not influence each other. Each mechanism has its own burgeoning jurisprudence, however, which is not always in harmony with that developed by others.

This can be illustrated by the divergent approaches taken by different monitoring bodies to the question of whether the 'death row' phenomenon is itself an example of inhuman or degrading treatment. In the *Soering* case, the European Court of Human Rights concluded that, on the facts of the case, the extradition of the applicant to a jurisdiction in which he would face death row would have violated Article 3 of the ECHR.[35] In the similar case of *Kindler v Canada*,[36] the HRC came to the opposite conclusion, distinguishing the decision of the Court in the *Soering* case on the grounds of the age and mental state of the applicant and the different prison conditions in which he would be held. In the subsequent case of *Ng v Canada*,[37] the HRC distinguished its own decision, taking the view that extradition to a state in which the death penalty was administered by gas asphyxiation would amount to a violation of Article 7 of the ICCPR. None of these cases go as far as the Privy Council in *Pratt and Morgan v AG of Jamaica*[38] which held that prolonged delay, of nearly 14 years in this instance, in administering a death sentence amounted to inhuman treatment, irrespective of the particular circumstances of the case. Despite the

---

[33] See below, Chapter 4, pp. 112–15.   [34] See below, Chapter 4, p. 112 n 38.

[35] *Soering v UK*, Judgment, 7 July 1989, Ser A, No 161. This contrasts with the Commission which, by a 6–5 majority, was of the view that there was no violation of Article 3 in this case. See Comm Rep, 19 Jan 1989, paras 110–54. Subsequent developments are considered below at pp. 94–7.

[36] HRC Comm No 470/1991, (30 July 1993) 14 HRLJ 307.

[37] HRC Comm No 469/1991, 15 HRLJ 149.   [38] [1993] 4 All ER 769.

similar wording of the relevant standards, very different interpretations compete with each other.[39]

The differences between the standards and approaches adopted by the various international mechanisms are beyond the scope of this text. We are concerned with the operation and practical impact of the ECPT. Since the ECPT is designed to assist states realize the obligations they have assumed under Article 3 of the ECHR, and since this provides the context within which the CPT functions,[40] the following sections of this chapter will examine, first, the background to that provision and, secondly, the understanding placed upon it by the ECHR organs.

2 ARTICLE 3 OF THE ECHR: DRAFTING THE TEXT

The origins of the ECHR lie in a draft Convention prepared by the Legal Committee of the European Movement and presented to the 1st Session of the Consultative Assembly of the Council of Europe in August 1949. The Legal Committee of the Assembly considered the proposal in detail and its work culminated in the Teitgen Report of 5 September 1949. This formed the basis of Assembly Recommendation No 38 which formally proposed that the Committee of Ministers draw up a Convention. From the outset, it was understood that a European Convention should not diminish the impact of the UDHR and there was some concern that, in proposing the adoption of a legally binding instrument which was to be complemented by mechanisms for implementation, the Council of Europe would be anticipating the work of the UN Commission on Human Rights. On the other hand, a part of the impetus behind the drawing up of a European Convention lay in the delays surrounding the adoption of the UN Convention and the desire to hasten the adoption of a legal instrument guaranteeing the most basic rights as a bulwark against their erosion with the onset of the cold war in Europe.

Although the final shape of the ECHR was a carefully crafted compromise of competing concepts of rights and of national priorities and

---

[39] For an examinination of these cases and the confusion they create, see Schabas, W (1994) 'Soering's Legacy', 43 ICLQ 913.

[40] It also provides the basis for considering whether the CPT and the Court and Commission share a common understanding of the reach of Article 3. This is not to say that other articles of the ECHR have no relevance to the work of the CPT. As will be seen below, the CPT has embraced a series of procedural safeguards designed to enhance the *'cordon sanitaire'* surrounding detention, all of which are intended to reduce the risk of ill-treatment from occuring. This brings the CPT into the proximity of the jurisprudence relating, *inter alia*, to Articles 5 and 6 of the ECHR where similar issues of congruence arise. This will be examined alongside the analysis of the CPT's standards.

sensibilities,[41] the adoption of what is now Article 3 of the Convention provoked little controversy. The very first of the list of rights to be gauranteed in the draft drawn up by the European Movement was 'Security of life and limb'.[42] This was reformulated in the draft appended to the Teitgen Report so as to read 'Security of person, in accordance with Articles 3, 5 and 8 of the Declaration of the United Nations'. The relevant article of the UDHR were set out in an annex.[43] The Teitgen Report was considered by the Assembly from 5–8 September 1949 and a British member of the Assembly, Seymour Cocks, made an impassioned attempt to introduce a direct reference to the prohibition of torture into the text.

Cocks proposed that Article 1 of the draft should contain the following statement:[44]

The Consultative Assembly takes this opportunity of declaring that all forms of physical torture, whether inflicted by the police, military authorities, members or private organizations or any other persons are inconsistent with civilized society, are offences against heaven and humanity and must be prohibited.

It declares that this prohibition must be absolute and that torture cannot be permitted by any purpose whatsoever, neither by extracting evidence for saving life nor even for the safety of the State.

The Assembly believe that it would be better even for society to perish than for it to permit this relic of barbarisim to remain.

Cocks argued that it was necessary to give greater emphasis to the condemnation of torture, which he thought was mentioned 'almost casually' in the Report. He considered 'the most terrible event in my lifetime in this century has been that torture and violence have returned . . . and that in some countries people are even becoming accustomed to it'. He pleaded that:[45]

this Assembly should condemn in the most forthright and absolute fashion this retrogression into barbarism. I say that to take the straight beautiful bodies of men and women and to maim them and mutilate them by torture is a crime against high heaven and the holy spirit of man. I say it is a sin against the Holy Ghost for which there is no forgiveness. I declare that it is incompatible with civilization.

Therefore I ask the Assembly to announce to the whole world that torture is wholly evil and absolutely to be condemned and that no cause whatsoever—not even the life of a wife, a mother or a child, the safety of an army or the security

---

[41] See Council of Europe, (1977–1984) *Collected Edition of the travaux préparatoires of the European Convention on Human Rights*, 8 vols, (Strasbourg: Council of Europe), (hereafter *CETP*). For a general account of the drafting, see Robertson, AH and Merrills, JG (1993) *Human Rights in Europe* (Manchester: Manchester University Press), 3rd edn, ch 1. Fawcett, JES (1987) *The Application of the European Convention on Human Rights* (Oxford: Clarendon Press) 2nd edn integrates the *travaux préparatoires* with an examination of the earlier jurisprudence of the Strasbourg organs.

[42] Draft European Convention on Human Rights, Article 1(a), *CETP*, Vol I, 296.

[43] Teitgen Report, *CETP*, Vol I, 216.   [44] *CETP*, Vol II, 36.   [45] ibid, 36–40.

of a State—can justify its use or existence. I say that if a State, in order to survive, must be built upon a torture chamber, then that State should perish.

The drafters of the Report, whilst applauding the sentiment, argued that it would distort the text to place such an emphasis on this single issue and that the substance was already covered by the reference to Article 5 of the UDHR. As a compromise, it was suggested that the Assembly should consider adopting a separate resolution which could be adopted at the same time as the Report itself. Mr Cocks accepted this and not only withdrew his proposal, but also withdrew his proposed amendment to Article 2(1) of the draft, which had added:

In particular no person shall be subjected to any form of mutilation or sterilisation, nor to any form of torture or beating. Nor shall he be forced to take drugs nor shall they be administered to him without his knowledge and consent. Nor shall he be subjected to imprisonment with such an excess of light, darkness, noise or silence as to cause mental suffering.

The substance of his proposals were amalgamated into a single motion which provided:

The Consultative Assembly solemnly declares that any use of torture by public authorities or individuals is a crime against humanity. It can never be justified even to extract information, to save life or to protect the interests of the State on any grounds whatsoever.

The Assembly records its abhorrence at the subjection of any person to any form of mutilation, sterilization or beating.

The first paragraph was uncontroversial, but the reference to 'sterilization' in the second was unacceptable to the Scandinavian members whose countries permitted the sterilization of sex offenders. A UK member also expressed concern over the reference to 'beatings', given the existence of corporal punishment for some offences. Although Mr Cocks was willing to withdraw the second paragraph, others felt this implied an acceptance of these practices and in this state of disarray it was decided to refer the entire text to the Legal Committee and reconsider the matter at the next session of the Assembly.[46] The Assembly then adopted Recommendation No 38, retaining the wording of Article 2(1) originally proposed in the Teitgen Report, and requesting the Committee of Ministers to produce a draft Convention. The Committtee agreed to this but, rather than utilize the Assembly's text, decided to convene a Committee of Experts to undertake the task.[47]

---

[46] *CETP*, Vol II, 238–46.
[47] *CEPT*, Vol II, 288–96. It was decided, at the suggestion of Ernest Bevin, not to consult with the Assembly over the composition of the Committee of Experts. It was also agreed that it should be comprised of jurists: the Italian member, with whom the chairman agreed, arguing that 'it would not be useful, for example, to appoint philosophers because they would lay down a basis not really suitable for drafting a useful convention on Human Rights' (ibid, 294).

The Committee of Experts was divided on the question of whether to adopt an 'enumeration of rights' approach (version A, favoured by France), along the lines of the UDHR and the Teitgen Report draft, or a 'definition of rights' approach (version B, favoured by the UK) which would be more akin to the approach being adopted for the UN Convention. The Committee submitted a series of proposals built around these alternatives to the Committee of Ministers. As regards the prohibtion of torture, however, there was little difference between the competing versions. The Committee of Experts thought it best to utilize the wording of the UDHR in the 'enumeration' model, rather than simply make reference to it, and so the relevant article of version A provided that: 'No one shall be subjected to torture or to cruel, inhuman or degrading treatment or punishment'. The UK's proposed version, adopting the 'definitional approach' was similar but shorter, providing: 'No one shall be subjected to torture or to inhuman treatment or punishment'.[48] Rather than choose between the variants the Committee of Ministers decided to convene a Conference of Senior Officials to consider the matter. The Conference based its work around version B and its final draft of what was now Article 3 added the reference to 'degrading' found in version A, and so provided: 'No one shall be subjected to torture or to inhuman or degrading treatment of punishment'. There is no record of this wording being a matter of particular discussion: it resulted from a melding of the two versions.[49] The ommission of the word 'cruel' and the addition of the word 'degrading' were not seen as being of particular significance by the proponents of either version. The text of Article 3 attracted no further attention and passed unaltered into the final text of the Convention.

The prohibition in Article 3 is absolute: it is not subject to any form of limitation, specific or general.[50] This also was uncontroversial. The Teitgen Report draft contained a general limitation clause that would have applied to the freedom of 'security of life and limb'. But both drafts drawn up by the Committee of Experts excluded this possibility, either expressly or by implication[51] and this was not subsequently challenged.

---

[48] Report of the Committee of Experts to the Committee of Ministers, 16 March 1950, *CETP*, Vol III, 2 at 52 and 58.

[49] See Report of the Conference of Senior Officials to the Committee of Ministers, *CETP*, Vol IV, 242 at 258.

[50] Article 3 is expressly excluded from the scope of Article 15, which permits derogations in times of war or national emergency threatening the life of the nation and contains no equivalent to the second subsections of Articles 8–11 which place certain bounds upon the the enjoyment of the rights they contain. The 'absolute' nature of this prohibition will be explored further below.

[51] The prohition of torture was expressly excluded from the scope of Article 2, the general derogation clause relating to war or public emergency, in version B. Article 6 of version A permitted limitations on all of the rights in the Convention, including the freedom from torture in Article 2(1)(a), in the interests of the rights of others, the just requirements

It is true to say, then, that the Convention gives effect to the substance of the sentiments eloquently expressed by Mr Cocks in the Consultative Assembly. However, the Assembly itself did not pursue the question of a separate motion specifically condemning torture to stand alongside the Convention.

3 UNDERSTANDING ARTICLE 3 OF THE ECHR: 'THREE IN ONE' OR 'ONE IN THREE'?

Although Article 3 of the Convention prohibits torture, inhuman or degrading treatment or punishment, the drafting history confirms that there was no clear understanding of what was meant by those terms. It is well established that the Convention is a living text, to be interpreted in accordance with the understandings current within European society at the time of the alleged violation, and not limited to what was within the contemplation of the drafters of the Treaty.[52] To that extent, the preventive mechanism established by the ECPT is built on sand. On the other hand, it means that there are no immutable propositions that circumscribe its range of activities. The Strasbourg jurisprudence may, at any given moment, reveal the current understanding of the key terms in Article 3 but it does not, and cannot, point to their limits. In consequence, the CPT remains free to test those limits by exploring—and revealing—the range of circumstances which potentially might be considered as within its ambit.

There is, however, a more general question which, although capable of evolution over time, is a more stable factor and informs the manner in which Article 3 is applied in practice. This concerns the nature of the relationship between the terms employed in Article 3. An understanding of this is not just a question of semantics. It has a profound influence over the forms of treatment or punishment likely to be found to violate Article 3. The CPT has shown itself to be very careful in its use of terms and any mismatch between its understanding of the relationship between them and that of the Court and of the Commission would potentially be more serious than would a 'simple' disagreement over whether a certain set of circumstances revealed a violation. The remainder of this chapter will be spent exploring the manner in which the Court and Commission have

of public morality and order, national security and territorial integrity, the smooth working of administration and justice. However, since under Article 8(2) of the draft no derogation could be made from Article 2(1)(a) in times of war or public emergency, it is difficult to see how any limitation could, in practice, have been justified under this draft.

[52] See in general, Merrills, JG (1993) *The Development of International Law by the European Court of Human Rights* (Manchester: Manchester University Press), 2nd edn, 78–81, Jacobs, FG and White, RAC (1996) *The European Convention on Human Rights* (Oxford: Clarendon Press), 2nd edn, 26–38.

conceptualized Article 3, highlighting some of the difficulties which flow from their approach. Given the essentially judicial nature of their functions this approach may well be appropriate. However, their conceptual apparatus is not necessarily appropriate for the work of the CPT, whose task is essentially preventive in function. The different, though complementary, functions of the ECHR organs and the CPT might go some way to explain the tensions between their approaches to Article 3. Certainly, neither appears comfortable when confronted with the output of the other. The point to be made is not that the approach currently adopted by the Court is wrong: even if this could be sustained, the principles developed by the Court now permeate the entire international approach to the outlawry of torture under other human rights instruments and cannot easily be rewritten. Rather, it is that the approach taken by the Court and Commission to Article 3 has been the product of choice, and that it is not inevitable that the CPT should adopt precisely the same approach when developing its preventive mandate.

Although the *traveaux préparatoires* suggest otherwise, Article 3 is normally broken down into three component parts and 'torture', 'inhuman', and 'degrading' are each invested with their own significance.[53] A complex jurisprudence has emerged around each of these terms. The origins of this approach lie in the opinion adopted by the European Commission on Human Rights in the *Greek* case in 1969 and subsequently refined in *Ireland v UK* by the Commission (1976) and Court (1978). Moreover, the approach taken by the Commission in the *Greek* case subsequently influenced the development of the 1975 UN Declaration and, through this, the 1984 UN Convention against Torture.

In the *Greek* case the Commission expressed the view that:

It is plain that there may be treatment to which all these descriptions apply, for all torture must be inhuman and degrading treatment, and all inhuman treatment also degrading.

The notion of inhuman treatment covers at least such treatment as deliberately causes severe suffering, mental or physical, which, in the particular situation is unjustifiable.

The word 'torture' is often used to describe inhuman treatment which has a purpose such as the obtaining of information or confessions, or the infliction of punishment, and it is generally an aggravated form of inhuman and degrading treatment.

Treatment or punishment of an individual may be said to be degrading if it grossly humiliates him before others or drives him to act against his will or conscience.[54]

---

[53] cf Harris, O'Boyle and Warbrick (1995), 55–89, who draw distinctions not only between 'torture' and 'inhuman' and 'degrading' treatment but also between 'treatment' and 'punishment' with regard to each.
[54] *Greek* case, Comm Rep, 5 Nov 1969, (1969) 12 *ECHRYb* 186.

The second statement was the object of much criticism, chiefly because it suggested that circumstances might render what might otherwise amount to inhuman treatment justifiable. Some argued that this amounted to allowing a derogation from Article 3, a situation incompatible with Article 15(2) of the Convention. In *Ireland v UK* the Commission sought to explain itself, recognizing that its use of the term 'unjustifiable' had 'given rise to some misunderstanding' and confirming that 'there cannot be any justification for treatment in breach of that provision'.[55] This had been confirmed in recent cases which have emphasized the absolute nature of the obligation contained in Article 3:

Even in the most difficult of circumstances, such as the fight against organized terrorism and crime, the Convention prohibits in absolute terms torture or inhuman or degrading treatment or punishment . . . even in the event of a public emergency threatening the life of the nation.[56]

Whatever the merits of this view, it fails to make it clear that what amounts to ill-treatment must always be subject to assessment in the light of the relevant circumstances.[57] This was acknowledged by the Court in *Ireland v UK*:

ill treatment must attain a minimum level of severity if it is to fall within the scope of Article 3. The assessment of this minimum is, in the nature of things, relative; it depends on all the circumstances of the case, such as the duration of the treatment, its physical or mental effects and, in some cases, the sex, age and state of health of the victim, etc.[58]

This has since become a standard recital used in almost all cases which raise novel or difficult issues under Article 3. To claim that Article 3 offers an unqualified protection against torture, inhuman or degrading treatment or punishment is, then, misleading. There can be no justification for such conduct but, as will be seen below, justification still has a role since it plays an—albeit rarely acknowledged—part in determining whether certain forms of action fall within the scope of Article 3 in the first place.

The real point at issue, then, concerns the range of factors that might be relevant to that assessment and the nature of the relationship between those factors and the treatment or punishment concerned. There may be some forms of ill-treatment which will always be deemed torture, in

---

[55] See *Ireland v UK*, Comm Rep, 25 Jan 1976, Ser B, No 23-I, 388–90.

[56] *Aksoy v Turkey*, Judgment, 18 Dec 1996, para 62. See also *Aydin v Turkey*, Judgment, 27 Sept 1997, para 62 and *Chahal v UK*, Judgment, 15 Nov 1996, considered below, pp. 95–6.

[57] See eg, Jacobs and White (1996), 51 who point out that the imposition of penalties appropriate for serious crimes could violate Article 3 if imposed for petty offences and, to that extent, inhuman treatment is a relative notion.

[58] *Ireland v UK*, Judgment, 18 Jan 1978, Ser A, No 25, para 162.

which case the contextualizing factors have no importance.[59] Conversely, there may be some forms of ill-treatment or combination of circumstances that, no matter how generally unpleasant or uncomfortable their consequences in a particular case, are never likely to pass into the sphere of Article 3.[60] However, as is evident from the case-load of the European Commission and Court of Human Rights, there will be some fine judgments to be made in many cases both as regards whether a situation falls within the scope of Article 3 and as regards the category in which it is placed. These decisions will often depend on the attendant circumstances.

It is worth pursuing further the nature of the relationship between 'torture' and 'inhuman' and 'degrading' since, despite the clear statements of the Strasbourg organs, there remains a question mark over the merits of the approach that has been adopted, not least because the UN Human Rights Committee adopts a rather different approach to the interpretation and application of the similarly worded Article 7 of the ICCPR. Although the HRC acknowledges in its General Comments on Article 7 that the distinction between the categories depends on 'the nature, purpose and severity of the treatment applied', it emphasizes that: 'The Covenant does not contain any definition of the concepts covered by article 7, nor does the Committee consider it necessary to draw up a list of prohibited acts or to establish sharp distinctions between the different kinds of punishment or treatment.'[61] The most important reason for pursuing this enquiry is, however, the difficulty in reconciling the actual practice of the Strasbourg organs with the theory of application which they espouse. An alternative view may be of value.

In the *Greek* case, the Commission first addressed the question of what amounted to inhuman treatment before moving on to consider how torture and degrading treatment might be understood. Inhuman treatment provided the starting point. What served to differentiate torture from

[59] eg the methods employed in the *Greek* case itself, and see also *Aydin v Turkey*, Comm Rep, 7 Mar 1996 and Court, Judgment, 27 Sept 1997, considered below, pp. 83–5. But cf *Cyprus v Turkey*, Comm Rep, 10 July 1976, in which the Commission concluded that an isolated case of rape did not violate Article 3. See also Addo, M and Grief, N (1995) 'Is There a Policy Behind the Decisions and Judgments Relating to Article 3 of the ECHR?', 20 ELRev 178, 189.

[60] The claims advanced in *Lopez Ostra v. Portugal*, Judgment, 9 Dec 1994, Ser A, No 303-C might provide an example. See below, p. 104.

[61] General Comment No 20/44 (3 Apr 1992). This is a more robust rejection of the need to categorize the nature of acts than in its previous General Comment on Article 7, which had observed that 'It *may* not be necessary to draw sharp distinctions . . .' (General Comment No 7/16 (27 July 1982), para 2 (emphasis added)). One reason for this might be that, unlike the ECHR, the ICCPR has a separate article, Article 10, which is directly concerned with conditions of detention. See below, n 65 for the similar approach of the CAT and the SRT. But cf Nowak, M (1993) *UN Covenant on Civil and Political Rights: CCPR Commentary* (Kehl am Rhein: NP Engel), 129, who claims there is now a greater willingness to differentiate under Article 7 itself than previously. Nowak also comments on the lack of precision in the jurisprudence relating to Article 7. See also McGoldrick (1991), 371.

inhuman treatment was not the degree of suffering involved but the fact that it was inflicted in order to achieve a purpose. Although it also observed that torture was often an 'aggravated' form of inhuman treatment, this was not an essential prerequisite. Torture was the purposive use of inhuman treatment.[62]

Although this approach has subsequently been refined, neither the Commission nor the Court has ever questioned the distinction first set out in the *Greek* case. Nevertheless, the prevailing view is that there is an hierarchical progression between three separate categories of ill-treatment and that the threshold between them is based on the severity of suffering. The consequence is that the purposive element has been marginalized in European practice. Yet it has been argued that the *Greek* case established that torture must be both purposive and 'aggravated'[63] and this understanding was ultimately reflected in Article 1 of the 1975 UN Declaration which provides that:

1. For the purposes of this Declaration, torture means any act by which severe pain or suffering, whether physical or mental, is intentionally inflicted by or at the instigation of a public official on a person for such a purpose as obtaining from him or a third person information or confession, punishing him for an act he has committed or is suspected of having committed, or intimidating him or other persons. It does not include pain or suffering arising only from, inherent in or incidental to, lawful sanctions to the extent consistent with the Standard Minimum Rules for the Treatment of Prisoners.

2. Torture constitutes an aggravated and deliberate form of cruel, inhuman or degrading treatment or punishment.

The Declaration was based upon draft proposals drawn up by Sweden and the Netherlands, two of the countries that had launched the inter-state application against Greece under the ECHR: it is not surprising that they were influenced by the Commission's views in that case.[64] The Declaration served as a model for the definition of torture in the 1984 UN Convention and, although subject to a number of changes—including the ommission of the second sub-paragraph—the idea of torture as a purposive and aggravated form of inhuman treatment remains reflected in the reference to 'severe' pain or suffering.[65]

---

[62] This is resonant of the historical understanding of the concept of torture. See Chapter 1.

[63] This is a matter of some uncertainty. Rodley (1987), 73–4, takes the view that both must be present, defining torture as 'an aggravated form of inhuman treatment, inflicted for certain purposes'. Duffy, P (1983) 'Article 3 of the ECHR', 32 ICLQ 316, 317, argues that it may be necessary in some, but not in all cases, depending on the level of suffering involved. See further below at pp. 82–6.

[64] Rodley (1987), 72.

[65] One might expect the CAT to pay particular attention to where this line is to be drawn, since, under the 1984 UNCAT, and unlike the ECHR and ICCPR, different legal consequences flow from the distinction. However, this is not the case. The CAT has a number of very

It has been argued, however,[66] that it is difficult to see how treatment which is inhuman can be 'aggravated' and that torture can be considered a form of treatment or punishment 'even more inhuman' than inhuman treatment itself. On such a view, the real division between the elements of Article 3 do not turn on the severity of suffering at all. Rather, torture and inhuman treatment could be seen as co-existing on the same plane, distinguished only by the purposive element. Inhuman treatment would, of course, incorporate many shades of suffering but it would be unnecessary to engage in the invidious task of ascertaining whether the necessary threshold had been crossed. If greater emotive value is attached to the term 'torture' than to 'inhuman' conduct, then this reflects, perhaps, an instinctive feeling that the infliction of pain or suffering for predetermined purposes of interrogation or punishment is a greater wrong than the infliction of pain or suffering itself. It may well be that 'torture' is rightly considered more reprehensible than 'inhuman' treatment—but it is arguable that this ought not to flow from considerations of the severity of the suffering involved.

Such an approach places less emphasis on distinguishing between the three forms of ill-treatment and suggests that attention be focused upon the concept of 'inhuman' treatment or punishment, of which torture and degrading treatment are variants. The use of the word 'torture' would be reserved for forms of inhuman treatment deliberately employed to

different functions: monitoring compliance with formal obligations; considering individual complaints; and conducting investigations into situations involving the alleged use of torture. Article 11, however, tends to blur the distinction between examining allegations of torture and formal prohibitions by requiring that each state party keep under systematic review interrogation rules, instructions, methods, and practices as well as arrangements for the custody and treatment of persons subjected to any form of arrest, detention, or imprisonment in any territory under its jurisdiction, with a view to preventing any cases of torture.

It is against this background that the CAT has veered towards examining the totality of circumstances in which ill-treatment may occur and states do not seem to object to the UNCAT probing matters which do not relate to 'torture' *per se*. The 'severity of suffering' does not figure prominently in the CAT's approach to its tasks. Similarly, the mandate of the SRT is limited to questions relating to torture, as opposed to cruel, inhuman, and degrading treatment or punishment. However, the SRT has taken the view that the distinction between the categories is a matter of degree: torture and other forms of ill-treatment represent different points along a continuum and, as such, he is competent to consider questions relating to ill-treatment which seem to fall into the 'grey area' between the two (see Kooijmans (1991), 59–61). This has been recognized by the CHR which, when renewing the SRT's mandate in 1995, invited him to examine questions concerning 'conditions conducive to . . . torture' (CHR Res, 1995/37 B, para 4). The flexibility inherent in the 'thematic procedure' approach presents greater scope for the development of the standards applicable than those which are more closely tied to the text of a particular convention. Saudi Arabia has objected to the SRT, raising questions concerning corporal punishment sanctioned by law as being beyond his mandate (see E/CN.4/1997/7/Add 1, para 435) but the SRT has vigorously defended his practice (see E/CN.4/1997/7, paras 3–11) and has been confirmed in this by the CHR (see CHR Res 1997/38).

[66] Fawcett (1987), 45–6.

achieve certain purposes. Degrading treatment would describe treatment not necessarily inhuman but acquiring that quality because of its effect upon the individual in all the circumstances of the case. On such a view all forms of treatment prohibited by Article 3 would be inhuman.

This, of course, is not the approach that has been adopted by the European Court and Commission of Human Rights. It should, however, be remembered that even if Article 3 is understood as embracing three separate concepts—three in one, not one in three—it still prohibits them all in single measure: Article 3 is violated once the first threshold is crossed. Of course, there might be greater moral opprobrium attached to conduct which is 'inhuman' as well as 'degrading', or 'torture' as well as 'inhuman', but that does not alter the fact that Article 3 has already been breached at the 'lower' level. The advantage of the alternative model outlined above is that it places less emphasis on the thresholds of suffering and opens up the prospect of a much broader conception of what forms of treatment these terms can embrace. As far as the CPT is concerned, this more flexible approach seems more in tune with the preventive nature of its mandate. Since the CPT is not formally tied to the jurisprudence of the ECHR it is able to approach Article 3 from a different perspective and, like the CAT and SRT, move away from categorization in the context of its preventive functions. Such an approach finds further justification—if justification is needed—when the actual practice under the ECHR is examined.

4 THE THRESHOLDS OF SUFFERING IN THE JURISPRUDENCE OF THE ECHR

Although the Court and Commission continue to endorse the 'severity of suffering' approach it is not fully reflected in their practice. The following sections will look at the ways in which the three elements have been distinguished both from each other and from conduct which does not fall for consideration under Article 3 at all. This will highlight both the unsatisfactory nature of these points of distinction and the way in which justifications and policy factors unconnected with the theory of the 'severity of suffering' have shaped the application of the article as a whole.

(a) Differentiating torture

In April 1967 a military *coup d'etat* brought Colonel George Papadopoulos to power in Greece.[67] During the seven years that the colonels

---

[67] For the background, see Mavrogordatos GTh (1983) 'The Emerging Party System' in Clogg, R (ed), 70–91.

ruled Greece, the security forces under their control made extensive use of torture. Torture was initially employed to break the relatively small resistance movement. Accounts of torture began emerging from Greece soon after the 1967 *coup*. These accounts led Amnesty International to send investigatory missions to Greece in late 1967 and early 1968, the reports of which persuaded the governments of the Netherlands, Sweden, and Denmark to add breach of Article 3 to the application already submitted to Strasbourg in September 1967 for violation of eight articles of the ECHR.

Most of the evidence that follows, however, emerged from the trials of some of the torturers which took place after the restoration of democracy. There were several hundred trials. Torture was used by 'trained officers of middle rank from the gendarmerie, the civilian security police (*Asfaleia*), the navy, and the military police (*Elliniki Stratiotiki Astynomia—ESA*).'[68] A large variety of methods, both physical and psychological, were documented: *falanga*; sexual abuse (the beating of genitalia or the insertion of objects into the vagina or anus); near suffocation; beating with sandbags on the head or with knotted wires on the body; suspension by the *strappado* method, or what is often now called Palestinian hanging; jumping on the stomach; tearing out of hair; rubbing pepper into sensitive parts of the body; extraction of finger or toe nails; burning, particularly with cigarettes; and electric shock. Physical beatings 'as a method of intimidation and interrogation' were described by Amnesty as 'general'.[69]

[68] Mavrogordatos GTh (1983), 11.

[69] Amnesty International (1968) *Situation in Greece*, January, London, reproduced as Appendix C in Amnesty International (1977), *Torture in Greece: The First Torturers' Trial* (London: Amnesty International, International Secretariat), 80. Amnesty's analysis of the evidence given at the first of the major trials of torturers, in which all of the defendants were members of ESA, provides an overall picture of the procedures adopted by that agency throughout the Junta years. In addition to the extensive use of paid informers, disguised members of ESA's prosecution section attended public places and events for the purposes of surveillance. Arrests were usually made in the early hours of the morning and were often accompanied by a beating and threats of imminent severe violence. At the station the detainee might be shut in a room on the wall of which might be hanging clubs, whips, or canes and provided with pen and paper on which to write a confession. The precise interrogation technique would then be decided between the commanding officer and the interrogator. The opening gambit would comprise further threats to the prisoner and his family of extreme violence and this would often be reinforced by what was known as a 'tea party'—a severe physical beating with fists or clubs by a group of ESA guards. Systematic torture might last several days or weeks during the course of which prisoners were deprived of food and drink and when in the cells 'told to remain standing in the corner of their cell, sometimes on one foot but usually at attention'. They would not be allowed to change their clothes, to wash, or to smoke and sometimes not permitted access to sanitary facilities so that they stank. When food or drink was provided it was often laced with soap or salt to increase the prisoner's thirst. Prisoners so weakened would be made to feel completely powerless and isolated and these feelings would be reinforced by their being told that their friends had been arrested and that no one outside cared whether they lived or died. Prolonged deprivation often resulted in hallucinations and a powerful urge to commit suicide. The prisoners were often seen by a doctor and when whatever form of physical torture to which

It is againist this background that the Commission said in the *Greek* case that:

The word 'torture' is often used to describe inhuman treatment which has a purpose such as the obtaining of information or confessions, or the infliction of punishment, and it is generally an aggravated form of inhuman and degrading treatment.

This is to be contrasted with the case of *Ireland v UK*.[70] Recalling its opinion in the *Greek* case, the Commission concluded unanimously that the five techniques of applying pressure during interrogation employed by the British security forces in Northern Ireland[71] amounted to torture, chiefly because of their purpose in the context of the case. The Commission observed that the combined application of these techniques was 'designed to put severe mental and physical stress, causing severe suffering, on a person in order to obtain information from him' and that:

the systematic application of the techniques for the purpose of inducing a person to give information shows a clear resemblance to those methods of systematic torture which have been known over the ages.[72]

If there was a threshold criteria for the Commission, it did not relate to the severity of suffering experienced by the victims but the circumstances surrounding its application. Thus when considering whether physical assaults upon detainees during the course of RUC interrogation at the Palace Barracks—and which had caused injuries, some of which were severe—amounted to torture, the Commission concluded that:

whilst the injuries sustained . . . would indicate that they have been subjected to treatment showing a considerable degree of violence and even brutality, the acts found to be in breach of Article 3 of the Convention could not be qualified as torture as the term is being used here. The cases involved interrogation, and therefore this question could arise. However, although the violence has been deliberately applied for this purpose in the cases concerned, the evidence obtained does not disclose the application of such premeditated methods or techniques in the infliction of the ill-treatment or to such a degree as would be required in the opinion of the Commission to describe the treatment as torture.[73]

they were subject resulted in particularly serious injuries they were transferred to a military hospital where care was taken to ensure that they were treated under a false name (Amnesty International (1977), 16–17).

[70] The factual background to this case is considered in Chapter 2, pp. 32–41.

[71] See Chapter 2, p. 34.

[72] *Ireland v UK*, Comm Rep, 25 Jan 1976, Ser B, No 23–1, 410. The Commission accepted that, considered individually, some of the techniques, such as sleep deprivation or dietary restrictions, might not breach Article 3 at all, but this would 'depend on the circumstances and the purpose . . .' (ibid).

[73] ibid, 471–2. Other cases concerning severe ill-treatment inflicted by army personnel during arrest and interrogation, and causing very serious injuries, were also thought not to amount to torture (ibid, 477).

When the case was referred to the Court by the Irish Government the UK did not challenge the Commission's finding that the application of the five techniques amounted to torture.[74] However, the Court chose to re-open this question and said that the distinction between torture on the one hand and inhuman and degrading treatment on the other 'derives principally from a difference in the intensity of the suffering inflicted'. Further, the Court said that:

it was the intention that the Convention, with its distinction between 'torture' and 'inhuman or degrading treatment' should by the first of these terms attach a special stigma to deliberate inhuman treatment causing very serious and cruel suffering.[75]

It concluded that:

Although the five techniques, as applied in combination, undoubtedly amounted to inhuman and degrading treatment, although their object was the extraction of confessions, the naming of others and/or information and although they were used systematically, they did not occaision suffering of the peculiar intensity and cruelty implied be the word torture . . .[76]

It is not clear from this whether the Court thought that premeditated and purposive treatment was a necessary but insufficient component of torture, or whether it thought that even if such elements were present they could not contribute to the assessment of the level of suffering. Whatever the case, it is clear that the Court did not see any evidence of treatment sufficiently severe to be categorized as torture, despite the undoubted levels of pain and suffering endured by many of the applicants in the case.

Whatever view one takes of the threshold drawn by the Court between torture and other forms of inhuman treatment in the *Ireland* case the very fact that such a distinction was drawn had the effect of ensuring that Article 3 would thereafter be seen as encapsulating a progression, starting with degrading treatment which, once it reaches a certain threshold, becomes inhuman and, if particularly serious, torture. Torture stood at the apex of a pyramid of suffering.

This approach has a number of attractions. First, it accords with an intuitive notion that acts of torture are particularly serious. More importantly, focusing attention upon the level of suffering endured by the victim diverts

[74] Hampson, F (1989) 'The United Kingdom and the European Court of Human Rights', 9 *YEL* 121, argues that this was because the UK wanted the question to be deemed moot and prevent the Court pressing for members of the security forces to be placed on trial. As such, she argues, this concession was made to protect the agents of the State, rather than recognize the rights of those ill-treated.

[75] *Ireland v UK*, Judgment, 18 Jan 1978, Ser A, No 25, para 167. This has been confirmed by the Court on numerous occasions including *Aksoy v Turkey*, Judgment, 18 Dec 1996, para 63; *Aydin v Turkey*, Judgment, 25 Sept 1997, para 82.

[76] *Ireland v UK*, Judgment, 18 Jan 1978, Ser A, No 25, para 167.

attention from the need to consider whether it was inflicted for a purpose. This is important because it forestalls the argument that, viewed in the light of all the relevant circumstances, the purpose was such as to justify the use of torture. In short, the language of purpose lies in too close a proximity to the language of justification and so is best removed from the equation altogether. What this approach fails to acknowledge, however, is that some criteria are needed to differentiate between the categories and that, when this issue is probed, purpose or justification is rarely absent. Indeed, it cannot be excluded.

In the *Tyrer* case, Judge Fitzmaurice pointed out in his dissenting opinion that since the prohibition in Article 3 is absolute, if the intensity of pain were the only factor to be taken into account, then 'any infliction of pain severe enough in degree to amount to torture[77] would involve a breach whatever the circumstances'; there could be no room for exceptions based on consent or necessity (for example, medical emergency operations without anaesthetic). He concluded that:

the gloss that has to be placed upon the literal effect of the Article relates not only to what *constitutes* or amounts to torture, etc, but to what may in certain circumstances *justify* its infliction.[78]

In the context of torture, as opposed inhuman or degrading treatment, this thesis remains to be tested. However, Fitzmaurice was correct in foreseeing that factors other than the intensity of suffering would influence the decision to characterize an act as torture, rather than as inhuman.

This is well illustrated by the approach taken by the Commission in *Aydin v Turkey*. The Commission found that the applicant had been taken into custody for three days during which time she had been 'blindfolded, beaten, stripped, placed inside a tyre and sprayed with high pressure water, and raped'. The Commission did not consider it appropriate to analyse these individual elements in order to see which of them amounted to an act of either torture or inhuman or degrading treatment under Article 3 but chose to 'examine the treatment suffered by the applicant as a whole'.[79] It may be that once a single element of the application is deemed to be an act of torture, and no more serious violation of Article 3 can be found, there is no need to analyse the individual elements.[80] On the other

---

[77] And, *a fortiori*, inhuman and degrading treatment.

[78] *Tyrer v UK*, Judgment, 25 April 1978, Ser A, No 26, Dissenting Opinion of Judge Fitzmaurice, para 5, 'torture' here being used in the Court's sense as the infliction of pain beyond a certain threshold.

[79] *Aydin v Turkey*, Comm Rep, 7 Mar 1996, para 185.

[80] The Court adopted a similar approach in *Aksoy v Turkey*, Judgment, 18 Dec 1996, para 64, once it had concluded that subjecting the applicant to 'Palestinian hanging' was, on the facts of the case, torture for the purposes of Article 3. The Commission, however, had concluded that the evidence was insufficient to consider the other allegations (Comm Rep, 23 Oct 1993, para 166).

hand, and on the facts of the case, it is difficult to see why the Commission chose to base its conclusion on so comparatively limited a basis. Its reasoning was as follows:

The Commission notes that the applicant was aged approximately seventeen when she was taken into custody by the security forces. She was isolated from the other members of her family and blindfolded. She was in the circumstances in a highly vulnerable situation. The deliberate ill-treatment inflicted on her by beating and being placed in a tyre and hosed with pressurized water, combined with the humiliation of being stripped naked, falls within the scope of the prohibition contained in Article 3. Rape committed by an official or person in authority on a detained person must in addition be regarded as treatment or punishment of an extremely severe kind. . . . The nature of such an act, which strikes at the heart of the victim's physical and moral integrity, must be characterized as particularly cruel and involving actual physical and psychological suffering. This is aggravated when committed by a person in authority over the victim. Having regard to the extreme vulnerability of the applicant and the deliberate infliction on her of serious and cruel ill-treatment in a coercive and punitive context, the Commission finds that such ill-treatment must be regarded as torture within the meaning of Article 3 of the Convention.[81]

Clearly, the rape was deemed inhuman treatment and was aggravated by the context in which it was inflicted so as to elevate it into an act of torture. Few would question this conclusion but it is not apparent why the Commission did not feel it worthwhile to find whether the other inhuman actions visited upon the applicant were also to be considered acts of torture.[82] It is difficult to imagine them being otherwise. It may be that the Commission felt that the rape was the worst violation of the victim and it was unnecessary to go beyond this. The Court, on the other hand, felt no such inhibitions and when it considered the case concluded that 'the accumulation of acts of physical and mental violence inflicted on the applicant and the especially cruel act of rape to which she was subjected amounted to torture . . . Indeed the Court would have reached this conclusion on either of these grounds taken separately'.[83]

The reasons given by the Commission for concluding that the act of rape was an act of torture were that it occasioned extreme suffering, was upon a person in a highly vulnerable position, and was inflicted by

[81] *Aydin v Turkey*, Comm Rep, 7 Mar 1996, para 189.
[82] cf *Tekin v Turkey*, Comm Rep, 17 Apr 1997, paras 214–15, in which the Commission again failed to clearly express its views. Having found that 'the applicant was kept in a cold and dark cell, blindfolded and treated in a way which left wounds and bruises on his body in connection with his interrogation' the Commission concluded that 'the conditions of detention and the treatment to which the applicant was subjected constituted at least inhuman treatment within the meaning of Article 3 of the Convention'. This hesitancy possibly reflects uncertainties in the evaluation of the evidence (ibid, para 190).
[83] *Aydin v Turkey*, Judgment, 25 Sept 1997, para 86.

a person in authority over her in a coercive and punitive context. The two latter factors characterized both all aspects of the treatment endured by the applicant and those inflicted upon any person in detention of any sort. Moreover, neither factor causes any greater degree of *physical* suffering but might add to the degree of *mental* suffering and humiliation endured by the victim. The use of these factors to explain the 'aggravation' of inhuman treatment into an act of torture reintroduces the idea that the nature of the action and the purpose it is intended to serve are factors alongside the degree of suffering it causes, albeit presented in the language of the 'severity' of suffering. This implicit thinking was rendered explicit by the Court which pointed out that:

The applicant and her family must have been taken from their village and brought to the Derik gendarmerie for a purpose, which can only be explained on account of the security situation in the region and the need of the security forces to elicit information. The suffering inflicted on the applicant during the period of her detention must also be seen as calculated to serve the same or related purposes.[84]

It was 'Against this background' that the Court concluded that these acts amounted to torture.[85] It seems clear that, like the Commission, the Court would have found the act of rape to amount to torture in the circumstances of the case irrespective of its purpose. It is not clear whether it was the purposive nature of the other acts which caused the Court, unlike the Commission, to label them as acts of torture.[86]

This tension is evident in other recent cases and which suggest that the central issue remains unresolved: does the 'aggravation' which raises an inhuman or degrading act into an act of torture derive from the suffering endured, the circumstances of its infliction, the purpose of its infliction, or all of these? In *Aksoy v Turkey*, the Commission concluded that:

the applicant, during his detention, was subjected to ill-treatment which consisted of his being strung up by the arms. This caused injury for which he subsequently received medical treatment. The ill treatment of the applicant was of such a serious nature that it should be deemed torture within the meaning of Article 3.[87]

Like the Commission, the Court was of the opinion that the applicant had been subjected to torture, but their reasoning was somewhat different. Recalling that 'this distinction would appear to have been embodied in the Convention to allow the special stigma of "torture" to attach only

---

[84] ibid, para 85.   [85] ibid, para 86.
[86] cf Duffy (1983), 317, who argues that a purposive element can raise an otherwise 'inhuman' act into torture, other acts being capable of being classified as torture irrespective of purpose if sufficiently severe.
[87] *Aksoy v Turkey*, Comm Rep, 23 Oct 1996, para 165.

to deliberate inhuman treatment causing very serious and cruel suffering',[88] the Court said:

this treatment could only have been deliberately inflicted; indeed, a certain amount of preparation and exertion would have been required to carry it out. It would appear to have been administered with the aim of obtaining admissions or information from the applicant. In addition to the severe pain which it must have caused at the time, the medical evidence shows that it led to a paralysis of both arms which lasted for some time. The Court considers that this treatment was of such a serious and cruel nature that it can only be described as torture.[89]

Although the Commission clearly understood that all these elements were present, its formulation in *Aksoy* was more narrowly based. However, in both *Yagiz v Turkey* and *Sur v Turkey*, the Commission drew attention to both the purposive approach and the 'severity of suffering' approach to determining the 'aggravated' nature of the acts in question. The Commission concluded that acts of torture had taken place in both cases. In *Sur v Turkey* it was found that the applicant had been subjected to electric shocks in the course of questioning by the police and this conclusion is not controversial.[90] In *Yagiz v Turkey* the applicant, an auxiliary nurse in a maternity hospital, had been arrested on suspicion of involvement with abduction of a newborn baby. She claimed to have been beaten on the soles of her feet whilst blindfold and been subject to sexual harassment, resulting in psychological trauma.[91] The Commission noted that the applicant had been held in police custody without access to legal advice and was, therefore, particularly vulnerable.[92] This fed into their opinion that an act of torture had been committed and, as in *Aydin v Turkey*, suggests that contextual features can 'tip the balance'.[93] A similar point can be made regarding the decision to categorize certain forms of conduct as 'inhuman' or 'degrading' treatment, as will be seen below.

(b) Differentiating degrading treatment

Returning to the decision of the Court in *Ireland v UK*, it should be noted that the Court did not seek to draw any distinctions between inhuman and degrading treatment but saw them as a single notion. This might be because it considered the techniques in question to be, at the very least,

---

[88] *Aksoy v Turkey*, Judgment, 18 Dec 1996, para 63, recalling *Ireland v UK*, Judgment, 18 Jan 1978, Ser A, No 25, para 167.

[89] ibid, para 64.   [90] *Sur v Turkey*, Comm Rep, 3 Sept 1996, para 50.

[91] *Yagiz v Turkey*, Comm Rep, 16 May 1995, paras 16–27; Judgment, 7 Aug 1996, paras 7–17.

[92] *Yagiz v Turkey*, Comm Rep, 16 May 1995, para 45.

[93] ibid, para 55. The case was referred to the Court but, in the wake of other Court decisions, the Court accepted the Turkish Government's submission that it lacked jurisdiction *ratione temporis*. See *Yagiz v Turkey*, Judgment, 7 Aug 1996.

inhuman and therefore degrading. It is now generally accepted that 'inhuman' and 'degrading' represent different categories of ill-treatment and that they too are differentiated by a threshold of severity.

The question of what is meant by 'degrading' treatment or punishment has received extensive examination. Following on from the views of the Commission in the *Greek* case, it was argued in the *East African Asians* case that treatment was 'degrading' for the purposes of Article 3 'if it lowers [the victim] in rank, position, reputation or character, whether in his own eyes or in the eyes of other people'.[94] The Commission thought this too wide ranging and was of the view that:

the general purpose of this provision is to prevent interferences with the dignity of man of a particularly serious nature. It follows that an action, which lowers a person in rank, position, reputation or character can only be regarded as 'degrading treatment' in the sense of Art.3, where is reaches a certain level of severity.[95]

As to the level of severity, the Commission recalled with approval its observation in the *Greek* case that degrading treatment implied 'gross' humiliation.[96] Thus not every humiliation would be degrading treatment for the purposes of Article 3, which raises the question of where the threshold lies. It should be noted that the language used by the Commission in the *East African Asians* case is more objective in tone than that employed in the *Greek* case, lending greater weight to the nature of the action in question, rather than the effect it has on the individual concerned. In the *East African Asians* case the Commission concluded that:

publicly to single out a group of persons for differential treatment on the basis of their race might, in certain circumstances, constitute a special form of affront to human dignity; and that differential treatment of a group of persons on the basis of race might therefore be capable of constituting degrading treatment when differential treatment on some other ground would raise no such question.[97]

It must be remembered that the Convention does not prohibit racial discrimination *per se*, and this may be seen as an attempt to go some way towards filling a perceived gap in the Convention system. Be that as it may, no further reasons were advanced to show what circumstances other than the application of racially discriminatory legislation had occurred. The conclusion that degrading treatment had taken place flowed from the 'affront to human dignity' inherent in the practice rather than its actually having had a degrading effect (which is not to say that this might not also have been the case).

Similar concerns have attended the question of whether corporal punishment is to be regarded as degrading. The leading case is *Tyrer v UK*.

---

[94] *East African Asians v UK*, Comm Rep, 14 Dec 1973, para 189.
[95] ibid.   [96] ibid, para 195.   [97] ibid, para 207.

The applicant had, as a fifteen-year-old, been subjected to a judicial birching in the Isle of Man following his pleading guilty to an unlawful assault occasioning actual bodily harm to a senior pupil at his school. Although some aspects of his claim were directly based upon the mental anguish that the delay in carrying out the sentence had upon him, the general thrust of his argument was that the practice of judicial corporal punishment was widely recognized as inhuman and degrading. The Commission did not think 'that corporal punishment in the Isle of Man falls within the meaning of torture or inhuman treatment or punishment as understood in its previous jurisprudence or by any ordinary understanding of those terms', but accepted that: 'Judicial birching humiliates and disgraces the offender and can therefore be said to be degrading treatment or punishment'.[98] Once again, it was the nature of the practice rather than its effects in the particular case in hand that was decisive.[99]

Of course, all forms of punishment carry with them a degree of humiliation and the Court pointed out that 'it would be absurd to hold that judicial punishment generally, by reason of its usual and perhaps almost inevitable element of humiliation, is 'degrading' within the meaning of Article 3'. However, the Court went on to confirm that:

the humiliation or debasement involved must attain a particular level and must in any event be other than the usual element of humiliation [inherent in judicial punishment]. The assessment is in the nature of things, relative: it depends on all the circumstances of the case and, in particular, on the nature and context of the punishment itself and the manner and method of its execution.[100]

On the facts of the case, the Court concluded that this degree of severity had been reached, pointing out that this was an institutionalized infliction of physical violence, constituting an assault on the applicant's dignity and physical integrity, compounded by the aura of official proceedings and its being administered by strangers (police officers).[101]

The approach of the Court was the subject of a powerful dissent by Judge Fitzmaurice.[102] He pointed out that if one is to draw distinctions based upon the level of severity of the treatment 'the tribunal must consider such aspects as the age, general health, bodily characteristics and current physical and mental condition of the person concerned, or other actual features of the case, any one of which may either increase or diminish the intensity of the effect produced'.[103] In his opinion, the Court had

---

[98] *Tyrer v UK*, Comm Rep, 14 Dec 1976, paras 32, 35.

[99] This is confirmed in the pleading of the Commission's Principal Delegate in the case, as he himself recounts in Kellberg, L (1991) 'The Case-Law of the European Commission of Human Rights' in Cassese, 97, 108–10.

[100] *Tyrer v UK*, Judgment, 25 Apr 1978, Ser A, No 26, para 30.   [101] ibid, para 33.

[102] The inadequacy of the Court's legal reasoning was also criticized by Zellick, G (1978) 'Corporal Punishment in the Isle of Man', 27 ICLQ 665.

[103] *Tyrer v UK*, Judgment, 25 Apr 1978, Ser A, No 26, Separate Opinion of Judge Fitzmaurice, para 3.

not done this and it was 'perfectly plain that, for all practical purposes, it is not "the other circumstances of the punishment" at all, but the punishment itself, and as such, that the Court regards as degrading'.[104] Judge Fitzmaurice observed that:

Modern opinion has come to regard corporal punishment as an *undesirable* form of punishment. . . . But the fact that a certain form of punishment is undesirable form of punishment does not turn it into a degrading one.[105]

He concluded with the observation that:

The fact that a certain practice is felt to be distasteful, undesirable or morally wrong and as such ought not to be allowed to continue is not a sufficient ground in itself for holding it to be contrary to Article 3. Still less is the fact that the Article fails to provide against types of treatment or punishment which, though they may legitimately be disapproved of, cannot, considered objectively and in relation to all the circumstances involved, reasonably be regarded without exaggeration as amounting, *in the particular case*, to any of the specific forms of treatment or punishment which the Article does provide against. Any other view would mean using the Article as a vehicle of indirect penal reform, for which it was not intended.[106]

This, of course, is exactly what the Article has become—a vehicle for indirect penal reform. It is, however, instructive to compare the approach taken by the Commission and Court in the *Tyrer* case with that adopted in the subsequent case of *Campbell and Cosans*. This raised the question of whether the use of corporal punishment as a disciplinary measure in the schools attended by the applicants' children amounted to a violation of Article 3. Neither of their children had in fact been subjected to corporal punishment but the son of Cosans had been suspended because of his refusal to submit to such a punishment. The approach adopted by the Court was rather different from that it had taken in *Tyrer*. Once again, the Court stressed the need for degrading treatment to have caused the person concerned humiliation or debasement attaining a minimum level of severity 'either in the eyes of others or in his own eyes', and that this had to be assessed in the light of the circumstances of the case. However, the manner in which this was done was very different. The Court considered whether the practice was actually considered degrading within Scotland and gave weight to this when concluding that it was not.[107] The Court then considered whether the boys had been humiliated or debased in their own eyes and, in concluding that this was not the case, observed

---

[104] ibid, para 8. He later said that he could have understood it if the Court had concluded that the manner in which the punishment had been inflicted had caused, in this case, a greater level of degradation than that inherent in the practice, but it had expressly chosen not to base itself on this ground and had preferred to work on the basis that 'any judicial corporal punishment meted out to a juvenile is degrading' which he felt was too broad a proposition (para 11).

[105] ibid, para 11.   [106] ibid, para 14.

[107] *Campbell and Cosans v UK*, Judgment, 22 Feb 1982, Ser A, No 48, para 29.

that 'it has not been shown by means of medical certificates or otherwise that they suffered any adverse psychological or other effects'. It admitted that Cosans 'may well have experienced feelings of apprehension or disquiet when he came close to an infliction of the tawse but such feelings are not sufficient to amount to degrading treatment, within the meaning of Article 3'.[108]

The principal difference between the cases concerns the relevance of the contextual circumstances. In *Tyrer*, the Court was very much of the opinion that judicial corporal punishment was degrading *per se* and the precise circumstances of its application were of little relevance. In *Campbell and Cosans* the Court was not prepared to be so dogmatic and, in consequence, paid greater attention to the question of whether the practice was considered degrading in the eyes of others or in the eyes of the victim. It seems, therefore, that there were three relevant categories: treatment which is degrading in the opinion of the Commission or Court, in the eyes of others, and in the eyes of the victim. Once it has been accepted that the practice is degrading *per se*, the precise circumstances of its application become irrelevant. If it has not been so decided, the full range of contextual factors come into play—including, it should be noted, the degree of injury sustained, the purpose of the treatment or punishment and the justifications advanced for its use.[109]

This may be illustrated by a further case dealing with corporal punishment in schools. In a most revealing passage, the Commission explained in *Y v UK* that:

to date, it has not found that moderate corporal punishment in schools constitutes, as a general principle, institutionalized violence of the kind observed in the *Tyrer* case which would be in breach of Article 3 of the Convention. The Commission, like the Court has always assessed claims of the present kind on the basis of the particular circumstances of the individual case.[110]

It went on to find a violation of Article 3 in this case because of the degree of pain inflicted, noting that:

such injury to a teenage boy is unacceptable . . . the Commission sees no justification for treating the applicant in this way. In particular it can find no pedagogical reason for dealing with the applicant's bullying behaviour with a punishment on the same bullying level, i.e. the use of superior strength to hurt and degrade another. The Commission notes that little pedagogical justification was put forward . . .[111]

---

[108] *Campbell and Cosans v UK*, Judgment, 22 Feb 1982, Ser A, No 48, para 30.

[109] See also Duffy (1983), 319, who argues that there is a balance to be struck between what an applicant subjectively considers to be degrading and the reasonableness of that attitude in the circumstances of the case.

[110] *Y v UK*, Comm Rep, 8 Oct 1991, para 42.

[111] ibid, paras 43–4. This is to be contrasted with *Costello-Roberts v UK*, Judgment, 25 Mar 1993, Ser A, No 247-C, in which a seven-year-old boy was slippered three times on his buttocks through his shorts with a rubber soled gym shoe by the headmaster in private. Both

It concluded that there had been 'significant physical injury and humiliation which attained such a level of seriousness that it constituted degrading treatment and punishment.[112] This remarkably confused exposition leaves little doubt that a coherent approach to the threshold of degrading treatment cannot be located in the severity of suffering experienced by the victim.[113] It also suggests that *justifications* for the treatment or punishment are never far from the minds of the Commission.

This is not the place to consider in depth the jurisprudence relating to degrading treatment. The purpose of the foregoing discussion has been to illustrate that what is taken to be degrading treatment depends not only on whether a particular act was in fact degrading, either in the eyes of the applicant or in the eyes of others, but often turns on whether a particular practice is deemed to be degrading, irrespective of the particular circumstances.[114] This is very much a policy decision that lies in the hands of the Strasbourg organs.[115]

---

the Commission and Court concluded that there had been no violation of Article 3. The Court noted that there was no evidence of any 'severe or long lasting effects as a result of the treatment complained of' and, since the treatment had not reached the minimum threshold of severity required, there was no violation of Article 3. See Phillips, B (1994) 'The Case for Corporal Punishment in the United Kingdom. Beaten into submission in Europe?', 43 ICLQ 153, for an examination of the corporal punishment cases. See also *A v UK* , Comm Rep, 18 Sept 1997, paras 35–41, for a recent example of a case in which the Commission marginalized the importance of contextualizing factors outlined in *Costello-Roberts* given the relatively greater seriousness of the injuries sustained.

[112] Y v UK, Comm Rep, 8 Oct 1991, para 45.

[113] But cf Phillips (1994), 161, who argues that the severity of suffering is the only factor which differentiates 'inhuman' from 'degrading' treatment. He also appears to take a subjective approach to determining whether a threshold of severity has been crossed. Such an approach would prevent Article 3 being used as a vehicle for 'operational policies' in the manner identified by Addo and Grief (1995), 178. For an example of a subjective element to the determination of the severity of suffering see *A v UK*, Comm Rep, 18 Sept 1997, para 39, where the Commission drew attention to the applicant's assertion that his caning had 'hurt a lot'. Whether this could cause the level of suffering to cross any thresholds, or merely alter the impact of other contextualizing factors is unclear.

[114] For example, in *B v France*, Comm Rep, 6 Sept 1990, the Commission thought that the failure of the French authorities to allow a transsexual to alter her official documents to reflect her change of sex violated Article 8 but was not sufficiently degrading to be in breach of Article 3. Even though it accepted that it created 'embarrassment for her in respect of third persons to whom she is constantly forced to reveal her particular situation', the Commission did not think this could be construed as 'inhuman' and was 'not such as to cause the applicant feelings of fear, anguish and inferiority capable of humiliating and degrading her' beyond the level necessary to establish a violation of Article 8 (para 86). It is very difficult to justify this conclusion, particularly if one compares it to the standard of humiliation set in other contexts. Is it really so much more degrading for a school child to be given four strokes with a cane than for a woman to be officially identified as a man and repeatedly called on to explain her sexual history?

[115] See, for example, the views expressed by Louciades in his concurring opinions to the Reports of the Commission in *Costello-Roberts v UK*, Ser A, No 247-C, 81 and *A v UK*, Comm Rep, 18 Sept 1997, where he maintains that the nature of corporal punishment in itself is a sufficiently severe blow to and degradation of the personality of the individual as to amount to such treatment. The role of policy factors in relation to Article 3 is examined in greater detail by Addo and Grief (1995).

Where the practice is not deemed degrading by virtue of its very nature, then the purpose underlying it assumes a new relevance. In *Raninen v Finland* the applicant complained of his being handcuffed in the sight of supporters and during transportation to a military establishment, having been (re)arrested for failure to undertake military service when released from custody following sentencing after similar refusals. The Commission had previously expressed the view that handcuffing a prisoner in public was 'clearly not so serious a measure as to amount to degrading treatment within the meaning of Article 3.'[116] However, recalling the *East Africa Asians* case, it accepted that 'a measure which does not involve physical ill-treatment but which lowers a person in rank, position, reputation or character may constitute degrading treatment . . . provided it attains a minimum level or severity',[117] and, in order to determine whether this threshold had been met, observed:

In addition to the objective nature of the treatment and its effects on the person subjected to it, also the purpose of the authority which resorted to the measure may be of relevance in determining whether it fulfils the essential elements of treatment prohibited by Article 3. It is essential whether or not the treatment in question denotes contempt or lack of respect for the personality of the person subjected to it and whether it was designed to humiliate or debase him instead of, or in addition to, achieving other aims.[118]

The Commission, surprisingly, failed to consider whether this had in fact been the case. Rather, it recalled the views of the Court in *Ribitsch v Austria*[119] that, as regards those deprived of their liberty, any recourse to physical force rendered unnecessary by the conduct of the detainee diminished human dignity, and concluded that there had been no such need in this case—in which, moreover, the handcuffing had taken place in public—and that Article 3 had therefore been violated. The argument seems to be that the handcuffing was degrading because it was not necessary. This has nothing whatsoever to do with the actual degree of suffering caused by the action, the 'degrading' nature of which is deduced from the intention imputed to the military police by the unjustified nature of their actions. The Court took a more rigorous approach and did focus more closely on the consequences for the incident for the applicant. Whilst accepting that his feelings of humiliation were of some relevance, the Court concluded that he had not demonstrated that the handcuffing 'was aimed at debasing or humilitating him' and that there was no violation of Article 3.[120]

---

[116] App No 12323/86, Dec 3 June 1987 (unpublished, quoted in *Raninen v Finland*, Comm Rep, 24 Oct 1996, para 51).
[117] *Raninen v Finland*, Comm Rep, 24 Oct 1996, para 50.   [118] ibid, para 52.
[119] *Ribitsch v Austria*, Judgment, 4 Dec 1995, Ser A, no 336, considered below, pp. 100–1, 103.
[120] *Raninen v Finland*, Judgment, 16 Dec 1997, paras 57–9. The judgment as a whole rather suggests that the Court felt that the incident had caused no substantial problems for the applicant since it had not resulting in any physical injury nor had it been linked with his subsequently diagnosed 'undefined psycological problem' (ibid).

Nevertheless, this merely reasserts the need to exercise a degree of vigilance in assessing the facts at the entry threshold. It seems that at the threshold of entry into the gradations inherent in Article 3, the justification for—the purpose of—the action in question continues to play a significant role. It might also be argued that the threshold of entry has been pitched at so low a level that any form of treatment of those in detention deemed inappropriate by the Convention machinery can be considered as falling within the sphere of Article 3 as being, at the very least, 'degrading'.

(c) Inhuman treatment

It has already been pointed out that in the *Greek* case the Commission placed inhuman treatment at the heart of the practical application of Article 3 by providing a working definition and then looking at the ways in which torture and degrading treatment were to be distinguished from it. The Commission reiterated this view in *Ireland v UK* when it said that 'any definition of the provisions of Article 3 of the Convention must start from the notion of "inhuman treatment" '.[121] This is at odds with the 'severity of suffering' approach advanced by the Court in *Ireland v UK*, which requires each case to be examined in order to determine its place upon the spectrum. However, although the cases conform to the orthodoxy that the threshold between degrading and inhuman treatment is based on the severity of suffering, there are reasons to doubt if this is truly the case.

The notion of 'inhuman' treatment or punishment is, paradoxically, the least well developed of the three categories from a theoretical perspective. On the one hand, it stands as a residual category into which acts not 'crossing the threshold' and amounting to torture will fall. On the other hand, it is used as a point of reference when determining whether treatment is to be deemed degrading, in the sense that the level of suffering reached is not sufficient to be categorized as inhuman. In many cases, however, a finding that 'inhuman and degrading' treatment has taken place is made without any real consideration of which is the more appropriate label. This seems to suggest that, in practice, alleged breaches of Article 3 are presumed to raise questions of 'inhuman' treatment or punishment, which by that very fact alone will be deemed degrading. If a practice is not sufficiently serious to meet the threshold of 'inhuman' treatment, then it may be examined to see if it represents a form of degrading treatment. Nevertheless, the starting point will be the concept of 'inhuman or degrading' treatment, unless it is an example of a case, such as corporal punishment in a non-custodial context, which past practice has categorized as 'merely' degrading.

---

[121] *Ireland v UK*, Comm Rep, 25 Jan 1976, Ser B, Vol 23-I, 389.

What, then, is meant by 'inhuman' treatment? The Commission in the *Greek* case defined it as covering

at least such treatment as deliberately causes severe suffering, mental or physical, which, in the particular situation is unjustifiable.

As has been seen, the Commission subsequently accepted that no justification for inhuman treatment was possible and the Court went on to refer to the 'intense physical and mental suffering to the persons subjected thereto'.[122] In consequence, the critical decision to find a form of treatment or punishment inhuman is extremely open textured. Given that ideas of what amounts to severe or intense suffering will change over time, there is little to be gained by trying to gauge in the abstract where this threshold is to be set. However, as with the thresholds between the elements of Article 3, the range of factors are not limited to the severity of suffering but can also embrace more policy-oriented factors.

The *Soering* case illustrates this in a number of ways. *Soering* concerned the extradition of a German national to the United States to face a charge of murder, which carried the death penalty in the State of Virginia. Since Article 2(1) of the ECHR expressly permits the use of the death penalty, the Court concluded that its use could not in itself be deemed in breach of Article 3. However, the Court thought that:

The manner in which it is imposed or executed, the personal circumstances of the condemned person and a disproportionality to the gravity of the crime committed, as well as the conditions of detention awaiting execution, are examples of factors capable of bringing the treatment or punishment received by the condemned person within the proscription of Article 3. Present-day attitudes in the Contracting States to capital punishment are relevant for the assessment whether the acceptable threshold of suffering or degradation has been exceeded.[123]

Applying this to the facts of the case, the Court decided that given the length of time likely to be spent on death row was 6–8 years, that the applicant had been aged only eighteen and in a disturbed mental state at the time

---

[122] *Ireland v UK*, Judgment, 18 Jan 1978, Ser A, No 25, para 167. Judge Fitzmaurice put the case for an alternative approach. He argued that: 'the concept of "inhuman treatment" should be confined to kinds of treatment that (taking some account of the circumstances) no member of the human species ought to inflict on another, or could so inflict without doing grave violence to the human, as opposed to animal, element in his or her make up . . . something amounting to an atrocity, or at least a barbarity. Hence it should not be employed as a mere figure of speech to denote what is bad treatment, ill treatment, maltreatment, rather than, properly speaking, inhuman treatment' (ibid, Separate Opinion, page 125, para 26). This places the threshold of inhuman treatment at a much higher level and focuses upon the nature of the act and the person who commits it, rather than upon the victim and the intensity of suffering. This approach has found no favour.

[123] *Soering v UK*, Judgment, 7 July 1989, Ser A, No 161, para 104.

of the offences, as well as the possibility that he might have been extradited to Germany where he would not have faced a death penalty, extradition was in breach of Article 3. Despite statements to the contrary, the overwhelming impression left by the judgment is that the Court considered the imposition of the death penalty to be contrary to the spirit, if not the letter, of the Convention and the contextual circumstances were seized on as a way of circumventing the textual difficulties with which the Court was faced, difficulties that were absent in the *Tyrer* case where, as has been seen above, a similarly policy-oriented decision was adopted.

This is significant because the Court, quoting its well known statement in *Ireland v UK*, also argued that the determination of what amounted to a violation of Article 3 in the context of extradition and expulsion was governed by the same formula as applied in other situations, that is, 'all the circumstances' of the case. However, the Court pointed out that:

As movement about the world becomes easier and crime takes on a larger international dimension, it is increasingly in the interest of all nations that suspected offenders who flee abroad should be brought to justice. Conversely, the establishment of safe havens for fugitives would not only result in danger for the State obliged to harbour the protected person but also tend to undermine the foundations of extradition. These considerations must also be included among the factors to be taken into account in the interpretation and the application of the notions of inhuman and degrading treatment or punishment in the extradition context.[124]

The pain or humiliation suffered by an individual does not diminish because the efficacy of extradition as a tool in the fight against crime might otherwise be reduced. Indeed, the Court has roundly rejected the idea that the fight against crime can act as a justificatory factor once a suspect is in detention.[125] The introduction of such factors is incompatible with the view that a violation of Article 3 depends upon the severity of suffering that a treatment or punishment causes the victim.

This has been taken up in subsequent cases. In *Chahal v UK* the Court argued that these comments in the *Soering* case did not mean that there was 'room for balancing the risk of ill-treatment against the reasons for expulsion in determining whether a State's responsibility under Article 3 is engaged'.[126] The Court rejected the submission of the UK Government that it was entitled to take into account the threat posed to national security by the continued presence of the applicant within the UK. It took

[124] ibid, para 89.
[125] See eg, *Tomasi v France*, Judgment, 27 Aug 1992, Ser A, No 241-A, para 115; *Ribitsch v Austria*, Judgment, 4 Dec 1995, Ser A, No 336, para 38 and see below, pp. 100–1.
[126] *Chalal v UK*, Judgment, 15 Nov 1996, para 81.

the view that 'the activities of the individual in question, however undesirable or dangerous, cannot be a material consideration',[127] and therefore national security 'could not be invoked to override the interest of the individual where substantial grounds had been shown for believing that he would be subject to ill-treatment if expelled'.[128] Despite the presence of a sizable dissenting minority,[129] this approach was subsequently confirmed by a unanimous Court in *Ahmed v Austria*.[130]

At first sight, this might suggest that the Court is indeed concerned only with the severity of suffering. 'Expulsion' cases, however, do not really turn on the 'severity of suffering' at all:[131] rather, they turn on the risk of ill-treatment occuring at some point in the future should an expulsion take place.[132] To that extent, the Court is exercising a form of preventive jurisdiction. The standard of proof of 'substantial risk' itself can amount to little more than an impressionistic assessment of the situation prevailing in the country in question at the time of the threatened expulsion. This can appear more like a policy decision that a particular state is a 'bad risk' for certain categories of individuals than a genuine assessment of the risk actually run by a particular individual in all the circumstances of the case.[133] It is also worth observing that a more stringent approach

---

[127] *Chalal v UK*, Judgment, 15 Nov 1996, para 80.   [128] ibid, para 78.

[129] Seven of the nineteen Judges argued that 'a Contracting State which is contemplating the removal of someone from its jurisdiction to that of another State may legitimately strike a fair balance between, on the one hand, the nature of the threat to its national security interests if the person concerned were to remain and, on the other, the extent of the potential risk of ill-treatment of that person in the State of destination ... the greater the risk of ill-treatment, the less weight should be accorded to the security threat'.

[130] *Ahmed v Austria*, Judgment, 17 Dec 1996, para 41.

[131] In *Vilvarajah v UK*, Judgment, 30 Oct 1991, Ser A, No 215, para 107, the Court recognized the need for the ill-treatment to attain a minimum level of severity to fall within the scope of Article 3. This requirement was not mentioned in *Chahal v UK* and *Ahmed v Austria* (though doubtless the threshold was passed) but was recalled by the Commission in *Bahaddar v Netherlands*, Comm Rep, 13 Sept 1996, para 88 (iii), but was not specifically examined.

[132] cf *Nsoma v Netherlands*, Judgment, 28 Nov 1996, 1996-V RJD 1979. This concerned the manner in which the return of a nine-year-old girl to Zaire was handled by the Dutch authorities, rather than any threat of ill-treatment by the Zairean authorities on her return. The Court, recalling the need for a mimimum level of severity, concluded that her seven-day journey 'must have been a distressing experience' but was not treatment 'of such a nature as to make it "inhuman or degrading"' for the purposes of Article 3 (ibid, para 99).

[133] eg in *Chahal v UK*, Judgment, 15 Nov 1996, paras 104–5, the Court noted that, in addition to the threat posed by the Punjabi security forces, 'it also attaches significance to the fact that attested allegations of serious human rights violations have been levelled at the police elsewhere in India.... [T]he violation of human rights in certain members of the security forces in Punjab and elsewhere is a recalcitrant and enduring problem. See also *Ahmed v Austria*, Judgment, 17 Dec 1996, para 42: 'his activities in an opposition group and the general situation in Somalia gave grounds for fear that, if he returned there, he would be subject to persecution'; *Bahaddar v Netherlands*, Comm Rep, 13 Sept 1996, para 101: 'police in Bangladesh were reported routinely to employ psychological and physical torture and other abuse during arrests and interrogations'.

to expulsion cases has coincided with the increased rigour which many Council of Europe countries have brought to their asylum laws: and in *Chahal v UK* the Court observed that: 'The protection afforded by Article 3 is thus wider than that provided by Articles 32 and 33 of the UN 1951 Convention on the Status of Refugees',[134] which permit a State to expel a refugee on grounds of national security or public order. Once again, it seems as if the Court might be attempting to forge by the backdoor a right—this time a right akin to political asylum—which is not found within the Convention.[135] Whatever the truth of the matter, the 'severity of suffering' does not seem to be at the heart of the matter.

(d) Conclusion

It is clear, then, that although the European Commission and Court of Human Rights have embraced and continue to endorse an interpretation of Article 3 which is based upon the severity of suffering involved, this is not fully reflected in their practice. The other factors which are taken into account when determining the level of severity which has been reached are neither clear nor consistent either within or between the categories. This reinforces the tendency to consider what amounts to torture, or inhuman or degrading treatment in a rather impressionistic fashion.

Approaching Article 3 in this manner also has the paradoxical effect of lessening the impact of the finding that it has been breached: the conclusion that a person has been treated in a fashion which, although degrading and even inhuman, is not sufficiently serious as to amount to torture, tends to place the emphasis upon what has not been done, rather than upon what has. Yet inhuman or degrading treatment or punishment is as great a violation of Article 3 as is torture. Even if the Commission and Court are correct in seeking to differentiate between these terms on the basis of the severity of suffering, there should be no suggestion that a degrading or inhuman act is any less serious.

A final point concerns our understanding of what torture comprises. The focus upon the severity of the suffering must be placed alongside the reluctance to adopt a subjective approach to its evaluation,[136] thus avoiding the need to determine whether a particular form of treatment

---

[134] *Chahal v UK*, Judgment, 15 Nov 1996, para 80.

[135] See *Vilvarajah v UK*, Judgment, 30 Oct 1991, Ser A, No 215, para 102. This has been frequently endorsed by the Court, eg, *Chahal v UK*, Judgment, 15 Nov 1996, para 73 and *Ahmed v Austria*, Judgment, 17 Dec 1996, para 38.

[136] On subjectivity and the 'severity of suffering' see also Dinstein, Y (1981) 'The rights to Life, Physical Integrity, and Liberty' in Henkin, L (ed) *The International Bill of Rights—The Covenant on Civil and Political Rights* (New York, Columbia University Press), 123; Novak (1993), 130.

or punishment was 'torture' to a frail or elderly person, but inhuman or degrading to a fitter or younger person better able to endure it. In consequence, the term 'torture' is still most often used to describe forms of treatment which will occasion severe suffering irrespective of the particular characteristics of the victim. This renders it more difficult to categorize certain practices as acts of torture, such as, for example, extended periods of solitary confinement. Of course, it would not matter that such practices might be labled 'inhuman or degrading' if this was considered to be equally unacceptable. The reality, however, is that it is not. Indeed, how can it be, when a degree of opprobrium needs to be reserved for the more 'severe' form of treatment?

The Court and Commission have developed an extremely flexible and inclusive attitude to the question of what constitutes inhuman and degrading treatment, whilst retaining a much more formalistic approach to torture, based upon the severity of suffering. Perhaps the time has come for it to be recognized that this not only produces an incoherent jurisprudence, but that it runs the risk of downgrading the fight against ill-treatment by understating the evils of inhuman and degrading treatment or punishment.

5 ARTICLE 3 AND ILL-TREATMENT IN DETENTION

The purpose of the previous section has been to illustrate and develop the theme that, no matter how necessary it might be (or has become) for studies of Article 3 in the context of the ECHR, and of the general international outlawry of 'torture, inhuman or degrading treatment or punishment', to work from within the framework of the 'severity of suffering', it is not necessary to do so for the purposes of this study of the work of the CPT. Rather than look to the jurisprudence of the ECHR and other international bodies, the CPT ought to be looking to develop its own, autonomous understanding of the phemonema which it is attempting to prevent. Indeed, such an approach receives support from the recent developments in the jurisprudence of the Commission and Court relating to Article 3, outlined in the previous section, which emphasize that detention provides a specific context in which the application of Article 3 cannot be understood either solely or principally from the perspective of the 'severity of suffering'. This current section will explore this further. It should be stressed at the outset that the CPT need not necessarily take a similar approach. It is, however, likely that the approach which it does adopt will not be less expansive than that now taken under the ECHR.

In *Hurtado v Switzerland*, the Commission confirmed that:

the State has a specific positive obligation to protect the physical well-being of persons deprived of their liberty.[137]

There has yet to be a finding that the very fact that a person has been placed in custody amounts to a violation of Article 3, although in theory this is possible. There has, however, been a considerable number of cases which have called into question the manner in which persons in custody have been treated. The special position of those in detention has come to affect both the assessment of whether treatment meets the threshold of seriousness,[138] and establishing responsibility for physical injuries received, issues which pervade the work of the CPT.

(a) The threshold of seriousness for physical injury

In the *Greek* case, the Commission distinguished between acts prohibited by Article 3 and what it called 'a certain roughness of treatment' which it was felt most detainees not only tolerated but took for granted. These, it said, 'may take the form of slaps or blows of the hand on the head or face. This underlines the fact that the point up to which prisoners and the public may accept physical violence as being neither cruel nor excessive varies between different societies and even between different sections of them'.[139] In *Ireland v UK* the Court envisaged a situation in which morally reprehensible and illegal acts of violence need not necessarily attain the threshold of seriousness necessary to engage responsibility under Article 3.

However, there has since been an acceptance that the abuse of a position of superiority is a factor to be taken into account when assessing whether ill-treatment is inhuman or degrading. In the *Tyrer* case the Court said that:

The very nature of judicial corporal punishment is that it involves one human being inflicting physical violence on another human being. Furthermore, it is institutionalized violence, that is in the present case violence permitted by the law, ordered by the judicial authorities of the State and carried out by the police authorities of the State. Thus although the applicant did not suffer any severe or long-lasting physical effects, his punishment—whereby he was treated as an object in the power of the authorities—constituted an assault on precisely that which it is one of the main purposes of Article 3 to protect, namely a person's dignity and physical integrity.[140]

[137] *Hurtado v Switzerland*, Comm Rep, 8 July 1993, para 79.
[138] cf *Aydin v Turkey*, in which the fact of being in custody contributed to the finding that the acts in question amounted to torture, as opposed to inhuman or degrading treatment. See above, pp. 84–6.
[139] *Greek* case, Comm Rep, 5 Nov 1969, 12 *ECHRYb* 501.
[140] *Tyrer v UK*, Judgment, 25 Apr 1978, Ser A, No 26, para 33.

If institutionalized physical violence is degrading treatment, unauthorized physical violence meted out by those in authority must also fall within the bounds of Article 3. In *Tomasi v France* the applicant alleged that whilst in police custody he was slapped, kicked, and punched by police officers responsible for questioning him. The Commission observed that:

As far as the injuries are concerned, it should be noted that although they might appear to be relatively slight, they none the less constitute outward signs of the use of physical force on an individual deprived of his liberty and thus vulnerable and in a state of inferiority. Such treatment cannot be justified and, in the circumstances of the case, may be considered both inhuman and degrading.[141]

This clearly represents a very different approach that places little weight on the surrounding circumstances and focuses on the mere fact of physical force having been used. Before the Court the Government argued that it was necessary to take other factors into account, including 'Mr Tomasi's youth and good state of health, the moderate length of the interrogations ... "particular circumstances" obtaining in Corsica at the time and the fact that he had been suspected of participating in a terrorist attack which had resulted in the death of one man and grave injuries to another'.[142]

The Court's response was emphatic:

... the medical certificates and reports ... attest to the large number of blows inflicted on Mr Tomasi and their intensity; these are two elements which are sufficiently serious to render such treatment inhuman and degrading. The requirements of the investigation and particularly the difficulties inherent in the fight against crime, particularly with regard to terrorism cannot result in limits being placed on the protection to be afforded in respect of the physical integrity of individuals.[143]

This is a step back from the opinion of the Commission, since the Court still required a certain level of severity to be reached.[144] However, in *Ribitsch v Austria* the Court aligned itself with the views of the Commission in the *Tomasi* case and said that:

in respect of a person deprived of his liberty, any recourse to physical force which has not been made strictly necessary by his own conduct diminishes human dignity and is in principle an infringement of the right set forth in Article 3.[145]

This formula, which has been endorsed on numerous occasions, now forms the basis of the Commission's and Court's approach in cases concerning

---

[141] *Tomasi v France*, Comm Rep, 11 Dec 1990, para 105.

[142] *Tomasi v France*, Judgment, 27 Aug 1992, Ser A, No 241-A, para 114.

[143] ibid, para 115.

[144] Although Judge De Meyer argued in his Concurring Opinion that '*any* use of physical force in respect of a person deprived of his liberty, which is not made strictly necessary as a result of his own conduct violates human dignity and must therefore be regarded as a breach ...' (emphasis added).

[145] *Ribitsch v Austria*, Judgment, 4 Dec 1995, Ser A, No 336, para 39.

allegations of ill-treatment of detainees[146] and, as was mentioned above,[147] does not mention the severity of the injuries received at all. The only limitation upon the scope of Article 3 in this context no longer concerns the gravity of the injuries sustained but relates to their cause. This would normally be seen as going to the question of responsibility and will be considered in detail in the following section. However, it is worth noting in conclusion that the manner in which this caveat is phrased—force 'not made strictly necessary by his conduct'—though doubtless intended to cover cases such as forceable restraint in the face of violent behaviour[148] or to avoid self inflicted injuries, could potentially embrace justifications for ill-treatment in the mould of the Parker Report and the Landau Commission.

(b) Determining responsibility for physical injuries sustained in custody

The fact that ill-treatment occurs in police custody has important consequences as regards the assessment of the evidence. In *Ireland v UK* the UK had argued that it was for the applicant to prove the allegations of ill-treatment made against its security forces. The Commission, however, took the view that it was for the respondent government 'to produce evidence showing facts which cast doubt on the evidence given by the victim and supported by medical evidence'.[149] In *Tomasi v France* the Government accepted that the injuries attested by the medical evidence had occurred during the period of custody and this was sufficient for the Commission to conclude that: 'In the absence of any plausible alternative explanation . . . it established that the marks observed . . . were the result of ill-treatment for which the Government bears responsibility'.[150]

In consequence, once it has been established that injuries were sustained in custody, the state will be responsible under Article 3 if they reach

[146] For a recent example see *Assenov and others v Bulgaria*, Comm Rep, 10 July 1997, para 91.

[147] See above, p. 100.

[148] See eg, the very early case of *Zeidler-Kormann v FRG*, App No 2686/65, Comm Dec, 3 Oct 1967, (1968) 11 *ECHRYb* 1020. This concerned very rough handling by prison officers, leading to the applicant being restrained in a strait-jacket. The Commission decided that Article 3 had not been breached.

[149] *Ireland v UK*, Comm Rep, 25 Jan 1976, Ser B, No 23-I, 413.

[150] *Tomasi v France*, Comm Rep, 11 Dec 1990, para 99. This should be compared with *Diaz Ruano v Spain*, Comm Rep, 31 Aug 1993, which concerned the death in custody and alleged ill-treatment of a suspected terrorist. The Commission found that Article 2 of the Convention had not been violated since the policeman had been acting in self defence. However, it was also claimed that marks on the body indicated ill-treatment unconnected with the shooting itself. The Government argued that the marks on the body could have been made when the body was being dragged into a car after the shooting incident and concluded that it 'cannot take it as a fact established beyond all reasonable doubt that the marks in question were caused while he was in police custody'.

the threshold level of severity and if it cannot cast reasonable doubt upon the allegation that they were the result of ill-treatment. This has been confirmed in *Ribitsch v Austria*, which also decided that the fact that a police officer may have been acquitted of a charge in domestic criminal proceedings does not necessarily suffice to disprove the allegation. The Court took the view that since a domestic court was bound by the presumption of innocence and a high standard of proof was necessary to secure a conviction, this alone was not sufficient to prove that injuries sustained during police custody had not been caused by ill-treatment.[151] This goes some way towards clarifying the impact of the decision of the Court in *Klaas v Germany* which had been thought to cast some doubt on the approach taken in *Tomasi*. The *Klaas* case also illustrates the limits of the benevolent approach taken towards to those in custody.[152]

In the *Klaas* case the Commission took the view that 'such considerations likewise apply in cases where a person is arrested by police authorities and thereby subjected to their power'.[153] The Court, however, distinguished the situation from the *Tomasi* case on the grounds that the domestic courts had all concluded that the injuries could have been the result of her resisting arrest and that the use of force had not been excessive in the circumstances of the case. Since it was not the task of the Court to substitute its assessment of the facts for that of the domestic courts and no new material had been introduced to cast doubt on their findings, it decided that there had been no breach of Article 3.[154] This strongly suggested that *Tomasi* was wrongly decided. In the light of the *Ribitsch* case, it would seem that the true ground of distinction lies in the fact that *Klaas* concerned arrest rather than ill-treatment in custody.

This is borne out by *Hurtado v Switzerland* in which the Commission decided that the circumstances of the applicant's arrest did not give rise to a breach of Article 3.[155] The arrest had involved the use of a

---

[151] *Ribitsch v Austria*, Judgment, 4 Dec 1995, Ser A, No 336, para 34.

[152] A further limitation is the need to prove injury. This approach can only apply to forms of ill-treatment which leave sequelae. Other forms of ill-treatment must be proved by the applicant: in *Tomasi* the Commission noted the lack of evidence 'to confirm or refute the allegation that the applicant was stripped naked, deprived of food or threatened with a gun, or that threats were made against his family' and made no findings in relation to these allegations (*Tomasi v France*, Comm Rep, 11 Dec 1990, para 100). See also *Assenov and Others v Bulgaria*, Comm Rep, 10 July 1997, paras 92–8, in which there was insufficent evidence to support a finding that the injuries in question had been sustained during the period of police custody, rather than having been inflicted on the applicant by his father prior to arrest.

[153] *Klaas v Germany*, Comm Rep, 21 May 1992, paras 103–4. The applicant claimed that she had been ill-treated in the course of being arrested in connection with an alleged drink-driving incident. She claimed that her arm had been twisted and her head knocked against a window ledge, resulting in her losing consciousness. She suffered bruising and a long-term injury to her arm.

[154] *Klaas v Germany*, Judgment, 22 Sept 1993, Ser A, No 269, paras 29–30.

[155] *Hurtado v Switzerland*, Comm Rep, 8 July 1993.

stungrenade and the applicant had been forced to the ground, handcuffed, and hooded. He also alleged that he had been beaten. He suffered bruising and a fracture to the anterior arch of a rib. Had such injuries been sustained whilst in custody this would almost certainly have amounted to a breach.

(c) Other forms of ill-treatment

In addition to the allegation of ill-treatment on arrest resulting in physical injury, the *Hurtado* case also raised issues concerning treatment received in police custody and whilst on remand. In addition to his physical injuries, the police action had caused the applicant to defecate in his trousers and he had not been provided with clean clothes on the day of his arrest (if not for longer). The Commission concluded that this was 'humiliating and debasing for the applicant and therefore degrading within the meaning of Article 3 of the Convention'.[156] It also concluded that, given the circumstances of his arrest, the fact that he had not been examined by a doctor for eight days amounted to inhuman treatment.[157] The manner in which these complaints were dealt with certainly indicates that a different approach is taken when assessing violations which occur whilst in detention rather than during arrest. Otherwise, how can one sustain a decision that the act which causes a person to defecate (throwing the stun-grenade) is neither inhuman nor degrading but wearing the soiled trousers for an initial period in custody is. The only cogent explanation is that the use of force in the context of the arrest was justified[158] whereas there was no justification for not providing clean clothes to those under effective police control.

The key question, however, still concerns the threshold of ill-treatment. The *Ribitsch* case suggests that any use of physical force, unless necessitated by the detainee's own actions, will now reach the threshold of seriousness. There can be no question of a legitimate degree of 'rough handling' or 'illegal acts of violence' which fall short of Article 3. Other forms of ill-treatment, however, must still be assessed in the light of all the relevant circumstances in order to determine whether they reveal a violation, but the fact that they relate to, or have occurred in, places of detention is a critical factor.

---

[156] ibid, para 68.   [157] ibid, paras 79–80.

[158] Certainly, four members of the Commission dissented on the basis that the degree of force used was 'extravagant' in the sense of its being 'disproportionate to the exigencies of the situation' and involved techniques (hooding) which 'cannot objectively be justified as necessary'. They concluded that the treatment was 'so severe and unjustified' as to amount to inhuman treatment' (Dissenting Opinion of Louciades, Ermacora, Thune, and Rozakis). Justification is, however, not meant to be a criterion for the assessment of whether an action amounts to inhuman or degrading treatment.

For example, it might be a dreadful indictment of a state if those subject to its jurisdiction are through poverty or inability living in dirty and insanitary or otherwise unacceptable conditions but, no matter how 'inhuman' or 'degrading' the conditions, this does not necessarily engage the responsibility of the state under Article 3. However, should the state be responsible for the creation of those conditions, different considerations might apply. In its Report in the case of *Akdivar and others v Turkey*, the Commission concluded that 'the burning of the applicants' homes by security forces, resulting in their migration from Diyarkabir, and dire personal circumstances, little state assistance having been forthcoming, amounts to inhuman and degrading treatment within the meaning of Article 3 of the Convention'.[159] The Court did not pursue this aspect of the case since it had already found a violation of Article 8(1) and felt there was an 'absence of precise evidence concerning the specific circumstances in which the destruction of the houses took place'.[160] Similarly, in the case of *Mentes and others v Turkey* the Commission decided that villagers had suffered inhuman and degrading treatment when units of the Turkish armed forces had destroyed their homes, since it was 'an act of violence and deliberate destruction in utter disregard of the safety and welfare of the applicants and their children who were left without shelter and assistance in circumstances which caused them anguish and suffering'.[161] Once again, the Court declined to consider this aspect of the case, having found a violation of Article 8(1).[162] At the very least, these cases show that if the state by its own direct action causes a person to endure such conditions, then there may be liability providing the mimimum level of severity is reached.[163]

The case of *Lopez Ostra v Spain*[164] suggests an even wider sphere of application. In this case the applicant argued that the nuisance caused by emissions from a waste-disposal plant, including having to live next to a filthy sewer, was degrading for the purposes of Article 3. Both the Court and Commission found there to have been a breach of Article 8 which imposes positive obligations on the state, but thought that, although difficult, the conditions did not meet the level of severity required for Article 3. This suggests that had they been sufficiently serious then the

---

[159] *Akdivar v Turkey*, Comm Rep, 26 Oct 1995, para 224.

[160] *Akdivar v Turkey*, Judgment, 16 Sept 1996, para 91.

[161] *Mentes v Turkey*, Comm Rep, 7 Mar 1996, para 190. This Report was adopted before the judgment of the Court in *Akdivar v Turkey*.

[162] *Mentes v Turkey*, Judgment, 28 Nov 1997, para 77.

[163] In *Akdivar v Turkey* three members of the Commission took the view that, in all the circumstances, the mimimum level had not been attained, one of whom (Mr Ress) took the view that 'leaving the applicants without any help when their houses were destroyed cannot be regarded as treatment coming within the scope of Article 3'.

[164] *Lopez Ostra v Spain*, Comm Rep, 31 Aug 1993, paras 60–1, Judgment, 9 Dec 1994, Ser A, No 303-C, paras 59–60.

state would have been liable for its failure to prevent the continuation of the nuisance caused by the plant.

However, once a person is placed in detention by the state, it assumes full responsibility for his or her treatment and it then becomes a matter of assessment whether the conditions or treatment received are adequate given that special context. For example, the state may not be obliged to provide health care services freely and available to all, but it is obliged to ensure that those to whom it denies the freedom to seek health-care provision should be adequately provided for.[165] The availability or non-availability of such services in society at large is not the touchstone by which this is to be judged. The result is that the thresholds of ill-treatment must be worked out from within that context and the special circumstances relating to it. Since the CPT is a specialist body established by the Council of Europe to penetrate to the heart of standards of treatment in places of detention, it would be extremely odd for the Commission and the Court to pay no attention to the work of the Committee. As will be seen, a great deal of attention is given to it. In the light of this, it is preferable to explore the standards applied by the Court and Commission alongside consideration of the standards which the CPT has developed in the same field.

---

[165] The recent case of *D v UK*, Judgment, 2 May 1997, provides a striking illustration of this. It was decided that the UK would be in breach of Article 3 in removing a convicted drugs courier suffering from AIDS to his country of origin, St Kitts, following his release on licence from prison because he would be unable to continue to receive the same levels of health care that he was receiving in the UK and upon which his remaining quality of life depended. This was so, even though the general conditions and lack of medical facilities in St Kitts would not itself violate Article 3, and the source of the risk of ill-treatment lay in factors which did not engage the responsibility of the state. The basis of the UK's obligation lay in its having assumed responsibility for his treatment while in custody. The Court did, however, stress that this was a special case, turning on its very exceptional circumstances. For the approach of the CPT to this problem, see Chapter 6, pp. 251–3 and Chapter 8, pp. 314–15.

4

The Origins and Drafting of the European Convention for the Prevention of Torture and Inhuman or Degrading Treatment or Punishment

1 GAUTIER AND THE SWISS COMMITTEE AGAINST TORTURE

Almost every account of the origins of the European Convention for the Prevention of Torture (ECPT) has justly given pride of place to the pioneering efforts of one man, Jean-Jacques Gautier.[1] Gautier was a successful Geneva-based private banker who had a deep Christian commitment and believed it to be his duty to use his wealth to assist his fellow-man. During the latter years of his banking career he became involved in Third World development activities and challenged both public and private Swiss development policies.[2] But in 1973, having followed Amnesty International's world-wide Campaign for the Abolition of Torture,[3] and read about the detail of the *Greek* case in particular, he decided to devote himself to the struggle against torture. At the age of 61 he retired from his bank and began exploring ways and means more effectively to combat torture.

[1] See, for example: Anon (1989) 'In memoriam Jean-Jacques Gautier', 10 HRLJ 132; Burgers, JH and Danelius, H (1988) *The UN Convention Against Torture: A Handbook to the Convention Against Torture and Other Cruel, Inhuman or Degrading Treatment or Punishment* (Dordrecht: Martinus Nijhoff), 26–9; Cassese, A (1989) 'A New Approach to Human Rights: The European Convention for the Prevention of Torture', 83 AJIL 130 (French translation in (1989) *Revue générale de droit international public*, 5); Jenkinson, D (1993) *Torture? In Europe? A study of the European Convention for the Prevention of Torture and Inhuman or Degrading Treatment or Punishment* (Brussels: Quaker Council for Europen Affairs), 7; Cassese, A (1996) *Inhuman States: Imprisonment, Detention and Torture in Europe Today* (Cambridge: Polity Press), 5–6 (originally published in Italian (1994) *Umano-Disumano: Commissariati en prigioni nell'Europa di oggi* (Rome, Bari: Laterza)); Association for the Prevention of Torture (1995) *The Implementation of the European Convention for the Prevention of Torture and Inhuman or Degrading Treatment or Punishment (ECPT): Assessment and Perspectives after Five Years of Activities of the European Committee for the Prevention of Torture and Inhuman or Degrading Treatment or Punishment—Acts of the Seminar of 5 to 7 December 1994, Strasbourg* (Geneva: APT), 207–13. See also APT (1997), which carries the subtitle *recueil d'articles en l'honneur de Jean-Jacques Gautier.*

[2] Interview with Francois de Vargas, Secretary-General of the Swiss Committee against Torture (since 1992 the Association for the Prevention of Torture) from its establishment in 1977 to 1995.

[3] See Amnesty International (1973) *Report on Torture* (London: Amnesty International, International Secretariat).

In 1970 Werner Schmid, a member of the Swiss Parliament, had proposed that the Swiss Federal Council prepare an international convention for the protection of political prisoners.[4] This proposal had been supported by 76 of his parliamentary colleagues and in 1971 the Federal Council commissioned the Henry-Dunant Institute in Geneva to undertake a study of how it should be done. In 1975 Gautier was invited to contribute and he drafted the conclusions to the study, which were submitted to the Swiss Government in March 1976.[5]

Gautier accepted that the work of Amnesty International had raised the consciousness of the world to the existence of torture and its letter campaigns had done a great deal to ameliorate the conditions of many political prisoners. He also recognized that it was necessary to move beyond this and seek to make more effective the international legal prohibition of torture which, whilst widely accepted, had little practical impact. He noted that, with the exception of the ECHR, there was:

une grave lacune: l'absence de tout *contrôle*, à plus forte raison l'absence de sanctions à l'égard des Etats qui ne respectent pas leurs obligations.[6]

Gautier was struck by the fact that even during the Holocaust, Jewish prisoners of war were well treated by their German captors. He attributed this to the ability of the International Committee of the Red Cross (ICRC) to visit prisoner-of-war camps[7] and, basing himself on this model,[8] conceived the idea of establishing by a convention an impartial body of persons authorized to visit places of detention, and able to publish the results of their inquiries in the event of states breaching their international legal obligations not to torture.[9] He also noted that the Red Cross

---

[4] Gautier, J-J (1977) 'Le Proposition de Jean-Jacques Gautier' in *Contre La Torture: Une Arme Nouvelle* (Geneva: La Vie Protestante), 16.

[5] Vargas, F de (1979) 'History of a Campaign' in International Commission of Jurists/ Swiss Committee Against Torture, *Torture: How to Make the International Convention Effective* (Geneva: International Committee of Jurists and Swiss Committee Against Torture).

[6] Gautier (1977), 11–12. At the time Gautier was writing, the International Covenant on Civil and Political Rights, and its First Optional Protocol, had recently entered into force (on 23 March 1976: see 999 UNTS 171). These instruments established the Human Rights Committee and granted individuals the right of individual petition but this was very much in embryo.

[7] However, the ICRC was excluded from the civil concentration camps such as Auschwitz and Buchenwald and unable to intervene in the horrors that were perpetrated in them. The ICRC was admitted only to Theresienstadt, a sort of show-camp for foreign visitors (see Facez, J-C (1988) *Une Mission Impossible? Le CICR, les déportations et les camps de concentration nazis* (Lausannes: Editions Payot)). The ICRC was also excluded from Greece in 1969 following the withdrawal of Greece from the Council of Europe in anticipation of their condemnation for the use of torture by the European Court of Human Rights and moves to expel them from the Council.

[8] Henry Dunant, the effective founder of the ICRC, had himself been spurred to action following his witness of the horrors that followed the battle of Solferino in 1859: Facez, J-C (1988).

[9] Gautier (1977), 13.

had developed into an organization enjoying near universal support from comparatively modest beginnings[10] and concluded that if a few states initially agreed to submit themselves to a system of inspection aimed at the prevention of torture, public pressure could eventually be brought to bear on others to join.[11]

These ideas received considerable public support in Switzerland, including that of the former ICRC President Eric Martin,[12] and in 1977 Gautier formed the Swiss Committee Against Torture (SCAT) to realize his vision. A Committee of Experts was established under the chairmanship of Professor Christian Dominicé and produced a draft 'Convention for the Treatment of Persons deprived for their Liberty'.[13] The Swiss Government, however, did not lend their support, considering plans for a convention idealistic and potentially compromising to the position of the ICRC.[14] The Swiss Parliament, however, rejected the Government's lead and in December 1977 supported Werner Schmid's original motion.

At about the same time that these events were taking place within Switzerland, international recommendations regarding torture were being presented in Geneva at the United Nations. Moreover, there were other non-governmental developments: Gautier was part of a much wider stream of consciousness. For example, Action des Chrétiens pour l'Abolition de la Torture (ACAT) was formed by Hélène Engel and Edith du Tertre in France in 1974 and their lead was followed by the creation of similar groups in many countries (since 1987 grouped together in the Fédération Internationale de l'Action des Chrétiens pour l'Abolition de la Torture (FIACAT)). In 1977 the *Revue Internationale de Droit Pénal* devoted a special issue of the journal to the question of torture[15] and in the same year the World Council of Churches, meeting in Geneva, issued a six-page 'Statement on Torture' and Amnesty International organized a seminar on 'Torture and Human Rights' for NGOs in Strasbourg.[16]

Following the lead provided by Amnesty International's 1973 worldwide Campaign for the Abolition of Torture, which culminated in a Conference for the Abolition of Torture in Paris in December 1973, several governments brought the issue of torture before the United Nations General Assembly.[17] A draft resolution was presented according to which the

[10] It was originally based upon an agreement between eleven 'advanced' states (ibid, 13–14).
[11] ibid, 15.   [12] ibid, 31–2.
[13] Vargas (1979), 43. Dominicé said of the proposal: 'We are asking for a little and a lot at the same time. The authorization of visits is a small thing. But at the same time it is immense, since we are asking States to lift the veil from the very thing they are most anxious to hide' (ibid). cf Cassese (1989), 150: 'the mechanism . . . takes the element of supervision substantially further than it had previously been taken in relation to peacetime human rights'.
[14] Swiss Government response to the Henry-Dunant Institute's proposals, published in June 1977. See Vargas (1979), 43.
[15] Volume 1977, No 3/4.   [16] See Burgers and Danelius (1988), 24–5.
[17] For a comprehensive account of activities at the United Nations see Rodley (1987), 17–42.

General Assembly, 'gravely concerned that torture is still practised in various parts of the world', was invited to decide 'to examine the question of torture and other cruel, inhuman or degrading treatment or punishment in relation to detention and imprisonment as an item at a future session'.[18] The following year the General Assembly adopted a resolution[19] which requested the 5th UN Congress on the Prevention of Crime and the Treatment of Offenders, due to be held in September 1975, to consider a whole raft of matters which had been explored at various meetings of NGOs and professional bodies.[20] This initiative ultimately led to the adoption by the UN General Assembly of the *Code of Conduct for Law Enforcement Officials*[21] and the *Principles of Medical Ethics relevant to the Role of Health Personnel, particularly Physicians, in the Protection of Prisoners and Detainees against Torture and Other Cruel, Inhuman or Degrading Treatment or Punishment*.[22] These developments were complemented by the request made the following year that the Commission on Human Rights draft a *Body of Principles for the Protection of All Persons under Any Form of Detention or Imprisonment*.[23]

The Congress itself decided to give priority to drafting the text which was forwarded to the General Assembly which in December 1975 adopted the *Declaration on the Protection of All Persons from Being Subjected to Torture and Other Cruel, Inhuman or Degrading Treatment or Punishment*.[24] This was followed up in 1977 when the General Assembly asked the

[18] UNGA Res 3059 (XXVIII), adopted 2 Nov 1973. This had been proposed by Sweden, Austria, Costa Rica, the Netherlands, and Trinidad and Tobago. Amendments put forward by Denmark and Egypt were also accepted into the text.

[19] UNGA Res 3218 (XXIX), adopted 6 November 1974.

[20] See Heider, A and van Geuns, H (1976) *Professional Codes of Ethics* (London: Amnesty International, International Secretariat).

[21] In June 1975 Amnesty International held a seminar on an international code of police ethics, the results of which were made known to the 5th UN Congress in September. The task of drafting a code was passed by the General Assembly to the Committee on Crime Prevention and Control and its draft was adopted by the General Assembly in UNGA Res 43/169, adopted 17 Dec 1979. See Burgers and Danelius (1988), 20 and Rodley (1987), 37, 279–90.

[22] UNGA Res 3218 (XXIX) requested the World Health Organization (WHO) to submit outline proposals to the UN 5th Congress, but it was unable to do so. The General Assembly therefore invited the WHO to pursue this itself (UNGA Res 3453 (XXX), adopted 9 Dec 1975), drawing on earlier resolutions adopted by the International Council of Nurses and the Tokyo Declaration of the World Medical Association (WMA). In conjuction with the WMA and the Council for International Organizations of Medical Services (CIOMS) the WHO prepared a draft which was adopted by the General Assemby in UNGA Res 37/194, on 8 Dec 1982. See Burgers and Danelius (1988), 21–2; Rodley (1987), 37, 291–301.

[23] The request was made in UNGA Res 3453 (XXX). Progress on the *Principles of Detention* (responsibility for which was delegated to the Sub-Commission on Prevention of Discrimination and Protection of Minorities) was slow and was finally adopted by the General Assembly in UNGA 43/173, on 9 Dec 1988. See Rodley (1987), 36, 256–77; Burgers and Danelius 1988), 22–3 (both written before the adoption of the *Principles*).

[24] UNGA Res 3452 (XXX), adopted 9 Dec 1975. See Rodley (1987), 19–35 for a detailed account of the 1973–5 period. For a more general account, see Burgers and Danelius (1988), 13–25.

Commission on Human Rights to prepare a draft Convention Against Torture and Other Forms of Cruel, Inhuman or Degrading Treatment or Punishment.[25]

When the Commission met in February 1978 it had before it the texts of two draft conventions presented by the Swedish Government[26] and the International Association of Penal Law.[27] Both included a definition of torture before setting out measures—legislative, judicial, and administrative—that ratifying states would be obliged to take to prevent torture or persons in their jurisdiction being subjected to torture. Neither draft, however, provided for an enforcement mechanism: reliance was placed entirely on state parties reporting on the measures taken by them to comply with the convention, though the Swedish Draft provided for an enquiry procedure in the event of there being evidence of 'systematic torture'; an inquiry might include a visit to the country concerned, but it would only be with the country's consent.[28]

At the beginning of 1978, therefore, there were three draft conventions against torture circulating, two of them not providing for the system of inspection which Gautier and leading NGOs knowledgeable about the phenomenon of torture increasingly considered essential. The Swedish Government, like the Swiss Government, thought the Gautier idea of visits unrealistic and, it was argued, pursuing it might slow down or prejudice the acceptance of any Convention Against Torture within the United Nations. It was Niall McDermot, then Secretary General of the International Commission of Jurists (ICJ), who saw that there might nevertheless be a way of bringing these ideas together.

McDermot suggested to Gautier that his text might be converted into an Optional Protocol to the draft Convention considered by the Commission on Human Rights. This was formally proposed at a conference organized by the Swiss University at St Gall in June 1978[29] and the ICJ and the SCT went on to publish a widely-circulated pamphlet putting forward the text of a draft Optional Protocol.[30] Gautier argued that:

[25] UNGA Res 32/64, adopted 8 Dec 1977. See Rodley (1987), 39–40; Burgers and Danelius (1988), 34. For the most thorough and authoratative account of the drafting of the UN Convention against Torture, see Burgers and Danelius (1988), 31–113.

[26] UN Doc E/CN.4/1285 (1978). The text of the Swedish proposal is reproduced as Appendix 1 in ICJ/SCAT (1979).

[27] Reproduced as Appendix 2 in ICJ/SCAT (1979). Elements of this were subsequently incorporated in a revised version of Swedish text, which became the basis of the Commission's deliberations. Burgers and Danelius (1988), 26.

[28] Swedish Draft, Article 17.   [29] Vargas (1979), 45.

[30] The draft received the support of many NGOs including, *inter alia*, Amnesty International, Christian Action for the Abolition of Torture (ACAT), the World Council of Churches, the International Federation of Human Rights, the International League for Human Rights, Pax Christi and Pax Romana (ICJ/SCAT (1979), 49). Eric Martin also wrote an introduction (ibid, 14–15) although the ICRC, of which he was formerly President and which has a policy of not expressing any opinion about issues being considered in the political forum of the United Nations, was necessarily silent.

There is nothing to prove that a fresh undertaking by a State which has already violated treaty obligations will prevent it from repeating such violations. Indeed, there is a danger that, by multiplying the number of conventions without being able to check whether they are respected, harm is done to their credibility and even to the value of international law. Hence, there is legitimate reason to doubt the utility of a new convention if it does not strengthen the existing procedures for implementation.[31]

Gautier considered the existing implementation mechanisms adopted in human rights instruments, (and reflected in the Swedish proposal) to be 'quasi-judicial' and placed the state in the position of an accused.[32] He did not dismiss the well-established reporting and enquiry procedures within the United Nations and argued that the ICJ/SCAT proposals, modelled as they were on the practice of the ICRC, were 'another parallel system of verification, which is more speedy, less politicized and does not involve a State being put on trial'.[33] Gautier's proposal, according to his own account, was relatively simple:

an international committee elected by an assembly of the Member States of the Protocol would be empowered to send to the territory of each of these States on a regular basis delegates authorized to visit, without prior notification, any centre for interrogation, detention or imprisonment. The Committee will then inform the State concerned of the findings made by its delegates and will make an effort, if necessary, to bring about an improvement in the treatment of those in detention. In the event of disagreement as to the Committee's findings or as to the implementation of its recommendations, the Committee will be able to publish its findings.[34]

Gautier characterized the contrast between what he proposed and the existing implementation procedures as follows:

- instead of a dramatic enquiry, *routine visits* to which the state will agree to submit its territory;
- instead of a charge being made against a state, a system of *mutual assistance and collaboration* to improve the protection of prisoners;
- instead of a state being found guilty of a violation, stress will be laid on *prevention*;
- instead of a time-consuming procedure, full of pitfalls, a possibility of *swift action*;
- instead of clashes between governments, *a nucleus of committed states in the fight against torture*, determined to ensure full openness in the treatment of their prisoners.[35]

---

[31] Gautier, J-J (1979) 'The Case for an Effective and Realistic Procedure' in ICJ/SCAT (1979), 32.

[32] Not only was this a long and drawn out process but, in the context of the United Nations, could also became a heavily politicized process. Moreover, the 'absence of a procedure for investigating and verifying the allegations weakens considerably the procedure and makes it largely nugatory' (ibid, 32–3).

[33] ibid, 33–4.   [34] ibid, 34–5.   [35] ibid, 35.

However, it was not just the Swiss and Swedish Governments that had doubts about the draft protocol. Some governments were concerned that an Optional Protocol might complicate and retard the progress of the Convention whilst others were concerned that there might be moves to transfer to the Optional Protocol the basic implementation provisions that the Swedish draft currently contained.[36] Thus in March 1980, when the government of Costa Rica agreed to submit the Draft Optional Protocol to the Commission on Human Rights of which it was a member, it did so requesting that consideration of it be deferred until after the adoption of the Convention itself.[37] The UN Convention Against Torture was adopted in 1984 and at the time of writing, the prospects for the adoption of an Optional Protocol are still unclear.[38] However, in the meanwhile, the focus of attention shifted to the Council of Europe.[39]

2 THE COUNCIL OF EUROPE

In January 1981 the Parliamentary Assembly of the Council of Europe considered a Report drawn up by Mrs Meier, the Rapporteur of its Legal Affairs Committee, which examined the progress being made towards the adoption of the UN Torture Convention.[40] Echoing Gautier, the Report noted that the operative provisions of the Swedish Draft were 'quasi-judicial in nature and carried with them the usual drawbacks of complexity

---

[36] Burgers and Danelius (1988), 28.   [37] Vargas (1979), 46.

[38] Costa Rica put forward a new draft Optional Protocol to the UN Commission on Human Rights in 1991 (E/CN.4/1993/28) Commission Res 43/92, adopted 5 Mar 1992, and established an open-ended working group (WG 11) to prepare a text for adoption. This is continuing to meet annually. The reports of the Working Group are contained in UN Docs E/CN.4/1993/28; E/CN.4/1994/25, E/CN.4/1995/38, E/CN.4/1996/28, E/CN.4/1997/33. For an analysis of progress to the end of 1995 see APT (1996) *Working Group on the Draft Optional Protocol to the Convention against Torture and Other Cruel, Inhuman or Degrading Treatment or Punishment, Analytical Report of the Association for the Prevention of Torture* (Geneva: Association for the Prevention of Torture).

[39] We are grateful to the Council of Europe for granting us permission to consult the documentary sources concerning the evolution of the ECPT. Other accounts of the drafting history which draw on the *travaux préparatoires* are Cassese, (1989) and MacDonald, R St John (1992) 'The European Convention for the Prevention of Torture and Inhuman or Degrading Treatment or Punishment' in Bello, E and Ajibola, B (eds) *Essays in Honour of Judge Taslim Olawale Elias* (Dordrecht: Martinus Nijhoff), 399. Cassese was a member of the Italian delegation serving on the Steering Committee on Human Rights and the Committee of Experts which drafted the text of the Convention (see n 56 below) and was subsequently elected as a member and the first President of the Committee. MacDonald is a Judge of the European Court of Human Rights. See also Vigny, D (1987) 'La Convention européene de 1987 pour la prévention de la torture et peines ou traitements inhumains ou dégradants', 43 *Annuaire suisse de droit international* 62; Decaux, E (1988) 'La Convention européene pour la prévention de la torture et peines ou traitements inhumains ou dégradants', 34 *Annuaire français de droit international* 618; Vargas, F de 'Bref Historique du CSCT-APT' in APT (1997) and Evans and Morgan (1997a).

[40] AS/Jur (32) 22, 8 Dec 1980.

and slowness', that states accused of practising torture tended to politi-
cize the debate and, crucially, that there was no machinery to investigate
and verify the facts. The answer to these problems, she argued, lay in the
proposal for the Optional Protocol which was 'the right one for strengthening the effectiveness of the convention'.[41]

The essence of the then current ICJ/SCAT proposal, as understood by
the Meier Report, was that there would be a fairly small Committee elected
by the states parties which would send delegates on unannounced visits
to places of detention. The delegates would report back to the Committee
which would, on the strength of the findings, make recommendations to
the state. Although modelled on the system operated by the ICRC, it went
beyond it by allowing the publication of its findings if the state failed to
respond in a satisfactory fashion. The advantage of the system was considered to be that since it was, in principle, confidential, the state would
not be put on the defensive but encouraged to co-operate. Additionally,
the system was seen as facilitating rapid action, cutting across protracted
national and international procedures.

The only drawback was considered to be the risk that the proposed
system might delay the acceptance of the Convention itself, and that it
was unlikely to be accepted by governments which did practice torture.
Neither of these were considered to be significant objections. The Meier
Report proposed that this development be endorsed by the Council of
Europe and the Assembly proceeded to adopt Recommendation 909 (1981)
namely, that the Committee of Ministers:[42]

invite the governments of the member states of the Council of Europe represented
on the United Nations Commission on Human Rights to do their utmost to ensure
that the Commission gives detailed consideration to the draft Optional Protocol
as soon as the text of the draft convention has been submitted to the Economic
and Social Council of the United Nations with a view to strengthening the implementation of the convention.

Shortly afterwards, two motions were tabled for resolutions concerning torture in Council of Europe member states to be placed before the
Assembly.[43] In response, Noel Berrier, the French Chairman of the Legal
Affairs Committee submitted an Introductory Memorandum on the subject.[44] This Memorandum drew a distinction between traditional means of
combating torture by *a posteriori* judicial control and preventive methods
designed to ensure that an individual did not fall victim to torture. As

[41] ibid, para 13.
[42] Recommendation 909 (1981) on the International Convention against Torture, adopted
26 Jan 1981, para 9(ii).
[43] These both concerned the situation in Turkey. See Doc 4718(Rev) tabled by Mr Lidbom
and Doc 4730 tabled by Mr Jager.
[44] AS/Jur (33) 18, 9 Sept 1981.

regards the former, Berrier stressed the need for all member states to participate fully in the ECHR mechanisms[45] and drew attention to the possibilities afforded by the inter-state referral system, the right of the Secretary General to request information on a state's compliance with its Convention obligations under Article 57 of the ECHR, and the possibility of an individual petitioning the Assembly under Article 56 of its Rules of Procedure. As regards preventive mechanisms, Berrier recalled the support given in Recommendation 909 to the draft Optional Protocol. The Memorandum recounts that, since 'such a system cannot be expected to be put into swift and perfect operation at world level':[46]

The thought therefore occurred to me that the countries of Europe might set an example and institute such a system among themselves in the framework of the Council of Europe, without waiting for the proposal to be implemented at world level. Such a system would usefully supplement the means available through the Council of Europe to combat torture, means which come into play only after a prisoner has fallen victim to torture.

The draft of the Optional Protocol was included as an annex to the Memorandum and comments on the Memorandum itself and information regarding torture in Europe requested from a number of international organizations and NGOs, including the ICRC, the SCT, the ICJ, and Amnesty International. The ICJ and SCT, in a joint response, welcomed the initiative—noting that 'it could serve to establish the viability and value of the system in what is perhaps the least sensitive region of the world. Europe would once again lead the way, as it did with the ECHR'—and offered to draw up a regional convention or draft protocol to the ECHR.[47]

The offer made by the ICJ/SCT was taken up and they produced a draft text[48] which, along with an explanatory memorandum and the substance of his Introductory Memorandum, formed the body of the final Berrier Report. This was adopted by the Legal Affairs Committee in June 1983. On 28 September 1983 the Parliamentary Assembly adopted Recommendation 971 (1983), which called on the Council of Ministers to adopt the draft Convention.[49]

Article 1 of the draft Convention described the Convention as a 'supplement' to the ECHR procedures intended 'better to ensure respect for

[45] When this was written Cyprus, France, Greece, Malta, and Turkey did not recognize the right of individual petition under Article 25 of the ECHR (although France had announced its intention to do so) and Cyprus, Malta, and Turkey did not recognize the competence of the Court under Article 46.

[46] AS/Jur (33) 18, para 13.

[47] Letter of 23 April 1992 from McDermot, Secretary-General of the ICJ, to the Clerk of the Parliamentary Assembly (reproduced in AS/Jur (34) 2).

[48] International Commission of Jurists/Swiss Committee against Torture (1983) *The Draft European Convention Against Torture* (Geneva: ICJ/SCAT).

[49] For the text of Res 971 see (1983) 4 HRLJ 498.

and observe Article 3' with respect to detainees. Articles 4 and 5 established a Commission comprising five members serving in their individual capacities and who were to be elected by the Parliamentary Assembly. They would serve for six years and be eligible for re-election. Article 8(1) provided that:

The Commission may organize visits, by delegates chosen from among its members or other persons, to places within the jurisdiction of the Contracting Parties.

Article 8(2) then provided that: 'Apart from periodic visits in the territory of each Contracting Party, the Commission may organize such visits as appear to it to be required in the circumstances'. According to Article 9, notification of a visit to a country was to be provided, following which its delegates could visit at any time and at any place, the only exception being places regularly visited by the ICRC. Article 10 required the Commission to draw up a confidential Report, and to communicate its findings to the state. However, findings and recommendations could be released in a public statement 'by way of exception . . . if the Government concerned fails to co-operate or refuses to apply the recommendation'.

This followed the essential elements of the UN Optional Protocol. Among other points of detail were two interesting and important developments. Draft Article 10(1) provided that: 'The Commission may on its own initiative engage in consultations with the Contracting party with a view to improving the treatment of detainees', whilst Article 10(2) stipulated that: 'It must publish its findings and recommendations whenever requested to do so by the Contracting Party concerned.' Although both of these provisions might have been implicit in the draft Optional Protocol, the prominence which they now attained is reflective of the hallmarks of the system as it has ultimately developed in practice. In response to Recommendation 971, the Committee of Ministers requested the Steering Committee for Human Rights (CDDH) to consider the draft Convention and to submit to the Committee 'proposals for the possible follow-up to the Recommendation'.

With this, the first phase of development was complete. It is, then, worth emphasizing that the mechanisms of the proposed Convention were, at this stage, very different from those which finally emerged. It is also worth emphasizing that the focus was still very much on the practice of torture as a tool of government policy,[50] rather than on conditions of, and the circumstances surrounding, detention. There was little in what had been said that suggested that the work of the proposed Commission would be of direct concern to the majority of member states.

---

[50] It should also be remembered that throughout this period the Council of Europe was actively examining the situation in Turkey, then subject to martial law. See, for example, Assembly Resolution 822, 10 May 1984.

Although the Meier Report accepted that 'delegates appointed by the Committee would concern themselves not only with the problem of torture, but with any cruel, inhuman or degrading treatment',[51] it saw the Protocol mechanism primarily as a supplementary means of calling States to account for the practice of torture. Torture was considered to be 'a crime committed by public officials' and for which the State was responsible and seen as the preserve of totalitarian regimes: the Report noted that even if only those countries which did not practice torture ratified the Convention, 'political regimes can change at any time. If a democratic government ratified the Convention, it would be difficult for a totalitarian government which replaced it to denounce the convention subsequently'.[52] This was prompted both by the Greek experience and by reports of torture in Spain and Turkey. Recommendation 909 itself noted that:[53]

... the alarming reports concerning torture in some member states of the Council of Europe are such as to justify the establishment of a system of unannounced visits to places of detention.

This impression was reinforced by a Commentary published by the ICJ on the draft annexed to Resolution 971[54] which also stressed that 'usually torture occurs as an instrument of interrogation'. The ICJ also pointed out that:

The Commission will also have the power to arrange emergency visits. Thus, if it has reason to believe torture is being practised at a specific location, it can take action at once and organize an ad hoc visit with a view to bringing immediate relief to the victims concerned.

Although the ICJ pointed out that 'on the spot visits . . . cannot but have a salutary effect on conditions of detention', this is a mere aside in comparison to the focus upon torture:[55]

Torture does still exit in Europe and in recent years there have been serious allegations of such practices in Turkey, Greece, Northern Ireland, Italy, Portugal and Spain. Even if this were not the case, merely because at any particular time there have been no obvious cases of torture in a region is not a sufficient reason to deny that region the means to prevent or fight such an occurrence in the future. Given certain conditions, torture can break out anywhere. If it is looked on as a disease then we can continue the comparison by saying that no single state can

---

[51] AS/Jur (32), para 18.   [52] ibid, paras 11–12; 21.
[53] Recommendation 909, para 8.
[54] (1983) 31 *ICJ Review* 50. This was reproduced and circulated within the Legal Affairs Committee of the Council of Europe (AS/Jur (36) 2).
[55] ibid.

claim a natural immunity to that disease. However, it is hoped that the European Convention Against Torture can provide Europe with, at least, an effective prophylactic.

3 DRAFTING THE CONVENTION

The Steering Committee for Human Rights (CDDH) took up the question of the draft Convention in 1984. Detailed work was delegated to its Committee of Experts (DH-EX), which itself was assisted by a smaller drafting group.[56] At this stage, the chief preoccupations concerned the relationship between the proposed Convention with, on the one hand, the text being considered by the UN and, on the other, with the ECHR itself. These matters were probed by the Committee of Experts at its meetings in May and October 1984.

(a) The advisability of adopting a new convention

A principal concern was that a European initiative could slow down or jeopardize progress at the UN, signalling, perhaps, a lessening of interest in the UN instrument. Other concerns were that a European instrument might be construed as an element in an attempt to impose a European model at the global level. There was certainly the danger of European states being faced with two texts which were not necessarily mutually compatible. However, it was widely thought that little progress was likely at the UN level and so these fears carried little weight. Moreover, there was a belief that such a mechanism might work best at a regional rather than global level and that a European convention would serve as a prototype.[57]

A further question hung over the efficacy of the proposed body: could a Committee of five members prevent torture in thousands of prisons and similar establishments in Europe? This was thought not to be a problem since the democratic nature of the majority of Council of Europe member states, the need to act with a certain reserve, and the possibility of the Committee being assisted in its work by delegates, in a similar fashion to the ICRC, would all combine to produce a modest workload that

---

[56] The Committee of Experts met in May and October 1994 and again in March and May 1985. The Drafting Committee met over the summer of 1985 and submitted its report to the Committee of Experts in August. This report formed the basis of the Committee of Experts' work at a further meeting in October. The Steering Committee reviewed progress in November 1995. The Committee of Experts held further meetings in February and July 1986 and the Steering Committee completed its consideration of the text in October 1996. See Cassese (1989), 132.

[57] ibid, 133.

should not be exaggerated.[58] No serious challenge was made to the principle of the Convention after 1984[59] and the subsequent work of the Committee focused on the second major issue of principle, before yielding to points of detail concerning the shape and structure of the supervisory body and its operational paramenters.

(b) The relationship with the European Commission and Court of Human Rights

The concern that was uppermost in the minds of most Committee members was the danger that the body to be established under the new Convention[60] would produce interpretations of Article 3 of the ECHR at variance with those adopted by the Court and Commission of Human Rights themselves.[61] Since this danger came about because the draft text expressly referred to Article 3, some argued that the reference be removed. Others argued that the problem could be addressed by establishing some form of connection between the new body and the ECHR organs. At one end of the spectrum this could take the form of an informal consultation mechanism; alternatively, the new body could have a relationship with the Court substantially similar to that of the Commission on Human Rights, and to which both the state and the new body might be able to refer questions for a final determination.[62] This would have made the system much more judicially orientated and empahsized the primacy of the judical mechanisms of the ECHR.[63]

It was against this background that by the end of 1984 an altogether different means of insulating the ECHR organs from the work of the new

[58] Although raised in the context of the debate on the advisability of the Convention, this exchange touched upon deeper questions of organization and mandate to which the Committee was to return. It is, however, worth noting that the Committee saw the new body as having only a marginal role to play in the majority of European states.

[59] The adoption of the UN Convention in 1984 caused some to wonder whether the initiative was still a live issue, it being suggested that the discussions at the European level had been induced in order to encourage progress at the UN level, and since that had been achieved the project had no further purpose. This, of course, failed to recognize that the UN Convention did not contain a visit mechanism.

[60] At various stages of the drafting process the new body was referred to as, first, the 'Commission' and later as the 'Committee'. The following account uses the expression 'new body' in order to lessen confusion.

[61] See Cassese (1989), 135–7.

[62] A particular problem with this approach was that it begged the question of whether the state concerned accepted the jurisdiction of the Court of Human Rights. At the time several of the states considered most likely to receive the close attention of the new Commission did not do so.

[63] Another possibility was that the new Convention be framed as an Optional Protocol to the ECHR. Such an approach would have made the arguments in favour of a formal link between the new body and the ECHR organs more compelling. There was, however, very little support for this approach and it was not pursued.

body emerged. This was to lay stress on the preventive and non-judicial nature of its work, thus delineating their spheres of competence and avoiding the need to create linking mechanisms to preclude a clash of jurisprudence. It would have the limited function of initiating dialogue with national authorities in order to recommend improvements in the treatment of detainees but it would have no competence to establish whether violations of Article 3 had occurred. Cassese characterized the work of the Committee thus:[64]

The Committee will be concerned only with fact finding investigations carried out in a humanitarian and practical manner and leading only to non-binding recommendations. Its aims will be to enlist the cooperation of national authorities in protecting persons deprived of their liberty, rather than to make legal assessments of those authorities' conduct or accuse them of violations of the relevant rules.

Having resolved the matter in this fashion, the Committee felt able to move on and undertake a detailed examination of the Parliamentary Assembly's draft.

Even within this scheme the reference to Article 3 of the ECHR in the text of the draft Convention proved controversial.[65] This held out the possibility of conflicting interpretations and possibly acted as a constraint, preventing the new body from drawing inspiration from sources. Similar issues arose in connection with Article 9(6) of the Assembly's draft, which provided that: 'During each visit, the delegates shall ascertain that detainees are being treated in conformity with Article 3 of the ECHR.' This was seen as an invitation to find a violation of Article 3, which would be at odds with the Convention's preventive functions.

A direct reference to Article 3 in either the text or the preamble was seen by some members as unnecessary since the new body would not be engaged in its interpretation or application when carrying out its functions. Others saw the Convention as an alternative route for securing the fulfilment of Article 3, and this meant that the new Commission should be bound by the case-law of the ECHR (and that a state found by the new body to have breached Article 3 be able to place the matter before the Court). Clearly, these were very different conceptions of the purpose of the Convention, but they share the common aim of securing the primacy of the Court as the custodian of the ECHR standard.

Unsurprisingly, both the Commission and the Court took the view that the new body should not undermine the authority of the existing institutions. The Commission on Human Rights did not see the need for a

---

[64] Cassese (1989), 136.

[65] Article 1 of the Parliamentary Assembly draft provided that the aim of the Convention was '. . . better to ensure respect for and observe Article 3 of the ECHR . . .', thus rendering it the legal basis upon which the work of the new body would be founded.

reference to Article 3, given the limited scope of the new body's functions. If, however, there was to be such a reference, the Comission felt
that there should be some form of institutional link and that the new body
should be purely fact-finding and conciliatory in function and have no
powers of legal assessment. The Commission, moreover, did not think
the new body should be called a 'Commission'. The Court took a very
similar view. It thought it appropriate that Article 3 be mentioned in the
Preamble but not in the text, and that other UN texts could also be cited.
Like the Commission, it felt that the function of the new body would be
to carry out inquiries in a pragmatic and humanitarian, rather than judicial, fashion without making findings of compliance or lack of compliance with the legal standards. Unlike the Commission, the Court felt that
this would render formal links between the bodies unnecessary.

Discussions of what can appear to be fairly obtuse points often mask
points of a fundamental significance and so it turned out in this case. In
an effort to make progress a Drafting Group was established which produced a draft text and Explanatory Report in August 1985. This included
two alternative versions of Article 6(6), as Article 9(6) had now been
renumbered. Version (A) provided:

During its visits, the Commission shall see that persons deprived of their liberty
are not subject to acts of torture or inhuman or degrading treatment or punishment as defined in Article 3 of the ECHR.

Version (B) provided:

During its visits, the Commission shall examine the conditions of detention and
the possible need for improving the protection of persons deprived of their liberty from torture and from inhuman or degrading treatment or punishment.

Version (A) suggested that the chief purpose of the Convention was to
assist in the implementation of Article 3 by means other than the ECHR
organs. Version (B) was premised upon the Convention being primarily
concerned with fact-finding, dialogue, and technical assistance. When these
alternatives were considered by the Committee of Experts in October 1985,
version (B) was adopted as a starting point for further discussion.[66]

This was consistent with the policy of distancing the work of the new
body from the judicial functions of the ECHR organs. However, it also
raised a new problem. The use of the phrase 'conditions of detention'
brought with it the risk of creating a commission for penal reform in states

[66] This probably reflected a coalition between those who wanted the new body to have
more flexibility and not be restricted by Article 3 and those who thought that any mention
of Article 3 could result in the new body's recommendations being construed as a finding
of a violation. For further consideration of the legal basis of the Convention, see Cassese
(1989), 137–9.

parties. In order to make it clear that any examination of conditions of detention should be undertaken for the sole purpose of improving the protection of persons concerned and that this was not a distinct head of activity for the new body, the wording was altered to:

For the purposes of this Convention, there shall be established a Commission which, during its visits, shall examine the conditions of detention with a view to improving, if necessary, the protection of persons deprived of their liberty from torture and from inhuman or degrading treatment of punishment.

Even this was not considered satisfactory, and the expression 'conditions of detention' was removed altogether and replaced with the word 'treatment'. It seems clear that the new body was not to focus upon conditions of detention but was intended to touch upon them only when pertinent to the 'treatment' of detainees, 'treatment' having the narrow meaning of 'physical' treatment. The centrality of this provision was underlined by its becoming Article 1 of the draft and, although subsequently remodelled, its substance was not subsequently called into question.

The CDDH considered the draft text in November 1985 and confirmed the approach taken by the Committee of Experts concerning the relationship between the two instruments, although it was suggested that the draft of the Explanatory Report be reconsidered in order to add further distance between the new body and the application of the jurisprudence of the Court. It was suggested that the scope of the new convention be broadened so as to cover not only cases of torture and inhuman or degrading treatment or punishment but other types of situations covered by the ECHR—such as correspondence, family life, and hygiene—which could be examined by a body visiting places of detention. This was thought to go beyond the CDDH's terms of reference and would also distract attention from the fight against torture and inhuman and degrading treatment or punishment. The suggestion did, however, have a certain attraction for those who wished to underscore the differences between the two instruments in order to reduce its impact upon Article 3.

In order to strike a balance and keep the work of the new body at a suitable distance from the judicial application of Article 3, whilst at the same time keeping it safely within its orbit, it was decided to include a reference to Article 3 in the preamble. This would serve as a point of reference and a general framework within which the new body could concern itself with situations liable to give rise to cases of torture or inhuman or degrading treatment or punishment. Similarly, it was thought that the non-judicial preventive function could be emphasised by inserting the word 'Prevention' into the Convention's title. The principal function of the new body would be fact-finding and it should not make interpretations based directly on Article 3. Although the subject was raised sporadically, this question received no further detailed examination and the substance of the drafts passed into the final text with no significant changes.

It is, then, clear that the new body was not meant to have any influence over the interpretation and application of Article 3, which was insulated from its work by the stress placed upon the different functions of the two instruments. This spirit of 'progressive distancing' resulted in the tasks of the new body coming to be described in terms of 'concerning itself with situations liable to give rise to torture'. This terminology has, paradoxically, fostered the view that 'conditions of detention' should be subject to scrutiny by the body, despite the hostility shown to this suggestion during the drafting process.

(c) The composition of the new body

Once the relationship of the new body to the ECHR began to emerge, the focus of attention shifted to its composition and the manner in which it would carry out its functions. This raised a number of closely related issues, including the method by which the members would be elected, their terms of office, the qualifications for membership, the size of the body and, crucially, its use of experts.

The draft text adopted by the Parliamentary Assembly in Recommendation 971 provided for a commission of five members, serving in their individual capacities and known for their 'competence in the field of human rights or in the fields covered by the convention'.[67] They were to be elected by the Parliamentary Assembly from lists of three persons nominated by member states of the Council of Europe,[68] serve for six years and be eligible for re-election. Three of the five, selected by lot, would have their initial terms of office reduced to three years in order to provide for an even turnover in membership.[69] Visits were to be conducted 'by delegates chosen from among its members or other persons'.[70]

The model finally adopted was very different.[71] One of its most problematic elements concerned the use of delegates to conduct visits. Some thought that the members of the new body itself should conduct the visits, accompanied by experts if they wished. Others considered this impractical and thought visits should be entrusted to delegates.[72] There was general agreement that if delegates were used, then their nationality, the method of appointing them, and the possibility of a state refusing

---

[67] Draft Article 4.

[68] This followed the model used for electing judges of the European Court of Human Rights. See ECHR, Article 39.

[69] Draft Article 5.   [70] Draft Article 8(1).   [71] See Cassese (1989), 146–9.

[72] It was also suggested that a system of 'national correspondents' be established, who could act on behalf of the new body in emergencies and report back to them.

them permission to carry out a visit, needed clarification, the fear being that it might be possible to circumvent the restrictions placed by a national authority on certain individuals or groups visiting a prison by the simple expedient of nominating them as its delegates.

The Committee of Experts decided that the new body should comprise seven members, increasing to eleven once the Convention had been ratified by fifteen states. They would be elected by the Committee of Ministers, from a list of three candidates nominated by the national delegations in the Consultative Assembly,[73] to a four-year term of office, with the possibility of being re-elected once only in order to ensure a degree of rotation in membership between nationals of the states parties. As to qualifications, one school of thought was that the convention should spell out the nature of the relevant experience, such as in medicine or in prison administration, in some detail. However, the more widely-held view was that there were other qualities that could make a candidate suitable and so detailed qualifications ought to be avoided. The Committee agreed that the statement of the qualifications looked for in members should be couched in general terms but that the need for competence in the areas covered by the convention, such as specialists in medicine and in prison regimes, would be emphasized in the Explanatory Report. Members should always conduct visits but other experts would be able to assist. To that end, a panel of 'qualified persons' would be established, consisting of individuals nominated by the new body and serving for periods of two years. States party to the Convention would be notified of the names and a state could, under certain circumstances, object to the participation of a particular person in a visit.

The ICJ, the ICRC, and the SCAT urged that this model be abandoned in favour of that used by the ICRC, arguing that it was inappropriate for members of the new body to undertake visits themselves, except in exceptional circumstances. Rather, members should rely for their information on the reports of delegates and restrict themselves to the task of negotiating with states on the basis of the facts as reported to them. Delegates, they argued, should be professional, all should attend special courses to ensure a common approach, and at least ten should work full time for the Commission. Nevertheless, it was decided to retain the broad outlines of the existing scheme built around the model of a small body elected by the Committee of Ministers and participating in all visits. Nor

---

[73] That is, by the method used for electing members of the European Commission of Human Rights. See ECHR, Article 21. If members were elected by a political body it was felt that it would be unnecessary to provide for the possibility of their being refused permission to conduct a visit. Cassese concluded that 'considerations relating to sovereignty prevailed in the end over demands more geared to respect for human rights'. See Cassese (1989), 145 and n 81.

was election by the Committee of Ministers or the statements concerning the relevant qualities to be looked for in members subject to further change at this stage. Similarly, the participation of members in all visits (not, however, necessarily in all its aspects) was affirmed. The chief controversy surrounded the use of 'qualified persons', with some members suggesting that they be nominated by the states themselves rather than by the new body, and institutionalizing the right of states to refuse entry, albeit on limited grounds.

The CDDH reviewed progress in November 1985 and endorsed the approach adopted by the Committee of Experts, agreeing that the body be small in size and elected by the Committee of Ministers. However, it was felt that the qualifications and role of qualified persons needed further refinement. When the Committee of Experts met again in in February 1986 the question of whether each state should have a member was raised but not pursued, given that the CDDH had endorsed the proposal for a small body. Contrary to the views of the CDDH, the Committee of Experts thought that the text on the function of the Panel of qualified persons was sufficiently clear, but the Explanatory Report was amended so as to clarify the underlying purpose of supplementing the expertise of the members in relation to particular countries, especially when visits were being carried out.

It was at this late stage in the development of the text that the entire concept of an institutionalized 'panel' of persons to assist the new body was called into question. It was argued that if each state party were to have a member of the new body it would have sufficient expertise to dispense with external assistance in all but exceptional circumstances. In July 1986 the 'one state one member system' was accepted by the Committee but the panel system of experts was retained, albeit with a downgraded role. This became a focus of debate, with the ICJ still pressing for full-time employed experts engaging in fact-finding visits on the body's behalf, whilst other voices, including the European Commission on Human Rights,[74] called for the abandonment of the panel system.

These points were considered by the CDDH in October 1986. The Committee thought that members of the new body need not be drawn solely from those with particular expertise in the subject matter of the convention, but it agreed with the Commission's comments concerning the use of experts. This was reflected in the final version of the text, which deleted all reference to the panel of experts from the convention and replaced it with the laconic provision that when conducting visits, 'The

[74] The Commission argued that the new body must comprise experts in their own right, and that this expertise be more specialized than 'human rights', but relate specifically to the matters covered by the Convention. The Commission felt that the new body would always be able to seek the opinion of other experts in exceptional cases and on technical points.

Committee may, if it considers it necessary, be assisted by experts and interpreters'.[75]

In conclusion, it seems clear that the use of experts was considered to be the exception rather than the rule,[76] although the final draft was not so restrictive as some of the proposals. At the outset of the drafting process, a small supervisory committee was envisaged, receiving reports from its experts and using them as a basis for dialogue: a mere 12 months before the text took on its final shape the ICJ and SCT were pressing the importance of its members *not* participating in visits at all. This model was abandoned at a late stage for an alternative in which the members of the new body would themselves be the experts, supplemented as necessary by external assistance of a predominantly technical nature.

These developments can sustain a variety of interpretations, some charitable, others not. For all the worthy language within which they were couched, it is difficult to avoid the impression that they represent a further playing out of concerns over the possible impact of the new body on the ECHR and were intended, once again, to minimize the potential for conflict. Thus the stress laid on the new body comprising experts in the fields covered by the Convention instead of being made up of human rights specialists (by which was meant lawyers) was probably intended to ensure that the new body did not seek to operate in a judicial fashion and compete with the Commission. The decision to increase the size of the Committee was driven by the desire to reduce its dependance on other experts, as was the insistence that experts be sparingly called upon. Yet minimizing the formal status of experts has, paradoxically, facilitated their extensive usage. *De facto*, there is, as we shall see, something approaching a panel of experts, but its composition is not open to scrutiny by member states. Experts have also accompanied virtually every visit of the Committee. Because the final version of the Convention failed to render explicit what was implicit in the minds of the drafters, it has been applied in practice in a manner quite different from the intentions underlying it.

4 THE PERCEIVED SCOPE OF THE CONVENTION

Similar observations can be made with regard to another crucial element of the Convention framework: the range of places of detention subject to

---

[75] ECPT, Article 7(2). The Explanatory Report, para 51 takes this a little further, saying: 'If the Committee considers it necessary, it may be assisted by experts and interpreters. The underlying idea is to supplement the experience of the Committee by the assistance, for example, of persons who have special training or experience in humanitarian missions, who have a medical background or possess a special competence in the treatment of detainees or in prison regimes and, when appropriate, as regards young persons.'

[76] Cassese (1996), 12 says: 'We also decided that each delegation could, *on occasion*, appoint experts' (emphasis added).

the visit mechanism. This might seem strange, given that Article 2 of the Convention provides that:

Each Party shall permit visits, in accordance with this Convention, to any place within its jurisdiction where persons are deprived of their liberty by a public authority.

Moreover, the Explanatory Report expands on this:[77]

Visits may be organized in all kinds of places where persons are deprived of their liberty, whatever the reasons may be. The Convention is therefore applicable, for example, to places where persons are held in custody, are imprisoned as a result of conviction for an offence, are held in administrative detention, or are interned for medical reasons or where minors are detained by a public authority. Detention by military authorities is also covered by the Convention.

This extremely generous remit[78] attracted little attention. It is particularly noteworthy that potential practical problems associated with conducting visits to police stations received almost no consideration at all. This is surprising since all the evidence suggests that it is in initial police custody that detainees run the greatest risk of physical abuse and that access to police facilities is the most likely to prove contentious. It is made all the more surprising in the light of the detailed consideration given to the problems of access to psychiatric hospitals and military establishments and raises the question of whether the routine application of the Convention to policing was fully appreciated.[79]

Article 9(1) of the original Assembly draft made an express reference to the power of delegates to visit 'police stations and civil and military interrogation centres', and Article 2 of the draft stressed that the Convention applied to 'persons held in provisional, administrative or re-educative detention, persons accused of, or sentenced for, any offence whatever . . .'. The Committee of Experts elided these two articles and, in the process, the final phrase, 'including police stations and civil and military establishments' was omitted. The reasoning behind this is unclear[80] but was probably not intended to be a change of substance, given that the Explanatory Report continued to provide that each party 'must supply

[77] Explanatory Report, para 30. This wording was used in the first draft and was not subject to subsequent alteration.

[78] MacDonald (1992), 399 suggests that this even extended to 'places in which a house arrest is under way'.

[79] It should be remembered that torture, as opposed to other forms of ill treatment, also was uppermost in the minds of the drafters, and that at the time the most recent and well publicized examples of torture being employed by the state had been in military or prison facilities, for example in Greece, Northern Ireland, and Chile. See Amnesty International (1984).

[80] For example, it might have been thought redundant given the all-embracing scope of the remaider of the text.

the committee on request with a list of the places under its jurisdiction where persons deprived of their liberty are being held, stating the nature of the establishment (prisons, police station, hospital, etc)'.[81] This seems conclusive. However, that comment was subsequently amplified:[82]

It is understood that in supplying a list, the state concerned may provide a general description of places where persons are capable of being held from time to time, for example, all police stations or all military barracks, in addition to a specific list of permanent places were persons are deprived of their liberty, such as prisons and mental health institutions. It is envisaged that the committee will eventually request a comprehensive list of places within a particular area which it intends to visit within the jurisdiction of the state.

This suggests that whilst prisons and psychiatric hospitals would always be liable to inspection visits, police stations and military barracks would only be liable to visits if, at the relevant time, they contained persons deprived of their liberty. It might be argued that police stations would, *de facto*, always fall into this category. Nevertheless, the implication is that a particular police station could only be visited if it was known that a person was being deprived of their liberty within it, given that they did not fall into a category of institutions where this was presumed to be the case. This is underscored by the belief, already considered above, that the convention did not empower inspections directly focusing upon the conditions in which persons might be held.[83] This view receives support from the response to the ICJ's suggestion that the wording of Article 2 be altered to make it clear that a visit could take place even if only a single person was being held. The Explanatory Report was altered to specify that a visit could be conducted in places where 'one or more' persons were deprived of their liberty. This certainly suggests that no visit would be possible unless it was known, or at least reasonably believed, that a detainee was being held there.

Irrespective of the merits of either view, it is clear that little thought was given to the application of the Convention to policing. Whether this was an oversight or deliberate is difficult to tell. Oversight seems implausible, given the discussions surrounding the possibility of excluding interrogations in situations of national emergency from the purview of the Committee. Perhaps it was thought that it would be all but impossible to secure acceptance of the Convention if its application to policing rather than penal institutions was highlighted. Such a well-ordered conspiracy against the Committee of Ministers by its own experts seems

---

[81] Explanatory Report, para 62.   [82] ibid.

[83] Indeed, an even more restrictive interpretation would be that police and military establishments could only be visited if they were being used to house detainees who would normally be held in a prison or analogous institution (eg a remand or convicted prisoner who was being held in a police station due to overcrowding, security, or other reasons).

wholly implausible. Whatever the reason, it is easy to see why some states have been taken aback by the powers of the CPT to probe so deeply into policing matters: there is little in the drafting process to suggest that this would be the case and much to imply that the new body's principal areas of activity would lie elsewhere.[84]

5 RESTRICTIONS UPON THE RIGHT OF VISIT

The freedom of the new body to visit places of detention was whittled down but, perhaps surprisingly, to only a comparatively small degree. The first of the following subsections will look at a restriction found in the original proposal. The following subsections will look at other restrictions which were introduced during the drafting process.

(a) The 'Red Cross' clause

The draft text adopted by the Assembly in Recommendation 971 contained only one fetter upon the freedom of the new body to visit places of detention. Draft Article 9(2) (subsequently adopted as Article 17(3) of the Convention) provided that:

The delegates may not inspect places which representatives or delegates of Protecting Powers or the International Committee of the Red Cross are entitled to visit under the Geneva Conventions of 1949 and the Protocols of 1977 thereto and which they do in fact visit regularly.

This 'Red Cross' clause caused some controversy but was resolved on the understanding, reflected in the Explanatory Report,[85] that in times of international armed conflict the ICRC, working under the Geneva Conventions, should have primacy over the new body. Similarly, the ICRC should enjoy primacy as regards non-international armed conflict, in situations where its delegates did in fact visit places of detention by special arrangement. Visits conducted by the ICRC in peacetime to 'political' prisoners, however, would fall outside the scope of Article 9(2) and the question of which body was best placed to carry out an inspection could best be determined on an *ad hoc* basis.[86]

---

[84] The Committee of Experts also referred to its draft as 'the convention for prison visits'. At the very least, this suggests that the principal thrust of the convention was seen as lying in that direction.

[85] Explanatory Report, para 93. See also MacDonald (1992), 411–12.

[86] It was pointed out that if the work of the ICRC should be shielded from intrusions by the new body, there was an equally compelling argument that its competence should be ousted if the Court or Commission of Human Rights was seised of a situation under the ECHR. Whatever the merits of the debate, however, it was always likely that the work of the ICRC would be insulated from the new body, given its proximity to the prime movers (see above, pp. 108, 110 n 30, 114).

(b) Detention by a public authority

As has been seen, Article 2 of the original draft provided that 'This convention shall apply in all circumstances and all places to all persons deprived of their liberty'. From the outset, it was understood that this was too broad a definition and that the mandate of the new body should be restricted to detention by a decision of public authorities. A suggestion that the right be limited to places under the control of public authorities, thus excluding private institutions, was rejected since it provided an easy means of evading scrutiny.[87] The text was therefore amended:

Each Contracting State shall, in all circumstances, permit visits, in accordance with the terms of this convention, to any place within its jurisdiction where persons are deprived of their liberty by decision of a public authority.

The phrase 'in all circumstances' was subsequently deleted[88] and the words 'by decision' removed at the suggestion of the European Court of Human Rights[89], making it clear that the Convention extended to cases of unauthorized, *de facto*, detention by a public authority. In this form, it was utimately adopted as Article 1 of the Convention. The Convention does not extend to individuals who have voluntarily entered state institutions, such as psychiatric hospitals or drugs or alcohol rehabilitation units but there was concern over the position where committal took place with the consent of the family but not the person concerned. The Explanatory Report therefore provides that 'it should be possible for the Committee to satisfy itself that this was indeed the wishes of the patient concerned'.[90]

(c) National emergencies

The prohibition of torture and inhuman or degrading treatment or punishment is so fundamental that it is non-derogable even in times of national emergency.[91] This was reflected in the Costa Rican Draft Optional Protocol tabled at the UN, which expressly provided that 'Exceptional circumstances, such as a state of war, state of seige, state of emergency or the passing of emergency legislation shall not suspend the application

---

[87] This is spelt out in the Explanatory Report, para 32.

[88] These words were considered to be unnecessary. In fact, they were somewhat misleading, given the retention of the 'Red Cross' clause and the other restrictions upon the right of visit found in the text and considered in this section.

[89] See MacDonald (1992), 400.

[90] Explanatory Report, para 32. See also Cassese (1989), 140; MacDonald (1992), 401–2. MacDonald considers the distinction between voluntary and involuntary detainees to be 'arbitrary'.

[91] See, for example, ECHR, Article 15 and Oraá, J (1992) *Human Rights in States of Emergency in International Law* (Oxford: Clarendon Press), 96.

of the present Protocol'.[92] Thus the original Parliamentary Assembly draft provided that: 'This convention shall apply in all circumstances . . .'. However, in response to concerns over the possibility of visits being conducted in military establishments[93] the draft of the explanatory report[94] said: 'this does not prevent the Commission from being accompanied[95] by an official from the visited State, for reasons of security in certain cases, and, more generally, in order to assist with the visit'.[96] However, it was subsequently decided to include the substance of this provision in a text which provided:

Exceptionally, in places which are secret for reasons of national defence, or which enjoy special protection for reasons of national security, the Committee may only carry out a visit if accompanied by an official of the State party Concerned, and then only in places where persons are deprived of their liberty.

At the following meeting a much more restrictive proposal was made, that:

For the purposes of safeguarding national security, the prevention and detection of serious crime and the protection of health, Parties may lay down limited conditions in relation to visits.

This latter proposal threatened to subvert the entire purpose of the text, since it could have resulted in the new body being denied access to places of detention in precisely those circumstances when torture was most likely. The ICJ was approached and it recommended that the new proposal be rejected, but suggested that the explanatory report might include a statement that the Committee should have regard to the representations of the governments concerning which places or persons should be visited in the light of the circumstances prevailing. The ICJ was, however, prepared to accept the previous suggestion requiring visits to be accompanied, provided that interviews could be conducted in private.

In the end an entirely different approach was adopted which, drawing on the wording in the ECHR,[97] permitted visits to a particular place or

[92] Draft Optional Protocol, Article 2.

[93] It has already been seen that the express reference to such visits was deleted from the final text. See above, pp. 126–7.

[94] Commenting on draft Article 6(3)(b), providing for 'unlimited access to any place where persons are deprived of their liberty, including the right to move inside the place of detention without restrictions'.

[95] However, no official would be permitted to be present when interviews with detainees were being conducted.

[96] The ICJ, the SCAT, and the ICRC suggested the inclusion of a special provision permitting the new body to visit only those parts of a military establishment in which persons were detained. The state could refuse to allow visits altogether if it formally declared that it would not hold detainees at military establishments. Although this proposal found favour when presented to the Committee of Experts, it was not reflected in subsequent drafts.

[97] See ECHR, Articles 8(2), 9(2), 10(2), and 11(2).

person to be delayed for short periods of time where necessary in a democratic society in the interest of national defence or public safety or the prevention of serious crime in these fields. The ICJ took the view that the final decision on whether to conduct a visit should lie with the new body, rather than with the state and opposed the idea that the state should be able to delay a visit to a detainee, even for a short time. The deadlock was not resolved until the end of 1986 when what became Article 9 was agreed as a compromise which sought to balance the legitimate interests of the state against the concerns of the Committee.[98] Article 9 provides that:

1. In exceptional circumstances, the competent authorities of the Party concerned may make representations to the Committee against a visit at the time or to the particular place proposed by the Committee. Such presentations may only be made on grounds of national defence, public safety, serious disorder in places where persons are deprived of their liberty, the medical condition of a person or that an urgent interrogation relating to a serious crime is in progress.
2. Following such representations, the Committee and the Party shall immediately enter into consultations in order to clarify the situation and seek agreement on arrangements to enable the Committee to exercise its functions expeditiously. Such arrangements may include the transfer to another place of any persons whom the Committee proposed to visit. Until the visit takes place, the Party shall provide information to the Committee about the person concerned.

This was close to the proposals of the ICJ, in that the final determination lay with the Committee rather than the state and a visit could not be delayed.[99] *De facto*, the requirement that there be discussions, and that information be provided on any person concerned, meant that some delay would be inevitable. Moreoever, it is clear, once again, that the visit was to focus on the treatment of the individual rather than the conditions in which detention took place, since transfer to another location for interview is expressly mentioned as an acceptable outcome.

(d) Objections to experts

The Costa Rican draft also permitted states to refuse entry to certain members of the proposed panel of experts who would assist the Committee in fulfilling its tasks. Although there was no equivalent in the Parliamentary Assembly draft, there was general agreement that as long as the choice of 'delegates' or 'experts' lay with the new body, states should have

---

[98] See Cassese (1989), 142–4.
[99] For consideration of what might amount to 'exceptional circumstances', and other problems in applying this article, see MacDonald (1992), 408–10. There is no evidence to suggest that Article 9 has ever been invoked.

the capacity to prevent experts from participating in a visit.[100] It was initially decided that a state 'may exceptionally, and for reasons given confidentially to the Commission,[101] declare that a member of the Panel ... may not be allowed to take part in a visit', it being understood that a refusal could only be made on the basis that the person did not fulfil the requirements of panel membership, such as being biased, not observing rules of confidentiality, or making political statements.

Though the panel system was subsequently abandoned and the role of experts downgraded, the substance of these provisions was retained. Article 14(3) of the Convention simply provides:

A State may exceptionally declare that an expert or other person assisting the Committee may not be allowed to take part in a visit to a place within its jurisdiction.

In order to take account of the fact that the state to be visited could not know the identities of the experts to accompany the Committee prior to the notification of the visit, the Explanatory Report calls on the state to be visited to make such a declaration 'at the earliest opportunity'.[102] The reasons for exclusion remain the same, but the exclusion of an expert at short notice does not have the same disruptive potency as under the original system.[103] Given that its experts were to be used exceptionally and the key 'expertise' would be provided by Committee members themselves, it is possible that, had there been more time, the grounds for refusing entry might have been relaxed, since it no longer went to the heart of the Convention. States might also have lost interest in this aspect of the Convention following this change. As it was, the limited nature of the state's right to exclude experts, inherited from the earlier systems, has probably enhanced their status and contributed to their being assigned a greater practical role than was envisaged when the Convention was adopted.

(e) Reservations

A final means through which states sought to insulate themselves from some aspects of the work of the new body was by permitting reservations

[100] Restrictions upon members participating in visits to a country were unnecessary since they would have been elected by the Committee of Ministers (which, presumably, could be trusted not to elect as members those deemed undesirable by other parties).

[101] The obligation to provide reasons was watered down to the extent that the Explanatory Report merely suggested that the reasons for an exclusion might be requested, since this might prove helpful to the new body when appointing future panel members.

[102] Explanatory Report, para 84.

[103] Moreover, if an objection is made once the visit has begun, the Committee is merely required to 'take all measures' which it, the Committee, deemed appropriate. This need not extend to preventing the expert continuing to participate in the visit. See Explanatory Report, para 86 and MacDonald (1992), 411.

to be made to the Convention. Article 14 of the Parliamentary Assembly draft provided that: 'No reservations may be made in respect of the provisions of this Convention.' This wording remained unchanged and was ultimately adopted as Article 21 of the Convention. Though this was not uncontroversial, the principle of no reservations became something of an article of faith for the Swiss in particular, and compromises were made on the substantive content of other articles in order to preserve it.

Since, in the absence of such a provision, the terms of the Vienna Convention on the Laws of Treaties would apply, under which, and in the absence of the common consent of all contracting states, only those reservations which are compatible with the object and purposes of the Convention would be permitted.[104] The advantage of such an approach was that it would allow states a degree of flexibility which might be helpful, having regard to specific situations (for example, foreign military establishments within their territory) which might otherwise pose problems for states seeking to ratify. It was finally decided to retain the provision, particularly in the light of the concessions made to the needs of national security and military establishments in Article 9.[105] However, the Explanatory Report is low key and, rather than declare the fundamental incompatibility of reservations with a treaty mechanism of this kind,[106] merely notes that the option of excluding reservations was chosen.[107]

6 OTHER ISSUES

A number of other matters that received considerable attention during the drafting process are considered in the following sections. Broadly speaking, they fall into two categories: first, issues associated with the mechanics of carrying out a visit and, second, matters relating to the Reports to be produced. In addition, there are pervasive concerns relating to confidentiality.

---

[104] Vienna Convention on the Law of Treaties, Art 20(2), following the principles established by the International Court of Justice in *Reservations to the Convention on Genocide*, Advisory Opinion, ICJ Reports, 1951, p. 15. See Sinclair, I (1984) *The Vienna Convention on the Law of Treaties* (Manchester: Manchester University Press), 2nd edn, 51–77.

[105] Although it has been argued above that these concessions were not very great.

[106] The extent to which the general rules of international law concerning reservations apply to human rights instruments is a matter of some controversy. The UN Human Rights Committee in General Comment No 24(52) (adopted 2 Nov 1994) argued the case for the adoption of a more rigorous approach. (For text, see (1995) 15 HRLJ 464). This has been contested by, *inter alia*, the USA and the UK (see (1995) 16 HRLJ 422). For analysis of the General Comment and its implications see Novak, M (1995) 'The Activities of the UN Human Rights Committee from 1 August 1992 through 31 July 1995', 16 HRLJ 377, 380–2; Redgwell, C (1997) 'Reservations to Treaties and Human Rights Committee General Comment No 24(52)', 46 ICLQ 390.

[107] Explanatory Report, para 96.

(a) Notification of visits

It is a mistake to characterize the Convention as providing for visits 'without notice'. The Parliamentary Assembly draft Article 9(1) (subsequently adopted as Article 8(1)) made it clear that visits would take place 'without prior notice and at any time' *following the notification of the State by the Committee that a visit was impending.*[108] This left open the period which might elapse between the initial notification and the actual visit and whether the delegation should itself provide further notice of its plans once the visit was under way. The experience of the ICRC was that satisfactory visits required a degree of advance notification: this helped establish a conducive atmosphere in which to conduct a dialogue. The ICJ/SCAT memorandum envisaged that the state would be notified of the date on which a visit was due to commence and given details of the proposed delegation. The list of places to be visited would be given to the authorities once the delegation had arrived in the country, following which the state would provide the delegation with full information regarding those places. A liaison officer would introduce the delegates to the establishments, which would normally be told that a visit was to take place 24 hours beforehand.

In the face of considerable disagreement,[109] it was decided to delete the words 'without prior notice' from the draft text and to require that the new body specify the period of notice to be given in its rule of procedure. It is against this background that the, admittedly opaque, Explanatory Report should be read.[110] It seems likely that the Committee thought that it would be only in unusual circumstances that a particular institution would *not* receive a minimum of 24-hours notification, although this is not explicitly stated in either the Convention or the Report. In practice, the need to provide a certain degree of notice in order to ensure efficiency has meant that the vagaries of the Explanatory Report have not been exploited to the full.[111] Nevertheless, as will be seen later, it is not the normal practice for the visiting delegation to give 24-hours notice of its arrival at a particular place of detention.

---

[108] But cf the Preamble, para 5, which called for 'regular visits without notice'. For further consideration of the notice requirements, see MacDonald (1992), 404–6.

[109] It should be noted that the concern expressed over giving 24-hours notice of a visit again reflects the view that the Convention was primarily concerned with the physical treatment of individuals. If the primary focus was upon conditions in which detainees were held, then providing further notification beyond that contained in the general announcement of the visit was likely to make little real difference. Of course, certain alterations—the removal of apparatus for example—is possible in the shortest of time-frames.

[110] The Explanatory Report in paras 55–6 does not draw a clear distinction between notification of an intention to conduct a visit and notification to specific institutions that they were shortly to receive a visit (it always being accepted that the body could visit any place with no notice at all in exceptional circumstances).

[111] See Cassese (1989), 141; Cassese (1996), 9–11, where the arguments based on the experience of the ICRC were described as 'utterly convincing'.

(b) Access to information and data protection

The question of whether the new body should have access to all information concerning persons in detention was raised fairly late in the development of the Convention but quickly attained prominence and led to disagreements that remained unresolved. It was proposed that the new body should be provided with the 'information which is necessary' for the new body to carry out its tasks, this being understood to include, *inter alia*, the results of medical examinations. This met with powerful resistance on the grounds that the right of access to such information should be subject to pre-existing domestic statutory provisions regarding access and data protection, and that the consent of the detainee should be obtained for the disclosure of personal files, both medical and relating to criminal proceedings. Particular attention was drawn to the problems of disclosure as regards psychiatric institutions.

As an alternative to placing a formal limitation upon the right of access to information, it was suggested that the right should be exercised in accordance with national law and accepted rules of professional practice, it being accepted that this might result in the degree of access varying from one country to another. This proposal found favour but, rather than amend the text, was reflected in the Explanatory Report, which provided:

[Article 8(2)] Subparagraph (d) obliges parties to provide the Committee with information available to them which is necessary for the Committee to carry out its task. Access to information will clearly be of great importance to the Committee. At the same time, it is acknowledged that particular rules concerning disclosure of information may be applicable in member states. Accordingly, the Committee is for its part obliged, when seeking information from a Party, to have regards to particular rules of medical secrecy and professional ethics (in particular rules regarding data protection and rules of medical secrecy). *For example, it is expected that the Committee will not normally override rules of national law or professional ethics which protect the rights of individuals concerning the confidentiality of information of a personal nature, or legal restrictions on the disclosure of information relating to criminal investigations.* It is envisaged that possible difficulties in this field will be resolved in the spirit of mutual understanding and co-operation upon which the Convention is founded.

However, for reasons that are not apparent, the final version of the Explanatory Report does not contain the italicized words.[112] This omission has the effect of lessening the onus on the Committee to respect the national laws of the states concerned. Whilst this might be at odds with

---

[112] Explanatory Report, para 64. See MacDonald (1992), 414, who points out that the Convention does not provide a sanction for non compliance with a request for information. Whilst this is true, in practice the Committee can publicize this 'lack of cooperation' in its reports.

the delicate balance struck during the drafting process, it *is* in accord with the subsequent practice of the Committee.

(c) The presentation and publication of the Report

The concerns regarding data protection were a particular manifestation of the more general issue of confidentiality, which was at its most acute in the deliberations surrounding the manner in which the new body would draw up, adopt, and publish its reports. Article 10 of the Parliamentary Assembly draft provided that:

1. After each visit, the commission shall draw up a report, setting out its observations and recommendations. On the basis of this report, the commission shall inform the Contracting Party concerned of its findings and, if necessary, make recommendations. The commission may on its own initiative engage in consultations with the Contracting party with a view to improving the treatment of detainees.
2. As a rule, the reports, findings, recommendations and consultations of the commission shall be confidential. By way of exception, however, if the government concerned fails to co-operate or refuses to apply the recommendations, the commission may decide to make a public statement on the matter, announcing its findings and recommendations. It must publish its findings and recommendations whenever requested to do so by the party concerned.

From the first, these proposals caused controversy. The following subsections will look at two distinct, but related, issues.

(i) Drawing up the 'report'

The initial view on this draft article was that it should allow the state an opportunity to respond to the conclusions arrived at by the new body before the report on a visit was finalized.[113] For some, this approach also tied into the question of the relationship between the new convention and the ECHR and it was suggested that the state should be able to ask the Court for an opinion if it disagreed with the draft of a report. Once the nature of that relationship had been settled, attention turned to the details of the text.

   The first paragraph of the draft article drew a distinction between the report to be drawn up by the new body and the findings and recommendations which were to be communicated to the state. Reflecting the practice of the ICRC, it was argued that the full report would take the

---

[113] It should be remembered that the members of the new body would have participated in the visit under the scheme then being considered.

form of a compilation of material acquired in the course of a visit and that this could not be transmitted to the state since it was likely to include factual information obtained in confidential interviews. Rather, the new body would inform the state of its general findings and recommendations. However, the text ultimately adopted as Article 10(1) of the Convention provides that:[114]

After each visit, the Commission shall draw up a report on the facts found during the visit, taking account of any observations that may have been submitted by the State party concerned. It shall transmit to the latter its report containing any recommendations it considers necessary. The Committee may consult with the State party with a view to improving the treatment of persons deprived of their liberty.

This text conflates the 'confidential' report with the 'findings' and 'recommendations', now also described as a 'report'.[115] Since it is inconceivable that the state should have had a role in determining the content of the 'confidential' report, and in the light of the blurring of the distinction between these two forms of 'report', the observations of the state have become subsumed within the general dialogue flowing from its transmission, even though it is expressly provided that the report shall be drawn up taking account of them.[116]

(ii) The publication of the report

The Parliamentary Assembly draft provided that the new body was obliged to publish the 'findings and recommendations' if requested to do so by the state. It also pointed out that the state might wish to publish the report itself and it was agreed that this would be possible, provided that it was published in its entirety.[117] Neither of these provisions was

---

[114] Also in the Explanatory Report, para 73.

[115] The Explanatory Report also makes it clear that this 'report' transmitted to the state would not necessarily include all the information found in the 'full' and confidential report. This would seem to be a legacy of the older model.

[116] cf MacDonald (1992), 422, who argues that 'the State appears to have an implicit right to make comments to the Committee before the latter draws up its report'. Although there is no formal mechanism through which this can happen, it is the practice of the Committee to make an oral presentation of its principal findings at the end of each visit (see further below, Chapter 5, pp. 195–6) and this can give a state the opportunity to express its views before the report is finalized. Evidence of a degree of dialogue at the earlier stage is found in Reports: eg Greece 1, para 24 where the results of an inquiry requested by the Committee into allegations of ill-treatment at Thessaloniki police headquarters at the conclusion of their visit in March 1993 (under Article 8(5) of the Convention) was fed into the report which was adopted by the Committee in December of that year.

[117] This is now reflected in Article 11(2) of the Convention and para 77 of the Report.

controversial but the ability of the new body to make public its findings *without* the consent of the state was, inevitably, the focus of much attention.

The Parliamentary Assembly draft permitted the findings and recommendations to be published: 'By way of exception . . . if the government concerned fails to co-operate or refuses to apply the recommendations, the commission may decide to make a public statement on the matter, announcing its findings and recommendations'.[118] When this was first considered a wide spectrum of possibilities was canvassed, ranging from publication in every case (along with the comments of the state concerned), to there being no publication at all, but with the findings and recommendation being transmitted in confidence to the Committee of Ministers or the European Court of Human Rights.

There was hesitation over permitting publication without the consent of the states concerned because this appeared to be a sanction which did not sit easily alongside a report which merely contained recommendations and was supposed to be part of a dialogue. Moreover, it was pointed out that the state might legitimately pursue approaches other than those recommended to bring about the desired improvements.[119]

In the light of these observations the grounds on which a public statement might be justified was changed from the 'refusal to apply' the recommendations to the 'refusal to improve the situation in the light of the Commission's recommendations'. Strict compliance was not necessary if the underlying rationale of the recommendations was accepted and acted on. In addition, the requirement that the public statement should 'announce the findings and recommendations' was dropppped, giving the Committee greater freedom in the choice of material it might decide to make public. This, however, was thought to give the Committee too much freedom, and invested their recommendations with too great an authority. It was suggested that the Committee of Ministers should be involved in making the decision. Though this proposal was not taken up it did usher in the idea that, by way of compromise, the decision to issue a public statement would have to be taken by a two-thirds majority. A further suggestion was that the state concerned should be given an opportunity to present its views to the Committee before a decision was taken. Both of these suggestions were reflected in the text of the Convention, which provides that:[120]

If the Party fails to co-operate or refuses to improve the situation in the light of the Committee's recommendations, the Committe may decide, after the Party has

---

[118] Parliamentary Assembly draft, Article 10(2).

[119] Indeed, it was also claimed that a state might be justified in not following the recommendations, or in not giving effect to them immediately, because of financial constraints.

[120] ECPT, Article 10(2).

had an opportunity to make known its views, by a majority of two thirds of its members to make a public statement on the matter.

The exceptional nature of a public statement is stressed in the Explanatory Report,[121] as is the need to give the state concerned an 'opportunity to make known its views'.[122] This suggests that once the Committee has decided that it is minded to make a public statement, it must warn the state concerned and provide an opportunity for it to present its case.[123] It is not enough for the decision to be based on the attitude of the state concerned towards the Committee's recommendations as evidenced in the dialogue based upon the reports. The decision to move towards a public statement ushers in a new phase in the relationship, and a new right for the state to be heard.[124]

7 CONCLUSION

Following its adoption by the Steering Committee for Human Rights, the Committee of Ministers decided in February 1987 to pass the texts of the draft Convention and Explanatory Report which accompanied it to the Parliamentary Assembly for consultation. The chairman of the Legal Affairs Committee, Mr Elmquist, drew up a Report which expressed the view that the proposed text was consistent with the key ideas found in the Parliamentary Assembly's draft. He proposed only two very modest changes,[125] which, despite being endorsed by the Parliamentary Assembly,[126] were rejected by the Committee of Ministers. The Convention was finally adopted on 26 June and opened for signature on 26 November 1987.

---

[121] The Report also picked up the point that when deciding whether or not to issue a statement the Committee 'should pay full regard to any difficulties' facing the state in responding to the recommendations.

[122] See now Explanatory Report, para 74.

[123] This is similar to the position under Article 20(5) of the UNCAT. Article 20 authorizes the CAT to enter into a dialogue with states if it has 'reliable information which appears to it to contain well-founded indications that torture is being systematically practiced' and which may result in a confidential inquiry. The CAT may, however, 'after consultations with the State Party Concerned' decide to include a summary account in its annual report. This has happened twice, with regard to Turkey (see A/48/44/Add.1; (1993) 14 HRLJ 426(1997); 4 *IHRR* 223: this decision having been delayed in the wake of the representations made— see A/49/44, para 177) and Egypt (see A/51/44, paras 180–222; (1997) 4 *IHRR* 235).

[124] But cf MacDonald (1992), 423, who takes the view that this is 'not necessarily a question of prior consultation'.

[125] These were that the terms of office of the Committee members be increased from four to six years and that the number of ratifications needed to bring the Convention into force be reduced from seven to five. (Given the speed with which the Convention entered into force, the discussion on this question has not been examined in this chapter.)

[126] See Parliamentary Assembly Opinion No 133 of 27 March 1987.

The Report adopted by the Parliamentary Assembly is of interest because it lends further support to the argument that the thrust of the Convention, as it has developed in practice, is very different from what was in the minds of the drafters (although well within the compass of the text itself). The Convention was primarily seen as concerning the practice of torture. Its conclusion stated that:[127]

It may appear pointless to adopt this draft Convention as a preventive measure against torture in a European Framework, that is in a part of the world which is the least affected by torture. In fact, past events testify that Europe is not immune to this evil. Even over the last 20 years there have been serious allegations of torture in several Council of Europe member states.

The Report went on to stress the 'pioneering aspects' of the Convention, and its importance as a model for other parts of the world.[128] This restates the understanding of the Convention's purpose held at the very outset of the drafting process, and it is evident that nothing had happened in the meanwhile to make any of the participants understand it differently. Be that as it may, a Convention seen as providing an inspectoral mechanism intended to combat the torture and physical mistreatment of detainees has been developed in a much broader fashion. It is, however, worth stressing the part played in this shift by the desire to distance the new Committee from the control mechanisms of the ECHR and to guard against any possibility of it making quasi-judicial determinations that might run counter to the Court's or Commission's understanding of Article 3 of the ECHR. By stressing its non-judicial and preventive function, the Committee has ironically been able to develop its work around the conditions of, and legal regime surrounding, detention, potentially carrying Article 3, as its prime legal basis, into areas hitherto considered beyond its scope. This has generated the potential for a clash which it was meant to prevent. There would have been less danger of innovation spilling over into the work of the ECHR organs had the Committee been granted a greater competence to make quasi-judicial determinations, since the argument that it should be subjected to scrutiny or control by the Court and/or the Committee of Ministers would then have been almost irresistible. The story of the drafting of the European Convention for the Prevention of Torture is the story of a text being progressively watered down and, according to its proponents, weakened.[129] The story of its

---

[127] Parliamentary Assembly Doc 5704, Report, para 18.   [128] ibid, para 19.
[129] See Cassese (1989), 152, where it is argued that 'those more concerned with the demands of state sovereignty . . . eventually got the upper hand'. But perhaps his experience as President of the Committee caused him to modify his opinion, since he subsequently wondered at the adoption of such a 'courageous, or imprudent' convention which laid bear 'the *sancta sanctorum* of each State' (Cassese (1996), 1).

subsequent development is of innovation and creativity resulting in an instrument of far greater potential than that which was originally conceived, not only by the drafters[130] but by Gautier himself.

[130] Cassese (1996), 7, suggests that 'the upper echelons of state bureaucracy . . . who had a hand in drafting . . . may not have understood its implications once it came into effect —these implications became apparant only gradually'. Given that Cassese was himself a member of the Committee of Experts and Steering Committee for Human Rights, this observation is significant. See also MacDonald (1992) who consistently gives the impression that the Convention is concerned with torture and little, if anything, else.

5

The CPT: Membership, Back-up Services, and Modus Operandi

The newly agreed Convention entered into force more rapidly than had been anticipated. No fewer than 19 of the then 23 member states of the Council of Europe signed the Convention before the end of November 1987, the month that the Convention opened for signature.[1] Two more states signed early in 1988,[2] and the remaining two member states signed in late 1989.[3] Ratifications followed signatures quickly in 1988, and on 1 February 1989 the Convention came into force.[4] By the beginning of 1990 the Convention was in force with respect to 15 countries, increasing to 19 countries by the end of that year. Early in 1989 a small secretariat was appointed.[5] The first members of the CPT were elected by the Committee of Ministers in September 1989, following which the newly constituted Committee elected its first President and Vice-Presidents. Late in 1989 training sessions for members were embarked on, and in May 1990 the CPT conducted its first visit, to Austria. At the time of writing, December 1997, the Convention is in force for 35 of the 40 member states of the Council of Europe, a figure that will rise to 37 in February 1998,[6] the Committee comprises 29 members and the Secretariat is now 13 persons strong. Further ratifications are in the pipeline, further members are due to be elected in respect of recently ratifying states, and the indications are that the Secretariat will be further strengthened in order to cope with the additional burdens of work that this expanded membership will bring. The recent practice of the Parliamentary Assembly of the Council of Europe has been to require ratification of the ECPT within a year from accession to the Council of Europe and, although this has not been fully complied

---

[1] Austria, Belgium, Cyprus, Denmark, France, Germany, Greece, Iceland, Italy, Liechtenstein, Luxembourg, Malta, the Netherlands, Norway, Portugal, Spain, Sweden, Switzerland, and the United Kingdom. See Appendix 4A.

[2] Ireland and Turkey.

[3] San Marino and Finland.

[4] In accordance with ECPT Article 19(1) the Convention entered into effect on the first day of the month following the expiration of three months after the date on which seven member states consented to be bound by it.

[5] Mr Trevor Stevens as Committee Secretary, and Mrs Genevieve Mayer-Fabian as Administrative Officer, supported by three administrative and secretarial staff.

[6] See Appendix 4A. The Convention enters into force for Croatia and Moldova on 1 February 1998, having ratified the Convention in October 1997. Latvia, Lithuania, and Russia have signed the Convention but are yet to ratify.

with, it is reasonable to suppose that the Convention will be in force with respect to some 40 countries at the end of 1998.[7]

In this chapter we will chart this rapid expansion of activity by considering in detail: the composition of the CPT; the Committee's support mechanisms; and the Committee's *modus operandi*, namely, how it conducts its main business by planning a programme for visits, preparing for visits, conducting visits, reporting on visits, and engaging in dialogue with member states following visits. As we shall see, some of the CPT's procedures were settled early on in the Committee's life and have been modified little since. But other aspects of the Committee's life are changing in relation to its growing pressure of work. We can reasonably anticipate that further changes will shortly become necessary.[8]

1 THE PEOPLE INVOLVED

Whatever 'effectiveness' is taken to mean, international conventions are or are not effective for a variety of reasons prominent among which is the quality of the core groups of persons whose task it is to breathe life into the Convention—to make it work. This aspect of the operation of conventions has been relatively under-explored by students of public international law. Their focus has traditionally been on the texts themselves, attributing potency largely to the legal powers established under conventions. Little attention has been given to the group ethos, established or not established as the case may be, by those persons we may describe as convention 'enforcers'. Nor has the day-to-day practical situation within which 'enforcers' operate been much considered. This approach to the analysis and evaluation of conventions we can characterize as a 'politico-cultural' approach as opposed to the dominant 'legal-bureaucratic' approach.[9]

[7] See Council of Europe, Parliamentary Assembly, Committee on Legal Affairs and Human Rights (1997) *Report on strengthening the machinery of the European Convention for the Prevention of Torture and Inhuman or Degrading Treament or Punishment*, Parl Ass Doc 7784, 26 March (hereafter CLAHR Report (1997)), para 16. Signature and ratification was required of Andorra and Latvia upon their accession to the Council of Europe, but no time-limits were set. The one-year time-limit has been added in the case of the subsequent accessions of Albania, Moldova, 'TYFRO Macedonia', Ukraine, the Russian Federation, and Croatia (ibid, para 13). With the exception of Albania, all failed to meet the one year time limit. See also Chapter 9, pp. 334–6.

[8] This has been indicated by the CPT in Gen Rep 7, paras 20–3.

[9] See, for example, McGoldrick (1991), whose acclaimed study largely comprises an analysis of the Committee's paper record, the brief analysis of the membership and their working methods not being central to the study. A more politico-cultural approach is adopted by Opsahl (1992). This distinction is similar to that made in the policing literature—see Reiner, R (1992) *The Politics of the Police* (Hemel Hempstead: Wheatsheaf), 2nd edn, Part II; McConville, M, Leng, R and Sanders, A (1991) *The Case for the Prosecution: Police, Suspects and the Construction of Criminality* (London: Routledge).

In the case of the CPT the 'enforcers' are particularly critical. The Convention establishes no new legal norms. It creates a Committee with unprecedented powers of access to places of detention within member states. The work of the Committee revolves entirely around the highly practical tasks of conducting visits and communicating with state governments on the basis of the findings, recommendations, and requests for further information arising out of visit reports. Moreover, in framing the standards it will apply, and forming judgments about what it finds, the Committee is not bound by the jurisprudence of the European Commission and Court of Human Rights. It may draw on a much wider body of codes and instruments between which there are considerable differences of background, methodology, and purpose.[10] The Committee exercises a broad discretion and the manner in which that discretion is exercised is necessarily dependent on the ethos which the members of the Committee develop and the manner in which they respond collectively to the operational practicalities encountered during visits. In developing this ethos the Committee will certainly be influenced by two support groups: first and foremost the CPT Secretariat; secondly, and not to be discounted, the expert advisers that the Committee almost invariably employs to assist them when conducting visits and preparing reports. Before examining the available evidence about these three groups we need first to note a few things about the relationships between the groups and the extent that we are able to know about them.

The CPT, more so than most treaty-based human rights bodies, conducts the bulk of its business behind closed doors. Unlike the CAT and the HRC, for example, it does not question state officials concerning the content of reports in public at formal hearings that analysts may observe. When CPT members interview detained persons they do so in locations not generally accessible to outside observers. Moreover they do so out of the sight and hearing of custodians and the Committee does not subsequently reveal in its reports the names of those detainees interviewed. Information is never attributed to individuals. Indeed individuals are never named in CPT reports unless the Committee wishes to refer to cases already identifiable within the public domain and which are the subject of ongoing investigations and publicity.[11] Even when making contact with

---

[10] For the background to this see Chapter 4, pp. 118–22, the Explanatory Report, paras 25, 27, 91–2 and Gen Rep 1, paras 2.2–6, 45–51. The details of the standards applied are examined in detail in Chapters 7 and 8.

[11] For example, the 1992 Dutch report (para 18) named a Turkish national about whom the CPT had received allegations of ill-treatment. Mr Köksal, of whom the CPT delegation heard after they completed their visit, had reportedly died in custody following his arrest. The 1990 Danish report made reference (para 19) to 'a recent case in which serious ill-treatment was allegedly inflicted' on a man who, though not named, was said to be Gambian and aged 29. This was clearly Mr Babading Fatty whose alleged ill-treatment had

NGOs during the course of visits the CPT has adopted the practice of not naming in their reports the representatives of the organizations with whom they have met, nor of repeating what advice they have been given or what allegations might have been passed on to them. The whole process takes place not so much in secret as in strict confidence, and when written up the information that the CPT has gleaned is depersonalized and made virtually anonymous.[12] It is of course open to those who have acted as informants to the CPT to repeat whatever they have said to others. But NGO representatives with whom we have spoken have indicated that even this disclosure is discouraged. At meetings with the CPT during the course of visits to member states informants are given the impression by CPT delegations, if not asked explicitly, that the CPT would be grateful if they would treat the exercise as confidential and not subsequently communicate to the media and others what has taken place.

Whether this strict code of confidentiality about information given to the CPT should be so tightly enforced is a matter we discuss in Chapter 9. Suffice it to say that member states not infrequently request the CPT to say who the alleged victims of ill-treatment are so that they can take up those cases and investigate them more effectively. At least one CPT member has said publicly[13] that he sees no reason why this should not usually be done. The collective CPT view, however, is that this should not be done, not least lest it leave the complainant open to retaliation and possible further ill-treatment. The confidentiality of all information is preserved, leaving it to informants to decide whether they wish to break cover.

The rest of the Committee's work, that is the work that takes place *between* visits to member states, is conducted *entirely* behind closed doors. The plenary meetings of the CPT, which are held at the headquarters of the Council of Europe in Strasbourg, are closed meetings as required by the Convention.[14] They are not even attended by the experts who have accompanied the Committee on the visit and who have contributed to the reports which are to be finalized and adopted. There are no witnesses to the Committee's deliberations other than the Secretariat, which has developed a strict code of security and confidentiality about its work which

been widely reported in the Danish press and elsewhere (see Amnesty International (1995c) *Denmark: Summary of Concerns.* EUR 18/01/95 (London: Amnesty International, International Secretariat)).

[12] However, this cloak of anonymity may be fairly penetrable and when the CPT conducts short visits to interview certain groups of detainess their identity is, of course, obvious.

[13] Constantin Economides, the member for Greece (1991–) expressed this view at a seminar on the work of the CPT organized by the Marangopolous Foundation in Athens in December 1996.

[14] Article 6(1).

is enforced with regard to Council of Europe colleagues and is well recognized in Strasbourg.[15]

It follows that outside their visits to member states there are no witnesses to CPT procedures and discussions other than those persons—the members of the Secretariat and the expert advisors—who are themselves as strictly bound by the rule of confidentiality as CPT members. They may not speak about what they observe, report who has argued what, or indeed what arguments have taken place. They may only speak of that material which has already been revealed in authorized publications. To date, this rule of confidentiality, which is emphasized by members having to give a solemn undertaking before taking up their duties,[16] appears to have been respected to a remarkable degree.[17]

This means that the ethos of the CPT, arguably so important, is also relatively impenetrable. In this study we have made contact with some of the NGOs with whom the CPT has had meetings during the course of country visits. We have asked to speak to the particular representatives of those organizations who have met with the CPT and whenever that proved possible we have asked them, *inter alia*, what impressions they formed of the CPT delegation. Did the members seem well informed? Did they appear to have an accurate understanding of the law or of the principal problems relating to custody prevailing in the country? Did they ask penetrating questions? Was their attention focused on particular issues? And so on.

We think that the answers we obtained from these questions are valuable, not least because they point to the credibility of the CPT with local NGOs. However, the answers to these questions provided us with very little material about the CPT. NGO representatives often have a hazy recollection of what took place at meetings which, in most cases, occurred several years previously.[18] It follows that we have little basis on which to judge the relative merits and contributions of the different core groups that, collectively, produce the reports on which the major part of the reputation of the CPT rests. We are able only to draw broad inferences from the formal information provided by the Council of Europe about

[15] This is both symbolically and practically reinforced by the physical segregation of their offices, at the end of a cul-de-sac corridor within the Human Rights Building at Strasbourg.

[16] See Rule 2 of the Committee's Rules of Procedure, reproduced in Appendix 3.

[17] Some might contend that Cassese (1996) contains information representing a breach of CPT confidentiality. However, to the extent that that case can be sustained, it appears to be a rare and marginal breach. The book certainly contains reportage of country visits over and above that contained in CPT reports and though the countries concerned are not named, no great detective skill is required to identity the countries concerned.

[18] For example, they could generally not recall, even when prompted with the sight of a published report containing details of the make-up of the delegation, precisely who had been met and whether the persons with whom they spoke were CPT members, the Secretariat, or accompanying experts.

the personnel involved and the extent to which they have been involved in CPT activity. The survey of that evidence that follows should be read with these caveats in mind.

(a) The Torture Committee

(i) *The election mechanism and tenure of office*

The final text of the Convention, as we saw in Chapter 4, represented a significant departure from that initially envisaged. The original draft envisaged a small committee elected for six years (though some members could have their initial terms reduced to three years so as to provide for an even turnover of membership) and eligible for re-election. Moreover the burden of conducting visits was to fall as much on a panel of experts assisting the Committee as on Committee members themselves. In the event the Convention provided for one member per state, the idea of a formal panel of assisting experts was abandoned, and the task of conducting visits was to fall primarily on the Committee members themselves. These changes were not accompanied by sensible amendment of the provisions for members' tenure of office, however, and in autumn 1993, when the shortcomings of the Convention became readily apparent, a Protocol—Protocol No 2—providing for the more orderly renewal of Committee members and the possibility for them to be re-elected twice, was opened for signature.[19] To enter into force Protocol No 2 must be ratified (or signed without reservation as to ratification) by all state parties to the Convention. At the end of 1997 Protocol No 2 had been signed by 34 of the 37 states which have ratified the ECPT but the protocol has itself been ratified (or signed without reservation as to ratification) by only 31 of the 35 state parties.[20] The consequence was that in September 1997 an important block of five experienced members, including the then President of the Committee, had to leave the Committee when their second terms of office expired.[21]

The confusion arising from the unamended Convention arises because of the provisions of Article 5, according to which Members are elected

---

[19] For the text of Protocol 2 see Appendix 1C and for comment see Evans and Morgan (1994).

[20] The states which must sign and ratify before Protocol No 2 can enter into force are Andorra, Croatia, and the Ukraine. Italy and Portugal have signed but are yet to ratify. In addition, Latvia, Lithuania, and Russian have signed but not ratified the Protocol. Since these three states have not as yet ratified the ECPT, this does not stand in the way of the Protocol's entering into force. See Appendix 1C.

[21] The members for Austria, Denmark, Luxembourg, the Netherlands, and the United Kingdom. See Appendix 6B.

for periods of four years and may only be re-elected once. However, in accordance with Article 5(3), three of the original members of the Committee chosen by lot had their terms of office reduced to two years,[22] the purpose being to provide for a more orderly turnover of membership. This provision made sense given a small Committee but less and less sense as the Committee grew in size.

An even greater problem is that the term of office of each member runs from the date of their election, rather than from a fixed point in the year. This means that every time a new state becomes a party to the Convention another cycle of office is superimposed on the Committee. It also means that if an existing member resigns from the Committee the new member elected to replace him or her serves a full four years from their date of election rather than the unexpired portion of their predecessor's term of office.[23] In addition, there may also be delays in holding an election brought about by states not submitting a list of candidates in time to prevent a break in the continuity of its membership of the Committee.[24] Whenever any of these situations arise, the orderly cyle of elections is further impaired. In consequence, after only eight years a remarkably inconvenient schedule of elections had been built up. This is

[22] The members for Cyprus, Ireland, and Italy.

[23] This has happened on several occasions. For example, Leopoldo Torres Boursault was elected as member for Spain in September 1989 and was therefore due for re-election in September 1993. However, he resigned as a member in 1990 and was replaced in April 1990 by José Mohedano, who himself resigned in May 1993 when Torres Boursault was immediately re-elected to the Committee. Interestingly, this seems to have been treated as a 'new' membership since Torres Boursault was considered eligible for re-election to the Committee in May 1997. In September 1991 Antonio Lopes Rocha, first elected as member for Portugal in June 1990, resigned following his election as a Judge of the European Court of Human Rights: in September 1992 José Viera Mesquita was elected member for Portugal. In September 1993 Nicolo Amato was elected to represent Italy (Antonio Cassesse, previously President of the CPT, having not stood for election to a second term of office), but he resigned in December 1994 and not until June 1995 was Vitaliano Esposito elected to replace him. Likewise Tonio Borg, member for Malta, originally elected in June 1990 and re-elected in June 1994, resigned in May 1995 on being appointed Minister of Justice for Malta. Not until January 1996 was Maria Sciberras elected as the new member for Malta. All these resignations have altered the election cycle beyond that dictated by when states became party to the Convention.

[24] This was the case during the Autumn 1997 regarding the UK, for example. Stefan Terlezki was not eligible for re-election in September 1997, but not until December 1997 was Silvia Casale elected as his replacement because the British Government failed to submit a slate of candidates sufficiently early to ensure continuity. Under Rule 1 of the 1991 Rules of Procedure, a member elected (or re-elected) to fill a vacancy brought about by the expiring of a term of office had their own term of office calculated from the day following the expired term. In effect a 'late' replacement was back-dated, resulting de facto in a shorter term of office. In March 1997 Rule 1 was amended by the removal of this requirement (see Appendix 3). In consequence, members elected to fill vacancies occasioned by the lapsing of office are now treated in the same way as vacancies occasioned by resignations. Although this might be seen as correcting anomaly, it adds a further disrupting element to the electoral cycle.

Table 5.1 Schedule of elections to CPT as at April 1997

Name	Country	Office expires	Eligible for re-election
Leopoldo Torres-Boussault	Spain	03.05.1997	Yes
Claude Nicolay	Luxembourg	19.09.1997	No
Ingrid Lycke Ellingsen	Norway	19.09.1997	Yes
Bent Sørenson	Denmark	19.09.1997	No
Stefan Terlezki	UK	19.09.1997	No
Rudolf Machacek	Austria	19.09.1997	No
Nadia Gevers Leuven-Lachinsky	Netherlands	19.09.1997	No
Safa Reisoğlu	Turkey	19.09.1997	Yes
Ivan Zakine	France	19.09.1997	Yes
Gisela Perren-Klinger	Switzerland	19.01.1997	Yes
Günther Kaiser	Germany	21.06.1998	No
John Olden	Ireland	21.03.1999	Yes
Florin Stănescu	Romania	21.03.1999	Yes
Mario Benedettini	San Marino	21.03.1999	Yes
Pirrko Lahti	Finland	21.06.1999	Yes
Vitaliano Esposito	Italy	21.06.1999	Yes
Jogoda Poloncová	Slovak Republic	21.06.1999	Yes
Christina Doctare	Sweden	19.09.1999	Yes
Lambert Kelchtermans	Belgium	08.01.2000	Yes
Constantin Economides	Greece	30.11.1999	No
Demetrios Stylianides	Cyprus	30.11.1999	Yes
Adam Laptaś	Poland	30.11.1999	Yes
Maria Sciberras	Malta	09.01.2000	Yes
Jón Bjarman	Iceland	26.03.2000	No
Miklós Magyer	Hungary	03.04.2000	Yes
Zdeněk Hájek	Czech Republic	11.09.2000	Yes
Arnold Oehry	Liechtenstein	13.01.2001	No
Emilia Drumeva	Bulgaria	17.03.2001	Yes

well illustrated by considering the schedule of forthcoming elections and necessary departures of members which confronted the Committee in April 1997 (Table 5.1).

The purpose of Protocol No 2 is described as being to make 'provision . . . for members of the [Committee] . . . to be placed in one of two groups for election purposes, the aim being to ensure that one half of the Committee's membership is renewed every two years'.[25] To this end Article 1(2) of the Protocol amends Article 5 of the Convention by adding two new sub-sections which provide:

---

[25] Council of Europe Press Release, Ref 454(93).

4. In order to ensure that, as far as possible, one half of the membership of the Committee shall be renewed every two years, the Committee of Ministers may decide, before proceeding to any subsequent election, that the term or terms of office of one or more members to be elected shall be for a period other than four years but not more than six and not less than two years.
5. In cases where more that one term of office is involved and the Committee of Ministers applies the preceding paragraph, the allocation of the terms of office shall be effected by the drawing of lots by the Secretary General, immediately after the election.

We presume that the intention is that the elections be consolidated so as to take place biennially, with new terms of office commencing in September. Both the Parliamentary Assembly and the CPT places a high value on the Protocol's entry into force at the earliest opportunity.[26] However, given that the Protocol, which is modelled on Articles 22(3) and (4) of the European Convention of Human Rights, has already been open for signature for more than four years, it seems likely that the relentless schedule of elections facing the Committee of Ministers will continue for the foreseeable future, with all its disruptive consequences for the work of the CPT.

(ii) The membership of the Committee

The advantage of arrangements which provide for an orderly and staggered turnover of members is that the Committee is not robbed of too much experience on a single occasion. This danger first arose in September 1993 when ten of the then 22 members were required to seek re-election.[27] Moreover, two members not due for re-election decided to take this opportunity to resign.[28] This meant that the Committee could have lost up to 12 members at a stroke, including nearly all of its most experienced members. However, only four of those members eligible for re-election either decided not to stand again, or were not nominated by

---

[26] See CLAHR Report (1997), para 7(ii) and CPT Gen Rep 7, para 17. Protocol No 1 to the ECPT, adopted at the same time as Protocol No 2, was intended to facilitate the work of the CPT in non-Council of Europe states. The growth in membership of the Council of Europe to include virtually all the states of Central and Eastern Europe has rendered this all but redundant. Protocol No 1 brought with it serious political and cost implications, whilst No 2 did not. A perceived 'linkage' between the two protocols was possibly a reason why No 2 has made such slow progress towards entry into force, and states are now being urged to ratify No 2 alone. So far, France had been the only state to do so. See Appendices 4B and 4C. For the text of Protocol No 1, see Appendix 1B. See also Chapter 9, pp. 335–6.

[27] The members for Austria, Denmark, France, Luxembourg, the Netherlands, Norway, Sweden, Switzerland, Turkey, and the United Kingdom, all of whom had been first elected on 19 September 1989.

[28] The members for Ireland and Italy.

their governments, or were not re-elected,[29] and the new members elected in September 1993 included persons whose expertise appeared to match that which was lost. September 1997 was the next significant test: 10 out of the 28 members' terms expired, five of whom were not eligible for re-election. In the event all those members eligible for re-election were re-elected. Moreover, now that the Committee has grown in size, the danger of losing a disproportionate amount of experience and expertise in a single occasion is lessened.

Despite the Convention currently being in force for 35 states, there are at present only 29 members of the CPT. No members have yet been elected for five relatively new member states[30] and replacements have yet to be elected for two states.[31] This is the usual situation. Some time generally elapses—occasionally a considerable period of time—between the Convention coming into force in relation to new State Parties and members of those countries being elected.[32] Moreover, there is not infrequently a delay of several months before a member is elected to replace someone who has resigned. Throughout its life the CPT has typically had several members fewer than the number of State Parties.[33]

It is difficult to assess, from the relatively cryptic *curriculum vitae* issued by the Council of Europe Directorate of Information when announcing the election of new members, how well members satisfy the requirement that they be 'persons of high moral character, known for their competence in the field of human rights or having professional experience in the areas covered by this Convention',[34] or the degree to which they satisfactorily 'serve in their individual capacity', are 'independent and impartial', and 'serve the Committee effectively'.[35] What is clear is that the drafters of the Convention considered that members 'do not have to be lawyers', indeed that it would be 'desirable that the Committee should include members who have experience in matters such as prison administration and the various medical fields relevant to the treatment of persons deprived of their liberty'.[36] Such a mix of experience would, argued the framers of the Convention, 'make the dialogue between the Committee and the states more effective and facilitate concrete suggestions from the

---

[29] The members for France, Norway, Switzerland, and Turkey were not re-elected. It is not known which, if any, of them offered themselves and were nominated for re-election.

[30] Albania, Andorra, 'TFYRO Macedonia', Slovenia, and the Ukraine. See Appendix 6A.

[31] Portugal, whose member resigned in October 1996.

[32] For example, the Convention came into force with respect to Bulgaria on 1 September 1994, but it was not until 17 March 1997 that its first member, Emilia Drumeva, was elected.

[33] See Gen Rep 4, Appendix 2 (four seats unfulled: Hungary, Ireland, San Marino, and Slovenia); Gen Rep 5, Appendix 2 (five seats unfulled: Bulgaria, Hungary, Malta, Poland, and Slovenia); Gen Rep 6, Appendix 2 (three seats unfulled: Bulgaria, Czech Republic, and Slovenia); Gen Rep 7, Appendix 2 (five seats left unfilled: Andorra, Albania, Estonia, Portugal, and Slovenia).

[34] Article 4(2).   [35] Article 4(4).   [36] Explanatory Report, para 36.

Committee'.[37] This argument served to emphasize the fact that the Committee is not a judicial body, but is concerned with the practical task of fostering arrangements best calculated to make ill-treatment less likely.

The *curriculum vitae* published for members provides a maximum of three briefly stated qualifications or appointments for each, a selection no doubt made by the members themselves. From these minimal career details it is not possible to divine much more than the general professional orientation of members, which is not necessarily a good guide to the potential contribution of a member to the work of the Committee.[38] The external observer is able to do little more than analyse the professional balance, age, and sex of the members making up the CPT, though it may be possible to infer something more about the capacity of the Committee as a whole from other aspects of its operation.[39]

When first established in 1989 the Committee was able to use some members with specialist knowledge for the training of their colleagues.[40] Yet the Committee nevertheless made it plain that they needed among their number more members with non-legal backgrounds, particularly 'medical doctors and experts in penitentiary systems', persons needed to 'play a decisive role in the Committee's operation, especially in the course of visits'.[41] This plea was re-emphasized after two years operation:

unless more members are elected with professional experience in the (medical and penitentiary) areas, there is a risk that the influence of asisting 'experts' (cf Article 7(2) of the Convention) over the CPT's activities will become greater than that envisaged by the authors of the Convention.[42]

---

[37] Explanatory Report, para 36.

[38] For example, a senior prisons administrator may never have governed a prison, let alone have walked the landings of a cell-block as a prison guard; a lawyer may never have been in a police station or prison; not all doctors have a good 'bedside manner'. On the other hand, persons with no obvious professional qualifications might have considerable practical or pastoral experience which could be of value.

[39] See section on use of *ad hoc* experts below.

[40] Gen Rep 1, para 37. We can reasonably speculate that these members included the three members elected by the newly formed Committee to constitute their Bureau. The founding President of the Committee, Antonio Cassesse, member for Italy, was from 1983 to 1986 a member of the Council of Europe's Committee of Experts charged with the task of drafting the Convention. He would have been ideally placed to advise his colleagues as to what purposes lay behind the various provisions of the Convention and the Explanatory Report and why one approach had been adopted as opposed to another. Jacques Bernheim, member for Switzerland, and elected First Vice-President, had formerly been a psychiatrist within the Swiss prison system: he was ideally placed to advise his colleagues on the realities of custodial life. Bent Sørensen, member for Denmark and elected Second Vice-President of the Committee in 1989 might also have been asked to share his experience with his new colleagues. Mr Sørensen, a retired Professor of Surgery, had been a member of the United Nations Committe Against Torture since its formation in 1986 and was also an active member of the internationally-reputed Centre for the Rehabilitation of Torture Victims in Copenhagen. He had lectured and written extensively on the phenomenon of torture and its consequences, psychological as well as physical, for victims.

[41] ibid, para 87.   [42] Gen Rep 2, para 27.

After three years the Committee apparently felt that the problem was recognized and was being addressed by the Committee of Ministers, though it is difficult to see why. Although four additional members were elected in 1992, two of them were lawyers,[43] one was a parliamentarian,[44] and one was a cleric. Only the latter, as far can be judged, had any practical experience of penal institutions.[45] The Committee nevertheless thanked the Committee of Ministers for taking action in relation to their shortage of members with penitentiary experience.[46] No thanks were offered in 1994. Quite the reverse. Though six new members were elected in 1993, the best that can be said is that the new members replaced the non-legal expertise that had been lost with members retiring in 1993.[47] The Committee bewailed the fact that 'the changes in the CPT's membership during 1993 cannot be said to have remedied [the] problem' previously raised.[48] The Committee also drew attention to the 'rather low' number of women on the Committee and hoped that 'these matters will be kept in mind in the course of the procedure to fill the vacant seats', then six in number.[49]

There were no changes in membership in 1994 and the President, Claude Nicolay, told a seminar in December 1994 that the Committee had 'not yet reached a balanced composition . . . it still needs more members with a specialised professional background in the different areas to which the ECPT applies, Moreover, we still have too few women'. He also observed that 'it should also be considered that the CPT's activities are a physical strain', a comment that must surely be taken to be a reference to the relatively advanced age of several Committee members.[50] Moreover, in its 5th Annual Report the Committee added, darkly, that

---

[43] Arnold Oehry (1992–), the member for Liechtenstein, a former judge and Jose Vieira Mesquita (1992–6), the member for Portugal, a lawyer and former Member of Parliament.

[44] Nora Staels-Dompas (1992–5), the member for Belgium, was a former Vice-President of the Parliamentary Assembly of the Council of Europe.

[45] Jón Bjarman (1922–), the member for Iceland, is currently a hospital chaplain of the National Church of Iceland. He has previously served in the same capacity as a prison chaplain.

[46] Gen Rep 3, para 23.

[47] Jacques Bernheim (1989–93), the member for Switzerland, and Astrid Heiberg (1989–93), the member for Norway, were both psychiatrists. They were replaced by Ingrid Lycke Ellingsen (1993–), the member for Norway, and Gisela Perren-Klinger (1993–), the member for Switzerland, also both psychiatrists. Other retiring members were Antonio Cassese (1989–93), the member for Italy, the CPT's founding President, and an international lawyer; Lydie Dupuy (1989–93), the member for France, a parliamentarian; José Mohedano (1990–93), the member for Spain, a lawyer; and Ergun Özbudun (1989–93), the member for Turkey, an academic lawyer. They were replaced by Nicolò Amato (1993–5), the member for Italy, a Professor of Law and Director General of Italian Prisons and Remand Centres; Ivan Zakine (1993–) the member for France, a former Director of Prison Administration; Leopoldo Torres Boursault (1993–) the member for Spain, a lawyer; and Safa Reisoğlu (1993–) the member for Turkey, an academic lawyer.

[48] Gen Rep 4, para 16.   [49] ibid, para 16.   [50] See APT (1995), 225.

'in the light of recent experience' they had to 'underline the importance of electing members who are both in a position, and ready, to serve the Committee effectively (cf Article 4, para 4, of the Convention)'.[51] The nature of the 'recent experience' was not stated. But we can speculate that it is a reference to the recent member for Italy who, for whatever reason, had taken part in not a single visit.[52] It seems clear from this reference, therefore, that failure to participate in visits—some members, as we shall see, make fewer visits than others—is not always the consequence of not being asked.

In 1995, however, the Committee felt able to suggest that their by now regularly intoned 'message has been heard'.[53] Nine new members were elected during 1995, among their number two women, one a medical doctor[54] and the other a lawyer.[55] Further, among the new male members was a psychotherapist,[56] a forensic pathologist,[57] a serving prison governor,[58] and a retired civil servant with experience of prisons administration.[59] Moreover, two of the new members were among the youngest ever to be elected to the Committee.[60] During 1996 the Committee's wishes were further met with the election of two new members, one a man and the other a woman, both of whom were doctors.[61] The Committee felt able to record with pleasure 'that the medical component of its membership has been reinforced considerably over the last eighteen months'. However they reiterated their continued need for more 'prison specialists' and they noted, again, that the number of women members (7 out of 27) remained 'rather low'.[62]

If three census points are adopted—1 January 1990, 1994, and 1998—then the changing composition of the CPT can be charted as follows. Membership grew from 16 to 21 to 29. The breadth of experience within

[51] Gen Rep 5, para 26.

[52] Nicolò Amato, a Professor of Law and Director General of Italian Remand Prisons, elected September 1993, resigned January 1995.

[53] Gen Rep 5, para 26.

[54] Christina Doctare (1995–), the member for Sweden. Mrs Doctare was elected to replace Love Kellberg (1989–95).

[55] Jagoda Poloncová (1994–), the member for Slovakia.

[56] Mario Benedettini (1994–) the member for San Marino.

[57] Florin Stănescu (1994–), the member for Romania.

[58] Adam Laptaś, the first member for Poland, was deputy Director of the Myslowice Remand Prison when elected.

[59] John Olden (1994–), the member for Ireland. The other new member elected in 1994 was Vitaliano Esposito (1995–), the member for Italy and a public prosecutor, who filled the vacancy cause by the resignation of Nicolò Amato in January 1995.

[60] Mario Benedittini and Adam Laptaś were 41 and 42 years old respectively when elected.

[61] Miklós Magyar, first member for Hungary, a psychiatrist, and Maria Sciberras, a medical doctor, the new member for Malta, replacing Tonio Borg who resigned in May 1995 on being appointed Minister of Justice for Malta.

[62] Gen Rep 6, para 22.

the Committee increased. In 1990 the Committee was dominated by lawyers (9 members out of 16, albeit with a wide range of experience[63]), the next largest professional group being the medics (four members, two of them psychiatrists). There was also a civil servant with experience of penal administration and two parliamentarians. No significant change had occurred by 1994. The lawyers still dominated (12 members out of 21), the medical group remained the same, but there was now a psychologist, a former prison chaplain and still two parliamentarians. By 1998, however, there had been a significant change. The lawyers remained only just a majority of the Committee (15 members out of 29) but three of them now had direct experience of penal administration.[64] Moreover the number of medics had grown from four to eight, including four psychiatrists and a pathologist. Further, the medical group was now supplemented by two psychotherapists.[65] The para-medical group therefore almost rivalled the legal group in size (10 members out of 29). Almost as significant was the net increase in the number of penal administrators. In addition to the two lawyers mentioned above there was also a former prison chaplain,[66] a retired civil servant with experience of penal policy,[67] and a criminologist advisor to a prison service and prison inspectorate.[68] There was now only one serving parliamentarian.[69] There had been a marginal improvement in the gender balance of the Committee: there were three women members in 1990, five in 1994 and nine in 1998, approaching a third of the Committee. However, gender representation within the Committee has always been skewed professionally. At the beginning of 1998, five of the women were medics or para-medics and only three were lawyers, not an ideal situation for constructing delegations balanced in terms of both gender and profession.

Given the relatively low continuity of membership within the Committee—only ten out of the 29 members in place in January 1998 had continuously been members since before 1994[70]—we should not expect a marked upward drift in the average age of members: there has been ample opportunity to balance the unavoidable increase in the ages of the core of long-standing members with newly appointed more youthful colleagues. But this has not been the case. In 1990 the average age of members was

[63] Some were in private practice, some were academics, some were judges, others had experience of diplomacy or politics. None, however, had experience of running prisons.

[64] A former director of prison administration, an advisor to a prison service and a serving prison governor, the members for France, the Czech Republic, and Poland respectively.

[65] The members for San Marino and Finland.

[66] The member for Iceland.   [67] The member for Ireland.

[68] The member for the United Kingdom.   [69] The member for Belgium.

[70] One member, Leopoldo Torres Boursault, the member for Spain, has had three periods of membership. Elected in September 1989 he resigned from the Committee in 1990, but was re-elected in May 1993 and again in September 1997.

54.4 years. This had risen to 60 by 1994, but reduced to 59 years in 1998. In 1990, four out of 16 members were 65 years or over, by 1994 and 1998 this had risen to eight out of 21 members and 11 out of 29 members respectively. This is not a gratuitously ageist observation. Visits by CPT delegations are onerous.[71] Though older members may well be as energetic as younger members, and though some older members are undoubtedly among the most experienced and hardworking, it is difficult to resist the conclusion that a Committee containing as many elderly members as the CPT may be more reliant on its generally more youthful secretariat and expert advisers than is necessary. Some countries continue to appoint members who, by the time they gather substantial experience of the Committee's work, are well into their 70s.[72]

It seems clear, from the number of visits that different members make, and their allocation by the Bureau to visiting delegations likely to encounter more or less difficulties (and thus to require more or less experience and expertise), that some members are judged by the Secretariat and Bureau to be more able to make a contribution than others. During the first two years of the Committee's life, for example, it was noticeable that some members took part in a large number of visits, whereas other members were relatively little used.[73] Those members used most were those most obviously experienced and well qualified.[74] These distinctions, however, were particularly stark during the first year or two when the whole Committee was finding its feet and there was an understandable premium on using members thought to have safe and experienced pairs of hands derived from their experience before joining the Committee. Analysis of the visits made during the first three calendar years following their election by *all* the members elected since 1989 and who have served at least three years demonstrates that such dramatic distinctions have not, with one or two notable exceptions, persisted. As of January 1998 there had been 26 past and present members with at least three years experience. During the first three years after the year in which they were appointed—a reasonable period of assessment given that a certain period of time typically elapses before a new member is asked to undertake a visit—the majority of these members (19 out of 26) undertook five

---

[71] A point emphasised, in relation to members' age, by the CLAHR Report (1997), para 44

[72] Arnold Oehry, the member for Liechtenstein, was 72 when he was appointed in November 1992. It may be significant that in the following three years he was the member of only three visiting delegations. Demetrios Stylianides, the member for Cyprus, was 68 when he was appointed in November 1995.

[73] Of the 20 members in place by December 1991—that is at least two years after most of them had been apointed—five had yet to make a visit (three because recently appointed), three had conducted one visit, two had made two visits, four three visits, two four visits, three members five visits and one member had made six visits (see Evans and Morgan (1992), 604).

[74] For example, Antonio Cassesse, Jacques Bernheim and Bent Sørensen (see n 40 above).

or more visits.[75] It is apparent, therefore, that most members who initially undertook few visits thereafter made up for their slow start, and those who were initially heavily burdened were subsequently relieved. Though there remain one or two conspicuous exceptions to this pattern, most members take part in on average two visiting delegations per annum though a minority take part in three.[76] Members given a particularly onerous schedule of visits in one year have invariably had a light load the previous year, or are given a light load the following year. The principal exceptions to this rule are members of the Bureau, the President of the CPT, and the 1st and 2nd Vice-Presidents,[77] though members with medical qualifications, particularly those who were appointed in the early days of the Committee when medically-qualified members were few in number, have tended also to make above average numbers of visits. The need for balanced delegations demands both that some members are inevitably called on more frequently than others. It is also clear that the services of all members are called on, irrespective of the contribution they are able to make.[78] Finally, and significantly, as we shall see below, it is apparent that most CPT members have considerably less experience of undertaking visits than most members of the Secretariat and a small core of *ad hoc* experts. Of the 29 CPT members on 1 January 1998, only eight had been on six or more visits.[79]

(iii) The CPT Bureau

The first task that the newly elected Committee set about in autumn 1989 was the formulation of their Rules of Procedure which were adopted in

[75] Three members undertook two visits, two members two visits, two members four visits, five members five visits, six members six visits, six members seven visits, and two members eight visits.

[76] The assertion, by Carol Mottet of the APT, that members have to make on average three to four visits per year, is therefore a considerable overstatement of the burden placed on CPT members to date (see APT (1995), 179).

[77] Thus Antonio Cassese, member for Italy from 1989–93 and the founding President of the CPT, undertook four visits in 1991. Bent Sørensen, member for Denmark from 1989–97 and Vice-President of the CPT from 1989–95 (2nd Vice-President from 1989–93 and 1st Vice-President from 1993–5) undertook five visits in 1991. Claude Nicolay, member for Luxembourg from 1989 and President of the CPT from 1993–7, undertook three visits in 1991 and again in 1994. Ingrid Lycke Ellingsen, member for Norway since 1993 and elected 1st Vice-President in 1995, undertook four visits in 1996.

[78] The CLAHR Report (1997), para 55 predicts that all members will soon be required to spend 55 days directly on CPT work. The CPT foresees an increase in the number of days spent on visits conducted each year from the current 120 to 200 (Gen Rep 7, para 21). Should this happen, the simple availability of members will become an increasingly important factor.

[79] Six recently appointed members had yet to go on a visit, 11 members had been on one, two or three visits, and four members had undertaken four or five visits. At the experienced end of the continuum, one member had undertaken six visits, one member seven, and two members had each done nine, ten and twelve visits respectively.

November 1989 and have been subject to a number of modifications.[80] The Rules provide that the work of the CPT shall be directed collegially by a Bureau comprising three members, a President and a First and Second Vice-President, elected every two years by secret ballot by a majority of members. Members may be re-elected to the Bureau.[81]

The CPT President chairs the Committee when it meets in plenary session[82] and the Bureau directs its work.[83] The Committee has decided that the need for plenary meetings, each of which represents a considerable drain on the CPT's budget as well as members' time, is less now than in the early days when the Committee was having to decide how to interpret its mandate and conduct its business. In 1990, 1991, and 1992, for example, there were six, five, and four plenary meetings respectively.[84] Four meetings remained the pattern until 1996 when it was decided to reduce the number to three following reorganization of the manner in which country visit reports are dealt with.[85] This means that relatively more of members' time can now be devoted to visits and meetings directly related to visits. It follows that the work of the Bureau, which meets regularly,[86] has become relatively more important for steering the work of the Committee.[87] With the assistance of the Secretariat the Bureau prepares proposals to be put to plenary sessions of the Committee as regards, *inter alia*: the programme of visits; the leadership and make-up of visiting delegations; and other business to be laid before the Committee.

Membership of the Bureau is therefore of strategic importance for the work of the Committee. The Bureau elected in 1989 and re-elected in 1991 comprised three members conspicuously experienced, in different ways, to lead the Committee during its formative years.[88] It seems likely, now that the CPT has found its operational and jurisprudential feet, that election to the Bureau will in future depend increasingly on political factors as well as the personal qualities seen by colleagues to be required for administrative leadership. The Bureau will almost certainly have to be seen to represent the varied interests and origins of the growing membership of the CPT. To date the Bureau has always been led by

---

[80] The Rules were amended in March, May and November 1990, January and September 1991, and March 1997. They are reproduced in their current form in Appendix 3.

[81] For the decision to establish a Bureau, see Cassese (1991), 135, 143.   [82] Rule 6(1).

[83] Rule 10(2).   [84] See Gen Rep 1, para 9; Gen Rep 2, paras 8 and 13.

[85] See below, pp. 198–9, and Gen Rep 7, para 22.   [86] Gen Rep 6, para 8.

[87] The burden of work on Bureau members has already increased to the point that they are paid a substantial 'retainer' for work-days in excess of 55 per annum up to a maximum of 77 days per annum. In 1996 the President and the First Vice-President were already making heavy use of this allowance with the President falling not far short of the maximum (CLAHR Report (1997), para 54 and n 33, and formal interview with the Bureau and Secretary of the Committee, Sept 1996).

[88] Antonio Cassese, Jacques Bernheim, and Bent Sørensen, the members for Italy, Switzerland, and Denmark respectively (see above, n 40).

a lawyer[89] and has always included a medically-qualified member.[90] Since 1993 it has always included a woman.[91] There has also been a discernible balance within the Bureau hitherto of predominantly Francophone and Anglophone members, the two official languages of the Council of Europe. This has tended also to mean reasonable representation of both the north and the south of Europe. With the accession of Eastern European states to the Convention, it will be surprising if, in future, the Bureau does not also include a member from the eastern block of state parties. The need to ensure adequate representation, in addition to the burden of work carried by the Bureau, suggests that it may be necessary to increase its size to four or five members.

(b) The Secretariat

The CPT is served by a Secretariat provided by the Secretary General of the Council of Europe.[92] In recognition of the rule of confidentiality surrounding the operation of the Convention the Secretary General has determined that the Secretariat should comprise a distinct section of the Council of Europe's Directorate of Human Rights.[93] The Secretariat is housed in the Human Rights building in Strasbourg, where the CPT meets in plenary session and where a separate library and information system for the use of the Committee is maintained.

The effective and efficient working of the CPT depends on the effectiveness and efficiency of the Secretariat. It is the task of the administrative officers within the Secretariat to: arrange and prepare for visits; accompany and provide administrative support to members during the course of visits; draft reports following visits; clerk all meetings of the Committee and Bureau and; implement the decisions of the Committee regarding dialogue with member states. The dependence of the Committee on an adequate Secretariat has become a constant refrain in the annual reports of the CPT. The Secretariat, initially five strong,[94] had grown, by 1997, to thirteen staff,[95] and further enlargement is envisaged in the near future.

The need for this build-up of Secretariat strength has repeatedly been emphasized. The growth in the number of state parties and their

---

[89] Presidents Antonio Cassese (1989–93), Claude Nicolay (1993–7), and Ivan Zakine (1997–).

[90] Jacques Bernheim (1989–93), Bent Sørensen (1989–95), Ingrid Lycke Ellingsen (1995–).

[91] Nora Staels Dompas (1992–5) and Ingrid Lycke Ellingsen (1995–).

[92] Article 6(3).   [93] Gen Rep 1, para 8.

[94] The Secretary to the Committee, Trevor Stevens, an administrative officer, an administrative assistant and two secretaries.

[95] The secretary and deputy secretary, seven administrative officers (one of whom is responsible for administrative and budgetry arrangements), an archivist and information officer, a senior clerk, and two secretaries (Gen Rep 7, Appendix B).

geographical spread, and the need to maintain a dialogue with countries subject to both *periodic* and *ad hoc* visits, has generated a 'heavy workload [which] is gradually taking its toll in terms of a lengthening gap (currently some four to five years) between periodic visits to a given country and a weakening of the ongoing dialogue following a visit. As a result, both the credibility and effectiveness of the CPT are being put at risk'.[96] The visiting potential of the Committee, for which budgetary allowance had been made, has not always being exploited to the full,[97] the lack of capacity within the Secretariat resulting in the cancellation of planned visits.[98] This clearly remains a serious issue and is likely to become more acute as new states parties present the Committee with problems of a different order than those hitherto encountered.[99]

As far as CPT members are concerned it is those Secretariat staff who accompany them on country visits who are most intimately involved with members in fulfilling the CPT mandate.[100] These are also the Secretariat members with whom NGOs have contact when seeking advice about CPT affairs or transmitting information to the CPT about alleged ill-treatment. They are also the persons with whom official liaison officers and other civil servants within member states have contact when visits are being arranged. Our interviews with both officials and NGO representatives suggest that the Secretariat are almost universally considered to exhibit the highest professional qualities: that they are skilled, multi-lingual, 'correct' in all their dealings—and extremely well informed. If there is a criticism it is that they have hitherto been excessively scrupulous in their interpretation of the confidentiality rule. The senior members of the Secretariat are generally considered to be the principal bearers of the ethos and tradition of the CPT.

That this is so is not suprising when the record is closely examined. Remarkably, none of the senior administrative staff have yet left the Secretariat. This means that those members of the Secretariat who accompany CPT members during visits and who draft CPT reports are typically

---

[96] Gen Rep 5, para 28.   [97] Interview with Bureau, Sept 1996.

[98] In 1995, for example, the planned *periodic* visit to Switzerland was postponed until 1996 for want of Secretariat staff both to engage in visits and sustain in a timely manner the work resulting from visits.

[99] One of the most recent members of the Council of Europe, the Russian Federation, for example, is not just a huge country geographically: it is also estimated to contain in excess of one million prisoners, more than those in all the other Council of Europe member states combined. The Ukraine presents a lesser but still formidable inspectional problem.

[100] Currently eight officers (the Secretary, Deputy Secretary, and six Administrative Officers) comprising five lawyers, one senior ex-police officer with a legal background, one member with wide administrative experience, and one member with a political science background. Three are women, five are men and they include a diversity of nationalities: two British, one French, one Belgian, one Spaniard, one Pole, one Bulgarian, and one Macedonian-American. They collectively command a wide variety of European languages.

much more experienced and knowledgeable about established CPT procedures, methods, and 'jurisprudence' than the members of the Committee they advise and serve. This relative depth of experience, which is of course a commonplace aspect of the relationship between civil servants and elected politicians or appointed executive officers within states, became even more pronounced with the retirement of the founder members of the Committee in September 1997. Most members of the Secretariat now have substantially more experience of CPT visits than most of the Committee members they accompany.[101]

(c) The *ad hoc* experts

The final text of the Convention provided that the members of the Committee should themselves be the experts responsible for carrying out visits of inspection. The use of *ad hoc* experts should, like the support role of interpreters, be resorted to only if considered 'necessary' by the Committee.[102] The underlying idea, according to the Explanatory Report, was to:

supplement the experience of the Committee by the assistance, for example, of persons who have special training or experience of humanitarian missions, who have a medical background or possess a special competence in the treatment of detainees or in prison regimes, and, when appropriate, as regards young persons.[103]

This suggests that the use of *ad hoc* experts was intended to be occasional rather than routine. It also suggests, given the supplemental role of *ad hoc* experts, that the extent to which they are used, and the characteristics of the *ad hoc* experts used, is an indication of the adequacy of the Committee itself, both as to numbers, qualities, experience, and expertise. Indeed, this symbiotic relationship between the characteristics of the CPT membership, and the degree to which *ad hoc* members are used, has repeatedly been stressed in the annual reports from the Committee when indicating to the Committee of Ministers what sort of members are needed.

In its first General Report the Committee pointed out that whenever the Committee was itself unable to provide members with particular

---

[101] It is difficult to determine precisely how many visits Secretariat staff have been engaged in because, until late 1996, the press releases issued by the Council of Europe following CPT visits simply recorded how many members of the Secretariat were involved in delegations, but not who. These details have always been recorded in CPT reports, however. It follows that until late 1996 it was possible to establish which members of the Secretariat were involved in visits only if the reports of those visits were published. Most have been. From these reports it is clear that senior members of the Secretariat have typically been involved in two, three, or four visits a year since they were first appointed, typically a higher rate of engagement than CPT members. By the close of 1997 the four most senior administrative members of the Secretariat had all accompanied 20 or more delegations, approximately twice as many as the most experienced CPT members.

[102] Article 7(2).　　　[103] Explanatory Report, para 51.

professional backgrounds in the make-up of visiting delegations, it could draw on 'experts'. It was implied, however, that this was not entirely satisfactory because *ad hoc* experts would not be able to participate in 'all stages' of the Committee's work.[104] The point was made again, more bluntly, the following year: 'Unless more members are elected with professional experience . . . there is a risk that the influence of assisting "experts" (cf Article 7(2) of the Convention) over the CPT's activities will become greater than that envisaged by the authors of the Convention'.[105] The Legal Affairs Committee of the Parliamentary Assembly has also highlighted the risk of *ad hoc* experts exercising unforseen influence over the work of the Committee, commenting: 'Were all CPT members to possess the necessary knowledge and experience, the need to resort to outside experts would be far less than at present.'[106]

This statement goes beyond pointing out that the balance of expertise within the Committee is not satisfactory. It is tantamount to saying that some CPT members are less than expertly qualified for the tasks of the Committee to which they have been appointed and that *ad hoc* experts are being resorted to as a consequence. For the fact is that during the first seven years of the Committee's operation, *ad hoc* experts have not been used occasionally *as and when necessary* to assist visiting delegations, they have been employed *routinely* to assist visiting delegations, we must presume because the Committee has considered it *routinely* 'necessary'.

By the end of 1997, the CPT had made use of 37 different experts to accompany delegations. Between them these 37 experts accompanied 120 missions, an average of rather less than two on each of the 68 missions undertaken by that date. In fact a few missions have included as many as four experts.[107] Only five visits have been undertaken without the assistance of experts.[108] It is clear, therefore, that the CPT has hitherto regarded the presence of accompanying experts to be essential to their work and it is notable that since the end of 1994, only one of the 31 CPT delegations was unaccompanied by an *ad hoc* expert.[109] There appears

---

[104] Gen Rep 1, para 88.   [105] Gen Rep 2, para 27.

[106] CLAHR Report (1997), para 44.

[107] For example, the visits to Greece, 1993, the United Kingdom, 1994, and Romania, 1995, included four *ad hoc* experts.

[108] The first two visits to the United Kingdom were made without experts (in July 1990 and July 1993), though on the second occasion this was not by design but because the intended expert was taken ill late in the day and no substitute could easily be arranged. The other three were very brief visits. One was of only three days duration to follow up a situation with which the CPT was already familiar, namely, conditions at the principal remand prison in Stockholm in August 1994. The second was a three-day periodic visit to Liechtenstein in April 1993 and the third was a brief follow-up visit to a mental hospital in Greece in November 1996.

[109] On three ocasions during this period there was one, on eleven occasions there were two, on two occasions there were three and on one occasion there were four experts.

to be no suggestion, therefore, that as the Committee and Secretariat becomes collectively more experienced so the services of experts can be dispensed with.

In terms of numbers used, accompanying experts are overwhelmingly medically qualified, with a particular emphasis upon psychiatric expertise.[110] The residue has been made up of academics with practical legal knowledge of police powers and procedures or penal administration and persons with operational experience of police or penal administration.[111] However, the latter two groups have been less of a minority than their numbers indicate. Some of their number have been used much more frequently than most of the medics. Very recently, and notably, the Committee has made use of a previous member as an *ad hoc* expert. In October 1997 the outgoing President of the Committee, Claude Nicolay, accompanied the Committee for its second *periodic* visit to Turkey, presumably because of his specialist knowledge of the ongoing dialogue with Turkey.[112]

The extensive use of *ad hoc* experts by the Committee poses the question debated by the Council of Europe Committee of Experts when drafting the Convention and Explanatory Report. Should there be a permanent panel of experts on whose regular services the Committee can draw? Or should the Committee be free to use whichever experts they find useful on the basis of experience and on whichever occasions they consider the presence of experts necessary? As we saw in Chapter 4, the latter course was adopted and it is noteworthy that whereas some experts have been used repeatedly—five of them on ten or more occasions—almost half, 18 out of 37, have been used only once. Some of the latter have only recently been employed and may be used again, but no fewer than eleven experts were used on a single occasion during the period 1990–4 and have not been called on since. Some of these individuals may of course not wish to assist the CPT again, or may be too busy to do so, but it seems likely that several have not been invited again because, for one reason or another, the CPT has not thought it appropriate. Conversely a few experts have been repeatedly used and are more experienced mission participants than most current CPT members. It cannot be said that the CPT has *de facto* generated a panel of *ad hoc* experts. However, current CPT routine reliance on a few tried and tested expert assistants is, for whatever reason, closer to the practice originally

---

[110] Twenty-six of the 37 experts used during the period 1990–7 were medics, 19 of them psychiatrists.

[111] Five of each respectively.

[112] See CPT Press Notice, 23 Oct 1997. The reverse is also the case. The current member for Denmark, Ole Rasmussen, accompanied two missions, in 1992 and 1994, as an *ad hoc* expert.

recommended by the ICRC, ICJ, and SCAT than was envisaged by the framers of the eventual Convention.

Given the CPT complaint of there being too few female CPT members, it is somewhat surprising that the *ad hoc* experts used have been overwhelmingly male.[113] Moreover, they have been drawn disproportionately from particular countries and parts of Europe.[114] With the exception of Switzerland, where the experience of so many doctors working with the International Committee of the Red Cross is almost certainly a contributory factor, experts have so far come overwhelmingly from North Western Europe. This factor should be borne in mind when thinking about the standards promulgated by the CPT: if *ad hoc* experts have exercised undue influence over the work of the Committee, as the CPT has suggested might be the case,[115] then that influence has been of an overwhelmingly medical hue and has been disproportionately Anglo-Saxon, Benelux, and Scandinavian.

2 THE ORGANIZATION OF VISITS

The framers of the Convention stipulated that the CPT should carry out a programme of *periodic* visits 'as far as possible . . . on an equitable basis', though it was recognised that if the Committee was to be effective it would 'inevitably have to take into account the number of places to be visited in the States concerned' and might 'even accord a certain priority to *ad hoc* visits which appear to it to be required in the circumstances'.[116] Precisely what circumstances might require *ad hoc* visits is not spelt out in the Convention, and thus a considerable degree of leeway is given to the Committee in deciding how to fulfil its obligation under Article 1 to conduct visits 'with a view to strengthening, if necessary, the protection of [persons deprived of their liberty] from torture and from inhuman or degrading treatment or punishment'. What is clear is that it is for the full Committee to determine its programme of visits and that once it has decided to carry out a visit, notification must be given to enable the state to be visited to make adequate preparations to assist the Committee in its visit.[117] In the sections that follow we shall look at the manner in which the Committee has carried out its visiting programme.

---

[113] Thirty-one of the 37 experts used during 1990–7.

[114] Nine from the Benelux Countries (five from Belgium, three from the Netherlands and one from Luxembourg), eight from the United Kingdom, seven from Switzerland, five from Scandinavia (3 Danes, one Norwegian and one Finn), four from France and two from Ireland. By contrast the Mediterranean and German-speaking regions have been poorly represented, with just one Italian and one Austrian expert used. No Eastern European was used at all.

[115] See n 87 above.   [116] Explanatory Report, para 48.   [117] Article 8(1) and (2).

(a) The programme of visits

The size of the Committee's programme of visits is constrained by the financial and human resources available to it, and which permit, in effect, so many 'visiting days' per annum to be planned. When Committee members are engaged on work for the Committee—be that formal preparation for visits,[118] conducting visits, or attending plenary and other meetings to discuss issues arising out of visits—they are paid a *per diem* allowance which, when away from home either in Strasbourg or in a member State, is more than sufficient to cover their expenses. In addition their travelling expenses are fully met. Moreover, visiting delegations usually include two members of the Secretariat whose travelling and living expenses must also be met. Finally, there are the fees and expenses required for accompanying *ad hoc* experts and interpreters. A visit lasting twelve days costs several tens of thousands of pounds.

In 1996 the CPT's human and financial resources permitted roughly 100 'visiting days' *per annum*. This was notionally apportioned as 70 days for *periodic* visits and 30 days for *ad hoc* or *follow up* visits, though the Bureau was confident that in the event of an *ad hoc* visit being judged urgently necessary then funding for supplementary 'visiting days' would be provided. In 1997 this figure was increased to 120 days.[119] The principal constraint was the capacity of the Secretariat. If additional 'visiting days' were used then other tasks falling on the Secretariat—drafting reports, corresponding with States in the wake of reports, and so on—would inevitably fall behind. Until now it has been the limited size of the Secretariat rather than the size of the budget allocated for visits which serves to limit the CPT's visiting programme. Table 5.2 shows the number of days spent on visits during the years 1990–7.

There has been a discernible shift in the balance of visits since 1993 towards *ad hoc* visits. This change of policy, which is in accordance with what the framers of the Convention envisaged, was announced in 1994. The Committee reflected that during its first four years of operation the need to make the first round of *periodic* visits had 'absorbed practically all the Committee's available resources'. Henceforth the Committee wished to 'be careful to avoid a situtaion in which an unduly onerous programme of scheduled visits'—and it should be noted that scheduled visits will include *follow-up* visits—'undermines its capacity to react expeditiously to events as they happen'.[120] In future they wished to leave more room to manoeuvre. The scheduled programme for 1994 absorbed

---

[118] This does not include 'homework' which members may spend better acquainting themselves with the background to the countries and places to be visited.

[119] Interview with Bureau, Sept 1996 and Gen Rep 7, para 21.

[120] Gen Rep 4, para 21.

Table 5.2 CPT programme of visits: 1990–7

Year	Periodic visits	Ad hoc/Follow up visits	Total
1990	4 (37 Days)	1 (13 days)	5 (50 days)
1991	5 (57 days)	1 (10 days)	6 (67 days)
1992	7 (66 days)[a]	—	7 (66 days)
1993	7 (62 days)	1 (10 days)	8 (72 days)
1994	4 (56 days)	7 (37 days)[b]	11 (93 days)
1995	7 (85 days)	—	7 (85 days)
1996	6 (73 Days)	5 (20 days)	11 (93 days)
1997	7 (83 days)	6 (33 days)	13 (116 days)

[a] The visit to San Marino is treated as a separate visit lasting three days even though it took place during the course of the visit to Italy and only involved personnel who were a part of that delegation.

[b] The visits to Netherlands Antilles and Netherlands Aruba are counted as two visits, but are calculated as lasting seven days in total in order to avoid double-counting the day on which the delegation moved from the first to the second visit.

approximately 60 days, leaving '25 visiting days . . . set aside for visits to be organised . . . in the light of information received'.[121] We must conclude that this policy was only temporarily knocked off course in 1995 because of the unusually large number of new member states to which *periodic* visits had necessarily to be made. It may be that 1998 will also show a relative decline in the number of *ad hoc* visits for similar reasons: the CPT has announced plans to conduct ten periodic visits.[122] This underlines the importance of the Committee's stated aspiration of achieving 200 visiting days by the turn of the century.[123]

(i) Periodic visits

In order to underline its impartiality the CPT decided in 1989 that its obligation to visit states party as far as possible on an equitable basis would initially best be satisfied by deciding the order of the first round of *periodic* visits by drawing lots.[124] Austria was the first country visited in May 1990 and the first round of *periodic* visits was completed when Belgium was visited in November 1993, just before the first of the Central and Eastern European states began the process of signing and ratifying the Convention in 1993/4.[125] The Committee then committed itself to

[121] Gen Rep 4, para 22.

[122] In a Press Release dated 16 Dec 1997, the Committee announced its intention to visit Andorra, Croatia, Finland, Iceland, Ireland, Moldova, Spain, Sweden, 'TFYRO Macedonia', and the Ukraine during 1998.

[123] Gen Rep 7, para 21.   [124] Gen Rep 1, para 19.

[125] Hungary ratified the Convention in November 1993 and Bulgaria, Poland, Romania, the Slovak Republic, and Slovenia followed suit in 1994. See Appendix 4A.

giving priority to new member states when organizing the programme of *periodic* visits[126] and in every case they have been visited either in the same year they ratified the Convention or shortly therafter.[127]

The process of selecting countries to be visited by lot has been abandoned for second *periodic* visits. We must presume that both the principle of equity *and* consideration of 'the number of places to be visited in the States concerned'[128] is now determining visiting priorities. Indeed the Committee has conceded that visits to countries 'with small populations' are likely to be less frequent than those to larger countries.[129] What is clear is that, given the number of new states parties either coming on stream or which will shortly come on stream, combined with the Committee's commitment to reserve a sizeable proportion of 'visiting days' each year for *ad hoc* visits, the CPT's early aspiration that states be visited roughly every two years[130] is practically impossible.[131] By 1997 it had become clear that the best that the Committee might achieve was a *periodic* visit on average once every four years, with countries exhibiting particular problems receiving additional *ad hoc*, including *follow-up*, visits. This the Committee has now recognized.[132] Yet even this modest objective may not be fully realized, and at the end of 1997 eight long-standing member states will have received only one *periodic* visit by the end of 1997, that is after eight years of CPT operation.[133]

(ii) Ad hoc *visits*

The Convention speaks of *periodic* visits and such other visits as the Committee may wish to organize 'as appear to it to be required in the

---

[126] They should be visited within 'a matter of months' of ratifying the Convention (Gen Rep 4, para 23).

[127] Thus Hungary was first visited in November 1994, 12 months after ratifying the Convention, Bulgaria, Romania, the Slovak Republic, and Slovenia were first visited in 1995 (to the detriment of *ad hoc* visits elsewhere in Europe), Poland was first visited in 1996, and the first visits to Albania, the Czech Republic, and Estonia have been carried out in 1997. Predictably, the five states which ratified the Convention in the course of 1997 are included in the list of countries to be visited during 1998, these being Andorra, Croatia, Moldova, 'TFYRO Macedonia', and the Ukraine.

[128] Explanatory Report, para 48.   [129] Gen Rep 4, para 24.

[130] Gen Rep 2, para 29.

[131] We must presume that the fact that the Committee continued in August 1994 to aspire to visits to states parties every 'two or three years' (Gen Rep 4, para 24) reflected an overly optimistic assumption that the Committee of Ministers would provide the Committee with Secretariat resources on a scale greatly in excess of those that have been provided—we estimate that it would require a Secretariat almost twice as large.

[132] Interview with Bureau, Sept 1996 and Gen Rep 7, para 21.

[133] Namely, Finland, Iceland, Ireland, Leichtenstein, Luxembourg, Norway, San Marino, and Sweden. However, none of these eight countries has a very large population and two have received *follow-up* visits (Sweden, 1994 and Norway, 1997) and one received a comparatively lengthy six-day *ad hoc* visit (Luxembourg, 1997). Finland, Iceland, and Ireland are now scheduled to receive a periodic visit during the course of 1998.

circumstances',[134] referred to as *ad hoc* visits in the Explanatory Report. Two situtions are envisaged: first, when individuals or groups communicate to the Committee that ill-treatment is occurring in a particular place or jurisdiction, though the Committee is reminded that it 'should not be concerned with the investigation of individual complaints (for which provision is already made, e.g. under the European Convention of Human Rights)'; secondly, when a state party requests that the Committee undertake a visit 'in order to investigate certain allegations and to clarify the situation'. In all instances, however, the Committee 'enjoys discretion as to when it deems [such visits] necessary and as to the elements on which its decision is based'.[135] This point was reinforced in 1996 when the CPT refused to act on information provided by the Council of Europe's Committee on Legal Affairs and Human Rights regarding the conditions of detention of IRA prisoners in UK mainland prisons.[136] Despite the importance of this visit being stressed formally by the Bureau of the Parliamentary Assembly, the CPT also declined subsequently to visit these institutions in 1997: an *ad hoc* visit was made to the UK in September 1997, but high-security mainland prisons were not included in the schedule.[137]

Visits at the request of a member state seem never to have been considered likely and only one has occurred to date. This was to Turkey in August 1996 when a four-day visit was made to Eskisehir Special Type Prison where a widely-reported hunger strike by prisoners was underway, one of the principal causes of which was apparently the transfer to the prison of remand prisoners suspected of terrorism.[138] The outcome of this visit is unlikely to have encouraged the CPT to repeat the exercise. During the course of the visit reports appeared in the Turkish media, presumably placed by the Turkish authorities, to the effect that the CPT had commented favourably on the situation at Eskisehir Prison. These reports the CPT delegation subsequently described as 'figments of the imagination'[139] and shortly thereafter an *ad hoc* visit was conducted at the instigation of the Committee.[140]

From the very beginning the CPT envisaged that *ad hoc* visits 'triggered by serious and consistent allegations of grave abuses in a particular

---

[134] Article 7(1).   [135] Explanatory Report, para 49.

[136] CLAHR Report (1997), para 29 and n 10.

[137] Council of Europe Press Release, 22 Sept 1997.

[138] Press Release 454(96). While in Turkey the delegation took the opportunity to visit another prison under construction.

[139] ibid.

[140] The Turkish authorities may nevertheless have achieved their public relations purposes as far as news available within Turkey was concerned. Whereas the August visit recieved due publicity, representatives of Turkish NGOs have informed us that neither CPT Public Statements regarding Turkey or Council of Europe Press Releases regarding other CPT visits to Turkey—before or since—have been reported in the Turkish press.

country' would be a vital part of their operation[141] and the Committee used the device with respect to Turkey in September 1990, within five months of becoming operational. The Committee emphasizes that their purposes in these circumstances are distinguishable from those of a judicial body like the Commission and Court of Human Rights, though in practice the distinction may be—and, from the standpoint of a member state, may appear to be—slender. The CPT stresses that their fact-finding method 'must be geared to forestalling possible acts or practices' of ill-treatment. Their purpose is 'not the minute and punctilious establishment of whether or not serious abuses have actually ocurred'—that is, a judicial finding—but is rather 'to verify on the spot whether or not . . . allegations are well-founded' in order to 'ascertain whether . . . there are specific conditions or circumstances that are likely to *degenerate into* torture or inhuman or degrading treatment or punishment'.[142]

Whenever an *ad hoc* visit focuses on a specific case or specific cases of alleged ill-treatment, and where the Committee concludes that ill-treatment has occurred or has probably occurred, the state concerned may feel that this distinction has come perilously close to being lost. For its part, the CPT will presumably point to the part which such *ad hoc* visits play within the overall sequence of visits to, and the ongoing dialogue with, the state concerned. An *ad hoc* visit focused entirely on a single grave allegation of ill-treatment in a country which, as far as can be judged, generates few such allegations, and which has many or most of the safeguards recommended by the CPT in place, would appear difficult to justify and contrary to the spirit of the Convention. However, such a visit to a country where allegations of grave ill-treatment are the pattern, and fundamental safeguards are lacking, would appear quite a different matter. In the circumstances the CPT could reasonably maintain that the likelihood of a situation degenerating into torture has to be tested when suitable opportunities arise, and this may not be within the context of a long-planned *periodic* or even *ad hoc* visit.

By the close of 1997 the CPT had made twenty-one *ad hoc* visits of which five were described as *follow-up* visits.[143] If the *ad hoc* visit by invitation to Turkey in 1996 is excluded, the remaining fifteen visits appear to have been prompted solely by reports of ill-treatment from unknown individuals, groups, or bodies. Several of these visits have resulted in published reports some of which shed a little light on the background to the visits.

During the period 1990–3 only three *ad hoc* visits were undertaken, two to Turkey and one to Northern Ireland. The Turkish authorities have so

---

[141] Gen Rep 1, para 46.   [142] ibid, paras 45–6.
[143] *Follow-up* visits are considered in detail in the following sub-section.

far not authorized the publication of a single CPT report including that resulting from a further *ad hoc* visit made in 1996. But it is scarcely necessary to speculate about the sources of reports of torture and other forms of ill-treatment in Turkey that will have been received by the CPT. Such reports were legion throughout the period 1990–7, and would have been submitted to the CPT from both Turkish and international human rights NGOs.[144] The CPT's visit to Northern Ireland in July 1993 was prompted, according to the Committee, by the following considerations:

Since the Committee was first established in November 1990 [sic], it has received a number of reports containing allegations of ill-treatment of persons suspected of offences related to terrorism by the security forces in Northern Ireland, both at the time of their arrest and in the course of their detention in the police offices known as 'holding centres' (located at Castlereagh in Belfast, Gough Barracks in Armagh and Strand Road in Londonderry).

The allegations related to both physical and psychological forms of ill-treatment, allegations of the later form of ill-treatment being more prevalent in recent times.[145]

By November 1991 the CPT was sufficiently concerned by these reports of ill-treatment in Northern Ireland that it asked the UK authorities for information about the situation[146] and was informed about preventive measures which the UK authorities were taking with a view to 'allaying fears and ensuring that adequate safeguards exist for the individual'.[147] On this basis:

Taking into account, on the one hand, the fact that the CPT continued to receive allegations of ill-treatment and, on the other hand, the positive developments outlined above, it appeared to the Committee that the time was ripe to visit Northern Ireland in order to examine the treatment of persons deprived of their liberty by the security forces, and, in particular, persons held in relation to terrorist activities.[148]

---

[144] Amnesty International published a stream of 'Urgent Action' bulletins regarding detainees in Turkey as well as some major reports outlining the pattern of allegations and findings (see, for example: Amnesty International (1989) *Turkey: Torture and Deaths in Custody* (London: Amnesty International, International Secretariat); Amnesty International (1996d) *Turkey: No Security Without Human Rights* (London: Amnesty International, International Secretariat). Many of Amnesty's reports are based on two Turkish NGOs, the Turkish Human Rights Association and the Human Rights Foundation of Turkey, both of which have also produced a mass of documentation during the period. In addition there have been major external investigative documents such as: Physicians for Human Rights (1996).

[145] UK 2, para 5.

[146] By invoking Rule 30 whereby: 'Before deciding on a particular visit, the Committee or, if appropriate, the Bureau may request information or explanations as regards the general situation in the State concerned, as regards a given place, or as regards an isolated case concerning which it has received reports'.

[147] Quoted in UK 2, para 6.   [148] UK 2, para 7.

The background to the *ad hoc* visit to Northern Ireland is fairly transparent. There are several NGOs in Northern Ireland that concern themselves with human rights and the treatment of detainees, prominent among which is the Northern Ireland Committee for the Administration of Justice. This organization sent a series of reports of ill-treatment of detainees in the so-called 'holding centres' for persons detained under the Prevention of Terrorism Act to Strasbourg in the period preceding the 1993 visit,[149] and representatives of the organization met with the CPT delegation during its visit to Northern Ireland.[150] The Committee also acted as go-between for the CPT in arranging interviews with persons recently held in custody by the security forces.[151] The CPT also met with other governmental and non-governmental bodies concerned with human rights in Northern Ireland, including the Standing Advisory Committee for Human Rights (which produces an annual report which the CPT had no doubt seen) and the recently appointed Independent Commissioner for the Holding Centres, Sir Louis Blom-Cooper.[152] It is quite clear that the Northern Ireland *ad hoc* visit was the culmination of a long gestation period during which allegations were made and assurances were given that the Committee felt could only fully be evaluated by means of a visit and the collection of evidence first-hand.

It seems likely that the CPT planned both the content and timing of the Northern Ireland visit in much the same way as they would a *periodic* visit, one of which had already taken place to the UK, albeit to England only, in August 1990. Indeed, it should be remembered that until November 1993, when the first round of periodic visits to existing member states was completed, the CPT carried out its *periodic* visits on the basis of lots. Categorizing these visits to known trouble spots as *ad hoc* was certainly a way in which both a visit to Turkey could be advanced up the order, and also a visit made to Northern Ireland which could not otherwise have taken place until the following year at the earliest.[153]

The completion of the first round of *periodic* visits to the first wave of member states gave the Committee more flexibility and, while some *ad hoc* visits are doubtless planned long in advance, it is clear that others take place at very short notice indeed. Moreover, the CPT clearly considers it important that those individuals and organizations with information about ill-treatment that would be valuable to the CPT understand

---

[149] Interview with the Northern Ireland Committee for the Administration of Justice, Belfast, June 1995.

[150] UK 2, para 12.

[151] Interview with Committee for the Administration of Justice, Belfast, June 1995.

[152] UK 2, para 12.

[153] Of course, this does not explain why the Committee decided not to visit Northern Ireland in the context of its *periodic* visit to the UK in 1990.

that the CPT has the capacity and will to undertake visits without delay when necessary.[154] In June 1994, for example, only two months after carrying out a *periodic* visit, the CPT undertook an *ad hoc* visit to Spain in order to interview a number of persons recently held in custody.[155] This visit was organized within a matter of days. It was triggered, according to the CPT, by 'information received at the beginning of June 1994 containing allegations of severe ill-treatent of persons who had very recently been arrested in the Basque Country by the Civil Guard, as presumed participants in terrorist-related activities'.[156]

We can be even more precise about the background circumstances in this case. Spain represents a considerable dilemma for the CPT. Several NGOs in Spain, a number of them Basque-based, annually generate hundreds of allegations of torture at the hands of the Spanish security forces—most of them relating to persons suspected of terrorist offences, many relating to the Basque nationalist terrorist organisation *Euskadi ta Askatasuna* (ETA). These allegations, individual and assembled as annual bound volumes, are routinely sent by the Spanish NGOs to the CPT Secretariat in Strasbourg and other international human rights bodies.[157] The allegations are difficult to evaluate. Many emanate from 'human rights organisations' that are commited to Basque autonomy and are widely perceived to be front organisations for ETA. The allegations are numerous and the Spanish authorities maintain that it is the policy of regional terrorist organizations in Spain to instruct their members to allege that they have been tortured or otherwise ill-treated whenever they are held in custody by the Spanish security forces.[158] The fact that most of the numerous serious allegations of torture generated in Spain have in recent years not been dignified with repetition by such organisations as Amnesty International, suggests that reputable international human rights NGOs have doubts about the veracity of many of the allegations emerging

[154] Emphasis was placed in Gen Rep 5 on the June 1994 visit to Spain being 'carried out at very short notice' (para 2). The point was further emphasized by Mr Jan Malinowski, a member of the CPT Secretariat, at a meeting of NGO representatives from the Mediterranean countries organized by the Association for the Prevention of Torture in Onati, Spain, in April 1997.

[155] Press Release Ref 290(94), 21 June 1994.

[156] Spain 3, para 3. The visit, undertaken by two members of the Committee accompanied by an *ad hoc* medical expert and two members of the Secretariat (including the Secretary to the Committee), began on 10 June and lasted five days.

[157] Interviews with Spanish NGOs carried out in 1994 and 1996. See, for example, Torturaren Aukako Taldea (1995) *Informe Anual 1994* (Bilbao: TAT); Euskadiko Amnistiaren Aldeko Atzordeak (1995) *Euskal Herrian, Tortura: Monografico 1994* (Hernani, Gipuzkoa, Spain: Gestoras Pro-Amnistia de Euskadi); Comissió de Porteveus dels presos i encausats independentistes (1995) *Denúncies de Tortures Acció Popular i Particlar (annex 1 'Dossier Tortures'* (Barcelona).

[158] See Spain 3, para 5.

from Spain.[159] Certainly the CPT, during *periodic* visits to Spain in 1991 and 1994 received many allegations of severe torture.[160] However, given the Committee's tentative finding—that 'it would ... be premature to conclude that the phenomena of torture and severe ill-treatment have been eradicated'[161]—we must conclude that, to cite the words employed following the *ad hoc* visit in 1994, many of the allegations were of a 'stereotyped nature' and were incapable of verification.[162]

The Spanish situation involves a dilemma which must preoccupy the CPT, as all other human rights organizations. In a country where torture has in the past undoubtedly been used by government agents, where the legitimacy of the government is contested by armed and other groups, and where members of groups opposed to the established authorities regularly allege torture as a credible tactic to undermine the legitimacy of the government, it is at least possible that law-enforcement agents will occasionally use torture believing that they can do so with virtual impunity because of the general disinformational 'noise' that is circulating. In these circumstances great circumspection will be required in the evaluation of reports of ill-treatment.

On 3 June 1994 the Basque-based organization *Torturaren Aurkako Taldea* (TAT) sent the CPT and other international human rights organizations a fax concerning several persons recently arrested by the *Guardia Civil* in the Basque country (in one case allegedly handed over to the *Guardia Civil* by the French police on the French/Spanish border). TAT alleged that the suspects were being tortured while being held *incommunicado*, and requested 'urgent intervention'.[163] Clearly, the substance and currency of these allegations were judged worthy of investigation by the CPT because, within a week, a CPT delegation arrived in Spain. During the course of a five-day visit the delegation interviewed the three principal suspects for whom TAT had requested urgent intervention,[164] and all three repeated their allegations. These allegations TAT subsequently published

---

[159] The annual reports of Amnesty International's International Secretariat for the period 1990–7, for example, record in some detail judicial inquiries into the 'dirty war' waged against ETA by the Spanish authorities in the 1980s and the trial of members of the Spanish security forces for the ill-treatment of suspects then and since. Few new cases of ill-treatment are outlined however, certainly very few cases compared to the hundreds publicized by NGOs within Spain.

[160] See Spain 1, paras 17–26 and Spain 2, paras 16–21.

[161] Spain 1, para 25, repeated in Spain 2, para 20.   [162] Spain 3, para 29.

[163] Interview with TAT, Jan 1996, Bilbao, Spain during which copies of correspondence were provided.

[164] Interviews with two of the suspects conducted in the Basque region in February 1996. Both claimed to have been interveiwed by the CPT on 11 June 1994 following their release from custody. According to TAT the third suspect was seen by the CPT while still in custody.

in a dossier containing 114 case studies of alleged torture.[165] During the course of the visit the CPT interviewed a total of eight persons who had recently been held at both the San Sebastian and Madrid premises of the *Guardia Civil* and all eight alleged ill-treatment in such a detailed and concordant manner that, from a technical standpoint, their accounts were judged credible.[166]

It is apparent, therefore, that this *ad hoc* visit to Spain, undertaken rapidly in response to current information, led the CPT to harden its recommendations to the Spanish authorities. They were asked 'to carry out, without delay, a general investigation of a thorough and independent nature into the methods used by the members of the Civil Guard when holding and questioning persons arrested as presumed participants in one or more offences' under Spain's current provisions for responding to terrorism and organized crime.[167]

A three day *ad hoc* visit to Turkey in September 1996 may well have involved procedures not dissimilar to those decribed for Spain in 1994. The Committee had been in Turkey only a month earlier at the invitation of the Turkish Government[168] and yet returned with a small but powerful delegation which included the CPT's President, the Secretary to the Committee, and two *ad hoc* medical experts. The delegation visited several police stations and went to three prisons to interview 'certain persons who had very recently been in police custody in Adana and Istanbul'.[169] This visit, it should be noted, was part of a continuing dialogue with the Turkish authorities which by the end of 1997 included seven visits and two Public Statements.

(iii) Follow-up *visits*

The *follow-up* visit represents a halfway house between a *periodic* and an *ad hoc* visit though the distinction between them is not always clear. Although the Committee anticipated the use of *follow-up* visits from the beginning,[170] they first emerged as part of the Committee's methodology during 1994 when the first of such visits, to Sweden and France, were undertaken. Subsequently, what might be called 'pure' follow-up visits have been conducted to Portugal in 1996 and the Netherlands Antilles in 1997. As a device the *follow-up* visit is an efficient use of the Committee's discretion to conduct 'such other visits as appear to it to be required in

---

[165] Torturaren Aurkako Taldea (1995).

[166] Spain 3, para 14. Though the Committee considered that some of the accounts could have been exaggerated, they were in several instances consistent with sequelae discovered by medically-qualified members of the delegation and the allegations were found to have 'the ring of truth to them': ibid, paras 29–33.

[167] Spain 3, para 34.   [168] See above, p. 168.

[169] Press Release Ref 517(96), 24 Sept 1996.   [170] Gen Rep 1, para 89.

the circumstances',[171] the circumstances being the Committee's ongoing concern about a situation or institution already investigated, and its inability either to conduct sufficiently frequent *periodic* visits or to spend too much time on subsequent *periodoc* visits revisiting a site or situation previously investigated. Indeed in a country with only a limited number of causes for concern the focused *follow-up* visit is arguably one of the most effective ways for the Committee to fulfil its mandate.

During a *periodic* visit to Sweden in May 1991 the CPT discovered that a high proportion of remand prisoners housed in Stockholm's principal remand prison were subject to restrictions relating to their contact with the outside world (visits, correspondence, telephone calls, access to newspapers, and so on) and with fellow prisoners. With the exception of contact with their lawyers, some prisoners were in virtual isolation for long periods. These restrictions, which at that time could be determined by public prosecutors, could, when combined with the very limited out-of-cell activities offered in the Stockholm remand prison, have a prolonged and severe impact. The CPT concluded that the limited human contact allowed to many remand prisoners 'when accumulated led to wholly unacceptable conditions of detention for many of the prisoners' and reiterated its previously expressed view[172] that 'solitary confinement can, in certain circumstances, amount to inhuman and degrading treatment'.[173] The CPT recommended that the Swedish authorities take steps that restrictions on remand prisoners' contacts be applied for as short periods as possible and be resorted to only in exceptional circumstances. They also recomended, *inter alia*, that decisions to impose restrictions be reviewed at regular intervals and be subject to appeal by an independent body.[174] Statistics on the use made of remand restrictions in recent years were requested.[175]

In their reply, transmitted to the CPT in August 1992, the Swedish authorities reported the findings of a review of the remand restrictions conducted by a former ombudsman. The review found that the system generally operated in a well-balanced fashion though it recommended that since restrictions might be applied by prosecutors in rather too routine a fashion, the courts should decide, when remanding a suspect in custody, whether the circumstances were such that the prosecutor should be allowed to impose contact restrictions.[176] This recommendation was adopted and became law in January 1994.[177] The fact was reported to the CPT as part of the ongoing written dialogue between the CPT and the Swedish authorities.[178] The CPT, however, continued to receive

---

[171] Article 7(1).   [172] Denmark 1, para 29.
[173] Sweden 1, paras 68–70.   [174] ibid.   [175] ibid, para 69.
[176] Sweden 1 R 2, 24–5.   [177] Sweden 2, para 21.
[178] Interview with Ministry of Justice, Stockholm, Sweden, 1995.

information—it is not known from whom—which suggested that conditions at the Stockholm remand prison had not improved.[179] Further, since 'Sweden was not one of the countries selected to receive a *periodic* visit in 1993 or 1994' it was 'decided to carry out a short visit of a follow-up nature' to the situation of remand prisoners, an odd roundabout way of saying that it had been decided to substitute a *follow-up* visit for a *periodic* one. The visit took place in August 1994, lasted only four days, involved no *ad hoc* expert, and focused entirely on the Stockholm remand prison, in particular on those remand prisoners subject to restrictions.

The 1994 visit to France provides a parallel case. France was also the subject of a *periodic* visit in 1991. Among the establishments visited was the *dépôt* of the Paris Police *Préfecture* employed to detain foreigners under immigration legislation. The CPT considered the accommodation at the *dépôt* 'completely unsatisactory' by virtue of its 'seriously unhygienic and insanitary' condition.[180] The cramped cells—six for men and one for women:

were very dirty and cleaning materials were not made available. The state of the bedding also left a lot to be desired. In principle, each detainee received a clean sheet and blanket on arrival, but the delegation saw a number of detainees without sheets, and the blankets and mattresses were filthy. In addition, detainees told the delegation that they were given no basic toiletries (soap, towel, etc) and that they were denied access to a change of clothing.

The location of the cells was far from ideal (in the basement, with dirty windows near the ceiling giving only a feeble light). In addition this part of the dépôt was particularly infested with cockroaches.

Detainees had no means of passing the time—they were not provided with television, books or any area for recreation. In addition, detainees seen at the time of the visit alleged that they had no opportunity for out-door exercise. At first, the officials who were asked about this denied it, but they then admitted that outdoor exercise was not feasible because of the acute shortage of staff.

Finally, a number of detainees said that the food was very poor—which was confirmed by observation on the spot.[181]

These concerns were immediately communicated to the French authorities by using the Article 8 procedure.[182] The French authorities acknowledged that the *dépôt* facilities 'were old and run down and indicated that a programme of modernisation and expansion was scheduled'. In turn the CPT recommended that this work be given 'the highest priority' and that 'immediate measures be taken to put right the deficiencies' identified.[183]

Fourteen months later in January 1993, when these findings and the French Government response were simultaneously published, conditions

---

[179] Sweden 2, para 5.
[180] France 1, paras 70–71 (translation from the French by Jennifer Monahan).
[181] ibid, para 71.   [182] ibid, para 7.   [183] ibid, para 72.

at the *dépôt* had scarcely changed. It was said by the French authorities that detainees could now take outdoor exercise in a courtyard but no mention was made of the major improvements sought by the CPT as a matter of urgency.[184] In fact a support group organized by lawyers for immigrant detainees judged in 1993 that conditions at the *dépôt* were now worse than when the CPT visited: they claimed that there was still no outdoor exercise.[185] This assessment was presented to a French Administrative Tribunal in November 1993 and lawyers representing immigration detainees subsequently sought an injuction from the *Tribunal de Grande Instance* against the Paris *Préfet de Police* ordering a judicial inspection of conditions at the *dépôt*.[186] The *Préfet* in turn went to the *Tribunal des Conflits* which decides disputed claims between *l'administration* and the judiciary, and in April the *Tribunal* ruled in favour of the *Préfet*. Conditions of detention fell solely within the jurisdiction of *l'administration* unless an act of violence (*voie de fait*) could be proved: if the detention itself was legitimate, and no act of violence had been demonstrated, the judiciary had no jurisdiction. The separation of powers doctrine (*séparation des pouvoirs*) was used to deny immigration detainees the judicial protection available to criminal suspects under the French Penal Code.

By 1994, therefore, the Paris *dépôt* had become something of a national scandal: on two occasions in 1994–5 the Paris *Procureur de la République* (the senior state prosecutor) publicly voiced his concerns about its state, questioning whether use of the facility was compatible with European human rights law. It was in this context that the CPT *follow-up* visit of July 1994 took place. Though the CPT's damning report (finding inhuman and degrading treatment) was not published until January 1996,[187] the CPT's findings were leaked to the French press in 1995.[188] The leak came shortly after two cases attracting widespread attention in the French press: in March the suicide at the *dépôt* of a young Moroccan, and in April the alleged beating by eight policemen of an Algerian detainee. The judge before whom the latter appeared (reportedly with an arm in a sling and his face puffy and bruised) decided, as was his right, to inspect the *dépôt* but the complainant's lawyers were denied permission by the police to accompany him. The judge therefore ordered that the complainant be released,

---

[184] France 1 R 1, para 187.

[185] Groupe d'Information et de Soutien des Travailleurs Immigrés (1995) Briefing Document, Paris.

[186] Immigration detainees are held under the jurisdiction of *l'administation*, in this case the police. The judiciary has no role in deciding why or whether a foreigner should be detained, only on prolonging or ending detention within the permitted limit. Judges' rights and duties to control conditions for immigrant detainees in police custody is hotly contested by the police. Moreover, neither lawyers nor journalists have been granted access to the *dépôt*, in contrast to the position in French prisons.

[187] France 2, again published simultaneously with the French response.

[188] *Le Monde*, 27 April 1995.

citing in his judgment the CPT findings of 1991 and arguing that, according to the evidence available to him, the CPT's recommendations had still not been implemented.[189] The judge released a large number of other *dépôt* detainees on the same grounds,[190] a decision against which the *Préfet* unsuccessfully appealed. When the press leak of the damning *follow-up* CPT report appeared nine days later, the French authorities announced that the *dépôt* had been closed for complete refurbishment.[191] The *dépôt* reopened in September 1995, reportedly now complying with all of the CPT's recommendations.[192]

Subsequent *follow-up* visits have been made to Greece,[193] Portugal,[194] and Italy[195] in 1996 and the Netherlands Antilles in 1997.[196] In all four cases the institutions returned to had been heavily criticized in one or more prior published reports. Not all so-called *follow-up* visits are quite so focused, however. The visit to Turkey in October 1994, for example, lasted thirteen days—the duration of a typical major *periodic* visit—and though some of the establishments visited had been visited previously, some of them three times previously,[197] a good many police stations, gendarmerie establishments and prisons were visited for the first time.[198] It is difficult to see what distinguishes this *follow-up* visit from many *periodic* visits which involve returning to sites previously seen combined with visits to places of detention not previously seen.[199] At best the distinction between some *follow-up* visits and some *periodic* visits is only a matter of degree, the term employed apparently having more to do with the fact that *periodic* visits are said to be precisely that—periodic and, as we have seen, rationed according to the Committee's scarce resources to at best once every four years. Thus Turkey, which by the end of 1996 had been visited on no fewer than

[189] Judge François Sottet, *Ordonnance*, 20 Apr 1995.
[190] The number was variously reported in the French press as 18 or 21.
[191] Subsequently confirmed in the French response published in January 1996 (France 2 R 1, 24).
[192] France 2 R, paras 24–6.
[193] Specifically to visit the Attica State Mental Hospital for Children, first visited in 1993 (see Press Release 628(96)).
[194] Specifically to consider conditions at the Oporto Prison, one of the institutions visited in 1995 (see Press Release 605(96)).
[195] Specifically to visit the Milan Remand Prison (San Vittore) previously visited in 1992 and 1995 (see Press Release 696(96)).
[196] Previously visited in 1994.
[197] The Ankara Police Headquarters and Central Closed Prison, and the Diyarkabir 1 Prison, Police Headquarters and Interrogation Centre of the 1st Section of the Diyarkabir Police were all visited in 1990, 1991, and 1992 (see Gen Rep 1, Appendix 3, and Gen Rep 2, Appendix 3, Gen Rep 3, Appendix 3).
[198] See Gen Rep 5, Appendix 3.
[199] The second *periodic* visit to the United Kingdom in 1994, for example, involved the CPT returning to Leeds and Wandsworth Prisons, both of which were visited during the previous *periodic* visit in 1990. Four other prisons visited in 1994 had not previously been visited, however (see Gen Rep 1, Appendix 3 and Gen Rep 5, Appendix 3).

six occasions, had nevertheless received only two *periodic* visits. The other five visits were described as *ad hoc* or *follow-up*.

(b) Planning and preparing for visits

Unlike the European Commission and Court of Human Rights the CPT is not dependent for action on being petitioned through applications from states or individuals. It is not a judicial but a preventative body. It does not have substantive treaty provisions to apply and interpret. It has been set up to prevent ill-treatment and it may act on the basis of information received from any number of sources. In deciding when, where, and how to visit a member state, it may proactively scan mass media sources or gather official reports. It may also react, *inter alia*, to information received from other official sources, national or inter-governmental, NGOs, and individual informants, both those who claim to be the victims of ill-treatment or those who act on their behalf. It is one of the central tasks of the Secretariat to collect, process and bring to the attention of CPT members information received which is relevant to the Committee's mandate. It is on the basis of this material that plans for visiting programmes are laid, initially by the Bureau, but ultimately determined by the Committee in plenary session.

(i) Gathering information

During the autumn of 1989 and the spring of 1990, when the CPT began preparing to undertake its first visits, knowledge of its existence was very limited. Those organizations intimately concerned with the genesis of the Convention—such as the Swiss Committee Against Torture (SCAT, since 1992 the Association for the Prevention of Torture, APT), the ICJ, some senior members of the ICRC, and Amnesty International—were of course well informed and followed developments closely. But it is clear from the evidence that we have collected throughout Europe that most workers within most domestic NGOs concerned with the welfare of detainees or prisoners had either not heard of the Convention and/or did not appreciate the potential relevance of the Committee for their work. This situation has changed, but not as dramatically as may be imagined. During our visits to member states to gather views on the CPT's operations in 1995–7 we were reminded time and time again how misleading an impression can be gained in Strasbourg of knowledge about, and the perceived relevance of, the CPT. The number of well-informed persons, though growing steadily, remains small. There are many individuals and organizations throughout Europe whose human rights commitments might be expected to make knowledge of the CPT essential but who are largely ignorant of the Committee's methods and findings. This distribution of knowledge does of course effect the quantity and quality of the relevant information received by the Secretariat in Strasbourg.

The CPT is very coy about its external relations and maintains strict confidentiality about the sources and nature of the information it receives. Although the CPT acknowledges receipt of material specifically sent to it, it gives no indication of the usefulness of the information for its work, or any other form of feedback. The CPT has described its relations with information-providers as 'one way',[200] a phrase that some Committee members regularly repeat at public fora.[201] Whether the CPT need be so tight-lipped about its work, whether it might adopt a more open and encouraging posture with regard to actual and potential information-providers, is a matter for debate and a question to which we return in Chapter 9. For the present, we can merely describe the informational framework within which the Committee operates by piecing together some evidence from different sources.

Early in its life the CPT established 'working relations' with several bodies directly relevant to its operation. These included the European Commission and Court of Human Rights, the ICRC, the UNCAT, the UN Special Rapporteur on Torture and the UN High Commissioner for Refugees. It also included establishing 'contact' with 'certain [unnamed] non-governmental organisations',[202] among which was certainly the APT and Amnesty International.[203] The CPT has said nothing about these 'working relations' and 'contacts' since 1990, except to acknowledge that CPT representatives, either members or Secretariat, regularly attend and participate in fora concerning the ill-treatment of persons in custody in general, or the work of the CPT in particular.[204] Whatever the 'working relations' comprise they are exceedingly discreet. Indeed, within Strasbourg CPT Secretariat staff have established a reputation for secrecy wholly consistent with the strict confidentiality that the CPT publicly espouses.

It is clear, however, that CPT relations are not entirely as one-way and discouraging as the official picture may suggest. In the course of our research we have encountered NGO representatives, for example, who

[200] Gen Rep 1, para 43.

[201] The phrase was used more than once at the seminar convened by the Association for the Prevention of Torture in Strasbourg, December 1994, to discuss the work of the CPT (see APT (1995)).

[202] Gen Rep 1, para 42.

[203] Interviews at various times with Amnesty International and the APT.

[204] In addition to APT fora, for example, CPT representatives attended an Amnesty International conference on torture in Stockholm, September 1996. Participation in such meetings is from time to time acknowledged in CPT annual reports (see, for example, Gen Rep 6, paras 12–13), though the then President, Claude Nicolay, on more than one occasion argued that such involvement would have to be reduced for want of adequate time and resources (see APT (1995), 222–3).

described regular and 'helpful' contact with members of the CPT Secretariat in the course of which they were encouraged to supply information which was likely to be of benefit to the CPT in the near future—suggesting that a visit to a particular country or place was imminent. However, such encouragement was based on trust, and information-providers were generally requested to exercise confidentiality about the details of the exchange.[205]

One organization, the APT, merits particular mention with regard to the supply of information to the CPT. Because the APT, and its founder, Jean-Jacques Gautier (see Chapter 4), were instrumental in promoting and framing the Convention, the organization regards the effectiveness of and, in particular, the flow of information to, the CPT to be part of its mandate.[206] By the end of 1995 the APT had prepared and published thirteen reports specifically designed to call the attention of the CPT 'to certain situations' in countries due to be visited by the Committee.[207] Additional information had also been sent to the CPT relating to eight countries, three of them—Bulgaria, Cyprus, and Slovenia—not the subject of specific country reports.[208]

Hitherto the APT has adopted the procedure of sending its country reports in confidence to the CPT 'a few months before the CPT visits a particular country' and then publishing it, usually after the CPT has visited, 'expurgated of all confidential data' in order to protect the identity of those providing the APT with information.[209] The purpose of maintaining informants' confidentiality is to enable the CPT to follow up appropriate lines of inquiry. APT reports also identify custodial sites exhibiting

[205] An anonymous example will serve to illustrate the point. One NGO that monitors closely the treatment of detainees and has in the past regularly recorded ill-treatment, both physical and psychological, attended a session of the CAT deliberating the situation in his country. At that stage he knew nothing about the CPT. His organization had prepared a submission for the CAT. At the meeting a member of the CAT who was also a member of the CPT introduced himself to the representative, revealed his membership of the CPT, and suggested that such information would also be useful to it. The NGO thereafter prepared a submission for the CPT which was headed 'Submission from X to the CPT'. A member of the CPT Secretariat subsequently telephoned, thanked the NGO but asked if the document could be differently titled since it gave the impression that the CPT had commissioned it. With this request the NGO complied, further contacts ensued, the sending of further information was encouraged, and when, shortly thereafter, the CPT visited the country concerned, including the places of custody about which the NGO had complained, the CPT delegation met with representatives of the NGO at the start of their visit. Other NGOs have said that they have received advice from the CPT on the optimum way to submit information (interview with FIACAT, Sept 1996).

[206] The SCAT announced in 1987 that among its objectives was: 'To get the European Convention ratified by the 21 Member States of the Council of Europe, and to watch the efficiency of the system' (Swiss Committee Against Torture (1987) *Swiss Committee Against Torture* (Geneva: SCAT), 14).

[207] APT (1993) *Preventing Torture*, APT Newsletter No 3, 13.   [208] ibid.

[209] APT (1995) *Preventing Torture*, APT Newsletter No 6, 23.

particular problems which the CPT might visit and investigate. Two examples will serve to illustrate these patterns.

In September 1992 the CPT announced that it intended to conduct a *periodic* visit to Belgium in 1993.[210] In October 1992 an APT researcher visited Belgium for a week to collect material. Her 43-page report was sent to the CPT in the summer of 1993 and was published in the autumn, an annotated list of contacts comprising six pages having been deleted.[211] The APT report on Belgium comprises three parts. The first sets out the legal framework for custody and penal trends, the second identifies what APT believes to be the principal problems relating to custody,[212] whilst the third section identifies seven prisons exhibiting combinations of problems worthy of attention. The report is detailed and enables the reader to identify alleged quite specific deficiencies in resources, facilities, and regimes in particular institutions. We do not know what information about Belgium the CPT received from other sources prior to their 1993 visit and the APT report mentions a large number of places of detention. Nevertheless it is noticeable that two out of the three prisons which the CPT visited in Belgium in November 1993 are repeatedly mentioned in the APT report as those exhibiting the most serious probems.[213]

It was also announced in the September 1992 statement that Ireland would be receiving a periodic visit during the course of 1993 and the APT produced a report on Ireland following a brief visit to Ireland in June of that year.[214] This seems fortuitous, the result of a well calculated—or well-informed—judgment that their report would be ready before the CPT visit, which began in late September.[215] The APT report on Ireland is rather more prescriptive in tone than that on Belgium—the second section is entitled: 'Places of Detention that Ought to be Visited'—but is in most respects of a similar character. Given the relatively small Irish population

---

[210] Council of Europe Press Release (1992) *European Committee for the Prevention of Torture: visits during 1993*, Ref 354(92) (Council of Europe: Strasbourg). Since it was still awaiting its first periodic visit, this, in any case, was fairly predictable.

[211] APT (1993a) *Rapport Sur Les Conditions De Detention En Belgique* (Geneva: APT). The earlier, confidential, report also bears a different title making it explicit that it is 'A l'intention du CPT'.

[212] These being prison overcrowding, the use of preventive detention, drugs and AIDS in the prison system, the use of force by the police, particularly in relation to immigrants, various aspects of prison conditions and regimes, conditions in closed psychiatric hospitals, the treatment of minors, and the position of asylum seekers and foreigners awaiting deportation.

[213] The prisons at St Gilles and Lantin are mentioned no fewer than 20 and 16 times respectively in the APT report. Both prisons were visited by the CPT and found to exhibit serious problems. By contrast the prison at St Andries, the third prison to be visited by the CPT, is not mentioned at all in the APT report and was found by the CPT to provide generally good conditions compared to those seen elsewhere (Belgium 1, paras 116–46).

[214] APT (1993b) *Report on Detention Conditions in the Republic of Ireland* (Geneva: APT).

[215] Although the public version is dated October 1993, the confidential version was no doubt transmitted to the CPT before the visit took place.

(3.6 million) and the small number of penal establishments in the Republic (a dozen), it would be surprising were there not a fairly high level of concordance between the suggestions for visits made by the APT and the visiting decisions of the CPT, and this is indeed the case. The CPT visited three prisons and one juvenile detention centre in Ireland, all of them specifically identified as problematical by the APT and all of them found wanting by the CPT.[216]

The extent to which the CPT currently considers important, and encourages, the work of the APT is not known. What is clear is that the APT, which sees itself as the midwife of the CPT, has set itself the task of supporting the Committee and, with or without the provision of discreet advice from the CPT, has regularly succeeded in timing the production of its country reports to precede by a close margin CPT visits.[217] Certainly the value of the APT's early reports was acknowledged by the first President of the CPT.[218] It seems likely that in the future the CPT will find most useful any peparatory reports the APT is able to prepare on the new member sates in Central and Eastern Europe, not just because these countries have not previously been visited but also because the countries of the former Soviet bloc have poorly developed civil societies in the sense that they generally lack the professional, well-informed, and critical NGOs that in the long-established democracies are generally better developed. Indeed this highlights an important issue about which we can reasonably speculate. It seems likely that in those countries with well-developed NGOs and critical mass media the CPT Secretariat will by now be in regular receipt of a wealth of information, possibly more that it can adequately cope with and respond to. From other countries, however, it is likely that they have a dearth of information making it difficult to decide which institutions to visit and what priorities to attach to those countries.

All communications prepared for and sent specifically to the CPT are acknowledged by the Secretariat and notified to CPT members when meeting in plenary session. Receipt from NGOs of general mailing list material—that is, material that is distributed mechanically rather than

---

[216] See the comments of the APT on the prisons at Mountjoy, Cork, and Limerick and the juvenile centre at St Patrick, Dublin: ibid, 8–11. For CPT findings see Ireland 1, paras 58–113.

[217] For example: the APT 1991 report on Switzerland is dated May, the CPT visit took place in July 1991; their 1994 report on the United Kingdom is dated January, the CPT visit took place in May 1994; their 1994 report on Spain is dated February, the CPT visit took place in April 1994; their 1994 report on Austria is dated May, the CPT visit took place in September 1994; their 1994 report on Hungary is dated September, the CPT visit took place in November 1994. Indeed, this alignment appears to fail only when the CPT changes its plans. Thus the projected 1995 CPT visit to Switzerland, announced in September 1994, was postponed to 1996, presumably as a result of the decision to visit Romania, a visit not pre-announced. The APT's report on Switzerland was published in February 1995.

[218] Cassese, A (1994) 'The European Committee for the Prevention of Torture and Inhuman or Degrading Treatment or Punishment Comes of Age' in *Liber Amicorum HG Schermers*.

being brought personally to the attention of recipients to whom it is thought relevant—is not acknowledged[219] though, if it is judged important, it is brought to the particular attention of CPT members when meeting in plenary session. What is clear is that not even detailed briefing papers, such as those prepared by the APT, will necessarily be seen by members of the Committee, although they all will be aware of their existence.[220]

Generally speaking the CPT does not solicit information, though as we have seen there are exceptions, albeit discreet. When the requirements of equity with regard to *periodic* visits have been satisfied, it is on the basis of sifting this incoming information that the Secretariat is in a position to advise the CPT, and the CPT is in a position to decide, which countries should be visited, which custodial sites within countries should be seen, and under what circumstances.

There is one possible stage in the information gathering process which must be highlighted. In 1990 the CPT revised its Rules of Procedure to allow what is in effect a 'halfway house' between receiving information and deciding to conduct an *ad hoc* visit. Rule 30 now provides:

1. Before deciding on a particular visit, the Committee or, if appropriate, the Bureau may request information or explanations as regards the general situation in the State concerned, as regards a given place or as regards an isolated case concerning which it has received reports.
2. Following receipt of such information or explanations, details of remedial action taken by the national authorities may be requested.

This is an interesting provision. It is clearly designed to assist the Bureau or Committee decide whether it is necessary to undertake an *ad hoc* or possibly a *follow-up* visit. If, in the light of information received, it is decided not to arrange a visit, it appears that the intention is to allow the Committee to engage in a dialogue with the state concerning the matter, as if a visit had in fact occurred.

(ii) Notification of visits

The CPT is required to 'notify the Government of the Party concerned of its intention to carry out a visit', after which 'it may at any time visit any place referred to in Article 2',[221] that is 'any place . . . where persons are deprived of their liberty by a public authority'. The period of notification is not specified and the Explanatory Report provides little additional guidance, though the examples given (24 or 48 hours 'between the

[219] This was revealed by members of the CPT Secretariat at the seminar referred to in n 201 above. Such unacknowledged material is also not 'registered as received' by the Secretariat within their filing system (interview with Bureau, Sept 1996).

[220] The Secretariat provides each member of a visiting delegation with a dossier of material relevant to the country in question. This would usually contain such material. Those members not involved in a visit have access to this information if they wish.

[221] Article 8(1).

notification and the moment when the visit becomes effective') suggests that the framers of the Convention considered that the notification would normally be brief.[222] However, the CPT has decided, possibly influenced by advice from agencies like the ICRC, that rather more notice should generally be given.[223] Striking a balance between the need to allow a country to prepare for a visit[224] so as to make it possible for the CPT to carry out its inspectoral task effectively, and denying cynical states the opportunity to cover up abuses, is a delicate matter.

In addition, the Committee soon realized that in order to undertake its routine visiting task effectively, it would need information about the custodial situation in the country concerned that could only be obtained from the local custodial authorities. The Committee recorded that:

While debating its procedures and methods of work, the Committee felt that a means had to be found of inciting the receipt of relevant information concerning the country due to receive a periodic visit, but a means which at the same time allowed a certain measure of surprise as regards the actual carrying out of the visit to be maintained. The dilemma was resolved by deciding that the notification of a periodic visit to the country concerned, which under the Convention could be taken to consist of a single act, should instead be conceived of as a process.[225]

In consequence the CPT has devised a three-stage notification process which meets delegations' practical needs but which leaves scope for surprise when this is considered necessary. Experience suggests that this decision was vital but that, even so, the process has not always succeeded in 'inciting' states to provide the necessary information.[226]

Once the CPT has decided in the autumn of each calendar year what its programme of *periodic* visits is to be for the following year,[227] the Secretariat informs the countries concerned and shortly thereafter the Council of Europe issues a press release naming the countries. The exact timing of

[222] Explanatory Report, para 56. This impression is underlined by the suggestion that 'exceptional situations could arise in which the visit takes place immediately after the notification has been given'.

[223] ICRC officials doubt the efficacy of 'lightning strikes' and have advised the CPT as such (interviews with ICRC officials).

[224] For example, making satisfactory arrangements regarding the delegation's credentials and means of identification, informing agencies about the nature of the CPT, supplying information to the CPT about, for example, the precise location of places of detention, their size, typical population, and so on.

[225] Gen Rep 1, para 26.

[226] Thus in the case of Bulgaria in 1995, 'Although the CPT had requested [lists of police and National Investigation Service (NIS) places of detention] from the Bulgarian authorities well before the visit, it only received the list of police establishments three days before the start of the visit and a summary list of NIS establishments on the second day of the visit': Bulgaria 1, para 7.

[227] *Follow-up* visits are never notified in this way though, as we have seen from the Swedish and Northern Irish examples discussed above at pp. 175–6 and 170–1, some *follow-up* visits, and probably some *ad hoc* visits, are almost certainly planned as far in advance as *periodic* visits.

visits is kept secret. Secondly, about two weeks before the visit is due to take place the official liaison officer of the country concerned is informed of the proposed date and duration of the visit, as well as the identities of the Committee members, experts, and interpreters making up the delegation. This stage satisfies the requirement that: 'The names of persons assisting the Committee shall be specified in the notification'[228] thereby giving the state party the opportunity 'exceptionally' to declare that such persons 'may not be allowed to take part in a visit to a place within its jurisdiction'.[229] Thirdly, a few days before the visit commences, a provisional list of places to be visited is sent to the country. This procedure is designed to give the country time to: make the necessary practical arrangements; collate and transmit information about the institutions notified; and fix meetings with officials. The latter notification period is, arguably, too short to allow the authorities time to make significant changes to physical conditions or the regime at the places to be visited. However, it should be noted, the CPT always reserves the right to visit places not notified and almost invariably does so (see Section 3 below).[230]

In conclusion it should be noted that 'exceptionally' (as in the case of exclusion of persons assisting the Committee) a state may argue for the postponement of a visit on specified grounds, namely national defence, public safety, serious disorder in places of detention, the medical condition of the person, or progress of an urgent interrogation relating to a serious crime.[231] This provision gives a wide—though not unfettered—margin of appreciation to the state concerned. It seems likely that the provision is intended to operate in relation to visits arranged in the light of special circumstances relating to particular locations. *Periodic* visits will tend to focus on general custodial conditions and it is unlikely that the factors listed in Article 9(1) could justifiably be invoked, though an exception might be a state of civil war or general unrest, as, for example, occurred in Albania in 1997.[232] Particular circumstances leading to an *ad hoc* visit are more likely to arise in the context of the type of extenuating circumstances cited in Article 9(1). Moroever, it is not unreasonable to suppose that *ad hoc* or *follow-up*, as opposed to *periodic*, visits may also be made to particular individuals.[233]

---

[228] Article 14(1).   [229] Article 14(3).

[230] Most visits, with the exception of *follow-up* visits focused on one or two institutions, typically involve the delegation going to places of custody not notified.

[231] Article 9(1).

[232] Albania was one of the countries scheduled for, and notified of, a *periodic* visit in 1997. It was originally intended that this visit should take place early in the spring but—doubtless due to the civil unrest in Albania at that time (including the release by opposing factions of prisoners from the main prison) which would have made the visit hazardous, impractical, and unlikely to be worthwhile—it was postponed and in fact took place in December 1997.

[233] As in the case of the *ad hoc* visit to Spain in June 1994 (see above, pp. 172–4).

As far as we can ascertain Article 9(1) has not yet been invoked. Were it to be invoked, then the CPT and the state concerned are required immediately to consult the other 'in order to clarify the situation and seek agreement on arrangements to enable the Committee to exercise its functions expeditiously'.[234] Where the requested postponement relates to a person, the Committee wishes to see that these 'arrangements may include the transfer to another place' and 'until the visit takes place, the Party shall provide information to the Committee about any person concerned'.[235] These circumstances are most likely to arise once a visit has been embarked on and would not, therefore, involve postponement of a delegation's arrival since, as far as we are aware, the Committee's interpretation of its rule of confidentiality normally precludes telling state authorities which persons the Committee wishes to see in advance of immediately seeing them. Though the CPT has frequently had cause to complain about not being given immediate access to prisoners they wished to see, the obstacles have always been operational (for example, officials not being aware of the Committee's identity or rights) and not because of Article 9(1).

(iii) The composition of delegations

It is the Bureau, together with the Secretariat, which formulates a plan for the timing and duration of all visits and the composition of visiting delegations, including their leadership.[236] Once this visit plan has been approved by the CPT meeting in plenary session, the members selected to form the delegation meet and begin to plan the detail of the visit. They decide such matters as: the duration of the visit; which institutions to visit; whether the delegation will need to be assisted by experts, and, if so, by what sort of expert and whom; whether specific NGOs should be approached with a view to meeting their representatives during the course of the visit; whether the delegation should split up during the visit so as to enable different parts of the country to be visited; and so on. To assist Committee members in this task the Secretariat prepares a dossier of information received about the country on the basis of which proposals are made as to which institutions should be visited.

Aside from the first two years when the Committee was finding its feet and a few members were heavily relied on, the work of the Committee—preparing for visits, taking part in visits, and agreeing reports following visits—is more or less equally shared between Committee members, with most members undertaking an average of two visits per year.

---

[234] Aricle 9(2).   [235] ibid.   [236] Interview with Bureau, Sept 1996.

It follows that the Bureau, advised by the Secretariat, have the difficult task of putting together balanced and harmonious delegations appropriate to the country being visited. Among the considerations they take into account are:

- the inclusion of a leader capable of representing the work of the Committee and communicating the preliminary findings of the Committee at high level meetings with ministers or senior officials at the beginning and end of the visit;
- the inclusion of a blend of expertise among members (or *ad hoc* experts), particularly legal and medical expertise;
- the inclusion of a blend of recently elected and long-standing members, so that experience is gained and shared;
- at least one man and woman;
- ensuring that members are generally able to communicate with each other in the same language (which, given that French and English are the working languages of the Council of Europe, results in delegations being predominantly Anglo or Francophone), ideally a language likely to be understood within the country without constant use of interpretators;
- ensuring that members are compatible and likely to be able to work well as a team during what may be an arduous week or two.

If every member is to be able to contribute more or less equally to the programme of visits then not all delegations can be made up of members whose characteristics cover all the above considerations. The balance has to be made up by asking experts, particularly medical experts, to accompany delegations. Furthermore, neither English nor French—nor indeed other languages such as Spanish, German, or Italian with which one might expect a minority of members to have at least a passing familiarity—is widely spoken in many countries visited. Only rarely are delegations able wholly to dispense with the services of interpreters[237] and sometimes whole delegations are made up of persons unable to speak the local language so that there are occasionally almost as many interpreters as members and experts.[238]

The size of delegations varies according to the nature of the country being visited and the length of the visit. Visits to large, complex, or difficult countries normally last two weeks and generally include five CPT

---

[237] It would appear that the delegations to Malta in 1990 (see Malta 1, para 2) and the United Kingdom in 1990 (UK 1, para 2) were not accompanied by interpreters, though it is possible that these early reports did not record the fact.

[238] The delegation for the visit to Greece in March 1993, for example, comprised five CPT members and four experts, none of them nationals from countries where Greek is spoken, accompanied by six interpreters (see Greece 1, para 2).

members. Shorter or potentially less difficult visits generally include four or fewer CPT members.[239] Small delegations also characterize some highly focused *ad hoc* or *follow-up* visits.[240]

In the early years, the majority of delegations included, and were led[241] by, a member of the Bureau. Delegations to large, complex, or potentially problematical countries have, at least until recently, invariably included a Bureau member, and sometimes two.[242] Delegations not including a Bureau member were generally, though not invariably, the shorter *periodic* visits to smaller countries,[243] brief *ad hoc* or *follow-up* visits,[244] or visits to countries which we can reasonably presume the CPT considered unlikely to present major problems.[245] Since 1995, and as the number of member states to be visited has grown in proportion to the size of the Bureau, it has become clear that, unless Bureau members are regularly to undertake many more visits than other CPT members, or the Bureau is increased in size, it will become necessary for more potentially difficult visits to be conducted without either their leadership or presence.[246] Whether a

[239] Thus, for example, the three-day *periodic* visit to San Marino in March 1992 was undertaken by only two CPT members (accompanied by one expert) and the three-day *periodic* visit to Liechtenstein in April 1993 was undertaken by only three CPT members without the assistance of an expert.

[240] Thus the week-long *ad hoc* visit to France in July 1994, during which attention was primarily focused on the Parisian *depôt* for alleged illegal immigrants previously visited by the CPT in November 1991, was undertaken by a delegation that included only three CPT members. The four-day long visit to Spain in June 1993 solely to interview persons recently held in custody was undertaken by only two CPT members, accompanied by a medical expert. Likewise the four or three-day long visits to Portugal in October 1996, Greece in November 1996, and Italy in November 1996 involved delegations of three, three, and two members respectively.

[241] On a few occasions delegations including a Bureau member have been led by non-Bureau members, but in all but one instance this was because the first First Vice-President of the CPT (Jacques Bernheim, member for Switzerland and First Vice-President 1989–93) declined to lead a delegation.

[242] The visit to the UK in July–Aug 1990, for example, included all three members of the Bureau and was led by the President. The same was true of the visits to Turkey in Sept 1990, Sept–Oct 1991 and Nov–Dec 1992. The visits to Spain (Apr 1991), France (Oct–Nov 1991), Greece (Mar 1993), the UK (July 1993), Turkey (Oct 1994), and France (Oct 1996) included 2 Bureau members.

[243] Examples include Malta (July 1990), Switzerland (July 1991), San Marino (Mar 1992), Luxembourg (Jan 1993), Liechtenstein (Apr 1993), Iceland (July 1993), and Malta again (July 1995).

[244] As, for example, to Spain (June 1994), Sweden (Aug 1994), Portugal (Oct 1996), Italy (Nov 1996), Spain (Jan 1997), Norway (Mar 1997) and Luxembourg (Apr 1997).

[245] Examples might include Denmark (Dec 1990), Finland (May 1992), the Netherlands (Aug–Sept 1992) and Norway (June–July 1993).

[246] Recent examples include the first periodic visits to Slovakia (June 1995, led by Love Kellberg, member for Sweden 1989–95), Romania (Sept 1995, lead by Constantin Economides, member for Greece since 1991), and the Czech Republic (Feb 1997, led by Bent Sørensen, member for Denmark 1989–97), and the second periodic visit to Germany (Apr 1996, also led by Bent Sørensen). Of the 13 visits conducted in 1997 only two were headed by a current Bureau member.

member of the Bureau or not, heads of delegation are always experienced and senior members of the Committee.[247]

Delegations *always* include someone, either a CPT member or an accompanying expert, with medical qualifications. It seems clear that the Committee considers this vital not least because, as we observe in Chapter 6, the Committee has never unequivocally found torture to have occurred without corroborative medical *sequelae* being discovered. The number of medically-qualified personnel included in delegations varies greatly. There are most commonly one or two medics, but there are occasionally as many as four or five.[248]

Almost every CPT delegation has hitherto also included a lawyer, and it is noteworthy that on two occasions when none of the CPT members were lawyers a legally qualified expert accompanied the delegation.[249] Should the proportion or number of CPT members who are medics further increase it will arguably be less necessary to rely on *ad hoc* medical experts than on persons with legal or legal-custody expertize, though it should be remembered that the majority of the CPT Secretariat,

---

[247] The Committee's Rules of Procedure incorporate detailed rules about the precedence of members according to length of time in office and age (Rule 3), in the event of Bureau members being unable to carry out their functions (Rule 8), or when Bureau members are required to stand down (Rule 9, when a report is being considered on the state party by which he or she was elected). Thus when Bent Sørensen ceased being a member of the Bureau in September 1995, he nevertheless enjoyed precedence as well as experience, and continued heading delegations on major *periodic* visits. In the early life of the CPT, Love Kellberg, though never a member of the Bureau, was nevertheless head of all but two of the delegations of which he was a member. He had previously been a member of the European Commission of Human Rights, and also enjoyed high precedence in terms of both appointment and age. Since Kellberg's resignation in 1995, Constantin Economides, the member for Greece since 1991, has come to occupy a similar position with regard to the leadership of delegations.

[248] It is not altogether appparent why some delegations include so many medical personnel. Visits to Turkey, for example—the member state which, to date, all the evidence suggests exhibits the greatest problems regarding the use of torture—had by the end of 1997 been visited on seven occasions, and delegations always included either two or three medically-qualified personnel. The delegations to France in 1991 and Bulgaria and Romania in 1995 included four doctors and the delegations to Greece and the UK in 1993 included no fewer than five doctors. It seems likely that the explanation for this very substantial gathering of medical expertise—which in the case of the UK in 1993 and Romania in 1995 involved the recruitment of three and four medical experts respectively—lay not in the anticipated likelihood of finding evidence of torture, but in the planned visit of psychiatric hospitals where difficult medical issues of care, treatment, and decision-making would be encountered. Even so, the relative weight given to medical personnel in some delegations is difficult to understand unless it is because medically-qualified members of the Committee lacked relevant expertise for the task in hand. In none of the above countries were more than two hospitals visited in the course of two-week long visits during which many non-medical institutions were inspected.

[249] Jim McManus, an academic lawyer, since appointed Complaints Adjudicator for the Scottish Prison Service, participated in the related visits in June–July 1994 to the Dutch and French overseas territories of the Antilles, Aruba, and Martinique.

two of whom usually accompany delegations, are qualified lawyers.[250] Finally, it would appear that some effort is made to ensure that delegations include a woman member, and that a female expert is included when no female CPT member is involved.[251] However, this has not always been done.[252]

3 CONDUCTING VISITS[253]

Two persons occupy strategically central positions in the conduct of visits: the Head of the delegation—who, as we have seen, is selected well in advance of the visit and presides over the planning arrangements— and the senior accompanying Secretariat member. Whilst the role of the Head of Delegation is formally acknowledged,[254] that of the accompanying Secretariat members is more shadowy. It seems likely, however, that the senior Secretariat member assigned to the delegation occupies a vital and crucially influential position: assembling evidence of ill-treatment gleaned from various sources; suggesting custodial sites to be visited and the priority to be attached to them; recommending whether the delegation should split up during the course of the visit and which members should accompany each other; proposing which *ad hoc* experts might be used to assist the delegation; contacting the authorities in the country concerned to ask for advance information about custodial institutions, their capacity, and occupancy rates; arranging meetings; acting as secretary during formal meetings; preparing briefs for the Head of delegation; taking responsibility for all the practical matters (accommodation, travel, meeting rooms, instructing interpreters, and so on) on which any sizeable delegation will depend; and, in the aftermath of the visit, collating the

---

[250] See n 100 above.

[251] As was the case for the visit to Sweden in May 1991 when Randi Rosenquist, a Norwegian psychiatrist, accompanied the all-male CPT delegation, and for the visit to Ireland in September–October 1993, when Marianne Kastrup, a Danish psychiatrist, accompanied an all-male CPT delegation.

[252] Six of the 68 delegations (Committee members and *ad hoc* experts) organized up to the end of 1997 were all-male, these being the missions to Malta in July 1990, Portugal in Jan 1992, San Marino in Mar 1992, the United Kingdom in July 1993, France in July 1994, and Italy in Nov 1996. On only one of these occasions was the delegation accompanied by a female member of the Secretariat (Malta, 1990). It should be recalled that only six of the 37 *ad hoc* experts employed by the CPT up to the end of 1996 were women (see above, p. 164).

[253] The CPT has revealed something about the practical conduct of visits (see Gen Rep 1 and Evans and Morgan (1992), 605–7). Other information has been gained or deduced from interviews with officials and NGO representatives in various countries.

[254] The Head 'is in charge of relations with the national authorities of the country visited and organises, as well as oversees, the drafting of the delegation's report': Gen Rep 1, para 58.

delegation's fieldnotes and preparing the first draft of the ensuing report. Given, as we have noted, that all the senior members of the Secretariat are much more experienced in the conduct of visits, and thus in the 'jurisprudence' of the CPT, than most Committee members, it would be very surprising were Committee members, including most Heads of Delegation, not to defer to the advice of the senior Secretariat member regarding most of these matters.

The position of *ad hoc* experts within delegations is much more ambiguous and seems likely to vary a good deal depending on the degree to which they have previously assisted the CPT, know Committee and Secretariat members, and are versed in the ways of the CPT. The Convention is obscure on their role not least because, as we have shown,[255] it was intended that *ad hoc* experts should not be relied on as often as they have been. The text of the Convention grants them little practical involvement during visits but it seems likely that there is a wide divergence between a strict interpretation of the text and the practice of the Committee. The Convention draws a distinction between the Committee members and the *ad hoc* experts in that, though the latter are members of the visiting delegation and enjoy the same privileges and immunities as CPT members,[256] they are not equals. They are 'assisting the Committee'[257] and 'shall act on the instructions and under the authority of the Committee'.[258] Further, it is unclear whether the Convention extends to *ad hoc* experts the Committee members' crucial freedoms to interview in private persons deprived of their liberty, or to communicate with any person who the Committee believes can supply relevant information.[259] What is clear is that the Committee has decided that *ad hoc* experts can do so and, as far as we are able to ascertain, no state has yet attempted to deny or restrict these facilities.

Visits generally begin on a Sunday with private meetings with local NGO representatives or individuals who it is felt can advise the delegation about recent developments that the delegation may wish to take into account when deciding to make last-minute alterations to their programme. These meetings typically take place in the hotel where the CPT delegation is staying and, though their content may influence the choice of custodial sites to be visited (generally police stations and immigration detention facilities *not* notified), it is doubtful that they influence to any significant extent the direction of the visit generally. Such meetings

---

[255] See Chapter 4 and Section 3 above.

[256] Article 16. The privileges and immunities enjoyed by Committee members (and *ad hoc* experts assisting the Committee during the course of visits) are set out in the Annex to the Convention and reproduced in Appendix 1A. They include 'immunity from personal arrest or detention and from seizure of their personal baggage' and 'exemption from any restrictions' on 'entry into and exit from the country in which they exercise their functions' (paras 2(a) and (b)). This includes the need for visas.

[257] Articles 7(2) and 14(1).   [258] Article 14(2).   [259] Article 8(3) and (4).

appear to be arranged at short notice (generally a few days before the visit takes place) and it seems that delegations do not deviate greatly from the visit programme to institutions notified, and of which the NGO representatives are unaware.[260]

On the following day, usually a Monday, meetings are generally held with ministers and high-ranking officials responsible for the institutions to be visited.[261] But most members of delegations are only briefly involved in these formal exchanges. Delegations quickly get on with the principal business of visits—namely, going to places where persons are held in custody—police stations, prisons, youth detention facilities, closed psychiatric hospitals, immigration detention centres, and so on—looking closely at the conditions in which detainees are held, scrutinizing custody records, and, above all, talking to prisoners about their experience in custody, both where they are currently held and also other places where they may have been since their initial arrest or detention. During this, the central stage of the visit, the delegation often splits 'into sub-groups',[262] particularly when the countries are large and institutions in different regions are included.

The CPT enjoys considerable powers when carrying out a visit. The Committee has: unlimited access to the territory of the state concerned and the right to travel without restriction; unlimited access to any place where people are deprived of their liberty, including the right to move inside such places without restriction; access to full information on places where people deprived of their liberty are being held, as well as other information, including medical records, available to the state which is necessary for the Committee to carry out its task;[263] the right to interview in private any persons deprived of their liberty,[264] though such persons may of course refuse; and the right to communicate freely with anyone else who the Committee believes can supply relevant information about the treatment of persons deprived of their liberty[265] (Article 8(4)).

The Committee sets great store by having immediate and unrestricted access to places of detention, and all areas within them, and published CPT reports testify to the fact that the Committee is insistent on compliance with this letter of the Convention.[266] References are made from time

---

[260] Various interviews. See also Shaw, S (1995) 'The Role of NGOs in Assisting and Promoting the Work of the CPT' in APT.

[261] Gen Rep 1, para 64.   [262] ibid, para 65.

[263] Article 8(2)(a)–(d). The latter provision is qualified by the stipulation that 'the Committee shall have regard to applicable rules of national law and professional ethics' (Article 8(2)(d)).

[264] Article 8(3).   [265] Article 8(4).

[266] These problems are perhaps understandably often met during first visits to member states as, for example, in the case of Bulgaria in 1995. Here a Regional Public Prosecutor, responsible for a Regional Investigation Service place of detention, denied all knowledge

to time to difficulties which the Committee has encountered. The CPT's
first General Report, for example, cited a 'certain amount of reticence'
met in police stations[267] and the following year the Committee reported
that 'there were some isolated examples (in both police and prison establishments) of access to a place that a delegation wished to visit being
delayed'.[268] These minor difficulties have continued. Thus the 6th Annual
Report notes problems relating to delayed access and to officials sometimes instructing that detainees should not be seen without the prior
authorization of judges or public prosecutors, instructions which the
CPT has unequivocally stated to be 'in clear breach of the Convention'.[269]
Whenever delegations encounter obstacles to their access it appears from
published reports that they are adamant about their rights and to date
seem always to have prevailed.[270]

The CPT concentrates its attention on relatively few places of custody which are looked at relatively thoroughly.[271] Delegations spend 'on
average one-and-a-half to two days in a moderately-sized to large institution (400+ detainees)' and 'much less time' at police stations—to which
visits are 'on occasion carried out at night'—and alien holding centres at
airports.[272] During the course of a two-week-long *periodic* visit a CPT delegation will typically visit perhaps half a dozen police stations (some of
which will have been notified, but others not), two or three prisons, a psychiatric hospital, a youth facility, and an immigration holding centre. The
precise balance of institutions visited depends on the country, the problems it presents, and whether it has previously been visited. During the
visits 'delegation members take notes as they proceed' but 'refrain from
using tape-recorders or taking photographs'.[273]

Precisely how many prisoners CPT delegations aim to interview, or
do interview, during a typical visit has neither been disclosed generally

of the CPT, said that letters of introduction carried by the delegation which had been issued
by the Bulgarian national authorities were insufficient for her to admit the delegation, and
claimed that it was in any case too late in the day for the delegation to meet detainees. The
problem was sorted out and the delegation admitted the following morning (Bulgaria 1,
para 9). However, in some countries, problems of access have continued. During the CPT's
second and third visits to Spain, for example, the Committee suffered delays in gaining access
to police stations (Spain 2, para 10) and information essential for carrying out their mission
(Spain 3, para 9).

[267] Gen Rep 1, para 69.   [268] Gen Rep 2, para 21.   [269] Gen Rep 6, para 6.

[270] A particularly telling example is provided in the report on the first visit to Greece in
1993. While at Thessaloniki police station, a station not notified in advance, the delegation
requested that police officers' private lockers be opened, a request that was vigorously resisted.
The Committee stood firm and eventually got their way. This proved to be a strikingly important example because when eventually opened one of the personal lockers was found
to contain an electric shock device of a type which former detainees had alleged had been
used against them in that police station (Greece 1, paras 20–2). See also below, Chapter 6,
p. 219.

[271] For comparison with the practice of other international monitoring agencies, see
Morgan and Evans (1994).

[272] Gen Rep 1, para 66.   [273] ibid.

nor are figures given in visit reports.[274] It is implausible, except in relation to very brief visits, to imagine that the number is small, such as could be counted on the fingers of two hands. Delegations are typically seven or eight strong, if *ad hoc* experts and Secretariat are included. They split up. We must assume that they all engage in data collection, and that this includes interviewing detainees. When discussing the numbers of allegations of ill-treatment received during the course of visits the Committee has developed in its reports a form of numerical continuum which ranges from 'none' to 'numerous' or even 'an extremely large number'.[275] Moreover to describe their findings the Committee uses the language of 'risk' of ill-treatment, once again employing a linguistic continuum which stretches to a 'risk not negligible' to 'a serious risk'. These usages would be inappropriate were delegations not seeing several score of prisoners during the course of a visit, which is certainly a practical possibility.

Finally, visits end as they formally begin, with a meeting, if possible attended by the whole delegation,[276] with ministers and senior officials responsible for the places visited. At this meeting the Head of Delegation 'comments on the circumstances surrounding the visit and the manner in which it has been conducted' and provides 'tentative first impressions of the places of detention visited',[277] that is, the Committee's preliminary findings. This practice, similar to that adopted by other inspectoral bodies,[278] sounds rather low-key, but can scarcely be so. The Head of Delegation's oral statement is carefully scripted and is the result of extensive consultation between members of the delegation.[279] It would scarcely enhance the Committee's credibility with national authorities were the Head of Delegation to offer a 'first impression' which was not subsequently reflected in the Committee's written report.

Moreover, these final talks, and the 'first impressions' may include 'immediate observations'[280] required, in the Committee's judgment, by the 'urgent need to improve the treatment of persons deprived of their liberty' in situations encountered during the visit.[281] This procedure, which is used only in 'exceptional cases',[282] is not a substitute for subsequently

---

[274] An exception to this rule was the *ad hoc* visit to Spain in June 1994, when the Committee went specifically to interview persons recently held in custody, of whom eight were seen (Spain 3, para 12).

[275] See Chapter 6, pp. 222–30.   [276] Gen Rep 1, para 67.   [277] ibid.

[278] For example, the Inspectorate of Prisons for England and Wales (see Morgan, R (1985) 'Her Majesty's Inspectorate of Prisons' in Maguire, M, Vagg, J and Morgan, R (eds), 117.

[279] Gen Rep 1, para 68.   [280] Article 8(5).   [281] Explanatory Report, para 70.

[282] ibid. Because not all CPT reports have been published it is not known on how many occasions Article 8(5) has been invoked. But it was used in Spain in April 1994, the United Kingdom in May 1994, Hungary in November 1994, and Bulgaria in April 1995. The UK example is typical of the procedure. The Committee were concerned about the practice of holding remand and convicted prisoners in the Main Bridewell Police Station in Liverpool in 'grossly overcrowded' and inadequate facilities. They recommended that 'urgent action be taken . . . to end the practice' (UK 3, paras 11–13).

reporting in writing on the matter. On the contrary,[283] the procedure underlines the importance of there being close correspondence between what
is said at the final talks and the content of the Committee's written report.
The final talks are, in effect, another step in the formal dialogue which
has by that stage already begun between the Committee and the state
party.

4 THE CPT AND THE MASS MEDIA

Shortly after the delegation has left the country the CPT issues a press
release announcing that the visit has taken place. The development of this
policy is worth noting because it illustrates the difficulty that the CPT has
had squaring the rule of confidentiality—and the Committee's interpretation of that rule—with the close interest that the mass media occasionally
show in the CPT's work.

The CPT has revealed that at the beginning of its life the Committee decided 'to refrain from having any contact whatsoever with the
media'.[284] It is not entirely clear what that meant, but it suggests: that
Committee members would not speak to journalists about the work of
the Committee; that visits would not be directly revealed to the media,
even after the event; that no comment would be made on any stories
relating to the Committee's activities; and so on. If that was the case, the
policy was naïve. Not only did it underestimate the interest of the media
in CPT affairs,[285] it also failed to acknowledge the educative power of
the media and the interplay between the media and NGOs whose well-
informed knowledge of the CPT is arguably vital to the Commitee's
effective operation. In addition, it did not anticipate the capacity of governments and groups to create and manipulate news stories in order to
present CPT-related issues to their own advantage. Ultimately, despite
all the fine words about the prevention of ill-treatment of detainees and
the spirit of co-operation between the CPT and state parties, CPT delegations are external inspectors and critics, and the judgments at which they
arrive call into question national and agency reputations. CPT reports
sometimes comprise the stuff of national, or even international, scandal.
As such, CPT activities are on occasion bound to be the subject of moral
entrepreneurial activity and attract considerable mass-media attention.

By the end of 1990 the CPT realized that its vow of complete media
silence was neither sensible nor practical. Newspaper articles appeared
in several countries 'purportedly disclosing confidential material'. Leaks,

---

[283] Explanatory Report, para 70.   [284] Gen Rep 1, para 78.   [285] ibid.

real or imagined, appeared[286] and the Committee observed that: 'Erroneous statements about what the delegation was supposed to have seen in a particular prison' had been published.[287] The Committee adopted a three-pronged media policy in an attempt to forestall this early trend. First, all information interpreted as not covered by the rule of confidentiality was in future to be channelled to the media.[288] This included issuing each autumn a press release listing countries to receive *periodic* visits during the following year and releasing, shortly after the end of each visit, a brief press release announcing the starting date and duration of the visit, the membership of the delegation and the places visited, but containing no reportage of the Committee's findings. The CPT Secretariat also 'maintains informal contacts with representatives of the media on a regular basis'.[289]

Secondly, though it was decided that 'visiting delegations should avoid contact with the media during the course of a visit', members were to be allowed to give interviews on an '"on the record" attributable basis' on condition that they disclose no confidential information and that a copy of the interview record be lodged with the CPT's Secretariat.[290] This is a topic to which we return in Chapter 9. The Committee has no policy on whether members should individually undertake ambassadorial work on behalf of the Committee—such as writing articles, giving lectures, attending meetings where CPT-related matters may be discussed —in order that the work of the CPT might become better known.[291] A few members do this, but many do not.[292]

Thirdly, the CPT decided that whenever inaccurate information appears in news stories about the Committee's activities then the Bureau will issue a correction. Furthermore, should it be alleged by the media that a state party has disclosed confidential information then the Bureau will immediately draw the attention of the authorities to the allegation and 'insist that the rule of confidentiality applies also to States'.[293] Corrections have been issued in accordance with this policy, though it is unclear whether national authorities have ever been involved.[294]

---

[286] A leak, subsequently shown to be fairly accurate, appeared in the *Salzburger Nachtrichten* on 7 January 1991 from the report on the very first visit carried out by the CPT, to Austria in May 1990.

[287] Gen Rep 1, para 79.   [288] ibid, para 80.   [289] ibid, para 81.

[290] ibid, para 82. This policy is backed by disciplinary procedures for members who breach the Committee's rule of confidentiality (see Rules 47 and 48 of the Rules of Procedure).

[291] Interview with the Bureau, Sept 1996.

[292] Certain members—Antonio Cassese and Claude Nicolay, the first two Presidents of the Committee, and other leading members (Love Kellberg, Bent Sørensen, and Constantin Economides, for example)—have on several occasions lectured at various fora on the work of the CPT or the phenomenon of torture and its prevention.

[293] Gen Rep 1, para 82(v).

[294] See above, p. 168 regarding the *ad hoc* visit to Turkey in August 1996.

5 REPORTING ON VISITS

The CPT is required to draw up a 'report on the facts found during the visit'.[295] This suggests that *ad hoc* experts who have assisted the Committee delegation in conducting the visit are excluded from the process, since *ad hoc* experts are not, even temporarily, members of the Committee and are therefore excluded from the plenary meetings of the Committee, which meet *in camera*.[296] However, this is only partially the case. The procedure, which has evolved since 1990 to make more efficient the increasing burden of report preparation as the number of member states and annual visits has grown, is as follows.

Before delegation members go their separate ways at the end of a visit they agree, as we have seen, on their tentative findings so that the Head of the Delegation can report them at the final talks. They also agree 'an outline of the report prepared by the Head of the Delegation and to allocate responsibility for the drafting of specific sections'.[297] Although this might have been the intention, in practice the task of preparing a draft report is delegated to the Secretariat.[298] This draft is then presented to members, including *ad hoc* experts, of the visit delegation at a reconvened meeting of the delegation which, for the sake of convenience, generally takes place in Paris a few months after the visit has taken place. This draft is based on the agreed 'first impressions' which the Head of Delegation has given orally at the final talks, and is filled out on the basis of the fieldnotes which members of the delegation are required to take during the course of the visit and which they subsequently transmit to the Secretariat. Thereafter the procedure for agreeing the report has changed substantially since the early days of the Committee.

Initially, the visiting delegation submitted to the CPT meeting in plenary session a 'distinct delegation report' which, following discussion and, if thought appropriate, amendment, was transmitted as the Committee's 'draft report' in order that the government concerned be given the chance to comment before the report was finalized.[299] The report was further discussed, and possibly amended in the light of these observations and

[295] Article 10(1).

[296] Article 6(1). However, Rule 18(2) states that: 'Apart from members of the Committee, only members of the Committee's Secretariat, interpreters and persons providing technical assistance to the Committee may be present at its meetings, unless the Committee decides otherwise.' It follows that *ad hoc* experts can attend whenever invited, for whatever purpose the Committee deems appropriate.

[297] Gen Rep 1, para 68.

[298] The Head of Delegation 'organises' and 'oversees' the drafting of the report (see Gen Rep 1, para 58).

[299] Article 10(1) of the Convention provides that when drawing up the Report the Committee should take 'account of any observations which may have been submitted by the Party concerned'.

consultations, at the next plenary meeting of the Committee, after which it would then be transmitted in confidence as the final report of the Committee to the government concerned. This original procedure was 'cumbersome and time-consuming' and after having being used only twice was abandoned in favour of a more streamlined two-stage approach.[300]

Under the revised procedure the delegation was asked to prepare a draft report, accompanied 'if appropriate by additional background material for the Committee's consideration', which would then be considered and adopted within the space of a single plenary meeting following a paragraph by paragraph examination.[301] This procedure operated from 1990 until 1996 when a further refinement was adopted to speed up the Committee's business. The current arrangement is that the draft report prepared by the delegation is circulated to all members roughly two weeks in advance of a plenary meeting and is formally agreed without discussion at the meeting unless a member gives notice requesting discussion of a particular paragraph. This procedure has reduced the average discussion time devoted to individual reports from one to two hours to five to ten minutes[302] and has certainly assisted the CPT in acheiving its aim to transmit visit reports to the governments concerned within six months of visits taking place.[303] This target was until 1995 honoured more often in the breach,[304] but seems now to be within the Committee's capability.

Although more efficient, the current procedure significantly reduces the likelihood of CPT members being conversant with reports other than those that they have been involved in preparing. Conversely, it probably means that *ad hoc* experts are more fully involved in the preparation of the report that will finally be transmitted. It is not known how often CPT members question the reports now submitted to plenary sessions for formal approval, but there must be a suspicion that the plenary body is becoming little more than a rubber stamp and that this procedure transfers even more influence and control into the hands of the Secretariat.

The current procedure is held to satisfy the requirement that the Committee take account of any observations that the state party may have on the Committee's preliminary findings, since the state will have been told of them at the conclusion of the visit (including any immediate observations under Article 8(5)) and—as many published reports

---

[300] Gen Rep 1, para 70.   [301] ibid.

[302] Interview with Bureau, Sept 1996.   [303] Gen Rep 1, para 71.

[304] The average delay between completing visits and transmitting reports to the governments concerned was 8.5 months in 1990, 8 months in 1991, 10 months in 1992, 8.1 months in 1993, 7 months in 1994 (if two very brief *ad hoc* reports are excepted) and 5.6 months in 1995.

testify—states do frequently correspond with the CPT before the visit report is adopted.[305]

Reports are transmitted in confidence to states party and may only be published if publication is authorized by them,[306] in which event the Committee is obliged to publish the report 'together with any comments of the Party concerned, whenever requested to do so by that Party'.[307] When the ECPT first came into force it was widely anticipated that few of the Committee's reports would ever see the light of day, since few governments would authorize publication. This pessimism has proved to be unjustified. Because some time typically elapses between the CPT undertaking a visit and transmitting its report, and the State party authorizing publication, it is never possible to be certain whether and when reports will be published until publication occurs. However, of those long-standing CPT state parties that are now in the course of receiving second or subsequent visits, only Turkey has so far failed to authorize publication of its reports, although Cyprus did so very belatedly.[308] Moreover, of those Central and East European members which have ratified the Convention since 1993, the trend is to follow the dominant precedent already established.[309] Publication has become the norm, which means that all eyes, and thus suspicion, is focused on those few countries that fail, or protractedly delay, publication.

The manner in which reports have been published varies widely and we can distinguish four responses to date: first are those states which authorize publication very soon after they receive the report, normally some six to nine months after the visit;[310] second are those states which

---

[305] Thus, to take two recent examples: the prison authorities in England and Wales wrote to Strasbourg in June 1994—that is within a month of the Committee's second *periodic* visit and six months before the CPT agreed its report—saying that all Home Office prisoners had been removed from Liverpool Bridewell (see n 282 above) and reporting that all police forces had been written to requesting that they avoid holding prisoners three-to-a-cell (UK 3, para 12); the Bulgarian authorities informed Strasbourg in June 1995—that is, two months after the CPT's first *periodic* visit to Bulgaria, and three months before the CPT agreed their report on Bulgaria—of a number of measures taken in response to the delegation's immediate observations (Bulgaria 1, para 13).

[306] Article 11(1).   [307] Article 11(2).

[308] Cyprus was visited in November 1992 and again in May 1996. Not until May 1997, however, were the reports from both visits pubished.

[309] By the end of 1997 reports on Bulgaria, Hungary, and Slovakia had been published. Romania, however, has not authorized publication of the Report arising from the CPT's visit in Sept–Oct 1995. If it does not appear soon, the publication of the Report on the visit to Poland in June–July 1996 might also be considered increasingly unlikely, despite it having been reported to the CAT on 20 Nov 1996 that Poland had 'no reason not to authorize publication' of the report which it had clearly already received (CAT/C/SR.277, para 16).

[310] Some states have adopted the stance of asserting that their commitment to open government is such that they undertake, during the course of CPT visits, to publish immediately any CPT report sent to them, irrespective of its contents. Sweden adopts this position (interviews with officials, Stockholm, June 1995).

authorize publication simultaneously with their response, which may take place a considerable time (eighteen months to two years after the visit is typical);[311] third are those states which for reasons that are usually obscure and no doubt vary, authorize publication of the CPT report, and possibly their response, long after they were received from Strasbourg and their responses submitted to Strasbourg;[312] and finally there are those countries that after a very long interval have not authorized publication —currently only Turkey—though, given the third category, it is always possible that Turkey may yet authorize publication.

If a state party fails to co-operate or refuses to improve the situation found by the CPT in the light of the Committee's recommendations, the Committee may decide to make a Public Statement on the matter, but only if there is a two-thirds majority of the Committee in favour of doing so.[313] In these circumstances it is not the report itself which is made public, but a statement concerning the failure to co-operate or improve the situation: the report itself remains confidential.[314]

The Public Statement is the only official sanction that the Committee weilds, but the Committee may only resort to this 'exceptional' measure 'after the State concerned has had an opportunity to make known its views'. Moreover, before deciding to issue a Public Statement the Committee 'should pay full regard to any difficulties' which might contribute to the state's refusal to improve the situation.[315] These requirements imply that the CPT must allow sufficient time for the state concerned to respond to, or take action in response to, the Committee's 'recommendations', which raises the question as to how the Committee's recommendations fit into the structure of CPT reports.

The form of CPT reports has changed very little since the first were written and published in 1990–1. Reports are clearly written with a view to publication. Virtually all *periodic* reports open with a summary overview of the CPT and its procedures (including the principal differences

[311] This group includes the UK whose officials argue that simultaneous publication ensures that journalists and other interested parties are thereby in receipt of both the CPT's findings and recommendations *and* the Government's *considered* responses to those findings and recommendations (interviews with British Foreign Office and English Home Office officials at various times).

[312] In the case of Spain publication took place five years after the first periodic visit. The reports resulting from the first three visits to Spain—in 1991, 1994, and 1994 respectively— were not published until March 1996, and were published in a single volume together with the Spanish Government's responses to the 1994 visits. This was done shortly after the change of government which resulted from the Spanish General Election in February 1996 and was probably motivated by domestic political factors. See also Cyprus, n 308 above.

[313] Article 10(2).

[314] The CPT has a 'wide discretion in deciding what information to be made public' (Explanatory Report, para 75), which presumably means that the discretion could stretch to revealing the conclusions of the report, if not a substantial proportion of text itself.

[315] Explanatory Report, para 74.

between the CPT and the European Commission and Court of Human Rights) and a section setting out the details of the visit, including the institutions visited and an enumeration of those individuals or goups with whose representatives consultations were held (now generally included in an Appendix). The level of co-operation exhibited by the state custodial agencies with whom the delegations dealt is always described and there is customarily a section setting out the relevant administrative and legal provisions relating to custody in the country concerned (sometimes provided in an Appendix). The meat of the report—the findings leading to the recommendations—now takes the following order. First, in relation to police[316] custodial establishments: torture and other types of physical ill-treatment; conditions of detention; and safeguards against the ill-treatment of persons deprived of their liberty, including access toa lawyer, the conduct of interrogations, medical screening, and so on. Much the same trajectory is then pursued in relation to prisons (though here, following the sections on torture and other types of ill-treatment, and custodial conditions, the range of issues covered is rather less regimented than is normally the case in relation to police custody), psychiatric hospitals, young offender detention facilities, holding centres for aliens, military establishments, or whatever other type of institution has been visited. Reports following *ad hoc* and *follow-up* visits draw on the relevant elements of this presentational framework.

All of these report sections describe in some detail what the Committee has found, reiterates what the Committee expects to find or wishes to see in place—that is to say, the substance of the matters discussed in Chapters 6 to 8—and moves then to what we may term the Committee's 'operative' elements—labelled 'recommendations', 'comments', and 'requests for information'—which are always reiterated in an Appendix to the Report. The distinction between these three operative terms is important because the Convention refers only to 'recommendations'—failure to respond to which might trigger the Article 10(2) procedure and result in the issuing of a Public Statement—whereas 'comments' and 'requests for information' have a lesser status: the Committee *hopes* that the member state will respond positively to them. The Article 10(2) procedure is only resorted to when co-operation breaks down and (as intended) has so far only been used exceptionally—twice, on both occasions in relation to Turkey.[317] Whereas visit reports are in most instances lengthy documents of up to 100 or more pages (though brief *ad hoc* visits typically result in commensurately brief reports), the two Public Statements so far issued

---

[316] 'Police' is here taken to include security forces that may have a variety of names, including gendarmerie, militia, civil guards, and various types of detective or investigative agencies.
[317] December 1992 and December 1996.

have been short documents[318] tersely setting out the facts of the grave ill-treatment found and the failure of the state party to implement the central recommendations made in an effort to prevent it.

6 DIALOGUE CONDUCTED FOLLOWING VISITS

The ECPT is designed to prevent ill-treatment through co-operative dialogue between the CPT and the member states. Thus the Committee sees the transmission of visit reports to states as the beginning rather than the end of a process[319] and it has decided that the best way to proceed thereafter is to request the government of the country concerned to report back to the CPT on the measures taken to implement the Committee's recommendations:

The State concerned is expected to give an account not only of any legislative and administrative measures taken, if any, but also of the implementation, in actual practice, of the Committee's recomendations.[320]

In fact, as we have observed throughout this chapter, state/CPT dialogue of a sort precedes visits, is engaged in during the course of visits, and is often embarked on through correspondence before the CPT drafts or agrees visit reports. Indeed, because issues are pressed by presence of a delegation and the imminent timing of the report, this latter stage in the process may be the most effective in gaining a response. Nevertheless the substance of the dialogue begins with the government's response to visit reports.

Following a *periodic* visit, states are requested to submit an *interim* response within six months of receipt, to be followed by a *final* response within twelve months.[321] There is some variation in practice with regard to reports arising from *ad hoc* and *follow-up* visits, presumably reflecting the nature of the concerns that motivated the visits and what it revealed.[322] It is within the context of the timetable thus established that the CPT

---

[318] Ten pages (Turkey PS1) and six pages (Turkey PS2) respectively.
[319] Gen Rep 1, para 33.   [320] ibid, para 32.   [321] ibid, para 33.
[322] For example, following the 1994 visits to Spain and France and the 1997 visits to Sweden and Norway, the Committee requested a single response, to be submitted within six months of receipt of the report (see the letters of transmission published in France 2, Spain 3, Sweden 2, and Norway 2). In the wake of its 1992 visit to Spain, the Committee asked for an initial response within three months, to be followed by a second response at twelve months (letter of transmision, Spain 2). In other instances, the standard request for an interim report at six months and a follow-up report after twelve months has been made (eg France (Martinique) 1, Netherlands Antilles 1, Netherlands Aruba 1, and UK 3—although in this latter case the UK decided to submit only a single, 'Final' response (UK 3 R)). It seems that the practice of requesting a single response within six months of an *ad hoc* or *follow up* visit emerged in 1994 when the number of such visits increased dramatically with the ending of the first round of *periodic* visits. It is reasonable to speculate that many (but not necessarily all) of subsequent and unpublished *ad hoc*-visit reports make similar requests.

engages in the (ideally) co-operative dialogue with member states which is at the heart of the ECPT methodology.

As at the end of 1997, 44 visit reports, 38 interim reports and 17 follow-up reports have been published.[323] Analysis of the extent and quality of post-report dialogue between the CPT and the member states is difficult because, as these figures suggest, although virtually all states have authorized publication of visit reports and have revealed elements of the post-report responses and communication, less than half have published both their *interim* and *final* responses[324] and only six have published other correspondence relating to CPT reports and their own responses.[325] It follows that the quantity and the quality of the dialogue between a considerable number of states and the CPT is largely hidden and in most cases it is partially so.

It is apparent from responses that have been published that most states have met the deadlines set by the CPT for *interim* and *final* responses. However, a minority have failed to do so, some conspicuously so.[326] The CPT has described this as particularly unsatisfactory when it concerns an *interim* report since this is sometimes the first official response of any kind. The Committee has warned that 'an excessive delay in providing an interim report' could lead the Committee to issue a public statement under Article 10(2).[327] In fact this appears not to have occurred. Only two public statements have been published, both relating to Turkey. Though Turkey has failed to authorize for publication any documents (the CPT's or their own), both public statements seem to have been triggered by the CPT's repeated findings of torture and other forms of ill-treatment and the *content* of the Turkish response—that is, the authorities' failure to take preventive actions—rather than their failure to submit responses.

---

[323] See Appendix 5A and 5B.

[324] Of those countries visited up to the end of 1995 (the publication of whose materials might reasonably be expected) only Turkey and Romania have not authorized publication of reports; San Marino and Cyprus have published reports but no responses, and Austria, Spain, Germany, Portugal, Italy, the Netherlands, Luxembourg, Leichenstein, UK, France, and Malta have on at least one occasion published only one response to a visit. See Appendix 5A and 5B.

[325] See Table 5.3 below. In 1995–6 we visited or wrote to every CPT liaison officer in countries which had been visited as part of the first round of CPT visits in 1990–4 requesting copies of *interim* or *final* responses not then published, or correspondence from or to Strasbourg relating to the CPT report on their country. Only three governments—Norway, Denmark, and Germany—responded with hitherto unpublished material. Norway provided copies of correspondence still not published. Denmark provided copies of responses and correspondence: the former have since been published. Germany provided a copy of their *final* (or *follow-up* response) which remains unpublished: the German explanation for not publishing this document was that they did not think it sufficiently interesting. We must presume that governments are just as likely to refuse to make either unpublished formal responses or correspondence available to interested domestic NGOs as they were to us.

[326] See also Gen Rep 5, para 10; Gen Rep 6, para 10.   [327] Gen Rep 6, para 10.

Three aspects of the dialogue in which the CPT engages need high-lighting. First, the extent of the hidden nature of much of the dialogue. Secondly, the variable quality of the response of state parties. Thirdly, the less than adequate CPT response to state responses.

(a) The hidden dialogue

As outlined above, the record of publication of state responses to CPT reports is one of less than complete openness. The extent of the dialogue between most governments and the CPT is partially hidden and in a few cases it is largely so. However, because the CPT drafts its reports in the light of, and as part of, an ongoing dialogue and flow of information, it is possible to discern more of the dialogue than is deliberately revealed. For example, if the Committee undertakes an *ad hoc* visit because information has been received that ill-treatment is occurring in a particular place of custody, then that trigger is invariably cited at the beginning of the report.[328] Equally, if the CPT is returning to follow up a concern established as a result of an earlier visit, and because the Committee is not satisfied either that the government concerned is taking the situation sufficiently seriously, or that whatever initiatives may have been adopted are insufficient to remedy the situation, then those developments and concerns are typically cited in the report.[329] It follows that even if the government concerned has not authorized publication of an earlier part of that ongoing dialogue, that dialogue nevertheless informs, and is frequently cited in, the subsequent CPT report which invariably *is* published. It would of course be more satisfactory were all state parties to make available the whole of the dialogue, but the assiduous observer is usually able to discern the principal contours of this hidden landscape.

[328] For example, the CPT's visit to Northern Ireland in 1993 was triggered by receipt of 'a number of reports containing allegations of ill-treatment of persons suspected of offences related to terrorism by the security forces'. In 1991 the Committee was sufficiently concerned by these reports to invoke Rule 30 and: 'There followed an exchange of correspondence in the course of which the Committee was inter alia made aware of measures taken by the United Kingdom authorities with a view to "allaying fears and ensuring that adequate safeguards exist for the individual".' Further reports containing allegations of ill-treatment were received, however, and thus the decision was made to conduct an *ad hoc* visit (UK 2, paras 4–7).

[329] Thus the *follow-up* visit to Sweden in 1994 to further investigate the use of restrictions on pre-trial detainees at the Stockholm Remand Prison had been preceded by an 'ongoing dialogue with the Swedish authorities on these matters—a dialogue which has been facilitated by the submission to the Committee of a response and follow-up report by the Swedish Government . . . nevertheless, [the Committee] continued to receive information which suggests that conditions in Stockholm Remand Prison had not improved to the extent which the Committee would have wished' (Sweden 2, para 5). It is apparent, therefore, that the dialogue with the Swedish authorities comprised more than the published Swedish response and follow-up reports.

Cyprus is a case in point. As will be seen in Chapter 6, Cyprus was visited in 1992 and substantial evidence of severe ill-treatment and torture was uncovered. The political embarrassment attending this finding doubtless influenced the decision not to publish the first CPT report until five years later, together with the much more favourable second CPT report arising out of the visit in 1996. Despite the fact that the responses to the first visit have not been published, the second CPT report makes repeated references to either the content of the Cypriot responses to the first report, or to actions taken as a result of that first report, or to the CPT's reactions to the Cyprus Government's responses to the first report.[330]

Of course, it is entirely possible that the substance of an unpublished report, or of the government's response to a report, may enter the public domain via another route. Once again, Cyprus provides a good example. The bulk of the section of the CPT's report concerning police custody was leaked to the Cypriot press and printed verbatim. Moreover, the second periodic report of Cyprus to the UNCAT contains a section headed 'Action taken in response to recommendations of the European Committee for the Prevention of Torture'.[331] Admittedly, this report was submitted just after publication of the CPT Report on its first visit had been authorized, but it is illustrative of the cross-fertilization of information flows that can come about and which may develop in the future.[332] In at least one case, a statement before the UNCAT has revealed something of an unpublished report: the representative of Poland observed that the unpublished CPT report 'had not noted any systematic practice of

---

[330] For example, the CPT had recommended that there be established an independent inquiry into the allegations of torture uncovered, (Cyprus 1, para 22). This was done, and we know that the CPT was informed of its contents, since the report, upholding the CPT's findings, is quoted in the second CPT report (Cyprus 2, para 9). Or, to take another example, in its first report the CPT had made a number of recommendations concerning fundamental safeguards for persons held in police custody. In the second report the Committee considered that 'the responses of the Cypriot authorities . . . did not remove all the doubts entertained by the Committee in this field; consequently, these issues were pursued further by the CPT during the second periodic visit' (Cyprus 2, para 36). It is evident that the Cypriot authorities had responded to the Committee's recommendation that a code of conduct for police interrogations be drawn up by referring to 'Administrative Instructions which are the subject of lectures at the Police academy' because the second CPT report records that the CPT found that these 'administrative instructions did not appear to be widely known' (ibid, para 44). To take a more positive example, in its first report the CPT had recommended the introduction of comprehensive custody records for use in police stations. We know that the Cypriot authorities replied that such a record had been formulated and introduced in July 1994 (ibid, para 46) as the Committee noted that this was indeed so (ibid, para 47).

[331] CAT/C/33/Add.1, para 40.

[332] For example, Sweden referred to the CPT's criticism of conditions at the Krononberg Remand Prison before the UNCAT (see CAT/C/SR.292, para 13) and Denmark submitted the (already published) Report of the CPT on its visit to Denmark in Sept–Oct 1996 to the UNCAT alongside its third periodic report in 1997 (see CAT/C/SR.287, para 3).

torture or ill-treatment during its mission'.[333] Although these collateral sources might throw some light on the content and response to CPT reports, it is the process of dialogue between the CPT and the state which is critical to an evaluation of the ECPT as a mechanism and which must be examined in its own right.

(b) The quality of state responses

To the extent that they are known, the formal written responses of member States to CPT reports have been of extremely variable quality. Some governments have met the CPT's time limits for interim and final responses and have produced systematic and detailed replies to almost every recommendation, comment, and request for information made by the Committee. Other member states have been tardy in their replies and the content of some has scarcely been worth the wait.[334] There is no simple way of classifying all government responses, but a number of examples will serve to illustrate the qualitative range involved.

The Scandinavian governments tend to pride themselves on their openness and all have published their responses to all CPT visits in full. The viewpoint expressed by Swedish Ministry of Justice and Foreign Affairs officials with whom we have met is probably typical. Their ministers had given undertakings to the CPT that publication of the report would be authorized upon receipt, irrespective of its content. This course of action has indeed been followed by Sweden after both the first *periodic* visit[335] and following the second brief *ad hoc* visit in August 1994.[336] The Swedish responses to the first visit were very detailed. The *interim* response to the 1991 report, for example, comprises sixty-five pages and contains subheadings and answers to every recommendation, comment, and request for information contained in the CPT report. Moreover, the answers to many of the requests for information contain statistics, or make references

[333] CAT/C/SR.277, para 16, 20 Nov 1996.

[334] Outstanding examples of published responses which are quite inadequate are the responses to the first visits to Greece and Bulgaria, both of which simply ignore findings of risks of ill-treatment.

[335] The report arising out of the visit to Sweden in May 1991 was adopted by the Committee and transmitted to Stockholm in February 1992. It was published in March 1992 and in August 1992 the Swedish authorities submitted their written response which was published by the Council of Europe in October. A follow-up report from the Swedish authorities was transmitted to the CPT in February 1993 and published the following month. See Table 5.3 below.

[336] On this occasion the CPT took seven months to complete and transmit their report— a surprisingly long delay given that it was only 17 pages in length—and the Swedish authorities' undated and even briefer response (14 pages of double-spaced script) was published seven months afterwards in October 1995.

to statutory or procedural provisions which go to the heart of the CPT's concerns. The Swedish authorities have attached importance to the CPT's reports: they clearly see it as their obligation to answer criticisms and questions promptly and with due seriousness.

A similar approach has been taken by the British government, albeit the sequence of response and publication has been different. The British authorities take the view that it is inappropriate to authorize publication of their CPT reports—of which there have now been three[337]—before the response has been carefully considered and is also ready for publication.[338] The publication of CPT reports on the United Kingdom has therefore taken place between one and two years after a visit has taken place[339] with the responses being published at the same time. The British responses have been if anything longer and more and detailed than those of Sweden. They are replete with statistics, administrative details, and references to legal provisions and, as is noted elsewhere in this text, they sometimes challenge the CPT's use of terminology and on occasion argue why a particular recommendation cannot or should not be implemented.[340]

A rather different response is exhibited by the German example. Germany was visited in December 1991, the CPT report transmitted to the German authorities ten months later in October 1992, but not published until July 1993 when the German authorities also made available their response.[341] No further response has been published, but a follow-up report was sent to Strasbourg in May 1994 (some seven months after the date by which its submission had been requested). This report, which is of almost derisory length,[342] was given to us by Federal officials in Bonn in autumn 1995 who explained that it was unpublished not because it was regarded as confidential but because it was thought unlikely to be of any interest to anyone. If this is to be understood as suggesting it was not worthy of publication, it is a judgment with which it would be hard to disagree.

The initial German response is, however, little better. Although at seventy-seven pages it is relatively long and formally addresses all the recommendations and requests posed by the CPT, several German commentators have noted that it does little more than go through the motions,

[337] A fourth CPT visit to the United Kingdom took place in September 1997. No report had appeared at the time of writing.
[338] British officials with whom we have spoken argue that they must be in a position to answer in full any criticisms within the reports that are likely to attract questions from the mass media as and when those questions are put.
[339] The delays were 15 months, 16 months, and 22 months respectively in the case of the visits in August 1990, July 1993, and May 1994.
[340] See, for example, Chapter 7, pp. 278 n 126, 279, 289 n 205, 291 n 219 and 294 n 241.
[341] The German response was first published by the Council of Europe in German and eight months later, in March 1994, in English.
[342] Nine double-spaced pages with large sub-headings and wide margins.

skirting round rather than answering many points.[343] This reaction would appear to reflect two factors. First, many of the policy issues posed by the CPT are for the *Länder* to decide and are matters about which the Federal ministries have little knowledge or interest. To that extent, Federal officials had merely collated material sent to them from the *Länder* officials.[344] In other cases the Federal Government merely passed on the opinions apparently transmitted to them by *Länder* officials, or report different *Länder* practices.[345] However, in addition to an apparent inability to reply responsibly to the CPT there also appears to be an undercurrent of hostility to CPT procedures and resistance to the Committee's findings

---

[343] See Feest, J and Wolters, C (1994) *Verhutung von Folter und unmenschlicher Behandlung oder Strafe—Ergebnisse einer Bestandsaufnahme und zugleich Enschätzung des Berichtes des CPT über seinen ersten Besuch in Deutschland und der dazu vorliegenden Stellungnahme der Bundesregierung* (Geneva: Asociation for the Prevention of Torture); Bank, R (1996) *Die internationale Bekämpfung von Folter und unmenschlicher Behandlung auf den Ebenen der Vereinten Nationen und des Europarates—Eine vergleichende Analyse von Implementation und Effektivität der neuen Kontrollmechanismen*, Doctoral Thesis, Max Planck Institute for Foreign and Inernational Penal Law, Freiburg; Bank, R (1997) 'International Efforts to Combat Torture and Inhuman Treatment: Have the New Mechanisms Improved Protection?', 8 EJIL (forthcoming). Thus, for example, with reference to the practice of punishing prisoners with loss of exercise following disciplinary proceedings in contravention of the European Prison Rules, Rule 86, a practice regarded as unacceptable by the CPT (Germany 1, para 159), the German response, in a masterpiece of equivocation, maintains that: 'commentators understand [the disciplinary provision for] "deprivation or restriction of time spent outdoors" . . . to mean not deprivation or restriction of all outdoor exercise, but rather limitation of *communal* outdoor exercise with other prisoners . . . [the] restriction could be satisfied by the hour of individual outdoor exercise. This view is not, however, without its dissenters.' (Germany 1, R 1, 39). Who the 'commentators' are, and who the 'dissenters', is not elaborated. One German expert we interviewed interpreted this explanation as follows: 'Most of the Länder agree that this disciplinary punishment is inappropriate and they don't use it. But one Land disagrees—everyone knows that that Land is Bavaria, though it is not named —because Bavaria thinks the punishment is useful education. So the German Federal authorities are not going to do anything about it. That is the usual Bonn stance. Bonn is little more than a mail box.'

[344] Thus in response to the CPT's customary request for information about the number of complaints of ill-treatment at the hands of the police made in Germany during recent years, and disciplinary or criminal proceedings taken as a result (Germany 1, para 20), the German authorities maintain that 'seven Federal Länder report neither complaints of ill-treatment . . . nor corresponding disciplinary or criminal proceedings' and provide details of a small number of disciplinary proceedings against, or criminal convictions of, police officers in the nine other *Länder*. However, no information is provided as to how many complaints led to these proceedings, nor are the time periods within which the proceedings were brought indicated, nor are the *Länder* concerned identified (Germany 1 R 1, 3–6).

[345] Thus, for example, with reference to the CPT's oft-repeated right of suspects detained in police custody to be examined by a doctor of their choice, and for medical examinations preferably to be conducted out of the sight and hearing of police officers (Germany 1, paras 36–8), the German authorities report that 'the doctors appointed by the police can be relied on' though 'some Länder permit—*after* the examination by the police doctor—on the detainees request, examination by a doctor of the detainee's choice and at his own expense' (Germany 1 R 1, 8). As for examinations out of sight or hearing, security considerations determine that 'a general rule does not seem to be appropriate and is unanimously rejected in practice' (ibid, 9).

and recommendations in the German response.[346] It is unclear whether this resistance has its origins in Bonn or at *Länder* level.The response to the CPT's Report on its second periodic visit to Germany, published in July 1997 is, perhaps, more systematic but is equally uncompromising in its rejection of key recommendations.[347]

(c) The Response of the CPT

The third critical factor concerns the contribution of the CPT to the post-reporting dialogue. This is the area about which least is known but the CPT has confessed that it is 'far from satisfied with its own record as regards the on-going dialogue'.[348] The Committee maintains that the explanation lies in the inadequacy of its Secretariat resources. The Committee admits that it does not respond as rapidly as it thinks it should to the *interim* and *follow-up* reports from governments and, when combined with the increasing interval between visits, this delay may undermine the credibility of the Convention. The appearance is created that there is little stress placed on monitoring whether recommendations are implemented or not. Thus, the Committee suggests, 'in the absence of a sustained post-visit on-going dialogue, the momentum for change generated by a visit will almost certainly be frittered away.'[349] The Council of Europe Parliamentary Assembly, clearly prompted by the CPT, has recently underlined the problem.[350]

The difficulty with this self-confessed shortcoming is that it is not clear to what degree the follow-up by the Committee to state responses is deficient either in terms of timeliness, quantity, or quality. Because few countries have authorized the publication of, or been willing to make

---

[346] For example, with regard to the CPT's repetition of allegations made to the delegation of ill-treatment of prisoners in Tegel and Straubing Prisons (Germany 1, paras 64 and 66) the response noted that the delegation did not raise these allegations during its visit, which would have enabled immediate investigations to be carried out and would have given the authorities the opportunity to report the results of inquiries already completed (Germany 1 R 1, 2) With regard to the CPT's recommendations regarding the fundamental rights of detainees in police custody, it is asserted that 'it seems neither possible nor practicable to compile a list of all possible constellations of cases' in which third-party notification of custody might be denied or delayed (ibid, 7) when it is clear that such an elaborate exercise is not being requested (Germany 1, para 35). There are other examples of what appear to be almost perverse misunderstandings.

[347] Substantive aspects of the German response to CPT recommendations are considered at relevant points in Chapters 7 and 8.

[348] Gen Rep 5, para 10.   [349] ibid.

[350] 'As a result of workload problems at the level of its Secretariat, the Committee has continued to experience great difficulties in responding in good time to interim and follow-up reports presented by states. In the Committee's view this is all the more worrying given the fact that the interval between periodic visits is considerably longer than the Committee would wish' (CLAHR Report (1997), para 23).

Table 5.3 Sample schedules of CPT visit reporting

Country	Visit	Report	R 1	CPT comments	R 2
Denmark	Dec 1990	July 1991	Jan 1992[a]	Sept 1993	July 1992[b]
UK	July–Aug 1990	Mar 1991	Sept 1991	Oct 1992[c]	Mar 1993
Sweden	May 1991	Mar 1992	Aug 1992	Jan 1993	Feb 1993
France	Oct–Nov 1991	June 1992	Jan 1993	June 1993	Jan 1994
Finland	May 1992	Feb 1993	Aug 1993	Dec 1993	Feb 1994
Ireland	Sept–Oct 1993	June 1994	Nov 1995	Apr 1996	Sept 1996

[a] In Mar 1992 the Danish authorities also submitted copies of independent judicial inquiry reports into the deaths of two prisoners, as originally requested by the CPT.

[b] In Sept 1994 the CPT reminded the Danish authorities by letter that their Sept 1993 report contained questions to which no answers had yet been received. The letter also requested information on a recent matter not arising out of the 1990 visit.[351]
In Jan 1995 the Danish authorities sent to Strasbourg information supplementary to their interim and follow-up reports in reply to CPT's letters of Sept 1993 and Sept 1994. This incuded information on a matter not arising out of the 1990 visit.

[c] Although this letter is dated 6 Oct 1992, UK 1 R 2, para 1 says it was received in November 1992.

available, their intermittent correspondence with the CPT,[352] few reliable conclusions can be drawn from that part of the record that has been made available. Table 5.3 sets out a number of known patterns relating to *periodic* visits.

In addition to the deadlines for *interim* and *final* responses stipulated in all CPT reports—responses in which state parties are asked how they intend to implement the CPT's recommendations—it seems to be general practice for the CPT to send comments on *interim* responses before *final* (or *follow-up*) reponses are recieved. Why this did not happen in the case of Denmark is not clear: it is possible that the practice had not become established at that early stage in the life of the Committee.[353] Because we

[351] This concerned police use of the so-called 'leg lock' for the restraint of arrestees and is likely to have arisen out of a report from Amnesty International, *Denmark: Police Ill-Treatment* (London: International Secretariat) published in June 1994 which was also a focus of discussion when Denmark's second periodic report (CAT/C/17/Add.13) was considered by the UNCAT in Nov 1994 (see CAT/C/SR.228, paras 21 and 34–5).

[352] Examples of such correspondence is included as an Appendix to the follow-up reports of the following *periodic* visits: UK 1 R 2, France 1 R 2, Sweden 1 R 2, Finland 1 R 2, Denmark 1 R 2, and Ireland 1 R 2. The documents sent to us by the Norwegian authorities, which have not been published, suggest that the sequence with respect to that country was similar to that for Denmark, Norway also having fully complied with the CPT's request that an *interim* and *follow-up* response be sent to Strasbourg within six and twelve months respectively.

[353] A full 14 months elapsed—a period longer than that given to state parties—before the CPT transmitted formal comments (we have no evidence of informal contacts having taken place in the interim, although it is quite possible that this was the case) on the Danish interim and follow-up reports.

do not have the evidence we do not know how exceptional the Danish sequence is, or indeed how typical are the other sequences recorded in Table 5.3. The following regular features are noteworthy, however. First, the CPT's reports arising out of visits are produced relatively slowly and, given their standardized format and, as we shall see in Chapters 6, 7, and 8, because large substantial chunks of them comprise routine repetition of CPT core standards, they could and should be produced, agreed, and transmitted much faster. Secondly, the authorities which have authorized full disclosure of information have usually responded in detail but frequently not within the time-scale requested by the CPT. Given that the CPT's own comments on *interim* responses are not swiftly dispatched following their receipt, and given that state parties might be expected— or, indeed, requested—to respond to issues raised, this is not surprising. It might also explain why the Committee has been reluctant to criticize some states which have overshot the suggested time-limits for delivery of responses: the CPT's own performance is at best no better and at worst might be a factor contributing to the delay.

Once the *final* response has been received, there are few indications of the extent to which a further round of dialogue occurs, Denmark's unusual example being the only one in the public domain.[354] It is possible that no further communication takes place prior to the next visit. Of course, it is also possible that an *ad hoc* or *follow-up* visit might become superimposed on the dialogue arising out of a *periodic* visit, in which case a more complex picture emerges. But even in these cases the nature of the second visit might be such that the dialogue arising out of it does not have an impact on the bulk of the concerns raised in the pre-existing dialogue: it may comprise a parallel rather than a complementary exercise, though it is to be expected that the threads of all ongoing dialogues will be picked up in the subsequent *periodic* report. Nevertheless, the lengthening gap between such visits can mean that these threads are left dangling for a considerable period of time. If the CPT, in saying that it is dissatisfied with its own performance regarding the degree of follow-up

---

[354] In the case of Denmark, where the letter was sent after receipt of the follow-up report, the CPT placed no great stress on receiving a further response at all: at seven points in the letter it was said that the CPT would like to be informed of any developments or would like a copy of some document when it appears, with no suggestion of a time-scale. It is not surprising, therefore, that a year later the Danish authorities had not replied. We speculate, furthermore, that the CPT might not have sent a reminder letter a year later had a new issue and concern not arisen, an issue about which there had been international publicity. In fact the Danish authorities sent within four months a further detailed response answering all the original points and the new ones but, as far as we can ascertain, no further communication was exchanged until the CPT visited again, 18 months later, in early autumn 1996.

to state implementation of recommendations, is commenting both on the delay before it reacts, and possibly on its failure to react at all, then we agree wholeheartedly. On what is perhaps the most important of the formal criteria against which the work of the Committee can be assessed, it does not score particularly well.

6

Findings of Ill-Treatment

1 CPT REPORTS: THE POLITICAL REALITY

The first CPT report which is sent to a state begins with a preface re-printed from the First General Report of the Committee.[1] This stresses, *inter alia*, the following. First, that the CPT is not a judicial body and so it is not concerned with establishing as a matter of fact that breaches of treaty obligations regarding torture or inhuman or degrading treatment or punishment have occurred. Secondly, that the ECPT aims for 'conflict avoidance' not 'conflict solution' and so the CPT is concerned with pre-vention through a process of co-operation. Thirdly, it is stressed that the CPT is not bound by the case law of judicial or quasi-judicial bodies acting in the same field, though it can use that case law as a point of reference when assessing the treatment of persons in custody. Nevertheless, the questions which most readers of CPT reports initially have uppermost in their minds are: 'Did the Committee find torture?' or 'Did the Com-mittee conclude that there was inhuman or degrading treatment?' To this can be added the almost inevitable question: 'Which countries in Europe have the worst record for torture or inhuman or degrading treatment according to the CPT?'[2]

This is not surprising. Most NGOs concerned with aspects of custody spend much of their time dealing with complaints of ill-treatment from persons in custody and in many countries they face an inscrutable wall of silence or categorical denial from officials. In consequence, they look to the CPT for confirmation of what they have long suspected or believed. If the CPT finds that there is torture, or concludes that custodial condi-tions are 'inhuman or degrading', this is powerful evidence which serves to legitimate claims which they might have been making for some time but with little impact. For officials, parallel considerations apply. If a CPT report contains any suggestion that allegations of torture may be well-founded, or concludes that aspects of custody are, in the CPT's judgment, unacceptable, then pressure mounts. Certainly the NGOs, probably prac-tising lawyers and possibly parliamentarians, may use CPT reports as a

[1] Gen Rep 1, paras 1–6.
[2] Interviews conducted with NGO representatives and officials throughout Europe, as well as questions asked by lecture audiences, convincingly showed the truth of this observation.

tool which cannot easily be ignored. If, however, there are no such critical conclusions, observers pay CPT reports less attention and the matter becomes less critical for officials. Thus what most consumers of CPT reports seek to know is whether country X been given a clean bill of health or not? Was the 'T-word' used? Was anything 'I&D' found? CPT findings of ill-treatment are therefore critical for understanding the politics of the chain reaction which CPT reports do or do not evoke.[3]

Given the crucial nature of these findings, a number of subsidiary questions arise on which the attention of professional and lay readers of CPT reports is undeniably focused, irrespective of their 'non-judicial' character. These questions concern the manner in which the Committee arrives at its findings and the benchmarks it has set when assessing the circumstances it encounters. It may be that the Committee itself does not consider these questions, drawn as they are from the sphere of judicial reasoning, to be of particular importance given the Committee's preventive and non-judicial functions. However, the answers to these questions are not only important in their own right, but also have an impact upon the co-operation and dialogue with states which the Committee itself asserts to be central to its rationale and methodology.

As regards the first of these questions—the 'evidential' question of whether an act has taken place—the Committee has developed a set of criteria on the basis of which it determines the credibility of allegations of ill-treatment that it hears. However, it then turns this evaluation into a generalized risk assessment which is next weighted against the numbers of allegations in order to produce the all-important finding regarding the general risk of ill-treatment. In doing so it has produced what can be called a 'risk continuum' which is both difficult to penetrate and not particularly cogent or constructive since it introduces terminological nuances which are not understood by recipients and users of reports. Examining this continuum does help clarify the overall patterns of findings of ill-treatment found by the Committee and it is for this reason that it will be examined in section 3 of this chapter. However, in numerous instances the findings are qualified by a variety of factors which impair its usefulness even for this purpose, and this again calls the utility of the exercise into question. The general assessment criteria will be considered in section 2 and the 'allegation and risk continuum' in section 3. For reasons which will subsequently be explained, the 'risk continuum' is

---

[3] In this respect the reception given to CPT reports is no different from that given to reports emanating from other inspectorates. The broader purposes of the audit or inspection may be said to involve 'constructive dialogue' about 'good practices' and 'raising standards', but those persons most intimately involved are more concerned with the immediate out-turn and the consequences for their and their institution's reputation. Not to be given a stamp of approval causes challenge, disruption, and trouble.

chiefly used with regard to police custody; other approaches are adopted in other custodial settings and these will be considered in section 4.

As regards the second question—what forms of treatment or circumstances of detention are to be categorized as amounting to 'torture' or as being 'inhuman or degrading'?—the Committee has followed an equally unorthodox approach which, whilst reconcilable with established jurisprudence of the Court and Commission of Human Rights on given sets of facts, is in theoretical terms wholly at variance with them. It was argued in Chapter 3 that a determination based upon the 'severity of suffering' does not provide an appropriate framework for the CPT to develop its preventive mandate and is not in fact truly reflective of European jurisprudence in any case. To that extent, it is entirely appropriate that the CPT should have departed from this framework. However, it seems to have constructed an alternative which is equally inappropriate. This needs to be remembered when the findings of the CPT are drawn on by judicial bodies: the language may be the same but the usage is very different. This will be considered in sections 5 and 6 of this chapter. The final section will look at a number of particular problems of classification which have faced the CPT, and which might in part be a creation of its own methodology.

2 ESTABLISHING ILL-TREATMENT

Although the CPT has not given any public indication of its methodology as regards establishing ill-treatment, it is possible to deduce certain criteria from the published reports. One important factor, which will be considered further in section 3 of this chapter, concerns the allegations of ill-treatment which have been made. But allegations by themselves prove nothing and it is apparent that the CPT is not prepared to find that there is a risk of ill-treatment—in particular a risk of 'severe ill-treatment' or 'torture'—without a good deal of corroborative evidence. The Committee appears to adopt what may be termed a triangulation methodology: that is, they approach the question of ill-treatment from several angles, and if several indicators cross-check then the Committee is willing to be correspondingly firm in its finding. Where such evidence is lacking, the Committee's conclusions are typically couched in much more tentative terms.

In addition to the published reports, the description given by its first President, Antonio Cassese, sheds considerable light on the Committee's practice and, given his authority, deserves quoting at length. He writes, with regard to torture:[4]

----

[4] Cassese (1996), 76–9.

Decisive factors are: the details that prisoners can give on the methods their tormentors adopted; the accuracy of the account of the mental and physical reactions; whether they can give a description of the premises where they were ill-treated and specifically indicate the equipment in the room where they were subjected to torture. The degree of precision of these accounts, together with the prisoners' attitude while they recount their experience (facial expression, body language, and other particulars that will not escape the careful observer) may all contribute to an impression of veracity, or may reveal instead that the description is based on the experiences of others, or even on the fantasies of a lively imagination. Another valid test of truthfulness may lie in the concordance of separate accounts given by various inmates of the same prison, the same town and the same country. . . . The volume of these testimonies, and the details they may contain constitute compelling indicators, if not conclusive proof, of torture . . .

Naturally, each time we collected circumstantial evidence, we always tried to corroborate it by getting our doctors to make a careful examination of the victim. As a rule we subjected testimonies to minute and rigorous inquiry to ascertain their truthfulness. In many cases in which we were persuaded of this veracity, our doctors could find no physical trace of torture: this is quite normal since . . . police officers know how to inflict torments that leave no marks. In many other cases, however . . . our doctors found traces that concurred with the detainees' allegations. To be one hundred per cent certain that we had reached the right conclusions, every time one of our doctors stated that traces and symptoms that corroborated the prisoner's statement had been found, I called in at least one other doctor from our delegation (often two) to make a separate examination and accepted the findings of the former only if the others agreed with it. . . .

We also gave not a little credit to certificates issued by the medical officers of the countries we visited . . . In numerous cases these certificates confirmed the statements of the detainees . . .

Needless to say, and without much hope of success, we always searched for the places and instruments or torture . . . We were hardly ever successful. Yet in some specific cases, we managed to put our hands on something tangible.

Although it might be wondered whether so rigorous an approach is in truth either practical or, indeed, necessary for making a non-judicial finding, it is clear that the basic contours rather colourfully painted by Cassese are reflected in numerous examples found in published reports. A number of examples will be given which both confirm and amplify the approach taken.

(a) Austria

The CPT has produced two reports, from visits in 1990 and 1994, relating to Austria and to which reference has already been made. Both reports refer to 'considerable numbers' of allegations of ill-treatment and find the risk of ill-treatment to be 'not inconsiderable' or 'serious'. The evidence adduced in support of this conclusion was as follows:

1. A good many of the allegations were detailed and consistent and *independently* identified the site of much of the alleged ill-treatment, namely the interrogation holding cells of the Vienna Security Bureau (*Sicherheitsburo*) immediately adjacent to the Vienna Police Jail.[5]

2. In 1994 several of the prisoners alleging ill-treatment *independently* described their being threatened with electric shocks during questioning at the *Sicherheitsburo* offices and *all* of them *independently* described the same type of 'portable device, of the size of an electric razor with two electrodes at one end, which a police officer apparently carried in a personal bag'.[6]

3. The delegation visited the offices of the *Sicherheitsburo* and found two cells of the sort described by prisoners; although the cells were said by the police to be used exclusively for interrogation purposes, in fact the walls bore a considerable amount of elaborate graffiti, the only explanation for which, according to the police, was that prisoners might occasionally be left briefly alone while officers made telephone calls.[7]

4. In 1994 two prisoners alleging ill-treatment at the *Sicherheitsburo* and who were examined by one of the delegation's doctors bore 'marks and other medical signs' consistent with their allegations.[8]

5. The medical records of several prisoners alleging ill-treatment at the *Sicherheitsburo* in both 1990 and 1994 showed that they carried marks or injuries on their bodies at the relevant times consistent with their allegations.[9]

6. In 1990 the prison records at the Vienna Police Jail showed that two of the prisoners alleging ill-treatment at the *Sicherheitsburo* bore no visible injuries when released back into the custody of the police for further questioning, but did bear injuries when received back into the prison, and in 1994 several of the prison admission records showed that prisoners received from the *Sicherheitsburo* bore injuries consistent with their allegations.[10]

This evidence is multi-layered and relates to the number and quality of the allegations, the independence and precision of the descriptions, the medical *sequelae* found first-hand by the delegation's doctors, the corroborative evidence from medical records and, last but not least, the precise chronological support provided by some of the prison medical records, namely that the prisoners were not injured when released into the custody of the police, but were injured when they were re-admitted to the prison. In this instance the only type of evidence lacking was evidence unequivocally supporting ill-treatment that was manifest torture—

[5] Austria 1, para 42; Austria 2, para 13.   [6] Austria 2, para 15.
[7] Austria 1, para 47.   [8] Austria 2, para 17.
[9] Austria 1, para 45, Austria 2, para 17.   [10] ibid.

namely finding instruments of torture at the offices of the *Sicherheitsburo*, and marks on the bodies of any prisoners consistent with the allegation of being electrically shocked. This gap in the evidence would appear to explain why the CPT concluded that there was a serious risk of persons being 'ill-treated' in custody in Austria, but not 'tortured', since the record suggests that the CPT never comes to the latter conclusion without unequivocal medical evidence to support the contention.[11]

(b) Greece

The sort of evidence lacking in Austria *was* found in Greece in 1993.[12] During this visit the CPT interviewed separately five prisoners who alleged they had received electric shocks in a particular police station. Two of these prisoners described the device used as being 'a rod . . . some 40–50 cm in length with two small points at one end'.[13] When the delegation visited the police station concerned, and following a lengthy process of what can only be interpreted as prevarication by officers in the station, it discovered in the personal locker of an officer 'who had been identified to the delegation as someone who had inflicted electric shocks . . . a 29 cm long plastic rod equipped with two small electrodes at one end. The pressing of a button in the middle of the rod resulted in a spark passing between the electrodes'.[14] During the same mission to Greece allegations were also received of beatings with wooden sticks, and two detainees were found by medical members of the delegation to have 'contusions consistent with the allegations' of beating. It was significant, therefore, that the delegation discovered in the different offices of one police station:

a variety of wooden sticks and batons as well as a baseball bat. Police officers present offered a number of conflicting explanations for the presence of these objects. By the time of the delegation's second visit two days later, all the above-mentioned items had disappeared, a situation for which, once again, different reasons were proffered.[15]

In Greece, therefore, all the evidential ingredients sought by the CPT were present for a finding of a 'significant risk of being ill-treated, and that on occasion resort might be had to methods of severe ill-treatment/torture'.[16] In addition, the CPT has also made a similar finding in relation

---

[11] See below.
[12] Cassese (1996), 86–90, gives a fulsome account of this incident though without mentioning it as having taken place in Greece since, at the time it was written, the Greek Report had not been published. His account is so full of the contempt which he acknowledges he felt for those concerned, and whom he labels as torturers, that the general tenor of the Report regarding this discovery is easy to account for.
[13] Greece 1, para 21.   [14] ibid, para 22   [15] ibid.   [16] ibid, para 25.

to Cyprus and Bulgaria where, once again, the evidential ingredients which it sought were all in place.[17]

(c) Spain

Spain highlights most acutely the evidential test that the CPT appears to apply. In spite of there being many allegations of torture—allegations involving treatment that, if proved, everyone would undoubtedly agree is torture—the Committee was not persuaded that there was a risk of torture. In Spain the critical evidential elements for such a finding were lacking, at least until the third visit.

During their first visit to Spain in 1991 the CPT heard, in addition to allegations of torture, 'an extremely large number of allegations of *less severe forms of ill-treatment*'.[18] Two prisoners were found by the delegation's doctors to have injuries consistent with such 'rough treatment' (they had allegedly been kicked or hit with truncheons).[19] However, an interview with a prisoner alleging torture 'did not enable the delegation to reach a firm conclusion as to the veracity of his allegations',[20] and an inspection of those places of detention where torture had allegedly taken place 'offered little guidance as to the possible veracity of those reports'.[21] It seems clear that the Committee found no incriminating objects, that whatever circumstantial evidence might have been provided by these inspections came to nothing, and that none of the prisoners alleging torture offered corroborative medical evidence either first-hand or from records. As a result the CPT hedged its bets. The Committee acknowledged that during the fascist period there had been frequent recourse to: 'torture and severe ill-treatment when interrogating suspects' in Spain; and the Committee was 'satisfied that recourse to torture or other forms of severe ill-treatment . . . is no longer common practice'. However allegations of torture continued to be made and it would 'therefore be premature to conclude that the phenomena of torture and severe ill-treatment have been eradicated'.[22]

This conclusion was repeated following a further visit to Spain in April 1994. Further allegations of torture were received and, even though

---

[17] Cyprus 1, paras 13–21; Bulgaria 1, para 27. Once again, Cassese (1996), 79–82, provides a graphic account of the findings in Cyprus, without mentioning the country by name.

[18] Spain 1, para 21, emphasis in the original.   [19] ibid, paras 22 and 26.

[20] ibid, para 20; cf Cassese (1996), 77, who notes, without referring to Spain, that 'in one country, we were able to establish that the numerous claims of "political prisoners" to have been tortured, which—it is worth noting—were all made by people of the same persuasion, were highly suspect. In this case all the accounts were stereotyped, and the prisoners were unable to furnish us with any convincing details and particulars such as to give each story its "individual" character'.

[21] Spain 1, para 23.   [22] ibid, para 25.

some were supported by medical reports, the allegations were sufficiently stale for first-hand medical evidence not to be available to the delegation's doctors, and the written medical reports received were equivocal: the evidence was weak and did not fully support what was alleged.[23] Two months later, in what was the first visit of its type to any country, the CPT returned briefly to Spain to examine former detainees who alleged torture and who had very recently been in custody. After examining these persons closely, the Committee reported that the allegations were not 'stereotyped'—which, by implication, suggests that many previous allegations had been—and some first-hand medical evidence was found consistent with allegations which, though possibly 'somewhat exaggerated', had 'the ring of truth' about them.[24] For example, one prisoner who claimed he had been electrically shocked 'by means of a cylindrical device' applied to his 'left temple' had on his left temple:

two reddish and punctiform marks, surrounded by a slight desquamation, between 3 and 4 mm in diameter and about 12 mm apart. They were situated slightly above and towards the back of the left eyebrow. In aslant light, they were particularly visible. The two marks, of an entirely different character to the acneform marks which the person concerned also bore, were highly indicative of the application of electrodes.[25]

However, despite this and other medical evidence, the Committee remained cautious. The Committee was aware 'that persons arrested in relation to terrorist offences may make false allegations of ill-treatment'.[26] Moreover:

for many of the types of ill-treatment alleged, it is very difficult to obtain medical evidence of their use. For example, to demonstrate recourse to asphyxiation by the placing of a plastic bag over the head would require performing an arterial gasometry immediately after the event—an unlikely scenario. Similarly, the application of electric shocks will not necessarily leave physical marks, if carried out expertly. Nor will making someone stand for a prolonged period or perform physical exercises leave clearly identifiable traces of such treatment. Even blows to the body may leave only slight marks, difficult to observe and which quickly disappear, especially if inflicted with an open hand.[27]

The Committee therefore returned no finding as to the risk of being severely ill-treated or tortured in Spain and recommended that the Spanish authorities 'carry out, without delay, a general investigation of a thorough and independent nature into the methods used by the Civil Guard when holding and questioning persons arrested as presumed participants' in offences covered by the Spanish anti-terrorist preventive detention provisions.[28]

---

[23] Spain 2, paras 16–20.   [24] Spain 3, para 29.   [25] ibid, para 21.
[26] ibid, para 29.   [27] ibid, para 30.   [28] ibid, para 34.

(d) Turkey

It would be impossible to conclude this section without drawing on the findings of the Committee in Turkey, and which have led to two public statements. Although the gravity of the findings is not formally the trigger for making a public statement, it is evident that the decisions to make the public statements have been taken against the background of the allegations and evidence at the Committee's disposal and not simply the perceived lack of progress in the dialogue. The Committee collected such overwhelming first-hand evidence—including finding locations and instruments of torture as well as first-hand medical evidence—that it has returned a finding that torture in Turkey is 'widespread'.[29] The Committee records that on its first visit it was 'struck by the extremely large number of allegations . . . the wide range of persons making those allegations and their consistency. . . . The CPT's medical findings must also be emphasised . . . a considerable number of persons examined . . . displayed physical marks or conditions consistent with their allegations'.[30] The second visit to Turkey yielded similar findings and was crowned by the 'highly incriminating material evidence found in police establishments'[31] during the third visit at the end of 1992, being[32]

a low stretcher-type bed equipped with eight straps (four each side) fitting perfectly the description of the item of furniture to which persons had said they were secured when electric shocks were administered to them. No credible explanation could be proffered for the presence of this bed in what was indicated by a sign as being an 'interrogation room'.

In Diyarbakir, the delegation found the equipment necessary for suspension by the arms in place and ready for use.

Similar findings in subsequent visits underpinned the second public statement on Turkey in December 1996.[33]

3 PHYSICAL ILL-TREATMENT IN POLICE CUSTODY: THE ALLEGATION AND RISK CONTINUA

Most official bodies that regularly employ the written word develop a linguistic code which is well understood by those who write the documents but which is often lost on the outsider or casual reader, and the CPT is no exception. In addition, most officials and national NGOs only concern themselves with the CPT report or reports on their own country, and in consequence can scarcely be aware of the subtle gradations of meaning

---

[29] Turkey PS 1, para 21. The background and further colour is provided in Cassese (1996) 82–5 (without mentioning Turkey by name).

[30] ibid, paras 5–6 and p. 10.   [31] ibid, para 19.

[32] ibid, para 20.   [33] Turkey PS 2, paras 3–4.

embedded within them.[34] These gradations are most marked in the context of findings of ill-treatment.

In Chapter 5 it was concluded that the members of a CPT delegation probably interview several score prisoners during the course of a typical *periodic* visit.[35] The previous section has charted how the material collected is evaluated and translated into findings as regards the risk of physical ill-treatment in police custody. However, and despite the fact that several facilities would normally be visited, findings regarding prisons are not presented in a generalized fashion but in an institution-specific fashion. Since other forms of places of detention—such as hospitals and detention centres for aliens—are usually visited to an even more limited extent than prisons, it is not surprising that findings regarding risk of ill-treatment again tends to be institution-specific rather than general in nature. This does mean, however, that the overall assessment of a country's 'position' in the 'league table of ill-treatment', is principally dictated by findings relating to police custody, since these are the findings which are presented in a generalized fashion.[36]

In one sense, the data collected by the CPT lends itself to this approach. CPT delegations conducting *periodic* (and most *ad hoc*) visits *always* visit several police stations and virtually every person in custody that the CPT interviews, no matter where they are accommodated at the time—prison, youth reformatory, detention centre for aliens, even persons involuntarily detained in a closed psychiatric hospital—will at an earlier point in their custodial career have been detained by the police. CPT reports make it clear that prisoners are asked about their experience from the point of their first being taken into custody,[37] and delegations also speak, when it is judged appropriate, with persons at liberty who have recently been in custody.[38] It follows that in terms of the sheer quantity of material, the

[34] In our interviews with officials and NGO representatives throughout Europe we have regularly asked the question: Do you see, or have you read, CPT reports on countries other than your own? We have encountered a few ministry officials who have made it their business to collect CPT reports on other countries, though most of them confess to not having looked at many of these reports. But most respondents replied that the only CPT report they had seen or read was the one concerning their own jurisdiction and about which they had a responsibility to think or respond.

[35] See Chapter 5, pp. 194–5.

[36] It also suggests that the CPT is more willing to assume that members of the police force within a country are more likely to exhibit common characteristics and practices than are prison and other custodial staff.

[37] Thus, with respect to its first *periodic* visit to the UK, the CPT reported that it had spoken to detainees in each of the 5 police stations visited and, further, that 'no complaints were heard in the [5] prisons visited about the manner in which prisoners had been treated while in police custody' (UK 1, para 206). Sometimes the CPT visits prisons with the 'express purpose of speaking with prisoners on remand about their treatment by the police' (Portugal 2, para 11).

[38] The *ad hoc* visit to Spain in June 1994 was conducted largely for this purpose (Spain 2, paras 3–4). The *ad hoc* visit to Northern Ireland in 1993 included interviews with 'persons then at liberty who had recently been detained by the police' (UK 2, para 26).

CPT should have the greatest wealth of data relating to police custody. However, since the bulk of this material will be derived from persons who are no longer in police custody, the Committee will be unearthing not evidence of ill-treatment but allegations of ill-treatment: most respondents will no longer be in police custody, their accounts will be historical and, to the extent that their allegations are true, any evidence of medical *sequelae* will likely have faded. It is probably for this reason that CPT findings relating to ill-treatment at the hands of the police have typically been presented along two generalized dimensions. First, the number of allegations and, secondly, a finding of the risk of ill-treatment based on the number and nature of allegations, evaluated in the light of whatever other evidence the CPT has been able to amass. On both dimensions the CPT has developed a linguistic continuum to convey its findings. It needs to be stressed however, that in most cases the conclusions drawn by the CPT represent the Committee's assessment of the risk of ill-treatment, rather than 'findings' that the alleged ill-treatment occurs.

The continuum that the CPT employs to summarize allegations of ill-treatment ranges from: 'none' or 'virtually none'; to 'hardly any' or 'a few'; to 'a number' or 'a certain number'; to 'a significant number', 'fairly large number', or 'large number'; to 'numerous', 'a considerable number', or 'extremely large number'. We present these categorizations—culled from all reports made on the basis of *periodic* reports and those *ad hoc* reports where it seemed appropriate,[39] published up to July 1997—in Table 6.1 below. They are cross-tabulated with the second dimension that the CPT typically employs—an assessment of the general risk of ill-treatment of persons held in police custody. Here the continuum of risk ranges from: 'none' or 'little'; to a 'small risk' or 'a risk'; to a 'risk not to be discounted' or 'risk not negligible'; to a 'significant risk' or the suggestion that ill-treatment is 'relatively common'; to a 'not inconsiderable risk' or a 'serious risk'.[40] What is risked ranges from 'ill-treatment', to 'severe ill-treatment', to 'torture'.[41]

[39] Where *ad hoc* visits were either very brief, or focused on a specific long-term custodial institution such as a prison or hospital, or where the delegation did not visit police stations or concern themselves with policing, it was not considered appropriate to categorize the visits.

[40] One could argue whether a 'not inconsiderable risk' is a greater or a lesser risk than one that is 'significant' or 'relatively common'. The phrase 'not inconsiderable' is particularly ambiguous (or even mealy-mouthed). We have chosen to interpret it as 'considerable'. In a letter to the French Government following the submission of their interim response to the CPT's Report on the first *periodic* visit to France in 1991, Cassese, writing as President of the CPT, noted that 'la Comité a choisi à dessin l'expression 'risque non négligeable' par opposition à celle de 'risque sérieux' dans un souci de relativisation de sa conclusion' (Letter of 1 June 1993, reproduced in France 1, R 2, Addendum).

[41] The latter terms have been used on only a few occasions and have generally been only a tentative conclusion due to the high evidential standard which it is clear the Committee has set for reaching the most serious of the ill-treatment findings that it can record. These evidential standards are considered in section 5 below.

Before considering these data some complexities require discussion. Not all reports include *generalized* or *unqualified* risk assessments. For some countries the typification regarding both allegations and risk assessment are qualified by police force, place, type of institution, type of suspect, or different stages in custodial process. A few illustrations will serve to make the point. We shall consider each of these qualifications in turn.

(a) Qualification as to the type of police force

In most European countries there is not one police force but several or even many. These police forces are not necessarily of the same type, in terms of organization, function, or public reputation. Thus municipal, county, regional, or federal police distinctions may be cross-cut by civil as opposed to militarized police forces (or gendarmerie) in addition to whatever division of labour—uniformed or plain-clothes, general patrol as opposed to detective bodies, and so on—may have been developed within each force. In some countries these distinctions have been made by CPT informants and prisoner interviewees and have sometimes been corroborated by medical and other evidence leading to a delegation's assessment of the risk of ill-treatment. The result is sometimes a pin-pointed risk assessment. In Portugal, for example, there are three distinct police forces, the Judicial Police (*Polícia Judiciaria*), the Public Security Police (*Polícia de Segurança Publica*), and the National Republican Guard (*Guarda Nacional Republicana*). The CPT received 'a considerable number' of complaints of ill-treatment regarding the Public Security Police, 'comparatively few' regarding the Judicial Police, and only 'a number of allegations of rough treatment' regarding the Republican Guard. Corroborative evidence was found supporting the allegations against the Public Security Police. Suspicious objects—including clubs, *nunchaku* sticks[42] and baseball bats —of the sort that might have been used to ill-treat detainees, were found in Security Police stations and some of the detainees making allegations bore injuries consistent with their allegations. The overall CPT conclusion is that ill-treatment of persons in police custody is a 'relatively common phenomenon' in Portugal, 'especially insofar as the Public Security Police is concerned'.[43] Several CPT reports are qualified in this way.

(b) Geographical qualification

In a number of cases, the finding of risk has been limited to particular geographical locations. In Ireland, for example, 'a certain number of those interviewed alleged that they had been physically ill-treated whilst in police custody in Dublin', though it should be noted that the delegation visited

---

[42] A Japanese martial arts weapon comprising two rods joined by a chain or strap.
[43] Portugal 2, paras 9–27.

both *Garda* stations and prisons in Cork, Dublin, Limerick, and Shannon.[44] The Dublin-related allegations were in several instances supported by the Committee finding a 'large number of non standard-issue weapons' in a Dublin police station cited in several allegations, some prisoners bore injuries consistent with their allegations, and the CPT noted an out-of-court settlement regarding another person who alleged he had been ill-treated in another Dublin police station. On this basis the CPT found that persons in police custody 'run a not inconsiderable risk of being physically ill treated . . . in certain police establishments . . . particularly in Dublin'.[45] A very similar conclusion was reached in Hungary regarding Budapest, though in this case it cannot be said that the CPT found Budapest to be distinctive: it was simply that the delegation scarcely went anywhere else.[46]

(c) Qualifications relating to specific institutions or circumstances

The CPT occasionally relates ill-treatment to specific police institutions or to certain sets of localized circumstances. This was the case in the UK in 1994. Though the CPT on this occasion visited eleven police stations in several cities in England and Scotland they encountered 'no allegations of torture . . . and hardly any allegations were heard of other forms of ill-treatment' at the hands of the police,[47] a situation similar to that which prevailed during the Committee's first *periodic* visit to England in 1990.[48] However the Committee 'did hear a number of allegations that *prisoners* [that is, prisoners normally referred to as 'Home Office' prisoners who, in ordinary circumstances, should be held in a prison] held at the Main Bridewell Police Station [Liverpool] had been ill-treated by police officers', and the delegation found that two prisoners' allegations that they had been kicked and punched 'were consistent with the details which the delegation had seen in official records there'.[49] On the basis of this and other evidence the CPT concluded 'that remand and convicted prisoners held at the Main Bridewell Police Station run a not inconsiderable risk of physical ill-treatment by police officers'.[50]

(d) Qualification by category of detainee

CPT reports also provide occasional indications that the Committee considers ill-treatment to be particularly likely with regard to certain

---

[44] Ireland 1, paras 2 and 13.   [45] ibid, paras 13–20.
[46] Hungary 1, para 22, a point criticized by some Hungarian commentators.
[47] UK 3, para 16.   [48] UK 1, para 206.   [49] ibid, paras 18–20.
[50] ibid, para 22. Indeed, because other aspects of the regime at the Main Bridewell in Liverpool were judged unsatisfactory, the delegation made immediate observations to the British authorities under Article 8(5) (ibid, paras 11–13).

categories of suspects or, conversely, indicate that a perception that certain offenders are *not* vulnerable is misplaced. For example, the 1992 Public Statement on Turkey emphasizes that, contrary possibly to the impression given by other international human rights bodies, 'both ordinary criminal suspects *and* persons held under anti-terrorism provisions' are the victims of the 'widespread' use of torture in Turkish police stations.[51] Much the same point, albeit made in relation to ill-treatment rather than torture, was made in the 1991 report on Spain.[52] In Belgium, the risk of ill-treatment that the delegation felt unable 'to discount' applied particularly to foreign immigrants,[53] whereas in Greece, interestingly, the CPT noted a contrary tendency—'very few' allegations of ill-treatment were received from 'foreign nationals . . . in the temporary placement centre' visited compared to the numerous allegations heard elsewhere. In Greece the 'significant risk of being ill-treated' while in police custody applied to 'certain categories of persons . . . in particular, persons arrested for drug-related offences; persons arrested for serious crimes such as murder, rape, robbery, etc.'[54]

(e) Qualification with reference to the stages of police procedure

Finally, the CPT has occasionally drawn attention to the incidence of ill-treatment at a particular stage of the police custodial process. The *ad hoc* visit to Northern Ireland in 1993, for example, focused as much on allegations relating to arrest—particularly the alleged practice of members of the security forces 'standing on the backs of the legs of arrested persons while they were in a kneeling position'—as it did on treatment in the holding centres for suspects detained under the Prevention of Terrorism Act.[55] In Austria in 1990, and again in 1994, the 'majority of the allegations of ill-treatment heard by the delegation concerned the Vienna Security Bureau (*Sicherheitsburo*)', including several prisoners held in the Vienna Police Jail and temporarily transferred back into the custody of the *Sicherheitsburo* for the purposes of further questioning. In this instance some of the allegations, and the corroborative evidence, concerned 'very serious ill-treatment amounting to torture'.[56]

It follows from these various qualifications that not all CPT reports can be categorized in terms of broad statements relating to allegations and the degree of risk of ill-treatment at the hands of the police. Such generalizations would often do a disservice to sections of the police as

---

[51] Turkey PS 1, para 21.   [52] Spain 1, para 25.

[53] '. . . le CPT a été amené à conclure que le risque pour une personne, notamment d'origine étrangère, d'être maltraitée pendant sa détention par les force de l'ordre ne saurait être écarté' (Belgium 1, para 21).

[54] Greece 1, para 25.   [55] UK 2, paras 28–30.   [56] Austria 1, para 14.

well as to individual officers who perform their tasks in a professional manner which respects the rights of suspects. Yet in a sense this outcome is inevitable. When visiting all but the smallest of states[57] the CPT can never hope to go to more than a small proportion of custodial sites, chosen on the basis of their being representative of either certain alleged problems or a particular type of custody. Any general assessment will inevitably be made on the basis of relatively few observations and this must be remembered, albeit bearing in mind the various qualifications cited above, when considering the data in Table 6.1 which has been based on published reports.[58]

Three general observations arise from the data displayed in Table 6.1. First, it is to be expected that most observations would lie on the diagonal or above it, and this is indeed the case. This is so because, although some prisoners may exaggerate the degree to which they are ill-treated (and for any number of reasons some prisoners may lie about what was done to them) it seems probable that in most countries the risk of ill-treatment coincides broadly with the numbers of allegations made. The converse may occur—namely, that some in custody will for various reasons (such as intimidation or fear of future ill-treatment) not be prepared to divulge information about their ill-treatment. However, because the CPT is able to gather information from any number of sources, including media reports, NGOs, lawyers acting on behalf of prisoners, and former detainees now at liberty, and is able to interview prisoners confidentially, it would be unusual for the Committee to find other indications which suggest levels of ill-treatment—and thus establish a degree of risk of ill-treatment—greater than that alleged. The very fact that most observations *do* lie on the diagonal indicates that the CPT attaches considerable weight to the number of allegations made when assessing the risk of ill-treatment. This is sometimes made explicit. In Spain in 1991, for example, although the CPT came to extremely cautious conclusions regarding the allegations of torture received, observing that 'it would . . . be premature to conclude that the phenomena of torture and severe ill-treatment have been eradicated', it concluded that 'the sheer number of the allegations [of general rough treatment] lends them credibility'.[59]

[57] For example, San Marino and Liechtenstein.

[58] Turkey has been located within the framework on the basis of the first Public Statement on Turkey which asserted that the Committee was 'struck by the extremely large number of allegations of torture and other forms of ill-treatment by the police received during the course of the visit' and concluded that 'torture and other forms of severe ill-treatment . . . remains widespread in Turkey' (Turkey PS 1, paras 4 and 21). The second Public Statement, following three further visits, confirmed that 'resort to torture and other forms of severe ill-treatment remains a common occurrence in police establishments in Turkey' (Turkey PS 2, para 10). It follows that there is little problem locating Turkey in Figure 1.

[59] Spain 1, paras 25–6.

Table 6.1 Allegations and risks of physical ill-treatment in policy custody in published CPT Reports 1990–1997

Allegation of ill-treatment \ Risk of ill-treatment	'None' or 'little'	'Small' or 'a risk'	A risk not to be 'discounted' or 'not negligible'	'significant risk' or 'relatively common'	A 'not inconsiderable risk' or 'serious risk'
'numerous', 'a considerable number', or 'extremely large number'				Slovakia Bulgaria Greece	Spain Austria Portugal Hungary France Turkey Cyprus
a 'significant number', 'fairly large number', or 'large number'			Italy		
'a number' or 'certain number'			Belgium Sweden		
'hardly any' or 'a few'		Netherlands			
'None' or 'virtually none'	UK 90 San Marino 92 Luxembourg Denmark Malta Norway Sweden Germany Iceland Finland				

However, it is the 'consistency' of the allegations,[60] or their 'detailed' nature,[61] which appears to be as important as the 'sheer number'.

The second aspect of Table 6.1 worthy of note is that the observations cluster at either ends of the continua. In terms of the rather crude questions posited at the beginning of this chapter, there is a large group of countries that are given a relatively clean bill of health and there is another, smaller, group of countries that generate 'numerous' allegations and for which the CPT assesses there is a 'significant', 'considerable', or 'serious' risk, either of 'torture', 'serious ill-treatment', or 'ill-treatment'. Equally noteworthy is the fact that there are few cases between these extremes.

[60] See, for example, Hungary 1, para 17.   [61] Portugal 1, para 13.

The third and most sensitive aspect of the data is that the countries within these two clusters are to a large extent also clustered geographically. The countries given a more or less clean bill of health with regard to physical abuse at the hands of the police—though not, as we shall see, necessarily with regard to psychological pressure that might be considered to be ill-treatment at the hands of either the police or other decision-makers—are predominantly North West European countries, whereas the countries found wanting are overwhelmingly from the Mediterranean and Central or Eastern European area. There are exceptions to this observation but they are few in number. The overall pattern is remarkably consistent.

4 PHYSICAL ILL-TREATMENT IN NON-POLICE SETTINGS

Though the CPT typically visits several prisons during the course of a *periodic* visit, and probably interviews several score prisoners, the Committee refrains from offering a generalized estimation of the likelihood of physical ill-treatment in penal establishments, and normally particularizes the number of allegations of physical ill-treatment to specific institutions. This is no doubt because penal institutions differ more in their atmosphere and regime than do the processes undertaken in police stations and because many prisoners' experience of prisons is confined to one or few prisons. Whatever the reason, the result is that it is not possible graphically to map the Committee's findings of physical ill-treatment in penal establishments in the manner in which we did with regard to police custody.

It is clear that the CPT has so far encountered remarkably few allegations of torture in prisons and only once in a published report to date —with regard to Spain in 1991—has the Committee heard allegations of ill-treatment in a prison which, in the Committee's opinion, 'could amount to torture'. Even in Turkey, where the Committee has found torture to be widespread in police custody, there is, in the CPT's view, no problem of torture in prisons.[62] The Spanish case is worthy of examination in detail.

In 1991 a CPT delegation visited five prisons and at one of them, in Madrid,[63] they heard 'a considerable number of allegations that

[62] 'The Committee has heard very few allegations of ill-treatment by prison staff in the different prisons visited over the last two years, and practically none of torture. Certainly, there are problems which need to be addressed in Turkish prisons, but the phenomenon of torture is not one of them' (Turkey PS 1, para 22).
[63] The Alcalá-Meco Prison.

prisoners . . . had in the past been subjected to physical ill-treatment by prison officers . . . [which] could in some instances have well amounted to torture'.[64] Though the CPT's informants suggested that the incidence of physical ill-treatment at the Madrid prison had in recent years subsided, further serious allegations were heard when the Committee returned to Spain in 1994, and the nature of the allegation was strikingly similar. Moreover, elsewhere in 1991 the delegation heard 'numerous' allegations of physical ill-treatment.[65]

The alleged ill-treatment was that an 'incapacitating gas would be sprayed into the prisoner's cell, following which officers equipped with anti-gas helmets would enter the cell and beat the prisoner; the prisoner would be handcuffed or chained to his cell bed or table, metal rings under these fittings being exploited for this purpose'. These forms of ill-treatment were said often to be combined.[66] Metal rings were found in prisoners' cells, use of incapacitating sprays was officially authorized, and in 1994 two prisoners at the same prison alleged, and had formally lodged complaints with the Spanish authorities, that they had been beaten with truncheons. One of them alleged that he had also been incapacitated by means of gas, and the other that he had been handcuffed overnight to a metal ring under his cell table.[67] There appears to have been no corroborating medical evidence in either of these instances and no assessment of general risk of ill-treatment was reached, but it appears that in this instance the combination of methods applied *could* amount to torture, the purpose presumably being to discipline the prisoners concerned.

Elsewhere, however, the CPT has refrained from using the word 'torture' even when faced with what appears to be evidence of severe violence at the hands of prison officers. In Bulgaria in 1995, for example, the Committee reported finding 'no evidence of torture in the two prison establishments visited and heard no allegations of such acts in other prisons'.[68] However 'many' prisoners complained about 'verbal abuse and rough treatment . . . occasional kicks, slaps and punches' and two prisoners 'held under a reinforced security regime . . . made more serious allegations'. They claimed that they had 'on occasion been severely beaten' and one of them had a scar on his head compatible with his allegation that he had been hit on the head with an iron bar nine months previously.[69] At another prison a prisoner alleged he had been severely beaten in the isolation unit by a prison officer because he had taken bread from the canteen.

---

[64] Spain 1, para 91.
[65] At the Puerto de Santa Maria Prisons I and II in Cadiz (see Spain 1, para 95).
[66] ibid, para 91.   [67] Spain 2, para 103.
[68] Bulgaria 1, para 103.   [69] ibid, para 104.

The prisoner claimed that he was hit, inter alia, on the front of the neck, as a result of which he could not speak for approximately three months. On examination the prisoner was found to be missing a piece of the cartilage on the left side of the pharynx, and to display atrophy of the right trapezius muscle, marked atrophy of the interosseous muscles and the thenar and hypothenar muscles, and reduced sensibility of four fingers of the right hand.[70]

Another prisoner alleged he had been beaten with a truncheon by an officer a week before the CPT visit. He had large haematomas on his left shoulder and upper arm.[71] The delegation also noted, and were critical of, the tendency of officers to brandish their truncheons in detention areas.[72] However, the Committee neither reached findings of ill-treatment or employed the terminology of 'severe ill-treatment' or 'torture': they simply recommended that the governors of the prisons concerned deliver to staff 'the clear message that both physical ill-treatment and verbal abuse is not acceptable and will be dealt with severely', a recommendation which suggests that either staff do not know that already, or that such behaviour is not currently dealt with severely.[73]

Use of violence or rough treatment by prison officers to control or discipline prisoners—kicks, punches, slaps, and blows with batons—the CPT has heard alleged, and has sometimes found evidence for, in some prisons in several countries. However, as in Bulgaria, the CPT has generally expressed its disapproval in a more qualified or reserved way than is typically the case in relation to police violence in police custody. Wherever possible the Committee has made use of the prison authorities' concerns. Thus in Ireland in 1993 'a number' of prisoners at Mountjoy prison alleged that they had been punched or kicked by staff,[74] and senior staff both at Mountjoy and Limerick prisons acknowledged there was a problem of ill-treatment by staff.

At Mountjoy prison, the Governor [said] . . . there were some prison officers . . . whose services he would prefer not to retain . . . he advanced that he had no effective control in matters of staff discipline . . . At Limerick Prison, the Governor said that, in some cases, no action had been taken in over two years on his recommendations to the Ministry of Justice that disciplinary measures be taken against certain prison officers. He believed that, in consequence, a 'hard core' of basic grade officers who had resorted to ill-treatment of prisoners had come to feel that they were 'invincible and immune to any instruction' from management.[75]

Such an admission of a problem is rare, however, although similar patterns of alleged violence, some of it corroborated by medical evidence, has been found in several penal locations.[76] Moreover, the CPT often receives

---

[70] Bulgaria 1, para 105.   [71] ibid.   [72] ibid, para 108.
[73] ibid, para 106.   [74] Ireland 1993, para 63.   [75] ibid, para 65.
[76] See, for example, the accounts concerning the segregation unit at Larissa Prison, Greece in 1993 (Greece 1, para 99), or the reception unit at Lisbon Judicial Police Prison, Portugal in 1993 (Portugal 2, para 71).

reports of incidents of violence in prisons, generally prior to or following a visit. When that occurs the Committee invariably either requests that the prison authorities look into these reports or, if an enquiry has already been established, requests that Strasbourg be informed of the enquiry's findings.[77]

5 THE USE OF TERMS: THE TORTURE THRESHOLD

The above findings lead us from the question of evidence to the question of what the Committee considers to be torture, as opposed to ill-treatment or severe ill-treatment. The discussions in the previous section are also interesting because they concern what might be called 'pressure points' with regard to the Committee's underlying presumptions, if not with its formal usage. Again, the Committee has not issued any formal guidance on its use of the term 'torture', but there seems to have been a number of general influences at work which have set the Committee's jurisprudence on an unorthodox path, and which will be explored in this section and in section 6. Without being formally committed to this division, it seem that the Committee tends to see torture as something which primarily occurs in the course of police custody, rather than in prisons and elsewhere, not because torture cannot be inflicted by prison staff, but because torture is the purposive, deliberate application of pain and, whatever other forms of ill-treatment might be experienced in other custodial settings, it is unlikely to be of this order.

Once again, Cassese provides a clear indication of the Committee's thinking—although it must be stressed that there is no verification of this from other members, and aspects of his description of how this 'definition' came to influence the Committee seem inherently implausible. He writes:[78]

Without any discussion among ourselves, we agreed that torture was any form of coercion or violence, whether mental or physical, against a person to extort a confession, information, or to humiliate, punish or intimidate that person. In all cases of torture, inhuman treatment is deliberate: one person behaves towards another in such a way as to hurt body or mind, and to offend that person's sense of dignity. In other words, torture is intended to humiliate, offend and degrade a human being and turn him or her into a 'thing'.

---

[77] See, for example, CPT requests for information from the German authorities regarding alleged incidents at Straubing Prison, Bavaria in August 1990 and Tegel Prison, Berlin, on an unspecified date in the report arising out of the 1991 visit (Germany 1991, paras 64–6). A similar request is made of the French authorities concerning an alleged incident at Marseille-Baumettes Prison in October 1991, some three weeks before the CPT visited France (France 1, para 86).

[78] Cassese (1996), 47.

The full force and significance of this description will become apparent when, in the following section, Cassese's understanding of 'inhuman' or 'degrading' treatment is considered, but at this point it is important to complement this quotation with his conclusion that:[79]

What I have seen and heard leaves me in no doubt: torture is carried out in the police stations and gendarmeries of certain countries; prison authorities and other state-run detention centres never use such cruel methods.

This is echoed in the approach taken by Bent Sørenson, a Vice President of the CPT from 1989–95 who has written that 'torture is generally perpetrated during police investigation, while inhuman and degrading treatment occurs more frequently in prisons'.[80] Although this seems a more nuanced and less categoric approach than Cassese's, he goes on to present a rather crude typology according to which 'torture' occurs in police custody, whereas 'inhuman or degrading treatment or punishment occurs in prisons.[81] It may well be that these conclusions flowed from the observations made in the course of visits. It is certainly probable that these views, expressed by founding members of the CPT Bureau, have had an impact upon the approach adopted by the Committee, and this is reflected in its reports. This must be remembered when examining the published reports in order to see what forms of ill-treatment have been alleged to the CPT, what its response to these allegations has been, and what sort of ill-treatment the Committee has found detainees to be at risk of receiving in police custody.

One further point needs explaining at the outset, and which further corroborates the claim that the CPT has adopted unorthodox terminological usages. It is striking that the CPT does not ever appear to have employed the term 'inhuman and degrading' to refer to physical ill-treatment at the hands of the police. For the CPT, it appears, ill-treatment may be 'severe ill-treatment' or it may be 'torture' and these terms appear to have been reserved for suffering of an aggravated kind imposed deliberately and purposively. The CPT may take the view that all physical ill-treatment, severe or otherwise, and all torture, is also inhuman and degrading, but the term 'inhuman and degrading' has not been used in this respect.

(a) The characterization of the allegations

As regards allegations of physical ill-treatment in police custody, two types of ill-treatment are normally reported: allegations of torture and

[79] Cassese (1996), 66.
[80] Sørenson, B (1995) 'Prevention of Torture and Inhuman or Degrading Treatment or Punishment: Medical Views', in APT, 259.
[81] ibid, 264.

allegations of physical ill-treatment not amounting to torture. These terms are not defined, except by way of illustration. Moreover, it is not entirely clear with regard to torture whether it is what interviewees *describe as* torture or what the CPT *considers to be* torture which is reported in answer to questions from members of (what is usually described as) the 'European Torture Committee'. However, as the following examples suggest, it seems likely that the CPT reports as 'allegations of torture' only those allegations which it considers would be judged torture were they proven. Lay usages of the term 'torture' are not reproduced in order to minimize semantic confusion.[82] The following examples illustrate this.

In the Netherlands in 1992 the CPT reported that the 'delegation heard no allegations of torture and few allegations of other forms of ill-treatment in police or gendarmerie establishments'. Moreover the delegation found 'no other indication of such treatment'.[83] It seems likely in this instance that although 'a few' allegations of ill-treatment were heard, they were not of a serious nature—perhaps some verbal abuse or physical rough handling—and that the complainants did not describe what was done to them as torture so that the question of the CPT endorsing interviewees' usages probably did not arise.

In Ireland the situation may have been a little different. Here:

a certain number of those interviewed alleged that they had been physically ill-treated whilst in custody in Dublin. Their allegations were consistent as regards the forms of ill-treatment involved (slaps, punches and/or kicks by police officers).[84]

In this instance there is no reportage of what term—'torture' or mere 'physical ill-treatment'—interviewees employed, or what term the CPT considered appropriate to describe the ill-treatment that interviewees alleged. But in Ireland it seems at least possible that interviewees alleged torture. To the extent that that is the case, the CPT avoids repeating the term.[85]

The third and fourth cases provide an interesting contrast in reports where the word torture *is* used. In Spain, as is widely known, allegations of torture are commonplace and not surprisingly they have repeatedly been made known to the CPT.[86] Thus the first CPT report on Spain straightforwardly reports, quite clearly employing the terminology

---

[82] At the same time, this sheds some light on the Committee's understanding of the term, which is considered further in section 5(6) of this chapter.

[83] Netherlands 1, para 16.   [84] Ireland 1, para 13.

[85] Both at this point in the report and later, having found medical evidence consistent with allegations of ill-treatment, the CPT moves to its conclusion that 'persons held in certain police establishments in Ireland . . . run a not inconsiderable risk of being physically ill-treated', not tortured. Ireland 1, para 13.

[86] See Chapter 5, pp. 172–4.

of interviewees, that 'a number of allegations of *torture and other forms of severe ill-treatment* by the police or the Civil Guard were made'.[87] Given what was alleged—the placing of a plastic bag over the head, electric shock treatment, immersion of the head in water, suspension by the wrists or feet, and so on[88]—the CPT had no problem about repeating the term torture even if, as the CPT subsequently discovered, it is extremely difficult in Spain to establish whether such allegations are true and whether prisoners do indeed run a significant risk of being gravely ill-treated or tortured. But such forms of ill-treatment would, if proved, certainly be found to constitute torture by both domestic and international courts.

In contrast to Spain, the situation and usages in Bulgaria are less well known, at least to non-Bulgarians.

During its visit, the delegation received numerous allegations of ill-treatment by the *police* of persons suspected of criminal offences. In certain cases, the severity of the ill-treatment alleged could be considered to amount to torture . . . The allegations of ill-treatment by the police related to both the time of apprehension and the subsequent period of up to 24 hours in police custody. They mainly concerned kicks, punches, slaps and stamping. Certain persons complained of blows struck with wooden objects or metal or plastic pipes. The most serious allegations concerned blows struck on the soles of the feet (better known as *falaka*) and the infliction of electric shocks.[89]

In this instance, what interviewees termed their ill-treatment is quite clearly set on one side. Whatever prisoners called it, and it is unlikely that they used neutral terminology, the CPT judges that some of what was alleged *could* be considered to amount to torture.

(b) Crossing the threshold: relevant factors

The manner in which the CPT presents and characterizes the allegations which it hears can, then, reveal something of what forms of ill-treatment it considers to amount to torture. This may indicate the CPT's agreement or rejection of the assessment of others, but it does not shed light on what forms of ill-treatment will cross the terminological threshold. As can readily be seen from Table 6.1 above, physical ill-treatment falling short of what the CPT regards as torture at the hands of the police has been found by the CPT to be either commonplace, or certainly not rare, in a relatively large proportion—about two-fifths—of European states. The bulk of such allegations fall into two categories: first, verbal abuse and rough physical treatment which, either at the time of apprehension or during questioning back at the station, extends to some robust physical

---

[87] Spain 1, para 18, emphasis in the original.
[88] ibid, para 19.   [89] Bulgaria 1, paras 17–18.

encouragement to 'co-operate' with the police; secondly, casual violence reflecting a degree of contempt on the part of officers for their charges. In the light of what has been said of the attitude of senior CPT members, one would expect the second category of allegations to amount to ill-treatment but, since it has no specific function (other than general humiliation), would not have the potential to be 'elevated' into an act of torture. Rather, such allegations (if proven in accordance with the criteria considered in section 2) would, combined with their quantity, result in a 'risk assessment' of ill-treatment. This process is well illustrated in the report on France, following the CPT's first *periodic* visit in 1991, and is not atypical of the situation in other countries.[90] The Committee recorded:[91]

The delegation heard a large number of allegations of ill-treatment, some of them serious . . . The allegations related to the police in particular. The allegations included: punches and slaps; blows on the head with telephone directories; psychological pressure; verbal abuse; and deprivation of food and medicine. The allegations concerned: males and females; foreigners, young persons and other vulnerable detainees; and they related to police stations in both Paris and the provinces. The allegations were corroborated from so many sources that they merited belief.

In the light of this, the Committee concluded that there was a 'not inconsiderable risk' of detainees being ill-treated by the police. Clearly, some of these allegations concerned purposive activities, and so it is evident that the mere fact of having a purpose is not sufficient to translate ill-treatment into the CPT's own classifications of 'severe ill-treatment' or 'torture'. An examination of CPT practice suggests that 'torture' is reserved for cases in which ill-treatment is not only purposive but premeditated in the sense that it employs certain methods which can loosely be described as 'exotic'. This can be illustrated by comparing a number of reports.

In Hungary the Committee heard 'numerous', 'remarkably consistent' allegations as to the 'precise form of the ill-treatment'. This combination the delegation found 'striking', we must presume with no pun intended.

In most cases, the persons concerned alleged that, after their hands had been handcuffed behind them (or their ankles attached to an item of furniture), they had been struck with truncheons, punched, slapped or kicked by police officers. The delegation found that, in a number of cases, the allegations made were supported by medical evidence.[92]

Several such cases are described in the report. In one case the victim had allegedly had his hands handcuffed behind and had then been struck by

---

[90] For example, almost identical allegations were made and conclusions reached regarding Italy, both with respect to the *Carabinieri* and the police (see Italy 1, paras 18–23).
[91] France 1, para 11. Translated from the French by the authors.
[92] Hungary 1, para 17.

a group of officers with their truncheons. The victim also claimed to have been punched in the stomach and threatened with a pistol. A doctor from the state forensic medical service had recorded extensive marks and injuries which he concluded had been inflicted about eight hours previously—that is, at roughly the time that the prisoner claimed to have been beaten by the officers—and could 'not rule out . . . that they were caused with a blunt force impact'.[93] There are other cases of a similar nature detailed in the CPT report.

In Hungary, therefore, the Committee found extensive evidence supporting the contention that when arrested persons are taken to police stations for questioning, they are not infrequently rendered physically vulnerable and unable to defend themselves by handcuffing their hands behind them, and then a considerable degree of violence is purposefully inflicted on them—punches, kicks, blows with batons, and so on—in order, we presume, to elicit information or confessions. This, however, the Committee does not deem severe ill-treatment or torture because neither expression is used in connection with either what is alleged or found.

In Bulgaria, by contrast and as we have seen earlier, the terms 'severe ill-treatment' and 'torture' *were* used by the CPT, in connection both with what was alleged and found in 1995. Again the complaints were 'numerous' and the delegation found 'noteworthy' the fact that many of their interviewees who said they had not been ill-treated attributed that to the fact 'that they had not yet been questioned by the police, had immediately confessed to the offences of which they were suspected or had supplied other information sought by the police',[94] that is, their time had not yet come or they had 'co-operated'. As in most countries where ill-treatment has been found to occur in police custody, most of the allegations concerned 'kicks, punches, slaps and stamping', and some interviewees 'complained of blows struck with wooden objects or metal or plastic pipes'.[95] However 'the most serious allegations concerned blows struck on the soles of the feet (better known as *falaka*) and the infliction of electric shocks.'[96]

Falaka or *falanga*—beating the soles of the feet with rods or batons—is a well-established method of torture[97] which can almost be described as traditional. Its use in Eastern Mediterranean countries in the twentieth century has repeatedly been documented. It involves extreme pain[98] and it can lead to long-term tissue damage which can result in impaired

---

[93] Hungary 1, para 18.   [94] Bulgaria 1, para 17.   [95] ibid, para 18.   [96] ibid.
[97] See Amnesty International (1984), 21–6; Peters (1996), 169–76.
[98] 'Each blow of the rod is felt not just on the soles of the feet, painfully flexed upward as the club smashes the delicate nerves between the heel and the balls of the foot; the pain shoots up the stretched muscles of the leg and explodes in the back of the skull. The whole body is in agony and the victim writhes like a worm' (from Gage, N (1983) *Eleni*, 521, quoted in Peters (1996), 174).

walking. This also is well documented.[99] About the use of electric shock treatment, however inflicted, little need be said. Thus, whereas bruises or other injuries resulting from the blow of a fist or baton *might*—and might is the vital operative word—have been the outcome of a legitimately inflicted physical restraint, or might have been caused in a variety of ways, the application of *falaka*, and the injuries resulting from *falaka*, almost irrefutably involve the purposeful and deliberate application of severe pain because any other cause is highly unlikely. The prisoner has to be prepared for the exercise by removing his shoes and socks. His body has to be strapped or held by others so that the sole of his foot is presented to the torturer. It is a process about which, if the injuries are clearly established, there can be little doubt. And the same applies to the use of electric shocks. They do not happen by chance or accident. They are invariably inflicted with an instrument made or adapted for the purpose.

In Bulgaria medical members in the CPT delegation examined several prisoners alleging that they had been subjected to *falaka* and found that they displayed 'physical marks or other medical conditions consistent with their allegations'.[100] No hard evidence, medical or otherwise, supporting the electric shock allegations appears to have been found. In Greece, in 1993, the reverse was the case. There, both *falaka* and the use of electric shocks was also alleged, but whereas both medical marks consistent with having been electrically shocked were seen, and a purpose-made electric-shock device was discovered in the police station where the ill-treatment was said to have happened, no medical evidence supporting *falaka* was revealed. The outcome, however, was the same as in Bulgaria. The CPT found that 'on occasion resort might be had [by the police] to methods of severe ill-treatment/torture'.[101]

It is clear, therefore, that the CPT regards both *falaka* and the use of electric shocks to be 'severe ill-treatment/torture'. It remains unclear whether the severity of their application in a particular case is relevant or whether the purposive application of such methods amounts to 'severe ill-treatment'/'torture' *per se*. It will be recalled that in Hungary the beating of a prisoner with batons while his hands are handcuffed behind him was, apparently, neither. It may be that this was because no case was discovered in Hungary where the medical evidence suggested that the beating had been severe enough to qualify as 'severe ill-treatment' or 'torture'. On the other hand, it could be that beating with fists or truncheons does not normally qualify as 'severe ill-treatment' or 'torture' and thus the occasional severe beating will not raise the general statement as to risk in a given country to include 'severe ill-treatment' or 'torture'.

---

[99] See, for example, Rasmussen, OV and Skylv, G (1993) 'Signs of *falanga* torture', 3 *Torture* 16.

[100] Bulgaria 1, paras 19–20.   [101] Greece 1, para 25; Bulgaria 1, para 27.

There may be an alternative explanation, relating to evidential issues: namely, that conventional beatings are inherently ambiguous in a way that *falaka* and electric shocks are not.

Since the CPT has not explained its reasoning, and is unlikely to do so, these questions cannot be answered definitively. What seems clear, however, is that the use of what can be termed conventional violence—blows with fists or feet or batons or other weapons—even when purposefully inflicted with the intention of causing pain in order to elicit confessions or information, or generally to intimidate, and no matter to what degree such violence may subjectively cause severe pain or serve to intimidate to a degree at least as great as that resulting from more specialized or exotic forms of violence, is generally deemed insufficient by the CPT to justify use of the terms 'severe ill-treatment' or 'torture'. The latter terms are generally reserved for the less ambiguous specialized or exotic forms of violence. This is well illustrated in the first report on Spain where seven 'forms of torture and severe ill-treatment' were listed:

asphyxiation by the placing of a plastic bag over the head; electric shocks, applied usually to the genitals, mouth or feet; immersion of the head in water; severe beating with truncheons while covered in a blanket; striking of the head with a heavy book (usually a telephone directory); . . . suspension from the wrists or feet; threats of execution or serious injury to the detainee or others.[102]

In Cyprus in 1992 four forms of 'serious ill-treatment/torture' were described, and all the evidence found to substantiate a finding that there was 'a serious risk of severe ill-treatment/torture':

suspension by the legs with the head just a few centimetres above the ground; the application of electric shocks to various parts of the body (including the penis); the placing of a metal bucket on the head and then striking it with blows from wooden sticks; blows struck with truncheons or wooden clubs.[103]

In these lists the conventional beating with truncheons is included, but in Spain it becomes specialized or exotic because the victim is covered in a blanket, a technique presumably designed to protect the identity of the officers involved or reduce the likelihood that abrasions will result, and in Cyprus the officers inflicting the ill-treatment are said to have had their faces covered.[104] In consequence, the only conventional form of violence included in these lists is the use of the telephone directory, a nondescript and apparently innocent everyday object the use of which has been alleged in several countries,[105] and which it is difficult to see as different from the use of any other heavy weapon to strike the head.

---

[102] Spain 1, para 19.   [103] Cyprus 1, para 15.   [104] ibid, para 16.
[105] See, for example, Austria 1, para 42; France 1, para 11; Portugal 1, para 12.

Turkey, the only country in which the CPT has so far found torture and severe ill-treatment to be 'widespread', presents the ultimate example of the reserved use of the terminology. The following methods were alleged 'time and time again':

suspension by the arms; suspension by the wrists which were fastened behind the victim (so-called 'Palestinian hanging', a technique apparently employed in particular in anti-terror departments); electric shocks to sensitive parts of the body (including the genitals); squeezing the testicles; beating of the soles of the feet ('falaka'); hosing with pressurised cold water; incarceration for lengthy periods in very small, dark and unventilated cells; threats of torture or other forms of serious ill-treatment to the person detained or against others; severe psychological humiliation.[106]

All these examples combine to reinforce the suggestion that the CPT considers severe ill-treatment/torture to be purposive, premeditated, and involving the use of particular techniques for the extraction of information or attainment of other specific ends: the equipment or instruments used may be mundane, but their usage is not and goes beyond the casual or even callous ill-treatment of detainees.[107]

6 THE USE OF TERMS: INHUMAN AND DEGRADING TREATMENT

The point has already been made that the CPT does not use the terms 'inhuman' and 'degrading' to refer to physical ill-treatment at the hands of the police. This suggests that it has wished to reserve these terms for a different category of ill-treatment, and it appears to be the case that the CPT has to date used them almost exclusively to describe environmental custodial conditions, generally in relation to the more physical and social aspects of what some sociologists have described as the custodial regime.[108] Moreover, the Committee has tended to use the terms in a

---

[106] Turkey PS 1, para 5.

[107] This is generally confirmed by Cassese (1996), 63–6 who gives the following as examples of torture found in the course of (his) visits: falaka, electric shocks, and Palestinian hanging. Cassese also includes the use of 'innocent' objects as potential means of inflicting torture, such as placing boiling eggs under armpits, asphyxiation with a plastic bag, beating the head with telephone directories, hosing with freezing water, and the 'five techniques' categorized by the European Court of Human Rights in the *Ireland v UK* case as 'inhuman or degrading', rather than as acts of torture (see Chapter 3, pp. 81–2). Although not using specialized equipment, the relevant reports from which these examples must have been culled (including Spain and Turkey) place them within the context of other premeditated and purposeful techniques of more 'exotic' ill-treatments, rather than more serious examples of conventional forms of ill-treatment.

[108] That is, 'the more or less varied application and use of the rules, routines and resources that are designed to govern the lives of prisoners' (see King, RD and Elliott, K (1977) *Albany: birth of a prison—end of an era* (London: Routledge and Kegan Paul), 190).

cumulative manner, in the fashion of the US courts, with reference to 'the totality of prison conditions'.[109] This means that conditions or restrictions that might not in themselves be deemed inhuman or degrading, become so when combined with others.

Once again, Cassese gives an accurate overview of what a study of the reports reveal. He draws the distinction between 'torture' (and, presumably ill-treatment) which are seen as 'single acts against an individual' whereas the incidence of 'inhuman' or 'degrading' treatment refer to *situations*.[110] He says that:[111]

these situations are the result of numerous acts and circumstances combined. They are often caused by the cumulative effect of the behaviour of many different persons . . . In cases of 'inhuman' or 'degrading' treatment, the intent to humiliate, offend or debase the victim is almost always absent. Although such situations are, in effect, contrary to one's sense of what is human, it is often hard to discern a malevolent purpose in the perpetrators.

Cassese goes on to identify three 'loose categories', these being[112]

(1) situations that are not intrinsically unacceptable, but which could become so, either because they *combine with other factors*, or because they can *degenerate*. . .
(2) situations which *are inadmissible* because they are not compatible with the concept of respect for the basic human rights of the individual;
(3) situations that are *inhuman or degrading*.

In essence, the first of these categories touch upon the basic standards (procedural and relating to conditions) which the CPT has regard to as a facet of its preventive mandate. These are examined in detail in Chapters 7 and 8. It is of course possible that the Committee encounters situations in which these standards have not been reached and the result might be, in Cassese's parlance, 'inadmissible'. It is only where 'inadmissible' situations have attained a certain degree of seriousness, however, that the threshold is crossed and the Committee deems them 'inhuman' or 'degrading'. Cassese explains:[113]

The difference between categories (2) and (3) . . . is one of gravity and degree; sometimes we came across conditions of detention that, though unacceptable, were not such as could be described as utterly repugnant to our sense of human dignity.

Once again, one might wonder whether the threshold criterion applied in practice is really pitched as high as 'utterly repugnant'—and if it is, it would be difficult to square, in terms of both theory and outcome, with

---

[109] For a discussion, see Morgan, R and Bronstein, A (1985) 'Prisoners and the courts: the US experience' in Maguire, M, Vagg, J and Morgan, R (eds), 264.
[110] Cassese (1996), 48.   [111] ibid.
[112] ibid, 48–9, emphasis in the original.   [113] ibid, 49.

the work of the European Commission and Court of Human Rights who, as was seen in Chapter 3, adopt a seemingly less rigorous threshold but apply it in a manner which excludes findings of violations of Article 3 in situations where the CPT does seem to see inhuman and degrading treatment. Be that as it may, it is clear from the reports that there is a threshold approach and this will now be explored.

(a) Inhuman or degrading situations

The first occasion on which the CPT used the term 'inhuman and degrading' in a published report concerned the UK, and the example well illustrates the pattern now established. In 1990 the CPT visited five prisons in England, two of which were judged generally satisfactory,[114] but the remaining three—Brixton and Wandsworth in London, and Leeds Prison—were not. Those three prisons are large nineteenth-century establishments and in 1990 were in substantial need of refurbishment. All three are radial prisons with relatively large cells originally designed for single occupancy under the 'silent' system.[115] In 1990 all three were greatly overcrowded, with many prisoners held two or three to a cell. The cells lacked integral sanitation and prisoners were confined to them for up to 23 hours each day. This meant that prisoners were obliged to meet calls of nature by using pots, without privacy from their cell-mates, which then had to be 'slopped out' at a communal 'slopping-out sink' whenever they were unlocked. These conditions, in combination, the CPT found inhuman and degrading:[116]

Overcrowding, lack of integral sanitation and inadequate regime activities would each alone be a matter of serious concern; combined they form a potent mixture. The three elements interact, the deleterious effects of each of them being multiplied by those of the two others. It is a generally recognised principle that people are sent to prison as a punishment, not for punishment.[117] However, many prisoners met by the CPT's delegation understandably perceived their conditions of detention as being in themselves a form of punishment. In the CPT's view, the cumulative effect of overcrowding, lack of integral sanitation and inadequate regimes amounts to inhuman and degrading treatment. This is a matter that needs to be addressed with the utmost urgency.

[114] Bullwood Hall and Holloway, both prisons for women (UK 1, paras 114–40).
[115] That is, prisoners were kept more or less separate from each other and had to remain silent when in each other's company (see Ignatieff (1978), ch 4; McConville, S (1981) *A History of English Prison Administration, Vol 1 1750–1877* (London: Routledge), chs 5–6).
[116] UK 1, para 57. See also Cassese (1996), 49–50 for an amplified commentary on this finding.
[117] A dictum first enunciated by the English prison administrator Alexander Paterson (see Ruck, SK (1951) *Paterson on Prisons: Prisoners and Patients* (London: Hodder and Stoughton), 23).

One element in this combination of circumstances the Committee found to be degrading in and of itself:

The CPT considers that the act of discharging human waste, and more particularly of defecating, in a bucket or pot in the presence of one or more other persons, in a confined space used as a living area, is degrading. It is degrading not only for the person using the bucket or pot but also for the person(s) who are obliged to hear and smell his activities.[118]

In this instance it seems clear that the Committee was satisfied that the prisoners themselves found the system embarrassing and degrading,[119] but it is doubtful that prisoners' subjective feelings of degradation are a precondition for the Committee's finding of degrading treatment. A prerequisite of subjectivity would be difficult to establish, and is likely to lead to culturally relative, and therefore unstable, applications.

The Committee's finding of inhuman and degrading custodial conditions in England was the first to become publicly known, but the judgment was swiftly replicated with regard to other countries. Very similar reasoning and conclusions were reached with regard to two prisons in France in 1991,[120] and two prisons in Italy in 1992.[121] Moreover, the finding that conditions in some parts of the Modelo Prison, Barcelona in 1994 were 'inhuman and degrading'[122] suggests that if overcrowding is acute (on two galleries at Modelo the delegation suggests that the level of overcrowding was 'outrageous') then it can be 'degrading' as well as 'inhuman' on the basis of overcrowding alone.[123] With respect to two prisons in Portugal in 1995 the CPT found a situation involving fourth elements to add to overcrowding, lack of integral sanitation, and an absence of

---

[118] Ruck, SK (1951) *Paterson on Prisons: Prisoners and Patients* (London: Hodder and Stoughton), 23, para 47. Elsewhere the practice of 'slopping out' has also been said to be 'debasing for the prison staff who have to supervise it' (Ireland 1, para 100).

[119] 'Prisoners informed the delegation that they would turn their back to someone who was defecating' (ibid, para 47). They also explained that they would do their best not to defecate in their cells but were sometimes 'caught out'. When 'caught out' it was their custom to wrap their faeces in an article of clothing or paper and throw it out of the window (para 45). Moreover in their report on Ireland in 1993 the Committee asserted, with reference to 'slopping out', that 'such a situation is certainly degrading for the prisoners concerned' (Ireland 1, para 104).

[120] The prisons at Marseille-Baumettes and Nice (France 1, paras 93, 97, and 102).

[121] Regina Coeli, Rome and San Vittore, Milan (Italy 1, para 77).

[122] At the Modelo prison all cells had integral sanitation and all prisoners were out of their cells for much of the day (10 hours). However, some 10m² cells were occupied by 5 prisoners, were rather 'dirty and unhygienic (which is scarcely surprising in view of the level of overcrowding) and a considerable number were in a poor state of repair' (Spain 2, paras 113–14 and 129).

[123] In view of this judgment it is interesting to note that the CPT did not earlier find 'inhuman and degrading' the condition of some prisoners at Korydallos Prison, Athens in 1993. Here also some prisoners were grossly overcrowded (there were instances of five prisoners occupying cells of 9.5m²) in ill-ventilated, poorly-repaired accommodation. However it was said that they had ready access to showers and well-proportioned exercise courtyards (Greece 1, paras 105–7).

regime activities for prisoners outside their cells. At Oporto Judicial Police Prison there was a 'complete denial of outdoor exercise' and in one wing of Oporto Prison the 'prisoners lived in a potentially perilous environment as a direct result of ineffective staff supervision'. These 'additional elements rendered the position of the prisoners even more objectionable', certainly 'inhuman and degrading'.[124]

The CPT has also found environmental circumstances to be inhuman but has not described them as being degrading, but it is unclear whether this is meant to have any significance. In Greece in 1993 conditions at the Piraeus Transfer Centre were considered 'inhuman'; the Centre was overcrowded, 'unhygienic . . . badly lit, dirty and a poor general state of repair' and the ventilation was inadequate. There were no facilities for outdoor exercise and no toilet paper, soap, or towels were provided.[125] In Bulgaria in 1995 the CPT considered the situation of prisoners being punished in the disciplinary unit of Stara Zagora Prison. One prisoner was undergoing punishment of 14 days isolation and was being held in a very 'small (approximately $2m^2$), dark and unventilated cell'. His conditions the Committee found 'deplorable'. Two other prisoners were described as being in slightly better conditions—'their cells did have a window giving access to natural light and air'—but none of them was allowed outdoor exercise and the situation for all three was judged to constitute 'inhuman treatment'.[126] It is difficult to imagine these not being also deemed to be 'degrading'.

(b) 'Unacceptable' conditions of detention

When the CPT encounters conditions that lie on the borderline of those which it considers to be ill-treatment, or situations about the designation of which it wishes to be cautious, it has adopted the tentative phrasing: '*x could* be considered to be *y*'. This would seem to equate with those situations described by Cassese as 'unacceptable', although the CPT has adopted this alternative terminology. This device is used in respect of situations the character of which is likely to be contested by the custodial authorities and NGOs. As such they are of particular interest for analysts. By their very nature, such sets of circumstances are borderline in terms of well-established but multi-dimensional CPT judgments. This is well illustrated by the situation for remand prisoners encountered at Stara Zagora Prison in Bulgaria in 1995. The prisoners were held in cramped dormitories (an important element given that the CPT has been rather more categorical about the acceptable size of cells designed for single occupancy than rooms designed for multiple occupancy),[127] the

---

[124] Portugal 2, para 95.   [125] Greece 1, para 76.
[126] Bulgaria 1, paras 109–10.   [127] See Chapter 8, pp. 307–9.

heating was inadequate, the dormitories were dirty and in a poor state of repair, and there was no integral sanitation. However, some prisoners were working and were therefore not confined to the dormitories for much of the day, and those prisoners who were not working could go to a lavatory on their way to the refectory to which they went thrice daily for meals. At night they were obliged to use a bucket. It appeared that bed-sheets were seldom laundered, personal hygiene products were inadequately supplied, and showers were available infrequently. With regard to several of these issues the prison authorities claimed arrangements and provisions superior to those of which some of the prisoners complained.

In this instance the CPT found that the conditions 'could be considered to be inhuman and degrading',[128] and several aspects of the situation described make the case borderline. First, the building blocks making for 'inhuman and degrading' treatment elsewhere are only partially in place (for example, there is *some* access to sanitation, *some* prisoners are out of their cells for regime activities, and *all* prisoners go to a refectory for meals). Secondly, the accounts are in some respects contested (for example, the prisoners say that it is not uncommon for showers to be available only once a month, whereas the prison authorities claim that prisoners can shower once a week). Thirdly, it is clear that the prison administration is operating under severe financial constraints yet have a plan for remedying some of the defects identified. What the balance is between these three contextual factors is unclear, but the appellation 'inhuman and degrading' is applied in a cautious or restrained fashion: the conditions *could* be considered inhuman and degrading; they are not categorically said to be so.

There is one instance where the Committee has found conditions to be 'akin to inhuman and degrading treatment', this imprecise halo-term being used because of the particular character of the custodial population concerned. This was found to be the case at Attica State Mental Hospital, Greece in 1993. The Hospital had a 'meagre' nursing staff some of them inadequately trained, the living conditions were generally poor and some were 'appalling' (much of the accommodation was 'bleak, impersonal and devoid of privacy'), bedding and mattresses were sometimes lacking, broken, or unclean, some wards had no heating, some incontinent patients lay in their excrement and sanitary provisions were generally rudimentary and, last but not least, means of restraint that were physically dangerous (padlocked straps to arms and legs, for example, or ligatures made from gauze bandages), and which were inappropriate in terms of the patients' mental condition and treatment needs, were used on difficult patients.[129] In this instance the CPT's medical members

---

[128] Bulgaria 1, paras 113 and 120–5.   [129] Greece 1, paras 202–60.

identified a catalogue of defects which they judged globally to be 'akin to inhuman and degrading' given the mentally-disordered character of the population being dealt with.

7 SOME SPECIFIC PROBLEMS

The previous sections have illustrated the approach adopted by the CPT to the categorization of treatment and situations as either 'torture' or as 'inhuman' or 'degrading'. There are a number of recurring sets of circumstances which do not seem easily to fit within their framework and which seem to be proving difficult to classify within CPT terminology. These will be described below, and the CPT's current approach to them outlined.

(a) Pre-trial isolation of remand prisoners

In successive visits to Denmark, Sweden, and Norway, the Committee has encountered the use of pre-trial isolation for remand prisoners. To the extent that this is purposive, it could qualify as an act of torture but the focus of the debate has in fact concerned whether the situation in which these prisoners find themselves can be described as inhuman or degrading. Although the Committee adopts a marked critical stance and makes many recommendations for change, it stops short of saying that the situation described *is* inhuman and degrading. Rather, it has observed that conditions 'could amount to inhuman and degrading punishment'. It is unclear under what circumstances the Committee would judge the situation to move beyond this and become inhuman and degrading.

In Denmark in 1990—the first CPT examination of this peculiarly Scandinavian phenomenon—the Committee noted that suspects remanded in custody could be subject to a court order, on request from the prosecution, either totally or partially prohibiting their contact with fellow prisoners or persons in the community, in order to safeguard evidence or prevent intimidation or collusion.[130] The CPT was informed that: restrictions were routinely authorized in certain types of cases without particular justification; the resulting isolation could be prolonged (one case was encountered of solitary confinement for 21 months); and that prolonged isolation under these circumstances could involve an 'isolation syndrome' involving 'psychological destruction'. Several prisoners said that they regarded their isolation as 'nothing less than psychological torture' used by the police as a deliberate means of putting pressure on suspects to obtain statements.[131] Though the Committee found some

---

[130] Denmark 1, Appendix 2, para 11.   [131] ibid, paras 23–7.

evidence to support the claim that the system did sometimes have adverse psychological consequences,[132] it did not find that it amounted to 'inhuman and degrading treatment' let alone 'psychological torture'. Nor did the Committee suggest that the system *could* amount to psychological torture, only that 'in certain circumstances, solitary confinement could amount to inhuman and degrading treatment'.[133] A number of recommendations were made designed better to ensure that the Danish authorities' use of pre-trial isolation be justified by the exceptional and particular circumstances of the case, that the isolation be as short as possible, and that isolated prisoners' medical and psychological conditions be reviewed whenever requested. This issue was examined closely again when the CPT returned to Denmark in 1996, their conclusions remaining much the same.[134]

The same issue has arisen during the course of two visits each to Sweden and Norway, albeit the procedural basis for determining isolation or restrictions during pre-trial custody is in both countries slightly different from that in Denmark. In Sweden in 1991, for example, the public prosecutor was empowered to impose restrictions on prisoner contacts without the authorization of the court, an arrangement that was changed before the CPT's second visit to Sweden in 1994. Nevertheless the crux of the issue has been the same with respect to both countries, and the CPT has expressed concerns about the situation of pre-trial-isolated prisoners in Sweden and Norway in terms almost identical to those expressed with regard to Denmark. In the Stockholm remand prison, for example, the very limited out-of-cell activities available for all remand prisoners had even greater impact when prisoners were not allowed by the prosecutor or court to have contact with fellow prisoners, or were prohibited from receiving phone calls, letters, or visits at all or from certain persons. Staff at the prison told the CPT that 'restrictions were applied too frequently and [they] expressed disquiet about the effects of the isolation that flowed from them'.[135] In Norway, where restrictions had always to be

---

[132] 'Suicidal tendencies, repetitive dreams, a loss of appetite and weight, and depression liable to result in the development of paranoid ideas' (ibid, para 25).

[133] ibid, para 29. Cassese (1996), 54–7, clearly labels solitary confinement as 'inhuman or degrading'.

[134] Denmark 2, paras 54–61. The CAT has also raised this with Denmark and has recently recommended that: 'Except in exceptional circumstances where the safety of persons or property is involved, the Committee recommends that the use of solitary confinement should be abolished, particularly during pre-trial detention, or at least that it should be strictly limited and specifically regulated by law (maximum duration, etc) and that the possibility of judicial supervision should be introduced' (Recommendation to Denmark, 1 May 1997, CAT/C/SR.288, 8.

[135] Sweden 1, paras 63–8. As with Denmark, the CAT has recently pressed for the abolition of solitary confinement, particularly during pre-trial detention. See Recommendation to Sweden, 6 May 1997, CAT/C/SR.294/Add.1, 3.

authorized by the court, the police nevertheless had discretion to relax them, a power which it was suggested the police exploited 'as a means of exerting pressure on detainees with the aim of advancing their inquiries'. Indeed prisoners alleged that police officers conducting investigations against them had 'explicitly stated that *"forbud/kontroll"* measures would be eased or lifted if they co-operated'.[136] Prisoners subject to isolation experienced the regime as psychologically oppressive and the delegation's medical experts encountered two prisoners who exhibited serious medical symptoms 'arising from solitary confinement'.[137] With respect to both Sweden and Norway the CPT reiterated its view that solitary confinement 'can, in certain circumstances, amount to inhuman and degrading treatment' and argued that 'under no circumstances would it be acceptable to apply restrictive measures . . . in order to exert psychological pressure on a detainee'.[138]

(b) Disciplinary or preventative isolation in penal settings

CPT strictures regarding the use of pre-trial isolation or social restrictions lies on the boundary between police and penal custody. It can take place, and sometimes does, in police stations[139] *or* prisons. Moreover, whatever the legitimate legal purposes that justify such practices, they are capable of being manipulated, as we have seen, by the police or prosecutorial authorities in order to pressurize suspects into giving evidence, confessing, or otherwise assisting the police in the construction of the prosecution file. It is this purposive potential which makes the practice open to the suggestion that it constitutes a form of torture. But the use of isolation or segregation, for either disciplinary, preventive, or control purposes, is a feature of most penal systems, and the question arises as to whether there are limits to be applied here also, and whether it is appropriate to use the terminology 'inhuman' or 'torture' when acceptable limits are breached.

Many allegations of physical ill-treatment in penal institutions arise in relation to segregation units used either administratively to contain high-security-risk or high-control-risk prisoners[140] or as places in which

---

[136] Norway 1, para 60.

[137] These included suicidal feelings, psychosomatic disorders, and depression (ibid, para 64).

[138] ibid, para 65.   [139] See, for example, Finland 1, paras 10 and 52–3.

[140] High-security-risk prisoners are those who might be escape-prone and whose escape would endanger the community at large or cause grave embarrassment to the authorities by virtue of the prisoners' offences or notoriety. High-control-risk prisoners are those who threaten the safety of fellow prisoners or the good order of the establishment. The two groups to some extent overlap, but not necessarily so. Many long-term prisoners who have committed grave offences are model prisoners, whereas many prisoners whose behaviour is highly

prisoners in breach of prison disciplinary codes are serving punishments of isolation, reduced privileges, or restricted regime.[141] That allegations arise out of such a setting is scarcely surprising. Though most prisons are orderly most of the time, prisons are ultimately coercive establishments in which physical restraint may from time to time be necessary. It is precisely when coercion is applied against prisoners who have allegedly broken the rules, in loci that are physically set apart, that prisoner vulnerability is greatest, prison-staff power is most overwhelming, and abuse, or allegations of abuse, most likely to arise. These contestations are illustrated in several CPT reports.

The CPT repeatedly emphasizes that it pays particular attention to prisoners detained in conditions akin to solitary confinement for all the reasons outlined above. The Committee has from the beginning argued that:

the principle of proportionality requires that a balance be struck between the requirements of the case [be it the prisoners' 'dangerousness' or their 'troublesome behaviour' or vulnerability] and the application of a solitary confinement-type regime, which is a step which can have very harmful consequences for the person concerned. Solitary confinement can, in certain circumstances, amount to inhuman and degrading treatment; in any event, all forms of solitary confinement should be as short as possible.[142]

Phrases from this general statement have been repeated in many CPT reports, not least, as we have seen, with regard to pre-trial isolation. But they have also been applied to strictly penal isolation settings.

Regarding the Helsinki Central Prison, Finland, for example, the CPT was critical not just of the material conditions for segregated prisoners, but also the daily regime in the isolation unit. There was little for them to do—no work, no group association, no sporting facilities:

To sum up, the vast majority of prisoners spent their time alone in their cells, with little to occupy them. Given the extended periods for which prisoners may be held under voluntary or non-voluntary segregation, the regime which was offered to them cannot be regarded as acceptable.[143]

The Committee went on to point out that the absence of mental and physical stimulation could in these circumstances have long-term damaging effects with regard to both mental faculties and social abilities. They found that the Helsinki isolation unit 'did not provide such stimulation',[144] but

---

disruptive within prison are serving short or medium sentences (for discussion, see Morgan, R (1997) 'Imprisonment: Current Concerns and a Brief History since 1945' in Maguire, M, Morgan, R and Reiner, R (eds) *The Oxford Handbook of Criminology* (Oxford: Clarendon Press), 2nd edn.

[141] See, for example, above p. 245 and below p. 255 regarding a disciplinary unit in Bulgaria.
[142] Gen Rep 2, para 56.   [143] Finland 1, para 72.   [144] ibid, para 73.

they did not find that conditions there were 'inhuman'. The CPT has made similar observations elsewhere.[145]

In Spain prisoners considered by the Spanish prison authorities to be 'dangerous or unadapted to an ordinary prison regime' are designated Grade 1 prisoners and subjected to regime restrictions applied in three phases involving progressive relaxation. In the first phase the prisoners' regime is very restrictive indeed—22 hours each day in their cells, no association with other prisoners, and limited visits.[146] In 1991 the delegation found that Grade 1 prisoners could occupy phases one and two for very long periods (more than a year), were often provided with little or nothing to do in their cells, and complained of feeling 'abandoned'. There was little to distinguish their condition from a punishment of solitary confinement and there was no maximum time-limit for the imposition of this regime. This situation the Committee considered 'inhuman treatment'.[147]

Later in 1991, possibly as a result of the CPT's criticisms, the number of phases for Grade 1 prisoners was reduced from three to two, but no alleviation of the impoverished and 'harsh' regime for phase one prisoners seems to have taken place, so that when the Committee returned to Spain in 1994 they found again that the 'combination of long periods of isolation, austere material conditions of detention and absence of activities amount[ed] . . . to inhuman treatment'.[148]

(c) Prisoner safety and prison authorities' duty of care

The relative impoverishment of the regimes provided for segregated prisoners in many countries is particularly ironic, given that many prisoners are in isolation at their own request, though the suggestion that they request isolation voluntarily does less than justice to the forces that impel their drastic remedy. It has often been said that the worst thing about being in prison is that one has to live with fellow prisoners, and some analysts have described the loss of security which imprisonment involves as one of the pains of imprisonment.[149] The situation in Helsinki Prison, to which reference has already been made, is a case in point.

In Helsinki Prison in 1992, whereas the CPT delegation heard no allegations of torture, and very few allegations of other types of physical ill-treatment at the hands of prison staff, they heard 'numerous' allegations 'of frequent and severe acts of violence between inmates'.

Such attacks seemed most often to take the form of beatings, with occasional incidents of slashing the face or body of a victim with a knife (the blade of which

---

[145] See, for example, references to solitary confinement facilities in Germany (Germany 1, paras 75–80).
[146] Spain 1, para 110.   [147] ibid, paras 112–13.   [148] Spain 2, para 109.
[149] Sykes, G (1958) *The Society of Captives* (Princeton, NJ: Princeton Univeristy Press).

might be partially bound with tape in order to reduce the chances of the injury proving fatal). It was also stated by prisoners, and confirmed by staff, that a variety of drugs (including cannabis, amphetamines, cocaine and heroin) were available in the prison. Those who incurred drug-related debts to other detainees were said to be most at risk of attack. The delegation were told that inter-prisoner attacks sometimes went undetected by staff and that, when they were discovered, little effective action was taken. Members of staff . . . recognised that inter-prisoner violence was a significant problem.[150]

The consequence was that 15 per cent of the prisoner population at Helsinki Prison were in 'voluntary' isolation and the CPT argued that its mandate to strengthen the protection of prisoners from torture and inhuman or degrading treatment or punishment extended to preventing the development of a 'prison culture which is conducive to inter-prisoner violence'. The duty of care owed by custodial staff to prisoners included the responsibility to protect prisoners from other prisoners wishing to cause them harm.[151] The staff had to be alert to signs of trouble and be trained to be prevent trouble. Management had to support basic-grade prison officers in this task.

The same problem came to the CPT's attention in another Scandinavian country, Denmark, in 1996. At two Danish prisons[152] the delegation learnt of inter-prisoner violence and intimidation, said by the governor at one prison to be recently 'on a scale, and of a ferocity, which he had never previously encountered'. In these prisons approximately 30 per cent of the prisoners had sought 'voluntary' isolation involving a regime much more restrictive than that offered on normal location. There was a waiting list of prisoners seeking isolation and once again the driving force appeared to be the trade in drugs and the debts resulting from drug use. The CPT recognized that the Danish authorities were aware of the problems confronting them but implicitly suggested that the appropriate balance had not been struck 'between prisoners' privacy and supervision, and between prisoner choice and regime restrictions'. There was need for the activities of intimidating and violent prisoners to be curtailed without having an adverse effect on the population at large. There might need to be greater effort 'to ensure that potentially incompatible categories of prisoners are not accommodated together'.[153]

In one prison in Portugal in 1995, as we have already noted, inter-prisoner violence and intimidation[154] and inadequate staff supervision

---

[150] Finland 1, para 60.   [151] ibid, paras 62–3.
[152] Western Prison, Copenhagen, and Horsens State Prison.   [153] ibid, para 53.
[154] Oporto Prison: 'Many of the newly-arrived prisoners interviewed by the CPT's delegation stated that they lived in daily terror of a small group of powerful inmates, who held sway in the wing. These claims were borne out by the delegation's own observations' (Portugal 2, para 94).

was combined with overcrowding, a lack of integral sanitation, and an absence of regime activities, so as to constitute, in combination, 'inhuman and degrading' conditions.[155] In 1996 the CPT returned to Oporto Prison for an *ad hoc* visit, presumably to investigate this toxic mix more closely. The Portuguese authorities have yet to authorize publication of the resulting report, but it is clear that in some prisons there is a possibility that the CPT may find that breach of a prison authority's duty of care may involve such a low level of inter-prisoner safety that that factor alone is judged to constitute either inhuman or degrading treatment.

8 CONCLUSIONS REGARDING THE CPT'S FINDINGS AND USE OF THE TERMS 'TORTURE' AND 'INHUMAN OR DEGRADING'

This review of CPT findings allows us to come to some general conclusions regarding the Committee's 'jurisprudence.' We do not know whether, at any stage, the Committee has systematically determined how the key terms in the Convention should be deployed and the anecdotal evidence is that it has not. It seems clear, however, that the Committee is using 'torture', 'inhuman', and 'degrading' to a large extent in a 'branched' rather than a 'linear' manner. That is to say, the terms reflect not so much a hierarchy of severity of ill-treatment as different types of ill-treatment more or less closely linked.

Torture has clearly been reserved to describe the deliberate and purposive use, to date almost exclusively by the police, of severe ill-treatment to elicit information, or a confession, or to intimidate, punish, or humiliate. Moreover, the word has been reserved for what we have described as 'exotic' or 'specialized' methods of ill-treatment which involve a degree of determined preparation such as disguising the identity of the officers taking part, of using implements which have no legitimate purpose in a custody area, or preparing the prisoner by removing clothing or securing parts of the body. The consequence is that, if viewed in the context of 'severity', a very high threshold has been set. Severe beatings with batons or fists, even in cases where the prisoner has been rendered defenceless by having his hands handcuffed behind his back, have not been designated torture. Relative to the jurisprudence of the European Commission and Court, considered in Chapter 3, the CPT's usage of the key terms in the Convention has, then, been markedly different. A further result has been to set—one suspects largely for evidential reasons —the severity threshold higher for deliberate individual physical ill-treatment and lower for general environmental ill-treatment.

[155] ibid, para 95.

By contrast the terms 'inhuman' and 'degrading', used either separately or in combination, have been reserved for forms of environmental ill-treatment where the purposive element, at least in individual terms, is lacking or disguised. All detainees or prisoners in a given class or location are treated in this way, because that is the treatment historically and culturally deemed appropriate. This is either because they are deemed to deserve such treatment or because, relative to other citizens dependent on public expenditure, they enjoy a low priority, and resources have not been found to make their situation better.

Because the terms 'inhuman' and 'degrading' have been reserved exclusively for environmental ill-treatment, the result has been to leave the Committee with only one term—'torture'—to describe physical ill-treatment of a purposive individual nature and this has been reserved for manifestly severe physical ill-treatment, with 'ill-treatment' or 'severe ill-treatment' being introduced as new terms of art unknown to—and potentially unrecognized by—ECHR jurisprudence. Problems of evidence have also intruded. Many allegations of physical ill-treatment are made to the Committee, though relatively few are accompanied by corroborative evidence, and even when evidence of medical *sequelae* is present, it is generally ambiguous—it could have resulted from legitimate police use of force. The Committee has therefore reserved the term 'torture' to describe exotic or specialized physical ill-treatment which could not have been legitimate. The outcome, however, is that very severe forms of purposive physical ill-treatment, involving beating with batons or fists or feet, are likely not to be described as torture or as inhuman or degrading. This has the paradoxical effect of placing CPT findings outside of the familiar linguistic continuum of the ECHR jurisprudence and can lead —erroneously—to a supposition that the CPT does not equate certain forms of ill-treatment with a breach of the convention standard.

The CPT's evidential problem to some extent arises from its custom hitherto of trying to align two potentially related dimensions—allegations of physical ill-treatment and assessments of risk of physical ill-treatment. Though both dimensions involve an evidential component—a judgment has to be made as to whether allegations are sufficiently credible (made in a serious manner, by persons able to describe the detail of what happened, in an independent manner) to be worthy of repetition—it is the assessment of risk of physical ill-treatment that most critically depends on corroborative evidence capable of being systematically tested by persons applying independent expertise. The fact that the CPT has set so high a threshold for physical ill-treatment prompts two questions. First, should the Committee not more clearly separate the two dimensions it has chosen to employ to categorize physical ill-treatment? Is it, for example, appropriate for the Committee to use the formulation, as it has done on several occasions, that 'the severity of the ill-treatment alleged *could* be considered to amount to torture'?[156] Why *could*? Is it because the Committee has not decided where the threshold for torture lies? Or is it because—as we suspect is principally the case—the Committee wishes to be cautious about using the term 'torture' too readily in circumstances where the evidential issues (both regarding the credibility of the alleged victim and corroboration) are cloudy? But if the latter be the case, the Committee could make the issues clearer by adopting a different formulation: by asserting that the 'ill-treatment alleged would, if proved, constitute torture'. This formula would underline the fact that an *allegation*, not a proven fact, was involved. It would also enable the Committee to describe as torture the deliberate and purposive use of severe pain involving methods (beating, asphyxiation by means of water or plastic bags, threats, and so on) for which unambiguous evidential support is typically lacking.

The second question is whether the Committee has been wise to develop a continuum of risk assessment at all, particularly given the relatively small number of cases on which such an assessment must rely? Would it not be better more clearly to delineate the pattern of credible allegations, with the Committee more precisely indicating whether such physical ill-treatment would, *if proved*, and in its opinion, constitute torture or inhuman or degrading treatment, and then simply laying out any corroborative evidence which the delegation has found lending credence to the allegations made? This assessment could then conclude that corroborative evidence of a given weight had been found supporting the allegations made, thereby leading the Committee into its conclusions that existing safeguards for the prevention of ill-treatment were inadequate. Tendentious and controversial assessments of risk, some of them relying disproportionately on one or two cases in which strong corroborative evidence had been found, could thereby be avoided.

In the case of general environmental conditions involving ill-treatment, no such evidential complexities arise, which is possibly why the CPT has been willing to employ the 'inhuman' and 'degrading' labels more readily than the Commission and Court would probably have done. Here the evidence is not in doubt. Unlike the Commission and Court, the CPT routinely sees these environmental conditions at first hand—is able to measure the cells, smell the fetid impact of insanitary arrangements and poor ventilation, hear the noisome consequences of overcrowding and inadequate supervision—and is able to gauge their combined corrosive impact and make systematic comparison with environmental conditions and regimes elsewhere. Under these circumstances it is scarcely

---

[156] For example, Bulgaria 1, para 17 (emphasis added).

surprising that the CPT has been less conservative—as appears to be the case—than the Commission and Court. At the same time, the CPT seems to have locked itself into a set of conventions which make it difficult to categorize circumstances which straddle the boundary between purposive ill-treatment of individuals and environmental factors. The question whether solitary confinement is, on the facts, an act of torture or whether it is inhuman or degrading is a thorny question on which there is no consensus, but this is precisely the sort of problem which the CPT should have been able to avoid by virtue of its preventive mandate and its not being tied to the jurisprudence of international instruments. Instead, it appears to have become bogged down by its own linguistic usages. Above all else, however, stands the disquieting truth that, even if the CPT fully understand the logic of their use of the key convention terms, it is highly unlikely that the recipients of the Reports appreciate their full implication.

7

Police Custody: Procedural Safeguards

1 THE PRINCIPAL SAFEGUARDS

Perhaps the most well attested and least flexible of all the standards applied by the CPT are the procedural safeguards surrounding those taken into initial police custody, the phase during which, all the evidence suggests, vulnerability to physical ill-treatment, including torture, is greatest. This stands in marked contrast to the position under other internationally binding legal instruments, which have little to say directly on these matters. The standards set out in the relevant non-binding codes of conduct provide more concrete guidance and have been used as benchmarks against which state practice is assessed by the HRC with respect to Article 10 of the ICCPR,[1] by the UN Special Rapporteur on the Prevention of Torture,[2] and by the CAT.[3] The CPT has been able to go even further by refining

---

[1] HRC Gen Com No 21(44), 6 April 1992, para 4, 'States parties are invited to indicate in their reports to what extent they are applying the relevant United Nations standards applicable to the treatment of prisoners.' The background to these codes of conduct has been sketched in Chapter 4, pp. 108–9.

[2] See, for example, E/CN.4/1990/17, paras 261–70 and E/CN.4/1994/31, para 667 in which the SRT stressed the significance of the Declaration on Principles of Detention and the recommendations contained in the reports of the SRT arising out of his recent visits to Chile (E/CN.4/1996/35/Add.2, para 76), Pakistan (E/CN.4/1997/1/Add.2, paras 95 and 104) Venezuela (E/CN.4/1997/7/Add.3, para 85). The Annual Report of the SRT to the CHR for 1995 contains a compilation of recommendations, amounting to a summary statement of the principle standards which are currently applied by the SRT (see E/CN.4/1995/34, para 926, affirmed in subsequent Reports (E/CN.4/1996/35, para 196; E/CN.4/1997/7, para 217). For an earlier, but similar compilation of standards see E/CN.4/1990/17, para 272.

[3] See, for example, A/45/44, paras 73 (France), 265 (Cameroon), 355 (Chile), 413 (Turkey); A/47/44 para 227 (Bulgaria), 105 (UK). Unlike the HRC and the SRT, the CAT has not made any general statements interpreting the Convention. Such an understanding must be gleaned from the records of their consideration of State Reports. In early years, these were in cast in a 'question and answer' format which tended not to shed much light on the specific content of the obligations contained in the convention text. The introduction of formalized 'concluding observations' and issuing of views on individual communication has made this task somewhat easier, but it remains the case that while the concern of the CAT with preventive safeguards is clear, it is difficult to discern many fixed points in their thinking. The work of the CAT will not be referred to in detail, therefore, but will be drawn on as appropriate. It should, however, be noted that the standards set by the CPT have increasingly been reflected in the work of the CAT, particularly in the observations of Bent Sørensen, a member of both the CPT and the CAT, who clearly draws on his CPT experience when addressing states under the UNCAT. See eg, the advocacy of systematic procedural safeguards, which owes more to the CPT than previous CAT work (CAT/C/SR.245, para 20

the basic provisions in the light of its preventive mandate and its practical experience. All CPT reports arising from *periodic* visits include the standard recital that now reads:

The CPT attaches particular importance to three rights for persons detained by the police:
— the right of those concerned to have the fact of their detention notified to a close relative or third party of their choice,
— the right of access to a lawyer,
— the right to a medical examination by a doctor of their choice (in addition to any medical examination carried out by a doctor called by the police authorities).

The CPT considers that these three rights are fundamental safeguards against the ill-treatment of persons in detention, which should apply from the very outset of custody (i.e. the moment when those concerned are obliged to remain with the police).

Moreover, it considers it equally fundamental that detained persons be informed without delay of all their rights, including those mentioned above.[4]

The Committee recognizes, however, that strict adherence to even these most basic of requirements can be delayed 'in order to protect the interests of justice' provided that such limitations be 'clearly defined and their application strictly limited in time'.[5] The following sections will examine these standards in greater detail. Since they have not been developed in a vacuum, outlines of more general internationally-approved standards will be given where relevant. A detailed comparison of the standards applied by the CPT in the light of these other indicia is beyond the scope

(Armenia)). This is not necessarily reflected in the comments of other CAT members and, given the relatively generalized nature of the concluding observations, means that it is difficult to be certain whether there is, or what represents, a CAT standard in the sense that is being considered in the following sections.

[4] The essential elements of this formula were first set out in Gen Rep 2, paras 36–7, but the precise wording has evolved over time. Attention will be drawn to significant developments in the context of the detailed examinations of these standards later in this chapter. It should be noted that in the bulk of the English language reports the final paragraph has been given as reading: 'Furthermore, in the view of the CPT, persons taken into police custody should be expressly informed without delay of all their rights, including those referred to [above]'. The version quoted in the text is taken from Malta 2, para 25 (adopted Dec 1995) and is similar to that used in Germany 1, para 30 (adopted Sept 1992). At first sight there might seem to be a change of nuance. However, it appears to represent a more accurate reflection of the French version which has been used consistently and provides: 'De plus, il considère tout aussi fondamental que les personnes détenues soient informées san délai de tout leurs droits, y compris ceux mentionnés ci-dessus'. See also below at n 167.

[5] ibid, para 37. For example, there may well be circumstances in which it is inappropriate to reveal immediately that a person has been taken into custody. Nevertheless, the CPT has suggested that the interests of both the authorities and the detainee could be balanced by allowing, exceptionally, 'lawyers and doctors to be chosen from pre-established lists drawn up in agreement with the relevant professional organizations' (ibid).

of this work.[6] However, it is important to bear in mind that, in so far as the standards set by the CPT are merely reflective of those already required of states by existing legally-binding international instruments, or clearly set out in the non-binding codes, compliance cannot be attributed solely to the work of the CPT.

(a) Notification of custody[7]

The international community signalled its particular concern with the practice of incommunicado detention when in 1980 the Commission on Human Rights established the first of its 'thematic' procedures, the Working Group on Enforced or Involuntary Disappearances, followed up in 1982 by the establishment of the Special Rapporteur on Summary or Arbitrary Executions. It is perhaps surprising, therefore, that no international treaty expressly prohibits incommunicado detention. The inability to inform a third party of the fact of detention can, however, result in a violation of other treaty obligations, such as the right to challenge the legality of detention or the right to a fair trial.[8] In addition, under both the ICCPR[9] and the ECHR,[10] the detainee has a right to be brought 'promptly' before a judicial authority which is itself an important safeguard against ill-treatment. The benchmark set by the European Court of Human Rights in *Brogan v UK*[11] suggests that an initial appearance should, under normal circumstances, occur within four days of detention, whilst the HRC has limited itself to saying that 'delays must not exceed

[6] For comparisons of CPT standards see Bank, R (1997) 'Preventive Measures Against Torture: An Analysis of standards set by the CPT, CAT HRC and Special Rapporteur' in Association for the Prevention of Torture (1996) 20 *Ans Consacrés à la réalisation d'une idée* (Geneva: APT), 129–43; Bank, R (1998).

[7] In early CPT reports this was referred to as the right not to be held incommunicado (Malta 1, para 84; UK 1, para 217). Spain 1, paras 45–6, drew a distinction between notification of custody and detention incommunicado (the latter being on the basis of judicial decision). Subsequently this terminology was abandoned by the Committee.

[8] ICCPR, Articles 9 and 14 and ECHR Article 5 and 6. See also SRT, E/CN.4/1991/17, para 289 and Rodley (1987), 263–70; Cook, H (1992) 'Preventive Detention—International Standards and the Protection of the Individual' in Frankowski, SJ and Shelton, D (1992) *Preventive Detention: a comparative and international law perspective* (Dordrecht: Martinus Nijhoff), 34–5.

[9] Article 9(3) provides: 'Anyone arrested or detained on a criminal charge shall be brought promptly before a judge or other officer authorized by law to exercise judicial power and shall be entitled to trial within a reasonable time or to release. . . .'

[10] Article 5(3) provides: 'Everyone arrested or detained in accordance with the provisions of paragraph 1(c) of this Article shall be brought promptly before a judge or other officer authorised by law to exercise judicial power and shall be entitled to trial within a reasonable time or to release pending trail. Release may be conditioned by guarantees to appear for trial'.

[11] *Brogan v UK*, Judgment, 29 Nov 1988, Ser A, No 145–B.

a few days'.[12] This still leaves a considerable period during which the detainee might be 'out of sight' and during which the risk of ill-treatment is greatest.

The SRT has called for the outlawing of incommunicado detention[13] whilst the HRC has found that, where the period of detention in question has been considerable, it falls short of the requirements of humane treatment and, in consequence, amounts to a violation of Article 10(1) of the ICCPR.[14] The European Commission of Human Rights has shown some virtuosity in determining that an inability to communicate the fact of detention to one's wife for much shorter periods can violate Article 8 of the ECHR.[15] The CAT views periods of over 24 hours with suspicion[16] and, indeed, has recommended that the right of third-party notification be available 'at all stages' of detention.[17] It will, however, be rare for incommunicado detention to amount to a violation of Article 7 of the ICCPR, or, indeed, of Article 3 of the ECHR without the addition of other factors.[18] Nevertheless, in its General Comment on Article 7 issued in 1992 the HRC said that 'Provisions should also be made against incommunicado detention',[19] indicating the importance of such measures in the prevention of ill-treatment.

The difficulty in establishing a general right of immediate third party notification of detention is well illustrated by the non-binding codes and

[12] HRC Gen Com 8(16), 27 July 1982, para 2. Cf the CAT, A/47/44, para 295, where it probed Luxembourg on the possibility of suspects being held for periods in excess of 24 hours, it being unclear on their rights to legal and medical advice and to notify a third party. Cf CAT/C/SR.245, para 20 (Armenia) where, against a background of similar uncertainty the view was expressed that 'a period of 72 hours might be acceptable as a strict maximum'.

[13] eg SRT Annual Report, 1989, E/CN.4/1989/15, para 239: 'a formal prohibition of incommunicado detention would greatly reduce the number of cases of reported torture'; Annual Report, 1995, E/CN.4/1995/34: 'Incommunicado detention should be made illegal and persons held incommunicado should be released without delay'.

[14] See eg, periods of: 6 weeks in *Drescher Caldas v Uruguay*, Comm No 43/1979 (21 July 1983), para 14, 2 *SD* 80, 82; 15 days in *Gilboa v Uruguay*, Comm No 147/1983 (1 Nov 1985), para 14, 2 *SD* 176, 178; for longer periods running into several months, see eg, *Cubas v Uruguay*, Comm No 70/1980 (1 Apr 1982), para 12, 1 *SD* 130, 132; *Marais v Madagascar*, Comm No 49/1979 (24 Mar 1983), 2 *SD* 82, 86; *Vasilskis v Uruguay*, Comm No 80/1980 (31 Mar 1983) 2 *SD* 105, 108; *Machado v Uruguay*, Comm No 83/1981 (4 Nov 1983) 2 *SD* 108, 111; *Muteba v Zaire*, Comm No 124/1982 (24 July 1984), 2 *SD* 158, 160; *Conteris v Uruguay*, Comm No 139/1983 (17 July 1985), 2 *SD* 168, 171.

[15] See *McVeigh, O'Neill and Evans v UK*, App Nos 8022/77, 8025/77, 8027/77, Comm Rep, 18 Mar 1981, 25 *DR* 15.

[16] eg A/47/44, para 99 (UK) in which the ability of the police to hold suspects incommunicado for up to 48 hours provoked criticism (reiterated in CAT/C/SR.234, para 26).

[17] See A/50/44, para 101 (with regard to Libya).

[18] Novak (1993), 187 gives incommunicado detention as 'a typical example of a violation of Article 10 that in and of itself does not represent inhuman treatment within the meaning of Art. 7'. But cf *El-Megreisi v Libyan Arab Jamahiriya*, Comm No 440/1990 (23 Mar 1994) A/49/40, Annex IX(T), in which being held incommunicado for three years was said to violate Article 7.

[19] Gen Com No 20(44), para 11.

Declarations which, although tending to go beyond the Conventions, still fall well short of such a position. The most comprehensive statement is Principle 16 of the Declaration on Principles of Detention which provides:

1. Promptly after arrest and after each transfer from one place of detention or imprisonment to another, a detained or imprisoned person shall be entitled to notify or to require the competent authority to notify members of his family or other appropriate persons of his choice of his arrest, detention or imprisonment or of the transfer and of the place where he is kept in custody.
2. If a detained or imprisoned person is a foreigner, he shall also be promptly informed of his right to communicate by appropriate means with a consular post or the diplomatic mission of the State of which he is a national or which is otherwise entitled to receive such communication in accordance with international law or with the representative of the competent international organization, if he is a refugee or is otherwise under the protection of an intergovernmental organization.
3. If a detained or imprisoned person is a juvenile or is incapable of understanding his entitlement, the competent authority shall on its own initiative undertake the notification referred to in the present principle. Special attention shall be given to notifying parents or guardians.
4. Any notification referred to in the present principle shall be made or permitted to be made without delay. The competent authority may, however, delay a notification for a reasonable period where exceptional needs of the investigation so require.

The potential impact of sub-section (4) is reduced by Principle 15, which provides that, this limitation notwithstanding, 'communication of the detained or imprisoned person with the outside world, and in particular his family or counsel, shall not be denied for more than a matter of days'. The *Principles on the Effective Prevention and Investigation of Extralegal, Arbitrary and Summary Executions*[20] and the *Declaration on the Protection of All Persons from Enforced Disappearance* also reinforce this standard.[21] The SRT adopts a more rigorous stance, arguing that: 'In all circumstances, a relative of the detainee should be informed of the arrest and place of detention within 18 hours'.[22] A more stringent standard is set by the SMR which provides that:

---

[20] ECOSOC Res 1989/65, 24 May 1989, para 6, provides that: 'Governments shall ensure that persons deprived of their liberty are held in officially recognized places of custody and that accurate information on their custody is promptly made available to their relatives, lawyer or other persons in confidence'.

[21] UNGA Res 47/133, 18 Dec 1992, Article 10(2), which provides that: 'Accurate information on the detention of [any person deprived of liberty] and their place or places of detention, including transfers, shall be made promptly available to their family members, their counsel or to any other persons having a legitimate interest in the information unless a wish to the contrary has been manifested by the persons concerned.'

[22] Annual Report 1995, E/CN.4/1995/24, para 926(d). Cf Annual Report 1990, E/CN.1990/17, para 272(C) which simply repeated the call for this to occur 'promptly'.

An untried prisoner shall be allowed to inform *immediately* his family of his detention and shall be given all reasonable facilities for communicating with his family and friends, and for receiving visits from them, subject only to such restrictions
and supervision as are necessary in the interests of the administration of justice
and of the security and good order of the institution.[23]

The thrust of this concerns prisoners who have been remanded in custody, 'untried prisoners' being defined as 'persons arrested or imprisoned
by reason of a criminal charge against them, who are detained either in
police custody or in prison custody (jail) but have not yet been tried and
sentenced'.[24] By virtue of Rule 95,[25] this rule also applies, inter alia, to 'persons arrested or imprisoned without charge'. However, this provision
still does not reach those who are detained but have not been formally
arrested or charged and it is on this point that the CPT's otherwise not
particularly innovative standards mark a significant advance.

The CPT has made it clear that the right of the person taken into custody[26] to have a relative or third party informed of this fact should be
expressly guaranteed.[27] A number of states do not accept the need for this
procedure to be guaranteed by law[28] whilst others, though not hostile to
giving the right a legal basis, seem to think it unnecessary.[29] The response
of the CPT to this reaction suggests that in the final analysis it is the
binding nature of the provision rather than its exact form that matters.[30]

---

[23] SMR, Rule 92 (emphasis added).   [24] SMR, Rule 84(1).

[25] Added to the SMR by ECOSOC Res 2076 (LXII), 13 May 1977.

[26] Custody for this purpose meaning the moment when those concerned are obliged to
remain with the police.

[27] eg Greece 1, para 37; Malta 1, para 84; Malta 2, para 27; France 1, para 39; Netherlands
1, paras 37–8; Portugal 1, para 40; Portugal 2, para 52; Netherlands Antilles 1, paras 45–6;
Liechtenstein 1, para 23; Cyprus 2, paras 37–8. However, the CPT has been satisfied with
provisions falling somewhat short of this. For example, it noted that although the Slovenian
Code of Criminal Procedure formally limited notification to close relatives, in practice it
was applied more liberally. Welcoming this, the CPT called upon the authorities to ensure
that 'detainees should be expressly informed of these possibilities', but did not specifically
recommend that the code be amended to provide for this (Slovenia 1, para 29).

[28] eg Denmark 1 R 1, 53–4; R 2, 177–8: Denmark accepted that arrested persons were
permitted to get in contact with the outside world so far as this was compatible with the
purposes of the arrest and with regard for law and order. Whilst it was prepared to issue
instructive regulations to this effect, it was not prepared to introduce legislative guarantees, although pressed by the CPT to do so. Such measures were put in place. See further,
n. 30 below. But cf, eg, Iceland 1 R 1, 7 and Luxembourg 1 R 1, 4 for an acceptance of the
legislative approach.

[29] The favoured method of giving effect to the CPT's recommendation is to issue circu-
lars or amend Codes of Practice: eg Malta 2 R 1, 12; Netherlands 1 R 1, 20–1; Netherlands
Antilles 1 R 1, 14; Finland 1 R 1, 13–14.

[30] eg CPT letter to Denmark in furtherance of its Responses, published in CPT/Inf (96)
14, 157–8, and in its report arising from the second periodic visit to Denmark in 1996 the
call for legislation seems to have been dropped. However, the CPT called into question
the extent to which these rights were enjoyed in practice and called for the guide lines to
be re-drafted in order to stress there was a 'positive presumption in favour of granting the
right' (Denmark 2, paras 27–9).

This should extend to third parties of the detainee's choice[31] as well as family members. Foreign nationals should be entitled to have their consulates notified with their consent[32] and, indeed, the Committee has said that 'foreign nationals should be provided with the address and telephone number of the consular authorities of their country'.[33]

The mode and amount of information that the detainee is entitled to communicate is unclear. Several early reports took the view that this right is to be exercised by detainees in person, rather than by the authorities on their behalf.[34] The state responses reflect a variety of views on whether the principal responsibility for giving the notification should rest with the detainee,[35] with the police[36] or with either, depending on which is appropriate in the circumstances.[37] Recent reports, however, suggest that the CPT has modified it's position and sees the safeguard extending only as far as ensuring that the authorities make the notification requested.[38] When the responsibility for notification rests with the authorities, the Committee is aware that, *de facto*, delays might well occur in giving effect to the detainee's request. Where there is evidence of this, the Committee requests the comments of the authorities and urges

---

[31] cf UK 3, para 286, questioning the restriction of the right to a person 'reasonably' named.

[32] cf Spain 1, para 54, where the Committee expressed concern about notification being made against the wishes of foreign nationals.

[33] Greece 1, para 37.

[34] The report on the first visit to Germany recommended that 'persons apprehended by the police be entitled . . . to inform . . . a family member or a third party of their detention' (Germany 1, para 35), but this was against the background of a system in which a person already enjoyed such a right upon 'arrest' but not upon 'apprehension'. It subsequently stressed that 'it is most important for persons apprehended by the police—regardless of the legal category or form of detention under which they are placed' (Germany 2, para 27). The report on the first visit to Greece says that the detainee has the right to inform another person (para 37: 'the right of the person taken into custody to immediately inform a relative or third party'). The report on the first visit to Finland is particularly confused. An arrested person had the right to have the fact of arrest notified to a third person. The Committee stressed that, as in Germany 1, 'an apprehended person be expressly guaranteed the right to inform without delay' (Finland 1, para 28). However, it then went on to speak of the right to 'have the fact of . . . custody notified' (paras 29–30). See also Netherlands 1, para 38; Spain 2, para 60 for the same confusion.

[35] eg Slovakia 1 R 1, 16, 'the law only lays down [that the police] give the detained person a possibility to notify . . .'; Bulgaria 1 R 1, 109; France 1 R 1, 34 (specifying that this be done by telephone).

[36] eg Netherlands 1 R 1, 21, 'notification will be given on their request . . .'; Malta 2 R 1, 12; Slovenia 1 R 1, 15; Belgium 1 R 1, 14 (stressing that this is a police function and that the police 'doit faire un effort normal et raisonnable afin d'avertir la personne en question'.

[37] eg Denmark 1 R 1, 54; cf Austria 2 R 1, 17, where the police give notification with regard to those detained under S 46(1) of the Police Act, whereas the detainee exercises this right if detained under the Code of Criminal Procedure.

[38] eg Ireland 1, para 40: 'the right of an arrested person to have a friend or relative informed of the fact'; Slovenia 1, para 29: that the notification requested by the detainee be carried out without delay; Bulgaria 1, 83, Netherlands Antilles 1, para 46, Netherlands Aruba 1, para 213, in which the form of the recommendation indicated that the third party be notified 'either directly or through a third party'.

compliance.[39] Moreover, the reports do not make it sufficiently clear that the right of notification extends to the place of detention.[40]

It is clear that some countries, in order to obfuscate the question of notification, draw on the distinctions between the various phases of their legal procedures. They are thereby able to pay lip-service to the principle while preserving a period during which the fact of detention remains uncommunicated.[41] In other states the rights which exist upon being taken into detention, and which may include the right to inform a third party, do not apply to those taken into police custody for identification purposes[42] or may not be generally enjoyed in practice.[43] However, the published responses suggest that states generally accept the basic thrust of the CPT's standard,[44] including the provision that it may be necessary to withhold notification for a period of time. Where this is the case, the Committee has stressed the need for further safeguards, namely: that the grounds of restriction are closely defined;[45] that it is for a strictly limited

[39] eg Norway 1, para 3; Slovakia 1, para 39. But cf Slovenia 1, paras 29–31, where the Committee noted that the 'criminal investigation officers have up to 24 hours within which to give effect to a detainee's wish'. As a general rule, this would be unacceptable and, as a specific measure in exceptional circumstances, would need to be surrounded by the safeguards outlined above.

[40] For example, Spain 2, adopted in December 1994, refers to a communication in March 1994 in which the CPT mentioned the right 'to notify the fact and place' of detention.

[41] See, for example, Sweden 1 R 1, 7–8. The right to notify a third party exists from the moment of arrest, rather than from the outset of custody. The Swedish authorities were 'not convinced that such amendments were required' and, whilst agreeing to examine the matter, thought that 'in this context police interests must be given considerable weight so that an obligation to provide notification does not occur in situations which may put the investigation of the crime at risk'. The CPT subsequently pressed them on this and elicited the formalistic response that the question would be studied 'in more detail' (Sweden 1 R 2, 5). Cf the very different attitude of Finland, which accepted that there was no reason why an apprehended person should not enjoy the same right as an arrested person, and was prepared to amend the law accordingly (Finland 1 R 1, 13–14 and R 2, 4).

[42] eg Portugal 2 R 1, 17–18, where under Art 250 of the Code of Penal Procedure persons can be held for up to 6 hours for identification but are not formally in the state of detention which would trigger the applicability of the relevant procedural safeguards. But cf Luxembourg 1 R 1, 4, where the position of those taken in for identity verification was more precise than those detained on other grounds.

[43] eg Denmark 2, para 28, where the CPT noted that, in practice, the enjoyment of this right varied from one police station to another.

[44] An exception being Slovakia which, in the case of persons taken to a police station under Art 17 of the Act on the Police Corps in order to explain their non-appearance at a police station when requested to do so, argued that this was unnecessary since 'in some cases, the notification could take more time than giving the explanation itself'(Slovakia 1 R 1, 16). See also Bulgaria 1 R 1, para 8, in which the view was expressed that since there was a right of access to a lawyer—and a close relative was allowed by law to act as an attorney—there was no need for an explicit duty to permit notification in the case of adults (there being such an obligation as regards under-age detainees). Also Leichenstien 1 R 1, 3.

[45] Italy 1, para 42, where delays were frequent (to avoid collusion) but this was not provided for in law. In addition, vaguely worded grounds are questioned: eg UK 3, para 288 ('in the interests of the investigation or the prevention of crime or the apprehension of offenders') as regards general notification to a third party; and Italy 1, para 46 ('des raisons exceptionnelles et spécifiques de circonspection' as regards access to a lawyer of the detainee's choosing).

period of time, this being no longer than is absolutely necessary,[46] and that other procedural safeguards are in place. The latter include the provision that 'such delay . . . be recorded in writing together with the reasons therefore and to require the approval of a senior officer or public prosecutor',[47] subsequent reports referring to the approval of judicial authorities,[48] judges or magistrates,[49] courts or public prosecutors.[50]

As regards what amounts to a reasonable period of time, the Committee has expressed reservations concerning periods of incommunicado detention for periods of five days[51] and has subsequently indicated that 'a period up to a maximum of 48 hours would strike a better balance between the requirements of investigation and the interests of detained persons'.[52] There are also clear disagreements on other points of detail. The CPT's requests that the occasions upon which this right can be delineated with greater precision, accepted by Finland,[53] has been expressly rejected by several states, including Germany [54] and the UK (Scotland),[55] and by implication by other states, which have indicated that future provisions will be subject to very generally-worded exceptions.[56] A further area of debate concerns whether the decision not to permit notification should be made by the police involved in the investigation (and reviewable on first appearance before a Court),[57] by higher police authorities, or by a public prosecutor, this being the CPT's preferred option.[58]

---

[46] These may often go hand in hand: eg, Sweden, where the broad discretion enjoyed by the authorities to hold a person for up to 96 hours without giving notification attracted criticism (Sweden 1, para 22).

[47] Portugal 1, para 41: see also UK 3, para 288 (senior officer).

[48] eg San Marino 1, para 22; Liechtenstein 1, para 23.   [49] Belgium 1, para 40.

[50] Netherlands Antilles 1, para 46; Hungary 1, para 43.   [51] Spain 1, para 48

[52] Spain 2, para 60. Cf UK 1, para 217; UK 2, para 54, in which maximum periods of 36 hours or 48 hours for those detained under the Prevention of Terrorism Act did not attract comment.

[53] eg Finland 1 R 1, 15–16; Iceland 1 R 1, 7; Netherlands Aruba 1 R 1, 65.

[54] Germany 1 R 1, 7: 'The exception to the right of the accused to inform someone, where notification would endanger the purpose of the investigation or the deprivation of liberty suffices for the principle of legal certainty. It seems neither possible nor practicable to compile a list of all possible constellations of cases'. The CPT pressed the point in their second report and it was once again rejected as unnecessary (Germany 2, para 32, and R 1, 88).

[55] UK 3 R, 60: 'the Govenement considered that the present arrangements [under the Criminal Justice Scotland Act (1980)] work well and do not propose to change them'.

[56] eg Netherlands 1 R 1, 21, notification on request 'except when it is considered to be prejudicial to the interests of the investigation'.

[57] This was the view expressed in eg Finland 1 R 1, 4–5; Luxembourg 1 R 1, 4; Norway 1 R 1, 10.

[58] See eg, CPT Response to Finland 1 R 1, in Finland 1 R 2, Appendix, 3. Spain 2 R 1, 135–6 reveals a bizarre position in which incommunicado detention is to be authorized by judicial authorities. Since the fact of this decision is often made public, Spain has said that, for those 'detentions' which become common knowledge, the authorities would request that the order be lifted and third-party notification occur. Of course, this still means that the detainee is unable to notify a third party prior to the initial court appearance at which the decision is made and which might itself be as long as 72 hours.

(b) Access to a lawyer

In addition to third-party awareness that a person has been taken into custody, it is important that detainees be able to receive legal assistance. The express right of arrested and detained persons to have access to a lawyer or to another legal representative, and adequate opportunity to communicate with that lawyer or representative, is well established under the international legal instruments and codes. In both the ICCPR[59] and the ECHR[60] this is linked with the right to a fair trial. It is clear that those who do not have a lawyer are entitled to have effective legal representation assigned to them,[61] and that this be provided free of charge 'where the interests of justice so require'. However, there is no explicit right to have access to a lawyer immediately upon being taken into detention[62] and the linkage with the right to a fair trial once again inhibits any attempt to develop this from the texts. The HRC has found violations of Article 14(3)(b) and (d) only when access has been denied for considerable periods of time,[63] and in *Imbrioscia v Switzerland* the European Court of Human Rights rejected the argument that Article 6(3) of the ECHR was of general application at the pre-trial phase. Rather, it stressed that it:

[59] Article 14(3) provides: 'In the determination of any criminal charge against him, everyone shall be entitled to the following minimum guarantees, in full equality: . . . (b) To have adequate time and facilities for the preparation of his defence and to communicate with counsel of his own choosing; . . . (d) To be tried in his presence, and to defend himself in person or through legal assistance, of his own choosing; to be informed, if he does not have legal assistance, of this right; and to have legal assistance assigned to him, in any case where the interests of justice so require, and without payment by him in any such case if he does not have sufficient means to pay for it.'

[60] Article 6(3) provides: 'Everyone charged with a criminal offence has the following minimum rights: . . . (c) to defend himself in person or through legal assistance of his own choosing or, if he has not sufficient means to pay for legal assistance, to be given it free when the interests of justice so require.

[61] eg *Artico v Italy*, Judgment, 13 May 1980, Ser A, No 37, in which the appointment of a lawyer who then took no part in the case was held not to satisfy Article 6(3) (c); *Trevor Collins v Jamaica*, HRC Comm No 356/1989, (25 Mar 1993), para 8.2: 'measures must be taken to ensure that counsel, once assigned, provides effective representation in the interest of justice'.

[62] See Cook (1992), 38.

[63] eg *Penarrieta v Bolivia*, Comm No 176/1984, (2 Nov 1987) 2 SD 201, 205 (44 days). Clearly, denial of access for periods which justify a finding of incommunicado detention in violation of Article 10(1) also violate Article 14(3)(b) and (d), some of the many examples of which are given above in n 14 (including in *Gilboa* a period of 15 days). The limited role that Article 14 can play in securing early access is well illustrated by *Sawyers and M and D McLean v Jamaica*, Comm No 226/1987 and 256/1987, (11 Apr 1991) A/46/40, Annex XI (B), para 13.6, in which the HRC concluded that Art 14(3)(b) had not been breached when none of the applicants had met their lawyers more than twice before their trial, since this did not in itself mean 'that the lawyers were unable to properly prepare the case for the defence'. See also *Kelly v Jamaica*, Comm No 153/1987 (8 Apr 1991), ibid, Annex XI (D), para 5.9, 5.10, in which Article 14(3)(d) (but not (b)) was breached by the failure of counsel to consult with the applicant over his decision not to pursue an appeal, not that they only had a perfunctory

may . . . be relevant before a case is sent for trial if and insofar as the fairness of the trial is likely to be seriously prejudiced by the initial failure to comply.[64]

The right of pre-trial access under the ECHR can, therefore, only be determined on a case by case basis and turns on the potential effect that the denial of such access might have upon the outcome of the trial. Thus in *John Murray v UK* the Court found the UK to have violated Article 6(3)(c) by refusing the applicant access to legal advice during initial interrogations in the 48 hours following detention, when exercising the right to silence could lead to adverse inferences being drawn at trial. The Court said:

National laws may attach consequences to the attitude of an accused at the initial stages of police interrogation which are decisive for the prospects of the defence in any subsequent criminal proceedings. In such circumstances Article 6 will normally require that the accused be allowed to benefit from the assistance of a lawyer already at the initial stages of police interrogation. However, this right, which is not explicitly set out in the Convention, may be subject to restrictions for a good cause. The question, in each case, is whether the restriction, in the light of the entirety of the proceedings, has deprived the accused of a fair hearing.[65]

It is clear, then, that there is no automatic right to legal advice for those taken into custody[66] and even where, *prima facie*, this is the case, it may be subject to restriction. It is also clear that right of access to a lawyer does not necessarily mean access to the lawyer of one's choice, provided that such a restriction is justified and the alternative provision adequate. However, when access does occur it must take place in conditions of confidentiality.[67]

As with third-party notification, the non-binding codes go further but do not speak with one voice. Principle 17 of the Principles of Detention substantially mirrors Article 14(3) of the ICCPR in providing that:

15 minute meeting on the day of his trial (for murder). Cf *Little v Jamaica*, Comm No 283/1988 (1 Nov 1991) A/47/40, Annex IX (J), paras 8.3, 8.4, in which a meeting of 30 minutes before and during the course of a trial for murder was held to violate Art 14(3)(b).

[64] *Imbrioscia v Switzerland*, Judgment, 24 Nov 1993, Ser A No 275, para 36.

[65] *John Murray v UK*, Judgment, 8 Feb 1996, 1996-I *RJD* 30, para 63.

[66] But cf Stavros, S (1993) *The Guarantees for Accused Persons Under Article 6 of the ECHR* (Dordrecht: Martinus Nijhoff), 72–3, who argues that under the ECHR a person becomes 'charged' for the purposes of Article 6 when 'he is substantially affected by the suspicions against him' (see *Deweer v Belguim*, Judgment, 27 Feb 1980, Ser A, No 35, para 44) and since this includes arrest on suspicion, this could be taken to guarantee access to counsel on arrest. He accepts, however, that decisions, such as App No 12391, *Di Stefano v UK*, 60 DR 182 (1989), stand against this (a complaint in which a denial of access for 2½ hours was declared inadmissible), and the *Murray* case would reinforce these objections.

[67] See *S v Switzerland*, Judgment, 28 Nov 1991, Ser A No 220, in which the Court concluded that there had been a breach of Article 6(3)(c) when consultations between a remand prisoner and his lawyer were required to be held within earshot of prison officers.

1. A detained person shall be entitled to have the assistance of a legal counsel. He shall be informed of his right by the competent authority promptly after arrest and shall be provided with reasonable facilities for exercising it.
2. If a detained person does not have a legal counsel of his own choice, he shall be entitled to have a legal counsel assigned to him by a judicial or other authority in all cases where the interests of justice so require and without payment by him if he does not have sufficient means to pay.

The principal advance in this formulation is the addition of the fairly opaque requirement that this entitlement be exercisable 'promptly after arrest', which is itself further qualified by Principle 18(3), which provides that this right:

may not be suspended or restricted save in exceptional circumstances, to be specified by law or lawful regulations, when it is considered indispensable by a judicial or other authority in order to maintain security and good order.

This sets a fairly high threshold for interference with the right, which is further buttressed by Article 15, which provides that communication with counsel 'shall not be denied for more than a couple of days'. In 1990 the Eighth UN Congress on the Prevention of Crime and the Treatment of Offenders adopted the *UN Basic Principles on the Role of Lawyers*, which goes beyond the Principles of Detention by providing that:

Governments shall further ensure that all persons arrested or detained, with or without criminal charge, shall have prompt access to a lawyer, and in any case not later that forty-eight hours from the time of arrest or detention.[68]

Even so, this still envisages a considerable period of time within which the detainee need not be in receipt of legal assistance. Given that the thrust of the ECHR and ICCPR is aimed towards ensuring the fairness of the trial, rather than with the prevention of ill-treatment in detention, this is not necessarily surprising. Nor is it surprising that, given the preventive rather than the procedural imperatives of their mandates, the CPT, the SRT, and the CAT have sought to reduce—or close—the gap between the commencement of detention and of right of access to a lawyer. The approach taken by the SRT is that: 'Legal provision should ensure that detainees be given access to legal counsel within 24 hours of detention. In exceptional circumstances, under which it is contended that prompt contact with a detainee's lawyer might raise genuine security concerns, and where restriction of such contact is judicially approved, it should at least be possible to allow a meeting with an independent lawyer, such as one recommended by a bar association.'[69] The CAT calls for access to a

[68] Principles of Lawyers, Principle 7.
[69] Annual Report, 1995, E/CN.4/1995/24, para 926 (d).

lawyer, but is not particularly consistent in its approach: in recent times it has recommended that all detainees have immediate access to legal advice (though not necessarily a lawyer of their choice),[70] yet has failed to criticize a situation in which a suspect could be held for up to 48 hours, with his family informed so that they (the family) could consult a lawyer on his behalf.[71]

The CPT standard is without doubt the most exacting of the various formulations in existence. The Committee sees the right of access to a lawyer from the outset of police custody as a potent safeguard against ill-treatment. It is firmly of the view that access to a lawyer is a right, and not a privilege,[72] that is to be enjoyed from the moment when a person is obliged to stay with the police[73] and is additional to the right to inform a third party.[74] However, the different meanings placed on words such as 'custody', 'arrest', 'apprehension', and 'detention', coupled with distinctions between criminal and administrative detention, provide—as has already been seen in the context of the right to notify a third party —opportunities to provide answers which are at best confusing and at worst misleading. For example, some government responses seek to draw a veil over the fact that the right of access comes into being at the first appearance before a judicial authority rather than at the outset of detention,[75] or at other points subsequent to the initial detention,[76] whilst others point to formal provisions which are known to be, in practice,

---

[70] eg A/49/44, para 132 (Switzerland); A/50/44, para 101 (Libya).

[71] CAT/C/SR.277, para 12 (Poland).

[72] For example, it has taken exception to the Dutch practice of permitting access within the first 6 hours of police custody whilst refusing to enshrine this in law, emphasizing that it 'considers it essential that a detainee's right to have access to a lawyer be guaranteed from the very outset of his detention' (Netherlands 1, para 41). See also Netherlands Antilles 1, para 48; Netherlands Aruba 1, para 215; France 1, paras 41–2; Switzerland 1, paras 120–1; Belgium 1, paras 41, 44.

[73] eg Liechtenstein 1, paras 24–8, where the position as regards access to a lawyer is similar to the German position concerning notification of a third party (n 34 above); Slovakia 1, para 41, where the right was applicable once the detainee was placed under the control of the investigation service, rather than upon apprehension.

[74] cf Slovakia 1 R 1, 16, in which Slovakia rejected the need to notify a lawyer as well as a relative, arguing that the relative could notify the lawyer or vice versa. In Luxembourg 1 R 1, 5, the Government rejected the suggestion that those apprehended for the purposes of verifying their identity should have this as an additional right to that of informing a person of their choice.

[75] eg Greece 1 R 1, 17: 'The right to communication [sic] of persons arrested by the police with a counsel of their choice, which is absolutely safeguarded in article 100 of the Code of Criminal Procedure, shall be exercised by them immediately after their formal appearance (referral) before the competent Police Authority'.

[76] The failure of some responses to give a clear answer creates this impression even if it is not justified; eg Sweden 1 R 1, 8, says that 'a suspect is entitled to engage defence counsel as soon as the investigation of his case has reached a stage where it may be said to be directed against him in the sense that he is suspected of a crime'. The CPT was left unclear whether this was applicable at the pre-arrest stage.

rarely operable.[77] In consequence the Committee frequently now asks for 'clarification of the precise moment at which the right of access to a lawyer becomes effective; does it always apply from the very outset of custody . . . or, in certain cases, does it only take effect at some later stage of police custody?', even when the report does not suggest that the position is otherwise.[78]

Some states, including Austria and Malta, which do not currently permit access have said that they will consider the issue, but subsequently provided no evidence that they had done so between the first and second visits of the CPT.[79] Other states have openly disagreed with the CPT's recommendations. In Germany, for example, a person apprehended by the police on *suspicion* of having committed a criminal offence (a *Verdachtiger*) has no right of access to a lawyer and is rarely allowed access. Not until the suspect becomes the *subject* of a criminal inquiry (a *Beschuldigter*)— that is, at the start of the first interrogation—does a suspect have the right to consult a lawyer.[80] The German Federal Government has bluntly said that they see little need to alter this arrangement:

It does not seem necessary to generally extend the right to presence of a lawyer because [the] interests of the person concerned worthy of protection do not seem to be placed in danger to an unacceptable extent if the interrogation is carried out without a lawyer.[81]

One of the most forthright rejections has come from the Netherlands. In response to the CPT's recommendation that those held for interroga-

[77] eg Finland 1 R 2, 23; Bulgaria 1 R 1, 109. Cf Turkish law, which guarantees a general right (with the exception of persons suspected of collective offences) of access to a lawyer during police detention but there is a considerable body of evidence that even the limited legal guarantees for suspects are ignored and police powers abused: 'These long detention periods are, according to the reports, a major factor in the continued use of torture [in Turkey] . . . lawyers are reportedly constantly denied by the police or security forces an opportunity to see their clients . . . in practice relatives spend days trying to learn the whereabouts of a detainee and are neither informed about the place of detention nor helped by the authorities in their search for such information' (SRT, Annual Report, 1993, E/CN.4/1993/26, para 480).

[78] Hungary 1, para 44; Bulgaria 1, para 84.

[79] Malta 2, para 28 and R 1, 12; Austria 1, para 44 and R 1, 15–16. In both cases a period of approximately 5 years had elapsed between visits.

[80] Further, it appears that persons held only on suspicion are rarely allowed to inform third parties of their detention, and suspects who are the subject of criminal inquiries are allowed to have a near relative or a third party informed only 'if this is considered compatible with the needs of the inquiry'. Germany 1, paras 32–3, Germany 2, para 28.

[81] Germany 1 R 1, 7. The views of the CPT and of the Federal Government remain unaltered. See Germany 2, paras 29 and 32 and R 1, 86–7. See also Denmark 1 R 1, 66–7 which, whilst accepting that the wishes of the detainee would normally be respected, took the view that it was inappropriate to expressly grant a right for detainees to contact a lawyer prior to formal questioning by the police (during which a lawyer could be present).

tion be entitled to have access to a lawyer from the very outset of their deprivation of liberty,[82] the Dutch Government pointed out that whilst there was an unequivocal right for suspects to be assisted by legal counsel 'during interrogation by the public prosecutor or his deputy preceding possible remand in police custody', this was preceded by an initial period of six hours during which police interrogation could take place. It was argued that:

There are often practical difficulties in finding a lawyer who is available at short notice. Moreover, it is not considered desirable for the legal counsel to be present during the police interrogation, when the investigating officer is intent on creating an atmosphere in which the person concerned is prepared to co-operate in establishing the facts and clarifying his role in the suspected crime. The presence of legal counsel at this stage could have the effect of lessening his willingness to co-operate, which would oblige the police to make more frequent use of other measures to establish the truth such as searching the premises of third parties. As measures of this kind take more time than interrogation, it could mean prolonging the period of pre-trial detention. There is no evidence to suggest that the police make improper use of interrogation procedures.[83]

Other countries which have rejected immediate access as a matter of principle include Switzerland,[84] Belgium,[85] Luxembourg,[86] and France.[87]

Where there is a right of access to a lawyer from the start of police detention, further issues arise. The Second CPT General Report said that 'Access to a lawyer for persons taken into police custody should include the right to contact and to be visited by the lawyer (in both cases under conditions guaranteeing the confidentiality of their discussions) as well as, in principle, the right for the person concerned to have the lawyer

---

[82] Netherlands 1, para 41.

[83] Netherlands 1 R 1, 23–4. From our conversations with Dutch officials, the Dutch view can be paraphrased as follows: 'We do not have torture in the Netherlands. Our police are professionals and subscribe to a code of professional ethics. Further, the police are not the prosecutors in our system. The police are impartial and are concerned to get at the truth. The situation is not as in the Anglo-Saxon adversarial system. There is no concern about this issue of suspects' initial access to lawyers in the Netherlands. There is no real public debate about it. The position is different elsewhere and we appreciate that. But there is no real case for us to change Dutch law or practice. We don't think it appropriate for lawyers to be present during the initial stage of detention here.'

Cf Netherlands Antilles 1 R 1, 15–17 and Netherlands Aruba 1 R 1, 65. In the context of the same proceudural structures, the responses seem designed to obscure the question of access during the 6-hour pre-arrest phase, involving police questioning, rather than investigation.

[84] Switzerland 1 R 1, 11, pointing out that this was not required by the Swiss Federal Constitution or by the European Court of Commission of Human Rights

[85] Belgium 1 R 1, 15.   [86] Luxembourg 1 R 1, 5.

[87] France 1 R 1, 36, indicated that a restricted form of access would be introduced but this was subsequently replaced with a 20-hour period in which access was denied (see France 1 R 2, 22 and p. 278 below).

present during interrogation'.[88] This drew on the experience of the Committee in Spain[89] where, although a detainee had the right to the presence of a lawyer when making statements—and this was officially understood to include questioning—in practice, access was often denied until the detainee was ready to make a formal statement following interrogation. The Committee observed that 'the core of the notion of access to legal assistance for persons in police custody is the possibility for a detainee to consult in private with a lawyer, and in particular during the period immediately following his loss of liberty'.[90] Not all states agree that such discussions should be private[91] whilst others place curbs upon it.[92]

As with third-party notification, the CPT accepts that it may be necessary to withhold access to a lawyer of the detainee's choosing for a period of time, and where this is the case the Committee stresses the need for application of the same range of safeguards: that the grounds of restriction are closely defined; that it is for a strictly limited period of time, this being no longer than is absolutely necessary; that such delay be recorded in writing together with the reasons for the decision; and that approval be given by a senior officer or public prosecutor.[93] Unlike third-party notification, however, the CPT takes the view that there is no justification for totally denying access to a lawyer during this period since it should be possible to arrange access to an independent lawyer 'who can be trusted

---

[88] Gen Rep 2, para 38. Malta 1, adopted in 1990, had merely recommended that the Authorities 'explore the possibilities of this latter right as a medium term measure' (Malta 1, para 87. Malta 2, paras 28–31 recalled this, but then restated the now standard phraseology and called for the necessary steps to be taken, 'without further delay'). The CAT has also expressed concern where a suspect lacks the entitlement to the presence of a solicitor during interrogation in Northern Ireland (A/47/44, para 125).

[89] See also A/46/46, para 62, where the CAT expressed similar concerns, based on Amnesty International source material.

[90] Spain 1, paras 49–50. See UK 3, paras 290–1, where there was no legal obligation to permit an arrested person to have a private interview until the person was due to be taken to court.

[91] Germany, for example takes the view that whilst in police custody 'the detainee can reasonably be expected to accept the presence of an officer' during meetings with counsel (Germany 1 R 1, 8). In the UK (Scotland), the Government had 'reservations about an obligatory right of confidential discussions between solicitors and clients at all stages of an inquiry' (UK 3 R, 58). See also Slovenia 1, R 1, 16, where 'in practice' no private meetings occur, and Bulgaria 1 R 1, 109, where it is acknowledged that this might be the case when appropriate facilities are lacking.

[92] In France, it was proposed that the lawyer be restricted to a 30-minute consultation, the content of which is to be recorded in writing and was not to be revealed during the period of detention or used to provide advice on the case itself (France 1 R 1, 36, referring to Arts 63–64 of the Code of Criminal Procedure, as amended on 4 Jan 1993). This proposal never entered into force, and was replaced by a 20-hour period, after which the 30-minute consultation could take place. See France 1 R 2, 22. Cf Sweden, where a public defence counsel can consult in private, but a private defence counsel can only do so with the permission of the person responsible for the investigation, although this appears to be rare, despite the lack of guidelines outlining the criteria for a refusal (Sweden 1 R 1, 14–15).

[93] See above, p. 265 for further details.

not to jeopardise the legitimate interests of the police investigation'.[94] If a detainee is being held incommunicado, then the right to legal representation is fulfilled by the presence of an officially appointed lawyer.[95] The right to such assistance should, the Committee believes, be the subject of express guarantee.[96]

The right of access does not imply that a detainee can insist on interrupting an interview in order to consult the lawyer before answering a question. Indeed, although the Committee says that this right, in principle, includes the presence of a lawyer during an interview, this has been seen as desirable, rather than central to the safeguard. In its second report on the UK (which focused on Northern Ireland) the Committee said that the key element was the 'possibility for the detainee to consult in private with the lawyer as from the very outset of his custody' and classified 'the right to have the lawyer present during interrogation' as 'a useful supplementary safeguard'[97] and recommended that this possibility be explored.[98] More recent reports suggest a somewhat stronger line regarding the importance of this safeguard.[99] Nevertheless, a number of states continue to place restrictions on the presence of lawyers during questioning.[100]

[94] Greece 1, para 40. See also Netherlands Antilles 1, paras 49–50 and Netherlands Aruba 1, paras 216–17 for 'concerns' over provisions preventing an officially appointed lawyer from having private discussions with a detainee for a period of up to 6 days. Cf UK 2 R 1, 12, in which the Government rejected the argument that the right of access to an independant lawyer, applicable elsewhere in the UK, should apply in a similar fashion in Northern Ireland.

[95] Spain 1, para 52.

[96] eg the CPT thought that the 'established practice' of permitting a person denied the right to consult his own lawyer to have access to a member of the Finnish Bar Association should be the subject of express legal provisions (CPT letter in response to Finland 1 R 1, in Finland 1 R 2, Appendix, para 13). Finland agreed that the Ministries of Justice and of the Interior would issue an order to this effect (Finland 1 R 2, 5). See also UK 3 R, 12, in which the UK agreed to upgrade the provision in the Notes for Guidance appended to the PACE Code of Practice into a full provision of the Codes in due course.

[97] UK 2, para 63.

[98] Ireland 1, para 43. See also Malta 1, para 87; Switzerland 1, para 121, where the authorities were recommended to explore the possibility of allowing the presence of a lawyer during interrogations as a medium term measure.

[99] eg Portugal 2, para 54: 'Preferably, they should benefit from the presence of a lawyer during questioning'. Practice is not consistent, however. In Slovenia 1, para 31, the CPT requested information on whether the right of access included the right to the presence of a lawyer during interrogation. In Leichtenstein, where this was neither sanctioned by law nor did it happen in practice, the Committee went further than usual and recommended that the right, in principle, be granted (Liechtenstein 1, para 28).

[100] eg as regards interviews with suspects held under the Prevention of Terrorism Act, the UK said: 'It is felt that the presence of a lawyer would inhibit interviews and lead to a reduction in information about serious crime given by detainees' (UK 2 R 1, 15). See also Ireland which, in the light of the CPT's recommendation that it explore this possibility, undertook to give the matter 'careful consideration' (Ireland 1 R 1, 16). See also Netherlands Antilles 1 R 1, 16–17: 'the presence of counsel during police interrogations presents problems from the point of view of legal proceedings'.

Hand in hand with the right of access to a lawyer is the question of information regarding providers of legal services. The Committee has welcomed schemes requiring lists of solicitors to be made available to detainees.[101] Even more important, of course, is the provision of legal services to those unable to pay for them and, without being prescriptive, the CPT frequently requests information on the availability of criminal legal aid and invites states to review their provisions,[102] recently expressing the view that: 'It goes without saying that if the right of access to a lawyer is to be exercised effectively there must be a system of legal aid for detained persons'.[103] It is clear, however, that this is an aspiration rather than a reality in many states visited.[104] As with other aspects of the right of access to a lawyer, as well as the other procedural safeguards considered in this chapter, the problem is often not so much with the standard adopted by the CPT or with the manner in which it is reflected in the relevant legislative provisions of the states concerned, but with the actual practice. Many CPT reports bear witness to the extent to which many provisions rarely operate in practice.[105]

(c) Access to a doctor of the detainee's choosing

Both third-party notification and access to a lawyer are valuable safeguards against physical ill-treatment in the early stages of detention. Perhaps the most important safeguard, however, is that the detainee be medically examined at the earliest possible opportunity, in order that any signs of ill-treatment be recorded, and that the physical condition of the detainee be authoritatively established and recorded, providing a basis against which any subsequent allegations of ill-treatment can be tested. The legally-binding instruments do not address this issue, but the SMR provides that in penal institutions: 'The medical officer shall see and

---

[101] Ireland 1, para 44.

[102] eg Germany 1, para 35: 'the CPT would like to receive information on any legal aid system for persons in police custody which might exist in Germany' (but not returned to in Germany 2); Ireland 1, para 45. Cf Portugal 2, para 54, where concern was expressed that indigent detainees could only be awarded legal assistance in the course of a court appearance.

[103] Bulgaria 1, para 87.

[104] eg Austria 1 R 1, 11: 'basic conditions for introducing such services in the near future are currently lacking'. Cf Netherlands Aruba 1 R 1, 65, which states: 'The right to legal aid is enshrined in the Constitution. A suspect is entitled to legal aid from the moment he is arrested'. However, an Annex to the Response notes that there are too few lawyers available, partly because the sums paid are too low (ibid, 95).

[105] See, for example: Finland 1, para 34; Portugal 1, para 44; Luxembourg 1, para 30; Italy 1, para 46; Bulgaria 1, paras 85–6; Demark 2, paras 31 and 34 (where it was noted that the possibility of those subsequently convicted having to refund the costs of their defence was used to put pressure on those not suspected of serious offence to forego this right).

examine every prisoner as soon as possible after his admission and there-after as necessary',[106] whilst prisoners under arrest or awaiting trial in police custody or prison 'shall be allowed to be visited and treated by his own doctor or dentist if there is reasonable ground for his application and he is able to pay any expenses incurred'.[107]

Clearly, these provisions do not reach back to the commencement of detention and are not intended to put in place systems of medical super-vision as a guarantee against ill-treatment. The position is not taken much further by the Declaration on Principles of Detention, which provides:

A proper medical examination shall be offered to a detained or imprisoned person as promptly as possible after his admission to the place of detention or imprison-ment, and thereafter medical care and treatment shall be provided whenever necessary. This care and attention shall be provided free of charge.[108]

A detained or imprisoned person or his counsel shall, subject only to reason-able conditions to ensure security and good order in the place of detention or imprisonment, have the right to request or petition a judicial or other authority for a second medical examination or opinion.[109]

The fact that a detainee or imprisoned person underwent a medical examina-tion, the name of the physician and the results of such an examination shall be duly recorded. Access to such records shall be ensured. Modalities therefor shall be in accordance with relevant rules of domestic law.[110]

Though this provides for an examination 'as promptly as possible', it does not provide a right to an independent examination, only the right to request it.[111] Even this, however, is in advance of the position adopted by the SRT.[112] Equally significant is the failure to specify who might have access to the records of examinations. The weakness of these provisions is underlined by comparing them with the draft articles originally adopted for inclusion in the Principles by the UN Sub-Commission on Prevention

---

[106] SMR, Rule 24.

[107] ibid, Rule 91. See above p. 262 for the application of this section of the Rules to persons arrested or imprisoned without charge.

[108] Principle 24.   [109] Principle 25.   [110] Principle 26.

[111] See also the Code of Conduct for Law Enforcement Officials (UNGA Res 34/169, 17 Dec 1979), Article 6, which provides that: 'Law enforcement officials shall ensure the full protection of the health of persons in their custody and, in particular, shall take immedi-ate action to secure medical attention whenever required'. The commentary to this article adds that: 'medical attention shall be secured when needed or requested'.

[112] See Annual Report, 1995, E/CN.4/1995/34, para 926 (d): 'at the time of arrest, a person should undergo a medical inspection, and medical inspections should be repeated regularly and should be compulsory upon transfer to another place of detention'. Although an improvement as regards the point of time ('arrest') there is no mention of a right to inde-pendent medical examination. This seems to be based on SMR Rule 24 (see E/CN.4/ 1988/17, para 68) and should be enlarged on. Of course, the rigorous application of the UN codes of conduct for health professionals should, in theory, render this unnecessary.

of Discrimination and Protection of Minorities but which were subsequently watered down. In that draft the equivalent articles provided:[113]

The Medical officer at the place of detention shall see and examine a detained or imprisoned person promptly after his admission and thereafter as often as necessary. The official responsible for supervising the detention of a person needing medical care shall take immediate action to meet the needs of the person in custody for medical attention.

A detained or imprisoned person shall also have the right to be examined by a physician of his own choice available under the existing general system of health care, at his request or at the request of his counsel or of a member of his family, subject only to reasonable conditions to ensure security and good order in the place or detention and to avoid undue delay in the investigation.

The fact that a detained or imprisoned person underwent a medical examination, the name of the physician and the results of such examination shall be duly recorded and such records be made available promptly to the person examined, his counsel or a member of his family.

The CAT has moved towards a more advanced position, including a recommendation that there be a right to an examination by a doctor of the detainee's choice, 'at all stages of detention'.[114] The standards applied by the CPT have more in common with this position, and with the earlier draft of the Principles of Detention, than with the final form of Principles 24–26.

On its very first visit, to Austria, the Committee found there to be no systematic medical examination of persons taken into police custody' and that a 'detainee had no right to be examined by a private doctor'.[115] A similar situation was revealed on its second visit, to Malta.[116] The reports on both of these visits recommended that 'in addition to examination by a police doctor, a person should have the right to be examined if he so wishes by a doctor of his own choice'.[117] This, however, does not go so far as to require the state medically to examine all detainees.[118] To the extent that this was implicit in the Austrian Report, it was soon recanted and the Second General Report refers to 'the right to request a medical

---

[113] Res 5C(XXXI), 13 Sept 1978, Draft Principles 21 and 22.

[114] See CAT A/50/44, para 101 (Libya).   [115] Austria 1, para 61.

[116] Malta 1, para 88. This situation remained unchanged at the time of the second visit. Malta 2, para 33.

[117] Austria 1, para 64; Malta 1, para 88.

[118] eg Sweden 1, paras 30–1, where (as in Malta) detainees were examined on request or if they appeared to be in need of examination. This was not in itself singled out for criticism. See also Rodley (1987), 260, who says that requiring a medical examination before and after every interrogation session might perhaps 'impose too heavy a burden on professional and financial resources'. Cf the ICJ which had raised this as a possible safeguard as far back as 1973. See *The Review*, Dec 1973, 23.

examination by a doctor of his own choice (in addition to any medical examination carried out by a doctor called by the police authorities).[119] It is also clear that it is the effective provision of medical supervision and care, rather than the organizational infrastructure through which it is delivered, which is important.[120]

It was the first Spanish report which probed more fully the detailed application of this standard. The Committee observed that where medical examinations were carried out by police or other state-employed doctors, the resulting reports were merely descriptive of the physical findings, not drawing any conclusions or recording the statements of the detainee regarding any injuries.[121] In light of this, the Committee recommended that 'all medical examinations of detainees be conducted out of the hearing, and preferably out of the sight, of police or Civil Guard officers' and that 'the results of all medical examinations as well as relevant statements by the detainee and the doctor's conclusions be formally recorded by the doctor and made available to the detainee.'[122]

A subsequent gloss was the acceptance of the right of the doctor not to be left out of sight of the police whilst conducting an examination.[123] This has now resulted in the standard formula the basics of which (modified as appropriate in the light of existing legal provisions and safeguards in the country concerned) have appeared in almost all first periodic reports,[124] providing that:[125]

The CPT recommends that specific legal provisions be adopted on the subject of the right of persons detained by the police to have access to a doctor. Those provisions should stipulate in particular:

—that a person taken into police custody has the right to be examined, if he so wishes, by a doctor of his choice, in addition to any examination carried out by a doctor called by the police authorities;

—that all medical examinations of persons in custody are to be conducted out of hearing and—unless the doctor concerned requests otherwise—out of the sight of police officers;

---

[119] Gen Rep 2, para 37. This now forms a part of the standard recital.

[120] Cf Germany 1, para 37, containing an explicit endorsement of a system in which examinations were carried out by doctors called by the police authorities.

[121] Spain 1, para 55.

[122] ibid, para 57. This formed the basis of the observations in Gen Rep 2, para 28.

[123] eg Ireland 1, para 47.

[124] The notable exception is the report on the first visit to Slovenia. Although the report stressed the importance of these factors, the Committee restricted its 'recommendation' to ensuring that the right of access to a doctor of the detainees choice was formally guaranteed (Slovenia 1, paras 35–6).

[125] The first report to carry the recommendation in this form was Malta 2, para 34. Previously, reference was made to 'detained persons' rather than 'persons taken into police custody'. Slovakia 1, para 44 and Bulgaria 1, para 89 also contain a slight variant, the reason for which—if any—is not obvious.

—that the results of every examination, as well as any relevant statements by the person in custody and the doctor's conclusions, are to be recorded in writing by the doctor and made available to the person in custody and his lawyer.[126]

Despite the emphasis which the CPT places upon this as a safeguard, the reaction of states has been cool. It is evident that a considerable number of states do not see the primary purpose of this recommendation to be as a safeguard against ill-treatment at all, but rather as pointing to a service which must be provided for those in need of medical assistance.[127] This perspective is further reflected in reactions to the requirement that the detainee be permitted access to a doctor of his own choosing. A number of states have rejected this out of hand, either directly,[128] or by implication,[129] whilst others are ambivalent.[130] France, having accepted the principle, subsequently changed its mind and left the choice of doctor with the authorities.[131] Other states which reject the need for a general rule to this effect offer a variety of reasons in support of their position, including problems of availability,[132] the limited benefit of the safeguard given the short time-scale of police custody, particularly when supplemented by other safegurads such as access to a lawyer,[133] and the observation that 'the police cannot examine the reliability of the doctors named in such a short time'.[134]

---

[126] This latter provision is not without difficulties. UK 2 raised a number of detailed points about the wording of the forms which those carrying out medical examinations at the holding centres were required to fill in, particularly where the detainee did not wish to record an allegation of ill-treatment but there were observable physical marks which would be consonant with such allegations (UK 2, para 71). Generally, the Committee took the view that the record drawn up by the police following a medical examination should contain: (i) an account of the statements made by the person concerned which are relevant to the medical examination (including his description of his state of health and any allegations of ill-treatment), (ii) an account of objective medical findings based on a thorough examination, and (iii) the doctor's conclusions in the light of (i) and (ii) (ibid, para 70).

[127] eg Denmark 1 R 1, 55 (but cf Denmark 2, para 36 where the CPT notes that such access was now granted); Sweden 1 R 1, 9 and R 2, 6 , where an examination requested by a detainee 'need not be carried out if it is clearly unncessary'; Greece 1 R 1, 17, referring to 'the option to call, in case he/she is ill, the physician of his choice . . .'.

[128] eg Switzerland 1 R 1, 11; Germany 1 R 1, 8: 'The doctors appointed by the police can be relied on to reach their conclusions to the best of their knowledge and conscience'.

[129] eg in response to the inadequacies noted in the CPT's report (Slovakia 1, para 43) the Government merely observed that existing procedures were 'effective and adequate' (Slovakia 1 R 1, 17). See similarly Hungary 1, para 48, and R 1, 85. Cf to the same effect Slovenia 1 R 1, 16: 'if the law enforcement officer . . . concluded that the detainee is ill or injured, he shall summon the duty doctor to the police premises, or see to it that the person is escorted to the nearest hospital . . .'.

[130] eg Austria 2 R 1, 16, impliedly rejects the right to a separate examination but accepts the more limited protection offered by allowing the detainee to request the presence of a doctor of his choice during an examination by a doctor appointed by the authorities, but provided that 'this does not seriously hold up the investigation'.

[131] France 1 R 2, 21.   [132] eg Luxembourg 1 R 1, 6.   [133] Iceland 1 R 1, 8.
[134] Germany 1 R 1, 8–9; Germany 2, para 35, and R 1, 88.

The cogency of such a standard in the broader context of the provision of medical services has also been questioned. Iceland, which had no particular objection to this 'if feasible or practical', pointed out that: 'When an Icelandic citizen urgently needs medical assistance he is not entitled to be served by a doctor of his choice, but must accept attendance by the doctor on duty at each particular time' and, in any case, doubted whether 'it would be ethical to impose the duty upon a doctor to provide medical consultation to an arrested person in every case when the arrested person requests this, particularly if there are no other grounds for his request than his desire to consult a doctor'.[135] These views have been echoed by others, pointing to the simple truth that the doctor requested to attend may choose not to do so.[136]

The underlying point of the standard is not of course that a particular doctor should be present, but that an independent doctor should be available. As with the other safeguards considered above, the CPT recognizes that it may not always be possible to permit such examinations to take place but it seeks clarity in provisions which might fetter its exercise.[137] As with access to a lawyer, it has also suggested that those being held 'incommunicado' (ie where contact is denied to third parties by operation of law) should be able to request an examination by a state-employed doctor and by a doctor chosen from a list 'drawn up in agreement with the appropriate professional body'.[138] A similar suggestion was made to the United Kingdom following the first periodic visit, but was rejected as 'unwarranted'.[139] This does not seem to have been pressed particularly hard and, given the general response of states, this is perhaps not surprising.[140] There is also the delicate question of the implied question mark which this 'safeguard' places on the professionalism of the police medical services (which has no direct comparator as regards the provision of legal advice to those in police custody) and it is possible to speculate that a Committee comprising a large number of medically-qualified members might feel uncomfortable working from overtly critical assumptions.

---

[135] Iceland 1 R, 1, 8.   [136] UK 3 R, 59.

[137] eg Ireland 1, paras 46–7: arrangements to be made 'if and as soon as practicable' came in for critical comment. See also Netherlands 1, para 46. In UK 2, para 67, the Committee questioned the practice of denying access to a detainee's own GP for a period of up to 48 hours, given that a medical officer would in any case have to be present to prevent discussion of other than medical matters.

[138] Spain 1, para 57. This was subsequently rejected on the grounds that, for the time being, it could not be set up in a way which permitted the reconciliation of the detainee's right to be informed of the indentiy of the doctor assisting him and the right of the doctor to safeguard his personal security *vis-à-vis* potential pressure from criminal organizations (Spain 2 R 1, para 20).

[139] See CPT letter to UK, para 37; UK 1 R 2, 21.

[140] France revealed that those doctors who had agreed to serve on such a panel turned out to be rarely available in practice. See France 1 R 2, 21.

There has also been some oscillation regarding the need for this safeguard to be prescribed in law. Early reports suggested that it was sufficient that this right be effectively enjoyed in practice.[141] Later reports, however, stress the need for legislative guarantees irrespective of whether, *de facto*, adequate provision is made[142] (and with some force where it is both absent and there is evidence of ill-treatment)[143] and this is now a part of the standard recital found in most reports, despite the reluctance by those states which did not already move in this direction.[144]

In contrast, the CPT seems to have modulated its views regarding the confidentiality of medical examinations by doctors of the detainee's choosing in the light of critical comments by states which question the appropriateness of requiring examinations to be conducted both out of hearing and out of sight of police officers. Several states have pointed out that the police are responsibile for the safety of doctors, the risk of hostage-takings, and attempted escape.[145] In response the CPT has indicated that privacy is preferable, unless the doctor concerned requests otherwise,[146] and this now forms part of the standard recital. This is still considered unacceptable by a significant number of states, which, whilst accepting that examinations should only be monitored where risk exists (or when requested, even if it does not), point out that 'only the police know whether the detainee has a potentially violent character or a criminal background, and what kind of motivation he might have to try to

---

[141] It is certainly sufficient for them to be covered by codes of practice, rather than guaranteed by legislative enactment. See eg, UK 1, para 220 and also Denmark 1, para 128, which recommended that the possibility of an arrested person having access to a doctor 'should be expressly provided for'.

[142] Finland 1, para 35 requested information on whether this right was guaranteed in law, and Greece 1, para 43 recommended that 'specific legal provisions be adopted on the subject of the right of all persons in police custody to have access to a doctor'. Also Italy 1, para 47; Iceland 1, para 36; Portugal 1, para 45; Norway 1, para 36; San Marino 1, paras 29–30; Belgium 1, para 47; Luxembourg 1, para 32; Liechtenstein 1, para 31; Netherlands Antilles 1, paras 52–3; Netherlands Aruba 1, para 221; Malta 2, para 34; Bulgaria 1, para 89; Hungary 1, para 48; UK 3, para 295; Slovenia 1, para 36.

[143] eg France 1, para 44: 'Le CPT considère cet amendement comme essential'.

[144] For example, Finland said that whilst there was no legal guarantee, 'the person to be examined is heard' when the decision regarding the choice of doctor was made, which could include the private doctor of the detainee, at his expense (Finland 1 R 1, 24). When the CPT pressed for a legal guarantee, this was rejected, on the grounds that it could lead to abuse (such as delaying investigations) and that 'given that an arrested person has in practice great freedom in choosing a doctor to examine him at his own cost, and that the entire public health care system in available to him at the state's expense, the kind of change in the law would seem inappropriate by Finnish standards.' (Finland 1 R 2, 6). Other states which have declined to place their practice (which generally conformed to the CPT's requirements) on a legal footing include Denmark 1 R 1, 55, and UK 3 R, 59. Cf Malta 2 R 1, 12, which agreed in principle to do so, but noting that 'in practice requests are very rare'.

[145] Finland 1 R 1, 19.

[146] CPT Letter to Finland, in Finland 1 R 2, Appendix, para 16.

escape or take a hostage'[147] It is understood, once again, that this safeguard will not be possible in all instances, but there are clearly differences remaining concerning how an appropriate balance should be struck between the considerations involved.[148] The CPT, perhaps surprisingly, has not expressly taken up the point made by Finland that the police personnel involved in monitoring medical examinations should be of the same sex as the detainee.[149]

Perhaps the least problematic element has been the suggestion that the detainee and lawyer have access to medical examination reports, though even here there is a wide spectrum of views ranging from: being a matter so obvious as to be not worth stating,[150] to reports being available on request,[151] to being a matter to be determined by the parties concerned,[152] to being 'at his own expense'.[153] It might also be noted that the fact that such examinations may be at the detainee's expense does not attract adverse comment, even though this may be a very real practical constraint,[154] and the lack of free provision of independent legal advice is, as has been seen, a cause of concern to the Committee.

The CPT has not delved deeply into what levels of provision are necessary to meet basic needs. This is not surprising, given the latitude given to states in determining the manner in which they will fulfil their obligation to ensure adequate medical facilities for detainees. In the report arising from its first visit to Finland, the Committee commented favourably on the level of provision at the police headquarters in Helsinki where there was a nurse present each day, a doctor on duty three days per week and a doctor permanently on call. That was contrasted with inadequate provision at a police-run detoxification centre where there was no nursing cover at weekends, the period of peak usage. The Committee recommended that this be rectified.[155] Certainly, a system in which a doctor is permanently 'on call' is seen as desirable,[156] as are schemes to alert police to the need to summon medical assistance,[157] whereas the failure to ensure that detainees are questioned about their health has come in for censure.[158]

---

[147] eg Finland 1 R 2, 7; UK 1 R 2, 21; UK 3 R, 59; Luxembourg 1 R 1, 6.
[148] cf Austria 2 R 1, 16, where it is said that the conditions in which examinations took place would be looked at, bearing in mind that 'politeness and decency should be preserved as far as the circumstances allow'.
[149] Finland 1 R 1, 19.   [150] Finland 1 R 2, 7.
[151] eg Luxembourg 1 R 1, 6.   [152] UK 1 R 2, 21.
[153] Germany 1 R 1, 9: 'he can have the result of the examination certified by the examining doctor at his own expense'.
[154] eg UK 1, para 220; Ireland 1, paras 46–7.   [155] Finland 1, para 39.
[156] eg Portugal, where the consideration of such a scheme being introduced to cover the Central Police Headquarters in Lisbon was described as an 'appropriate development' (Portugal 1, para 36).
[157] Germany 1, para 39, where such initiatives were described as 'particularly valuable and offer examples which could be more widely followed'.
[158] Norway 1, para 36.

(d) Notification of rights

The ICCPR provides that 'anyone who is arrested shall be informed, at the time of arrest, of the reasons for his arrest and shall be promptly informed of any charges against him'.[159] If subsequently charged with a criminal offence, this is supplemented by the right 'to be informed promptly and in detail in a language which he understands of the nature and cause of the charge against him'.[160] This differs slightly from the ECHR, which requires that: 'Everyone who is arrested shall be informed promptly, in a language which he understands, of the reasons for his arrest and of any charge against him'[161] and, if charged with a criminal offence, to be informed promptly, in a language which he understands and in detail of the nature and cause of the accusations against him'.[162] The chief difference is that under the ICCPR formulations the initial reasons must be given at the time of arrest, rather than promptly as under the ECHR, and this rules out any realistic prospect of requiring that the reasons be given in a language understood by the detainee in all cases. The gist of both provisions, however, is that the detainee be informed of the reasons for detention in a comprehensible fashion as soon as possible.[163]

Neither instrument, however, requires detainees to be informed of their rights as detainees once deprived of their liberty. Once again, this gap is partly addressed by the Principles of Detention, which provide that:

Any person shall, at the moment of arrest and at the commencement of detention or imprisonment, or promptly thereafter, be provided by the authority responsible for his arrest, detention or imprisonment, respectively with information on and an explanation of his rights and how to avail himself of such rights.[164]

Any person who does not adequately understand or speak the language used by the authorities responsible for his arrest, detention or imprisonment is entitled to receive promptly in a language which he understands the information referred to in principle 10, . . . and principle 13 and to have the assistance, free of charge, if necessary, of an interpreter in connection with legal proceedings subsequent to his arrest.[165]

Although this raises the issue of notification of rights, it still leaves open whether the notification is to be given 'immediately' or 'promptly'. When detainees do not understand the language of the responsible authorities, the requirement is, probably inevitably, one of 'promptness'. It is, however, unsatisfactory that the requirement of linguistic assistance extends only to legal proceedings arising out of the arrest. If the detainee cannot

---

[159] ICCPR Article 9(2). This is repeated *verbatim* in the Principles of Detention as Principle 10.
[160] ICCPR Article 14(3)(a).   [161] ECHR Article 5(2).
[162] ECHR Article 6(3)(a).   [163] See Cook (1991), 13.
[164] Principles of Detention, Principle 13.   [165] ibid, Principle 14.

communicate with a lawyer or doctor—or, indeed, does not have the linguistic skills required to request medical or legal assistance—then being informed of these rights in a comprehensible language is of little real value. It is also questionable whether the jurisprudence of the ECHR and the HRC has any relevance to the interpretation of 'promptly' in this context, since it has been developed primarily against the background of provisions intended to ensure that detainees have sufficient information to challenge the legality of detention and, if charged with a criminal offence, with the right to a fair trial.[166] Clearly, what might be sufficiently 'prompt' for these purposes may not be sufficient in the different circumstances presented by the practical exercise of procedural guarantees in a preventive context.

The CPT takes the view that 'it is equally fundamental that detained persons be informed without delay of all their rights, including those mentioned above'.[167] Indeed, the basic safeguards are rendered meaningless if detainees are unaware of them. It is, then, a little surprising that this requirement did not begin to feature prominently in CPT reports for some time. The report on the visit to Sweden carried out in May 1991 and adopted in February 1992 raised this issue, and the CPT recommended that:

a form setting out these rights be given systematically to [persons in police custody] at the outset of their custody. This form should be available in different languages. Further, the detainee should be asked to sign a statement attesting that he has been informed of these rights.[168]

The essence of this formula has been used in virtually all subsequent reports, even if this is currently the practice in the country or region in

---

[166] For example, in *Drescher Caldas v Uruguay*, Comm No 43/1979 (21 July 1983), para 13.2, 2 *SD* 80, 81, the HRC said that the purpose of this requirement was to enable the person 'to take immediate steps to secure his release if he believes that the reasons given are invalid or unfounded', and, in Gen Com No 13(21), 12 Apr 1984, para 8, that 'the right to be informed of the charge 'promptly' requires that information is given ... as soon as the charge is first made by a competent authority ... this right must arise when in the course of an investigation a court of a competent authority of the prosecution decides to take procedural steps against a person suspected of a crime or publicly names him as such'. See also Nowak (1993), 255. Under the ECHR the Court decided in *Fox, Campbell and Hartley v UK*, Judgment, 30 Aug 1990, Ser A, No 182, that a gap of several hours in perfecting the information was considered compatible with Article 5(2). Since this included information given out by the authorities in the course of interrogation, it clearly could not serve as a benchmark appropriate for the protection of the detainee from ill-treatment which might itself occur during the interrogation process. See also Harris, O'Bolye, and Warbrick (1995), 131, where cases in which the Commission has approved delays of up to 2 days are noted.

[167] The exact phraseology has varied over time. The version quoted is from Malta 2, para 25, and is similar to Germany 1, para 30, and is slightly changed from the formula in Gen Rep 2, para 37 and that used in most English language reports. See n 4 above. The principal change is that 'detained persons' replaces 'persons taken into custody'. This inverts the change made regarding access to a doctor (see above, p. 277). Since the French terminology seems to have remained constant in both contexts throughout ('personnes détenues), it seems unwise to extrapolate substantive observations from these linguistic alterations.

[168] Sweden 1, para 29.

question. Occasionally, the recommendation is limited to those rights which are not already adequately dealt with, this usually relating to medical examinations.[169] There have, however, been a number of interesting variations. It has been stressed that the form should set out those rights 'in a straightforward manner', the Committee having been concerned at the 'technical nature' of the wording in orally-communicated statements of rights to detainees in Portugal.[170] The Italian Report stressed the need to use a language understood by the detainee and that this be certified by him.[171] Both of these points were combined in the report on the visit to Finland: a booklet reproducing legal provisions and available only in Finnish also came in for criticism since 'the complexity of the language employed might render it obscure to many Finnish detainees and the booklet would be incomprehensible to foreigners'.[172] In consequence, it was recommended that forms be made available 'in an appropriate range of languages.'[173] Clearly, which languages are appropriate will depend on the local circumstances.[174] The report on the visit to Ireland illustrates a variant on this, confirming that forms should be available in a variety of languages, but also recommending that steps be taken to ensure that persons in police custody are informed of their rights in a language they understand.[175]

Thus it is not necessary to have forms in all relevant languages (indeed, this would be quite unreasonable) but it is necessary to ensure the effective communication of the detainee's rights, in either written or oral form. Some reports have required that the detainee 'certify' he has been informed of his rights, rather than spell out the manner in which this is to be recorded.[176] Recent reports draw on these elements and produce various permutations which might be intended to stress points of special relevance to the country concerned but which seem of little real significance.[177] The core, however, remains unaltered: detainees must be

---

[169] eg UK 2, para 72, where, acknowledging that written information was regularly given setting out rights to notify a third party and of access to a lawyer, the recommendation was limited to the right to seek independent medical examination. See also Ireland 1, para 49.

[170] Portugal 1, para 47.   [171] Italy 1, para 48. Also Luxembourg 1, para 34.

[172] Finland 1, para 42. See also Slovakia 1, para 46 (available in only one language).

[173] Finland 1, para 48; Slovakia 1, para 47.

[174] Perhaps surprisingly, the Committee did not mention the question of language at all in the report on its first visit to the Netherlands (Netherlands 1, para 48). This was raised, however, in Netherlands Antilles 1, 54 and Netherlands Aruba 1, paras 211, 223.

[175] Ireland 1, para 49. See also Belgium 1, para 48. Exceptionally, the report on the visit to Liechtenstein went beyond this, recommending the production of a brochure in various languages and the use of interpreters to ensure that foreigners in particular were made fully aware of both their rights and the legal procedures, and in a language understood by the detainee (Liechtenstein 1, para 32).

[176] Greece 1, para 44; Norway 1, para 37; Iceland 1, para 37; Malta 2, para 35.

[177] See, for examples, the subtle differences in UK 1, para 296; Netherlands Antilles 1, para 54; Hungary 1, para 49; Slovenia 1, para 37; Portugal 2, para 58.

made aware of their rights in an intelligible fashion. Forms setting out these rights must be available in an appropriate (but not comprehensive) range of languages, and detainees must record in some fashion the fact that their rights have been made known to them.

Most states seem happy to comply with the essence of these recommendations and the CPT can justifiably take credit for undertakings to produce leaflets and making them available in a wider range of languages than was previously the case.[178] Belgium, however, disagreed with the need to provide a form,[179] and, whilst confirming that information on rights was given, Germany observed that forms concerning access to lawyers existed 'in some Länder' without indicating any intention to take this further.[180] The UK thought it worth pointing out that 'many detainees or prisoners may refuse to certify or sign the form, either due to suspicion of what they might be signing, or from a desire to be obstructive'.[181] Attitudes concerning the range of languages in which such forms should be available also vary considerably, and this is only partly explained by the range of languages for which there might be a foreseeable need.[182] There is also some evidence of mild irritation with the stress laid upon communication being comprehensible, some states taking the view that it is patently obvious that this must be ensured, by the use of intepreters if necessary.[183]

2 OTHER PROCEDURAL SAFEGUARDS

The safeguards considered in the previous section take the form of rights which are to be granted to the detainee. The CPT also stresses the

[178] For leaflets compiled in order to give effect to CPT recommendations, see eg Finland 1 R 1, 21; Iceland 1 R 1, 8; Netherlands 1 R 1, 26; Malta 2 R 1, 14; Slovenia 1 R 1, 17; Sweden 1 R 1, 9; Luxembourg 1 R 1, 7; Austria 2, R 1, 18; Ireland 1 R 1 17; Netherlands Antilles 1 R 1, 15.

[179] A notable exception being Belgium, which thought it uncalled for given the terms of the ECHR (for which see above, p. 282), the relatively short period of police custody prior to an appearance before judicial authorities and the possibility of communication with a lawyer, who could inform them of their rights (Belgium 1 R 1, p. 18). Denmark also failed to act on this recommendation, which was reiterated in Denmark 2, paras 40–41.

[180] Germany 1 R 1, 8. In Germany 2 R 1, 87, the Federal Govenment said this would be considered, but it was noted that 'the problem will be that even a form in various languages will not be able to cover all relevant nationalities and language groups'. Portugal also appears less than enthusiastic, its response to the second CPT visit commenting that the question of information sheets was being studied (Portugal 2 R 1, 21).

[181] UK 3 R, 59. Signing the form was considered unnecessary in Netherlands Aruba 1 R 2, 135.

[182] eg UK 1 R 1, 43, notices available in 29 languages; Finland 1 R 1, 21, all EC languages and 'at least Russian and Estonian'; but Norway 1 R 1, 8, leaflets prepared in only Norwegian, English, and French.

[183] eg Finland 1, R 2, 8; Slovakia 1 R 1, 18.

significance of a number of other prodecural safeguards which, whilst not rights of the detainee, enhance the protective mantle cast around initial custody by regulating the conduct of law enforcement officers and subjecting them to independent scrutiny. The general prohibition of torture, ill-treatment, and inhumane treatment found in Articles 3 of the ECHR and 7 and 10 of the ICCPR provide a legal basis for these safeguards, but the level of specificity involved means that it is not worthwhile to try to locate the basis for the particular forms which these safeguards take within the legal instruments.

(a) Custody records

Keeping adequate custody records is an essential element of any protective framework. The HRC calls for 'the names [of detainees] and places of detention, as well as for the names of persons responsible for their detention, to be kept in registers readily available and acessible to those concerned, including relatives and friends'.[184] The SMR contain provisions on the keeping of a register[185] whilst Principle 12 of the Principles of Detention requires that:

1. There shall be duly recorded:
    (a) the reasons for the arrest;
    (b) the time of the arrest and the taking of the arrested person to a place of custody as well as that of his first appearance before a judicial or other authority;
    (c) the identity of the law enforcement officials concerned;
    (d) precise information concerning the place of custody.
2. Such records shall be communicated to the detained person, or his counsel, if any, in the form prescribed by law.

This is a fairly minimalist requirement and the CPT has gone much further, pressing for a single, comprehensive custody record which also includes medical reports. The CPT's standards concerning the keeping and content of custody records was developed in early reports and found its basic shape in the Second General Report which provided:

The CPT considers that the fundamental safeguards granted to persons in police custody would be reinforced (and the work of police officers quite possibly facilitated) if a single and comprehensive custody record were to exist for each person detained, on which would be recorded all aspects of his custody and action taken regarding them (when deprived of liberty and reasons for that measure; when told of rights; signs of injuries, mental illness, etc; when next of kin/ consulate and lawyer contacted and when visited by them; when offered food; when interrogated; when transferred or released, etc). For various matters (for

---

[184] Gen Com No 20(44), para 11.   [185] SMR, Rule 7.

example, items in the person's possession, the fact of being told of one's rights and of invoking or waiving them), the signature of the detainee would be obtained and, if necessary, the absence of a signature explained. Further, the detainee's lawyer would have access to such a custody record.[186]

This form of words (with minor modifications)[187] has been used consistently in virtually all[188] reports since adopted (and published), along with the recommendation that the relevant authorities examine the possibility of establishing such an individualized system where it does not exist[189] or highlighting areas in which existing provision is inadequate.[190] There has, however, been some variation in the reports on visits to some Central and Eastern European countries. Going beyond previous practice, this statement in its entirety was given as an express recommendation in the Hungarian Report.[191] On the other hand, the Slovenian, Slovak, and Bulgarian reports contained a modified statement, the principal difference being that the requirement that detainees' signatures be obtained is omitted, and was not given as a recommendation, but as a comment. The significance of the other alterations are not readily apparent but it seems that the force with which this standard is being advanced has been reduced as regards some eastern European countries.[192] Occasionally, the Committee has noted its satisfaction with the system in operation.[193] As a core minimum, the CPT lays particular stress on the importance of ensuring that a record must be made of the fact of detention without delay, irrespective of the purpose or length of time for which a person was detained.[194]

A small number of states have rejected the need for a single comprehensive custody record,[195] whilst others, though doubtful of it worth, have agreed to consider doing so.[196] Others, whilst not opposed to the

[186] Gen Rep 2, para 40. This list is a similar but expanded and more carefully phrased version of the list proposed in the very first report, Austria 1, para 69. See also Malta 1, para 92; Denmark 1, para 132; Spain 1, para 65; Sweden 1, para 32; Switzerland 1, para 129 (cf replacement of the reference to 'arrest' by a reference to 'deprivation of liberty').

[187] Including the eminently sensible decision to recommend the recording of all 'relevant' aspects of a detainee's custody.

[188] Portugal 1 being an exception. It was however, included in Portugal 2, para 62.

[189] eg France 1, para 50 (adopted June 1992).

[190] eg Slovenia 1, para 41.   [191] Hungary 1, para 53.

[192] See Slovenia 1, para 41; Slovakia 1, 52; Bulgaria 1, para 97, in each of which this gave rise to a 'comment', rather than a recommendation. But the previously used version was retained in Portugal 2, para 62, adopted subsequently, and gave rise to a recommendation.

[193] eg Ireland 1, para 53.

[194] eg Portugal 2, para 63, and cf Slovenia 1, para 42, where a backlog of seven detentions was noted and the Committee was told that records were not kept of periods of detention of under 6 hours.

[195] eg Switzerland 1 R 1, para 43; Germany 1 R 1, 10–11 (but cf Germany 2, para 39, where the CPT noted that such custody records had in fact been introduced, and welcomed this); Luxembourg 1 R 1, 8.

[196] eg Denmark 1 R 1, 60–1.

proposition,[197] have pointed to the added bureaucratic burdens which it creates. Many states not already keeping records in this form, however, appear quite willing to examine the matter and broaden the range of information recorded to meet the CPT's requirements.[198] Several states have introduced such forms as a consequence.[199] This appears to be an aspect of custody about which the CPT has been able to prompt a number of states into making changes in their practice.

(b) Conduct of interrogations

It is axiomatic that everyone charged with a criminal offence has the right 'not to be compelled to testify against himself or to confess guilt'[200] and the Principles of Detention provide that:

No detained person while being interrogated shall be subject to violence, threats or methods of interrogation which impair his capacity of decision or his judgment.[201]

Article 11 of the UNCAT provides that: 'Each State party shall keep under systemtic review interrogation rules, instructions, methods and practices ... with a view to preventing any cases of torture'. The CAT regularly questions states on their compliance with this requirement and has condemned the Israeli authorization of 'moderate physical pressure' in the wake of the Landau Report as 'completely unacceptable'.[202] This concern with interrogation practice has been echoed by the HRC which has specified that 'the time and place of all interrogations should be recorded, together with the names of all those present and this information should also be available for the purposes of judicial or administrative detention'.[203]

Principle 23 of the Principles on Detention adds further guidance, providing that:

1. The duration of any interrogation of a detained or imprisoned person and of the intervals between interrogations as well as the identity of the officials who conducted the interrogations and other persons present shall be recorded and certified in such a form as may be prescribed by law.

[197] eg Belgium, 1 R 1, 21; Spain 3 R, 133–4 (but cf the subsequent Spain 2 R 2, 64).

[198] eg Sweden 1, R 1, 13; Norway 1 R 2, 8; Iceland 1 R 1, 9–10.

[199] eg Spain 2 R 1, 64; Cyprus 1, para 62, Cyprus 2, paras 46–7.

[200] ICCPR Art 14(3)(g).   [201] Principle 21(2).

[202] See A/49/44, para 168. Israel was asked to submit to the CAT a special report on its interrogation tactics (see CAT/C/33/Add.2/Rev.1 (18 Feb 1997). This was considered by the CAT in CAT/C/SR.295–297 (15 May 1997) and led to a further condemnation. For a fuller discussion of the Landau report and Israeli practice see Chapter 2, pp. 41–51.

[203] Gen Com No 20(44), 2 Apr 1992, para 11. Its earlier General Comment on Article 7 had drawn attention to the preventive role played by 'measures of training and instruction of law enforcement officials' (Gen Com No 7(16) 27 July 1982, para 1).

2. A detained or imprisoned person, or his counsel when provided by law, shall have access to the information described in paragraph 1 of the present principle.

This transparantly malleable provision has been improved on by the SRT, who has argued that: 'Each interrogation should be initiated with the identification of all persons present. All interrogation sessions should be recorded and the identity of all persons present should be recorded in the records . . . The practice of blindfolding and hooding victims often makes the prosecution of torture virtually impossible, as victims are rendered incapable of identifying their torturers. Thus, blindfolding or hooding should be forbidden.'[204]

The CPT has adopted a similar approach to that found in the Principles on Detention, in that it points to matters which must be subject to regulation, but does not give specific guidance on their content. It covers, however, a much broader range of matters. Recent reports recommend that codes of practice be drawn up for police interrogations and that:

The code should address inter alia the following matters: the systematic informing of the detainee of the identity (name and/or number) of those present at the interview; the permissible length of an interrogation; rest periods between interviews and breaks during an interrogation; places in which interrogations may take place; whether the detainee may be required to stand while being questioned; the questioning of persons who are under the influence of drugs, alcohol, medicine, or who are in a state of shock. It should also be required that a record be systematically kept of the time at which interrogations start and end, of the persons present during each interrogation and of any request made by a detainee during the interrogation.

The position of particularly vulnerable persons (for example, the young, those who are mentally disabled or mentally ill) should be the subject of specific safeguards.[205]

The response of states has been at best lukewarm. Whilst some have been prepared to issue more detailed rules on interrogation practice[206] or

---

[204] SRT, Annual Report, 1995, E/CN.4/1995/34, para 926(d).

[205] The essence of this was set out in Gen Rep 2, para 39, but it has evolved over time. Its current form, quoted in the text, seems to have been settled towards the end of 1994 and is found, for example, in Netherlands Antilles 1, para 56; Netherlands Aruba 1, 225; Hungary 1, para 51; Slovenia 1, para 39; Slovakia 1, para 49, Portugal 2, para 59; Bulgaria 1, para 94 (last sentence omitted—in error?). Perhaps the most controversial change from the General Report formula has been the use of the word 'interrogation' in place of 'interview'. This provoked criticism from the UK on the grounds that it was pejorative (UK 3, R, 58–60, with reference to practice in Scotland).

[206] eg Iceland 1 R 1, 8; Malta 2 R 1, 11 (new guidelines issued in 1996, this not having been introduced following the first CPT visit in 1990); Austria 1 R 1, 9 (cf Austria 2, para 50, which noted that this had occurred but pointed to some inadequacies, notably the lack of a limit on the length of an interrogation, and of guidance for the question of specific categories of individual. In their response the Austrian authorities thought further action unnecessary for the time being (Austria 2 R 1, 17–18).

are prepared to consider doing so,[207] it appears that a considerable number consider it unnecessary to draw up specific codes of conduct, believing the existing patterns of police training and practice give adequate guidance,[208] and in some instances have held to this position despite the CPT prompting them to reconsider.[209] The impression is that the CPT's approach is generally considered to be unnecessarily formalistic.

Another issue related to the conduct of interrogations on which the CPT seems to be at variance with a considerable number of states concerns its views regarding the electronic recording of interviews.[210] At the outset the CPT formally *recommended* that states 'explore the possibility of making such recordings' where they do not already do so. The Committee argued that this is 'another useful safeguard against the ill-treatment of detainees (as well as having significant advantages for the police)',[211] subject to appropriate safeguards, for example 'one tape to be sealed in the presence of the detainee, the other used as a working copy'.[212] This now forms the basis of the formula used in almost all[213] reports.[214]

This suggestion has also prompted considerable opposition. As might be expected, some states consider it desirable—but potentially too costly seriously to contemplate.[215] Other states are prepared to give the matter further thought but are clearly dubious, doubting its practicality or utility, or questioning the cost.[216] A number of states, however, do not believe it to be appropriate as a standard practice, judging that it may hinder the general effectiveness of the interrogation process.[217] The CPT contests this view,[218] but it is clear that there is a degree of principled opposition to

[207] eg Slovenia, 1 R 1, 17; Slovakia 1 R 2, 80.

[208] eg Denmark 1 R 1, 56–9; Denmark 2, para 43; Finland 1 R 1, 21; Germany 1, R 1, 10–11; Germany 2, para 38 and R 1, 87; Sweden 1 R 1, 10–11 and R 2, 7; Netherlands 1 R 1, 26; Greece 1 R 1, 17–18, R 2, 19–20; Spain 3 R, 138; Belgium 1 R 1, 18; Luxembourg 1 R 1, 7; Cyprus 2, para 44; Portugal 2 R 1, 21–2.

[209] See Denmark 1 R 2, 179–80.

[210] Not only tape recording, but, exceptionally, even the use of video recording: UK 1, para 221. Cf UK 2, paras 76–81, where some concern was expressed over the use of CCTV to monitor police interrogations in the Northern Ireland holding centres. The CAT has also expressed concern over the failure to use video in Northern Ireland (A/47/44, para 125).

[211] Austria 1, para 67; Malta 1, para 90; Denmark 1, para 130; Gen Rep 2, para 39.

[212] Sweden 1, para 34.

[213] But not all. Electronic recording was not mentioned in the reports on the first visits to Portugal, San Marino, the Netherlands, and Italy. It was, however, raised in Portugal 2, para 61. This non-inclusion was possibly an oversight.

[214] eg France 1, para 49; Germany 1, para 43; Finland 1, para 48; Norway 1, para 40; Greece 1, para 47; Iceland 1, para 40; Luxembourg 1, para 36; Liechtenstein 1, para 34; Belgium 1, para 50.

[215] eg Spain 3 R, 138; Slovenia, 1 R 1, 17.

[216] eg Sweden 1 R 1, 11–12; Iceland 1 R 1, 9, R 2, 6; Norway 1 R 1, 9–10.

[217] eg Finland 1 R 1, 21: 'In most cases recording makes the person to be interrogated ... freeze and therefore results in the loss of a confidential atmosphere which police officers always try to creates'. See also Switzerland 1 R 1, 11; Belgium 1 R 1, 20; Luxembourg 1 R 1, 7.

[218] eg CPT letter to Finland in response to Finland 1 R 1, para 22.

the routine use of recording police interviews, a practice which seems not to exist in any European country except Britain, and the CPT has not so far been able to generate much support for the idea.[219] The fact that the CPT favours its widespread use does not seem to carry much weight and it appears that the Committee is no longer pressing the case as strongly as in the past: its recommendation to 'explore the possibilities' having been replaced by a comment carrying an 'invitation' to do so,[220] a clear downgrading.

(c) Complaints and inspectoral mechanisms

Both the ICCPR and the ECHR oblige states to ensure that those who claim that their rights under the conventions have been violated have an effective remedy,[221] whilst the UNCAT provides that the individual 'has the right to complain to, and have his case promptly and impartially examined by, its competent authorities'.[222] The need for effective complaints mechanisms is underlined by the HRC,[223] the SRT,[224] and the Principles of Detention.[225]

Alongside mechanisms for considering complaints of ill-treatment by detainees is the need for adequate mechanisms of inspection to deter and detect incidents of ill-treatment. The very existence of the ECPT, and the current discussions concerning the adoption of a draft protocol to the UNCAT to provide for such a mechanism at the international level, clearly bears this out. Mechanisms are also needed at the domestic level,

---

[219] eg Denmark 1 R 2, 180. See also UK 2 R 1, 18, with regard to the recording of interviews with suspects detained under the Prevention of Terrorism Act, where it was said that it could not be guaranteed that 'such a recording could not later come to be seen or heard by someone who had a punitive motive'. See also France 1 R 1, 37–8.

[220] eg Netherlands Antilles 1, para 57; Netherlands Aruba 1, para 226; Hungary 1, para 52; Slovenia 1, para 40; Slovakia 1, para 50; Portugal 2, para 61.

[221] ICCPR, Art 2; ECHR Art 13.

[222] UNCAT Art 12. In *Halimi-Nedzibi v Austria*, Comm No 8/1991 (18 Nov 1993), A/49/44, Annex V-A, 40, 45, a 15-month delay in instigating an inquiry was considered to violate Article 12. Article 11 further requires the state to investigate irrespective of a complaint having been made by the individual if it has reasonable grounds to believe that an act of torture has been committed. Article 16 extends both Articles 11 and 12 to other forms of cruel, inhuman, or degrading treatment or punishment.

[223] Gen Com No 20(44), para 14 makes the connection between Articles 7 and 2(3) stressing that: 'The right to lodge complaints against maltreatment prohibited by Article 7 must be recognized in the domestic law. Complaints must be investigated promptly and impartially by competent authorities so as to make the remedy effective'.

[224] SRT Annual Report, 1995, E/CN.4/1995/34, para 926(g): 'Independent national authorities, such as a national commission or ombudsman with investigatory and/or prosecutorial powers, should be established to receive and to investigate complaints. Complaints about torture should be dealt with immediately and should be investigated by an independent authority with no relation to that which is investigating or prosecuting the case against the alleged victim. See also E/CN.4/1988/17, paras 65 and 81(c), suggesting the institution of a panel of experts under the umbrella of the UN Advisory Services.

[225] Principle 33.

of course. The HRC has limited itself to requesting states to provide information on 'how impartial supervision' of penitentiary establishments is ensured'.[226] The Principles of Detention are more expansive, providing that 'places of detention shall be visited regularly by qualified and experienced persons appointed by, and responsible to, a competent authority distinct from the authority in charge of the administration of the place of detention or imprisonment.[227] It is, however, the SRT who has developed this most fully. In a passage worth quoting in full, he has expressed the view that:

Regular inspection of places of detention, especially when carried out as part of a system of periodic visits, constitutes one of the most effective preventive measures against torture. Inspections of all places of detention, including police lock-ups, pre-trial detention centres, security services premises, administrative detention areas and prisons, should be conducted by teams of *independent* experts. When inspection occurs, members of the inspection team should be afforded an opportunity to speak privately with detainees. The team should also report publicly on its findings. When official, rather than independent teams, carry out inspections, such teams should be composed of members of the judiciary, law enforcement officials, defence lawyers and physicians, as well as independent experts. Where such inspection teams have yet to be established, the International Committee of the Red Cross teams should be granted access to places of detention.[228]

The CPT, not surprisingly, takes the view that 'regular and unannounced visits by the prosecuting/judicial authorities to places where persons are detained by the police can have a significant effect in terms of preventing ill-treatment'.[229] In its report on the first visit to the UK the Committee 'noted with interest' the system of lay visitors[230] to police stations. In its Second General Report the Committee commented that 'the existence of an independent mechanism for examining complaints about treatment whilst in police custody is an essential safeguard'.[231] Its interest in these questions seems to have increased with the passing of time. Where the Committee feels that inspection is not always conducted in a conscientious fashion, it recommends that it be given a high priority.[232] The Committee now regularly seeks information on the relevant mechanisms in the countries visited, recommending that the establishment of such systems be explored where they do not exist[233] and examining the

---

[226] Gen Com No 21(44), para 6.   [227] Principle 29(1).
[228] SRT Annual Report, 1995, E/CN.4/1995/34, para 926(c).
[229] eg France 1, para 53; Italy 1, para 54; Finland 1, para 51; Liechtenstein 1, para 35; Luxembourg 1, para 38; Netherlands Antilles 1, para 67; Netherlands Aruba 1, para 230; Hungary 1, para 55; Slovenia 1, para 45; Denmark 3, para 45.
[230] UK 1, para 226.   [231] Gen Rep 2, para 41.
[232] Hungary 1, para 55; Malta 2, para 42, where is was an 'essential' safeguard, to be given a 'very high priority'.
[233] eg Ireland 1, para 57.

guarantees of their objectivity and independence where they do.[234] Information is also regularly requested on the use made of complaints and inspectoral mechanisms, and questions raised when there is a stark mismatch between the number of complaints investigated and the resulting number of disciplinary sanctions taken.[235] In this context, the Committee has also stressed the importance of ensuring that evidence obtained as a result of ill-treatment should not be admissible in legal proceedings.[236] Even so, the CPT has arguably developed fewer standards with respect to the accountability of custodial authorities than might have been expected, a topic to which we return in Chapter 9.

(d) Procedures relating to the removal of persons to another jurisdiction

It is now well established that a state might be in breach of its international obligations if it removes a person to another jurisdicition where there are substantial grounds for believing that he or she would be in danger of being subjected to torture, or inhuman or degrading treatment or punishment.[237] The HRC has said that states should inform it of the measures they have adopted to ensure that individuals are not exposed to such a risk 'upon return to a country by way of their extradition, expulsion or refoulement'[238] The CPT has raised this issue and, in a number of reports, has said that 'it would . . . like to receive information on the

---

[234] The Committee has questioned the composition of complaints boards and disciplinary tribunals where it considers them to be inadequate: eg Ireland 1, para 55, where criticism was made of a disciplinary tribunal in which one member was a senior officer in the police force to which the person facing charges belonged and the other members were drawn from the body which referred the complaint to the tribunal. See also UK 2, para 95; Denmark 2, para 44.

[235] eg UK 2, para 93. The Committee suggested that the burden of proof in such cases should be that used in civil (balance of probabilities) rather than criminal (beyond reasonable doubt) cases.

[236] Portugal 1, para 52. The Report refers to Article 15 of the UNCAT. Strictly speaking, this is inaccurate, since the UNCAT only bars the use of evidence obtained by acts of torture, as opposed to 'inhuman or degrading treatment'.

[237] eg *Soering v UK*, Judgment, 7 July 1989, Ser A, No 161, and see above, Chapter 3, pp. 94–7. Article 3 of the UNCAT expressly requires that this be so where the threat is of torture (as defined in the Convention), but not where the risk is of cruel, inhuman, or degrading treatment or punishment. The UNCAT has found states to have been in breach of this obligation in a number of individual communications. See eg, *Mutombo v Switzerland*, Comm No 13/1993 (27 Apr 1994), A/49/44 Annex V-B, 45; *Khan v Canada*, Comm No 15/1994 (15 Nov 1994), A/50/44, Annex A-a, 46. Cf also CAT/C/SR.234, para 38, in which a member of the Committee implied that the UK had violated Article 3 as regards Mr Chalal, even though the UK did not accept the optional individual petition procedure under Article 22 of the UNCAT and the case was pending before the European Court of Human Rights at the same time. The SRT believes that national legislation and practice should reflect the CAT's standard practice. See E/CN.4/1995/296, para (j).

[238] Gen Com No 20(44), para 9.

formal safeguards and practical arrangements which exist in order to ensure that aliens are not sent to a country where they run a risk of being subjected to torture or to inhuman or degrading treatment or punishment'.[239] If there has been some hesitancy it is probably because it lies towards the margins of the CPT's visit-based mandate. However, it appears that, as the subject matter has become an increasingly well established component of the jurisprudence of Article 3 of the ECHR, the CPT has adopted a progressively more robust approach,[240] and that states are generally willing to respond to such requests when made.[241]

These are difficult areas for the Committee. It has now acknowledged that the preventive role developed by the ECHR organs is better equipped to deal with instances of potential removal to a country where such a threat might exist, and has decided to pass any relevant material to the Commission of Human Rights, regardless of whether it has been submitted to the CPT or uncovered by it in the course of a visit, and thus raising questions regarding the confidentiality of material relating to visits.[242] For its part, the Committee 'is inclined to focus its attention on the question of whether the decision-making process as a whole offers suitable guarantees . . .' and, to that end:

will wish to explore whether the applicable procedure offers the persons concerned a real opportunity to present their cases, and whether the officials entrusted with handling such cases have been provided with appropriate training and have access to objective and independent information about the human rights situation in other countries. Further, in view of the potential gravity of the interests at stake, the Committee considers that a decision involving the removal of a person from a State's territory should be appealable before another body of an independent nature prior to its implementation.[243]

Obviously, states have not yet had an occasion to respond to this but it is likely to prove problematic, reaching as it does into the internal functioning and administrative decision-making processes within government departments which are not in themselves places of detention.

---

[239] Greece 1, para 51; Netherlands Antilles 1, para 61; Netherlands Aruba 1, para 232.

[240] eg Slovakia 1, para 66; Bulgaria 1, para 96, where the principle is described as 'axiomatic' and the CPT requests 'a detailed account of the precise practical steps taken . . . to ensure that such a situation does not occur'.

[241] It should be noted, however, that the level of detail provided varies greatly. For example, cf the lengthy explanation in UK 3 R, 38–50 with the much more general statements —of only a few lines—in Spain 2 R 1, 83–4, Austria 2 R 1, 22–3, and Greece 1 R 1, 19; Slovakia 1 R 2, 85 (a matter of six lines). It should also be noted that Bulgaria did not respond to the request at all.

[242] Gen Rep 7, para 33.   [243] ibid, para 34.

8

Conditions of Detention

An examination of the standards used by the CPT relating to conditions of detention is a complex undertaking and can be approached in a number ways, none of which is entirely satisfactory. At the heart of the problem lies the question of what actually is the purpose of the CPT's activities in this field. If the role of the Committee is to determine whether the conditions encountered amount to a violation of Article 3 of the ECHR, then the emphasis should be upon the cumulative impact of individual factors. This presents problems for an analysis of standards and of impact since, although general lessons can be distilled from the practice examined, it is very difficult to identify the thresholds of acceptability for each of the circumstances encountered. The possibility that differing combinations of the many factors at issue would lead to different conclusions further emphasizes the unique nature of each determination. At first sight it might seem appropriate to focus upon those situations in which the assessment is indicative of a violation precisely in order to facilitate this. This approach also has a certain sensationalist appeal. But it has a number of drawbacks.

The principal function of the Committee is to assist states to prevent ill-treatment rather than determine whether the conditions seen during a visit do or do not violate the ECHR Convention standard. As we saw in Chapter 6, the CPT has concluded in a considerable number of instances that conditions of detention can 'fairly be described' as inhuman or degrading—and in the light of the conditions encountered it is not difficult to agree with this assessment. Whilst it is hardly to be expected that the CPT could or would decline to comment in this fashion in such cases, it is important to remember that the jurisprudence in this area is not well developed, and so the Committee's findings are more likely to be seen by commentators as setting benchmarks than are similar findings relating to corporal ill-treatment.

The previous chapter examined the procedural safeguards which the Committee considers to be essential protections against ill-treatment in police custody, even though the failure to meet them might only amount to a violation of Article 3 in combination and in extreme circumstances.[1]

---

[1] Such as prolonged incommunicado detention. See Chapter 7, pp. 259–60.

Had the CPT, and the previous chapter, focused on the few instances in which this was the case, general improvements aimed at the protection of detainees, and the examination and analysis of them, would have suffered accordingly. It is, then, preferable to follow a more measured approach and focus upon a number of discrete aspects of conditions on each of which the CPT has offered guidance, albeit guidance of a more open-ended nature than that considered in the previous chapter and in consequence seldom possible to track in such detail.

The merits of this approach become apparant if one considers other international practice in this field. Unlike the ECHR, the ICCPR complements the prohibition on torture and ill-treatment by Article 10(1) which provides that:

All persons deprived of their liberty shall be treated with humanity and with respect for the inherent dignity of the human person.[2]

This goes further than Article 3 of the ECHR. Article 3, like Article 7 of the ICCPR, protects the individual from ill-treatment at the hands of the state. Article 10(1) obliges the state to adhere to minimum standards of humane treatment. This is a positive obligation[3] and 'cannot be dependent on the material resources available in the State party'.[4] Any situation which amounts to a violation of Article 7 will, in a custodial context, necessarily imply a violation of Article 10(1). But the converse does not apply. Not all incidents of inhumane treatment will necessarily be of sufficient intensity to warrant a finding of a breach of Article 7.[5] Thus if it is assumed that the limits of 'inhuman and degrading' treatment under Article 3 of the ECHR are coterminus with the limits of the similarly worded Article 7 of the ICCPR, this implies that there are circumstances which give rise to responsibility under the ICCPR but not under the ECHR. It is also possible, however, to see in Article 10(1) an alternative basis for a finding of a violation which might otherwise have fallen within an expansive interpretation of inhuman and degrading treatment. Certainly, most of the individual communications which have given rise to findings of a violation of Article 10(1) seem capable of being fairly described as 'inhuman or degrading treatment or punishment' and might have been so but for Article 10(1). For example a string of cases confirmed conditions in the 'Libertad' prison in Uruguay to be 'inhumane':[6]

---

[2] The substance of this is also reflected in the first of the UN Principles of Detention, which provides: 'All persons under any form of detention or imprisonment shall be treated in a humane manner and with respect for the inherent dignity of the human person.'

[3] Gen Com 21 (44), para 2.   [4] ibid, para 3.

[5] It has been concluded that 'inhuman treatment within the meaning of Article 10 evidences a lower intensity of disregard for human dignity than that within the meaning of Article 7'. See Nowak (1993), 186.

[6] eg *Cámpora Schweizer v Uruguay*, Comm No 66/1980 (12 Oct 1982) 2 *SD* 90, para 11: *Estrella v Uruguay*, Comm No 74/1980 (29 Mar 1983) 2 *SD* 93; *Bequio v Uruguay*, Comm No 88/1981 (29 Mar 1983), 2 *SD* 118; *Nieto v Uruguay* Comm No 92/1981, (25 July 1983)

... harassment and persecution by the guards, the regime of arbitrary prohibitions and unnecessary torments; the combination of solitude and isolation on the one hand and the fact of being constantly watched, listened to and followed by microphones and through peepholes on the other hand; the lack of contact with families, aggravated by worries about the difficulties, experiences and pressures exerted on their families; the cruel conditions in the punishment wing in which a prisoner might be detained for up to 90 days at a time;[7] the breakdown of physical and mental health through malnutrition, lack of sunshine and exercise, as well as nervous problems created by tension and ill-treatment.

Among the specific prison conditions recorded were: very small cells shared by two detainees for 23 hours per day;[8] prisoners being prevented from taking exercise at other times; prisoners being forbidden to lie on their beds from 6.30 am to 9.00 pm; and being allowed visits of only 45 minutes duration every two months.[9]

It is virtually impossible to discern any meaningful difference between those cases in which the HRC found that conditions violated Article 10(1) and those in which they violated Article 7, as is evident from those instances in which the HRC found violations of both Articles without distinguishing between them.[10] It is sufficient to note here that over a period of time it appears that the threshold at which conditions qualify for dual censure has been lowered somewhat.[11]

---

2 *SD* 126; *Cabreira de Estradet v Uruguay*, Comm No 105/1981 (21 July 1983) 2 *SD* 133; *Acosta v Uruguay*, Comm No 110/1981 (29 Mar 1984) 2 *SD* 148; *Lluberas v Uruguay*, Comm No 123/1982 (6 Apr 1984) 2 *SD* 155; *Conteris v Uruguay*, Comm No 139/1983, (17 July 1985) 2 *SD* 168; *Cariboni v Uruguay*, Comm No 159/1983 (27 Oct 1987) 2 *SD* 189. See also *Gilboa v Uruguay*, Comm No 147/1983 (1 Nov 1985) 2 *SD* 176, for similar conditions at female prisons and *Voituret v Uruguay*, Comm No 109/1981 (10 Apr 1984) 2 *SD* 146 (holding of a woman in solitary confinement in a cell with virtually no artificial light for 6 months in violation of Article 10(1)).

[7] This wing, known as 'La Isla' comprised 'small cells without windows, where artificial light is left on 24 hours a day'. See *Bequio v Uruguay*, Comm No 88/1981 (29 Mar 1983), 2 *SD* 118, para 10.3, where the HRC was of the view that Urguary had violated both Article 7 and 10(1) in holding the applicant in these cells for one month.

[8] In *Nieto v Uruguay*, Comm No 92/1981, (25 July 1993) 2 *SD* 126, para 1.7, these were recorded to be 2m by 3.5m.

[9] *Estrella v Uruguay*, Comm No 74/1980 (29 Mar 1983) 2 *SD* 93, paras 1.10–1.16.

[10] eg *Portorreal v Dominican Republic*, Comm No 188/1984 (5 Nov 1987) 2 *SD* 214, paras 2.2 and 11. The HRC was of the view that the applicant had been 'subjected to inhuman and degrading treatment and to lack of respect for his inherent human dignity during his detention' in violation of Article 7 and 10(1) following his being held for 50 hours in a cell 20 by 5 metres, holding in the region of 125 persons, in which 'owing to lack of space some detainees had to sit on excrement'. See also *Marais v Madagascar*, Comm No 49/1979 (24 Mar 1983) 2 *SD* 82 (solitary confinement in police cell measuring 2m by 1m for 20 months); *Wight v Madagascar*, Comm No 115/1982 (1 Apr 1985) 2 *SD* 151 (including solitary confinement in cell measuring 2m by 1.5m for three and a half months, chained to the floor with minimal food and clothing); *Muteba v Zaire*, Comm No 124/1982 (24 July 1984) 2 *SD* 158; *Herrera v Colombia*, Comm No 161/1983 (2 Nov 1987) 2 *SD* 192; *Jijon v Eucador*, Comm No 277/1988 (26 Mar 1992), A/47/40, Annex IX-I.

[11] eg *Conteris v Uruguay*, Comm No 139/1983, (17 July 1985) 2 *SD* 168, para 10, finding a violation of Article 7 'because of severe ill treatment ... suffered during the first three months of detention and the harsh and, at times, degrading conditions of his detention since then'.

To the extent that it is possible to provide a rough guide to the HRC's approach it might be that conditions of detention *per se* tend to fall for consideration under Article 10 unless there is evidence to suggest that conditions or regime features were part of a deliberate attempt to undermine the personality of the individual concerned and could therefore be considered ancillary to a principal purpose of inhumanity and degradation, rather than indicating a generalized lack of respect for the individual in question. This might explain why the HRC was of the view in *Griffin v Spain* that holding the applicant for a period of seven months in the following conditions in Melilla Prison violated Article 10 (1), but made no mention of Article 7:[12]

a 500 year old prison, virtually unchanged, infested with rats, lice, cockroaches and diseases; 30 persons per cell, among them old men, women, adolescents and an eight month old baby; no windows but only steel bars open to the cold and the wind; high incidence of suicide, self-mutilation, violent fights and beatings; human faeces all over the floor as the toilet, a hole in the ground, was flowing over; sea water for showers and often to drink as well; urine soaked blankets and mattresses to sleep on in spite of the fact that the supply rooms were full of new bedlinen, clothes, etc.

Such conditions are outrageous against any scale of standards. In addition, the HRC has been confronted with applications raising less extreme, but equally unacceptable, forms of inhumane treatment which have also been found to amount to violations of Article 10(1), including: cases of beatings by prison warders (which, amounting to violations of Article 7, are said to entail a violation of Article 10(1) also);[13] ill-treatment and deprivation of food;[14] internal banishment and internment in insanitary conditions;[15] detention for a week in a police lock-up, during which period only five minutes per day were allowed for basic hygiene and for exercise, meagre food supplies and alleged intimidation;[16] holding an applicant on

---

[12] *Griffin v Spain*, Comm No 493/1992 (4 Apr 1995), CCPR/C/57/1, 52, para 3.1.

[13] eg *Collins v Jamaica*, Comm No 240/1987 (1 Nov 1991) A/47/40, Annex IX-C, paras 2.12, 8.6; *Sutcliffe v Jamaica*, Comm No 271/1988 (30 Mar 1992), A/47/40 Annex IX-F, para 8.6; *Francis v Jamaica*, Comm No 606/1994 (25 July 1995) CCPR/C/57/1, 148, paras 4.5 and 9.2.

[14] *Wolf v Panama*, Comm No 289/1988 (26 Mar 1992), A/47/40, Annex IX-K, para 6.9 for a 5-day period. This was expressly said not to violate Article 7 and contrasts with *Tshisekedi v Zaire*, Comm No 242/1987 (2 Nov 1989) A/44/40 Annex X-I, para 13, in which 4 days of deprivation coupled with additional detention under 'unacceptable sanitary conditions' was said to violate Article 7 rather than Article 10(1).

[15] *Tshisekedi v Zaire*, Comm No 242/1987 (2 Nov 1989) A/44/40 Annex X-I; See also *Mpandanjila v Zaire*, Comm No 138/1983 (26 Mar 1986) 2 SD 164, for a finding of a violation in Article 10(1) in similar circumstances (and including inadequate access to medical assistance). It was the views expressed by the HRC in this earlier case which prompted the action which gave rise to the subsequent application.

[16] *Párkányi v Hungary*, Comm No 410/1990 (27 July 1992) A/47/40 Annex IX-Q, para 10. The HRC noted that 'legal provision should be made for both hygiene and exercise'. Cf *Vuolanne v Finland*, Comm No 265/1987 (7 Apr 1989) A/44/40 Annex X-J, where the HRC

death row in 'a cell measuring 10 x 10 feet, which was dirty and infested with cockroaches' and being 'only allowed out of his cell for a few minutes each day and sometimes remained locked up for 24 hours'; in addition to allegations of beatings and a lack of medical attention.[17] The HRC has, however, rejected the argument that being held on death row is inhumane *per se*.[18]

It is apparent that there is an almost limitless array of factors which may need to be taken into consideration when determining whether the conditions in which a person is detained are inhumane for the purposes of the Convention. Among the most important factors are: cell size and levels of occupancy; cleanliness; adequacy of food and drink; the regime to which detainees are subjected (such as out-of-cell time and exercise facilities); and contact with the outside world. Even this briefest of overviews of the work of the HRC under Article 10, however, is sufficient to show that studying findings of violations does not shed much light on what might be required of a state in fulfilling its obligation to provide a humane environment for detainees.

This, it seems, has been recognized by the HRC. In its latest General Comment on Article 10 the Committee chose not to explore the practical consequences of this obligation in detail. Rather, the HRC invited states 'to indicate in their reports to what extent they are applying the relevant United Nations standards applicable to the treatment of prisoners',[19] these being the SMR, the Principles of Detention, the Code of Conduct for Law Enforcement Officials (1979), and the Principles of Medical Ethics (1982).[20] These, then, provide the building blocks out of which the standard of humane treatment is to be constructed for the purposes of Article 10(1) of the ICCPR. It would seem apposite to adopt a similar approach when considering not only the content, but also the approach to the examination of the standards adopted by the CPT in relation to conditions of detention (the European Prison Rules[21] being added to the catalogue).

---

expressed the view that a 10-day period of solitary confinement in a cell measuring 2 by 3 metres (with 30 minutes out of cell each day) under a military discipline procedure did not violate Article 10.

[17] *Francis v Jamaica,* Comm No 606/1994 (25 July 1995) CCPR/C/57/1, 148.

[18] See eg, *Pratt and Morgan v Jamaica,* Comm No 210/1986 (6 Apr 1989); *Barret and Sutcliffe v Jamaica,* Comm Nos 270/1988 and 271/1988 (30 Mar 1992), A/47/40 Annex IX-F; *Kindler v Canada,* Comm No 470/1991 (30 July 1993); *Rogers v Jamaica,* Comm No 494/1992 (4 Apr 1995), CCPR/C/57/1, 168; *Simms v Jamaica,* Comm No 541/1993 (3 Apr 1995) CCPR/C/57/1, 185; *Johnson v Jamaica,* Comm No 588/1994 (22 Mar 1996) A/51/40, Annex VIII; *Edwards v Jamaica,* Comm No 529/1993 (28 July 1997), A/52/40, Annex VI-D; *Adams v Jamaica,* Comm No 607/1994 (30 Oct 1996), A/52/40, Annex VI-P.

[19] This is presumably an error: detainees must have been intended, given the inclusion of the Principles of Detention in the following list.

[20] Gen Com 21 (44), para 5.   [21] Recommendation No R (87) 3, adopted 12 Feb 1987.

The absence of an obligation equivalent to Article 10(1) of the ICCPR within the ECHR has not prevented the development of a jurisprudence relating to conditions of detention. However, it has arguably acted as a restraining factor and that jurisprudence is not well developed. Focusing upon the range of factors which can combine to produce a situation in violation of Article 3, rather than the nature of the combinations which do result in such a finding, is, then, an approach which remains true to the essence of the ECPT's role and function and is also well suited to assist in the development of that jurisprudence by providing a schematic account of what humane standards in detention are. The interpretation placed upon the interplay between those standards will always remain controversial, but, just as the HRC has brought the non-legally binding standards into the orbit of Article 10(1) through its General Comment, so the CPT can bring these and other standards into the orbit of Article 3 of the ECHR. Before examining the contribution of the CPT to this process, it will be useful, by way of background, to outline the nature and combinations of conditions of detention which the European Court and Commission of Human Rights has already acknowledged as being violations of Article 3.

The starting point must be the *Greek* case, where conditions of detention in the basement of the Bouboulinas Street police station, in the Averoff Prison in Athens, and at the Lakki Detention Camp on Leros were considered to be in breach of Article 3. The Commisson relied on a complicated combination of factors. In the police station these included: severe overcrowding; incommunicado detention for up to 30 days; no access to open air; limited light; no exercise; and, most critically, prolonged duration of detention in such conditions—in excess of 30 days in many cases (including one of up to nine months).[22] In the prisons the conditions included: gross overcrowding; no heating in winter; no hot water; limited access to sanitation; poor dental care; and severe restrictions to family contact.[23] The emphasis placed upon their cumulative impact makes its virtually impossible to determine whether any particular factor had a critical impact on this finding, or to construct a set of benchmarks against which to measure the acceptability of particular aspects of the condition in question.[24] It does, however, provide an important indication of those aspects

[22] Com Rep, 5 Nov 1969, (1969) 12 *ECHR Yb* 186, 468–80. Where similarly severe conditions were endured for shorter periods, the Commission did not find a violation of Article 3: eg 4th floor of Bouboulinas Street Police Station and at the security police headquarters in Pireaus; ibid, 480–1.

[23] ibid, 489.

[24] A similar observation can be made with regard to the recent finding of the Commission in *Tekin v Turkey*, Comm Rep, 17 Apr 1997, in which it was found that the applicant had been 'kept in a cold and dark cell, blindfolded and treated in a way which left wounds and bruises on his body in connection with his interrogation'. It was concluded that 'the conditions of detention and the treatment to which the applicant was subjected constituted

of detention which can fall for evaluation under Article 3, and in relation to which the CPT can legitimately be expected to develop standards as part of its preventive function.

Subsequent cases have confirmed that the conditions of detention can give rise to violations of Article 3 but have done little to clarify when this is likely to be the case. There are a number of situations in which such a finding seems likely. For example, in *Cyprus v Turkey* the Commission concluded that 'withholding of an adequate supply of food and drinking water and of adequate medical treatment' amounted to 'inhuman treatment'.[25] A further example relates to sanitation and hygiene. In *Hurtado v Switzerland* the Commission considered the manner in which the applicant had been treated to be 'humiliating and debasing for the applicant and therefore degrading within the meaning of Article 3' in that the authorities had 'neglected to take the most elementary hygiene measures by failing to make available to the applicant clean clothes to replace those soiled as a result of their action'.[26] In the light of this, it would seem that prolonged exposure to insanitary conditions would amount to degrading treatment irrespective of other factors, a conclusion supported by the opinion of the Commission in *McFeeley v UK*. In this case the Commission expressed the view that the condition of prison cells which had been smeared with excrement would have violated Article 3 but for the fact that these conditions were the consequences of the applicants' own actions.[27] Even in such cases as these, however, the assessment turns on the evaluation of the circumstances. This was made clear by the Commission in its Report in *Ireland v UK* when it said that the conditions of detention at Ballykinler police holding centre could not be regarded 'in the circumstances prevailing in Northern Ireland at the time' as violating Article 3.[28] This also may account for the finding of the Commission

at least inhuman and degrading treatment within the meaning of Article 3 of the Convention' (paras 214, 215). Here the difficulty is exacerbated by the linkage with physical ill-treatment. It is unlikely that the conditions of detention were considered as being 'at least' inhuman or degrading.

[25] *Cyprus v Turkey*, App Nos 5780/74 and 6950/75, Comm Rep, 10 July 1976, para 405, 4 *EHRR* 482, 541.

[26] Comm Rep, 8 July 1993, para 67. The applicant had been left wearing soiled clothes for 24 hours following his arrest.

[27] *McFeeley v UK*, App No 8317/78, Comm Dec, 15 May 1980, para 47, 20 DR 44, 80. Cf also *Guzzadi v Italy* in which the conditions of detention for those kept in a small area of the island of Asinara in 'compulsory residence' did not cross the relevant threshold, the Commission noting that the accommodation was 'uncomfortable' but thinking that this could have been due to the behaviour of the residents themselves (Comm Rep, 7 Dec 1978, para 82). The Court agreed that conditions were 'undoubtedly unpleasant and even irksome', but not in violation of Article 3 (*Guzzardi v Italy*, Judgment, 6 Nov 1980, Ser A, No 39, para 107).

[28] *Ireland v UK*, Comm Rep, 10 Mar 1976, Ser B, Vol 23-I, 479–80. It is unlikely that the conditions in question would have violated Article 3 in any event, these many being concerned with the unswept state of the floors and the absence of bedding for those who were yet to undergo interrogation.

in *B v UK*, in which the applicant complained of having been held in 'extremely slum conditions' whilst at Broodmoor hospital, in that the hospital was grossly overcrowded and the sanitary facilitites (both toilets and washing facilities) dirty and inadequate, that there was a prevailing atmosphere of violence, that he received no medical treatment, and that he was inadequately occupied. The Commission visited the Hospital and concluded that although there was 'deplorable overcrowding', the conditions observed did not breach Article 3, chiefly, it seems, on the basis that they considered the applicant to have exaggerated the situation.[29]

More recent cases continue to indicate a reluctance to characterize general conditions of detention[30] as 'inhuman'or 'degrading', even in circumstances where the CPT has expressed its opinion that this is the case. In *Delazarus v UK*[31] the applicant, a sentenced prisoner in Wandsworth Prison, was held in solitary confinement for 14 weeks pending a disciplinary hearing. During that time, he was kept in his cell with no integral sanitation for 23 hours per day. The Commission accepted that overcrowding, a lack of regime activities, and an absence of sanitary facilities could combine to produce a violation of Article 3—a combination of conditions so described by the CPT following their visit to Wandsworth Prison in 1990[32]—but decided that the application was inadmissible since the applicant could not complain of overcrowding, and the very fact of being in solitary confinement mitigated the impact of the lack of proper sanitation. The same issues were also raised in *Raphaie v UK*.[33] The applicant argued that being confined for 23 hours per day in an overcrowded cell (three in a cell intended for single occupancy) which had no internal sanitation was in violation of Article 3. Once again, the Commission found the application inadmissible, this time on the grounds that the situation of which the applicant was complaining ended upon his removal from Wandsworth Prison in December 1989 and that, since the application was submitted in January 1992, it did not comply with the rule requiring complaints to be made within six months of the alleged violation. Against this

---

[29] *B v UK*, App No 6870/75, Comm Rep, 7 Oct 1981, 32 *DR* 5, 29–30. For trenchant criticism of this case, arguing that the Commission failed to take account of the cumulative impact of the conditions encountered (a point made in the dissenting opinion of Mr Opsahl—later a member of the HRC), see Cassese, A (1993) 'Prohibition of Torture and Inhuamn or Degrading Treatment or Punishment' in MacDonald, R StJ, Matscher, F and Petzold, H, *The European System for the Protection of Human Rights* (Dordrecht: Martinus Nijhoff), 232–6.

[30] When more specific conditions—such as solitary confinement with a degree of sensory isolation—have been involved, both the Commission and ECHR have been reluctant to find a breach of Article 3. As Rodley (1987), 232 has put it: 'the task of balancing humane treatment with exceptional security needs is a difficult one, but it seems that, for the Commission, the balance can tilt a long way towards security concerns before Article 3 comes into play'.

[31] *Delazarus v UK*, App No 17525/90, Comm Dec, 16 Feb 1993.

[32] See Chapter Six, pp. 243–4.

[33] *Raphaie v UK*, App No 20035/92, Comm Dec, 3 Dec 1993.

background it is hardly surprising that if the CPT has visited an institution and has not characterized conditions of detention as inhuman or degrading, then the Commission is not likely to do so.[34]

The principal contribution of the CPT to the development of standards concerning custodial conditions lies less in the identification of relevant aspects deserving of critical scrutiny and more in the degree of specificity which it brings to its tasks. This presents a number of distinct problems for any analysis of standards and impact. The very nature of its visit-based operations brings the CPT into direct contact with physical conditions of detention. Inevitably, this means that the Committee moves beyond the generalism of the standards as set out in the SMR and the European Prison Rules. At the same time, two factors operate to reduce the more general impact of the CPT's work: the fact that the standards in question are developed in relation to specific premises or institutions visited means that it is often difficult to separate out points of general application from those points of detail the significance of which is partly or wholly related to the facility in question. This problem is exacerbated by the sheer number and complexity of the interrelating factors, which again tends to mean that the work of the Committee is more geared towards the problems of the particular places visited than with what they might indicate to be problems within the system as a whole. In consequence, the CPT's reports can be seen as having two elements: the restatement of primary standards, pitched at a level of generality not far removed from that set out in the non-binding Codes and Rules, and a series of institution-specific recommendations that reflect the CPT's perception of the shortcomings of the place in question in the light of all the relevant factors.

In consequence, the tasks of tracing the development of standards and of evaluating the impact of the CPT's work lead down separate paths. Unlike the case of the procedural standards considered in Chapter 7, the impact of the CPT cannot be traced by examining the acceptance or rejection of recommendations *as a matter of principle*, but must be done by considering the extent to which the particular changes requested have been made. However, examining the acceptance or rejection of specific recommendations relating to particular places of detention does not say a great deal about the acceptability of the basic standard which underpins the recommendation made. The very fact of developing the general standards in the context of focused, institution-specific recommendations fosters both the practical possibility of substantive developement of those standards and the near impossibility of gauging the extent to which even their

---

[34] In *Tosunoglu v Greece*, App No 21892/93, Comm Dec, 12 Feb 1996, the Commission took note of the CPT Report on Greece when determining that the general conditions of detention at Larissa Prison, which had been visited by the Committee, did not meet the threshold of seriousness necessary to render the application admissible.

implementation indicates indicates a generalized acceptance of that particular component of that recommendation, or, indeed, a more general compliance.

The statements of standards, their development and application by the CPT in reports, and the responses of states to them do not, then, combine in a fashion which permits conclusions to be readily or easily drawn. Rather than try to extract more from the material than it can reasonably bear, the following sections will limit themselves to setting out the basic standards which have been adopted by the CPT, indicating the degree to which the reports have added further clarity and definition which is of a general nature and which is not primarily the product of the interplay of factors at a particular place visited. This will be followed by a more general consideration of the responses to the recommendations made. This will not of itself indicate the degree to which states accept the developed standards applied by the CPT but it will give an impression of the degree to which states are willing to adopt the particular solutions suggested by the Committee for the particular problems observed in the places of detention in question.

2 THE STANDARDS APPLIED: POLICE CUSTODY

The SMR provide that:[35]

All accommodation provided for the use of prisoners and in particular all sleeping accommodation shall meet all requirements of health, due regard being paid to climatic conditions and particularly to cubic content of air, minimum floor space, lighting, heating and ventilation.

This deliberately open-textured provision is mirrored in the European Prison Rules, which provides in very similar terms that:[36]

The accommodation provided for prisoners, and in particular all sleeping accommodation, shall meet the requirements of health and hygiene, due regard being paid to climatic conditions and especially the cubic content of air, a reasonable amount of space, lighting and ventilation.

As might be expected, the CPT has added considerable detail to certain aspects of this.[37] The bulk of the CPT's work in this field is concerned with the overall quality of life within penal institutions, since this might not only lead to the creation of situations in which ill-treatment might occur but it may also amount to a form of ill-treatment in its own right.

---

[35] SMR, Rule 10.　　　[36] EPR Rule 15.

[37] As will be seen, however, this is not uniform. With regard to certain elements of this framework, such as lighting and ventilation, the SMR and EPR provide comparable levels of specificity.

Although this is also true for conditions of police detention, the primary risk in police custody is of physical ill-treatment. As regards prisons, although there is a risk of physical ill-treatment which must be guarded against, the principal concern is that the conditions encountered might cumulatively amount to a violation of Article 3.[38] The standards which the CPT seeks to bring to prison life are, then, intended to ensure that this does not occur and, in consequence, are more broadly drawn than the equivalent standards relating to police custody. They can be broken down into a number of discrete areas, and the following will be considered below: physical conditions; regime activities; outside contacts; complaints and grievance procedures.[39] The standards applied will vary depending on the type of institution in question. Comparison with the European Prison Rules shows that the CPT adopts and develops their basic structure in its recommendations[40] and the CPT has on several occasions expressly referred to the Rules when commenting on aspects of the conditions of detention it has encountered.[41] The extent to which the EPR underpin the work of the CPT is evident from the observation made in the first periodic report on Germany, when the Committee expressed the hope that, while renovating the Waldheim Prison in Saxony, 'the authorities will take full account, inter alia, of the relevant provisions of the European Prison Rules, in particular those in paragraphs 14 to 18'.[42] It has, however, also developed its own guidelines for police detention faciltities[43] and these will be considered first.

The CPT takes the view that:[44]

Custody by the police is in principle of relatively short duration. Consequently, physical conditions of detention cannot be expected to be as good in police establishments as in other places of detention where persons may be held for lengthy periods. However, certain elementary material requirements should be met.

---

[38] Of course, there are numerous instances in which the CPT has encountered conditions which it considers already to have breached this standard, as has been seen in Chapter 6, thus giving rise to the prospect of a direct clash with the jurisprudence under the ECHR.

[39] Special regimes of detention (eg segregation for disciplinary reasons or at the request of the prisoner) will not be considered here because of the extent to which they raise country specific issues.

[40] See Murdoch, J (1994) 'The Work of the Council of Europe's Torture Committee', 5 EJIL 220, 231–8.

[41] eg Sweden 1, para 43 (ventilation), Germany 1, para 90 (food).

[42] Germany 1, para 109. Articles 14–18 cover accommodation, sanitation, and hygiene.

[43] cf *Eggs v Switzerland*, App No 7431/76, Comm Dec, 11 Dec 1976, 6 *DR* 170, in which it was said that 'it is not established that the [European] "Minimum Rules" should be considered as principles to be applied by Member States . . . in all cases of persons [detained] for a short period on disciplinary grounds'. This case concerned a five-day disciplinary sanction imposed on a soldier engaged in national service.

[44] Gen Rep 2, para 42, and found in the introduction of most Reports since published. However, it was not used in Hungary, where the Committee found that police facilities were often used to house remand prisoners.

However, experience showed that this was not to be assumed. The longer the detainee is in police custody, the less acceptable the more basic forms of provision will be. The legal regime of police custody varies considerably from one country to another and, when account is taken of those countries in which it is not uncommon for remand prisoners to be housed in police facilities, it is evident that each situation must be assessed in the light of all the relevant and interrelated factors. It is possible nevertheless to identify core standards which will normally be insisted upon even if more, and occasionally less, stringent standards will sometimes be called for, depending on the use to which the particular facility is put.

Periodic reports currently provide that:[45]

Police cells should be clean, of a reasonable size for the number of persons they are used to accommodate, and have adequate lighting (i.e. sufficient to read by, sleeping periods excluded) and ventilation; preferably, cells should have natural light. Further, cells should be equipped with a means of rest (e.g. a fixed chair or bench), and persons obliged to stay overnight in custody should be provided with a clean mattress and blankets.

Persons in custody should be allowed to comply with the needs of nature when necessary in clean and decent conditions, and be offered adequate washing facilities. They should have ready access to drinking water and be given food at appropriate times, including at least one full meal (i.e. something more substantial than a sandwich) every day. Those detained for extended periods, 24 hours or more, should be allowed to take outdoor exercise.

It is difficult, if not impossible, to probe each of these factors separately and in the abstract in order to determine what is 'adequate'. This must be a matter of perception for the visiting delegation. However, it is clear that the Committee considers it necessary that detainees have access to toilet facilities at all times (and requests to use toilet facilities are responded to promptly, which implies an effective call system),[46] and thinks it preferable that showers should be available for their use. The reports give many examples of unacceptable conditions, illustrating the extent and degree to which the basic requirements set out above are not met. These will be returned to later.

The question of cell size can, however, be considered in greater detail since it has been illuminated and elaborated in both the general and visit reports in a manner which indicates a standard of more general application. Whilst admitting the difficulty of determining what is a reasonable size for a police cell (or equivalent), the Second General Report responded to the need expressed by delegations for a 'rough guideline' and continued:

---

[45] The basis of this was set out in Gen Rep·2 , para 42, and has been adapted in the light of experience. The principal alterations have been the addition of the final sentence and the reference to access to drinking water in reports adopted since the end of 1994 (see eg Netherlands Antilles 1, para 27; Netherlands Aruba 1, para 196; Austria 2, para 30; Slovenia 1, para 17; Slovakia 1, para 27) and in reports adopted since the end of 1995, the further requirement in the first line that police cells be clean (see eg, Slovakia 1, para 24; Malta 2, para 8).

[46] eg Spain 1, para 41.

The following criterion (seen as a desirable level rather than a minimum standard) is currently being used when assessing police cells intended for single occupancy for stays in excess of a few hours: in the order of 7 m², 2 or more between walls, 2.5 between floor and ceiling.[47]

In practice, the Committee has accepted that cells substantially smaller than this are acceptable, and it appears to have established a threshold of acceptability somewhere in the region of 4 and 4.5 m² for overnight stays.[48] Cells smaller than 4 m² have been judged acceptable only for holding detainees for a 'few' hours'.[49] The Committee has requested that very small holding-cells less than 2 m² be taken out of service, no matter how short their period of use.[50]

Standards relating to multiple occupancy cells are more difficult to elaborate. The CPT has, however said that 'cells of 6–7 m² should preferably accommodate not more that one person overnight, and never more than two, and that a cell of 10 m² should preferably accommodate not more than two persons overnight and never more than three.[51] Cells of 12 and 13 m² have been deemed acceptable for up to four prisoners overnight,[52] and cells of 15 m² should accommodate a maximum of five.[53] Where police facilities are used for longer periods of detention, more stringent criteria are applied.[54]

3 THE STANDARDS APPLIED: IMPRISONMENT

(a) Cell size and occupany

The SMR are premised upon the belief that single occupancy of cells is the ideal.[55] This is now widely regarded as outmoded[56] and this view is reflected in the EPR which provide that: 'Prisoners shall normally be

---

[47] Gen Rep 2, para 43.

[48] eg Belgium 1, para 26: 4 m² cells inappropriate for overnight stays; Spain 1, para 36: single occupancy cells of 'scarcely more than 4 m²' were thought to 'border on the unacceptable' for stays of over 24 hours.

[49] eg Spain 1, para 38; Italy 1, para 33, Belgium 1, para 26.

[50] eg Sweden 1, para 18 (1.45 m²); Belgium 1, para 29 (1.25 m²); France 2, para 25 (2 m²).

[51] Spain 2, para 44.

[52] In Athens and Pireaus cells of 12 and 13 m² respectively were considered suitable for at most 4 prisoners each for overnight use (rather than the 10 that they had recently held and which was 'unacceptable'), Greece 1, paras 54–9, 62.

[53] Spain 2, para 45.

[54] eg Hungary 1, paras 27–39, where the Committee found it 'a commonplace' for detainees to be held for extended periods. This also caused the Committee to raise questions of regime activities, not normally deemed relevant to police custody. See also Netherlands Antilles 1, para 15, where police facilities were used to house those held under the Aliens legislation.

[55] SMR, Rule 9(1).

[56] See eg Prison Reform International (1995) *Making Standards Work* (The Hague: PRI/UN), 60, pointing out that it is not necessarily undesirable to allow shared cells; Cassese (1996), 27–8, where is it argued that in southern Europe detainees 'would find separate cells, with little chance to socialize, inhuman'.

lodged during the night in individual cells except in cases where it is considered that there are advantages in sharing acommodation with other prisoners.'[57] The CPT has not taken a view on this,[58] but has chosen to focus on the levels of occupancy relative to the size of the cell or dormitory in question. Overcrowding is relevant to the CPT's mandate both because it affects the overall quality of life within an establishment and also because, in the Committee's opinion, it 'might be such as to be in itself inhuman or degrading from a physical standpoint'.[59] A prison population in excess of the official capacity, though never ideal, is not necessary unacceptable.[60]

In the report on its first visit to the UK, the Committee described as 'outrageous' the situation in Leeds Prison where up to three prisoners were held in cells of 8.6 m².[61] Single cells of 6 m² have been described as 'rather small', but acceptable if a significant portion of the day is spent out the cell.[62] Cells of 4 m² and smaller are considered to be altogether unacceptable, irrespective of their use.[63] It seems to have adopted a toleration threshold of around 9 m² for two-person cells,[64] below which conditions are considered 'cramped'.[65] Cells of 7 m² should hold no more than one prisoner.[66] A reasonably good indication of CPT thinking is given in the Report on the first periodic visit to Slovakia in which it was noted that at Bratislava Prison:[67]

In theory, there were three types of cells: two-persons (approximately 9–10 m²), three persons (about 12 m²) and four person (16–17 m²).

Although this was considered to be 'restricted', it appears to be an acceptable baseline. When the occupany levels of such cells increase, however, they become 'unacceptable'.[68]

---

[57] EPR, Rule 14(1).

[58] It does, however, incline towards single occupany as the most desirable option. See eg, Denmark 1, paras 39–40.

[59] Spain 1, para 117; Gen Rep 2, para 46.   [60] eg Austria 1, para 33.

[61] UK 1, para 39.   [62] Sweden 1, paras 46, 73 (Kumla Remand Centre).

[63] Finland 1, para 81; and see Hungary 1, paras 93, 97, where cubicles of 1.2 m² in a reception unit at Budapest Remand Prison were condemned outright.

[64] Spain 1, para 126; Ireland 1, para 78; Spain 2, para 113, where 10 m² for two inmates was described as 'just about adequate' and Austria 2, para 103, where the CPT stressed that 'cells of about 10 m²—even when fitted with a partitioned lavatory—are not of an ideal size for double occupancy'. Cf Greece 1, para 109, where the Committee urged that cells of 9.5 m² should hold no more that 3 prisoners and 'serious efforts' be made to reduce this to 2.

[65] UK 2, para 119.

[66] Hungary 1, para 97. The Committee had found instances of as many as 4 in a cell of this size in the Budapest Central Remand Prison, and up to 6 in cells of 14 m² (ibid, para 91). But cf Slovenia 1, para 63, where the dual occupancy of such cells was considered 'cramped' rather than unacceptable.

[67] Slovakia 1, para 75.

[68] In fact, the CPT noted that in Bratislava Prison, 'two-person cells often had three or four occupants, three-person cells four occupants and four person cells six occupants' (ibid).

In general, the CPT considers large-scale dormitory-style prison accommodation to be unsatisfactory, even if not overcrowded, because of the increased lack of privacy and risk of violence.[69] However, dormitories of 21 m² have been considered acceptable for five prisoners,[70] cells of 25 m² 'should accommodate an absolute maximum of six prisoners',[71] and it has said that 'a dormitory of 60 m² should never be used to accommodate more than 12 prisoners and one of 35 m² more than 7'.[72] Once again, the toleration threshold appears to be somewhat lower and the Slovak report indicates broad tolerance of the following official occupany levels at the Leopoldov Prison, it being accepted that it represents only 'a limited amount of living space':[73]

cells measuring 11–22 m²—up to three prisoners; cells measuring 21–29 m²— six or seven prisoners; cells measuring 25–38 m²—eight or nine prisoners; cells measuring 31–35 m²—ten prisoners; cells measuring approximately 40 m²— twelve prisoners; and cells measuring 51m²—sixteen prisoners.

(b) Hygiene and sanitation

Of course, cell size and occupancy form merely one aspect of the material conditions of detention. Amongst the other factors, the Committee pays particular attention to hygiene and sanitation. The EPR provide that: 'The sanitary installations and arrangements for access shall be adequate to enable every prisoner to comply with the needs of nature when necessary and in clean and decent conditions'.[74] The CPT has built on this and it was stressed in the Second General Report that:

regular access to proper toilet facilities and the maintenance of good standards of hygiene are essential components of a humane environment. In this connection, the CPT must state that it does not like the practice found in certain countries of prisoners discharging human waste in buckets in their cells (which are subsequently 'slopped out' at appointed times. Either a toilet facility should be located in cellular accommodation (preferably in a sanitary annex) or means should exist enabling prisoners who need to use a toilet facility to be released from their cells without undue delay at all time (including at night).[75]

---

[69] Spain 1, para 122.
[70] Greece 1, para 117—although it was made clear that a maximum of 4 would be preferable.
[71] Austria 2, para 66.   [72] Slovenia 1, para 63.
[73] Slovakia 1, para 86. Once again, however, actual occupany rates were in excess of the official levels, and 14 beds were noted in a 9-person unit of 35 m² which was considered 'quite unacceptable' (ibid, para 87).
[74] EPR, Rule 17. Cf SMR, Rule 12: 'The sanitary installations shall be adequate to enable every prisoner to comply with the needs of nature when necessary and in a clean and decent manner.'
[75] Gen Rep 2, para 49. This has formed the basis of observations made in a number of subsequent reports, including Finland 1, para 81 (Helsinki Central Prison); Norway 1, para 78 (Oslo Prison).

Indeed, it has already been noted that the CPT considers defecating into a bucket in the presence of another person in a confined area used as a living space to be degrading.[76]

Where sanitary facilities are not in a separate annex, proper screening arrangements should be made and the CPT has, rather bluntly, said that the result of installing unscreened lavatories in cells is that the inmate(s) concerned 'could be said to be living in a lavatory'.[77] This standard has been constantly reflected in the reports. Where there are no in-cell facilities, it appears that maximum waiting times of between 10 and 20 minutes to respond to a request to use a lavatory appear to be acceptable.[78]

As regards washing facilities, the CPT is of the view that:

prisoners should have adequate access to shower or bathing facilities. It is desirable for running water to be available within cellular accommodation.[79]

The SMR appear to be more specific in that they state that prisoners 'may be entitled and required to have a bath or shower, at a temperature suitable to the climate, as frequently as necessary for general hygiene according to season and geographical region, but at least once a week.'[80] The EPR add to this that: 'Wherever possible there should be free access at all reasonable times'.[81] However, the CPT expressly recalled EPR, Rule 18 when stating that 'access to bathing facilities at least once a week is an absolute mimimum requirement ... in any prison', and that: 'In an establishment where prisoners do not have ready access to either toilet facilities or running water, a shower once a week cannot be considered sufficient'.[82] Equally, in particularly warm weather, bi-weekly access may not necessarily be sufficient.[83]

(c) Other questions

The Committee is also concerned with the ventilation, lighting, and furnishing of cells, to include a bed, mattress, cupboard, table and chair, as well as the provision of adequate supplies of sheets and towels.[84] It is clear that the EPR provide the inspiration for the CPT, whose observations on

---

[76] See above, Chapter 6, pp. 243–4, and UK 1, para 47 and UK 2, para 120.

[77] UK 3, para 80; Portugal 2, para 99.

[78] Sweden 1, para 47. Netherlands 1, para 39. Cf Sweden 1, para 74, where night waiting times of up to one hour at Kumla Prison were considered unsatisfactory.

[79] Gen Rep 2, para 49.   [80] SMR, Rule 13.   [81] EPR, Rule 18.

[82] UK 1, para 74. The CPT condemned the facilities at Leeds and Wandsworth prisons as 'falling below the threshold of acceptability' (ibid).

[83] France 1, para 112.

[84] eg Spain 1, para 181: 'prisoners should be provided with two clean sheets and one or more clean towels every week, and that each new prisoner should be provided with a clean set of blankets'.

these questions are so particularized that it is not profitable to search for greater clarity in the standards than that set by the Rules themselves.[85]

(d) Regime

The CPT takes as its starting point the basic criterion that all prisoners should be allowed 'at least one hour of exercise in the open air every day' This applies to all prisoners, including those subject to disciplinary measures.[86] Moreover, 'it is axiomatic that outdoor exercise facilities should be reasonably spacious and whenever possible offer shelter from inclement weather'.[87]

Beyond this, the CPT takes the view that 'a satisfactory programme of activities (work, education, sport, etc) is of crucial importance for the well being of prisoners'.[88] It recognizes that it is not possible to offer as developed a programme of activities for remand prisoners as for sentenced prisoners. Nevertheless, the Committee takes the view that 'the aim should be to ensure that remand prisoners spend a reasonable part of the day (8 hours or more) outside their cells, engaged in purposeful activities of a varied nature (work, preferably with vocational value, education; sport; recreation/association)'.[89]

Sentenced prisoners should enjoy an even more favourable regime, in the sense that the activities offered should be geared more closely to the particular needs of the prisoner concerned. It is not possible to lay down in the abstract and with any precision the level of provision required of an establishment since this is a product of too great a number of variable factors (some general, some specific to the institution concerned). What is clear, however, is that out-of-cell time is no substitute for activity. Hence the Committee concluded of Greece that prison regimes were 'rich in out of cell time but poor in activities ... the activities of the great majority of prisoners consisted essentially of outdoor exercise, association and watching television in their cells. Such a regime is not adequate, and is

---

[85] The EPR provide:

'16. In all places where prisoners are required to live or work:

a. The windows shall be large enough to enable the prisoners, *inter alia*, to read or work by natural light in normal conditions. They shall be so constructed that they can allow the entrance of fresh air except when there is an adequate air conditioning system. Moreover, the windows shall, with due regard to security requirements, present in their size, location and construction as normal an appearance as possible:

b. Artificial light shall satisfy recognized technical standards

19. All parts of an institution shall be properly maintained and kept clean at all times.

24. Every prisoner shall be provided with a separate bed and separate and appropriate bedding which shall be kept in good order and changed often enough to ensure its cleanliness.

[86] Spain 1, para 48.   [87] ibid.   [88] ibid, para 47.

[89] Hungary 1, para 97; Slovenia 1, para 71. Also Gen Rep 2, para 47.

particularly undesirable for juveniles and for prisoners serving lengthy sentences'.[90]

By way of illustration, this might be contrasted with a programme of activities commended as 'very well developed':

Inmates who so wished—which is to say almost all prisoners—could work four days a week (up to a total of 140 hours per month) in one of 25 prison workshops (production of car parts, printing, shoe-mending, locksmithing, joinery, etc), a certain number of which also offered vocational training. . . . Moreover, a large number of educational and training activities were also available. Vocational train-ing leading to an examination and the award of a certificate covered such areas as car mechanics, baking, training as cooks and waiters, book binding, electrical work, men's clothing etc.[91]

It is important that the range of activities offered should be appropriate for the specific group of prisoners concerned. Thus young persons in cus-tody 'should be provided with a full regime of educational, recreational and other purposeful activities. Physical education should constitute a significant element in that regime. Moreover, the staff assigned to units accommodating juveniles should be carefully chosen and, more specific-ally, be persons capable of guiding and motivating young people'.[92] In this context, providing only one hour of formal teaching per week is 'man-ifestly insufficient in an establishment designed for the detention of school aged inmates'.[93]

(e) Outside contacts

The Committee takes the view that:

It is very important for prisoners to be able to maintain reasonably good con-tact with the outside world. Above all, a prisoner must be given the means of safeguarding his relationships with his family and close friends, in particular his wife/partner and children. . . . The guiding principle should be the promo-tion of contact with the outside world; any limitations upon such contact should be based exclusively on security concerns of an appreciable nature or resource considerations.[94]

The reports add some detail to this. Weekly visits from a family mem-ber and permission to use the phone regularly (ie at least once a week), coupled with free use of the mail (censored only in exceptional circum-stances)[95] and home leave arrangements are components of a satisfactory

---

[90] Greece 1, para 120.   [91] Austria 2, para 105 (comments on Stein Prison).
[92] Greece 1, para 116; Slovenia 1, para 76.   [93] Netherlands 1, para 116.
[94] Hungary 1, para 127. See also Ireland 1, para 158; Gen Rep 2, para 51.
[95] See also Ireland 1, para 164, in which the Committee 'invited' Ireland to consider abol-ishing its rule that all correspondence to or from a prisoner must be read by a prison officer.

level of provision.[96] Two hours of visits per month (with the possibility of further visits being authorized) has been deemed acceptable: one hour per month is not.[97] Even more unacceptable was the situation of remand prisoners in Ljubljana (Slovenia), when they were permitted a single, supervised, visit of 15 minutes per week.[98] The Committee accepts the need to control communications with remand prisoners. However, it also takes the view that 'granting prisoners the right to receive extended unsupervised visits in order to maintain family and personal (including sexual) relations would be a commendable step, provided that such visits took place in conditions which respected human dignity'.[99] In its report on the first visit to Norway the Committee remarked on the poor furnishings of the cells set aside for such visits—artificial lighting, a sofa, and a washbasin—and said that 'the aim should be for these visits to take place under home-like conditions, thereby promoting stable relationships'.[100]

In general, the Committee has said that it:

wishes to emphasise in this context the need for some flexibility as regards the application of rules on visits and telephones contacts viz-à-vis prisoners whose families live far away (thereby rendering regular visits impracticable). For example, such prisoners could be allowed to accumulate visiting time and/or be offered improved possibilities for telephone contacts with their families.[101]

The Committee has welcomed the installation of card phones, particularly where it was claimed that, since the authorities bore the expense of calls, their use had to be strictly limited.[102]

(f) Grievance and inspection procedures

As might be expected, the Committee considers effective grievance and inspection procedures to be fundamental safeguards against ill-treatment. To this end, it seeks to ensure that prisoners have:

avenues of complaint open to them both within and outside the context of the prison system, including the possibility to have confidential access to an appropriate authority. The CPT attaches particular importance to regular visits to each prison establishment by an independent body (eg a Board of Visitors or supervisory judge) possessing powers to hear (and if necessary take action upon) complaints from prisoners and to inspect the establishment's premises.[103]

---

[96] eg Greece 1, para 127.
[97] Hungary 1, paras 128–9. Also Ireland 1, para 161, visits of 30 minutes per week were 'adequate, although they could hardly be described as generous'.
[98] Slovenia 1, para 79.   [99] Ireland 1, para 161.   [100] Norway 1, para 109.
[101] Gen Rep 2, para 51; Netherlands Antilles 1, para 110.
[102] Ireland 1, para 165: one call of 5 minutes per week permitted, cost met by the State.
[103] Gen Rep 2, para 54.

In addition to such formal safeguards the Committee also encourages states to consider creating such mechanisms where they do not already exist:

a visiting committee composed of members of the public, acting in an independent capacity) for each prison establishment, with responsibility for undertaking regular visits (preferably weekly and at least monthly) and authority to enter all the premises and talk freely with any prisoner (in order to receive any complaints). Such a committee would no doubt submit reports to the director of the establishment, but should also be empowered, where necessary, to report directly to a higher level of authority.[104]

The Committee regularly examines the existing procedures in the light of these *desiderata*.

(g) Health care services in prisons

A final area where the Committee has elaborated its standards in detail concerns the provision of medical services. In its Third General Report, the Committee explained that this was 'a subject of direct relevance to the CPT's mandate' because 'an inadequate level of health care can lead rapidly to situations falling within the scope of the term "inhuman and degrading treatment" '.[105] This view is not altogether unproblematic. Without seeking to question the desirability of the standards promulgated, the principle of 'equivalence of care' with services provided outside of the penal system—said to be 'inherent in the fundamental rights of the individual'[106] —begs the question of the adequacy of such provision available outside of the institution. No matter how inadequate the health care provision within an institution, it will always be contentious to equate that provision with inhuman or degrading treatment, notwithstanding the duty of care owed by the State to those it deprives of their liberty,[107] if it is at least as good as that which would have been available to the person concerned outside of that system. Less controversial is the proposition that the health care service 'is well placed to make a positive impact on the overall quality of life in the establishment within which it operates'.[108] To this end, the Committee has elaborated a detailed set of standards in its Third General Report (1993) and this remains the template against which health care service provision is measured.

Rather than summarize the standards, the relevant sections of the Third General Report are set out in Appendix 7C. However, attention should be drawn to the way in which the standards overlap with other areas of concern and, as such, represent collateral means of achieving

---

[104] Italy 1, para 149; Greece 1, para 144.
[105] Gen Rep 3, para 30.   [106] ibid, para 31.
[107] For which see above, Chapter 3, pp. 99, 105, and Chapter 6, pp. 251–3, section 7(c).
[108] ibid.

certain results. For example, 'Preventive health care' embraces general hygiene standards, and 'insalubrity, overcrowding, prolonged isolation and inactivity may necessitate either medical assistance for an individual prisoner or general medical action vis-à-vis the responsible authority'.[109] Thus general concerns are 're-presented' from a health care perspective. A similar—and perhaps less convincing—example of the same technique concerns the promotion of social and family ties and, in particular, the need for 'properly equipped visiting areas'.[110] The heath care standards also 'emphasise that there is no medical justification for the segregation of an HIV+ prisoner who is well'.[111] It is the view of the Committee that this means that such prisoners should not be subject to any form of segregation[112] (except at the request of the prisoner).

The aspect of health care services which is, perhaps, connected most closely with the prevention of torture and inhuman or degrading treatment or punishment is the extent to which it 'can potentially play an important role in combating the infliction of ill-treatment, both in that establishment and elsewhere (in particular in police establishments)'.[113] To this end, it is the policy of the CPT to recommend that:

all newly admitted prisoners—sentenced or remand—should be seen without delay be a member of the prison health care service and, if necessary, given a medical examination. The medical screening on admission could be undertaken either by a doctor or by a qualified nurse reporting to a doctor. Moreover any signs of violence observed on admission should be fully recorded, together with any relevant statement by the prisoner and the doctor's conclusions; this information should be made available to the prisoner. The same approach should be followed whenever the prisoner is medically examined following a violent episode in the prison.[114]

Additional medical examinations should take place whenever a prisoner is readmitted to prison after having been returned to police custody for questioning.[115]

In a sense, this brings this overview of the CPT's core standards full circle and is a convenient place to bring this aspect of the discussion to a close. In what follows, the broad outlines of the response of European states to the mechanism and operation of the CPT, as set out in Chapter 5, and the standards it has developed and applied, which have been set out in Chapters 6, 7, and the current chapter, will be considered.

---

[109] ibid, para 53.   [110] ibid, para 63.   [111] ibid, para 56.
[112] eg Ireland 1, para 138.   [113] Gen Rep 3, para 30.
[114] eg Slovenia 1, para 74 and see Gen Rep 3, para 33.
[115] Hungary 1, para 110.

9
Current Assessment and Future Prospects

The purpose of this chapter is to draw together the issues that have been considered previously, to provide an evaluation of the ECPT and to present a number of suggestions based on this examination. The first section, recalling the questions raised by the overview of the history of torture presented in Chapters 1 and 2 and relating them to trends in contemporary European civil society, makes a general assessment of the need for the ECPT. The second section assesses the extent to which the ECPT is functioning effectively as an international instrument and doing so in accordance with the aspirations of the drafters. This draws on the material presented in Chapters 4 and 5. The material presented in Chapters 3 and 6–8 provides the background to the third section. This considers how the CPT is received and perceived by the other players in the quest to prevent ill-treatment: is there, to use the fashionable phrase, synergy between the various players on which successful prevention must ultimately depend? The answer to that question then leads into the final section which sets out our opinions regarding the strategy which the CPT should pursue in the foreseeable future with regard to a number of key issues which currently face it. In reaching our conclusions we have drawn heavily on the views of the many officials and NGO representatives that we have interviewed during our research conducted in a large number of states party to the ECPT over the past four years.

This chapter sets out our conclusions. But it is also a summary. Since it is possible that some readers might wish to gain a general view of the ECPT without, in the first instance, studying the details, we have written this chapter so as to be relatively self contained.

1 CUSTODIAL ILL-TREATMENT AND ACCOUNTABILITY IN CONTEMPORARY EUROPE: THE NEED FOR THE CPT

(a) Europe: exemplar or example of universal themes?

Jean-Jacques Gautier considered the principal justification for the ECPT to be that it provided an example for the rest of the world to follow. Although Europe needed to be on its guard, given the recent instances of dictatorial regimes employing torture in Greece, Portugal, and Spain (as well as by France in Algeria), those who pressed for the adoption of the ECPT did not see the member states of the Council of Europe in the 1980s as the prime beneficiaries of the Convention. Their sights were set on more distant and problematic prospects.

This viewpoint was not entirely wide of the mark, and the fact that the practice of torture by the authorities is almost certainly a relatively rare phenomenon in Europe has meant that the CPT has been able to focus on other issues, in particular conditions of custody, to which the progenitors of the Convention devoted little attention. But this is only part of the story. Since the drafting of the ECPT, Europe has been riven by nationalism and ethnic conflicts in the wake of the collapse of the Soviet Empire. To the slow-burning civil conflict in Turkey must now be added the horrendous events in the former Yugoslavia and the bitter conflicts in the Caucasus, Chechnya, and elsewhere in the former Soviet provinces. These conflicts have involved acts of unspeakable brutality by both state authorities and armed factions challenging the state, both on the field of battle and in custodial settings. The expansion of membership of the Council of Europe has brought many of these conflicts within the range of the ECPT, a situation quite unforseen in the 1980s.

Secondly, the collapse of dictatorships and authoritarian regimes seldom involves the sweeping away at a stroke of security apparatuses and personnel. Most police and prison officers remain in their previous employment, and change in legal frameworks, procedures, and cultural practices comes slowly. In consequence, public attitudes to the law enforcement agencies are also resistant to change: when insignia and uniforms are new but the faces are not, trust is difficult to establish. In countries that were formerly dictatorships there is evidence that continued ill-treatment is fuelled by the lack of legitimacy accorded by some to reformed political institutions.[1]

But ill-treatment is not confined to countries where democracy has shallow roots. Abuse of power from time to time by law enforcement officers is almost certainly a universal phenomenon. Studies of police culture emphasize that, although most police work is routine and tedious, the fact that the core characteristic of police agencies is their monopoly, or near monopoly, of the legitimate use of force,[2] and that police work is ultimately uncertain and occasionally involves danger, means that police officers are inclined to be conservative, suspicious, and socially distanced from the communities they police. Their culture is solidary, a reflection

[1] In Spain, for example, the passing of the Franco regime has unleashed regional separatist aspirations in pursuit of which terrorism has been employed and against which the state has employed counter-terrorist measures both lawful and unlawful. Ill-treatment of persons in custody has undoubtedly been part of this 'dirty war'.

[2] A definition emphasized by Bittner, E (1974) 'Florence Nightingale in Pursuit of Willie Sutton: A Theory of the Police' in Jacob, H (ed) *The Potential for Reform of Criminal Justice* (Beverly Hills, Calif: Sage), 35.

of the individual officer's dependence on the group to offer physical support in time of crisis and social protection when subjected to external threat. A good deal of police work is adversarial and is therefore inevitably controversial. Police officers are often under immense pressure to get 'results'. Moreover, since junior police officers are recognized as exercising the most discretion, and the manner in which they exercise that discretion is relatively difficult for their superiors to monitor and their critics to prove, it is scarcely surprising that short cuts are occasionally taken to get results, short cuts that may involve violence or other forms of ill-treatment against suspects.[3]

The term 'noble cause corruption' has been used to describe the use of illegitimate methods in pursuit of what the police take to be legitimate ends[4], and this provides the backcloth to much maltreatment of suspects in police custody. As was seen in Chapter 2, much maltreatment of suspects lies on the uneasy continuum between the pressure which all criminal justice systems permit by law as being the necessary corollary of police investigation and prosecutorial case construction (such as detention in the police station for a certain period, restrictions on contacts with outside persons, and police interrogation for possibly prolonged periods) and that unlawful pressure which the informal police culture may justify as necessary to do the job which the authorities, and possibly the public, expect them to do.

One analyst of police culture and working methods[5] has usefully distinguished between three sets of rules employed by the police—'working', 'inhibitory', and 'presentational' rules. 'Presentational' rules are those which have little or no bearing on what the police do in practice, but which must generally be satisfied when after-the-event accounts are given. They are typically the rules provided in statute law and criminal procedure. 'Inhibitory' rules are those formal rules that are effectively sanctioned and that must therefore be applied even if they are not accepted. 'Working' rules are those which are derived from informal police culture and which determine police practice. The fact that much police work is not naturally transparent means that 'working' and 'presentational' rules may diverge substantially.[6]

---

[3] For a general review of the literature on police culture, see Reiner, R (1992) *The Politics of the Police* (Hemel Hempstead: Wheatsheaf), 2nd edn. For a discussion of pressure applied by the police to induce confessions, see Gudjonsson, G (1996) 'Custodial Confinement, Interrogation and Coerced Confessions' in Forrest, D (ed) *A Glimpse of Hell: Reports of Torture Worldwide* (London: Amnesty International UK).

[4] This phrase was recently used by the Commissioner of the Metropolitan Police, Sir Paul Condon. See Morgan (1996).

[5] Smith, D, Gray, J and Small, S (1983) *Police and People in London* Vol IV (London: Policy Studies Institute), 169–72.

[6] Thus it is possible, particularly when there is social pressure to clear up some outrageous crime, to make decisions on the basis of what the police *know or believe to be the case* and subsequently to construct a justification for the action which satisfies the law, or the

The manner in which police 'working' rules operate may have an under-lying similarity with the 'presentational' rules that related to the applica-tion of judicial torture and which, as seen in Chapter 1, incorporated complex proportionality rules. There is, for example, considerable evidence that the most marginal groups in any society are most vulnerable to ill-treatment.[7] In ancient and medieval times torture could only generally be applied to slaves, aliens or non-citizens, or persons of low status. It also appears that severe ill-treatment is often reserved for those suspected of offences deemed particularly heinous, for example terrorism, the sexual abuse of children, and drug trafficking. Judicial torture, particularly in its most severe forms, could historically be employed only if the suspected crime was serious, and sufficient *indicia* were present.[8]

The evidence suggests that in spite of their prohibition, physical pressure and abuse, and occasionally methods that would generally be regarded as torture, are employed in some places by some police officers against some suspects in Europe. The phenomenon is more widespread than most governments would care to admit and, contrary to what some of the framers of the ECPT possibly thought, continues to be a problem in many parts of Europe.

Moreover, poor custodial conditions in both police stations and prisons cannot entirely be divorced from the instrumental use of physical ill-treatment of suspects. It is not by chance that the worst custodial con-ditions encountered by the CPT—be they degrading or restrictive and including those capable of exerting psychological pressure—have gener-ally been found in institutions for preventive detention. This pattern appears to be universal. International surveys as well as national studies have revealed that within most penal systems the worst custodial conditions tend to be reserved for those who are yet to be tried and who are subject to the presumption of innocence—prisoners who, legally and morally, are least eligible for them.[9] To the extent that their custodial conditions are unpleasant, this may serve to persuade prisoners held on remand to admit their assumed guilt, an instrumental device which is unlawful but which is too pervasive, in Europe as elsewhere, to be fortuitous. It is, then, clear

---

'presentational' rule. Likewise it is possible to exert illegitimate pressure, physical or other-wise, on a suspect because the police *know* him or her to be guilty, and subsequently to deny that incriminating confessional or other evidence was obtained by other than lawful means. It is often not difficult for the police to attribute allegations from suspects, whose moral credibility may by now be heavily tarnished, to malign motives and thus easily to discredit them.

[7] See Reiner, R (1997) 'Policing and the Police' in Maguire, M, Morgan, R and Reiner, R (eds) *The Oxford Handbook of Criminology* (Oxford: Clarendon Press), 2nd edn, 1010–12.

[8] Indeed remnants of this thinking still exist in the greater latitude accorded to the police in many countries under anti-terrorist or anti-organized crime legislation which such 'work-ing' rules merely mirror and build on.

[9] See Morgan, R (1993) 'Remand Prisoners: An awkward Anomaly' in Jenkins, M and Player, E (eds) *Prisons After Woolf* (London: Routledge).

that there remains a very real need for the CPT in Europe, and not merely as an example of 'best practice' for the rest of the world to follow.

(b) Growth in the use of incarceration and its consequences

Custodial conditions are also framed by the extent to which use is made of custody, and the trend has changed since the ECPT was envisaged and drafted. Except for a small number of central and eastern European countries which have only recently become members of the Council of Europe, capital punishment has been abolished, *de facto* if not *de jure*,[10] throughout Europe, and imprisonment is the most serious sanction that criminal courts can impose on offenders. Moreover, the prevailing trend during most of the twentieth century has been for imprisonment to be used in a declining proportion of criminal cases[11] and has increasingly been reserved for the most serious crimes or for recidivist offenders.[12] However, the last decade has seen some evidence of a reversal: in several European countries there has been proportionately greater use made of custody, and incarceration rates—that is, the number of prisoners in relation to the population generally—have risen.[13] The pattern is well exhibited by the data in Table 9.1 derived, for the most part, from those countries that made up the Council of Europe in the 1980s.

Of the 22 countries listed 15 had in 1995 significantly higher incarceration rates than a decade earlier, in several instances—France, Greece, Iceland, Ireland, Italy, Luxembourg, the Netherlands, Portugal, Spain, Switzerland, England and Wales, and Scotland—very considerably higher, albeit from

[10] Two long-standing Council of Europe member states, Belgium and Turkey, retain the death penalty for ordinary crimes, though both are *de facto* abolitionist. Four other states—Cyprus, Greece, Malta, and the United Kingdom—retain the death penalty for crimes against the State in time of war, but are also *de facto* abolitionist. Of the former Warsaw Pact states that are now members of the Council of Europe, most have abolished the death penalty. In Albania, Bulgaria, and Estonia the penalty has been retained but there is a moratorium on executions. In Russia and the Ukraine the penalty has been retained, albeit for a reduced number of offences, and continues in use. See Hood, R (1996) *The Death Penalty: A Worldwide Perspective* (Oxford: Clarendon Press), rev edn.

[11] In England and Wales, for example, see Bottoms, AE (1987) 'Limiting Prison Use: Experience in England and Wales', 26, 3 *Howard Journal* 177.

[12] This phenomenon, observed in many countries, has been termed 'bifurcation' in sentencing: the process whereby serious or 'dangerous' offenders receive longer custodial penalties, whereas less serious offenders receive community-based sanctions of various types. See Bottoms, AE (1977) 'Reflections on the Renaissance of Dangerousness', 16, 2 *Howard Journal* 70.

[13] The incarceration rate, by custom expressed as the number of prisoners per 100,000 population, is a crude measure of a country's use of imprisonment. It fails to distinguish between countries that sentence many offenders for short periods, as opposed to few offenders for long periods. Neither is it geared to the prevalence of serious crime, or the proportion of the population comprising young men, that section of the population typically responsible for most crime. For discussion, see Pease, K (1994) 'Cross-National Imprisonment Rates: Limitations of Method and Possible Conclusions' in King, R and Maguire, M (eds) *Prisons in Context* (Oxford: Clarendon Press).

Table 9.1 Incarceration rates (prisoners per 100,000 population) for Council of Europe Member States for selected years for which data are available

Country	1984	1987	1990	1993	1995
Austria	114	102	82	91	85
Belgium	72	69	66	65	75
Cyprus	39	38	38	25	25
Denmark	70	69	63	71	65
Finland	—	—	62	62	60
France	74	88	82	86	90
Germany	104	84	80	81	80
Greece	40	40	49	68	55
Iceland	32	37	41	38	45
Ireland	47	54	—	60	60
Italy	76	57	57	89	90
Luxembourg	78	90	94	109	115
Netherlands	31	36	44	51	65
Norway	48	50	56	60	55
Portugal	68	85	87	111	125
Spain	38	66	85	106	105
Sweden	55	57	58	66	65
Switzerland	62	—	77	81	80
Turkey	171	100	82	72	90
England & Wales	83	94	90	89	100
Scotland	89	109	109	115	110
N/Ireland	—	121	109	118	105

different base figures. The figures for several countries since 1995 show a further sharp trend upwards.[14]

Part of the explanation for the rising number of prisoners in Europe lies in the attempt to stem migration flows, particularly from Eastern Europe, Africa, and Asia—the 'Fortress Europe' phenomenon. This has allegedly been accompanied by widespread harassment of ethnic minorities, many of whose members are long-term residents in the countries concerned.[15]

[14] In October 1997 the prison population in England and Wales, for example, rose above 63,000—an incarceration rate of 123/100,000—an increase of more than 50 per cent since 1992. In Belgium the prison population rose to over 8,500 in 1997 representing an incarceration rate of 85/100,000. In the Netherlands, a country which 10 years previously had almost the lowest incarceration rate in Europe, the prison population has now reached 12,800, representing an incarceration rate of 88/100,000. This is a truly astonishing rate of growth. If the Dutch fill all the additional prison places they are currently building—and it is to be expected that they will—then they will have an incarceration rate well above the average in North West Europe.

[15] For a report on Germany, for example, see Human Rights Watch (1995a) *'Germany for Germans': Xenophobia and Racist Violence in Germany* (New York: Human Rights Watch).

Table 9.2 Percentage of foreigners in selected prison populations for selected years for which data are available

Country	1983	1985	1987	1989	1991	1995
Austria	7%	8%	9%	14%	22%	27%
Belgium	22%	28%	27%	31%	34%	41%
France	25%	26%	27%	28%	30%	28%
Greece	12%	16%	19%	27%	22%	—
Italy	8%	9%	9%	9%	15%	17%
Luxembourg	27%	43%	39%	41%	40%	54%
Netherlands	23%	15%	19%	24%	25%	—
Norway	6%	8%	11%	—	11%	14%
Spain	8%	11%	13%	15%	16%	16%
Sweden	17%	21%	22%	22%	20%	26%
Switzerland	32%	35%	36%	41%	44%	57%

The elimination of border controls between most member states of the European Union has also fuelled the demand that other forms of surveillance and intelligence gathering be stepped up against those involved in 'organized' crime, particularly the trade in drugs. The brunt of this effort bears down on visible ethnic minorities, 'foreigners' or otherwise, who are said disproportionately to be engaged in these activities.[16] In combination, these factors have generated a massive increase in the number and proportion of 'foreigners'[17] imprisoned. This is illustrated in Table 9.2.[18]

Analysts, not surprisingly, vary in the degree to which they attribute the over-representation of foreigners and ethnic minorities in criminal justice and prison population statistics to stereotyping and discrimination rather than to their over-representation among the offending population.[19] In a sense such arguments miss the important underlying point, which is that prisoners are drawn disproportionately from the ranks of the multiply-

[16] See Sim, J, Ruggiero, V and Ryan, M (1995) 'Punishment in Europe: Perceptions and Commonalities' in Ruggiero, V, Ryan, M and Sim, J (eds) *Western European Penal Systems: A Critical Anatomy* (London: Sage).

[17] 'Foreigner' is a poor guide to the heterogeneous population so designated and imprisoned: it includes second-generation migrants and long-term residents as well as short-term visitors and recently arrived migrant workers.

[18] Sources: Tomashevski, K (1994) *Foreigners in Prison* (Helsinki: European Institute for Crime Prevention and Control); Council of Europe (1997) *SPACE: Council of Europe Annual Penal Statistics—1995 Survey* (Strasbourg: Council of Europe).

[19] For a review of the evidence for the UK see Smith, D (1997) 'Ethnic Origins, Crime and Criminal Justice' in Maguire, M, Morgan, R and Reiner, R (eds) *The Oxford Handbook of Criminology* (Oxford: Clarendon Press), 2nd edn. For a collection of essays on the situation in France, Germany, the Netherlands, Sweden, Switzerland, and the UK, see Tonry, M (ed) (1997) *Ethnicity, Crime and Immigration: Comparative and Cross-National Perspectives* (Chicago: University of Chicago Press).

disadvantaged,[20] and in Europe the ethnic minorities fall overwhelmingly within the socio-economically dispossessed. This is reflected in the crimes in which they engage, and on which the police concentrate, and in their vulnerability in the exercise of discretion within the criminal justice system. The development of more 'flexible' labour markets, combined with immigration and 'organized' crime 'crackdowns', inevitably makes the position of members of marginal social groups even more precarious: the welfare safety net shreds and the criminal-justice keep-net tightens.

These processes, apparent in Western Europe, are, if anything, more acute in Eastern Europe and those countries that have joined the Council of Europe since the ECPT came into force. Indeed, when incarceration rates across the present member states of the Council of Europe are compared, three more or less distinct groups of countries emerge. At the top end of the incarceration continuum is the Russian Federation with approximately 700 persons per 100,000 (though a contemplated amnesty may sharply reduce this figure). At the opposite end of the continuum are the countries of Western Europe and the Mediterranean which, as we have seen, exhibit incarceration rates in the range of 40–120 persons per 100,000. The third group comprises those former Warsaw Pact states which were confronted, it might be said, with a clear choice as to whether to pursue the penal path still being taken by Russia or to follow that of the older Council of Europe states. This third group itself embraces a wide spectrum, ranging from the Ukraine and Belarus with 400–500 prisoners per 100,000, the Baltic states with figures in the 275–375 per 100,000 range, to countries such as the Czech Republic, Poland, and Romania with prison populations in the 150–250 per 100,000 range.

Over time, these groupings are already becoming less uniform and discrete. Some countries formerly within the Soviet sphere of influence have already reduced their prison populations below the level now prevailing in many Western European countries.[21] By contrast the prison populations of several Western European countries are moving, as we have seen, in the opposite direction: international co-operation through the agency of the Council of Europe and, more particularly, the European Union, is promoting harmonization in policing with consequences for penal policy. The important point as far the present study is concerned is that the ECPT

[20] For a survey and socio-economic analysis of the prison population in England and Wales, see Walmesley, R, Howard, L and White, S (1992) *The National Prison Survey 1991: Main Findings*, Home Office Research Study No 128 (London: HMSO).

[21] Finland, for example, has in recent years made a determined and successful bid to emulate Scandinavian practice and now has a prison population only marginally higher than Sweden. With 120 prisoners per 100,000 population Hungary currently has proportionately the same number of prisoners as England and Wales, and Slovenia with 25 prisoners per 100,000 has the lowest incarceration rate in Europe, on a par with Cyprus and significantly lower, for example, than Iceland with 45 per 100,000 population.

came into being at a time when custodial populations in western Europe were, in defiance of historic trends, about to increase and the Council of Europe was set to expand and embrace states which had historically relied on the use of custody to a far greater extent than was the case in Western Europe. In the light of both these factors, the adoption of the ECPT was timely for reasons beyond the contemplation of the Convention's proponents. As far as custodial conditions are concerned these trends have arguably led to a deterioration in two specific areas and, again, underline the continuing need for the ECPT mechanism.

(i) Overcrowding

Despite prison building programmes of an unprecedented scale in a number of states, there has been a growing problem of overcrowding. Of the 31 states for which prisons data were returned to the Council of Europe in 1995,[22] 12 recorded system overcrowding[23] and the present position is almost certainly far worse than these statistics suggest, not only because of continued growth in prison populations since 1995, but also because institutional overcrowding is inevitably often more acute than system figures indicate. It is likely that between one-half and two-thirds of all the prison systems in Europe contain some establishments that are overcrowded,[24] and that prison systems such as those in Spain and Italy, which according to Council of Europe data were 31 and 22 per cent system-overcrowded respectively in 1995, are likely to have some institutions that are grotesquely overcrowded.[25] In addition, governments may be estimating the capacity of their prison systems on a basis which might itself be unacceptable. This is certainly a major problem in certain Eastern European countries where public concern about rising crime is great, incarceration rates are high, and public expenditure resources few.[26]

---

[22] Several countries, for example Estonia, Greece, Poland, and Portugal, known to have prisons overcrowding problems, failed to return data.

[23] Council of Europe (1997), Table 1.

[24] A rough rule of thumb is that a prison system needs at least 5 per cent more spaces than prisoners to cope with routine refurbishment programmes, *ad hoc* repairs, loss of accommodation as a result of prisoner disturbances, and so on. A much larger margin is generally necessary to cope with the mismatch between the location of prison places and receipt of new prisoners: the available beds are often in the wrong places. Any prison system which is more than 90 per cent occupied is likely to exhibit overcrowding in some prisons.

[25] This is borne out by CPT reports, which generally make no reference to system population pressures. When the CPT visited Spain in 1994, for example, the Modelo Prison in Barcelona, the Madrid No 1 Prison for men and the Madrid Prison for women were 87, 70, and 73 per cent overcrowded respectively (Spain 2, paras 97–8). The visit to Italy's San Vittore Prison in Milan in 1992 revealed that 2,000 prisoners were being detained in accommodation said officially to have a capacity for 1,295 but, according to the Prison Director, was optimally suitable for 800—a level of overcrowding of between 60 and 150 per cent depending on whose word one takes (Italy 1, para 67).

[26] Russia, for example, described its prison system in 1995 as being a modest 4 per cent overcrowded. However, when the United Nations Special Rapporteur for the Prevention

(ii) The 'depth' of imprisonment

Imprisonment can be measured both by the extent of its use and its 'depth'. Imprisonment can take a variety of forms, ranging from detention in open camps involving few restrictions and from which prisoners may go out to work in paid employment in the community, to high security 'prisons within prisons' in which the regime for allegedly dangerous or subversive prisoners may be very restrictive indeed. In some European countries there is even provision for weekend imprisonment sentences or a queuing system whereby sentenced offenders are summoned to a nearby prison when a place becomes available for them.[27] It is notable that those countries with the lowest incarceration rates tend also to have the shallowest systems, that is a high proportion of prisoners in small, relatively open institutions with liberal regimes. Rising incarceration rates tend to be accompanied by the growth of more restrictive prison regimes. This is scarcely surprising since to the extent that growth in the use of imprisonment reflects a political will to get 'tough on crime', it is to be expected that 'toughness' will be extended to the provision of more restrictive regimes.[28] Once again, the work of the CPT provides supporting evidence of this.[29]

In the light of all of the above, we conclude that however effective the CPT may have proved itself in preventing ill-treatment during its short life, there are good grounds for thinking that the climate within which the Committee is operating has become more unfavourable. It may be that the achievements of the CPT should really be gauged by the extent to which

---

of Torture visited Russia in 1994 he was informed that the 160 remand centres (*sizos*) in the country provided accommodation for 167,000 persons but were currently occupied by 238,000 detainees (42 per cent crowded). At one prison in Moscow he found 6,300 prisoners occupying accommodation said to be capable of holding 3,500 (80 per cent crowded) and in one cell with dimensions of 6 × 12 metres said to be capable of holding 25 prisoners he found no fewer than 83 persons (152 per cent crowded). See *Report of the Special Rapporteur, Mr Nigel S Rodley: Visit to the Russian Federation*, E/CN.4/1995/34/Add.1. It is quite clear from the Special Rapporteur's description of the accommodation that the CPT would not find such cells suitable for 25 prisoners, let alone the 83 that occupied it.

[27] The Netherlands and Belgium.

[28] Thus the conjunction in the UK under the Conservative Government in the early 1990s between the doctrine of 'prison works' and the promulgation of more 'austere' regimes. See Morgan, R (1997).

[29] In 1992, for example, the Committee was critical of the 'unduly restrictive' conditions in two high security prison units in the Netherlands (Netherlands 1, para 91). The evidence suggests that Dutch high security provisions are now even more restrictive and that the next CPT report on the Netherlands is likely to be even more critical (see van Swaaningen, R and de Jonge, G (1995) 'The Dutch Prison System and Penal Policy in the 1990s: from Humanitarian Paternalism to Penal Business Management' in Ruggiero, V, Ryan, M and Sim, J (eds) *Western European Penal Systems: A Critical Anatomy* (London: Sage)). It should be noted that when we visited officials in the Dutch Ministry of Justice in 1995 they confessed that the regime in their high security units had become more rather than less restrictive since the CPT's visit. Similar developments have occurred in England and Wales since 1994/5— see Morgan (1997).

it has prevented the situation from deteriorating further, rather than by looking at the extent to which the situation has improved as a result of its work.

(c) The NGO patchwork quilt

A final factor that needs to be considered when assessing the need for the ECPT concerns the extent to which there are other mechanisms and agencies, national and international, which work for the same ends as the CPT, and the degree to which member states of the Council of Europe are rich or poor in terms of their presence and attention. Given that the CPT is able to visit member states on average only every four or five years, and then only a minute number of all the custodial sites that might be visited, do the activities of NGOs and other bodies complement the CPT—or eclipse it? It is our conclusion that the spread and focus of NGOs and other bodies is not sufficiently developed or potent to call into question the need for the Committee. At the same time, the effectiveness of the CPT is at least in part contingent on the existence of an effective NGO community in each ECPT member state. It is against this background that the following overview of the 'NGO patchwork quilt' must be read.

In addition to the United Nations Charter and treaty-based organs which were introduced in Chapter 3, there are international human rights agencies that seek to cover the whole of Europe, indeed the world. Foremost among these is the ICRC, which is uniquely placed between the inter-governmental organs and the NGOs and, as was seen in Chapter 4, to which the CPT is obliged to have regard when contemplating visits.[30] It is, however, clear that the ICRC does not and cannot fulfil a role equivalent to that of the CPT.

The ICRC has an inspectoral role regarding compliance with the four Geneva Conventions of 1949 (relating to field forces, combatants atsea, POWs, and civilians in time of war, respectively) and two additional Protocols of 1977 (relating to victims of international and non-international conflicts respectively), all of which unequivocally prohibit the infliction of torture, ill-treatment, or reprisals against persons protected by the Conventions. The ICRC has a mandate to visit POWs and civilian detainees in places of detention and does so with the agreement of parties to conflicts: the Geneva Conventions do not oblige states to permit this. Further, given the current resurgence of nationalism, the rise of religious fundamentalism, and the risk of civil wars in a number of states, it is important to note that the ICRC seeks access to prisoners in conflict situations not covered by the Geneva Conventions. In domestic circumstances which do

---

[30] Article 17(3).

not degenerate into open warfare, but which involve violence between more or less organized groups and governments, leading to the taking of emergency powers and widespread use of the army or police, the ICRC may offer its services: the Committee is concerned with persons arrested for offences with 'political connotations'. It is in precisely these circumstances that large numbers of persons are likely to be detained and labelled 'terrorists', 'collaborators', 'subversives', and so on, with a high risk of their being tortured or otherwise ill-treated.[31] However, the fact that the ICRC has to negotiate with governments to obtain access to detainees[32] means that many countries which might benefit from its involvement remain unvisited.[33] Moreover, such visits are undertaken on the basis of absolute confidentiality. Although the fact that the visit has taken place is in the public domain, the Committee's findings are transmitted only to the authorities concerned. The Committee maintains that this working method is 'not a sign of timidity or a wish to conceal ill-treatment', but is a pre-condition to gain access, making 'the ICRC's "interference" more palatable to the detaining authorities'.[34] This is no doubt so, but it means that other NGOs are unable to learn from the ICRC's experience. On both counts—the lack of activity in ECPT member states, and the strict confidentiality rule—neither the CPT nor any other non-State monitoring group has been able to derive much advantage from the ICRC within the Council of Europe area.

Several other international NGOs provide more scope for trading information about the extent and nature of ill-treatment. Of these the most well-known and best resourced is Amnesty International. Amnesty has both national sections which are membership based and an International Secretariat, based in London, comprising a large number of researchers organized into regional world sections (one of which covers Europe),

[31] ICRC (1988) 'ICRC Protection and Assistance Activities in Situations not Covered by International Humanitarian Law', *International Review of the Red Cross*, Jan–Feb, 9; Gasser, H-P (1988) 'A Measure of Humanity in Internal Disturbances and Tensions: Proposals for a Code of Conduct', *International Review of the Red Cross*, Jan–Feb.

[32] The Committee will only undertake visits if certain conditions are agreed to (access to all detainees, in all locations, permission to interview detainees freely without witnesses, permission to draw up lists of prisoners, to repeat visits and, if necessary, to distribute material aid).

[33] Turkey, for example, has repeatedly denied the ICRC access to its places of detention. Both Spain and Northern Ireland used to be visited regularly by the ICRC but the Committee decided to withdraw, presumably because its concerns were allayed, before the CPT became operational. As a consequence, according to the CPT Bureau, the question of the need to liaise closely with the ICRC regarding potential overlap between the two organizations had not, up to 1996, arisen, though it was conceded that the question might arise in parts of Eastern Europe (interview with CPT Bureau, Sept 1996). We can speculate that the question may since have arisen with regard to Albania and parts of the Russian Federation.

[34] ICRC (1992) *Visits by the International Committee of the Red Cross to Persons Deprived of their Freedom* (Geneva: ICRC), 9.

engaged full time in monitoring and publicizing human rights abuses falling within Amnesty's mandate. Amnesty is mandated to: seek the release of prisoners of conscience; oppose detention of political prisoners without fair trial; oppose the death penalty, torture, or other cruel, inhuman, and degrading treatment of all prisoners; and oppose extra-judicial execution or 'disappearances'.[35] Amnesty's researchers gather data from individuals and groups in the countries where the abuses are allegedly taking place and occasionally supplement these data by means of investigatory missions if the countries concerned will grant access to their territory, institutions, or victims.[36]

Amnesty's energies and resources have been largely absorbed challenging the widespread practice of imprisoning people on the basis of their political, religious, or other beliefs, and the extensive use of the death penalty and torture. Police violence is also a major preoccupation.[37] Amnesty has understandably been reluctant to delve deeply into the question of custodial conditions that might amount to cruel, inhuman, and degrading treatment[38] which is not only not a top priority, but presents a global organization such as Amnesty with difficult problems of definition and of cultural relativity. It follows that Amnesty largely concerns itself with prisoners rather than prisons and generally comments on conditions only if their consequences demonstrate clearly that they are cruel, inhuman, or degrading.[39] However, it is clear that Amnesty is a very important player alongside the CPT within Europe. Many European national Amnesty

[35] Amnesty International (1991) *Statute of Amnesty International—as amended by the 20th International Council, Yokohama, Japan* (London: Amnesty International, International Secretariat).

[36] Amnesty, like the CPT, has a policy of never using nationals to investigate their own country. Moreover, unlike Human Rights Watch (see below, pp. 329–30), Amnesty always informs governments that they are undertaking an investigatory mission. This means that from time to time Amnesty researchers are denied entry or visas. This was the case in Turkey, for example, in 1995–6. It goes without saying that Amnesty has no right of access to custodial institutions.

[37] An Amnesty report on Denmark, for example, drew attention to the use by the Danish police in street public order situations of a restraining 'leg lock' judged to involve excessive force and alleged to be potentially fatal for suspects with respiratory difficulties—Amnesty International (1994b) *Denmark: Police Ill-Treatment* (London: Amnesty International. International Secretariat).

[38] See Cook, H (1991) 'The Role of Amnesty International in the Fight Against Torture' in Cassese (ed).

[39] In 1980, for example, Amnesty published its concern about the use of solitary confinement or small group isolation for prisoners suspected or convicted of politically motivated crimes in West Germany, principally the '*Rote Armee Fraktion*'. The dossier provided details on the deteriorating mental and physical condition of four prisoners, said to be the consequence of prolonged isolation and sensory deprivation. The subjects of the report were not adopted by Amnesty as 'prisoners of conscience' but the German authorities were urged to adopt a more humane custodial policy (Amnesty International (1980) *Prison Conditions of Persons Suspected or Convicted of Politically Motivated Crimes in the Federal Republic of Germany: Isolation and Solitary Confinement*, EUR 23/01/80 (London: Amnesty International, International Secretariat)).

sections have large memberships, particularly in North West Europe. In spite of difficulties regarding the verification of allegations—difficulties faced by any organization which does not have a right of access— Amnesty reports enjoy a considerable reputation for thoroughness and accuracy,[40] and its publications generally attract considerable mass media attention. Amnesty reports are routinely sent to the CPT Secretariat and it would appear that they frequently influence the shape of CPT visits.[41] This influence is two-way in that CPT findings are frequently cited in Amnesty Reports,[42] with the result that Amnesty International provides a route for the widespread dissemination of CPT findings.

Another NGO with a global remit is Human Rights Watch which is the umbrella organization, based in the United States, and which links the operations of five regional organizations.[43] The origins of the entire organization lie in the regional Helsinki Watch organization which was founded in 1978 and which sought to monitor compliance with the human rights provisions of the Helsinki Final Act of 1975 within the states involved in the CSCE Process (now the OSCE), these being the countries of Europe and North America. In each of those countries, members of national Helsinki Watch Committees monitor local policy and practice regarding human rights and campaign for change. They are particularly concerned to document and denounce 'murders, disappearances, torture, arbitrary imprisonment, exile, censorship and other abuses of internationally recognized human rights'.[44] In addition to the work of the Helsinki Watch

---

[40] Within Europe Amnesty reports often encounter controversy regarding the priority attached to some allegations. In Denmark in particular, and Scandinavia in general, for example, there was widespread criticism, not least from Amnesty members (many of whom resigned), regarding the 1994 report on Danish police violence (see n 37 above). It was widely felt that when put in the scale of problems raised elsewhere in the world by Amnesty, the incidents described in the Danish report were scarcely worthy of the attention devoted to them.

[41] See Chapter 5, p. 170 n 144 and 211 n 351. The first CPT visit ever undertaken, to Austria in 1990, came 4 months after the publication of an extremely critical report on Austria from Amnesty International ((1990) *Austria: Torture and Ill-Treatment* (London: Amnesty International, International Secretariat)). So close were the two events that the Austrian authorities were originally disbelieving that they were unconnected. In fact Austria had been selected to receive the first visit by lot. That is not to say that the CPT delegation was uninfluenced by the Amnesty publication, however. Amnesty sent their report to the CPT Secretariat in Strasbourg and it is noteworthy that several of the Vienna police stations visited by the delegation were cited in the Amnesty report as sites where ill-treatment had occurred. Or, to take the more recent example of the 1994 Amnesty report on Denmark, the allegations regarding police use of the leg-lock (see nn 37 and 40 above) were reflected in the CPT visit to Denmark in 1996 (see Denmark 2, para 13).

[42] See, for example, Amnesty International (1996d), 34–5; and the entry on Austria in Amnesty International (1997) *Amnesty International Report 1997* (London: Amnesty International, International Secretariat), 79–81.

[43] These being Helsinki Watch, Africa Watch, Americas Watch, Asia Watch, and Middle East Watch.

[44] Taken from Human Rights Watch (1995a), p. iii.

Committees, the mother body, Human Rights Watch, has a specific Prison Project which was established in 1988. It follows that the Human Rights Watch/Helsinki Watch network serves a dual function in relation to the CPT in Europe. First, Helsinki Watch/Human Rights Watch have published a number of reports on European prison systems the contents of which traverse the same ground with which the CPT is concerned[45] and a limited number of reports on other aspects of national life with a bearing on the CPT's mandate.[46] These reports of the Human Rights Watch Prison Project contain background information which is potentially of considerable value to the CPT.[47] Secondly, national Helsinki Watch Committees, the size and quality of which vary greatly, have claims to local knowledge and expertise which the CPT has utilized during the course of visits.[48]

Other important international NGOs for the work of the CPT include the Geneva-based Association for the Prevention of Torture (APT)[49] and Prison Reform International. Both are member-based organizations, and the former, as we saw in Chapter 5, has made it its business over the years to prepare dossiers of information and contacts that might assist the CPT in the planning and preparation of its visits.[50] Both organizations have

[45] That is, physical ill-treatment, general living conditions, prisoner safeguards and general accountability mechanisms, and so on. See Reports on: *Prison Conditions in Poland, June 1988*; *Prison Conditions in Turkey, August 1989*; *Prison Conditions in Poland, January 1991*; *Prison Conditions in the United Kingdom, June 1992*; *Prison Conditions in Spain, April 1992*, all published by Human Rights Watch, New York.

[46] Such as the 1995 report—'*Germany for Germans': Xenophobia and Racist Violence in Germany*—on racist violence, some of it allegedly at the hands of the police, in Germany. Other examples include: regarding Hungary (1996) *Rights Denied: The Roma of Hungary*; regarding Russia (1995b) *Crime or Simply Punishment?: Racist Attacks by Moscow Law Enforcement*, (1997) *A Legacy of Abuse*; regarding Turkey (1992c) *Nothing Unusual: the Torture of Children in Turkey*, (1993a) *16 Deaths in Detention in 1992*, (1993b) *The Kurds of Turkey: Killings, Disappearances and Torture*, (1997) *Torture and Mistreatment in Pre-Trial Detention by Anti-Terror Police*.

[47] It is arguable that the Project has not realized is full potential. Human Rights Watch has chosen to rely largely on second-hand, particularly media, reports and when missions do visit and gain access to institutions, many sites seem to be covered in a remarkably short space of time. It is possible that they could have elicited a higher degree of co-operation from some national authorities which would have granted them access to institutions and enabled them to collect more information first-hand. See, for example, the report on *Prison Conditions in the United Kingdom, June 1992*. For further discussion of this and other methodological points see Morgan and Evans (1994).

[48] Meetings were held, for example, with national representatives of Helsinki Watch during the course of the visits to Bulgaria in April 1995 and Slovakia in July 1995.

[49] Formerly the Swiss Committee Against Torture.

[50] See Chapter 5, pp. 181–3. APT reports have been transmitted to the CPT Secretariat and subseqently published on: Austria (1994), Belgium (1993), Germany (1994), Hungary (1994), Ireland (1993), Portugal (1994), Spain (1993 and 1994), Switzerland (1991 and 1995), Turkey (1992 and 1994), and the United Kingdom (1994). Unpublished information has been sent to the CPT on Bulgaria, Cyprus, France, Germany, Greece, Italy, Slovenia, and Spain and in 1995 further reports were said to be in preparation regarding France, Greece, Italy, and Romania (see APT (1995) *Preventing Torture*, APT Newsletter No 6, 23). During its visit

magazines for their members which routinely include digests of published CPT reports. Moreover the APT has organized several conferences, Europe-wide and regional, to discuss the work of the CPT and make it better known to local NGOs.[51] These two organizations play a crucial role in spread-ing information regarding the CPT to national NGOs, in which many of APT and PRI members are also involved. PRI has also undertaken some developmental work with local NGOs and prison personnel in Eastern Europe, the focus being on improved human-rights-based commitments and good institutional practice in prisons.[52]

There are other international NGOs of relevance for the CPT. The Federation of International Associations of Christians Against Torture (FIACAT), for example, has grown out of the Paris-based Association of Christians Against Torture which in the 1980s worked closely with Jean-Jacques Gautier, Amnesty International, the ICJ, and the ICRC to press the case for the ECPT. FIACAT now comprises twenty-seven member-based autonomous national branches of ACAT with more than 30,000 members world-wide. Unlike the national sections of Amnesty, whose members are generally not allowed to campaign about issues within their own jurisdiction, ACAT branch members may and do campaign about issues at home and abroad and in some European countries appear to have played a significant role in following up and monitoring compliance with CPT recommendations.[53] The CPT has met with national ACAT groups in several countries during the course of visits.[54] Likewise the Lyons-based *Observatoire international des prisons* not only has strong local branches in France engaged in monitoring custodial conditions, but publishes an annual review of prison conditions world-wide.[55]

In most member states, however, it is to unfederated national NGOs, and in some cases to pioneering individuals such as motivated members of parliament or campaigning legal practitioners or academic researchers,

to Switzerland in July 1991 the CPT met with APT representatives, presumably to invite elaboration on the dossier of information on Switzerland that the Association had earlier transmitted to Strasbourg. See Switzerland 1, Appendix III).

[51] A general conference was held in Strasbourg in December 1994 (proceedings published as APT (1995)) and regional conferences in Onati, Spain in April 1997 (proceedings partly published in (1997) 1(3) *Mediterranean Journal of Human Rights* 159–276) and London, UK in September 1997.

[52] See PRI (1994).

[53] The CPT visit to France in 1991 resulted in serious criticism of conditions for prisoners at Marseilles-Baumettes Prison (see France 1, paras 91–120), conditions which French ACAT members in Marseilles have subsequently been actively involved in remedying (interview with FIACAT/ACAT, Paris, Sept 1996).

[54] For example, during the visits to: Spain in April 1991; Switzerland in July 1991; France in October 1991; and Belgium in November 1993.

[55] Like Amnesty, therefore, *Observatoire* is in a position to reproduce CPT findings and does so. See Observatoire international des prisons (1995) *Rapport 1995: les conditions de déten-tion des personnes incarcérées* (Lyon: Observatoire international des prisons).

to take up and follow up CPT findings and recommendations. There are few countries where such groups and individuals are not to be found, as is evidenced from the consultative meetings with non-state organizations and individuals with whom the CPT typically begins each *periodic* visit.[56] However, on the basis of our own forays to member states we conclude that the richness or paucity of NGO organizations and activity is one of the most important distinctions between member states, a differentiation which we would argue is of enormous importance for the long-term effectiveness of the CPT.

CPT reports themselves provide an impression of the scale of NGO activity within a given country. For example, during their first three visits to the United Kingdom the CPT met with no fewer than eleven penal or human rights pressure groups,[57] most of them well-known highly professional organizations with permanent staffs engaged in high profile campaigning work.[58] Moreover, it is notable that the CPT could have met with other pressure groups, and given the clear shift of the Committee's focus of attention towards allegations of ill-treatment against the police during the course of their fourth visit in September 1997, possibly did so.[59]

In other countries it may be relatively difficult—as we found ourselves, during the course of our fieldwork—for the CPT to track down monitoring NGOs with a degree of expertise and well-founded information about

[56] From CPT reports that have been published, only during the course of the 1992 visit to San Marino and the 1994 visit to Hungary does it appear that the CPT had no such meetings during a *periodic* visit.

[57] During their first visit, in addition to their meeting with representatives of the British Medical Association, the Committee met with representatives of 5 penal or human rights pressure groups, these being The Howard League, Justice, the National Association for the Care and Resettlement of Offenders (NACRO), the Prison Reform Trust (PRT), and the National Council for Civil Liberties (NCCL, now renamed Liberty) (see UK 1, para 7). On their second visit the delegation met with two further pressure groups, this time based in Northern Ireland, NACRO Northern Ireland and the Committee for the Administration of Justice (see UK 2, para 12). On their third visit, in addition to meetings with three of the pressure groups met on the first occasion, (The Howard League, Liberty, and NACRO) the delegation met with representatives of a further four pressure groups, The Asylum Rights Campaign, The Joint Council for the Welfare of Immigrants (JCWI), MIND, and the Scottish Council for Civil Liberties (SCCL) (see UK 3, Appendix II).

[58] For an overview of some of these organizations see: Ryan, M (1978) *The Acceptable Pressure Group: Ineqaulity in the Penal Lobby—a case-study of the Howard League and RAP* (Farnborough: Saxon House); Ryan, M (1983) *The Politics of Penal Reform* (London: Longman); and Downes, D and Morgan, R (1974) 'Dumping the "Hostages to Fortune"? The Politics of Law and Order in Post-War Britain', in Maguire, M, Morgan, R and Reiner, R (eds) *The Oxford Handbook of Criminology* (Oxford: Clarendon Press), 2nd edn 112–21.

[59] See Council of Europe Press Release, Ref 534a(97) which states that during the course of this fourth visit the delegation was concerned, inter alia, to examine 'the efficacity (sic) of existing legal remedies in cases involving allegations of ill-treatment by police officers'. Given that this visit followed several high profile cases involving deaths in police custody, it would have been surprising had the Committee not met with INQUEST, a pressure groups specifically concerned with deaths in custody visit (see Ryan, M (1997) *Lobbying from Below* (London: UCL Publishing)).

the situation in places of custody. In Germany, for example, there is not the network of professional NGOs, at least not at Federal level, to which the CPT can turn.[60] It was no doubt for this reason that the delegation sought out two academic specialists who had undertaken relevant research in places of custody, one of whom works closely with the APT.[61] A similar pattern was pursued during the visit to Germany in 1996.[62] This is not the place to speculate as to why there is a relative absence of independent well-resourced human rights NGOs in Germany concerned generally with policing and penal affairs, but it was put to us by those organizations that we contacted that a principal reason is the devolution of so much policy-making power to the *Länder*,[63] a point reflected in the official German government responses to the first *periodic* visit of the CPT.[64]

Elsewhere, the relative absence of national NGOs sometimes reflects historical factors. In many Eastern European countries, for example, the restoration of democracy is so recent, and the absence of openness by the policing and penal authorities so deep-seated, that a developed network of professional NGOs has yet to emerge.[65] A number of the Helsinki Committees and similar organizations are poorly resourced, lack effective organization and, most importantly, do not have members able to penetrate what are often the still largely closed worlds of the police and prison authorities. But this is not just an Eastern European phenomenon. In countries as far apart as Scandinavia and the Mediterranean we have followed up the individuals and organizations that we know the CPT to have met during visits, and we have formed the impression that many of these consultations are unlikely to have greatly benefited the Committee in identifying problems to investigate and troublesome institutions

---

[60] In 1991, for example, the CPT delegation met with representatives of three NGOs, but one was a professional association of police officers, another a lawyers' association, and the third was an independent NGO but concerned with the relatively narrow technical question of AIDS/HIV (see Germany 1, Appendix II).

[61] Professor Johannes Feest, University of Bremen.

[62] The delegation met with another academic prisons researcher as well as representatives of four NGOs concerned with the detention of immigrants or asylum seekers. No NGOs concerned generally with policing or prisons policy were contacted (see Germany 2, Appendix II).

[63] It is relatively difficult for national organizations in Germany to gather data about what is going on locally: activist citizens tend to be oriented to the *Länder* and not to Bonn and to the extent that there are NGOs within the *Länder* they are not the highly professional well-resourced organizations that are to be found within the honey-pot of London. This is characteristic of civil society in many federal jurisdictions.

[64] See above, Chapter 5, pp. 208–10 and Chapter 7, pp. 270, 285.

[65] In Hungary, for example, we have noted that the CPT met with no NGOs at all during the 1994 visit. In Slovenia in 1995 the fact that the CPT delegation met, inter alia, with two individual academics, suggests that there were no strong NGOs to contact. And though the Committee has, as we have also noted, met with Helsinki Committees in several Eastern European countries, our own experience suggests that in some states, which it would be invidious to mention, the CPT is unlikely to have been much enlightened by the contact.

to visit. Day-to-day policing, prisons, and immigration control practices are aspects of domestic policy which in many European countries attract little detailed attention from parliamentarians or civic groups of active citizens.

Moreover, apart from North West Europe—particularly Britain, the Low Countries, Scandinavia, and to some extent Germany—academic lawyers and social scientists have undertaken relatively little empirical research on criminal-justice policy of the sort which might provide them with an in-depth familiarity with the custodial policies that fall within the CPT mandate.[66] This paucity of independent experts, academic or otherwise, is reflected in the make-up of NGOs throughout much of Europe. Despite the presence of a number of professional and well-resourced NGOs, either operating or monitoring the situation, in a number of European states, it is clear that this is the exception rather than the rule. Not only does this further underline the need for the CPT as an institution, but it also points to a potentially serious gap in the spread of agencies which are in a position to complement the work of the Committee—by providing information and monitoring compliance with recommendations—in the majority of state parties to the Convention.

2 THE ECPT: AN OPERATIONAL ASSESSMENT

The need for the ECPT is established. The next question concerns the extent to which it can be said that the Convention and Committee is functioning effectively. Most commentators would agree that, according to most —but not all—of the technical criteria that one might wish to apply, it has been a success. In this sense the framers of the Convention should feel a high degree of satisfaction that this innovative human rights mechanism works. This section will consider its performance with regard to a number of formal, technical criteria that are implied in and derived from the Convention.

(a) Participation

At the time of writing, the Convention is in force for 35 states, a number that will shortly increase to 37. This includes all 23 states which were

---

[66] This fact is reflected in the nationality of the *ad hoc* experts on whom the CPT has chosen to rely to assist them with visits. The latter, as we noted in Chapter 5, p. 164, come overwhelmingly from North West Europe and if the medical experts are excluded the pattern is even more marked: Of the ten non-medical experts employed to date, four are British, three are from the Low Countries, two are Swiss, and one is Austrian. See also Morgan, R (forthcoming) 'The CPT and the Academy' in APT/British Institute of Human Rights, *The European Convention for the Prevention of Torture: Issues and Mechanisms for Preventing Torture and Ill-Treatment.*

members of the Council of Europe during the period 1983–7 when the Convention was being drafted, and 14 of the 17 states which have since joined the Council.[67] As a result of its expansion into central and eastern Europe and Russia the Council has in effect become the Council of a significant part of Eurasia: it extends from Iceland to Portugal, from Greece and Turkey to the borders of the Russian Federation on the Sea of Japan. In consequence the number and range of countries which have signed and ratified the ECPT has been beyond the reasonable contemplation of its framers. The more recently admitted members[68] have been required to give a commitment that they will become a party to the various human rights mechanisms of the Council of Europe, including the ECPT, within one year of their accession. To the extent that the rationale of the CPT lay in its symbolic significance for the rest of the world, the Europe now covered by the ECPT incorporates countries for whom that example was undoubtedly being set.

This is not to say that the process of ratification has gone entirely smoothly or that it is has been without cynicism. From the evidence collected not only by the CPT—and revealed in its two Public Statements—but by a whole host of other international human rights bodies and NGOs, it is evident that the first country to ratify the ECPT, Turkey, has one of the worst human rights records within the region, including the widespread use of torture. Moreover, not all of the Eastern Block countries that have joined the Council of Europe have so far lived up to the expectations that the organization had of them. Latvia, which joined the Council of Europe in February 1995, did not sign the Convention until October 1997. Lithuania, which joined the Council of Europe in May 1995 and signed the ECPT in September of that year, has still not ratified the Convention two years later. Moldova, which joined the Council of Europe in 1995, and Croatia, which joined in 1996, ratified outside of the one-year period required of them and Russia, which had undertaken to ratify by the end of February 1997, still has not done so.[69]

The response to the conclusion of the two Protocols to the ECPT has been equally disappointing. Neither is yet in force and, although Protocol 1 has lost much of its impact given the growth in CPT membership,[70]

---

[67] See Chapter 5, pp. 142–3 and Appendix 4A.

[68] That is, Albania, Croatia, Moldova, the Russian Federation, 'TFYRO Macedonia', and the Ukraine.

[69] As at 31 Dec 1997. See CLAHR Report (1997), paras 11–17; Evans and Morgan (1997); Appendix 4B.

[70] For Protocol No 1, see Chapter 5, p. 150 n 26 and Appendices 1B and 4B. The states most likely to be invited to accede should the Protocol enter into force are Belarus, Bosnia and Herzegovina, and Serbia/Montenegro. Israel might also be a potential invitee. Bosnia and Herzegovina are already within the orbit the the CPT by virtue of the Dayton Agreement on Implementing the Federation of Bosnia and Herzegovina, (1996) 35 ILM 170. Annex 6

the entry into force of Protocol 2 is of considerable significance for the smooth operation of the Convention mechanism.[71] Nevertheless, for 37 of the 40 Council of Europe member states to have ratified the ECPT is impressive, and it is believed that the Convention will shortly be in force for the remainder. It is too early to tell whether those states which are, in effect, being forced into the system will show the same degree of commitment and toleration to its operation as has, generally speaking, been displayed by those who contributed to its drafting and who were somewhat less dragooned into initial participation.

(b) CPT members and *ad hoc* experts

The CPT comprises one member per ratifying state. Some states have been rather slow to submit lists of candidates so that the Committee has generally had fewer members than state parties. Nevertheless, there has continuously been a working Committee since 1989. A more important point concerns the quality of the membership. According to the Convention, members serve in their individual capacity and are to be 'chosen from among persons of high moral character, known for their competence in the field of human rights or having professional experience in the areas covered by this convention'.[72] It is difficult to judge precisely how well these requirements have been satisfied and we would expect reaction to the calibre of membership to be nuanced rather than categorical.[73]

As was seen in Chapter 5, the General Reports of the Committee have repeatedly requested that the Committee of Ministers of the Council of Europe ensure the election of a Committee which is better balanced as far as gender and relevant experience is concerned, and the paper record suggests that this has come about. In addition to lawyers, the Committee today includes, as the framers of the Convention hoped that it would, a mix of personnel: medical doctors with different expertise, psychologists, a priest, parliamentarians (generally retired), and persons with experience of penal administration. Indeed, during its first eight years the Committee has included a sprinkling of genuinely international luminaries in the

---

(agreement on Human Rights) Chapter 3, Article XIII(4) provides that 'All competent authorities in Bosnia and Herzegovina shall cooperate with and provide unrestricted access to . . . the supervisory bodies established by any of the international agreements listed in the Appendix to this Annex.' That Appendix includes the CPT. It seems that if the CPT were requested to enter by authorities, this would provide the CPT with the basis to respond. It does not, of course, give the CPT authority to demand entry.

[71] See Chapter 5, pp. 149–50.   [72] ECPT, Article 4.

[73] As far as the public record is concerned there has been no scandal—no member has publicly been accused of behaving in an improper manner, disciplined or asked to resign— and this is a considerable achievement given the tensions existing between some member states and the potential propaganda value of the human rights evidence that the Committee collects in confidence.

fields of international human rights law and psychiatric medicine, and international experts in the identification and treatment of torture victims.

Paper qualifications are of course one thing: the practical skills involved in inspecting places of custody, talking to operational police and prison officers, and interviewing nervous prisoners unlikely to have much inkling of the nature a body comprising foreigners and going by the intimidating name of the European Committee for the Prevention of Torture, is quite another. Members may be lawyers or doctors. But have they ever spent time talking to newly arrested prisoners in police cells? Or long-term prisoners in high security units? Or frightened asylum seekers unexpectedly detained at an airport? Do they have the personal qualities necessary to elicit information in such unpromising and intimidating environments? It is impossible to know the answer to such questions from the curriculum vitae of members distributed by the Council of Europe. It is also worth remembering that experience does not necessarily imply competence, or vice versa.

What is clear is that the CPT, contrary to the expectations of those who framed the Convention, has from the outset relied heavily on the assistance of *ad hoc* experts. Rather than providing occasional supplementary assistance, *ad hoc* experts have accompanied the Committee on practically every mission. Moreover the repeated use of a small core of *ad hoc* experts, mostly forensic psychiatrists, means that the members of this group have considerably more experience of CPT missions than most Committee members. This was not anticipated, though ironically the arrangement accords with the advice offered by a number of NGOs—the SCAT, the ICRC, and the ICJ—when the Convention was drafted.

It is also clear from our interviews across Europe with officials and NGO representatives who have had meetings with visiting CPT delegations, that many of those who meet with the CPT in the course of a visit are unable to distinguish between CPT members, accompanying *ad hoc* experts, or members of the CPT Secretariat. CPT delegations generally make a favourable impression on those with whom they have contact in member states, but it is not clear whether any particular component of the delegation bears particular responsibility for this. What is clear is that, to the extent that CPT members lack those qualities or skills ideal for their visiting task, the lacunae are filled by those who support and assist them.

(c) The visiting programme

The work of the CPT revolves around visits to places of custody in member states and it is evident that the pace of the visiting programme has accelerated in successive years—from 5 visits occupying 50 days in 1990, to 11 visits occupying 93 days in 1996, and 13 visits occupying 116 days in 1997. In its latest General Report the Committee looks forward to the millennium when it anticipates the number of state parties will peak at between 40 and 45. The Committee would like to think it could be in a position to organize 200 days of visits per year by that time.[74] However, this barely keeps pace with the increase in the number of visits necessitated by the growth in the number of states parties.

More significant than the overall increase in the number of visits has been the change in the shape of the visiting programme. During the first four years the majority of visits were full-blown *periodic* visits lasting between one and two weeks, depending on the size of the country. In the second four years *periodic* visits gradually began to be balanced by shorter *ad hoc* or *follow-up* visits. This was entirely appropriate. Most of the visits during the early years were the first to the countries concerned and it was fitting that a good deal of time was devoted to formal meetings with officials and responsible ministers. By 1995/6, however, the majority of visits were return calls, in a few countries for the third or fourth time, and were increasingly focused on procedures or sites known (often from previous visits) to present problems in term of physical ill-treatment or poor custodial conditions. Whether the nature and organization of visits should change even more radically—indeed, whether the Committee should in the future be so dependent on making visits in order to gather information—is a matter which will be considered later.

The expanding scope of the visiting programme has of course only been made possible because of the budgetary resources made available to it. The Convention would be little more than a dead letter were the Committee not allocated a budget which permitted the appointment of an adequate Secretariat to support the work of the Committee and sufficient funds to enable it to carry out a full programme of visits, the cost of which are high. Few organizations are ever satisfied with their resources and there remain, as will be seen below, continuing signs of administrative strain. It must be considered a tribute to the reputation in Strasbourg of the CPT that, whilst the budget of the Council for Europe as a whole had doubled in the period 1990–97, the budget of the CPT has trebled.[75]

(d) CPT access to places of detention

Perhaps surprisingly, the process of undertaking visits has proved remarkably trouble-free to date. On one occasion early in the life of the

[74] Gen Rep 7, para 21.
[75] The Council of Europe's budget increased from 477 million to one billion French Francs during this period, whilst that of the CPT grew from 3.2 million to 9.6 million French Francs. This has made possible, in addition to the enlarged visiting programme, the recruitment of additional members of the Secretariat, which has grown from five in 1990 to being 13 strong in 1997 (speech by Trevor Stevens, CPT Secretary, APT Conference, London, Sept 1997).

Committee a delegation or a delegation member was required to have a visa, in contravention of the Convention.[76] This early diplomatic discourtesy appears not to have been repeated—or if it has, the Committee has chosen not to make a public fuss about it.[77] Furthermore, though many country reports, and a few General Reports, have drawn attention to continuing problems of access in the course of a visit—being kept waiting at the entrance of a police station from time to time, being denied access to particular prisoners for a few hours, not being initially allowed to see inside a locker or to read a particular medical file[78]—they have for the most part been comparatively minor and transitory impediments. Given that the CPT deals with one of the most secretive and sensitive inner portals of the modern state, and that many of the state parties have an unaccountable and authoritarian, not to say dictatorial, policing and penal recent past, it is little short of remarkable that the Committee has encountered so few access obstructions.

All the evidence indicates that despite occasional hiccups, hiccups generally borne of local officials' ignorance of the Convention and defensiveness rather than wilful obstruction, the CPT has been able to see what it wanted to see and talk to whomsoever it wished, in confidence and out of sight and hearing. Moreover, the Committee has been able to function in some extremely difficult circumstances.[79]

(e) Publication of reports

Although a press release containing general information is issued by the Council of Europe following every CPT visit, the details of a visit can only be known if publication of the Report on the visit is authorized by the state concerned. The fact that by the end of 1997 the publication of

[76] Although the identity of the country has never been revealed, no great detective skill is required to identify Turkey as the culprit.

[77] The previous incident resulted in an exchange with the Committee of Ministers which was published as an occasional paper by the Council of Europe (1993) *European Committee for the Prevention of Torture and Inhuman or Degrading Teatment or Punishment (CPT): Some issues concerning the interpretation of the European Convention for the Prevention of Torture and Inhuman or Degrading Treatment or Punishment*, CPT/Inf (93) 10 (Strasbourg: Council of Europe), 3–4 and 11–14.

[78] Access to medical records has proved the most difficult of the access issues and, as has been seen in Chapter 4, pp. 135–6, was already identified as a problem at the time of drafting the Convention and Explanatory Report. The question has repeatedly led to disputes with state parties during the course of visits (see Gen Rep 3, paras 4–6; Gen Rep 4, para 5; Gen Rep 5, paras 14–15).

[79] Delegations have visited, for example, police stations in isolated civil-war-torn towns in provinces under emergency rule in South East Turkey. It is true that the Committee postponed a visit planned to Albania in early 1997 but, given the literal anarchy reigning in that country at the time, and the fact that prisoners had reportedly generally been released, the visit would have been foolhardy and served little purpose. The visit was in fact undertaken in December 1997.

44 visit reports and 55 responses (38 interim and 17 follow up reports) had been authorized is possibly the greatest single indicator of the Convention's success. It has been said by CPT members[80] that the Committee is not concerned whether CPT reports are published or not: that this is a matter for state parties; that the Committee is concerned only with having constructive dialogue with governments in order that its preventive mandate be fulfilled. To the extent that this is a truly held belief, rather than a public position, we consider it naïve and wholly mistaken. Our reasons for this view will be explored more fully later in this chapter but at this point it needs to be emphasized that it is implausible that the CPT alone can prevent ill-treatment. Prevention requires the efforts of many actors, most of whom lack the forensic skills and unimpeded access enjoyed by the CPT. Were CPT reports not to be published those other actors would be unable to capitalize upon the CPT's detailed findings. For the Convention to work to its full potential, it is vital that as many sources of pressure as possible be brought to bear upon the state: and the CPT is not necessarily well placed to trigger action in the political arena which is usually necessary to achieve compliance.

It is certainly true that CPT reports have always been constructed and written in a manner which facilitates publication, being entirely self-contained. However, the letter[81] from the CPT President which accompanies reports to states does not even express the hope that the report will be published. Rather, it refers only to the principle of co-operation set out in Article 3 of the Convention and underlines the importance of the ongoing dialogue which the report sets in train and requests that there be a response or responses within the time limits routinely set by the Committee.[82] On the other hand, there is reason to believe that some CPT members acting in a private capacity have pressed the case for publication and, if the CPT has been coy in this regard, other international bodies have not. It is, for example, striking that the UN Committee against Torture has called upon states to publish CPT reports on a number of

[80] Unrecorded oral comments made at the APT Conference, Strasbourg, 1994.

[81] These letters appears as a sort of frontispiece to published reports.

[82] That the Committee does not subsequently apply pressure to publish is best illustrated by the circumstances leading to the publication of the government responses to the report arising out of the CPT visit to Denmark in December 1990, circumstances in which unwittingly we appear to have played a crucial role. Denmark, like its fellow Scandinavian countries, has a tradition of open government. We were surprised, therefore, that no responses had been published and raised this when we visited Copenhagen during Autumn 1995. The Danish officials were equally surprised, taking the view that the Danish responses had been published and were freely available on request. We were promptly given copies. Shortly afterwards, in March 1996, the Council of Europe published a compendium of five documents, the *interim* Danish response to the 1990 report, dated January 1992, the Danish follow-up report, dated July 1992 and, for good measure, letters from the CPT dated September 1993 and September 1994, together with supplementary information transmitted to Strasbourg from the Danish authorities dated February 1995.

occasions. Indeed, it has been suggested that whilst the CPT will not directly intercede with a state to publish, it has on occasions suggested that NGOs might like to apply pressure to this end.[83]

Whatever the truth of the matter, almost all states have decided to publish, although some have taken a long time to do so.[84] Many countries routinely take eighteen months to authorize publication because they wish to publish their response simultaneously. Since the CPT is itself not a speedy producer of reports—its target, still not always met, is six months between visit and transmission of report—and the co-ordination of what is typically several ministerial responses *within* states often takes a full year, the result can be grindingly slow. It follows that a considerable time must be allowed to pass before one can conclude that publication is unlikely.[85] It also follows that some CPT reports are more historical than contemporary documents by the time they see the light of day and of comparatively little use to the campaigning communities which might have benefited from earlier sight of them.[86]

Nevertheless, this unexpected openness, for which few commentators in the late 1980s dared hope, or considered likely, should be seen as a resounding success for the Convention.

(f) Dialogue with member states

It is the quantity and quality of the ongoing post-report dialogue with state parties which is arguably the least satisfactory aspect of the implementation of the ECPT to date. Though virtually all states who might reasonably be expected by now to have authorized the publication of reports received have done so—with the exception of Turkey and, possibly, Romania—and most of these have also published their interim responses, less than half have published their follow-up reports and even fewer have made ancillary correspondence available.[87] Moreover, a minority of state parties have failed to meet the CPT deadlines of six and twelve months

---

[83] Conversation with FIACAT, Sept 1996.

[84] Cyprus, for example, failed to publish the CPT report arising out of the visit in 1992 until 1997. Likewise Spain took 5 years to publish the report arising out of the visit in 1991. Both countries chose belatedly to reveal accumulated material from successive visits, material which was no doubt initially considered politically compromising.

[85] In consequence, it may still be too early to be wholly pessimistic about the prospects of the report arising out of the visit to Romania in September 1995 being published. It follows that Turkey, which alone has published neither CPT reports nor government responses arising out of 7 visits dating from 1990 to the end of 1997, may yet decide to publish—indeed there are rumours to that effect.

[86] An outcome with which no doubt some jurisdictions are content: it also enables them to claim that whatever the CPT has found no longer applies; that the report is largely irrelevant.

[87] For details see Chapter 5, pp. 203–4 and Appendix 5.

respectively for transmission of interim and final responses following receipt of a CPT report. This delay and lack of transparency makes it extremely difficult for national NGOs to know how seriously their governments are taking the CPT's findings, and undermines their capacity to monitor government implementation of CPT recommendations.

Regrettably, as the CPT itself and the Council of Europe Parliamentary Assembly has partially acknowledged, the fault does not lie entirely with State parties. The CPT, or the Council of Europe as the provider of CPT resources, has almost certainly contributed to any tardiness on the part of governments. Though the CPT, as a result of streamlining its plenary meeting procedures, is tending now to achieve its target of drafting, agreeing, and transmitting reports within six months of completing visits, this target is scarcely ambitious. Given that CPT reports mostly take a standardized form—though because of the narrow focus of some *ad hoc* visits, the resulting reports are sometimes distinctively different—and that CPT core standards have from the earliest days been so well settled, large portions of CPT visit reports can almost literally be pulled down from a computer disk and simply inserted in any country report. If Committee and Secretariat members are trained in the art of fieldnote taking and report drafting, and are provided with laptop computers so that they can efficiently record their observations during the course of visits—and it seems reasonable to assume that all this is done—then six months is a distinctly unambitious target.[88]

The relatively slow-moving aftermath for the CPT's visiting programme has two certain knock-on consequences and arguably a third. First, having allowed themselves six months to produce a report—a target which in the early years was frequently not met—the CPT was virtually constrained to give governments the same amount of time to produce both their interim and final responses, despite the fact that the principal ingredients in the CPT's report will, or should, have been communicated to senior officials and ministers during the visit final talks. Secondly, those governments (like the United Kingdom, France, and others) who take the not unreasonable view that nothing can be published until their detailed response has been prepared, have therefore been given a full year's grace before whatever the CPT has found will see the light of day, by which

---

[88] As a possible point of comparison, Her Majesty's Inspector of Prisons in England —a body which lacks the backing of agreed core standards—currently aims to transmit completed reports following week-long visits to a single establishment—admittedly a less complex inspection undertaking than that typically engaged in by the CPT—within weeks of a visit being completed (address by Colin Allen, Deputy Chief Inspector of Prisons to an APT Conference on the CPT, London, Sept 1997). This means that 6 months is the target in England for reports being published *together with* the response from the Prison Service (Her Majesty's Chief Inspector of Prisons (1996) *Report: April 1995–March 1996* (London: HMSO, 30)).

time they are able plausibly to claim or imply that the report has little relevance for the contemporary situation. The force of CPT reports is thereby undermined. Thirdly, in the context of this relaxed timetable, it is scarcely surprising that some states have failed conspicuously to meet the six and twelve month deadlines.[89] Urgency (except where the Article 8(5) procedure is invoked),[90] or even promptness, has been conspicuously lacking from the whole procedure.

The CPT has not said that its self-imposed six-month target for producing reports was determined by lack of Secretariat resources, though that may have been one of the factors explaining why the Committee failed often to meet its target. The Committee has admitted, however, that it is not satisfied with its own performance regarding the post-response dialogue with governments,[91] an admission that the Parliamentary Assembly has endorsed.[92] The explanation for this poor performance is that the workload borne by the Secretariat has been too great. We are not in a position to judge the validity of this explanation. So little of the correspondence between the CPT and state parties has been allowed into the public domain, that we do not know how great is the quantity or quality shortcoming. Nor, in consequence, do we know what increase in Secretariat resources would permit whatever deficit there is in the CPT's performance to be rectified. On one issue, however, there can scarcely be disagreement. Given the gradually widening gap between *periodic* visits, any failure by the CPT to monitor the implementation of recommendations by governments, and chase governments when progress is lacking, certainly puts at risk 'both the credibility and the effectiveness' of the Convention.[93] As the Committee has put it, 'the momentum for change generated by a visit will almost certainly be frittered away'.[94] How this situation might be remedied, without necessarily greatly increasing resources, is a topic to which we return.

What is clear is that some governments need chasing: the quality of government responses has varied greatly. Whereas some governments have promptly, meticulously, and fully answered every CPT *recommendation, comment*, and *request for information*, others have been tardy in their responses and have to all intents and purposes either ignored CPT findings and recommendations or brushed them aside. In a few countries, for example, the CPT has found prima-facie evidence of torture or other physical ill-treatment, and has concluded that suspects in police custody run a significant risk of physical ill-treatment. In some of these cases

---

[89] Gen Rep 5, para 10; Gen Rep 6, para 10.
[90] The communication of immediate observations to a state party during the course of a visit, generally to indicate that accommodation be no longer used.
[91] Gen Rep 5, para 10.   [92] CLAHR Report (1997), para 23.
[93] Gen Rep 5, para 10.   [94] ibid; CLAHR Report (1997), para 23.

the governments concerned have engaged in straightforward denial, not accepting that a prima-facie case has been made out or repudiating the suggestion that there is any risk. Elsewhere a wall of silence has been displayed: a failure to comment or institute an inquiry.

This does not mean that CPT recommendations have made no discernible impact on domestic policy. On the contrary. Though it is seldom possible to establish an unequivocal causal connection—CPT criticisms generally echo concerns already expressed domestically—we are persuaded that CPT findings and recommendations have had some impact on domestic policies. The evidence from successive CPT visit reports to Cyprus, for example—evidence that we were able to confirm from conversations during our own visit—suggests that the Cypriot authorities have taken measures to investigate, condemn, and prevent the serious physical ill-treatment of suspects in police custody and that the CPT's intervention played an important part in the process.[95] Or, to take a rather different case, the evidence suggests the CPT's strictures influenced the Swedish authorities' decision to institute legislative change so that the courts, as opposed to public prosecutors, now determine whether pre-trial suspects held on remand should be subject to restrictions regarding their contact with fellow prisoners and external visitors. It is also the case that no great change in the proportion of pre-trial prisoners subject to restrictions appears yet to have resulted, but the procedure is arguably now more subject to public scrutiny and pressure for reform.[96]

The balance of evidence indicates that the CPT has so far exercised at best a marginal influence on the domestic policy of member states, and then only in a very few cases. But it is not plausible to expect that it could be otherwise. In most states criminal law and procedure changes but slowly. Even when some scandal creates the demand and impetus for reform, and the scandalous events are investigated by an official high-level domestic inquiry, it is not uncommon for a decade or more to pass before new legislation or administrative procedures are agreed and resources made available so that day-to-day practice is effectively influenced. Though the CPT has a capacity to generate scandal through the publication of its findings, that capacity is very limited. The Committee is not a judicial body. The Committee's findings—when related to the physical ill-treatment of individuals—are couched in anonymous terms. The findings typically enter the public domain long after the alleged events have taken place. The findings are published in what is often a foreign language and are heavily encoded in rather dry legal-bureaucratic terminology. And, worst of all, they originate from a little-known Committee based in a distant bureacratic citadel—Strasbourg—about which

---

[95] See Chapter 5, p. 206.   [96] Chapter 6, p. 248.

in many countries there are deep public suspicions which at the very least call into question the legitimacy of the intervention. On the basis of our fieldwork experience, for example, it seems likely that at the time of writing—the close of 1997—many Turkish opinion-formers will, first, confuse the Council of Europe with the European Union and, secondly, dismiss or downgrade any judgment originating from the former because of the perceived hostility of the latter in rejecting Turkey's application to become an early candidate for membership of the Union. In the case of Turkey the confusion regarding European institutions (which we have repeatedly encountered in many state parties) would be unsurprising. Several senior spokespersons for European Union member states have repeatedly cited Turkey's human rights record as a principal reason for rejecting Turkey's candidature for the European Union, and the CPT's finding that torture is widespread in Turkey has been widely cited (albeit usually without mentioning the CPT) as supporting evidence. The case of Turkey is far from unique. The British popular press frequently publish dismissive jibes regarding Strasbourg interventions, in alleged defence of the national interest and sovereignty. The CPT is not well-placed to effect major structural change. It would be surprising were there much evidence of CPT influence on the shape of criminal justice and penal policy in member states.

In one area—the closure of pockets of seriously substandard accommodation—one can identify repeated CPT successes. A number of factors appear to have contributed to this outcome in several countries. First, the use of the Article 8(5) procedure is often involved: that is, immediate pressure is applied. At the conclusion of a visit the delegation makes an observation that in the opinion of the delegation the use of particular cells or rooms, either at all or for particular purposes, is unacceptable and should cease: the accommodation is too small or fetid, or insufficiently ventilated or lit by natural light, and so on. The recommendation is frequently acted on by the local authorities sufficiently speedily for the CPT to report the fact in their subsequent report. Secondly, the recommendation is precise and limited in scope. It is feasible practically. The amount of accommodation involved is normally small. The authorities are able, relatively easily, to do without it. Where whole blocks or institutions of disreputable accommodation are subject to criticism, either because they are inherently defective according to CPT space-standards, or because the accommodation is in a state of disrepair or is being too intensely used, a more complex or time-sensitive package of recommendations is typically offered. It generally follows, therefore—a third explanation—that CPT strictures about small pockets of substandard accommodation have not been preceded by similarly couched criticisms by NGOs at home. The poor quality of the accommodation appears to have been little known about, except by those who have occupied it. In this regard the CPT is often able to achieve immediate, albeit modest, improvement.

(g) Developing 'jurisprudence'

In Chapters 6, 7 and 8 we describe the corpus of usages and standards which the CPT has promulgated in successive country reports and, in summary form, annual general reports. Though the term is technically inappropriate, we have collectively described these usages (the circumstances in which the Committee has judged it appropriate to employ the key terms 'torture', 'inhuman', and 'degrading') and standards (the protective safeguards that the CPT routinely recommends should be in place, the minimum facilities which should be provided for prisoners, the procedures which should be applied, and so on) as the CPT's 'jurisprudence'. It would be otiose to reiterate the principal ingedients of this jurisprudence here, but it is relevant to pose, and attempt to answer, certain general questions, regarding it.

First, to what extent has the CPT's jurisprudence evolved as the Committee appears originally to have thought that it should and would? In its first year of operation the Committee explained that 'in spite of the wealth of material available . . . no clear guidance [could] be drawn from . . . an array of international standards on the treatment of persons deprived of their liberty . . . for the purpose of dealing with specific situations encountered by the Comittee'.[97] More general standards were needed and the Committee was 'feeling its way towards developing its own "measuring rods" '.[98] The Committee was 'considering the feasibility of the gradual building up of a set of general criteria for the treatment of persons depived of their liberty' and, if the Committee succeeded 'over the years, in distilling a body of such general standards, the CPT might at some future date decide to make them public, so as to offer national authorities some general guidelines'.[99] Subsequent annual general reports have on three occasions included significant statements of general standards,[100] and Trevor Stevens, Secretary to the Committee, has recently indicated that the Committee is contemplating publishing a compilation of its standards to date.[101]

Only a few aspects of custody, which were apparently initially little considered by the Committee, are now covered by CPT standards, and

[97] Gen Rep 1, para 95.   [98] ibid.   [99] ibid, para 96.

[100] The relevant sections of Gen Reps 2, 3, and 7, relating to police and prison custodial conditions and procedures, medical matters and provisions relating to persons detained, and immigration provisions respectively, are reproduced at Appendix 7.

[101] Speech by Trevor Stevens at an APT/British Institute of Human Rights conference on the work of the CPT at Kings College, London, Sept 1997.

the jurisprudence of the Committee has *evolved* only modestly. By this we mean that those aspects of custody which were early addressed—and the bulk of CPT jurisprudence was apparent in the country reports resulting from visits undertaken in 1990,[102] and was subsequently stated concisely in the Committee's Second General Report[103]—are stated today in terms very similar to those set out in the period 1990–2. That is, the standards have only marginally been qualified or amplified by time, place, person, or circumstance to reflect the nuances of custodial situations encountered since the early years.

Thus, to take some examples, the safeguard that suspects in police custody should have a right of access to legal advice from the outset of custody is routinely stated or elaborated today in terms almost identical to those employed during the initial period of the Committee's work,[104] albeit not all the constituent parts of the Committee's elaboration of this right are incorporated in the core statement of the right in the Second Annual Report.[105] Moreover, there are a good many aspects of this right which have not been commented on by the Committee.[106] Or, to take a very different aspect of the Committee's work, the Committee has insisted from the very beginning that all prisoners, irrespective of their legal status (remand or sentenced) or circumstances (undergoing disciplinary or other-wise) should have the possibility of outdoor exercise for one hour each day, and that wherever they are confined they should have access

---

[102] To Austria, Malta, the UK, Turkey, and Denmark, all of which reports, except that on Turkey, were published in 1991–2.

[103] Gen Rep 2, paras 35–60. See Appendix 7.

[104] Namely, that: the right of access to a lawyer should be from the outset of police detention, and any exceptions be clearly defined in legislation and regulations; that right of access should mean the right to contact a lawyer and be visited by a lawyer (under conditions guaranteeing confidentiality); that though it might be necessary, in the interest of justice, to delay right of access to a *particular* lawyer, this should not mean denying access to *a* lawyer trusted not to jeopardize the legitimate interests of the police interrogation; that the right should in principle include the lawyer's right to be present during interrogations; and that, to have meaning, right of access to a lawyer means some form of legal assistance for detainees without financial means. Not all these ingredients are incorporated in the statement in Gen Rep 2, but they can all be found in various country reports dating from 1992–3.

[105] See Gen Rep 2, para 38.

[106] For example, in England, where the right of suspects held in police stations to legal advice is provided for by the Police and Criminal Evidence Act 1984, there has been research, discussion, and case law on such issues as: what is to count as legal advice or access to a lawyer? (what of the use of para-legals, for example?); should the police be permitted to question suspects before they have had the benefit of the legal advice for which they have asked, either because the police regard the matter as urgent, or because the arrival of the lawyer is delayed?; and what use is made by the police of ploys to dissuade suspects from asking for legal advice, and to what extent should their use, and other forms of pressure, invalidate the subsequent use of evidence gathered in these circumstances? For reviews of these and other issues, see Ashworth, A (1994) *The Criminal Process* (Oxford: Clarendon Press), 99–124; Sanders, A and Young, R (1994) *Criminal Justice* (London: Butterworths), ch 4.

'without undue delay' to a lavatory 'at all times'.[107] There has been some evolution of accommodation-space standards—the gradual emergence of a threshold below which a cell is deemed too small to accommodate a prisoner overnight, for example, or the approximate number of prisoners large rooms in multiple use can reasonably be allowed to contain.[108]

On a good many issues the Committee has failed to develop or elaborate much jurisprudence, however. Thus, to take an issue which has greatly preoccupied the Committee, prolonged solitary confinement (in the sense that prisoners are not allowed visits or contact with fellow prisoners) may, the Committee has repeatedly asserted, 'in certain circumstances, amount to inhuman and degrading treatment'.[109] But the CPT has yet to explain, either definitively or by way of example, what these 'certain circumstances' are. Thus the answer to the second question to which we have moved—to what extent has the CPT devised a comprehensive jurisprudence?—must be answered in the negative. There remains a good deal to do.

The CPT devised most of its standard-setting building blocks early on, and allowed the material of which they were made to set fairly hard so that little evolution has since occurred or, to put the issue another way, little surface decoration has since been attempted. Further building *has* taken place, but only on a modest scale. Medical standards were extensively set out in the Third General Report and following a rather fallow period the Seventh General Report pulled together the Committee's standards regarding 'Foreign Nationals Detained Under Aliens Legislation'.[110] But there has been no equivalent statement regarding other categories of prisoners who arguably have particular needs—women or juveniles, for example[111]—nor has the CPT generated much jurisprudence regarding what we might term the public accountability of custodial systems —the publication of decision-making statistics, judicial oversight, independent inspectoral arrangements, complaints mechanisms, managerial accountability systems, appeal against prison disciplinary decisions, and so on—arguably a key aspect of any effective preventive structure.[112] Nor has the Committee had much to say about rules of evidence in criminal

---

[107] Police and Criminal Evidence Act 1984, ss. 48–9.   [108] See Chapter 8, pp. 307–9.
[109] See Chapter 6, p. 247.   [110] Gen Rep 7, paras 24–36, reproduced in Appendix 7c.
[111] The case for arguing that both categories of prisoners have special needs that should be reflected in their custodial arrangements is well set out, for example, in the thematic reports of Her Majesty's Chief Inspector of Prisons (1997a) *Women in Prison* (London: Home Office); and (1997b) *Young Prisoners* (London: Home Office).
[112] See, for example, Rouget, D (1997) 'Juges et Avocats, Acteurs Essentiels de la Prévention de la Torture' in APT. For an extended discussion, see Rouget, D (1995) *La Convention européenne pour la prévention de la torture et des peines ou traitements inhumains ou dégradants* (Univerisité de Lille).

proceedings, arguably another significant factor generating ill-treatment by the police.[113] We think there is certainly a case for the CPT publishing its accumulated jurisprudence in a brief consolidated form so that it is more accessible to commentators and NGOs than can be achieved by their trawling through the several score country and general reports where it currently lies. But we also think that the CPT has not yet fully realized its early promise that a code of 'measuring rods' or standards be set out that address in practical detail all aspects of custody. In 1997 the European Prison Rules, for example, looked more and more inadequate than they did in 1989–90. The Committee decided very early on what its 'fundamental safeguards' against torture and inhuman and degrading treatment were, and it has deviated scarcely at all from those early decisions. But it is at least debatable that the Committee's safeguards are fundamental and that other aspects of custody are not as important.

Thirdly, how consistently has the CPT applied the standards it has promulgated? Close reading of the whole corpus, or even a sample, of country reports—the sort of reading that few consumers of CPT reports have undertaken—throws up no glaring inconsistencies in the Committee's application of its core standards: these are everywhere stated in more or less identical terms. Moreover, when questioned, the CPT Bureau sets its face resolutely against any relative application of its standards on the basis, for example, of financial capacity, cultural tradition, or administrative legacy.[114] However, this apparently categorical rejection of relativism is belied by what we might term the *variable geometry* of the CPT's expectations regarding the *achievement* of standards: we detect the emergence of a doctrine, in effect, of same standards, different pace, and this bears out an aspect of the Committee's thinking revealed by Antonio Cassese, the first President of the CPT.

The question of whether absolute as opposed to relative standards should be applied was apparently the subject of a 'lively debate' within the Committee during its early days and the members were divided on the issue. According to Cassese it was finally decided (against the opinion of the medics within the Committee) that standards had to be judged within the context of the 'specific history and degree of economic

[113] Such questions as: the possibility of conviction on the basis of an uncorroborated confession taken by the police; or the application of the 'fruit of the poisoned tree' doctrine in invalidating evidence gathered under duress.

[114] Interview with Bureau, Strasbourg, Sept 1996. By way of example, it was said (we paraphrase): 'The fact that a country is so poor that citizens at liberty are having to live in holes in the ground would not make it acceptable for prisoners to live in similar conditions in a place of custody. When the state deprives a citizen of his or her liberty, it assumes responsibility for the citizen's welfare and this means meeting certain minimum standards which we shall everywhere apply.'

development of each state'. Though the central parameters (what is 'inhuman' treatment, for example) were universally to be applied,[115] there was to be recognition of contextual factors when interpreting how custodial conditions and procedures are subjectively interpreted locally and when formulating 'adequate and realistic recommendations'.[116] In fact, as Cassese's illustration of the Committee's alleged thinking makes abundantly clear, there is a contradiction here. What is subjectively interpreted as 'inhuman' or 'degrading' in one country may not be in another,[117] and presumably where such differences occur they influence whether the Committee considers it appropriate to apply the allegedly universal 'central parameter' terms. As for the formulation of 'adequate and realistic recommendations', this implies that governments that choose—and ultimately the size of any given penal population is a matter of political choice—to incarcerate a large number of citizens, but cannot financially afford to provide decent custodial conditions for that population, may benefit from the application of some understanding of relative 'socio-economic development'. In which case 'these two exceptions' make significant inroads into what Cassese describes as the Committee's aim—'to achieve the same level of civilized standards in the field of detention, throughout Europe'.[118]

   This aspect of the the CPT's jurisprudence has begun to become more apparent as reports on Eastern European states are published[119] and, to date, is best exhibited in the report on Bulgaria where, given the considerable shortcomings in the custodial conditions identified according to routine CPT standards, the Committee's recommendations are muted: they are pushed with discernibly less vigour than elsewhere in Europe,[120] and

---

[115] 'What is "human" or "inhuman" and "degrading" should always be the same. We could not accept the idea of Europe as a Neapolitan ice-cream of cultural levels and degrees of development; "mankind" and "human" are universal concepts' (Cassese (1996), 27).

[116] ibid, 28.

[117] Cassese's illustration is: 'a noisy and crowded dormitory in prisons in a country such as Spain or Turkey would be experienced in other countries (such as Norway and Finland) as an unbearable invasion of the inmates' privacy. By contrast, in Southern Europe such conditions are seen as a form of social relationship that are both acceptable and to be encouraged; detainees in these countries would find separate cells, with little chance to socialize, inhuman' (ibid).

[118] ibid.

[119] Though it is possible that, had the early reports on Turkey been published, similar issues might have arisen also. Some prisons in Turkey comprise old buildings in which very large numbers of prisoners are accommodated in communal areas, an arrangement that is certainly more culturally acceptable than in Western Europe, and an arrangement that would require considerable expenditure to change, were change considered desirable.

[120] The CPT description of police and NIS detention facilities in Bulgaria, for example, must count among the worst that the CPT has described in any published report. The Committee reports that the Bulgarian authorities received it's report constructively and agreed that 'the delegation's assessment was "objective and correctly presented"' but that the government's options for improving matters 'were limited by the country's difficult financial circumstances'. Thereafter the Committee recognizes 'that fundamental changes to the

contrast noticeably with the emphasis given to rather minor imperfections found in countries where custodial standards are higher and economic wealth greater.[121] Clearly there *is* a distinction to be made between applying different standards and applying those same standards in a manner and according to a timescale that is financially feasible, but, in the short-term at least, they both involve some acceptance of a 'two-speed' or culturally relative Europe. We think this is to some extent inevitable.

Finally, there is one aspect of the Committee's jurisprudence, or more properly its methodology, about which we have doubts. This concerns the use of the Committee's apparently calibrated estimation for any given country of the risk of physical ill-treatment that we describe in detail in Chapter 6. There are a number of problems which attend this approach. First, the apparently subtle linguistic distinctions between levels of risk —'little', 'small', 'a risk', 'a risk not to discounted', 'significant', 'not inconsiderable', and so on—are unlikely to be understood by readers who, for the most part, read only the report relating to their own country and, in that sense, the usages may well be *misunderstood*. Second, we have grave doubts whether such an implied statistical estimation of risk can be valid given the relatively small number of prisoners with whom the CPT can possibly speak and their unrepresentativeness of all the prisoners held in the country concerned. It may be said by the CPT that no such statistical inference is being made. But if that is true, it is difficult to see what other construction can be put on the clear relationship which we describe in Chapter 6 between the descriptions of risk and the apparently careful use of a similar linguistic continuum regarding the number of allegations of ill-treatment heard and reported. We think that the Committee *should* report, roughly if not precisely, whether a few or many allegations of ill-treatment are heard, and whether they are concentrated in particular groups of prisoners or locations: this is a vital piece of evidence. But we doubt that the Committee can, on the basis of such limited allegations—most of which, we presume, the Committee is incapable within the time available of cross-checking with other possible sources of evidence—reasonably arrive at either a global or partial estimation of the risk of ill-treatment. To that extent we understand that a few national authorities[122] might feel aggrieved at the justice of the estimates to which the Committee has hitherto come.

current situation will not be possible overnight' and suggests 'a number of steps that would not require major financial outlays' but which 'can and must be taken at once' (Bulgaria 1, para 62). A similarly sensitive approach is taken with regard to Bulgarian prisons where conditions are described which '*could* be considered to be inhuman and degrading' (ibid, para 113, emphasis added).

[121] See, for example, the Swedish 'Venetian blind' and English 'tea towel' examples cited below, p. 357.

[122] See the example of Greece below, p. 355.

3 PERCEPTIONS OF THE CPT

Even if it is concluded that, on balance, the CPT is performing tolerably well in terms of the technical criteria against which its operations can be judged, this is only part of the story. A factor of equal—if not greater— importance concerns the manner in which the Committee is perceived to operate. How is the CPT regarded by those which whom it comes into contact? Although there is no very reliable way of assessing what is necessarily a subjective question, we have attempted to form an impression of the impact made by the CPT and the manner in which it is regarded on the basis of conversations held during the period 1994–7 with a wide variety of individuals and groups,[123] typically focusing on a recent visit to gather views about the manner in which the Convention had been implemented.[124]

(a) General impressions of the CPT as a body

It would have been surprising had the persons with whom we made contact known little or nothing of the CPT: most, after all, were sought out precisely because they had met a visiting delegation from the CPT or had other reasons to come into contact with them. Yet it has to be said at once that we were struck by just how little many of our interviewees knew about the general nature of the CPT's work, its mandate and its standards. It would hardly be safe to assume that others would know more and it must be concluded that there is little general awareness of the CPT even within circles upon which its work impacts.

---

[123] We talked to individuals and representatives of organizations with whom the CPT had met during the course of visits, met with CPT liaison officers and other civil servants with responsibility for the areas of policy with which the CPT concerns itself, and met with academic researchers knowledgeable about custodial policy. In a few countries we also met with members of parliament, ombudsmen, and other relevant officials. During the course of these conversations we ranged, when appropriate, over virtually every aspect of the CPT's work: the interpretation of the Convention; the make-up of the CPT; the programme of visits; the manner in which visits are undertaken; the reports; and the responses of governments. We also sought opinions regarding the degree to which there is ill-treatment of persons in custody and the relative vulnerability of different groups of persons in custody.

[124] In addition to talking to persons in the UK, fieldwork visits were made to Austria, Belgium, Bulgaria, Cyprus, the Czech Republic, Denmark, France, Germany, Greece, Hungary, Ireland, Malta, the Netherlands, Poland, Slovakia, Spain, Sweden, Switzerland, and Turkey. One of us (Morgan) also assisted the CPT as an *ad hoc* expert during CPT visits to Austria (1990), Sweden (1991), Finland (1992), Turkey (1992), Norway (1993), Turkey (1994), Portugal (1995), Denmark (1996), Portugal (1996), Norway (1997), and Estonia (1997). Moreover, during APT organized conferences in Strasbourg in 1994, Onati, Spain in 1997, and London in 1997, we had the opportunity to talk to delegates from countries not visited about the work of the CPT.

Those that have come into contact with the CPT are overwhelmingly positive about the CPT as a body,[125] considering it well informed and professional in its conduct. Liaison officers were particularly complimentary about the Secretariat, the persons with whom they are principally engaged. They hold the Secretariat in high regard—describing its members as well briefed and professionally competent. Some interviewees expressed doubts about the qualifications of their own national members to serve on the CPT but in no case did these reservations appear to call into question their confidence in the CPT as a body.

The general perception, from NGOs and civil servants alike, is that the visiting programme is generally well organized and conducted, that visiting delegations appear to incorporate appropriate expertise, that by one means or another the Committee generally focuses on the principal problems that need to be confronted, and goes to those sites and institutions which most need to be visited.

This is not to say that there are no criticisms. Several NGO interviewees, for example, were unhappy with aspects of the Committee's arrangements for particular visits. A few said that the Committee did not always take sufficient time to explain themselves (their mandate, *modus operandi*, and so on) and took rather too much for granted regarding their interlocutors' knowledge and understanding of the CPT. One or two said that the timings and settings for meetings were not always appropriate.[126] There was inevitably occasional disagreement about the choice of places visited,[127] with it sometimes being said that advice had been ignored.[128] These criticisms were relatively marginal and unusual, however.

The overall judgment which we encountered in country after country was that, on a general level, the CPT was doing a valuable job on the basis

[125] We have already noted that many NGO representatives were unable to distinguish between members, experts, and the secretariat.

[126] The Committee tends to invite NGOs to meetings on Sundays at the very beginning of visits shortly after the delegation has arrived. This is not always judged convenient. And meetings invariably take place in the hotel in which the CPT delegation is staying. This is not always judged appropriate. In Northern Ireland in 1994, for example, the delegation's rather opulent hotel, situated in a Protestant area of Belfast, was thought by local intermediaries to be an insensitive place to invite former Republican prisoners to attend. The meeting was re-arranged at another location at the suggestion of local intermediaries.

[127] NGO representatives with whom we met in Hungary, for example, considered that the CPT had been mistaken in confining their visit almost entirely to Budapest in 1994. They claimed there were many problems of ill-treatment in the rural border areas of the south and west of the country.

[128] In the UK in 1997, for example, at least one NGO representative with whom the CPT met pressed the case that the delegation visit one of the high-security prison units which, ever since certain high profile escapes in 1994–5, had been the subject of policy changes to restrict the prisoners' regime. Controversy and prisoners' rights litigation had ensued. In the event the CPT, which the previous year had been pressed by the Council of Europe Parliamentary Assembly to mount an *ad hoc* visit to the UK to investigate the same issue (see CLAHR Report (1997), para 29), chose not to visit any of the high security units.

of methods that were a model for other monitoring bodies, domestic and international, to follow. With regard to only one issue was there a widely held, though by no means majority, critical edge—that concerned the manner in which the CPT interprets its rule of confidentiality. This is such an important and recurrent issue that we deal with it separately below.[129]

(b) CPT reports, findings, standards and recommendations

Very few activists and officials have face-to-face contact with the CPT. To the extent that the Committee's work is known, it is known by reading the Committee's reports, and it is clear that these reach a narrow, but gradually expanding, audience. How are CPT reports viewed? Before considering this, two preliminary points need to be made.

First, very few people have read CPT reports other than those on their own country. We did encounter official and other liaison officers[130] who had taken the trouble to collect CPT reports on countries other than their own, though few had read them closely. Even within the international NGOs like Amnesty International and Human Rights Watch, consumption of CPT reports tends to be devolved to country or region researchers so that it is rare to encounter commentators with a general perspective of the CPT's work. It follows that appreciation of CPT reports is almost entirely parochial.[131] This has at least one important consequence: it is simply not possible to gauge the reactions to the standards applied by the CPT *as a body of standards* because they are not considered in this way by those with whom the CPT engages.

Secondly, although the culture of civil servants differs somewhat from country to country, the general tendency is to be guarded and discreet. When asked their opinion about CPT reports, most of the civil servants we interviewed were not prepared to go much beyond the official line as stated in their government responses, responses which they had often been responsible for drafting. However, even in the space of comparatively short, 'cold' interviews a good many of our respondents were prepared

---

[129] See below, pp. 375–9.

[130] Every country designates a CPT liaison officer. However, in most countries there are officials in each ministry with responsibilities for custodial populations. This will typically include ministries of justice or internal (or home) affairs, health, social services, immigration, and the various branches of the armed forces. These ministerial liaison officers tend to have primary responsibility for drafting or collating responses to those sections of CPT reports concerned with their ministry responsibilities.

[131] There is nothing unusual about this phenomenon. It parallels the situation within countries. In England and Wales, for example, the Chief Inspector of Prisons doubts that there are more than a handful of people who read all or most of his reports on individual institutions. Most readers will read only that report for the institution or group of institutions for which they are directly responsible (interview with the Chief Inspector, Autumn 1995).

to set aside the veil of officialdom to a greater or less extent, with revealing consequences.

The overwhelming view we encountered, from officials and NGO representatives, was that CPT reports were written in a highly professional manner and were authoritative in that they were: generally accurate in their exposition of the law; revealed a thorough understanding about day-to-day practice; the standards implicit in findings were generally fair and appropriate; and most recommendations were reasonable and appropriate. NGO representatives, not surprisingly, tended to give higher marks under all these heads than officials, but we were struck by the generally positive view taken, not least because many officials had then to proceed to explain why many recommendations were unlikely, at least in the short term, to be implemented. Of course there were conspicuous exceptions to this appreciative response and it is worth considering one or two examples of hostility in some detail in order to explore the dynamics which may underlie some CPT–state relations.

Our visits to Greece and Austria were particularly interesting because in both countries the CPT had found evidence of grave ill-treatment, possibly amounting to torture, at the hands of the police. The variety of reactions to these findings was notable. In Greece we met with senior police officers in the Ministry of Public Order and discussed with them the CPT findings regarding the police generally. It soon became apparent that our respondents were extremely angry about the CPT report and that they felt that the CPT suggestion that prisoners had been subjected to electric shocks with a purpose-made baton by the police was unwarranted, unfair, and had unjustifiably besmirched the reputation of the Greek police.[132] This pattern of vigorous denial needs setting against the reaction to the same issue within the Ministry of Foreign Affairs: the civil servants with whom we spoke declined to comment on those sections

---

[132] It was accepted that an electric-shock baton had been found in a police officer's private locker, but they did not understand why the CPT had refused to accept the explanation offered for this (Greece 1, para 24: the officer had, we gather, apparently explained that the baton had been given to him as a present by a German police officer on holiday with his family in Greece). On the other hand, they reported that the officer had subsequently been fined by way of a disciplinary measure for allowing discredit to be brought on the Greek police by the finding of the baton. They rejected the suggestion implicit in the CPT report that the baton fitted into a broader pattern of evidence of ill-treatment, discounting the allegations of prisoners claiming to have been ill-treated by electric shock or otherwise and not accepting that the medical evidence cited by the CPT supported them. In general they resented the fact that the CPT had chosen to give credence to prisoners' accounts above those of officials. As far as they were concerned, the whole edifice of the CPT's general conclusion was built on a chance finding of an instrument that was the personal possession of an individual officer. On the contrary, whilst accepting that, as in every police force, ill-treatment would occur from time to time, it was vigorously asserted that there was no evidence that the Greek police employed torture as a means of investigation or that ill-treatment was a serious problem in Greece.

of the CPT concerning the police on the grounds that it was not their responsibility.

In Austria we met with senior civil servants in the Ministry of the Interior who conceded that there was a serious problem of ill-treatment of suspects by the detective branch of the Vienna police identified in successive reports by the CPT.[133] The CPT findings were not a surprise to them nor, they said, to other senior officials: ill-treatment was a recognized aspect of the police detective culture in Austria. Moreover there was an accompanying legal culture that tended not to call this into question. We learned that nothing by way of an official inquiry or disciplinary proceedings had been instituted in the wake of the CPT's findings and there was a political reluctance to challenge the police because one of the most powerful police unions, particularly strong in Vienna, was allied with the right-wing Freedom Party whose further rise the Government feared.

These examples demonstrate the variety of reactions to CPT findings that can occur within and between ministries.[134] Moreover, the fact that the dominant reaction is one of denial—expressed as rejection, obfuscation, or blanking silence in the Government response to the CPT, does not necessarily mean that there is not acceptance in some ministerial quarters that what the CPT has found and stated is without substance or can in practice be ignored. Several of our interviews have indicated that whatever the official government response may say, an inter or intra-ministerial debate may have been started and domestic challenges stimulated.

If reluctant acceptance, though masked by a wall of denial, is one response to CPT findings, the Swedish experience provides an example of a different reaction which might be termed benign toleration. The view was expressed in several countries in north west Europe that the CPT has to be seen not to be concentrating on the less well-resourced regions of Europe where problems of ill-treatment are greatest and, in consequence, the Committee was bound to find something to criticize in practically every country visited, and this was seen as probably not unreasonable. In Sweden, we talked to several senior servants in the Ministries of Justice and Foreign Affairs who generally spoke positively about the CPT, but who tempered their irritation at what they regarded as minor issues blown up out of critical proportion on the grounds that it was

---

[133] Austria 1 (1990) and Austria 2 (1994). See Chapter 6, pp. 217–18.

[134] We cite the examples of Austria and Greece *not* because they represent, in our view, contrasting cases and reactions to CPT findings. On the contrary we have no reason to believe that to be the case. Had we interviewed senior uniformed police officers in Vienna we think it likely that we would have encountered exactly the same wall of denial that we encountered in Athens. By the same token it seems likely that there are senior civil servants in Athens who, given the right circumstances, might have lifted the veil of discretion and revealed their doubts about aspects of police practice.

reasonable to expect something to be criticized. Examples cited to us included one prisoner who, because he had been transferred at a critical time, had not received a full meal during one half day at either the police station where he had initially been held or the remand prison where he was subsequently taken.[135] Another was the alleged inability of prisoners in the main Stockholm remand prison to control the venetian blinds in their double-glazed windows.[136] Even raising such matters in the report was regarded as fairly ridiculous, irritating, and disproportionate.

This reaction is given additional emphasis in circumstances where it is accepted on both sides that there are very real issues which need addressing, as illustrated by the 'tea towel' saga in the UK. Following its first visit to the UK in 1990, the CPT, as part of a general review of unhygienic prison conditions at three prisons, suggested that prisoners be given tea cloths in order to avoid having to use body towels to dry their eating and drinking utensils.[137] Given the then general inadequacy of sanitary arrangements in the prisons concerned—no integral sanitation, overcrowding, long lock-up periods, slopping out, and so on—this was considered by British officials a somewhat risible minor consideration and prompted the response that it was more hygienic to let utensils dry naturally.[138] The CPT chose to return to the issue in subsequent correspondence, apparently agreeing that letting utensils dry naturally was preferable, but doubted the hygiene of such a practice in an overcrowded prison, hence tea towels should be provided. The British Government disagreed[139] and it is clear from subsequent exchanges that the British took the view, like the Swedes in the example above, that the CPT was being disproportionate and a little silly to press the point.[140]

Other, less dramatic, examples occur in other reports. In Hungary, for example, officials in the Prisons Department were fairly bemused at the depth of criticism levied at prison dental care facilities. It was put to us that the level of care was far in excess of that generally available to the public and that our interviewee would rather be treated under the prison system than outside of it. It is clear, however, that such irritations are seldom allowed to cloud an overall positive appreciation of the CPT's work. Thus during the same interviews in Sweden, referred to above, it was agreed by senior officials in 1995 that a criticism more central to the CPT's report—the widespread use of custody with restricted contact

[135] See Sweden 1, para 19.
[136] Sweden 1, para 44. Alleged, because prison staff claimed that prisoners could ask for their blind to be adjusted.
[137] UK 1, para 77.   [138] UK 1 R 1, 15.   [139] UK 1 R 2, para 65.
[140] The tea towel saga was the subject of a ribald public exchange at an APT-organized seminar on the CPT in London in September 1997 between Trevor Stevens, Secretary to the CPT, and Andrew Coyle, who in 1990 had been the governor of Brixton Prison, one of the three prisons concerned.

pre-trial—was probably justified,[141] that the CPT was correct in thinking that recent legislative change had not had much impact, and that the issue should be looked at again.

Among NGOs, reactions to CPT reports vary, depending on how sophisticated a picture of custodial processes and conditions the NGOs have themselves been able to generate, which in turn depends on the openness and accountability of the authorities in the countries concerned and the experience and resources commanded by the NGOs. However, on one issue there was almost universal agreement: that CPT reports were valuable because they were authoritative and that if the CPT said something in a published report, it *had* to be taken seriously by the authorities. The CPT could provide unimpeachable corroboration of claims often made by NGOs but dismissed by governments as unreliable or partial. The differences between the NGO representatives we interviewed lay in the degree to which they claimed that CPT reports told them anything they did not already know, or had had a marked impact on domestic policy. One or two illustrations will once again serve to make the point.

In the UK, which has an abundance of well-resourced NGOs, the general view was that CPT reports had been useful but had not revealed anything that was not already known and, in consequence, were unlikely to have a major impact on policy. These claims seem plausible. The first CPT visit to the UK took place in 1990 and the Report was produced in 1991. In spring 1990 there occurred the fiercest and most prolonged spell of prison rioting in English penal history. The riots resulted in a major judicial inquiry headed by a senior judge and joined, during the second stage of the inquiry, by the Chief Inspector of Prisons. The report of the inquiry, 600 pages in length, was published early in 1991[142] following a process of consultation in which the leading penal reform NGOs were widely consulted.[143] Later in 1991 the Government published a White Paper providing a detailed response to the inquiry report.[144] At the time when the CPT began its work in the UK, the shortcomings of the penal system were a high profile issue, widely known and discussed. It was highly unlikely, therefore, that the CPT could have added new elements to the picture. The value in the Report lay in its adding an international voice to the chorus and, by describing conditions in three prisons to be 'inhuman and degrading',[145] gave

---

[141] Sweden 1, paras 63–9; Sweden 2, paras 21–7.

[142] Woolf Report (1991) *Prison Disturbances April 1990: Report of an Inquiry by the Rt Hon Lord Justice Woolf (parts I and II) and His Honour Judge Stephen Tumin (Part II)*, Cm 1456 (London: HMSO).

[143] For a discussion of the procedures adopted by the inquiry by a member of the inquiry, see Morgan, R (1991) 'Woolf: in retrospect and prospect', 54 MLR 713.

[144] Home Office (1991) *Custody, Care and Justice: The Way Ahead for the Prison Service in England and Wales*, Cm 1647 (London: HMSO).

[145] UK 1, para 57.

additional momentum to the process of change. But it did not affect the direction of changes on which the authorities were already embarked. Moreover—and this is a view which was widely held in several countries in north west Europe—neither the first nor subsequent CPT reports had prevented reformist agendas subsequently being knocked off course by other factors.[146] In short, the CPT was useful in that it lent legitimacy to the arguments of the penal reform lobby (as one Dutch NGO put it) but in the final analysis the direction of domestic policy regarding custodial arrangements and conditions were shaped by structural forces of a more long-term nature.[147]

Elsewhere, particularly where NGOs are less numerous, are less well-resourced, and attract less attention, or where human rights issues in relation to criminal justice has a comparatively low profile, the dynamics are different. In Greece, for example, the findings of the Committee were not widely known in NGO and academic circles and appeared to have had little impact on the authorities. Moreover, NGOs operated in an atmosphere of 'official discreditation'—that is, they were for the most part reportedly discounted by the authorities, had little or no access to institutions, and were not consulted by policy makers. This impression was confirmed by our meetings with academic specialists in criminal justice, whose focus was on the text of statutory provisions and penal theories. There was not the practical engagement with the operation of the system which, in countries where there is an established socio-legal empirical research tradition, brings academics and practitioners together with victims and complaints to form NGOs and monitoring and pressure groups. In such countries, CPT reports are potentially revelatory. The problem is that there is not a developed infrastructure of receptors for the revelations, though CPT reports may stimulate the growth of such an infrastructure.

(c) Confidentiality and confidence

Whereas the CPT's rule of confidentiality, and the manner in which the Committee and Secretariat have interpreted that rule, are undoubtedly reassuring to many officials, they represent the biggest difficulty in the Committee's relationship with NGOs, not least because they colour the way in which many NGOs perceive the CPT. Confidentiality, discretion, even secrecy, and certainly holding the mass media at arms length, are familiar and welcomed cultural values and practices for civil servants in

---

[146] For example, notorious crimes or prison security breaches, the toughening of the party political agenda on 'law and order' policy and the decline of custodial standards as a result of the rising prison population, overcrowding and the application of tighter security measures in prisons.

[147] For a discussion of some of these factors, see Downes and Morgan (1997).

most European countries. By contrast they are alien values and practices for most NGOs who devote much of their energy battling *against* the secrecy of the state. They seek to bring facts to light, to increase official accountability, and seek to *construct* public scandals by generating media publicity and enlisting public support in order that pressure be brought to bear on the authorities. It follows that for most NGOs, most of the time, publicity is the oxygen of their operations. This is not to say that NGOs do not understand the need for confidentiality in certain circumstances. They fully comprehend, for example, that the identity of informants may have to be protected and, in our experience, they have a sophisticated understanding of the need discreetly to trade information with officials who, from time to time, may be willing to assist them with leaked documents or information. Nevertheless the natural instinct of NGOs is for disclosure. It follows that human rights NGOs and a CPT committed to confidentiality as a working principle are not natural bedfellows: there were bound to be difficulties in their relationship.[148]

Representatives of several NGOs in the countries we visited did not understand why the CPT had, as they saw it, made such a fetish of the secrecy with which they surrounded their meetings. If meetings were to be conducted on the basis of mutual trust and confidence, why could NGOs not be given an indication of which institutions were to be visited so that the discussion could be more focused? Why was it not possible for meetings to take place before visits were undertaken so that material could be collected specifically for the purpose of assisting the Committee? Why, following a visit, could the Secretariat not contact NGOs which had assisted the Committee by providing information used in preparation for the visit, with some feedback as to its usefulness? At the very least why could they not ensure that the press release and, if published, the report was sent to them with an accompanying letter of thanks, possibly drawing attention to those parts of the report which addressed those issues about which the NGO had provided information? It is difficult to find significant objections to many of these points.

At the APT-organised conference on the working of the CPT in December 1994 there was much talk by NGOs working in 'partnership' with the CPT[149] and some disgruntlement with the suggestion that the NGOs could not, in truth, be partners with the Committee if being a partner meant operating on the basis of equality and openness.[150] The then President of the CPT emphasized that the CPT members present at the

---

[148] This was acknowledged in several of the contributions to the APT-organized conference on the CPT in December 1994. In particular, see Shaw (1995).

[149] See Mottet, C (1995) 'Preparatory Document', in APT, 187–92.

[150] See Murdoch, J (1995) 'Functioning of the CPT and Standard Setting' in APT, 281; Casale, S (1995) 'Conclusions and Suggestions of the Seminar' in APT, 303.

conference would be listening rather than participating in the discussion, because of the rule of confidentiality.[151] It was emphasized by one CPT member at the conference, though his remarks were not recorded, that the relationship of NGOs with the CPT would necessarily be one-way: NGOs could provide information but the CPT would not, and could not, provide any information in return. As far as NGOs were concerned the CPT would be operating not unlike an aircraft flight recorder 'black box': individual NGOs would know only about that information which they had themselves relayed to the CPT, but as to how it meshed with other information fed in, what conclusions had been drawn and what had been done on the basis of these bits of information, they would remain wholly ignorant. If the CPT's report was ultimately published the NGO could then surmise—but it would be no more than that—how their contribution might have contributed to the activities and thinking of the Committee.

Nevertheless, a number of NGOs were not critical of the CPT's interpretation of its framework of confidentiality. Generally speaking, however, these were the NGOs who had the greatest knowledge of the Convention and who, on the basis of what was clearly mutual trust, had established quite close working relationships with the CPT that seem to transcend the standard application of confidentiality. For example, an academic lawyer member of the Dutch Branch of the International Commission of Jurists learned, while working in Strasbourg for the European Commission on Human Rights, that the CPT was to visit the Netherlands during 1992. He informed his ICJ colleagues who decided to draw up a list of custodial institutions that they thought the CPT should visit. This list was sent to the CPT Secretariat and this was followed up with a meeting with the Secretariat. Further, the Dutch ICJ was one of the groups with whom the CPT delegation met in the course of its visit. The Committee visited virtually all the institutions the Dutch ICJ suggested.

Against such a background, it is not surprising to discover that the Dutch ICJ hold the CPT in high esteem and endorse the view that NGOs should accept that their relationship with the CPT will be be almost entirely one-way. The Dutch ICJ managed, on the basis of geographical convenience and personal familiarity and confidence, to arrange precisely the sort of personal advance meeting which other NGOs desire. We encountered similar positive reactions from one or two other NGOs who had been able to achieve a similar understanding with the CPT through extended telephone discussions with members of the CPT Secretariat well in advance of visits, though all maintained that during these conversations the members of the Secretariat were scrupulously careful not to divulge

---

[151] Nicolay, C (1995) 'Five Years of Activities of the CPT: And Now?' in APT, 221.

any information indicating the details or the timing of the forthcoming visit. We note also that when the APT has produced country briefings, they have rarely appeared at inappropriate times: we know not how this has been achieved, but the APT's reports have neatly coincided with the CPT's visiting programme.

In conclusion, most NGOs who complain that the CPT is secretive, remote, unhelpful, and unresponsive tend to be those that are least well informed about the ECPT and, we suspect, those that the CPT considers have least to offer the Committee in terms of detailed knowledge that might practically guide the CPT in its work. Nevertheless not all critics of the CPT's current interpretation of its confidentiality rule are ill-informed amateurs. It is not difficult to understand why many NGOs, particularly those which are small and poorly resourced, might feel that there is little to be gained by channelling their activities into supporting the work of a body evidencing such an unresponsive attitude. To the extent that the CPT can work effectively without the input of such bodies, this may not be a significant handicap, but to the extent that the practical impact of the CPT's recommendations are assisted by their being taken up by NGOs and used by them in their ongoing or developing dialogue with their national governments, any such alienation is regrettable. Since we consider that the development of effective NGOs is so vital to the long-term effectiveness of *any* effort aimed at preventing torture, we return to this topic in our final section.

4 THE FUTURE OPERATIONS OF THE CPT

The CPT is coming of age. At the time of writing it is eight years since the first Committee members were appointed and began implementing the Convention. A good deal has been written about the Convention, but most of that writing has been descriptive rather than analytical, and complimentary rather than critical. Most commentators have offered the sort of indulgence that befits youth: the Committee has been 'establishing itself', 'finding its feet', 'gaining credibility', and so on. As has already been seen in the earlier sections of this chapter, such comments are not unjustified. Moreover, it is only to be expected that in its early years the Committee will have been working under a largely benign gaze, not least because those observers knowing its operation best, tend to be those most close to it, people committed to its success and, thus, unlikely to voice any doubts that might undermine the reception of the Committee. But the CPT is now sufficiently well-established for us to take stock. In this text we hope to provide the sort of detailed scrutiny which might enable us, and others, to consider whether the future operation of the Committee should continue along the lines pursued hitherto. The remainder of this chapter seeks to pull some strands of analysis together and make some suggestions for modest change.[152]

(a) The strategic setting

A useful starting point is the 1997 report from the Committee on Legal Affairs and Human Rights of the Parliamentary Assembly of the Council of Europe 'on strengthening the machinery of the ECPT',[153] the recommendations of which were adopted by the Parliamentary Assembly in Resolution 1323 (1997).[154] The Committee paid tribute to the work of the CPT but identified developments which, in its judgment, necessitated changes to preserve the effectiveness and credibility of the CPT. The principal development highlighted in the report was the increasing work-load due to the rise in membership, and in particular the immense problems posed by the eventual accession of the Russian Federation and the Ukraine which would 'more than double the civil prisoner population which will be subject to the CPT's mandate'.[155]

The Committee also noted strains in the CPT's operation—the less than adequate awareness that some member states have of the CPT's mandate and methods (perhaps as a result of the CPT's inability to devote more of its resources to the organization of information seminars for new member states) resulting in difficulties in obtaining access to places, persons, and information; the reduced ambition represented by the four-year gap between *periodic* visits which is now the CPT's target;[156] the CPT's dissatisfaction with its capacity to engage in ongoing dialogue with member states following visits—and made proposals to remedy these difficulties. Moreover, there was indeed a danger that 'the absence of a sustained post-visit ongoing dialogue' would fritter away 'the momentum for change'.[157] The Committee recommended, inter alia, that the Parliamentary Assembly stress the need for:

(i) a more balanced composition of CPT membership, with regard to professional background, gender and age;
(ii) the rapid entry into force of the second protocol to the Convention, so that members be able to serve more than two terms; and

---

[152] A number of the issues raised in the following pages were raised and discussed at the APT/BIHR London Conference in September 1997 and are considered in Evans, MD (forthcoming) 'The CPT: Future Challenges' in Association for the Prevention of Torture/British Institute of Human Rights.
[153] CLAHR Report (1997).   [154] Adopted 21 Apr 1997.   [155] ibid, para 68.
[156] A country 'as large as the Russian Federation'—and involving so many other difficulties, it is implied—'should be visited far more frequently' than every four years (ibid, para 28).
[157] ibid, para 23, underlining a quotation from CPT Gen Rep 5, para 10.

(iii) for the Committee of Ministers to give 'favourable consideration to any request for further increase of the human and budgetary resources of the CPT'.[158]

Were the CPT to have more resources it could be able better to act on reports from the Parliamentary Assembly regarding 'the honouring of obligations and commitments by member states'[159] and exchange information and co-operate with the CAT. Whether the CPT would wish always to act on reports from the Parliamentary Assembly,[160] or indeed co-operate much more closely with the CAT,[161] are interesting questions. None the less, there is no doubt that the CPT would welcome additional resources to enhance other aspects of its performance. All of which prompts a return to a basic question which it may seem surprising to pose at this late stage: What is the CPT for?

(b) The emphasis on formal visits

The lay observer might assume that the function of a visits-based mechanism like the CPT is to enable inspectors to make on-the-spot findings concerning the practice or likelihood of ill-treatment occurring. There is little doubt that this is what the drafters of the Convention intended. There is also little doubt that they did not expect much evidence of ill-treatment to be found outside of a few recognized troublespots which were already under scrutiny by other legal or political mechanisms within the Council

---

[158] CLAHR Report (1997), Draft Recommendation, para 10. The Draft Recommendations contained in the Report were adopted unchanged by the Assembly in Recommendation 1323 (1997).

[159] ibid, Draft Recommendations, para 9. This reference is to an exchange which occurred between the Committee on Legal Affairs and Human Rights and the CPT in 1996. In May 1996 the Committee transmitted to the CPT reports of allegations of ill-treatment of Irish Republican prisoners in British mainland prisons (almost certainly arising out of tightened conditions in high-security units following certain notorious escapes in 1994/5). The Committee felt that the allegations were sufficiently serious to justify an *ad hoc* visit by the CPT to the prisons concerned. Correspondence resulted. The President of the CPT responded that no visit to the UK was envisaged in 1996 and that no information could be given regarding the proposed programme for 1997 (the programme for *periodic* visits not yet having been announced). Pressure on the CPT was exerted in the form of a proposal for a visit by the Bureau of the Assembly. This pressure was resisted. The CPT President replied that a visit to certain prisoners held in high-security units in England was 'not warranted at the present time' (see CLAHR, para 29). Moreover, it is notable that when the CPT made an *ad hoc* visit to the UK 16 months later (Sept 1997) the delegation did not visit any high-security prison units in England (Press Release 534a(97)).

[160] See Chapter 5, pp. 168, 179–80.

[161] Our own conversations both with people involved with the CPT and civil servants in Council of Europe member states, suggests that whereas the CPT—by which we mean the manner in which it operates—commands widespread admiration and credibility, the same cannot be said of the CAT. There is not space here to consider the work of the CAT —its membership, its *modus operandi*, its reports, and so on—but we encountered many criticisms of it. Indeed, some commentators observed to us that were the CAT to be given, by means by an optional protocol, a role and powers similar to the CPT, they would doubt the Committee's ability credibly to fulfil such a mandate.

of Europe, and that the chief element of the Committee's 'preventive' function would be fulfilled by the very fact of its existence. It was assumed that the CPT's ability to uncover and probe causes of concern as they arose would serve as a deterrent.

To the extent that this was true—and we believe it was—it was certainly naïve, if only bearing in mind the experience of the ECHR, which some states did not see as having any particular bearing upon them at the time of its adoption. Perhaps the virtually instantaneous nature of the way in which the CPT transformed itself into an inspectoral agency largely concerned with conditions of detention and the legal framework surrounding custody (which is what most of its proponents had always envisaged) makes it appear as if this was intended all along. It is, then, not surprising that the CPT has developed a corpus of standards which, as we have seen, is fairly formalistic, a template which can be applied as a first point of assessment to the situations which the Committee encounters. This being so, we need to ask whether it is necessary for the CPT to assess the congruence of the local legal order with sets of procedural safeguards which the CPT routinely applies in the context of elaborate and expensive *periodic* or *ad hoc* visits. Could not this legal order be established, and the gap between that legal order and the CPT's established code of standards be ascertained, by means other than a full-blown Committee visit? We do not know how much of this ground work is done by other means but it is clearly possible for it to be done by research conducted, either at arm's length in Strasbourg or by means of forays to the country, by a Committee or Secretariat member in advance of a visit. Moreover, when it is known that certain procedural safeguards are not in place, why is it necessary to wait for a *periodic* country visit in order to raise the issues with the state concerned? Why should dialogue on such matters have to 'hang' on a *periodic* visit report?

The relevance of this question becomes apparent when one considers the implications of the Committee's workload. At the time of writing the ECPT has been ratified by 37 states and, as noted earlier, this is expected to increase shortly to 40 states, and possibly beyond. Increasing participation creates more work than is offset by the consequential elections of new member to the Committee. It is generally accepted that the effective functioning of the Committee depends upon the Secretariat who organize the visits, accompany them, draft the reports and, in substance, conduct the dialogue that arises out of them. As has been seen, the real backlog of work clearly concerns the dialogue. At the same time, and in the light of the increasing time period between *periodic* visits, there is increasing need for the Committee to place further emphasis upon the post-reporting dialogue if, as the CPT has put the matter, the 'momentum for change' is to be maintained.

It is true that 'problem' states—those where severe physical ill-treatment is found to be prevalent—are likely to go on receiving *ad hoc* visits every year or two. But it is in precisely those other countries, the majority, where there are no such pressing issues but where there are clearly identifiable structural weaknesses leading, for example, to inhumanity in the form of overcrowding or prolonged isolation, that it will be most difficult to build any sort of momentum for change. It is certainly not likely to happen as a result of very infrequent *periodic* visits which, given the turnover in national bureaucracies, will probably constitute a new experience for many of the officials with whom the CPT deals. Moreover if the flow of correspondence between the CPT and member states is as intermittent as the available evidence suggests, such communications are likely to be regarded as occasional intrusions into normal working patterns rather than part of the ebb and flow of regular activities, certainly at the operational level. We think means have to be found, without expecting a significant expansion in the CPT's resources, to make the work of the CPT less an occasional voice from the wilderness and more an integral part of states' operational considerations.

Article 1 of the ECPT provides that: 'The Committee shall, by means of visits, examine the treatment of persons deprived of their liberty with a view to strengthening, if necessary, the protection of such persons . . .' But this does not mean that the Committee can *only* exercise its mandate though the means of visits, or visits of the sort envisaged by the Convention. Article 3, for example, provides that: 'In the application of the Convention, the Committee and the competent national authorities of the Party concerned shall co-operate with each other'. This would seem to provide a fairly convenient vehicle for developing a dialogue on matters of substance without having to inaugurate the topic in a visit report.

Indeed, a model is already provided for in the Rules of Procedure. Article 30 provides that:

1. Before deciding on a particular visit, the Committee or if appropriate, the Bureau may request information or explanations as regards the general situation in the State concerned, as regards a given place, or as regards an isolated case concerning which it has received reports.
2. Following receipt of such information or explanations, details of remedial action taken by the national authorities may be requested.

The purpose of the first part of this Rule is to allow the Committee to test the necessity for conducting a visit by referring the cause of concern to the state concerned,[162] whilst the second part enables the Committee to

---

[162] This procedure is similar to the manner in which the European Commission of Human Rights refers applications to Governments for comment before deciding on admissibility. Rule 30 was adopted at the suggestion of Love Kellberg, member of the CPT for Sweden 1989–93, who had previously served as a member of the Commission.

exercise its protective remit in relation to such a place or person without having to undertake a visit. A modest amendment to this rule, to include, for example, procedural safeguards, would give the Committee the powers needed to engage in constructive dialogue on a broad range of issues without having to relate back to matters expressly raised in a visit report.

We are not suggesting the CPT should abandon *periodic* or *ad hoc* visits as the principal working tool of the CPT. The prime purpose of the Convention is to subject states to the discipline of international inspection, it being axiomatic that the mere presence of legislative or administrative provisions guaranteeing minimum standards and legal safeguards does not mean that they exist in practice. The need for verification is obvious and it is precisely the CPT's capacity to undertake verification at first hand which makes the ECPT so innovative and powerful a human rights mechanism. What is not obvious, however, is that the current *reliance* of the CPT on visits by full-blown delegations is the best mechanism for establishing *all* the facts that the Committee needs to establish, or that dialogue with states parties need wait upon the findings from such visits. Although clearly well-designed to highlight certain general procedural inadequacies (including the failure to apply the law in practice), and identify particular instances of ill-treatment, many legal provisions could be established and commented on without the need for visits at all. Moreover, findings based on relatively short and infrequent visits will not always provide a sufficiently sound basis for conclusions that would normally need supporting by more sustained observation and research, a task for which the CPT is peculiarly ill-suited. In the light of the increasing workload with which the CPT is burdened, it seems at the very least questionable whether some aspects of the CPT's work need be conducted within the framework of formal visits as envisaged by the Convention. Other methods, more suited to certain tasks, could be developed. The Committee could, for example, consider allocating a country (not their own) to each member or several countries to certain members well qualified to examine legal provisions and procedures. That member could have the capacity to visit if necessary, but could conduct an examination of the legal safeguards (assisted, if necessary, by a member of the Secretariat or by an *ad hoc* expert—the Convention does not say that *ad hoc* experts can only be used during the course of a formal delegation visit) without making a visit. Salient points could be raised in the course of a subsequent *periodic* visit if the need arose.

This proposal, it seems to us, is in accord with changes in CPT practice already being pursued. First, the full-blown *periodic* visit is becoming increasingly infrequent. There has already been a move towards increased reliance on *ad hoc* and *follow-up* visits. The current form of *periodic* visits now appears too cumbersome for the variety of tasks that are identified as in need of attention by the Committee. For the future, a better model might be a fairly formal 'first' *periodic* visit for new states, establishing contact and making a general evaluation of concerns, to be followed by more frequent, short, thematic visits, focusing on different identified problems. These could be conducted on a much less formal basis than is currently the case. Secondly, in response to the problems posed by the expanding number of states parties, the CPT has suggested that the dialogue with governments 'should also encompass regular face-to-face discussion on matters of concern',[163] and this has already happened on at least one occasion.[164]

To sum up, the work of the CPT is 'based' on visits,[165] and its visiting mandate is now well established. But it may no longer be necessary for most of the activity of the Committee to revolve around visits in the way it has to date. Sections of the membership and the Secretariat could jointly develop other modes of specialist activity a good deal of which could be conducted by correspondence or small-scale forays to the countries concerned. Just as in a municipal legal system not all cases come to court, not all of the preventive work of the Committee needs a visit, although all its work would be conducted under the mantle of the visiting mandate. Such non-visit work could, of course, be chronicled in the Annual General Report. Were the future work of the Committee to move in this direction, it would have implications for all aspects of the Committee's composition and working methods.

(c) The membership

Without doubt the thorniest CPT question is that of the Committee's membership. What forms of experience are relevant to membership? What abilities are needed? How well have past and present members lived up to expectations? It has not been easy to examine these questions, partly because whatever shortcomings members may have are shielded from public view by the confidentiality rule and the fact that the Committee's plenary meetings are held in private. Moreover, no constructive purpose would likely be served by invidious examination of individuals. Nevertheless the quality of CPT members is critical for the work of the Committee, both in terms of what is done and what contribution members might make in future. The questions cannot be shrugged off.

The CLAHR Report calls for a 'more balanced composition with regard to professional background, gender and age', with greater participation

---

[163] Gen Rep 7, para 8.
[164] The visit by members of the Committee and Secretariat to Turkey in September 1992, prior to the issuing of the First Public Statement on Turkey, PS 1, paras 14–15.
[165] ECPT, Preamble.

of 'prison specialists and medical doctors with relevant experience, including forensic medicine', to which is added the need for 'availability'.[166] It is a matter of public record[167] that not all members have been used equally—or, indeed, at all—and this must be a matter of concern, be it because members are unable to participate or are deemed by the Bureau (who determine the composition of delegations) less 'useful'. Of course, the usefulness of members depends upon what one expects the purpose of a visit to be and it may be that some states, at least initially, chose certain members in good faith but on the basis of assumptions concerning the nature of the CPT's work which were not borne out in practice.

The received wisdom, which the CPT has encouraged in its annual reports, that more medical and prison specialists are called for, chiefly at the expense of lawyers, has arguably been pushed far enough. It needs to be emphasized that the CPT is a body conceived and created under the auspices of international law. It operates within the context of an inter-governmental organization and the Parliamentary Assembly Resolution itself calls upon it to take advantage of the work of the CAT, to which it might have added the UN Special Rapporteur, the ICRC, and many other bodies. Of course, the CPT does so already to a limited extent. The Committee's role as a preventive mechanism of a non-judicial nature means that it must be sensitive to the boundaries of the judicial and quasi-judicial functions. It must also have a keen awareness of the jurisprudence regarding Article 3 of the ECHR and of other concepts of torture and inhuman and degrading treatment or punishment. Failure to do so is likely to bring the CPT's work, which is conducted in proximity to that of other international bodies, into a position of conflict—a point which will be considered further below. For current purposes, the point that must be emphasized is that as with any international instrument, questions of interpretation and application will arise,[168] in addition to fine points concerning the domestic legal systems of the states concerned. On all these counts, the presence of respected jurists gives the views of the Committee an authority which they might otherwise lack in the circles to which they are addressed. This is very important if the assessments and understandings acquired by the Committee are to achieve a broader impact within the international system, thereby enhancing their overall effectiveness. There is of course no immediate danger of lawyers being under represented

---

[166] CLAHR Report, para 47.

[167] See Chapter 5; and Evans and Morgan (1997), 664–6.

[168] See, for example, Council of Europe (1993), which contains declassified correspondence between the Committee and the Council of Ministers concerning the application of visa requirements to CPT members, the need to give reasons for the exclusion of an expert under Article 14(3) of the Convention, and the legal status of the Explanatory Report.

on the Committee: as a group they account for some two-fifths of members. However, we consider that the range of legal specialisms within the Committee is as important as the spread of medical and prison specialisms, a point not given due weight in current debate on membership qualities.

Why might this be so? There are two plausible reasons. First, there is the familiar tendency of committees attempting to reproduce themselves. In its early days the CPT was numerically dominated by lawyers, but the high-profile medical minority (both of the Committee's Vice-Presidents were medics during the period 1989–93) was able successfully to draw on the text of the ECPT Explanatory Report which emphasized the desirability of the Committee including members with experience of prisons administration and medical matters in its advocacy.[169] Over the years the Committee of Ministers appears to have listened and there is now a formidable coterie of medical and para-medical experience and there is a general climate of opinion within the Committee which will not wish this aspect of the Committee's membership and work to decline in importance. For example, during plenary sessions the medical and para-medical members of the Committee meet as a sub-group to discuss medical issues.[170]

There may also be a second factor at work. The senior members of the Secretariat, among whom, as we noted in Chapter 5, there is yet to be any turnover, are overwhelmingly lawyers. It would be surprising were the Secretariat not to see themselves—rather than the legally qualified members within the Committee—as the essential guardians of the Committee's 'jurisprudence' and of the CPT's boundaries with relevant Council of Europe and other institutions. In this sense the Secretariat may be content to have the CPT membership taking the legal lead largely from the Secretariat rather than from legal experts within the Committee. This may be a natural tendency, but it may not be in the best interests of the CPT as an effective institution. There is a strong case, for the reasons that we have already begun to explore, for developing the capacity of members, particularly those with legal research skills and drafting experience, to take on more of the work of fact-finding and dialogue with member states. This potential role for members needs to be recognized when appointing members in the future.

On much the same grounds, we suggest that there is a role for experienced parliamentarians and diplomats, who may also be lawyers, within the CPT. Any analysis of effectiveness of international obligations will include the vital role that can—indeed, must—be played by pressure through political agencies. The political placement of members within the CPT is, of course, to be shunned, but that should not be allowed to rule out recruiting the insights and experience of people versed in the political

---

[169] Explanatory Report, para 36.   [170] Meeting with Bureau, Sept 1996.

process. Indeed, it is the basic building block of the Council of Europe itself. A balanced committee will embrace all these elements, in proportions relevant to the execution of its mandate—an issue to which we return below.

(d) Links with other international and intergovernmental bodies

One of the issues highlighted by the CLAHR Report concerns links with other bodies within the Council of Europe and with the CAT. The following subsections give an overview of the relationships between these bodies and the CPT in order to draw attention to areas of unresolved tensions.

(i) The Council of Europe

The Report suggests the desirability of the CPT drawing on the experience of the CLAHR and the Monitoring Committee of the Council of Europe.[171] This seems to have been inspired at least in part by the refusal, as we have seen, of the CPT to act on a formal proposal by the Bureau of the Assembly that the CPT conduct an *ad hoc* visit to the UK.[172] To the extent that political factors might influence such requests it is understandable that the CPT wishes to avoid being seen to be overly responsive to external direction. Without knowing more about the incident, it is impossible to draw further conclusions but it is obviously important that the Committee does not lose the confidence and support of the political organs of the Council.

Somewhat surprisingly the Report makes no mention of contacts with the ECHR supervisory mechanisms. From the outset of the drafting process, there has been concern that the CPT and ECHR might operate in too close a proximity for mutual comfort. The solution to this problem was seen initially to lie in emphasising the preventive and non-judicial function of the CPT, but in the light of the manner in which the CPT has developed its mandate, it is difficult to maintain this line. It is important to distinguish between two situations.

Conditions of detention

The CPT has established what we have termed a 'jurisprudence' concerning conditions of detention by which, for example, the combination of overcrowding, lack of regime activity and lack of appropriate sanitary facilities will be condemned as 'inhuman and degrading'. It requires too great a juristic refinement to expect such a CPT finding not to be translated by those subject to such conditions into an assumption that the conditions

---

[171] CLAHR Report (1997), paras 29–31.   [172] See Chapter 5, p. 168 and p. 364 n 159.

are indeed 'inhuman and degrading' for the purposes of an application under Article 3 of the ECHR. However, as we have repeatedly emphasized, this is not necessarily so: the CPT is free to draw inspiration from other sources and, in any case, its preventive function justifies its laying down markers which lie in advance of the threshold of Article 3 liability. However, it is not surprising that applications have been lodged which draw on CPT findings. It appears that, to date, the Commission has been able to avoid a head on clash by being able to distinguish these cases on the facts.[173]

An interesting variant of this problem recently arose in *Aertz v Belgium*, concerning whether the conditions of detention in a psychiatric hospital were in violation of Article 3. The CPT had visited the unit in question in the course of its periodic visit to Belgium in 1993 and concluded that prolonged detention in such conditions '*comporte un risque indéniable d'aggravation de leur état mental*'.[174] Drawing on the failure of the Government to address the situation, the majority of the Commission, some seventeen members, concluded that these conditions now amounted to a violation of Article 3.[175] At the same time, a minority of fourteen members disagreed, concluding that the conditions encountered did not cross the minimum threshold, and found it significant that the CPT had chosen not to describe the conditions as inhuman or degrading.[176] The *Aertz* case clearly underlines the care which the CPT must put into its conclusions. It also shows that the Commission can be heavily influenced by CPT findings but that the interpretation of reports may be, to say the least, unpredictable: in this instance the CPT's findings were taken by almost equal numbers of Commissioners to imply that conditions both were and were not in violation of Article 3. It might be preferable for the Commission to have an opportunity to clarify the value it places on a CPT opinion concerning detention conditions and 'clear the air'. Presumably, the only possible resolution is the acknowledgment that the CPT's views can influence, but not dictate, the views of the Commission, but this must be balanced by the Commission becoming more adept at handling the messages given in CPT reports, the approach taken in the *Aertz* case being overly simplistic. In particular, it must be realized that the CPT's approach to the key terms 'torture' and 'inhuman or degrading' and its methods of fact-finding and risk-assessment, are very different to that of the Commission and Court of Human Rights.[177]

---

[173] See, for example, *Delazarus v UK*, App No 17525/90, Comm Dec, 16 Feb 1993, in which it was concluded that since the applicant had been held in solitary confinement he could not complain of overcrowding, and *Raphaie v UK*, App No 20035/92, Comm Dec, 3 Dec 1993, which was declared inadmissible, having been submitted out of time.
[174] Belgium 1, para 190.   [175] *Aertz v Belgium*, Comm Rep, 20 May 1997, paras 81–2.
[176] ibid, 28.   [177] See Chapter 6, pp. 253–5.

Findings of physical ill-treatment.

The *Aertz* case was not the first in which the Commission and Court have taken note of CPT findings. Another interesting example is *Aksoy v Turkey* in which the CPT's findings, released in the first public statement of the Committee in December 1992, were seemingly used to add authority to allegations of ill-treatment and helped foster a climate in which some evidential shortcomings could reasonably be minimized.[178] On the other hand, it would be interesting to know the extent to which the CPT has adapted its practices in the light of the Court's Judgment in *Ribitsch v Austria* which, as was seen in Chapter 6, requires the authorities to disprove their responsibility for injuries sustained by detainees in police custody. A practical example is provided by allegations concerning the use of electric-shock equipment in Greece.[179] As has been seen, and very much to the chagrin of the Ministry of the Interior, the CPT gave very short shrift to the findings of an official investigation into the matter.[180] Had the persons making the allegations been in police custody at the time of the visit, it is difficult to see what more would be required for the Commission on Human Rights to have found a violation in accordance with the *Ribitsch* principles. Perhaps the separation of judicial from preventive functions should require the CPT to refrain from passing comment on explanations offered, as opposed to merely recording them, whatever the Committee's private view might be.

Other areas of intersection, less obvious, also come to mind, particularly the question of what amounts to a place of detention. The views of the Commission in *Amuur v France* must have sent shock wakes through the CPT. The Commission found that airport holding centres for aliens were not places of detention for the purposes of Article 5 of the ECHR,[181] and this presented states with a powerful tool to challenge the work of the CPT in relation to such places. The Court subsequently reversed this finding,[182] a decision duly emphasized by the CPT.[183] Though the Committee gave no such prominence to the Commission's view, it is noticeable that in the interim period there seems to have been less emphasis in CPT reports on visits to such places.

Perhaps the most important issue, however, concerns evidence relating to particular individuals. The CPT, as we have seen, will not, without their consent (since this would place them at risk), reveal either in reports or subsequent correspondence with states, details of individuals who appear to have allegedly been subject to ill-treatment. Similarly,

---

[178] *Aksoy v Turkey*, Comm Rep, 23 Oct 1995 (eg paras 52, 111, 114, 153, 159); Judgment, 18 Dec 1996.
[179] Greece 1, paras 21–2.   [180] ibid, para 24. See also above, p. 355 n 132.
[181] *Amuur v France*, Comm Rep, 10 Jan 1995, paras 44–50.
[182] *Amuur v France*, Judgment, 25 June 1996, paras 38–49.   [183] Gen Rep 7, para 25.

the principle of confidentiality has hitherto been taken to preclude the passing of information acquired in the course of a visit to other bodies. In consequence, it is entirely plausible that CPT field notes might contain vital evidence of physical injuries sustained during custody, and which would support a finding of a violation under Article 3 of the Convention. It is equally plausible that such an application might fall for lack of evidence (even if the Commission conducts a fact-finding visit). It is a matter of record that the CPT and Commission have trodden the same paths in Turkey, and it is believed that this scenario has occurred. Such situations may at best involve frustrating duplication: at worst they could amount to what many would regard as a humanitarian outrage caused by bureaucratic protectionism. In such a situation it might be worth considering whether the Commission could ask the CPT whether it holds information which might be pertinent to an application. If the CPT believed that it had, it could contact the state concerned and enquire whether it would be prepared to waive confidentially and allow transmission to the Commission of factual material.

This is not as radical a suggestion as it might seem. In its most recent General Report, the Committee has revealed that where it acquires information that leads it to suspect that a person faces the threat of being removed from the jurisdiction of a state party and into that of a country in which they run a risk of being subjected to torture or inhuman or degrading treatment—the *'Soering'* scenario[184]—then the Committee will pass relevant information to the European Commission of Human Rights, irrespective of whether that information came from a direct communication with the CPT or was gleaned in the course of a visit.[185] This acknowledgment of the Commission's greater preventive powers in such cases is to be welcomed, not least for the suggestion that the confidentiality of CPT materials is not necessarily absolute. In any event, this practice underlines the point that hard and fast divisions between the functions of the CPT and the ECHR organs, if sustainable in theory, are not sustainable in practice. It is clear that the clarification of the relationship between these bodies is a major issue for the future.

(ii) The CAT

Cordial relations and exchanges of information are no doubt beneficial to all concerned. There is, however, no reason to suppose that a state is more likely to respond to the prompting of the CAT to implement a recommendation than it is to that of the CPT itself—although the greater

---

[184] See *Soering v UK*, Judgment, 7 July 1989, Ser A, No 161, considered in Chapter 3, p. 94–7.
[185] Gen Rep 7, paras 32–4.

publicity attached to the CAT is probably a plus. This might also partly explain why the attention of many NGOs is more focused on the CAT than on the CPT. The CAT acknowledges the work of the CPT and, when considering reports from states parties, draws attention to its findings and has urged compliance with its recommendations. Moreover the CAT urges states to authorize publication of CPT reports, where this has not been done. This mutual support has undoubtedly been facilitated by the dual role of Mr Sørensen (the Danish representative on the CPT from 1989 to 1997) as a CPT and CAT member, but that has now terminated. Though dual membership of the two bodies clearly has some advantages, it does pose problems of confidentiality when a member of the CAT has had sight of an unpublished CPT report on a state which comes up for consideration in Geneva.

The current proposals to adopt an Optional Protocol to the UN Convention against Torture, which would establish a visiting mechanism similar to the CPT, is likely to throw these issues into stark relief. Would states be subject to two visit mechanisms? If so, how is the state to respond should the assessments of the two bodies vary? Almost inevitably, their priorities in terms of preventive mechanisms and prescriptions would be different, given the differing scope of their fields of operation. If both bodies work on the basis of confidentiality, there is little opportunity for them to co-ordinate action. It is equally possible that a state might wish to invite both bodies to conduct a joint visit. Would this be possible? And what would the modalities be for adopting a report and engaging in dialogue in such circumstances? These are only a few of a large number of potential problems which will need to be faced.

It is clearly unwise to speculate in the abstract about the nature of the relationship which the CPT will need to develop with a body which does not yet exist, and which is not likely to do so for a number of years to come. On the other hand, it would be shortsighted not to feed the experience of the CPT into the negotiations and to develop an idea of what a suitable form of interaction might be. At the very least, there is a need to signal whether it is desirable for states to be a party to both systems since this is likely to affect the range of compromise necessary to ensure the negotiation of a satisfactory text.

(e) Confidentiality and NGOs

The observations above lead us naturally back to the question left open earlier in this chapter and what is, for many observers and particularly the NGOs, the greatest single challenge to the future of the CPT—the principle of confidentiality. This has been an essential element in the history of the establishment of the CPT system. Without the confidentiality rule, it is doubtful that most states would have permitted the intrusion of the CPT into their 'darkest places', their *'sancta sanctorum'*.[186] The work of the Committee was in its earliest days surrounded by what many considered to be an excessive degree of secrecy. In recent years, however, a good deal has changed. There are signs of a more relaxed approach to certain aspects of the CPT's work. This has been characterized by the participation of Committee and Secretariat members in seminars and other discussions.[187] Some 'insiders' have also written about the work of the Committee.[188] Most of this lifting of heads above the parapet has, however, been geared towards generating a greater awareness of the work of the Committee. The central tenets of confidentiality remain relatively untouched.[189] We think it may be time for change.

The Convention text cannot of course be ignored. However, in common with so many international instruments, there are plenty of possibilities for pragmatic malleability. Publicity is the lifeblood of human rights, both in terms of norm creation and of implementation. Confidentiality has always been a price sought by states for the acceptance of international scrutiny and the history of virtually all human rights mechanisms has been the struggle to break through the restrictions imposed by the framers—the states themselves—of these limitations. If examples are wanted, they are easy to come by.[190] The general lesson, however, is that those bodies which have not embarked on the road to greater institutional and procedural independence and openness have withered on the vine, becoming out-moded and outflanked by more fruitful developments.

If the CPT has truly come of age, this ought to be marked by greater evidence of the Committee struggling to break the bonds by which it was bound and which hitherto it has been generally perceived—rightly or wrongly—as seeking to strengthen rather than weaken. It will be argued

---

[186] Cassese (1996), 1.

[187] In September 1997, for example, we organized a small three-day seminar at Bristol on the work of the CPT at which the current member for Eire, John Olden (elected 2nd Vice-President in November 1997), was a participating delegate.

[188] See, for example, Cassese (1996); Kelly, M (1996) 'Preventing Ill-treatment: the Work of the European Committee for the Prevention of Torture', EHRLR, Issue 3, 287.

[189] But cf above p. 374 above for signs of relaxation.

[190] For example, UN Special Rapporteurs, thematic and country, have developed their competency through incremental steps away from confidentiality and into an open, public dissemination of allegations and responses. The Human Rights Committee and other treaty-monitoring bodies moved slowly to break down the resistance of states to the acceptance of external material when considering country reports, and now routinely quizzes them on NGO allegations. The introduction of 'concluding observations' on state reports is another milestone, moving away from the restrictions of the non state-specific 'general comment'. The African Commission on Human Rights has been innovative in developing a right of individual petition outside the fetters imposed by the African Charter on Human And People's Rights. One might add the battles within the Council of Europe over the composition of the Monitoring Committee under the Framework Convention on National Minorities. The list could go on and on.

that states would resist any such attempt and that the work of the Committee would generally be impeded. There are reasons to doubt that would be the case. There is, for example, very little evidence of states successfully restraining over time the creative development of practice by human rights bodies when they are revealing and addressing matters of genuine concern. A more particular indicator of the likely response of states to a more nuanced application of confidentiality lies in the approach of states to the publication of CPT reports and responses. It is now the well-entrenched norm for reports to be published. Whatever caused this to come about, there is, as we have seen above, no evidence that the CPT has been particularly proactive in achieving this.[191] Now that the work of the CPT is firmly established on the human-rights map, states will be less willing and able to object to reasonable re-evaluations of previous practice without calling their good faith into question. Indeed, as was indicated earlier in this chapter, several of our interviews with officials suggest that some states are a good deal less concerned about the confidentiality of CPT material than the caution of the CPT would suggest.

We are firmly of the view that the long-term vibrancy and effectiveness of the CPT is likely to depend in large measure on the extent to which various partners—and we wish to employ that term in spite of our recognition that the partners have different statuses, resources, expertise, and interests, and cannot therefore be considered equals—engage with the Committee, providing it with information, reinforcing its message, and monitoring the progress of its recommendations. Rightly or wrongly, the current interpretation of confidentiality has an inhibiting effect on the positive development of these partnerships.

We doubt that this is currently a matter of great concern to the Committee or the Secretariat, and we understand the reasons why this may be so. The Committee and Secretariat is overwhelmed with work: there is precious little time for members, at least during the time that they are paid allowances for their services, or the Secretariat, to communicate with NGOs and other informants. Moreover, given this considerable burden of work, it is likely that the Secretariat will select for close contact only those NGOs, probably a small minority, which have detailed information and genuine experience of custodial conditions and procedures that the Secretariat lacks. It may be the pressure of time rather than the principle of confidentiality which causes the Secretariat to appear impatient with the many NGOs who lack the information and experience that could be of immediate benefit to the CPT and which truly dictates the largely one-way relationship which exists between the CPT and most NGOs.

---

[191] See, for example, the account given above, p. 340 n 82, regarding the publication of the Danish responses to the CPT report on the 1990 visit to Denmark.

Indeed confidentiality may be little more than a fig-leaf to cloak the CPT's perception that most NGOs in member states have little or nothing to teach it. The Committee may consider that to nurture most NGOs is, frankly, not worth the informational candle.

Moreover, as far as we have been able to discern, most Committee members do not see it as part of their CPT role, and have not been encouraged by any policy framed in Strasbourg to see it as their role,[192] to liaise with, or educate and encourage, NGOs in their own countries. Very few CPT members are active public propagators of the work of the CPT at home. Indeed some maintain, misleadingly, that the confidentiality rule precludes their engaging in such activity. During our fieldwork visits we heard accounts of several members who had on these grounds declined invitations to attend meetings in their own countries at which CPT related matters were to be discussed. There is of course no bar to CPT members engaging in public discussions of those CPT findings and recommendations which, because the relevant reports have been published, are in no sense confidential. The only thing they have to fear is their own indiscretion.

In the long term we suggest that a failure by the CPT to play its part in cultivating NGOs so that they are well informed about the work of the CPT will run the risk of prejudicing the development of that 'momentum for change' which the Committee says it is concerned to maintain. We think that the interest and support of NGOs is of critical importance to the effective functioning of the mechanism. Indeed, greater effectiveness may depend upon being able to foster more intimate connections with groups in member states who are better able to engage in continuous long term monitoring of the response to CPT recommendations. It is important that the foundations for such developments are well laid and laid promptly. As a practical expression of this, there is no very obvious reason why the Convention needs to be interpreted so as to prevent the Committee from giving general feedback to NGOs on the usefulness of the information it receives and the extent to which it was able to make use of it during a visit. The relevant information will often be in the public domain anyway (through Council of Europe press releases) and the Committee would be doing no more than drawing the connections which the NGO might otherwise not be aware of. Certainly, the CPT should ensure that NGOs receive copies of reports on visits which have taken up the concerns they, the NGOs, have raised with the CPT.

If the Council of Europe generally wishes to promote civil society infrastructures throughout member states it should surely be prepared to

---

[192] During our meeting with the CPT Bureau in September 1996, the then President, Claude Nicolay, made it clear that there was no CPT policy on this issue. The matter was left with individual members to decide.

ensure that the courtesies of providing feedback and publications to CPT informants is done more systematically and promptly than is currently the case. Were it so, we have no doubt that it would radically improve perceptions of the CPT.

(f) Dissemination of CPT concerns and jurisprudence

Continuing this line of argument, the CPT could use its general reports —which should routinely be sent out to all NGOs with which the CPT has had dealings—as a vehicle for expressing general observations on compliance and causes of concern, as it already uses them to make generalized comments on applicable standards. This would not conflict with the text of the Convention which merely provides that 'The information gathered by the Committee in relation to a visit, its report and its consultations with the Party concerned shall be confidential'.[193] The Seventh General Report suggests that the Committee is already moving in this direction: its exposition of its approach to 'Foreign Nationals Detained Under Aliens Legislation' is characterized by references to the experience of the CPT followed by the CPT's observations on what it deems desirable.[194] Even more encouragingly, and possibly controversially, the Report also points to the problems posed by prison overcrowding, originally raised in the Second General Report,[195] and casts doubt on the wisdom of addressing this issue solely by means of increasing prison capacity, noting that:

the existence of policies to limit or modulate the numbers of persons being sent to prison has in certain States made an important contribution to maintaining the prison population at a manageable level.[196]

This is a solid precedent on which the CPT might build. Future General Reports could emulate those of some national inspectorates[197] by including summaries of findings and trends, highlighting areas of general concern, or, of course, of general improvements. We also think there is a case for the CPT publishing as a separate document a concise statement, a digest, of the core standards (in effect, the Committee's 'jurisprudence') which the CPT applies during the course of visits or, if our proposal above is taken up, in the course of dialogues following fact-finding exercises. This digest, which would need regularly to be updated, could become a valuable guide for both new member states *and* for NGOs engaged in monitoring exercises. It would better ensure, for example, that a variety of human rights groups were singing from the same hymn sheet. Above all

---

[193] ECPT Article 11(1).   [194] Gen Rep 7, paras 24–36.
[195] Gen Rep 2, para 46.   [196] Gen Rep 7, paras 13–14.
[197] See, for example, the annual reports of Her Majesty's Chief Inspector of Prisons or Her Majesty's Inspectorate of Constabulary in England and Wales.

else, however, we think the Committee should be seeking to restrict the principle of confidentiality to the narrowest of bounds, whilst remaining faithful to the letter of the Convention text.

5 CONCLUSION

After eight years of operation, there are good grounds for substantially rethinking the working methods of the Committee in the light of the Committee's development and bearing in mind the magnitude of the problems posed by carrying on a dialogue both with so many member states and on so diverse a range of issues. To that extent, much of the current discussion about membership (particularly as regards members' expertise, age and, to a degree, availability) may be rather backward looking. If the work of the Committee developed along the variegated lines suggested above, it is not obvious that all members need be ideal candidates to take part in prolonged visits, provided they were actively engaged in other aspects of the Committee's functions. It is not necessary that all members be equally effective during visits and candidates who may not possess the physical and mental stamina to cope with midnight stand-offs with burly policemen in locker-rooms should not be excluded from consideration. People with track-records in legal research, drafting reports, and examining senior officials should also be considered: these are all important aspects of the CPT's work in which members, as well as members of the Secretariat, should ideally play a prominent part. We have doubts about whether the Secretariat need carry so large a part of the burden of the Committee's work as it appears, from all accounts, they do. The Committee needs able members, and the potential capacity of the membership needs fully to be realized. Indeed the future credibility of the CPT demands no less. If the Committee appears to be dominated by the Secretariat—an impression that some CPT members currently give and which an examination of their working practices tends to confirm—then it is unlikely that the Committee will maintain the stature that it gained in its early years. It will look more and more like an uninspired bureaucratic exercise. Members generally, and the Bureau in particular, need to adopt a higher and more professionally assured public profile.

The question remains: what is the Committee for? Is it to *discover* evidence of ill-treatment in the course of visits? Is it to *investigate* allegations of ill-treatment? Is it to *inspect* conditions in which people are detained? Is it to *seek* improvements in the legal protection of detainees? In the light of the CPT's work to date, the answer to all these questions and others beside must be yes. If that be the case, is it reasonable to expect all of these objectives to be met effectively and efficiently by the application of the same working methodology, and at the same time. Surely not.

Recent general reports provide evidence that the CPT is already adopting new working methods. The enormity of the tasks posed by the accession of the Ukraine and the imminent accession of the Russian Federation have made these questions unavoidable. The Sixth General Report remarked on the need to 'rationalise the CPT's working methods'[198] and this was fleshed out in the Seventh General Report, which reported the creation of working groups to deal with Russia and the Ukraine, medical confidentiality, solitary confinement, and the growing 'jurisprudence' of the Committee. The introduction of a 'streamlined' system for adopting reports and a reduction in the number of plenary sessions from four to three per year was also reported.[199] This complemented the Committee's principal response, which was to call for more visiting days per year— moving from the current 120 days per year towards 200 days per year by the millennium.[200] The aim, it appears, is to free up and acquire more resources for visits, albeit, if the trend in recent years continues, visits that are more often *ad hoc* or *follow-up* rather than *periodic* in nature.

We doubt whether these changes will prove sufficient to meet the challenges the Committee faces. We think that the problems that the Committee faces derive largely from 'the on-site nature of the Committee's activities'.[201] Rather than seek merely to extend the current concentration on delegation visits—and tinker at the edges—it is probably time for the CPT to reconceptualize itself, and alter its working practices in a far more fundamental fashion. There is need for more varied and flexible methods of data-collection so that member states can be more continuously engaged in critical dialogue. The visit mechanism is vital. It cannot and should not be abandoned: but it must also be remembered that it is a means to an end and not an end in itself.

These critical observations of what we regard as possibly ineffective methods are relatively minor, however, when weighed in the balance against the Committee's considerable achievements. Indeed we make our critical observations *because* the ECPT has, by any standard, been such a conspicuous success and because it is vital if that success is to continue for the Convention, and the Committee established under the Convention, to be a living body which adapts to the changing contours of Europe and the challenges resulting from those changes. In 1989 the coming into force of the ECPT represented a considerable innovation in international human rights protection. Now, eight years later, the Convention is not merely seen practically to work: no one in Europe rejects it. The Convention is

---

[198] Gen Rep 6, para 24.   [199] Gen Rep 7, paras 7 and 22.
[200] ibid, para 21.   [201] Gen Rep 6, para 24.

widely admired. Indeed the ECPT has become a model text, and the CPT a model mechanism, which many states and NGOs wish to see emulated both in regions other than Europe and within the United Nations. There can be no greater testimony to those who conceived and framed the Convention and whose vision we hope this text may help to perpetuate.

Appendix 1
Texts

A. EUROPEAN CONVENTION FOR THE PREVENTION OF TORTURE AND INHUMAN OR DEGRADING TREATMENT OR PUNISHMENT

The member States of the Council of Europe, signatory hereto,

Having regard to the provisions of the Convention for the Protection of Human Rights and Fundamental Freedoms,

Recalling that, under Article 3 of the same Convention, 'no one shall be subjected to torture or to inhuman or degrading treatment or punishment';

Noting that the machinery provided for in that Convention operates in relation to persons who allege that they are victims of violations of Article 3;

Convinced that the protection of persons deprived of their liberty against torture and inhuman or degrading treatment or punishment could be strengthened by non-judicial means of a preventive character based on visits,

Have agreed as follows:

Chapter I

Article 1

There shall be established a European Committee for the Prevention of Torture and Inhuman or Degrading Treatment or Punishment (hereinafter referred to as 'the Committee'). The Committee shall, by means of visits, examine the treatment of persons deprived of their liberty with a view to strengthening, if necessary, the protection of such persons from torture and from inhuman or degrading treatment or punishment.

Article 2

Each Party shall permit visits, in accordance with this Convention, to any place within its jurisdiction where persons are deprived of their liberty by a public authority.

Article 3

In the application of this Convention, the Committee and the competent national authorities of the Party concerned shall co-operate with each other.

Chapter II

Article 4

1. The Committee shall consist of a number of members equal to that of the Parties.
2. The members of the Committee shall be chosen from among persons of high moral character, known for their competence in the field of human rights or having professional experience in the areas covered by this Convention.
3. No two members of the Committee may be nationals of the same State.
4. The members shall serve in their individual capacity, shall be independent and impartial, and shall be available to serve the Committee effectively.

Article 5

1. The members of the Committee shall be elected by the Committee of Ministers of the Council of Europe by an absolute majority of votes, from a list of names drawn up by the Bureau of the Consultative Assembly of the Council of Europe; each national delegation of the Parties in the Consultative Assembly shall put forward three candidates, of whom two at least shall be its nationals.
2. The same procedure shall be followed in filling casual vacancies.
3. The members of the Committee shall be elected for a period of four years. They may only be re-elected once. However, among the members elected at the first election, the terms of three members shall expire at the end of two years. The members whose terms are to expire at the end of the initial period of two years shall be chosen by lot by the Secretary General of the Council of Europe immediately after the first election has been completed.

Article 6

1. The Committee shall meet in camera. A quorum shall be equal to the majority of its members. The decisions of the Committee shall be taken by a majority of the members present, subject to the provisions of Article 10, paragraph 2.
2. The Committee shall draw up its own rules of procedure.
3. The Secretariat of the Committee shall be provided by the Secretary General of the Council of Europe.

Chapter III

Article 7

1. The Committee shall organise visits to places referred to in Article 2. Apart from periodic visits, the Committee may organise such other visits as appear to it to be required in the circumstances.
2. As a general rule, the visits shall be carried out by at least two members of the Committee. The Committee may, if it considers it necessary, be assisted by experts and interpreters

Article 8

1. The Committee shall notify the Government of the Party concerned of its intention to carry out a visit. After such notification, it may at any time visit any place referred to in Article 2.
2. A Party shall provide the Committee with the following facilities to carry out its task:
    (a) access to its territory and the right to travel without restriction;
    (b) full information on the places where persons deprived of their liberty are being held;
    (c) unlimited access to any place where persons are deprived of their liberty, including the right to move inside such places without restriction;
    (d) other information available to the Party which is necessary for the Committee to carry out its task. In seeking such information, the Committee shall have regard to applicable rules of national law and professional ethics.
3. The Committee may interview in private persons deprived of their liberty.
4. The Committee may communicate freely with any person whom it believes can supply relevant information.
5. If necessary, the Committee may immediately communicate observations to the competent authorities of the Party concerned.

Article 9

1. In exceptional circumstances, the competent authorities of the Party concerned may make representations to the Committee against a visit at the time or to the particular place proposed by the Committee. Such representations may only be made on grounds of national defence, public safety, serious disorder in places where persons are deprived of their liberty, the medical condition of a person or that an urgent interrogation relating to a serious crime is in progress.
2. Following such representations, the Committee and the Party shall immediately enter into consultations in order to clarify the situation and seek agreement on arrangements to enable the Committee to exercise its functions expeditiously. Such arrangements may include the transfer to another place of any person whom the Committee proposed to visit. Until the visit takes place, the Party shall provide information to the Committee about any person concerned.

Article 10

1. After each visit, the Committee shall draw up a report on the facts found during the visit, taking account of any observations which may have been submitted by the Party concerned. It shall transmit to the latter its report containing any recommendations it considers necessary. The Committee may consult with the Party with a view to suggesting, if necessary, improvements in the protection of persons deprived of their liberty.
2. If the Party fails to co-operate or refuses to improve the situation in the light of the Committee's recommendations, the Committee may decide, after the Party

has had an opportunity to make known its views, by a majority of two-thirds of its members to make a public statement on the matter.

Article 11

1. The information gathered by the Committee in relation to a visit, its report and its consultations with the Party concerned shall be confidential.
2. The Committee shall publish its report, together with any comments of the Party concerned, whenever requested to do so by that Party.
3. However, no personal data shall be published without the express consent of the person concerned.

Article 12

Subject to the rules of confidentiality in Article 11, the Committee shall every year submit to the Committee of Ministers a general report on its activities which shall be transmitted to the Consultative Assembly and made public.

Article 13

The members of the Committee, experts and other persons assisting the Committee are required, during and after their terms of office, to maintain the confidentiality of the facts or information of which they have become aware during the discharge of their functions.

Article 14

1. The names of persons assisting the Committee shall be specified in the notification under Article 8, paragraph 1.
2. Experts shall act on the instructions and under the authority of the Committee. They shall have particular knowledge and experience in the areas covered by this Convention and shall be bound by the same duties of independence, impartiality and availability as the members of the Committee.
3. A Party may exceptionally declare that an expert or other person assisting the Committee may not be allowed to take part in a visit to a place within its jurisdiction.

Chapter IV

Article 15

Each Party shall inform the Committee of the name and address of the authority competent to receive notifications to its Government, and of any liaison officer it may appoint.

Article 16

The Committee, its members and experts referred to in Article 7, paragraph 2 shall enjoy the privileges and immunities set out in the Annex to this Convention.

Article 17

1. This Convention shall not prejudice the provisions of domestic law or any international agreement which provide greater protection for persons deprived of their liberty.

2. Nothing in this Convention shall be construed as limiting or derogating from the competence of the organs of the European Convention on Human Rights or from the obligations assumed by the Parties under that Convention.

3. The Committee shall not visit places which representatives or delegates of Protecting Powers or the International Committee of the Red Cross effectively visit on a regular basis by virtue of the Geneva Conventions of 12 August 1949 and the Additional Protocols of 8 June 1977 thereto.

Chapter V

Article 18

This Convention shall be open for signature by the member States of the Council of Europe. It is subject to ratification, acceptance or approval. Instruments of ratification, acceptance or approval shall be deposited with the Secretary General of the Council of Europe.

Article 19

1. This Convention shall enter into force on the first day of the month following the expiration of a period of three months after the date on which seven member States of the Council of Europe have expressed their consent to be bound by the Convention in accordance with the provisions of Article 18.

2. In respect of any member State which subsequently expresses its consent to be bound by it, the Convention shall enter into force on the first day of the month following the expiration of a period of three months after the date of the deposit of the instrument of ratification, acceptance or approval.

Article 20

1. Any State may at the time of signature or when depositing its instrument of ratification, acceptance or approval, specify the territory or territories to which this Convention shall apply.

2. Any State may at any later date, by a declaration addressed to the Secretary General of the Council of Europe, extend the application of this Convention to any other territory specified in the declaration. In respect of such territory the

Convention shall enter into force on the first day of the month following the expiration of a period of three months after the date of receipt of such declaration by the Secretary General.

3. Any declaration made under the two preceding paragraphs may, in respect of any territory specified in such declaration, be withdrawn by a notification addressed to the Secretary General. The withdrawal shall become effective on the first day of the month following the expiration of a period of three months after the date of receipt of such notification by the Secretary General.

Article 21

No reservation may be made in respect of the provisions of this Convention.

Article 22

1. Any Party may, at any time, denounce this Convention by means of a notification addressed to the Secretary General of the Council of Europe.

2. Such denunciation shall become effective on the first day of the month following the expiration of a period of twelve months after the date of receipt of the notification by the Secretary General.

Article 23

The Secretary General of the Council of Europe shall notify the member States of the Council of Europe of:
    (a) any signature;
    (b) the deposit of any instrument of ratification, acceptance or approval;
    (c) any date of entry into force of this Convention in accordance with Articles 19 and 20;
    (d) any other act, notification or communication relating to this Convention, except for action taken in pursuance of Articles 8 and 10.

In witness whereof, the undersigned, being duly authorised thereto, have signed this Convention.

Done at Strasbourg, the 26 November 1987, in English and French, both texts being equally authentic, in a single copy which shall be deposited in the archives of the Council of Europe. The Secretary General of the Council of Europe shall transmit certified copies to each member State of the Council of Europe.

ANNEX

Privileges and immunities

(Article 16)

1. For the purpose of this annex, references to members of the Committee shall be deemed to include references to experts mentioned in Article 7, paragraph 2.

2. The members of the Committee shall, while exercising their functions and during journeys made in the exercise of their functions, enjoy the following privileges and immunities:

(a) immunity from personal arrest or detention and from seizure of their personal baggage and, in respect of words spoken or written and all acts done by them in their official capacity, immunity from legal process of every kind;

(b) exemption from any restrictions on their freedom of movement on exit from and return to their country of residence, and entry into and exit from the country in which they exercise their functions, and from alien registration in the country which they are visiting or through which they are passing in the exercise of their functions.

3. In the course of journeys undertaken in the exercise of their functions, the members of the Committee shall, in the matter of customs and exchange control, be accorded:

(a) by their own Government, the same facilities as those accorded to senior officials travelling abroad on temporary official duty;

(b) by the Governments of other Parties, the same facilities as those accorded to representatives of foreign Governments on temporary official duty.

4. Documents and papers of the Committee, in so far as they relate to the business of the Committee, shall be inviolable. The official correspondence and other official communications of the Committee may not be held up or subjected to censorship.

5. In order to secure for the members of the Committee complete freedom of speech and complete independence in the discharge of their duties, the immunity from legal process in respect of words spoken or written and all acts done by them in discharging their duties shall continue to be accorded, notwithstanding that the persons concerned are no longer engaged in the discharge of such duties.

6. Privileges and immunities are accorded to the members of the Committee, not for the personal benefit of the individuals themselves but in order to safeguard the independent exercise of their functions. The Committee alone shall be competent to waive the immunity of its members; it has not only the right, but is under a duty, to waive the immunity of one of its members in any case where, in its opinion, the immunity would impede the course of justice, and where it can be waived without prejudice to the purpose for which the immunity is accorded.

B. PROTOCOL NO 1 TO THE EUROPEAN CONVENTION FOR THE PREVENTION OF TORTURE AND INHUMAN OR DEGRADING TREATMENT OR PUNISHMENT

The member States of the Council of Europe, signatories to this Protocol to the European Convention for the Prevention of Torture and Inhuman or Degrading Treatment or Punishment, signed at Strasbourg on 26 November 1987 (hereinafter referred to as 'the Convention'),

Considering that non-member States of the Council of Europe should be allowed to accede to the Convention at the invitation of the Committee of Ministers,

Have agreed as follows:

Article 1

A sub-paragraph shall be added to Article 5, paragraph 1, of the Convention as follows:

'Where a member is to be elected to the Committee in respect of a non-member State of the Council of Europe, the Bureau of the Consultative Assembly shall invite the Parliament of that State to put forward three candidates, of whom two at least shall be its nationals. The election by the Committee of Ministers shall take place after consultation with the Party concerned.'

Article 2

Article 12 of the Convention shall read as follows:

'Subject to the rules of confidentiality in Article 11, the Committee shall every year submit to the Committee of Ministers a general report on its activities which shall be transmitted to the Consultative Assembly and to any non-member State of the Council of Europe which is a party to the Convention, and made public.'

Article 3

The text of Article 18 of the Convention shall become paragraph 1 of that article and shall be supplemented by the following second paragraph:

'2. The Committee of Ministers of the Council of Europe may invite any non-member State of the Council of Europe to accede to the Convention.'

Article 4

In paragraph 2 of Article 19 of the Convention, the word 'member' shall be deleted and the words 'or approval,' shall be replaced by 'approval or accession.'.

Article 5

In paragraph 1 of Article 20 of the Convention, the words 'or approval' shall be replaced by 'approval or accession,'.

Article 6

The introductory sentence of Article 23 of the Convention shall read as follows:

'The Secretary General of the Council of Europe shall notify the member States and any non-member State of the Council of Europe party to the Convention of:'

In Article 23.b of the Convention, the words 'or approval;' shall be replaced by 'approval or accession;'.

Article 7

1. This Protocol shall be open for signature by member States of the Council of Europe signatories to the Convention, which may express their consent to be bound by:
> (a) signature without reservation as to ratification, acceptance or approval; or
> (b) signature subject to ratification, acceptance or approval, followed by ratification, acceptance or approval.

2. Instruments of ratification, acceptance or approval shall be deposited with the Secretary General of the Council of Europe.

Article 8

This Protocol shall enter into force on the first day of the month following the expiration of a period of three months after the date on which all Parties to the Convention have expressed their consent to be bound by the Protocol, in accordance with the provisions of Article 7.

Article 9

The Secretary General of the Council of Europe shall notify the member States of the Council of Europe of:
> (a) any signature;
> (b) the deposit of any instrument of ratification, acceptance or approval;
> (c) the date of entry into force of this Protocol, in accordance with Article 8;
> (d) any other act, notification or communication relating to this Protocol.

In witness whereof, the undersigned, being duly authorised thereto, have signed this Protocol.

Done at Strasbourg, this 4th day of November 1993, in English and French, both texts being equally authentic, in a single copy which shall be deposited in the archives of the Council of Europe. The Secretary General of the Council of Europe shall transmit certified copies to each member State of the Council of Europe.

C. PROTOCOL NO. 2 TO THE EUROPEAN CONVENTION FOR THE PREVENTION OF TORTURE AND INHUMAN OR DEGRADING TREATMENT OR PUNISHMENT

The States, signatories to this Protocol to the European Convention for the Prevention of Torture and Inhuman or Degrading Treatment or Punishment, signed at Strasbourg on 26 November 1987 (hereinafter referred to as 'the Convention'),

Convinced of the advisibility of enabling members of the European Committee for the Prevention of Torture and Inhuman and Degrading Treatment (hereinafter referred to as 'the Committee') to be re-elected twice;

Also considering the need to guarantee an orderly renewal of the membership of the Committee,

Have agreed as follows:

Article 1

1. In Article 5, paragraph 3, the second sentence shall read as follows:

'They may be re-elected twice.'

2. Article 5 of the Convention shall be supplemented by the following paragraphs 4 and 5:

4. In order to ensure that, as far as possible, one half of the membership of the Committee shall be renewed every two years, the Committee of Ministers may decide, before proceeding to any subsequent election, that the term or terms of office of one or more members to be elected shall be for a period other than four years but not more than six and not less than two years.
5. In cases where more than one term of office is involved and the Committee of Ministers applies the preceding paragraph, the allocation of the terms of office shall be effected by the drawing of lots by the Secretary General, immediately after the election.'

Article 2

1. This Protocol shall be open for signature by States signatories to the Convention or acceding thereto, which may express their consent to be bound by:
    (a) signature without reservation as to ratification, acceptance or approval; or
    (b) signature subject to ratification, acceptance or approval, followed by ratification, acceptance or approval.
2. Instruments of ratification, acceptance or approval shall be deposited with the Secretary General of the Council of Europe.

Article 3

This Protocol shall enter into force on the first day of the month following the expiration of a period of three months after the date on which all Parties to the Convention have expressed their consent to be bound by the Protocol, in accordance with the provisions of Article 2.

Article 4

The Secretary General of the Council of Europe shall notify the member States of the Council of Europe and non-member States Parties to the Convention of:
    (a) any signature;
    (b) the deposit of any instrument of ratification, acceptance or approval;
    (c) the date of any entry into force of this Protocol, in accordance with Article 3;
    (d) any other act, notification or communication relating to this Protocol.

In witness whereof, the undersigned, being duly authorised thereto, have signed this Protocol.

Done at Strasbourg, this 4th day of November 1993, in English and French, both texts being equally authentic, in a single copy which shall be deposited in the archives of the Council of Europe. The Secretary General of the Council of Europe shall transmit certified copies to each member State of the Council of Europe.

Appendix 2

Explanatory Report to the European Convention for the Prevention of Torture and Inhuman or Degrading Treatment or Punishment

I. Introduction

1. On 28 September 1983 the Consultative Assembly of the Council of Europe adopted Recommendation 971 (1983) on the protection of detainees from torture and from cruel, inhuman or degrading treatment or punishment. In this text, the Assembly in particular recommended that the Committee of Ministers adopt the draft European Convention on the Protection of Detainees from Torture and from Cruel, Inhman or Degrading Treatment or Punishment which was appended to the Recommendation.

The background to this initiative may be summarised as follows:

2. In January 1981, the Assembly adopted Recommendation 909 (1981) on the International Convention against Torture, in which it referred to the work undertaken in the framework of the United Nations and recommended that the Committee of Ministers invite Governments of member States to hasten the adoption and implementation of the draft Convention against Torture being prepared by the United Nations Commission on Human Rights. It also invited the Governments of member States represented on that Commission to do their utmost to ensure that it gave detailed consideration to the draft optional Protocol to the Convention (submitted by Costa Rica), as soon as the draft Convention itself had been submitted to the United Nations Economic and Social Council.

3. In March 1981 two motions for resolutions on torture in member States of the Council of Europe were tabled in the Assembly, one by Mr Lidbom (Doc 4718 rev) and the other by Mr Jõger (Doc 4730). These motions were transmitted to the Legal Affairs Commitee which decided to study them together.

4. Consideration by the Legal Affairs Committee resulted in a report (Doc 5099) drawn up on behalf of the Committee by Mr Berrier and adopted on 30 June 1983. This report contained the draft of a European Convention elaborated by the International Commission of Jurists and the Swiss Committee against Torture at the request of the Rapporteur.

In September 1983, the opinion of the Political Affairs Committee on the report was presented by Mr Dejardin (Doc 5123).

5. It is to be noted in this context that similar work was being conducted in the framework of the United Nations, and that the text of the Convention against Torture and other Cruel, Inhuman or Degrading Treatment or Punishment, referred to in Recommendation 909, was adopted by the General Assembly of the United Nations on 10 December 1984 and subsequently opened for signature. As to the

draft optional Protocol submitted by Costa Rica, it aims to establish a preventive mechanism of a similar nature to that foreseen in the draft Convention appended to the Assembly's Recommendation 971.

6. Subsequent to the adoption of Recommendation 971, the Committee of Ministers conferred the following terms of reference on the Steering Committee for Human Rights (CDDH) at the 366th meeting of the Ministers' Deputies, in January 1984:

'Consider Assembly Recommendation 971 with a view to submitting to the Committee of Ministers, after consultation of the European Committee on Crime Problems (CDPC), the text of a draft Convention or other legal instrument on the protection of detainees from torture and from cruel, inhuman or degrading treatment or punishment.'

7. The Committee of Experts for the extension of the rights embodied in the European Convention on Human Rights (DH-EX), a subordinate body of the CDDH, was instucted by the latter (15th meeting, March 1984) to implement this work under the authority of the CDDH.

8. The DH-EX considered the draft Convention appended to Recommendation 971 of its 19th to 25th meetings (May 1984 to June 1986). It took into account *inter alia* that:

—the Ministerial Conference on Human Rights (Vienna, 19–20 March 1985), in its Resolution No 2, 'urges the Committee of Ministers to have the work on a draft legal instrument on torture completed as rapidly as possible with a view to its adoption';

—the Final Communiqué of the 76th session of the Committee of Ministers (25 April 1985) said that the Ministers had 'supported the Conference's appeal';

—in the Assembly, three questions concerning the draft Convention were put to the Chairman of the Committee of Ministers, one by Mr Berrier in January 1985, the others by Mr Arbeloa in April and September 1985;

—in the Final Communiqué of its 77th session (20 November 1985) the Committee of Ministers reiterated its great interest in the early completion of the draft Convention.

9. During its work, the DH-EX had occasion to consult the European Commission and Court of Human Rights. It also organised a hearing with representatives of the International Commission of Jurists, the Swiss Committee against Torture and the International Committee of the Red Cross.

Other hearings took place with two experts in the psychiatric field. Before transmitting in June 1986 the preliminary draft Convention to the CDDH, the DH-EX took into account the opinions of the European Committee for Legal Co-operation (CDCJ) and the European Committee on Crime Problems (CDPC) which had been consulted by the CDDH.

10. In addition to the CDCJ and the CDCP, the CDDH also consulted the European Commission and Court of Human Rights. The text of the draft European Convention for the prevention of torture and inhuman or degrading treatment or punishment was finalised at the CDDH's 21st meeting in November 1986 and then transmitted to the Committee of Ministers.

11. After having consulted the Assembly (see Opinion No 133 of 27 March 1987), the Committee of Ministers adopted the text of the Convention on 26 June 1987. It was opened for signature by member States of the Council of Europe on 26 November 1987.

II. Reasons for the elaboration of a new Convention

12. Torture and inhuman or degrading treatment or punishment are prohibited in national law and by several international instruments. Experience shows, however, that there is a need for wider and more effective international measures, in particular to strengthen the protection of persons deprived of their liberty.
13. Within the Council of Europe, the supervisory system established by the Convention for the Protection of Human Rights and Fundamental Freedoms, of 4 November 1950, has achieved important results. It is considered that this system, which is based on complaints from individuals or from States claiming that human rights violations have taken place, could usefully be supplemented by non-judicial machinery of a preventive character, whose task would be to examine the treatment of persons deprived of their liberty with a view to strengthening, if necessary, the protection of such persons from torture and from inhuman or degrading treatment or punishment.
14. For these reasons the present Convention establishes a Committee which may visit any place within the jurisdiction of the Parties where persons are deprived of their liberty by a public authority.

III. Main features of the new system

15. As indicated in paragraphs 13 and 14 above, the Committee's function is to carry out visits and, where necessary, to suggest improvements as regards the protection of persons deprived of their liberty from torture and from inhuman or degrading treatment or punishment.
16. The members of the Committee will serve in their individual capacity and be chosen from among persons of high moral character, known for their competence in the field of human rights or having professional experience in the areas covered by the Convention. If the Committee considers it necessary, it may be assisted by suitably qualified experts.
17. It is not for the Committee to perform any judicial functions; it is not its task to adjudge that violations of the relevant international instruments have been committed. Accordingly, the Committee shall also refrain from expressing its views on the interpretation of those instruments either in abstracto or in relation to concrete facts.
18. When deciding whether there is a need for making recommendations, the Committee will, of course, have to assess the facts found during its visits. As the Committee is not competent to hear witnesses in conformity with general principles of judicial procedure, it will not have a sufficient basis for making recommendations if the facts are unclear and there is a need for further investigations. In such cases, the Committee may then inform the State concerned and suggest

that further investigations be conducted at the national level and request to be kept informed of the results of the enquiry.

19. As a follow-up, the Committee may arrange for fresh visits to the places already visited.

20. In the application of the Convention, the Committee and the State concerned are obliged to co-operate. The purpose of the Committee is not to condemn States, but, in a spirit of co-operation and through advice, to seek improvements, if necessary, in the protection of persons deprived of their liberty.

V. Observations on the provisions of the Convention

Preamble

21. The preamble sets out reasons which led member States of the Council of Europe to adopt this Convention and states its purpose (see Chapters I to III above).

22. The reference to Article 3 of the European Convention on Human Rights will provide the Committee with a point of reference for its consideration of situations liable to give rise to torture or inhuman or degrading treatment or punishment (see infra, paragraphs 26 and 27).

Article 1

23. This Article establishes the body which is to carry out the visits, and the purpose of the visits. In this way it describes the principal functions of the European Committee for the Prevention of Torture and Inhuman or Degrading Treatment or Punishment.

24. The notion of 'deprivation of liberty' for the purposes of the present convention is to be understood within the meaning of Article 5 of the European Convention on Human Rights as elucidated by the case law of the European Court and Commission of Human Rights. However, the distinction between 'lawful' and 'unlawful' deprivation of liberty arising in connection with Article 5 is immaterial in relation to the Committee's competence.

25. As already pointed out in paragraph 17, the Committee shall not perform any judicial functions: its members will not have to be lawyers, its recommendations will not bind the State concerned and the Committee shall not express any view on the interpretation of legal terms. Its task is a purely preventive one. It will carry out fact-finding visits, and, if necessary, on the basis of information obtained through them, make recommendations with a view to strengthening the protection of persons deprived of their liberty from torture and from inhuman or degrading treatment or punishment.

26. The prohibition of torture and inhuman or degrading treatment or punishment is a general international standard which, albeit differently formulated, is found in various international instruments, such as Article 3 of the European Convention on Human Rights.

27. The case-law of the Court and Commission of Human Rights on Article 3 provides a source of guidance for the Committee. However, the Committee's

activities are aimed at future prevention rather than the application of legal requirements to existing circumstances. The Committee should not seek to inter-
fere in the interpretation and application of Article 3.

Article 2

28. By this provision Parties to the Convention agree to permit visits to any place
within their jurisdiction where one or more persons are deprived of their liberty
by a public authority. It is immaterial whether the deprivation is based on a
formal decision or not.

29. Visits may take place in any circumstances. The Convention applies not
only in peace time, but also during war or any other public emergency. The Committee's competence is, however, limited as regards the places it may visit by the
provisions of Article 17, paragraph 3 (see infra, paragraph 93).

30. Visits may be organised in all kinds of places where persons are deprived of
their liberty, whatever the reasons may be. The Convention is therefore applicable, for example, to places where persons are held in custody, are imprisoned as
a result of conviction for an offence, are held in administrative detention, or are
interned for medical reasons or where minors are detained by a public authority. Detention by military authorities is also covered by the Convention.

31. Visits to places where persons are deprived of their liberty because of their
mental condition will require careful preparation and handling, for example as
regards the qualifications and experience of those chosen for the visit and the
manner in which the visit is conducted. In carrying out its visits, moreover, the
Committee will no doubt wish to have regard to any relevant Recommendation
adopted by the Committee of Ministers.

32. Visits may be carried out in private as well as public institutions. The
criterion is whether the deprivation of liberty is the result of action by a public
authority. Accordingly, the Committee may carry out visits only in relation to persons who are deprived of their liberty by a public authority, and not voluntary
patients. However, in the latter case, it should be possible for the Committee to
satisfy itself that this was indeed the wish of the patient concerned.

Article 3

33. As stated in the general considerations (see Chapters II and III above), the
present Convention institutes a non-judicial system of a preventive character.
It is not the task of the Committee to condemn States for violations, but to co-
operate with them in strengthening the protection of persons deprived of their
liberty. In order to indicate the spirit of the relationship between the Committee
and the Parties, Article 3 contains a general provision on co-operation.

34. The principle of co-operation applies to all stages of the Committee's activities. It is of direct relevance to several other provisions of the Convention, such
as Articles 2, 8, 9 and 10.

It is expected that the Committee will take advantage of national expertise made
available to it by the Parties to assist its task, particularly during visits (see also
infra, paragraphs 64 and 65).

Article 4

Paragraph 1

35. The Committee will be composed of a number of members amounting to the number of Parties to the Convention. This provision is inspired by the first part of Article 20 of the European Convention on Human Rights.

Paragraph 2

36. With regard to the qualifications of the members of the Committee it is stated in paragraph 2 that they shall be chosen from among persons of high moral character, known for their competence in the field of human rights or having professional experience in the areas covered by the Convention. It is not thought desirable to specify in detail the professional fields from which members of the Committee might be drawn. It is clear that they do not have to be lawyers. It would be desirable that the Committee should include members who have experience in matters such as prison administration and the various medical fields relevant to the treatment of persons deprived of their liberty. This will make the dialogue between the Committee and the States more effective and facilitate concrete suggestions from the Committee.

Paragraph 3

37. This provision corresponds to the last part of Article 20 of the European Convention on Human Rights.

Paragraph 4

38. This paragraph requires that members serve in their individual capacity and that they are independent and impartial, and are to be available to serve the Committee effectively. Accordingly it is expected that candidates who would have a conflict of interests or who otherwise might encounter difficulties in satisfying the requirements of independence, impartiality and availability will not be proposed or elected. It is also expected that a member of the Committee who might have such difficulties with regard to an individual situation would not participate in any activity of the Committee relating to that situation.

Article 5

Paragraph 1

39. The procedure for the election of members of the Committee is basically the same as that laid down in Article 21 of the European Convention on Human Rights for the election of members of the Commission.

Paragraph 2

40. It is considered appropriate that the same electoral procedure should be followed for filling casual vacancies (death or resignation).

Paragraph 3

41. The term of office has been fixed at four years, with the possibility of re-election only once.

42. Provision is made for the partial renewal of the Committee after an initial period of two years. The procedure laid down is inspired by the corresponding provisions of Articles 22 and 40 of the European Convention on Human Rights.

Article 6

Paragraph 1

43. Having regard to the specific characteristics of the Committee's functions as provided for in the present Convention, it is specified that the Committee shall meet in camera. This provision complements the principle contained in Article 11 that the information gathered by the Committee in relation to a visit, its report and consultations with the State concerned shall be confidential.

44. Subject to the requirements laid down by Article 10, paragraph 2, the decisions of the Committee shall be taken by a majority of the members present. The quorum has been fixed at a number equal to a majority of the members.

Paragraph 2

45. This paragraph provides, in accordance with international practice, that the Committee shall draw up its own Rules of Procedure. They will regulate organisational matters normally found in such rules, including the election of the Chairman.

Paragraph 3

46. This provision, specifying that the Secretariat of the Committee shall be provided by the Secretary General of the Council of Europe, is inspired by the usual practice of this Organisation.

Article 7

Paragraph 1

47. This paragraph provides that it is the responsibility of the Committee to organise the visits to places referred to in Article 2 of the Convention. It also indicates that the Committee may organise periodic visits as well as ad hoc visits.

48. With regard to periodic visits, if it is to be effective the Committee will inevitably have to take into account the number of places to be visited in the States concerned. The Committee should also ensure, as far as possible, that the different States are visited on an equitable basis. Furthermore, its programme of periodic visits should not imply, for practical reasons, systematic visits in all places where persons are deprived of their liberty. The Committee should even accord a certain priority to ad hoc visits which appear to it to be required in the circumstances.

49. With regard to such ad hoc visits the Committee enjoys discretion as to when it deems a visit necessary and as to elements on which its decision is based. Thus,

whilst the Committee should not be concerned with the investigation of individual complaints (for which provision is already made, eg under the European Convention on Human Rights), it should be free to assess communications from individuals or groups of individuals and to decide whether to exercise its functions upon such communications. It should enjoy similar discretion in the event of a Party expressing the desire that the Committee should conduct a visit to places within its jurisdiction in order to investigate certain allegations and to clarify the situation.

Paragraph 2

50. The visits themselves need not necessarily be carried out by the full Committee; it is indeed probable that a visit by the full Committee would arise only in exceptional situations. Provision is therefore made in paragraph 2 for the visits to be carried out, as a general rule, by at least two members of the Committee, acting in the name of the latter. Exceptionally, however, the Committee may be represented by only one member, eg in ad hoc visits of an urgent nature when only one member is available.

51. If the Committee considers it necessary, it may be assisted by experts and interpreters. The underlying idea is to supplement the experience of the Committee by the assistance, for example, of persons who have special training or experience of humanitarian missions, who have a medical background or possess a special competence in the treatment of detainees or in prison regimes and, when appropriate, as regards young persons.

52. When organising a visit, the Committee will take into account the need to have at its disposal sufficient knowledge of the State concerned and its language.

53. The member or members of the Committee chosen to carry out a visit will enjoy the necessary authority for the contacts with the national authorities. They will have responsibility for the general conduct of the visit and for the findings submitted to the Committee after the visit.

Article 8

54. With the exception of paragraph 1, in which the reference to 'Committee' means the plenary Committee, references to 'Committee' in this Article (as in Articles 3, 9, 14, paragraph 3 and 17, paragraph 3) include the delegation carrying out the visit on behalf of the Committee.

Paragraph 1

55. By ratifying the Convention, the States are under an obligation to permit visits to any place within their jurisdiction. The purpose of the present provision is to specify the modalities by which a visit is initiated. Before a visit can take place the Committee shall notify the Government of the Party concerned of its intention to carry out a visit (cf Article 15). After such notification it may at any time visit any place referred to in Article 2 of the Convention.

It will be essential for the Committee and each Party to arrive at satisfactory arrangements as respects the credentials and means of identification of each person belonging to a visiting team.

56. This provision does not specify the period of time which should elapse (for example twenty-four or forty-eight hours) between the notification and the moment the visit becomes effective. Indeed, exceptional situations could arise in which the visit takes place immediately after the notification has been given. However, as a general rule and taking into consideration the principle of co-operation set out in Article 3, the Committee should give the State concerned reasonable time to take the necessary measures to make the visit as effective as possible. On the other hand, the Committee should carry out the visit within a reasonable time after the notification.

57. In the same spirit of co-operation, in cases where the notification announces the intention of the Committee to visit a State, without specifying the date and place of arrival, it is expected that the Committee will provide such details subsequently, before the visit takes place.

58. The notification should, in addition to announcing the visit, contain the names of members of the Committee and identify the experts taking part in the visit, the interpreters and other accompanying staff, as well as the places which the Committee intends visiting. However, the fact that specific establishments are mentioned in the notification should not preclude the Committee from announcing that it also wishes to visit other establishments in the course of the visit.

59. Finally, it is expected that the Committee will bear in mind that visits to high security prison establishments may require careful preparation.

Paragraph 2

60. It is understood, in view of the particular nature of the visits which the Committee is required to make, that this paragraph applies equally before, during and after visits. The paragraph contains an exhaustive list of the facilities with which the Committee is entitled to be provided by the Party. It is, however, understood that the Party should render the Committee other necessary assistance to facilitate its work.

61. Under sub-paragraph (a), which must be read in conjunction with Articles 2 and 16, conditions prescribed by Parties with respect to immigration (eg visas) may not be invoked against members of the visiting team (subject to Article 14, paragraph 3 in respect of experts and other persons assisting the Committee). It is understood that the right to travel without restrictions does not give the Committee or its experts the general freedom to move within areas which are restricted for reasons of national defence (cf Article 9).

62. Under sub-paragraph (b), each Party must supply the Committee on request with a list of the places under its jurisdiction where persons deprived of their liberty are being held, stating the nature of the establishment (prison, police station, hospital, etc). It is understood that, in supplying a list, the State concerned may provide a general description of places where persons are capable of being held from time to time, for example, all police stations or all military barracks, in addition to a specific list or permanent places where persons are deprived of their liberty, such as prisons and mental health institutions. It is envisaged that the Committee will eventually request a comprehensive list of places within a particular area which it intends to visit within the jurisdiction of the State. On

the other hand, it is not necessary for the State to make a list of all detainees. If, for particular reasons, the Committee wishes to obtain information about a specific person (including his or her place of detention), it may ask for it under sub-paragraph (d) of this paragraph 2.

63. Sub-paragraph (c) emphasises the freedom of movement of the members of the Committee, particularly inside places referred to in Article 2. But this provision does not prevent the Committee from being accompanied by an official from the visited State, in order to assist with the visit (cf Article 15). The State may in particular require the Committee to be accompanied by a senior officer in places which are secret for reasons of national defence or which enjoy special protection for reasons of national security (cf Article 9). However, an accompanying person must not be present at the interviews in private mentioned in paragraph 3 of this Article.

64. Sub-paragraph (d) obliges Parties to provide the Committee with information available to them which is necessary for the Committee to carry out its task. Access to information will clearly be of great importance to the Committee. At the same time, it is acknowledged that particular rules concerning disclosure of information may be applicable in member States. Accordingly, the Committee is for its part obliged, when seeking information from a Party, to have regard to applicable rules of national law and professional ethics (in particular rules regarding data protection and rules of medical secrecy). It is envisaged that possible difficulties in this field will be resolved in the spirit of mutual understanding and co-operation upon which the Convention is founded.

65. It is understood that it is for Parties to decide the form (eg originals or copies of documents) in which the information requested by the Committee shall be communicated.

Paragraph 3

66. Under this paragraph the Committee may conduct interviews in private. For the purpose of such interviews it can choose its own interpreters and must not be subjected to any time-limits.

The Committee should take special care in connection with mentally disturbed patients over the number, qualifications and linguistic ability of the person or persons conducting the interview (cf paragraph 31 supra).

67. It is understood that a person deprived of liberty is not obliged to agree to enter into contact with the Committee. But the latter must be given the opportunity to satisfy itself that this is in fact the free decision of the person concerned.

Paragraph 4

68. When referring to persons with whom the Committee may communicate, those drafting the Convention had in mind in particular the families, lawyers, doctors and nursing staff of the persons deprived of their liberty. But no private individuals can be obliged to communicate with the Committee.

69. However, this right conferred on the Committee does not authorise it to organise formal hearings in the legal sense with all the procedural conditions that this would imply. For instance, no one would be obliged to give evidence on oath.

Paragraph 5

70. This paragraph enables the Committee to make certain observations during the visit itself. This possibility should only be made use of in exceptional cases (eg when there is an urgent need to improve the treatment of persons deprived of liberty). It will not absolve the Committee from making a subsequent report as provided for in Article 10.

Article 9

71. This Article recognises that, notwithstanding the obligations of a Party to permit visits by the Committee, certain exceptional circumstances may justify a postponement of a visit or some limitation of the right of access of the Committee as regards a particular place. Paragraph 1 specifies these exceptional circumstances, restricting the grounds on which the Article may be invoked on any particular occasion to:
　　—safeguarding national defence;
　　—safeguarding public safety which, it is envisaged, would include an urgent and compelling need to prevent serious crime;
　　—serious disorder in prisons and other places where persons are deprived of their liberty;
　　—cases where, having regard to the medical (including mental) condition of a person proposed to be visited, a visit at a particular time could prove detrimental to health;
　　—avoiding prejudicing an urgent interrogation, and consequential investigation, relating to a serious crime.
72. A Party which wishes to invoke the provisions of Article 9 is required to make representations as to the relevant circumstances to the Committee. The Committee and the Party would then be required by paragraph 2 to enter into consultations to elucidate the circumstances cited by the Party and their bearing on the proposals notified by the Committee pursuant to Article 8. The Committee and the Party are also required (and this is a particular example of the co-operation enjoined by Article 3) to seek agreement on ways in which the Committee will be able to perform its functions speedily and effectively. One possibility which is specified in the Article is that if, for example, representations are made on national security grounds against a visit to a particular place, any person who is deprived of his liberty in that place shall be transferred to another place where he may be visited by the Committee. This paragraph also provides that when a visit to any place is postponed, the Party shall ensure that the Committee is fully informed about the persons who are deprived of their liberty at that place.

Article 10

Paragraph 1

73. This paragraph deals with the report which the Committee has to draw up following each visit. This will be based on the facts found during the visit and will take account of any observations which the State concerned might wish to

make. The report will also contain the recommendations the Committee considers necessary, the object being in every case to strengthen the protection of persons deprived of their liberty. It is understood that the report transmitted to the State concerned will not necessarily contain all the information obtained by the Committee on the occasion of its visits (eg records of certain interviews).

Paragraph 2

74. In certain eventualities referred to in this paragraph the Committee may, after the State concerned has had an opportunity to make known its views, decide to make a public statement. The exceptional competence of the Committee to make a public statement can be used if the State fails to co-operate or refuses to improve the situation in the light of the Committee's recommendations. Given the importance of such a decision, it may only be taken by a qualified majority. Before using this remedy in the case of a State's refusal to improve the situation, the Committee should pay full regard to any difficulties in the way of doing so. 75. The Committee will have a wide discretion in deciding what information to make public, but will have to take due account of the need to secure that information passed over in confidence is not revealed. It should also take into consideration the desirability of not revealing information in connection with pending investigations.

Article 11

Paragraph 1

76. This provision establishes the principle of the confidential nature of the Committee's activities. The 'information gathered by the Committee' may consist of facts it has itself observed, information which it has obtained from external sources and information which it has itself collected.

Paragraph 2

77. This provision specifies that, whenever requested to do so by the State concerned, the Committee is required to publish the report and any comments the State wishes to make. If the State concerned itself makes the report public, it should do so in its entirety.

Paragraph 3

78. This paragraph provides that no personal data may be published without the express consent of the person concerned. But this might not exclude the publication of such data if the identity of the person concerned is not revealed or could not be discovered from the context.

Article 12

79. Every year the Committee shall submit a general report on its activities to the Committee of Ministers. The report, which will be transmitted to the Assembly

and made public, should contain information on the organisation and internal workings of the Committee and on its activities proper, with particular mention of the States visited. When preparing its report, the Committee must naturally comply with the provisions of Article 11 concerning the confidential character of certain types of information and data.

Article 13

80. In accordance with this provision, members of the Committee, experts and other persons assisting the Committee are required to observe confidentiality, even after their term of office has come to an end. It relates to all facts or information which may have come to the notice of the Committee members or such other persons during the discharge of their functions when visits are being effected, or at any other moment.

Article 14

Paragraph 1

81. This provision lays down the principle that the names of persons assisting the Committee shall be specified in the notification of a visit under Article 8, paragraph 1.

Paragraph 2

82. The experts shall be bound by the same duties of independence, impartiality and availability as the members of the Committee (cf Article 4, paragraph 4). They are subject to the instructions of the Committee and shall act under its authority.

Paragraph 3

83. This paragraph sets forth the conditions in which a State may refuse to a person assisting the Committee the possibility of participating in visits, or in a particular visit, to a place within its jurisdiction.

84. This right may be exercised only exceptionally and at the earliest opportunity. Thus a State, upon being given the relevant information, should only refuse such a person if, in its opinion, he fails to fulfil the requirements set forth in paragraph 2 of this Article or in Article 13. This might be the case if the person concerned has manifested a biased attitude towards that State or if, on other occasions, he has broken the rule of confidentiality.

85. When a State declares that a person may not take part in a visit, the Committee may wish to ask for the reasons, on the understanding that the enquiry and any response shall be confidential. Such an arrangement may be of assistance to the Committee in appointing other persons to assist it.

86. If, in the course of the visit, a person assisting the Committee behaves in a manner that the State concerned considers improper (for instance, if he makes political or similar public statements), it may request the Committee to take all the measures the latter deems appropriate.

Article 15

87. In order to facilitate the notifications under Article 8, paragraph 1 of the Convention, the present provision obliges Parties to inform the Committee of the authority to which such notifications should be sent. A Party must also inform the Committee of the name of any liaison officer it may appoint to facilitate the task of the Committee when making a visit.

Article 16

88. This Article deals with the privileges and immunities of the Committee, its members and experts. It is inspired by Article 59 of the European Convention on Human Rights and by the Second and Fourth Protocols to the General Agreement on Privileges and Immunities of the Council of Europe.

Article 17

Paragraph 1

89. This paragraph provides that the present Convention cannot be invoked as a justification for restricting the protection granted under other international instruments or at the domestic level. Indeed, the Convention is only one of several measures aimed at preventing torture and strengthening the protection afforded to persons deprived of their liberty.

90. The fact that national authorities may be empowered to conduct certain investigations in the places covered by the Convention is not sufficient to prevent the Committee from deciding to conduct a visit. But in the spirit of co-operation which is to govern the application of the Convention, the Committee may wish to enter into contact with such national authorities before making a decision (cf paragraphs 33 and 34 above).

Paragraph 2

91. This paragraph addresses the particular relationship between the new Convention and the European Convention on Human Rights, to which all member States of the Council of Europe are party and a connection with which is acknowledged in the preamble. The obligations of the Parties under the European Convention on Human Rights are not affected. Nor is the competence entrusted by that Convention to the Court and Commission of Human Rights and the Committee of Ministers. Accordingly, in respecting the established competence of these organs, the Committee set up by the present Convention will not concern itself with matters raised in proceedings pending before them, and will not itself formulate interpretations of the provisions of the European Convention on Human Rights.

92. In particular, the cardinal importance of the right of individual petition under Article 25 of the European Convention on Human Rights remains undiminished. Accordingly, it is not envisaged that a person whose case has been examined by the Committee would be met with a plea based on Article 27, paragraph 1 (b) of

the European Convention on Human Rights if he subsequently lodges a petition with the Commission of Human Rights alleging that he has been the victim of a violation of that Convention.

Paragraph 3

93. It follows from Article 2 that the Convention applies both in time of peace and in time of war. However, it appeared necessary to take account of the existence of other international instruments, in particular the Geneva Conventions of 12 August 1949 and the 8 June 1977 Protocols. In the case of armed conflict (international or non-international) the Geneva Conventions must have priority of application; that is to say that the visits will be carried out by the delegates or representatives of the International Committee of the Red Cross (ICRC).[1] However, the new Committee could proceed to visit certain places where (particularly in the event of non-international armed conflict) the ICRC does not visit them 'effectively' or 'on a regular basis'. On the other hand, visits to detainees made by the ICRC in time of peace in a specific country by virtue of bilateral agreements (outside the framework of the Geneva Convention) are not covered by this provision. In such cases the Committee must decide what attitude to adopt taking account of the situation and status of persons who might be the subject of a visit.

94. The drafters of the Convention decided to make a distinction with regard to the Geneva Conventions, not only because of the specific competence and experience acquired by the ICRC but also because the latter carries out functions and uses methods very similar to those of the new Committee. Thus it seemed particularly necessary to specify the respective competence of the two organs.

Articles 18 to 23

95. These Articles, which contain the final clauses of the Convention, correspond to the model adopted by the Committee of Ministers of the Council of Europe.

As for Article 21, it should be noted that the option excluding the possibility of making reservations has been chosen.

---

[1] See in particular Article 126 of the 3rd Geneva Convention and Article 143 of the 4th Convention.

Appendix 3
Rules of Procedure

(Adopted on 16 November 1989 and amended on 8 March 1990, 11 May 1990, 9 November 1990, 31 January 1991, 20 September 1991, and 12 March 1997)

The Committee,

Having regard to the European Convention for the Prevention of Torture and Inhuman or Degrading Treatment or Punishment (hereinafter referred to as 'the Convention');

Pursuant to Article 6, paragraph 2, of the Convention,

Adopts the present Rules:

TITLE I

ORGANISATION OF THE COMMITTEE

Chapter I

Members of the Committee

Rule 1 (Calculation of term of office)

1. The duration of the term of office of a member of the Committee shall be calculated as from his election, unless the Committee of Ministers stipulates otherwise when proceeding to the election (*).

2. A member elected to replace a member whose term of office has not expired shall be elected for a four year term of office.

(*) Paragraph amended by the Committee on 12 March 1997.

Rule 2 (Solemn declaration)

Before taking up his duties, each member of the Committee shall, at the first meeting of the Committee at which he is present after his election, make the following solemn declaration:

'I solemnly declare that I will exercise my functions as a member of this Committee honourably, independently, impartially and conscientiously and that I will keep secret all Committee proceedings'.

Rule 3 (Precedence)

1. Members of the Committee shall take precedence after the President and Vice-Presidents according to the length of time they have been in office.

2. Members having the same length of time in office shall take precedence according to age.

3. Re-elected members shall take precedence having regard to the duration of their previous term of office.

Rule 4 *(Resignation)*

Resignation of a member of the Committee shall be notified to the President, who shall transmit it to the Secretary General of the Council of Europe.

Chapter II

Presidency of the Committee

Rule 5 *(Election of the President and Vice-Presidents)*

1. The Committee shall elect from among its members a President and a first and second Vice-President.

2. The President and Vice-Presidents shall be elected for a term of two years. They may be re-elected. However, the term of office of the President or of a Vice-President shall end if he ceases to be a member of the Committee.

3. If the President or a Vice-President ceases to be a member of the Committee or resigns his office of President or Vice-President before its normal expiry, the Committee may elect a successor for the remainder of the term of that office.

4. The elections referred to in this Rule shall be held by secret ballot. Election shall be by a majority of the members present.

5. If no candidate is elected after the first ballot, a second ballot shall take place between the two candidates who have received most votes; in the case of equal voting, the candidate having precedence under Rule 3 shall take part in the second ballot. If necessary, a third ballot shall take place between the two candidates concerned. The candidate who receives the most votes in such a third ballot or, in the case of equal voting, who has precedence under Rule 3, shall be declared elected.

6. If there are only two candidates for a vacant office and neither of the candidates is elected after the first ballot, a second ballot shall take place. The candidate who receives the most votes in such a second ballot or, in the case of equal voting, who has precedence under Rule 3, shall be declared elected.

Rule 6 *(Functions of the President)*

1. The President shall chair the meetings of the Committee and shall perform all other functions conferred upon him by these Rules of Procedure and by the Committee.

2. In exercising his functions, the President shall remain under the authority of the Committee.

3. The President may delegate certain of his functions to either Vice-President.

Rule 7 *(Functions of the Vice-Presidents)*

The first Vice-President shall take the place of the President if the latter is unable to carry out his duties or if the office of President is vacant. The second Vice-President shall replace the first Vice-President if the latter is unable to carry out his duties or if the office of first Vice-President is vacant.

Rule 8 *(Replacement of the President and Vice-Presidents)*

If the President and Vice-Presidents are at the same time unable to carry out their duties or if their offices are at the same time vacant, the duties of President shall be carried out by another member of the Committee according to the order of precedence laid down in Rule 3.

Rule 9 *(Obstacle to the exercise of the functions of President)*

No member of the Committee shall preside when the report on a visit to the State Party in respect of which he was elected is being considered.

Chapter III

Bureau of the Committee

Rule 10

1. The Bureau of the Committee shall consist of the President and Vice-Presidents. If one or more members of the Bureau are unable to carry out their duties, they shall be replaced by other members of the Committee in accordance with the rules of precedence laid down in Rule 3.

2. The Bureau shall direct the work of the Committee and shall perform all other functions conferred upon it by these Rules of Procedure and by the Committee.

Chapter IV

Secretariat of the Committee

Rule 11

The Secretariat of the Committee shall consist of a Secretary and other staff members appointed by the Secretary General of the Council of Europe.

TITLE II

WORKING OF THE COMMITTEE: GENERAL RULES

Chapter I

Seat of the Committee and languages

Rule 12 (Seat of the Committee)

The seat of the Committee shall be in Strasbourg.

Rule 13 (Languages)

The official and working languages of the Committee shall be English and French.

Chapter II

Meetings of the Committee

Rule 14 (Holding of meetings)

1. The Committee and its Bureau shall hold such meetings as are required for the exercise of their functions.
2. Committee meetings shall be convened at dates decided by the Committee. The Committee shall meet at other times by decision of the Bureau, as circumstances may require. It shall also meet if at least one third of the members so request.
3. The Secretary shall notify the members of the Committee of the date, time and place of each Committee meeting. Whenever possible, such notification shall be given at least six weeks in advance.

Rule 15 (Agenda)

1. Following consultation with the Bureau, the Secretary shall transmit to the members a draft agenda simultaneously with the notification of the meeting.
2. The agenda shall be adopted by the Committee at the beginning of the meeting.

Rule 16 (Meeting documentation)

The Secretary shall transmit to the members of the Committee the working documents relating to the different agenda items, whenever possible at least four weeks in advance.

Rule 17 (Quorum)

The quorum of the Committee shall be the majority of its members.

Rule 18 (Privacy of meetings)

1. The Committee shall meet in camera. Its deliberations shall remain confidential.
2. Apart from members of the Committee, only members of the Committee's Secretariat, interpreters and persons providing technical assistance to the Committee may be present at its meetings, unless the Committee decides otherwise.

Rule 19 (Hearings)

The Committee may hear any person whom it considers to be in a position to assist it in the performance of its functions under the Convention.

Chapter III

Conduct of business

Rule 20 (Proposals)

A proposal must be submitted in writing if a member of the Committee so requests. In that case it shall not be discussed until it has been circulated.

Rule 21 (Order of voting on proposals and amendments)

1. Where a number of proposals relate to the same subject, they shall be put to the vote in the order in which they were submitted. In case of doubt, the President shall decide.
2. Where a proposal is the subject of an amendment, the amendment shall be put to the vote first. Where two or more amendments to the same proposal are presented, the Committee shall vote first on whichever departs furthest in substance from the original proposal, and so on until all the amendments have been put to the vote. However, where the acceptance of one amendment necessarily entails rejection of another, the latter shall not be put to the vote. The final vote shall then be taken on the proposal as amended or not amended. In case of doubt as to the order of priority, the President shall decide.
3. Parts of a proposal or amendment may be put to the vote separately.
4. In the case of proposals with financial implications, the most costly shall be put to the vote first.

Rule 22 (Order of procedural motions)

Procedural motions shall take precedence over all other proposals or motions except points of order. They shall be put to the vote in the following order:

(a) suspension of the meeting;
(b) adjournment of the meeting;
(c) adjournment of discussion on the item in hand;
(d) closure of discussion on the item in hand.

Rule 23 (Reconsideration of a question)

When a decision has been taken it is only re-examined if a member of the Committee so requests and the Committee accedes to this request.

Rule 24 (Voting)

1. Subject to the provisions of Rules 44 (paragraph 1), 47, 48, 50 and 51, the decisions of the Committee shall be taken by a majority of the members present.
2. In matters other than elections, a proposal shall be regarded as rejected if the majority referred to in paragraph 1 is not obtained.
3. Subject to Rule 5, paragraph 4, the Committee shall normally vote by show of hands. However, any member may request that a vote be taken by roll-call; in this event, the roll shall be called in the alphabetical order of the names of the Committee's members, beginning with the letter 'A'.
4. After a vote has commenced, there shall be no interruption of the voting except on a point of order by a member in connection with the actual conduct of the voting. Brief statements by members consisting solely of explanations of their votes may be permitted by the President before the voting has commenced or after the voting has been completed.

Chapter IV

Decisions and meeting reports

Rule 25 (Decisions)

At the end of each meeting the Secretary shall submit to the Committee for its approval a list of the decisions adopted during the meeting.

Rule 26 (Meeting reports)

1. A draft report of the Committee's deliberations at each meeting shall be prepared by the Secretary. The draft report shall be circulated as soon as possible to members of the Committee, who will be given the opportunity to submit corrections within a prescribed time-limit.
2. If no corrections are submitted, the meeting report shall be deemed to be adopted. If corrections are submitted, they shall be consolidated in a single document and circulated to all members. In this latter case, the adoption of the meeting report shall be taken up at the next meeting of the Committee.

Chapter V

Working parties

Rule 27

The Committee may set-up ad hoc working parties comprising a limited number of its members. The terms of reference of such working parties shall be defined by the Committee.

Chapter VI

Communications containing information submitted for the Committee's consideration

Rule 28

1. The Secretary shall bring to the Committee's attention communications received containing information submitted for the Committee's consideration, unless the information in question relates to matters which manifestly fall outside its field of competence.
2. Such communications received by individual members of the Committee shall be forwarded to the Secretariat.
3. The Secretary shall keep a register of all communications received.
4. The Secretary shall send an acknowledgement of receipt to the authors of such communications.

TITLE III

PROCEDURE CONCERNING VISITS

Chapter I

Basic rules

Rule 29 (The principle of visits)

Pursuant to Article 1 and 7 of the Convention, the Committee shall organise visits to places referred to in Article 2 of the Convention to examine the treatment of persons deprived of their liberty, with a view to strengthening, if necessary, the protection of such persons from torture and from inhuman or degrading treatment or punishment.

Rule 30(*) (Requests for information or explanations)

1. Before deciding on a particular visit, the Committee or, if appropriate, the Bureau may request information or explanations as regards the general situation in the

State concerned, as regards a given place, or as regards an isolated case concerning which it has received reports.

2. Following receipt of such information or explanations, details of remedial action taken by the national authorities may be requested.

(*) Rule inserted by the Committee on 8 March 1990.

Rule 31 (Periodic visits)

1. The Committee shall carry out visits of a periodic nature.

2. Before the end of each calendar year, the Committee shall establish a provisional programme of periodic visits for the following calendar year. In drawing up this programme the Committee shall ensure, as far as possible, that the different States Parties to the Convention are visited on an equitable basis, regard being had to the number of relevant places in each State Party (*).

3. The Committee may subsequently decide to modify the above-mentioned programme in the light of circumstances.

4. The Committee shall make public the names of the countries in which periodic visits are envisaged in a given year, after having informed the authorities of each of the States concerned of the likelihood of a visit (**).

(*) Paragraph amended by the Committee on 31 January 1991.

(**) Paragraph inserted by the Committee on 11 May 1990 and amended on 31 January 1991.

Rule 32 (Ad hoc visits)

1. In addition to periodic visits, the Committee may carry out such ad hoc visits as appear to it to be required in the circumstances.

2. When the Committee is not in session, the Bureau may, in case of urgency, decide on the Committee's behalf on the carrying out of an ad hoc visit. The President shall report to the Committee at its next meeting on any action which has been taken under this paragraph.

Rule 33 (Follow-up visits)

The Committee may carry out one or more follow-up visits to any place already visited in the context of a periodic or ad hoc visit.

Rule 34 (Responsibility for carrying out visits)

1. As a general rule, visits shall be carried out by a delegation of the Committee consisting of at least two of its members. Exceptionally, visits may be carried out by the full Committee or by a single member thereof.

2. The members of the Committee with responsibility for carrying out a visit shall act in the name of the Committee.

Rule 35 (Notification of visits)

1. The Committee or, if the Committee is not in session at the relevant time, its President shall notify the Government of the Party concerned of the intention to carry out a visit. The notification shall be sent to the authority referred to in Article 15 of the Convention.
2. The notification shall contain the names of the Committee members responsible for carrying out the visit and of all persons assisting the visiting delegation.
3. The notification shall indicate the places which the delegation intends to visit. However, this shall not prevent the visiting delegation from deciding to visit also places not indicated in the notification.
4. The notification of a visit in pursuance of paragraphs 1 to 3 may be given in stages. (*)

(*) Paragraph inserted by the Committee on 8 March 1990.

Rule 36 (Register of visits)

The Secretary shall maintain a register of all visits carried out by the Committee.

Chapter II

Visiting delegations

Rule 37 (Choice of members)

1. The members of the Committee to carry out a visit shall be chosen by the Committee or, in case of urgency when the Committee is not in session, by the Bureau. Due regard shall be had to the nature of the visit in question, and in particular to the type of place or places to be visited, when the composition of the delegation is determined.
2. The member of the Committee elected in respect of the State to be visited shall not be chosen as a member of the visiting delegation (*).
3. In consultation with the Bureau, the members of the delegation shall appoint one of their number as Head of the delegation (**).

(*) Paragraph inserted by the Committee on 9 November 1990.
(**) Paragraph amended by the Committee on 31 January 1991.

Rule 38 (Assistants)

1. The Committee or, in the case of an ad hoc visit under Rule 32, paragraph 2, the Bureau may decide that a visiting delegation shall be assisted by one or more experts or interpreters.
2. As a rule, a visiting delegation shall not be assisted by an expert who is a national of the State to be visited (*).

3. At least one member of the Secretariat of the Committee shall accompany each visiting delegation.

4. All persons assisting a visiting delegation shall act on the instructions and under the authoritiy of the Head of the delegation.

(*) Paragraph inserted by the Committee on 9 November 1990.

Rule 39 (Procedure for visits)

1. Visiting delegations shall carry out visits in accordance with any general or specific instructions or guidelines issued by the Committee or, as the case may be, the Bureau.

2. A visiting delegation may immediately communicate observations to the authorities of the Party concerned.

Rule 40 (Visiting delegation reports)

On the completion of its visit, a visiting delegation shall as soon as possible submit a report to the Committee. This report shall contain in particular:
   —a description of the different stages of the visit;
   —an account of the facts found during the visit and of consultations with the authorities of the Party concerned, that are of relevance for the Committee's report; (*)
   —proposals for any recommendations which the visiting delegation considers should be addressed to the Party.

(*) Indent amended by the Committee on 31 January 1991.

TITLE IV

POST-VISIT PROCEDURE

Chapter I

Reports and recommendations

Rule 41 (Preparation of the Committee's report)

1. After each visit the Committee shall draw up, in the light of the visiting delegation's report, a report for transmission to the Party concerned. This report shall set out the facts found during the visit and contain any recommendations which the Committee considers necessary with a view to strengthening the protection of persons deprived of their liberty.

2. When drawing up its report, the Committee shall take account of any observations which the Party concerned might submit to it following a visit. Further, the Committee may on its own initiative seek observations or additional information from the Party.

3. After its adoption, the report shall be transmitted to the Party concerned by the President.

Rule 42 (Confidential nature of the report)

1. The report transmitted to a Party following a visit is and, as a rule, shall remain confidential. However, the Committee shall publish its report, together with any comments of the Party concerned, whenever requested to do so by that Party.
2. If the Party itself makes the report public, but does not do so in its entirety, the Committee may decide to publish the whole report.
3. Similarly, the Committee may decide to publish the whole report if the Party concerned makes a public statement summarising the report or commenting upon its contents. (*)
4. Publication of the report by the Committee under paragraphs 1 to 3 of this Rule shall be subject to the provisions of Rule 45, paragraph 2. (**)

(*) Paragraph inserted by the Committee on 20 September 1991.
(**) Paragraph amended by the Committee on 20 September 1991.

Rule 43 (Subsequent consultations)

After transmission of the Committee's report, the Committee and the Party may hold consultations concerning in particular the implementation of any recommendations set out in the report.

Chapter II

Public statements

Rule 44

1. If a Party fails to co-operate with the Committee or refuses to improve the situation in the light of the Committee's recommendations, the Committee may decide, by a majority of two-thirds of its members, to make a public statement on the matter.
2. Before a decision to make such a statement is taken, the Party concerned shall be given an opportunity to make known its views.
3. Subject to the provisions of Rule 45, paragraph 2, the Committee shall be released from the obligation of confidentiality set out under Title V when making a public statement.

TITLE V

CONFIDENTIALITY

Rule 45

1. Subject to Rules 42 and 44, information gathered by the Committee in relation to a visit, its report on that visit, and its consultations with the Party concerned

shall be and shall remain confidential. The same shall apply to all Committee meeting reports and working documents.

2. No personal data shall be published without the express consent of the person concerned.

Rule 46

1. Members of the Committee, experts and other persons assisting the Committee are required, during and after their terms of office, to maintain the confidentiality of the facts or information of which they have become aware during the discharge of their functions.

2. A provision to the above effect shall be inserted in the contracts of experts and interpreters recruited to assist the Committee.

Article 47 (*)

If there are serious grounds for believing that a Committee member has violated the obligation of confidentiality, the Committee may, after the member concerned has had an opportunity to state his views, decide by a majority of two-thirds of its members to inform the Committee of Ministers of the matter.

(*) Rule inserted by the Committee on 9 November 1990.

Article 48 (*)

1. If there are serious grounds for believing that a member of the Committee's Secretariat or an interpreter has violated the obligation of confidentiality, the Committee may, after the person concerned has had an opportunity to state his views, decide by a majority of its members to inform the Secretary General of the Council of Europe of the matter and request that appropriate measures be taken.

2. If there are serious grounds for believing that an expert has violated the obligation of confidentiality, the Committee shall, after the person concerned has had an opportunity to state his views, decide by a majority of its members on the measures to be taken.

(*) Rule inserted by the Committee on 9 November 1990.

TITLE VI

ANNUAL GENERAL REPORT OF THE COMMITTEE

Rule 49

1. Subject to the obligation of confidentiality set out under Title V, the Committee shall every year submit to the Committee of Ministers a general report on its activities, which shall be transmitted to the Consultative Assembly and made public.

2. The report shall contain inter alia information on the organisation and internal workings of the Committee and on its activities proper, with particular mention of the States visited.

3. Whenever possible, the report shall be adopted at the first meeting of the Committee in a given calendar year and cover the whole of the preceding calendar year. The Secretary shall submit a draft report to the Committee in good time.

TITLE VII

AMENDMENTS AND SUSPENSION

Rule 50 (Amendment of the Rules)

These Rules of Procedure may be amended by decision taken by a majority of the members of the Committee, subject to the provisions of the Convention.

Rule 51 (Suspension of a Rule)

Upon the proposal of a Committee member, the application of a Rule may be suspended by decisions taken by a majority of the members of the Committee, subject to the provisions of the Convention. The suspension of a rule shall be limited in its operation to the particular purpose for which such suspension has been sought.

Appendix 4

Tables of Signatures and Ratifications (as at 31 December 1997)

A. EUROPEAN CONVENTION FOR THE PREVENTION OF TORTURE
AND INHUMAN OR DEGRADING TREATMENT OR PUNISHMENT

Member State	Date of Signature	Date of Ratification	Entry into Force
Albania	02.10.96	02.10.96	01.02.97
Andorra	10.09.96	06.01.97	01.05.97
Austria	26.11.87	06.01.89	01.05.89
Belgium	26.11.87	23.07.91	01.11.91
Bulgaria	30.09.93	03.05.94	01.01.94
Croatia	06.11.96	11.10.97	01.02.98
Cyprus	26.11.87	03.04.89	01.08.89
Czech Republic	23.12.92	07.09.95	01.01.96
Denmark	26.11.87	02.05.89	01.09.89
Estonia	28.06.96	06.11.96	01.03.97
Finland	16.11.89	20.12.90	01.04.91
France	26.11.87	09.01.89	01.05.89
Germany	26.11.87	21.02.90	01.06.90
Greece	26.11.87	02.08.91	01.12.91
Hungary	09.02.93	04.11.93	01.03.94
Iceland	26.11.87	19.06.90	01.10.90
Ireland	14.03.88	14.03.88	01.02.89
Italy	26.11.87	29.12.88	01.04.89
Liechtenstein	26.11.87	12.09.91	01.01.92
Luxembourg	26.11.87	06.09.88	01.02.89
Malta	26.11.87	07.03.88	01.02.89
Moldova	02.05.96	02.10.97	01.02.98
Netherlands	26.11.87	12.10.88	01.02.89
Norway	26.11.87	21.04.89	01.08.89
Poland	11.07.94	10.10.94	01.02.95
Portugal	26.11.87	29.03.90	01.07.90
Romania	04.11.93	04.10.94	01.02.95
San Marino	16.11.89	31.01.90	01.05.90
Slovak Republic	23.12.92	11.05.94	01.09.94
Slovenia	04.11.93	02.02.94	01.06.94
Spain	26.11.87	02.05.89	01.09.89

Member State	Date of Signature	Date of Ratification	Entry into Force
Sweden	26.11.87	21.06.88	01.02.89
Switzerland	26.11.87	07.10.88	01.02.89
'TFYRO Macedonia'	14.06.96	06.06.97	01.10.97
Turkey	11.01.88	26.02.88	01.02.89
Ukraine	02.05.96	05.05.97	01.09.97
United Kingdom	26.11.87	24.06.88	01.02.89

Member States of the Council of Europe yet to ratify the ECPT

State	Member of Council of Europe	Date of Signature of ECPT	Ratification of ECPT due by
Latvia	10.02.95	11.09.97	N/A
Lithuania	14.05.95	14.09.95	N/A
Russia	01.03.97	28.02.96	28.02.97

B. PROTOCOL NO 1 TO THE EUROPEAN CONVENTION FOR THE
PREVENTION OF TORTURE AND INHUMAN OR DEGRADING
TREATMENT OR PUNISHMENT

Member State	Date of Signature	Date of Ratification	Entry into Force
Albania	02.10.96	02.10.96	
Andorra		***	
Austria	04.11.93	31.04.96	
Belgium	04.11.93	12.09.96	
Bulgaria	04.03.97	27.10.97	
Croatia		***	
Cyprus	02.02.94	10.09.97	
Czech Republic	28.04.95	07.09.95	
Denmark	04.11.93	26.04.94	
Estonia	28.06.96	06.11.96	
Finland	04.11.93 (*)	04.11.93 (*)	
France	04.11.93	***	
Germany	04.11.93	13.12.96	
Greece	04.11.93	20.06.94	
Hungary	04.11.93 (*)	04.11.93 (*)	
Iceland	08.09.94	29.06.95	
Ireland	10.04.96 (*)	10.04.96 (*)	

Member State	Date of Signature	Date of Ratification	Entry into Force
Italy	30.10.96	***	
Latvia	11.09.97	***	
Liechtenstein	04.11.93	05.05.95	
Lithuania	14.05.95		
Luxembourg	04.11.93	20.07.95	
Malta	04.11.93 (*)	04.11.93 (*)	
Moldova	02.10.97	02.10.97	
Netherlands	05.05.94	23.02.95	
Norway	04.11.93 (*)	04.11.93 (*)	
Poland	11.01.95	24.03.95	
Portugal	03.06.94	***	
Romania	04.11.93	04.10.94	
Russia	28.02.96		
San Marino	04.11.93	05.12.96	
Slovak Republic	07.03.94	11.05.94	
Slovenia	31.03.94	16.02.95	
Spain	21.02.95	08.06.95	
Sweden	07.03.94 (*)	07.03.94 (*)	
Switzerland	09.03.94 (*)	09.03.94 (*)	
'TFYRO Macedonia'	14.06.96	06.06.97	
Turkey	10.05.95	17.09.97	
Ukraine		***	
United Kingdom	09.12.93	11.04.96	

(*) Signature without reservation as to ratification.
*** State whose ratification is needed for the Protocol to enter into force.

C. PROTOCOL NO 2 TO THE EUROPEAN CONVENTION FOR THE PREVENTION OF TORTURE AND INHUMAN OR DEGRADING TREATMENT OR PUNISHMENT

Member State	Date of Signature	Date of Ratification	Entry into Force
Albania	02.10.96	02.10.96	
Andorra		***	
Austria	04.11.93	31.04.96	
Belgium	04.11.93	12.09.96	
Bulgaria	04.03.97	27.10.97	
Croatia		***	
Cyprus	02.02.94	10.09.97	
Czech Republic	28.04.95	07.09.95	
Denmark	04.11.93	26.04.94	

Member State	Date of Signature	Date of Ratification	Entry into Force
Estonia	28.06.96	06.11.96	
Finland	04.11.93 (*)	04.11.93 (*)	
France	04.11.93	14.08.96	
Germany	04.11.93	13.12.96	
Greece	04.11.93	20.06.94	
Hungary	04.11.93 (*)	04.11.93 (*)	
Iceland	08.09.94	29.06.95	
Ireland	10.04.96 (*)	10.04.96 (*)	
Italy	30.10.96	***	
Latvia	11.09.97	***	
Liechtenstein	04.11.93	05.05.95	
Lithuania	14.05.95		
Luxembourg	04.11.93	20.07.95	
Malta	04.11.93 (*)	04.11.93 (*)	
Moldova	02.10.97	02.10.97	
Netherlands	05.05.94	23.02.95	
Norway	04.11.93 (*)	04.11.93 (*)	
Poland	11.01.95	24.03.95	
Portugal	03.06.94	***	
Romania	04.11.93	04.10.94	
Russia	28.02.96		
San Marino	04.11.93	05.12.96	
Slovak Republic	07.03.94	11.05.94	
Slovenia	31.03.94	16.02.95	
Spain	21.02.95	08.06.95	
Sweden	07.03.94 (*)	07.03.94 (*)	
Switzerland	09.03.94 (*)	09.03.94 (*)	
'TFYRO Macedonia'	14.06.96	06.06.97	
Turkey	10.05.95	17.09.97	
Ukraine		***	
United Kingdom	09.12.93	11.04.96	

(*) Signature without reservation as to ratification.
*** State whose ratification is needed for the Protocol to enter into force.

Appendix 5
Lists of CPT Visits and of Resulting Reports and Responses, 1990–97

A. IN ALPHABETICAL ORDER

Country	Date of Visit	Type of Visit	Report Published	Interim Report Published	Follow-Up Report Published
Albania	09.12.97–19.12.97	Periodic			
Austria	20.05.90–27.05.90	Periodic	03.10.91	03.10.91[a]	
Austria	26.09.94–07.10.94	Periodic	31.10.96	31.10.96[a]	
Belgium	14.11.93–23.11.93	Periodic	14.10.94	03.05.95	21.02.96
Belgium	31.08.97–12.09.97	Periodic			
Bulgaria	26.03.95–07.04.95	Periodic	06.03.97	06.03.97	06.03.97
Czech Republic	16.02.97–26.02.97	Periodic			
Cyprus	02.11.92–09.11.92	Periodic	22.05.97		
Cyprus	12.05.96–21.05.96	Periodic	22.05.97		
Denmark	02.12.90–08.12.90	Periodic	03.10.91	21.03.96	21.03.96
Denmark	29.09.96–09.10.96	Periodic	24.04.97	11.12.97	
Estonia	13.07.97–23.07.97	Periodic			
Finland	10.05.92–20.05.92	Periodic	01.04.93	26.08.93	25.02.94
France	27.10.91–08.11.91	Periodic	19.1.93	19.1.93	17.02.94
France (Martinique)	03.07.94–07.07.94	Ad Hoc	24.09.96	24.09.96	24.09.96

Country	Date of Visit	Type of Visit	Report Published	Interim Report Published	Follow-Up Report Published
France	20.07.94–22.07.94	Follow–up	23.01.96	23.01.96	N/A[b]
France	06.10.96–18.10.96	Periodic			
Germany	08.12.91–20.12.91	Periodic	19.07.93	19.07.93	
Germany	14.04.96–26.04.96	Periodic	17.07.97	17.07.97	
Greece	14.03.93–26.03.93	Periodic	29.11.94	29.11.94	21.02.96
Greece	04.11.96–06.11.96	Follow-up			
Greece	25.05.97–06.06.97	Periodic			
Hungary	01.11.94–14.11.94	Periodic	01.02.96[c]	18.04.96	
Iceland	06.07.93–12.07.93	Periodic	28.06.94	20.10.94	12.02.96
Ireland	26.09.93–05.10.93	Periodic	13.12.95	13.12.95	19.09.96
Italy	15.03.92–27.03.92	Periodic	31.01.95	31.05.95	
Italy	22.10.95–06.11.95	Follow-up	04.12.97	04.12.97	
Italy	25.11.96–28.11.96	Ad Hoc			
Liechtenstein	14.04.93–16.04.93	Periodic	23.05.95	23.05.95	
Luxembourg	17.01.93–25.01.93	Periodic	12.11.93	31.03.94	
Luxembourg	20.04.97–25.04.97	Ad Hoc			
Malta	01.07.90–09.07.90	Periodic	01.10.92		
Malta	16.07.95–21.07.95	Periodic	26.09.96	26.09.96	10.07.97
Netherlands	30.08.92–08.09.92	Periodic	15.7.93	20.12.93	
Netherlands (Antilles)	26.06.94–30.06.94	Ad Hoc	18.01.96	18.01.96	
Netherlands (Aruba)	30.06.94–02.07.94	Ad Hoc	03.10.96	03.10.96	03.10.96
Netherlands	17.11.97–27.11.97	Periodic			

Country	Date of Visit	Type of Visit	Report Published	Interim Report Published	Follow-Up Report Published
Netherlands (Antilles)	7.12.97– 11.12.97	Follow-up			
Norway	27.06.93– 06.07.93	Periodic	21.09.94	21.09.94	26.04.96
Norway	17.03.97– 21.03.97	Ad Hoc	05.09.97	N/A[b]	
Poland	30.06.96– 12.07.96	Periodic			
Portugal	19.01.92– 27.01.92	Periodic	22.07.94	22.07.94	
Portugal	14.05.95– 26.05.95	Periodic	21.11.96	21.11.96	27.11.97
Portugal	20.10.96– 24.10.96	Follow-up			
Romania	24.09.95– 06.10.95	Periodic[d]			
San Marino	25.03.92– 27.03.92	Periodic	12.10.94		
Slovakia	25.05.95– 07.07.95	Periodic	03.04.97	03.04.97	03.04.97
Slovenia	19.02.95– 28.02.95	Periodic	27.06.96	27.06.96	
Spain	01.04.91– 12.04.91	Periodic	05.03.96	05.03.96	
Spain	10.04.94– 22.94.94	Periodic	05.03.96	05.03.96	
Spain	10.06.94– 14.06.94	Ad Hoc	05.03.96	05.03.96	N/A[b]
Spain	17.01.97– 18.01.97	Ad Hoc			
Spain	21.04.97– 25.04.97	Ad Hoc			
Sweden	05.05.91– 14.05.91	Periodic	12.03.92	01.10.92	07.04.93
Sweden	23.08.94– 26.08.94	Follow-up	03.04.95	02.10.95	N/A[b]
Switzerland	21.07.91– 29.07.91	Periodic	27.01.93	27.01.93	08.06.94
Switzerland	11.02.96– 23.02.96	Periodic	26.06.97	26.06.97	
Turkey	09.09.90– 21.09.90	Ad Hoc			
Turkey	29.09.91– 07.10.91	Ad Hoc			

Country	Date of Visit	Type of Visit	Report Published	Interim Report Published	Follow-Up Report Published
Turkey	22.11.92–03.12.92	Periodic			
Turkey	16.10.94–28.10.94	Follow-up			
Turkey	19.08.96–23.08.96	Ad Hoc			
Turkey	18.09.96–20.09.96	Ad Hoc			
Turkey	05.10.97–17.10.97	Periodic			
UK	29.07.90–10.08.90	Periodic	26.11.91	26.11.91	15.04.93
UK (Northern Ireland)	20.07.93–29.07.93	Ad Hoc	17.11.94	17.11.94	
UK	15.05.94–31.05.94	Periodic	05.03.96	05.03.96ᵉ	
UK/Isle of Man	08.09.97–17.09.97	Ad Hoc			

ª Published as 'Comments', but forming the Interim Response.
ᵇ No Follow-up Report requested.
ᶜ Published with 'Comments'.
ᵈ The ECPT entered into force for Romania on 1 Feb 1995. This visit was not included in the list of periodic visits announced in September 1994 but resembled a periodic visit in form and so is listed as such.
ᵉ Described as 'Final Response'.

B. IN DATE ORDER

1990

Country	Date of Visit	Type of Visit	Report Published	Interim Report Published	Follow-up Report Published
Austria	20.05–27.05	Periodic	03.10.91	3.10.91ª	
Malta	01.07–09.07	Periodic	01.10.92		
UK	29.07–10.08	Periodic	26.11.91	26.11.91	15.04.93
Turkey	09.09–21.09	Ad Hoc			
Denmark	02.12–08.12	Periodic	03.10.91	21.03.96	21.03.96

ª Published as 'Comments'.

1991

Country	Date of Visit	Type of Visit	Report Published	Interim Report Published	Follow-up Report Published
Spain	01.04–12.04	Periodic	05.03.96	05.03.96	
Sweden	05.05–14.05	Periodic	12.03.92	01.10.92	07.04.93
Switzerland	21.07–29.07	Periodic	27.01.93	27.01.93	08.06.94
Turkey	29.09–07.10	Ad Hoc			
France	27.10–08.11	Periodic	19.01.93	19.01.93	17.02.94
Germany	08.12–20.12	Periodic	19.07.93	19.07.93	

1992

Country	Date of Visit	Type of Visit	Report Published	Interim Report Published	Follow-up Report Published
Portugal	19.01–27.01	Periodic	22.07.94	22.07.94	
Italy	15.03–27.03	Periodic	31.01.95	31.05.95	
San Marino	25.03–27.03	Periodic	12.10.94		
Finland	10.05–20.05	Periodic	01.04.93	26.08.93	25.02.94
Netherlands	30.08–08.09	Periodic	15.7.93	20.12.93	
Cyprus	02.11–09.11	Periodic	22.05.97		
Turkey	22.11–03.12	Periodic			

1993

Country	Date of Visit	Type of Visit	Report Published	Interim Report Published	Follow-up Report Published
Luxembourg	17.01–25.01	Periodic	12.11.93	31.03.94	
Greece	14.03–26.03	Periodic	29.11.94	29.11.94	21.02.96
Liechtenstein	14.04–16.04	Periodic	23.05.95	23.05.95	
Norway	27.06–06.07	Periodic	21.09.94	21.09.94	26.04.96
Iceland	06.07–12.07	Periodic	28.06.94	20.10.94	12.02.96
UK (Northern Ireland)	20.07–29.07	Ad Hoc	17.11.94	17.11.94	
Ireland	26.09–05.10	Periodic	13.12.95	13.12.95	19.09.96
Belgium	14.11–23.11	Periodic	14.10.94	03.05.95	21.02.96

1994

Country	Date of Visit	Type of Visit	Report Published	Interim Report Published	Follow-up Report Published
Spain	10.04–22.94	Periodic	05.03.96	05.03.96	
UK	15.05–31.05	Periodic	05.03.96	05.03.96[a]	
Spain	10.06–14.06	Ad Hoc	05.03.96	05.03.96	N/A[b]
Netherlands (Antilles)	26.04–30.04	Ad Hoc	18.01.96	18.01.96	
Netherlands (Aruba)	30.06–02.07	Ad Hoc	03.10.96	03.10.96	03.10.96
France (Martinique)	03.07–07.07	Ad Hoc	24.09.96	24.09.96	24.09.96
France	20.07–22.07	Follow-up	23.01.96	23.01.96	N/A[b]
Sweden	23.08–26.08	Follow-up	03.04.95	02.10.95	N/A[b]
Austria	26.09–07.10	Periodic	31.10.96	31.10.96[c]	
Turkey	16.10–28.10	Follow-up			
Hungary	01.11–14.11	Periodic	01.02.96[d]	18.04.96	

[a] Described as 'Final Response'.
[b] No Follow-up Report requested.
[c] Described as 'Comments', but forming the Interim Response.
[d] With 'Comments'.

1995

Country	Date of Visit	Type of Visit	Report Published	Interim Report Published	Follow-up Report Published
Slovenia	19.02–28.02	Periodic	27.06.96	27.06.96	
Bulgaria	26.03–07.04	Periodic	06.03.97	06.03.97	06.03.97
Portugal	14.05–26.05	Periodic	21.11.96	21.11.96	27.11.97
Slovakia	25.05–07.07	Periodic	03.04.97	03.04.97	03.04.97
Malta	16.07–21.07	Periodic	26.09.96	26.09.96	10.07.97
Romania	24.09–06.10	Periodic[a]			
Italy	22.10–06.11	Periodic	04.12.97	04.12.97	

[a] The ECPT entered into force for Romania on 1 Feb 1995. This visit was not included in the list of periodic visits announced in September 1994 but resembled a periodic visit in form and so is listed as such.

1996

Country	Date of Visit	Type of Visit	Report Published	Interim Report Published	Follow-up Report Published
Switzerland	11.02–23.02	Periodic	26.06.97	26.06.97	
Germany	14.04–26.04	Periodic	17.07.97	17.07.97	
Cyprus	12.05–21.05	Periodic	22.05.97		
Poland	30.06–12.07	Periodic			
Turkey	19.08–23.08	Ad Hoc			
Turkey	18.09–20.09	Ad Hoc			
Denmark	29.09–09.10	Periodic	24.04.97	11.12.97	
France	06.10–18.10	Periodic			
Portugal	20.10–24.10	Follow-up			
Greece	04.11–06.11	Follow-up			
Italy	25.11–28.11	Follow-up			

1997

Country	Date of Visit	Type of Visit	Report Published	Interim Report Published	Follow-up Report Published
Spain	17.01–18.01	Ad Hoc			
Czech Republic	16.02–26.02	Periodic			
Norway	17.03–21.03	Ad Hoc	05.09.97		N/A[a]
Luxembourg	20.04–25.04	Ad Hoc			
Spain	21.04–25.04	Ad Hoc			
Greece	25.05–06–06	Periodic			
Estonia	13.07–23.07	Periodic			
Belgium	31.08–12.09	Periodic			
UK/Isle of Man	08.09–17.09	Ad Hoc			
Turkey	05.10–17.10	Periodic			
Netherlands	17.11– 27.11	Periodic			
Netherlands (Antilles)	07.12–11.12	Follow-up			
Albania	09.12–19.12	Periodic			

[a] No Follow-up report requested.

Appendix 6
CPT Membership

Country	Member	Term expires
Albania	Vacant	
Andorra	Vacant	
Austria	Renate Kicker	20.09.2001[b]
Belgium	Lambert Kelchtermans	08.01.2000[b]
Bulgaria	Emilia Drumeva	17.03.2001[b]
Cyprus	Demetrios Stylianides	30.11.1999[b]
Czech Republic	Zdeněk Hájek	11.09.2000[b]
Denmark	Ole Rasmussen	20.09.2001[b]
Estonia	Andres Lehtmets	19.12.2001[b]
Finland	Pirrko Lahti	20.06.1999
France	Ivan Zakine (President, Nov 1997–)	20.09.2001
Germany	Günther Kaiser	21.06.1998
Greece	Constantin Economides	30.11.1999
Hungary	Miklós Magyer	03.04.2000[b]
Iceland	Jón Bjarman	26.03.2000
Ireland	John Olden (2nd Vice President, Nov 1997–)	21.03.1999[b]
Italy	Vitaliano Esposito	21.06.1999[b]
Liechtenstein	Arnold Oehry	13.01.2001
Luxembourg	Pierre Schmit	19.09.2001[b]
Malta	Maria Sciberras	09.01.2000[b]
Netherlands	Pieter Stoffelen	20.09.2001
Norway	Ingrid Lycke Ellingsen (1st Vice-President, Sept 1995–)	19.09.2001
Poland	Adam Laptaś	30.11.1999[b]
Portugal	Vacant	
Romania	Florin Stănescu	21.03.1999[b]
San Marino	Mario Benedettini	21.03.1999[b]
Slovak Republic	Jogoda Poloncová	21.06.1999[b]
Slovenia	Vacant	
Spain	Leopoldo Torres-Boussault (2nd Vice-President, Sept 1995–Nov 1997)	03.05.2001
Sweden	Christina Doctare	19.09.1999[b]
Switzerland	Gisela Perren-Klinger	20.09.2001

Country	Member	Term expires
'TFYRO Macedonia'	Vacant	
Turkey	Safa Reisoğlu	20.09.2001
Ukraine	Vacant	
United Kingdom	Silvia Casale	19.12.2001[b]

[a] Members for Croatia and Moldova will be due for election following the entry into force of the Convention for these states on 1 Feb 1998.

[b] Members eligible for re-election.

B. LIST OF PAST AND PRESENT MEMBERS AND THEIR AREAS OF EXPERTISE

Country	Members	Period of Office	Expertise
Austria	Rudolph Machacek	19.09.89–19.09.97	Lawyer/Academic
	Renate Kicker	19.09.97–	Lawyer/Academic
Belgium	Nora Staels-Dompas	08.01.92–08.01.96	Parliamentarian
	Lambert Kelchtermans	08.01.96–	Parliamentarian
Bulgaria	Emilia Drumeva	17.03.97–	Lawyer/Academic
Cyprus	Petros Michaelides	19.09.89–19.09.95	Lawyer/Parliamentarian
	Demetrios Stylianides	30.11.95–	Lawyer/Judge
Czech Republic	Zdeněk Hájek	11.09.96–	Lawyer/Civil servant
Denmark	Bent Sørensen	19.09.89–19.09.97	Medic/Surgeon
	Ole Rasmussen	19.09.97–	Medic
Estonia	Andres Lehtmets	19.12.97–	Medic/Psychiatrist
Finland	Pirrko Lahti	20.06.91–	Psychologist
France	Lydie Dupuy	19.09.89–19.09.93	Parliamentarian
	Ivan Zakine	19.09.93–	Lawyer/Judge
Germany	Günther Kaiser	20.06.90–	Lawyer/Academic
Greece	Constantin Economides	30.11.91–	Lawyer/Academic
Hungary	Miklós Magyer	03.04.96–	Medic/Psychiatrist
Iceland	Jón Bjarman	26.03.92–	Cleric/Prison Chaplain
Ireland	Michael Mellet	19.09.89–19.09.93	Civil Servant/Prison Administrator
	John Olden	21.03.95–	Civil Servant/Prison Administrator

Country	Members	Period of Office	Expertise
Italy	Antonio Cassese	19.09.89–19.09.93	Lawyer/Academic
	Nicolò Amato	19.09.93–19.01.95	Lawyer/Prison Administrator
	Vitaliano Esposito	21.06.95–	Lawyer/Prosecutor
Liechtenstein	Arnold Oehry	22.10.92–	Lawyer/Judge
Luxembourg	Claude Nicolay	19.09.89–19.09.97	Lawyer/Prosecutor
	Pierre Schmit	19.09.97–	Lawyer/Prosecutor
Malta	Tonio Borg	20.06.90–31.05.95	Lawyer/Parliamentarian
	Maria Sciberras	09.01.96–	Medic/General Practioner
Netherlands	Nadia Gevers Leuven-Lachinsky	19.09.89–19.09.97	Medic/General Practioner
	Pieter Stoffelen	19.09.97–	Lawyer/Parliamentarian
Norway	Astrid Heiberg	19.09.89–19.09.93	Medic/Psychiatrist
	Ingrid Lycke Ellingsen	19.09.93–	Medic/Psychiatrist
Poland	Adam Laptaś	30.11.95–	Lawyer/Prison Governor
Portugal	Antonio Lopez Rocha	21.06.90–27.09.91	Lawyer/Judge
	José Vieira Mesquita	24.09.92–24.09.96	Lawyer/Parliamentarian
Romania	Florin Stănescu	21.03.95–	Medic/Pathologist
San Marino	Mario Benedettini	21.03.95–	Psycotherapist
Slovakia	Jagoda Poloncová	21.06.95–	Lawyer/Ministerial Advisor
Spain	Leopoldo Torres Boursault	19.09.89–26.01.90	Lawyer/Prosector
	José Mohedano	19.04.90–15.02.93	Lawyer
	Leopoldo Torres Boursault	23.05.93–	Lawyer/Prosector
Sweden	Love Kellberg	19.09.89–19.09.95	Lawyer/Diplomat
	Christina Doctare	19.09.95–	Medic/General Practioner
Switzerland	Jacques Bernheim	19.09.89–19.09.93	Medic/Psychiatrist
	Gisela Perren-Klinger	19.09.93–	Medic/Psychiatrist
Turkey	Ergun Ozbudun	19.09.89–19.09.93	Lawyer/Academic
	Safa Reisoğlu	19.09.93–	Lawyer/Academic
United Kingdom	Stefan Terlezki	19.09.89–19.09.97	Parliamentarian
	Silvia Casale	19.12.97–	Criminologist

Appendix 7
CPT Statements of Standards

35. The CPT's role is essentially preventive in nature; its main purpose is to forestall torture or inhuman or degrading treatment or punishment rather than to establish that it has actually occurred (see further the 1st General Report, op cit Part IV). To fulfil that role, the Committee must explore a wide range of issues—rights possessed by persons deprived of their liberty; custody and interrogation procedures; disciplinary procedures; avenues of complaint; physical conditions of detention; regime activities; health care and standards of hygiene; etc—in order to assess not only whether there is an imminent risk of ill-treatment but also whether conditions or circumstances exist which could degenerate into ill-treatment. Further, these issues must be viewed both individually and cumulatively.

a. Police custody

36. The CPT attaches particular importance to three rights for persons detained by the police: the right of the person concerned to have the fact of his detention notified to a third party of his choice (family member, friend, consulate), the right of access to a lawyer, and the right to request a medical examination by a doctor of his choice (in addition to any medical examination carried out by a doctor called by the police authorities). They are, in the CPT's opinion, three fundamental safeguards against the ill-treatment of detained persons which should apply as from the very outset of deprivation of liberty, regardless of how it may be described under the legal system concerned (apprehension, arrest, etc).

37. Persons taken into police custody should be expressly informed without delay of all their rights, including those referred to in paragraph 36. Further, any possibilities offered to the authorities to delay the exercise of one or other of the latter rights in order to protect the interests of justice should be clearly defined and their application strictly limited in time. As regards more particularly the rights of access to a lawyer and to request a medical examination by a doctor other than one called by the police, systems whereby, exceptionally, lawyers and doctors can be chosen from pre-established lists drawn up in agreement with the relevant professional organisations should remove any need to delay the exercise of these rights.

38. Access to a lawyer for persons in police custody should include the right to contact and to be visited by the lawyer (in both cases under conditions guaranteeing the confidentiality of their discussions) as well as, in principle, the right for the person concerned to have the lawyer present during interrogation.

As regards the medical examination of persons in police custody, all such examinations should be conducted out of the hearing, and preferably out of the sight, of police officers. Further, the results of every examination as well as relevant statements by the detainee and the doctor's conclusions should be formally recorded by the doctor and made available to the detainee and his lawyer.

39. Turning to the interrogation process, the CPT considers that clear rules or guidelines should exist on the way in which police interviews are to be conducted. They should address inter alia the following matters: the informing of the detainee of the identity (name and/or number) of those present at the interview; the permissible length of an interview; rest periods between interviews and breaks during an interview; places in which interviews may take place; whether the detainee may be required to stand while being questioned; the interviewing of persons who are under the influence of drugs, alcohol, etc. It should also be required that a record be systematically kept of the time at which interviews start and end, of any request made by a detainee during an interview, and of the persons present during each interview.

The CPT would add that the electronic recording of police interviews is another useful safeguard against the ill-treatment of detainees (as well as having significant advantages for the police).

40. The CPT considers that the fundamental safeguards granted to persons in police custody would be reinforced (and the work of police officers quite possibly facilitated) if a single and comprehensive custody record were to exist for each person detained, on which would be recorded all aspects of his custody and action taken regarding them (when deprived of liberty and reasons for that measure; when told of rights; signs of injury, mental illness, etc; when next of kin/consulate and lawyer contacted and when visited by them; when offered food; when interrogated; when transferred or released, etc). For various matters (for example, items in the person's possession, the fact of being told of one's rights, and of invoking or waiving them), the signature of the detainee should be obtained and, if necessary, the absence of a signature explained. Further, the detainee's lawyer should have access to such a custody record.

41. Further, the existence of an independent mechanism for examining complaints about treatment whilst in police custody is an essential safeguard.

42. Custody by the police is in principle of relatively short duration. Consequently, physical conditions of detention cannot be expected to be as good in police establishments as in other places of detention where persons may be held for lengthy periods. However, certain elementary material requirements should be met.

All police cells should be of a reasonable size for the number of persons they are used to accommodate, and have adequate lighting (ie sufficient to read by, sleeping periods excluded) and ventilation; preferably, cells should enjoy natural light. Further, cells should be equipped with a means of rest (eg a fixed chair or bench), and persons obliged to stay overnight in custody should be provided with a clean mattress and blankets.

Persons in custody should be allowed to comply with the needs of nature when necessary in clean and decent conditions, and be offered adequate washing facilities. They should be given food at appropriate times, including at least one full meal (ie something more substantial than a sandwich) every day.

43. The issue of what is a reasonable size for a police cell (or any other type of detainee/prisoner accommodation) is a difficult question. Many factors have to be taken into account when making such an assessment. However, CPT delegations felt the need for a rough guideline in this area. The following criterion (seen as a desirable level rather than a minimum standard) is currently being used when assessing police cells intended for single occupancy for stays in excess of a few hours: in the order of 7 square metres, 2 metres or more between walls, 2.5 metres between floor and ceiling.

b. Imprisonment

44. In introduction, it should be emphasised that the CPT must examine many questions when visiting a prison. Of course, it pays special attention to allegations of ill-treatment of prisoners by staff. However, all aspects of the conditions of detention in a prison are of relevance to the CPT's mandate. Ill-treatment can take numerous forms, many of which may not be deliberate but rather the result of organisational failings or inadequate resources. The overall quality of life in an establishment is therefore of considerable importance to the CPT. That quality of life will depend to a very large extent upon the activities offered to prisoners and the general state of relations between prisoners and staff.

45. The CPT observes carefully the prevailing climate within an establishment. The promotion of constructive as opposed to confrontational relations between prisoners and staff will serve to lower the tension inherent in any prison environment and by the same token significantly reduce the likelihood of violent incidents and associated ill-treatment. In short, the CPT wishes to see a spirit of communication and care accompany measures of control and containment. Such an approach, far from undermining security in the establishment, might well enhance it.

46. Overcrowding is an issue of direct relevance to the CPT's mandate. All the services and activities within a prison will be adversely affected if it is required to cater for more prisoners than it was designed to accommodate; the overall quality of life in the establishment will be lowered, perhaps significantly. Moreover, the level of overcrowding in a prison, or in a particular part of it, might be such as to be in itself inhuman or degrading from a physical standpoint.

47. A satisfactory programme of activities (work, education, sport, etc) is of crucial importance for the well-being of prisoners. This holds true for all establishments, whether for sentenced prisoners or those awaiting trial. The CPT has observed that activities in many remand prisons are extremely limited. The organisation of regime activities in such establishments—which have a fairly rapid turnover of inmates—is not a straightforward matter. Clearly, there can be

no question of individualised treatment programmes of the sort which might be aspired to in an establishment for sentenced prisoners. However, prisoners cannot simply be left to languish for weeks, possibly months, locked up in their cells, and this regardless of how good material conditions might be within the cells. The CPT considers that one should aim at ensuring that prisoners in remand establishments are able to spend a reasonable part of the day (8 hours or more) outside their cells, engaged in purposeful activity of a varied nature. Of course, regimes in establishments for sentenced prisoners should be even more favourable.

48. Specific mention should be made of outdoor exercise. The requirement that prisoners be allowed at least one hour of exercise in the open air every day is widely accepted as a basic safeguard (preferably it should form part of a broader programme of activities). The CPT wishes to emphasise that **all prisoners without exception** (including those undergoing cellular confinement as a punishment) should be offered the possibility to take outdoor exercise daily. It is also axiomatic that outdoor exercise facilities should be reasonably spacious and whenever possible offer shelter from inclement weather.

49. Ready access to proper toilet facilities and the maintenance of good standards of hygiene are essential components of a humane environment.

In this connection, the CPT must state that it does not like the practice found in certain countries of prisoners discharging human waste in buckets in their cells (which are subsequently 'slopped out' at appointed times). Either a toilet facility should be located in cellular accommodation (preferably in a sanitary annex) or means should exist enabling prisoners who need to use a toilet facility to be released from their cells without undue delay at all times (including at night).

Further, prisoners should have adequate access to shower or bathing facilities. It is also desirable for running water to be available within cellular accommodation.

50. The CPT would add that it is particularly concerned when it finds a combination of overcrowding, poor regime activities and inadequate access to toilet/washing facilities in the same establishment. The cumulative effect of such conditions can prove extremely detrimental to prisoners.

51. It is also very important for prisoners to maintain reasonably good contact with the outside world. Above all, a prisoner must be given the means of safeguarding his relationships with his family and close friends. The guiding principle should be the promotion of contact with the outside world; any limitations upon such contact should be based exclusively on security concerns of an appreciable nature or resource considerations.

The CPT wishes to emphasise in this context the need for some flexibility as regards the application of rules on visits and telephone contacts vis-à-vis prisoners whose families live far away (thereby rendering regular visits impracticable). For example, such prisoners could be allowed to accumulate visiting time and/or be offered improved possibilities for telephone contacts with their families.

52. Naturally, the CPT is also attentive to the particular problems that might be encountered by certain specific categories of prisoners, for example: women, juveniles and foreigners.

53. Prison staff will on occasion have to use force to control violent prisoners and, exceptionally, may even need to resort to instruments of physical restraint. These are clearly high risk situations insofar as the possible ill-treatment of prisoners is concerned, and as such call for specific safeguards.

A prisoner against whom any means of force have been used should have the right to be immediately examined and, if necessary, treated by a medical doctor. This examination should be conducted out of the hearing and preferably out of the sight of non-medical staff, and the results of the examination (including any relevant statements by the prisoner and the doctor's conclusions) should be formally recorded and made available to the prisoner. In those rare cases when resort to instruments of physical restraint is required, the prisoner concerned should be kept under constant and adequate supervision. Further, instruments of restraint should be removed at the earliest possible opportunity; they should never be applied, or their application prolonged, as a punishment. Finally, a record should be kept of every instance of the use of force against prisoners.

54. Effective grievance and inspection procedures are fundamental safeguards against ill-treatment in prisons. Prisoners should have avenues of complaint open to them both within and outside the context of the prison system, including the possibility to have confidential access to an appropriate authority. The CPT attaches particular importance to regular visits to each prison establishment by an independent body (eg a Board of visitors or supervisory judge) possessing powers to hear (and if necessary take action upon) complaints from prisoners and to inspect the establishment's premises. Such bodies can inter alia play an important role in bridging differences that arise between prison management and a given prisoner or prisoners in general.

55. It is also in the interests of both prisoners and prison staff that clear disciplinary procedures be both formally established and applied in practice; any grey zones in this area involve the risk of seeing unofficial (and uncontrolled) systems developing. Disciplinary procedures should provide prisoners with a right to be heard on the subject of the offences it is alleged they have committed, and to appeal to a higher authority against any sanctions imposed.

Other procedures often exist, alongside the formal disciplinary procedure, under which a prisoner may be involuntarily separated from other inmates for discipline-related/security reasons (eg in the interests of 'good order' within an establishment). These procedures should also be accompanied by effective safeguards. The prisoner should be informed of the reasons for the measure taken against him, unless security requirements dictate otherwise, be given an opportunity to present his views on the matter, and be able to contest the measure before an appropriate authority.

56. The CPT pays particular attention to prisoners held, for whatever reason (for disciplinary purposes; as a result of their 'dangerousness' or their 'troublesome' behaviour; in the interests of a criminal investigation; at their own request), under conditions akin to solitary confinement.

The principle of proportionality requires that a balance be struck between the requirements of the case and the application of a solitary confinement-type regime, which is a step that can have very harmful consequences for the person concerned. Solitary confinement can, in certain circumstances, amount to inhuman and degrading treatment; in any event, all forms of solitary confinement should be as short as possible.

In the event of such a regime being imposed or applied on request, an essential safeguard is that whenever the prisoner concerned, or a prison officer on the prisoner's behalf, requests a medical doctor, such a doctor should be called without delay with a view to carrying out a medical examination of the prisoner. The results of this examination, including an account of the prisoner's physical and mental condition as well as, if need be, the foreseeable consequences of continued isolation, should be set out in a written statement to be forwarded to the competent authorities.

57. The transfer of troublesome prisoners is another practice of interest to the CPT. Certain prisoners are extremely difficult to handle, and the transfer of such a prisoner to another establishment can sometimes prove necessary. However, the continuous moving of a prisoner from one establishment to another can have very harmful effects on his psychological and physical well being. Moreover, a prisoner in such a position will have difficulty in maintaining appropriate contacts with his family and lawyer. The overall effect on the prisoner of successive transfers could under certain circumstances amount to inhuman and degrading treatment.

58. Health care services within prisons (including dietary matters and food in general) is, of course, an additional matter to which the CPT pays the closest attention. This is a vast subject, which the Committee hopes to explore in depth in a future general report. However, persons particularly interested in this subject can already refer to the relevant sections of the reports drawn up by the CPT following its visits to Austria, Denmark and the United Kingdom (as regards the publication of these reports, see paragraph 25). In this report, the CPT would only stress that it is highly desirable for prison medical services to be closely aligned with the mainstream of health care provision in the community as a whole.

59. Finally, the CPT wishes to emphasise the great importance it attaches to the training of law enforcement personnel [the expression 'law enforcement personnel' in this report includes both police and prison officers] (which should include education on human rights matters—cf also Article 10 of the United Nations Convention against Torture and Other Cruel, Inhuman or Degrading Treatment or Punishment). There is arguably no better guarantee against the ill-treatment of a person deprived of his liberty than a properly trained police or prison officer. Skilled officers will be able to carry out successfully their duties without having recourse to ill-treatment and to cope with the presence of fundamental safeguards for detainees and prisoners.

60. In this connection, the CPT believes that aptitude for interpersonal communication should be a major factor in the process of recruiting law enforcement personnel and that, during training, considerable emphasis should be placed on developing interpersonal communication skills, based on respect for human dignity. The possession of such skills will often enable a police or prison officer to defuse a situation which could otherwise turn into violence, and more generally, will lead to a lowering of tension, and raising of the quality of life, in police and prison establishments, to the benefit of all concerned.

B. HEALTH CARE SERVICES IN PRISONS

(EXTRACTED FROM GEN REP 3)

30. Health care services for persons deprived of their liberty is a subject of direct relevance to the CPT's mandate. An inadequate level of health care can lead rapidly to situations falling within the scope of the term 'inhuman and degrading treatment'. Further, the health care service in a given establishment can potentially play an important role in combatting the infliction of ill-treatment, both in that establishment and elsewhere (in particular in police establishments). Moreover, it is well placed to make a positive impact on the overall quality of life in the establishment within which it operates.

31. In the following paragraphs, some of the main issues pursued by CPT delegations when examining health care services within prisons are described. However, at the outset the CPT wishes to make clear the importance which it attaches to the general principle—already recognised in most, if not all, of the countries visited by the Committee to date—that prisoners are entitled to the same level of medical care as persons living in the community at large. This principle is inherent in the fundamental rights of the individual.

32. The considerations which have guided the CPT during its visits to prison health care services can be set out under the following headings:

a. Access to a doctor
b. Equivalence of care
c. Patient's consent and confidentiality
d. Preventive health care
e. Humanitarian assistance
f. Professional independence
g. Professional competence.

a. Access to a doctor

33. When entering prison, all prisoners should without delay be seen by a member of the establishment's health care service. In its reports to date the CPT has recommended that every newly arrived prisoner be properly interviewed and, if necessary, physically *examined* by a medical doctor as soon as possible after his admission. It should be added that in some countries, medical screening on arrival is carried out by a fully qualified nurse, who reports to a doctor. This latter approach could be considered as a more efficient use of available resources.

It is also desirable that a leaflet or booklet be handed to prisoners on *their arrival*, informing them of the existence and operation of the health care service and reminding them of basic measures of hygiene.

34. While in custody, prisoners should be able to have access to a doctor at any time, irrespective of their detention regime (as regards more particularly access to a doctor for prisoners held in solitary confinement, see paragraph 56 of the CPT's 2nd General Report: CPT/Inf (92)3). The health care service should be so organised as to enable requests to consult a doctor to be met without undue delay.

Prisoners should be able to approach the health care service on a confidential basis, for example, by means of a message in a sealed envelope. Further, prison officers should not seek to screen requests to consult a doctor.

35. A prison's health care service should at least be able to provide regular out-patient consultations and emergency treatment (of course, in addition there may often be a hospital-type unit with beds). The services of a qualified dentist should be available to every prisoner. Further, prison doctors should be able to call upon the services of specialists.

As regards emergency treatment, a doctor should always be on call. Further, someone competent to provide first aid should always be present on prison premises, preferably someone with a recognised nursing qualification.

Out-patient treatment should be supervised, as appropriate, by health care staff; in many cases it is not sufficient for the provision of follow-up care to depend upon the initiative being taken by the prisoner.

36. The direct support of a fully-equipped hospital service should be available, in either a civil or prison hospital.

If recourse is had to a civil hospital, the question of security arrangements will arise. In this respect, the CPT wishes to stress that prisoners sent to hospital to receive treatment should not be physically attached to their hospital beds or other items of furniture for custodial reasons. Other means of meeting security needs satisfactorily can and should be found; the creation of a custodial unit in such hospitals is one possible solution.

37. Whenever prisoners need to be hospitalised or examined by a specialist in a hospital, they should be transported with the promptness and in the manner required by their state of health.

b. Equivalence of care

(i) general medicine

38. A prison health care service should be able to provide medical treatment and nursing care, as well as appropriate diets, physiotherapy, rehabilitation or any other necessary special facility, in conditions comparable to those enjoyed by patients in the outside community. Provision in terms of medical, nursing and technical staff, as well as premises, installations and equipment, should be geared accordingly.

There should be appropriate supervision of the pharmacy and of the distribution of medicines. Further, the preparation of medicines should always be entrusted to qualified staff (pharmacist/nurse, etc).

39. A medical file should be compiled for each patient, containing diagnostic information as well as an ongoing record of the patient's evolution and of any special examinations he has undergone. In the event of a transfer, the file should be forwarded to the doctors in the receiving establishment.

Further, daily registers should be kept by health care teams, in which particular incidents relating to the patients should be mentioned. Such registers are useful in that they provide an overall view of the health care situation in the prison, at the same time as highlighting specific problems which may arise.

40. The smooth operation of a health care service presupposes that doctors and nursing staff are able to meet regularly and to form a working team under the authority of a senior doctor in charge of the service.

(ii) psychiatric care

41. In comparison with the general population, there is a high incidence of psychiatric symptoms among prisoners. Consequently, a doctor qualified in psychiatry should be attached to the health care service of each prison, and some of the nurses employed there should have had training in this field.

The provision of medical and nursing staff, as well as the layout of prisons, should be such as to enable regular pharmacological, psychotherapeutic and occupational therapy programmes to be carried out.

42. The CPT wishes to stress the role to be played by prison management in the early detection of prisoners suffering from a psychiatric ailment (eg depression, reactive state, etc), with a view to enabling appropriate adjustments to be made to their environment. This activity can be encouraged by the provision of appropriate health training for certain members of the custodial staff.

43. A mentally ill prisoner should be kept and cared for in a hospital facility which is adequately equipped and possesses appropriately trained staff. That facility could be a civil mental hospital or a specially equipped psychiatric facility within the prison system.

On the one hand, it is often advanced that, from an ethical standpoint, it is appropriate for mentally ill prisoners to be hospitalised outside the prison system, in institutions for which the public health service is responsible. On the other hand, it can be argued that the provision of psychiatric facilities within the prison system enables care to be administered in optimum conditions of security, and the activities of medical and social services intensified within that system.

Whichever course is chosen, the accommodation capacity of the psychiatric facility in question should be adequate; too often there is a prolonged waiting period before a necessary transfer is effected. The transfer of the person concerned to a psychiatric facility should be treated as a matter of the highest priority.

44. A mentally disturbed and violent patient should be treated through close supervision and nursing support, combined, if considered appropriate, with sedatives. Resort to instruments of physical restraint shall only very rarely be justified and must always be either expressly ordered by a medical doctor or immediately brought to the attention of such a doctor with a view to seeking his approval. Instruments of physical restraint should be removed at the earliest possible opportunity. They should never be applied, or their application prolonged, as a punishment.

In the event of resort being had to instruments of physical restraint, an entry should be made in both the patient's file and an appropriate register, with an indication of the times at which the measure began and ended, as well as of the circumstances of the case and the reasons for resorting to such means.

c. Patient's consent and confidentiality

45. Freedom of consent and respect for confidentiality are fundamental rights of the individual. They are also essential to the atmosphere of trust which is a

necessary part of the doctor/patient relationship, especially in prisons, where a prisoner cannot freely choose his own doctor.

(i) patient's consent

46. Patients should be provided with all relevant information (if necessary in the form of a medical report) concerning their condition, the course of their treatment and the medication prescribed for them. Preferably, patients should have the right to consult the contents of their prison medical files, unless this is inadvisable from a therapeutic standpoint.

They should be able to ask for this information to be communicated to their families and lawyers or to an outside doctor.

47. Every patient capable of discernment is free to refuse treatment or any other medical intervention. Any derogation from this fundamental principle should be based upon law and only relate to clearly and strictly defined exceptional circumstances which are applicable to the population as a whole.

A classically difficult situation arises when the patient's decision conflicts with the general duty of care incumbent on the doctor. This might happen when the patient is influenced by personal beliefs (eg refusal of a blood transfusion) or when he is intent on using his body, or even mutilating himself, in order to press his demands, protest against an authority or demonstrate his support for a cause.

In the event of a hunger strike, public authorities or professional organisations in some countries will require the doctor to intervene to prevent death as soon as the patient's consciousness becomes seriously impaired. In other countries, the rule is to leave clinical decisions to the doctor in charge, after he has sought advice and weighed up all the relevant facts.

48. As regards the issue of medical research with prisoners, it is clear that a very cautious approach must be followed, given the risk of prisoners' agreement to participate being influenced by their penal situation. Safeguards should exist to ensure that any prisoner concerned has given his free and informed consent.

The rules applied should be those prevailing in the community, with the intervention of a board of ethics. The CPT would add that it favours research concerning custodial pathology or epidemiology or other aspects specific to the condition of prisoners.

49. The involvement of prisoners in the teaching programmes of students should require the prisoners' consent.

(ii) confidentiality

50. Medical secrecy should be observed in prisons in the same way as in the community. Keeping patients' files should be the doctor's responsibility.

51. All medical examinations of prisoners (whether on arrival or at a later stage) should be conducted out of the hearing and—unless the doctor concerned requests otherwise—out of the sight of prison officers. Further, prisoners should be examined on an individual basis, not in groups.

d. Preventive health care

52. The task of prison health care services should not be limited to treating sick patients. They should also be entrusted with responsibility for social and preventive medicine.

(i) hygiene

53. It lies with prison health care services—as appropriate acting in conjunction with other authorities—to supervise catering arrangements (quantity, quality, preparation and distribution of food) and conditions of hygiene (cleanliness of clothing and bedding; access to running water; sanitary installations) as well as the heating, lighting and ventilation of cells. Work and outdoor exercise arrangements should also be taken into consideration.

Insalubrity, overcrowding, prolonged isolation and inactivity may necessitate either medical assistance for an individual prisoner or general medical action vis-à-vis the responsible authority.

(ii) transmittable diseases

54. A prison health care service should ensure that information about transmittable diseases (in particular hepatitis, AIDS, tuberculosis, dermatological infections) is regularly circulated, both to prisoners and to prison staff. Where appropriate, medical control of those with whom a particular prisoner has regular contact (fellow prisoners, prison staff, frequent visitors) should be carried out.
55. As regards more particularly AIDS, appropriate counselling should be provided both before and, if necessary, after any screening test. Prison staff should be provided with ongoing training in the preventive measures to be taken and the attitudes to be adopted regarding HIV-positivity and given appropriate instructions concerning nondiscrimination and confidentiality.
56. The CPT wishes to emphasise that there is no medical justification for the segregation of an HIV+ prisoner who is well.

(iii) suicide prevention

57. Suicide prevention is another matter falling within the purview of a prison's health care service. It should ensure that there is an adequate awareness of this subject throughout the establishment, and that appropriate procedures are in place.
58. Medical screening on arrival, and the reception process as a whole, has an important role to play in this context; performed properly, it could identify at least certain of those at risk and relieve some of the anxiety experienced by all newly-arrived prisoners.

Further, prison staff, whatever their particular job, should be made aware of (which implies being trained in recognising) indications of suicidal risk. In this connection it should be noted that the periods immediately before and after trial and, in some cases, the pre-release period, involve an increased risk of suicide.

CPT Statements of Standards

447

59. A person identified as a suicide risk should, for as long as necessary, be kept under a special observation scheme. Further, such persons should not have easy access to means of killing themselves (cell window bars, broken glass, belts or ties, etc).

Steps should also be taken to ensure a proper flow of information—both within a given establishment and, as appropriate, between establishments (and more specifically between their respective health care services)—about persons who have been identified as potentially at risk.

(iv) prevention of violence

60. Prison health care services can contribute to the prevention of violence against detained persons, through the systematic recording of injuries and, if appropriate, the provision of general information to the relevant authorities. Information could also be forwarded on specific cases, though as a rule such action should only be undertaken with the consent of the prisoners concerned.

61. Any signs of violence observed when a prisoner is medically screened on his admission to the establishment should be fully recorded, together with any relevant statements by the prisoner and the doctor's conclusions. Further, this information should be made available to the prisoner.

The same approach should be followed whenever a prisoner is medically examined following a violent episode within the prison (see also paragraph 53 of the CPT's 2nd General report: CPT/Inf (92) 3) or on his readmission to prison after having been temporarily returned to police custody for the purposes of an investigation.

62. The health care service could compile periodic statistics concerning injuries observed, for the attention of prison management, the Ministry of Justice, etc.

(v) social and family ties

63. The health care service may also help to limit the disruption of social and family ties which usually goes hand in hand with imprisonment. It should support— in association with the relevant social services—measures that foster prisoners' contacts with the outside world, such as properly-equipped visiting areas, family or spouse/partner visits under appropriate conditions, and leaves in family, occupational, educational and sociocultural contexts.

According to the circumstances, a prison doctor may take action in order to obtain the grant or continued payment of social insurance benefits to prisoners and their families.

e. Humanitarian assistance

64. Certain specific categories of particularly vulnerable prisoners can be identified. Prison health care services should pay especial attention to their needs.

(i) mother and child

65. It is a generally accepted principle that children should not be born in prison, and the CPT's experience is that this principle is respected.

66. A mother and child should be allowed to stay together for at least a certain period of time. If the mother and child are together in prison, they should be placed in conditions providing them with the equivalent of a creche and the support of staff specialised in post natal care and nursery nursing.

Long-term arrangements, in particular the transfer of the child to the community involving its separation from its mother, should be decided on in each individual case in the light of pedo-psychiatric and medico-social opinions.

(ii) adolescents

67. Adolescence is a period marked by a certain reorganisation of the personality, requiring a special effort to reduce the risks of long-term social maladjustment.

While in custody, adolescents should be allowed to stay in a fixed place, surrounded by personal objects and in socially favourable groups. The regime applied to them should be based on intensive activity, including socio-educational meetings, sport, education, vocational training, escorted outings and the availability of appropriate optional activities.

(iii) prisoners with personality disorders

68. Among the patients of a prison health care service there is always a certain proportion of unbalanced, marginal individuals who have a history of family traumas, long-standing drug addiction, conflicts with authority or other social misfortunes. They may be violent, suicidal or characterised by unacceptable sexual behaviour, and are for most of the time incapable of controlling or caring for themselves.

69. The needs of these prisoners are not truly medical, but the prison doctor can promote the development of socio-therapeutic programmes for them, in prison units which are organised along community lines and carefully supervised.

Such units can reduce the prisoners' humiliation, self-contempt and hatred, give them a sense of responsibility and prepare them for reintegration. Another direct advantage of programmes of this type is that they involve the active participation and commitment of the prison staff.

(iv) prisoners unsuited for continued detention

70. Typical examples of this kind of prisoner are those who are the subject of a short-term fatal prognosis, who are suffering from a serious disease which cannot be properly treated in prison conditions; who are severely handicapped or of advanced age. The continued detention of such persons in a prison environment can create an intolerable situation. In cases of this type, it lies with the prison

doctor to draw up a report for the responsible authority, with a view to suitable alternative arrangements being made.

f. Professional independence

71. The health-care staff in any prison is potentially a staff at risk. Their duty to care for their patients (sick prisoners) may often enter into conflict with considerations of prison management and security. This can give rise to difficult ethical questions and choices. In order to guarantee their independence in health-care matters, the CPT considers it important that such personnel should be aligned as closely as possible with the mainstream of healthcare provision in the community at large.

72. Whatever the formal position under which a prison doctor carries on his activity, his clinical decisions should be governed only by medical criteria.

The quality and the effectiveness of medical work should be assessed by a qualified medical authority. Likewise, the available resources should be managed by such an authority, not by bodies responsible for security or administration.

73. A prison doctor acts as a patient's personal doctor. Consequently, in the interests of safeguarding the doctor/patient relationship, he should not be asked to certify that a prisoner is fit to undergo punishment. Nor should he carry out any body searches or examinations requested by an authority, except in an emergency when no other doctor can be called in.

74. It should also be noted that a prison doctor's professional freedom is limited by the prison situation itself: he cannot freely choose his patients, as the prisoners have no other medical option at their disposal. His professional duty still exists even if the patient breaks the medical rules or resorts to threats or violence.

g. Professional competence

75. Prison doctors and nurses should possess specialist knowledge enabling them to deal with the particular forms of prison pathology and adapt their treatment methods to the conditions imposed by detention.

In particular, professional attitudes designed to prevent violence—and, where appropriate, control it—should be developed.

76. To ensure the presence of an adequate number of staff, nurses are frequently assisted by medical orderlies, some of whom are recruited from among the prison officers. At the various levels, the necessary experience should be passed on by the qualified staff and periodically updated.

Sometimes prisoners themselves are allowed to act as medical orderlies. No doubt, such an approach can have the advantage of providing a certain number of prisoners with a useful job. Nevertheless, it should be seen as a last resort. Further, prisoners should never be involved in the distribution of medicines.

77. Finally, the CPT would suggest that the specific features of the provision of health care in a prison environment may justify the introduction of a recognised professional speciality, both for doctors and for nurses, on the basis of postgraduate training and regular in-service training.

C. FOREIGN NATIONALS DETAINED UNDER ALIENS LEGISLATION

(EXTRACTED FROM GEN REP 7)

A. Preliminary remarks

24. CPT visiting delegations frequently encounter foreign nationals deprived of their liberty under aliens legislation (hereafter 'immigration detainees'): persons refused entry to the country concerned; persons who have entered the country illegally and have subsequently been identified by the authorities; persons whose authorisation to stay in the country has expired; asylum-seekers whose detention is considered necessary by the authorities; etc.

In the following paragraphs, some of the main issues pursued by the CPT in relation to such persons are described. The CPT hopes in this way to give a clear advance indication to national authorities of its views concerning the treatment of immigration detainees and, more generally, to stimulate discussion in relation to this category of persons deprived of their liberty. The Committee would welcome comments on this section of its General Report.

B. Detention facilities

25. CPT visiting delegations have met immigration detainees in a variety of custodial settings, ranging from holding facilities at points of entry to police stations, prisons and specialised detention centres. As regards more particularly transit and 'international' zones at airports, the precise legal position of persons refused entry to a country and placed in such zones has been the subject of some controversy. On more than one occasion, the CPT has been confronted with the argument that such persons are not 'deprived of their liberty' as they are free to leave the zone at any moment by taking any international flight of their choice.

For its part, the CPT has always maintained that a stay in a transit or 'international' zone can, depending on the circumstances, amount to a deprivation of liberty within the meaning of Article 5 (1)(f) of the European Convention on Human Rights, and that consequently such zones fall within the Committee's mandate. The judgement delivered on 25 June 1996 by the European Court of Human Rights in the case of Amuur against France can be considered as vindicating this view. In that case, which concerned four asylum seekers held in the transit zone at Paris-Orly Airport for 20 days, the Court stated that 'The mere fact that it is possible for asylum seekers to leave voluntarily the country where they wish to take refuge cannot exclude a restriction ("atteinte") on liberty' . . . and held that 'holding the applicants in the transit zone . . . was equivalent in practice, in view of the restrictions suffered, to a deprivation of liberty'.

26. **Point of entry holding facilities** have often been found to be inadequate, in particular for extended stays. More specifically, CPT delegations have on several occasions met persons held for days under makeshift conditions in airport lounges. It is axiomatic that such persons should be provided with suitable means for

sleeping, granted access to their luggage and to suitably-equipped sanitary and washing facilities, and allowed to exercise in the open air on a daily basis. Further, access to food and, if necessary, medical care should be guaranteed.

27. In certain countries, CPT delegations have found immigration detainees held in **police stations** for prolonged periods (for weeks and, in certain cases, months), subject to mediocre material conditions of detention, deprived of any form of activity and on occasion obliged to share cells with criminal suspects. Such a situation is indefensible.

The CPT recognises that, in the very nature of things, immigration detainees may have to spend some time in an ordinary police detention facility. However, conditions in police stations will frequently—if not invariably—be inadequate for prolonged periods *of detention.* Consequently, the period of time spent by immigration detainees in such establishments should be kept to the absolute minimum.

28. On occasion, CPT delegations have found immigration detainees held in **prisons**. Even if the actual conditions of detention for these persons in the establishments concerned are adequate—which has not always been the case—the CPT considers such an approach to be fundamentally flawed. A prison is by definition not a suitable place in which to detain someone who is neither convicted nor suspected of a criminal offence.

Admittedly, in certain exceptional cases, it might be appropriate to hold an immigration detainee in a prison, because of a known potential for violence. Further, an immigration detainee in need of in-patient treatment might have to be accommodated temporarily in a prison health-care facility, in the event of no other secure hospital facility being available. However, such detainees should be held quite separately from prisoners, whether on remand or convicted.

29. In the view of the CPT, in those cases where it is deemed necessary to deprive persons of their liberty for an extended period under aliens legislation, they should be accommodated in **centres specifically designed for that purpose,** offering material conditions and a regime appropriate to their legal situation and staffed by suitably-qualified personnel. The Committee is pleased to note that such an approach is increasingly being followed in Parties to the Convention.

Obviously, such centres should provide accommodation which is adequately-furnished, clean and in a good state of repair, and which offers sufficient living space for the numbers involved. Further, care should be taken in the design and layout of the premises to avoid as far as possible any impression of a carceral environment. As regards regime activities, they should include outdoor exercise, access to a day room and to radio/television and newspapers/magazines, as well as other appropriate means of recreation (eg board games, table tennis). The longer the period for which persons are detained, the more developed should be the activities which are offered to them.

The staff of centres for immigration detainees have a particularly onerous task. Firstly, there will inevitably be communication difficulties caused by language barriers. Secondly, many detained persons will find the fact that they have been deprived of their liberty when they are not suspected of any criminal offence difficult to accept. Thirdly, there is a risk of tension between detainees of different nationalities or ethnic groups. Consequently, the CPT places a premium upon the supervisory staff in such centres being carefully selected and receiving appropriate training. As well as possessing well-developed qualities in the field of interpersonal communication, the staff concerned should be familiarised with the different cultures of the detainees and at least some of them should have relevant language skills. Further, they should be taught to recognise possible symptoms of stress reactions displayed by detained persons (whether post-traumatic or induced by sociocultural changes) and to take appropriate action.

C. Safeguards during detention

30. Immigration detainees should—in the same way as other categories of persons deprived of their liberty—be entitled, as from the outset of their detention, to inform a person of their choice of their situation and to have access to a lawyer and a doctor. Further, they should be expressly informed, without delay and in a language they understand, of all their rights and of the procedure applicable to them.

The CPT has observed that these requirements are met in some countries, but not in others. In particular, visiting delegations have on many occasions met immigration detainees who manifestly had not been fully informed in a language they understood of their legal position. In order to overcome such difficulties, immigration detainees should be systematically provided with a document explaining the procedure applicable to them and setting out their rights. This document should be available in the languages most commonly spoken by those concerned and, if necessary, recourse should be had to the services of an interpreter.

31. The right of access to a lawyer should apply throughout the detention period and include both the right to speak with the lawyer in private and to have him present during interviews with the authorities concerned.

All detention facilities for immigration detainees should provide access to medical care. Particular attention should be paid to the physical and psychological state of asylum seekers, some of whom may have been tortured or otherwise ill-treated in the countries from which they have come. The right of access to a doctor should include the right—if a detainee so wishes—to be examined by a doctor of his choice; however, the detainee might be expected to cover the cost of such a second examination.

More generally, immigration detainees should be entitled to maintain contact with the outside world during their detention, and in particular to have access to a telephone and to receive visits from relatives and representatives of relevant organisations.

D. Risk of ill-treatment after expulsion

32. The prohibition of torture and inhuman or degrading treatment or punishment englobes the obligation not to send a person to a country where there are substantial grounds for believing that he would run a real risk of being subjected to torture or ill-treatment. Whether Parties to the Convention are fulfilling this

obligation is obviously a matter of considerable interest to the CPT. What is the precise role that the Committee should seek to play in relation to that question? 33. Any communications addressed to the CPT in Strasbourg by persons alleging that they are to be sent to a country where they run a risk of being subjected to torture or ill-treatment are immediately brought to the attention of the European Commission of Human Rights. The Commission is better placed than the CPT to examine such allegations and, if appropriate, take preventive action.

If an immigration detainee (or any other person deprived of his liberty) interviewed in the course of a visit alleges that he is to be sent to a country where he runs a risk of being subjected to torture or ill-treatment, the CPT's visiting delegation will verify that this assertion has been brought to the attention of the relevant national authorities and is being given due consideration. Depending on the circumstances, the delegation might request to be kept informed of the detainee's position and/or inform the detainee of the possibility of raising the issue with the European Commission of Human Rights (and, in the latter case, verify that he is in a position to submit a petition to the Commission). 34. However, in view of the CPT's essentially preventive function, the Committee is inclined to focus its attention on the question of whether the decision-making process as a whole offers suitable guarantees against persons being sent to countries where they run a risk of torture or ill-treatment. In this connection, the CPT will wish to explore whether the applicable procedure offers the persons concerned a real opportunity to present their cases, and whether officials entrusted with handling such cases have been provided with appropriate training and have access to objective and independent information about the human rights situation in other countries. Further, in view of the potential gravity of the interests at stake, the Committee considers that a decision involving the removal of a person from a State's territory should be appealable before another body of an independent nature prior to its implementation.

E. Means of coercion in the context of expulsion procedures

35. Finally, the CPT must point out that it has received disturbing reports from several countries about the means of coercion employed in the course of expelling immigration detainees. Those reports have contained in particular allegations of beating, binding and gagging, and the administration of tranquillizers against the will of the persons concerned.

36. The CPT recognises that it will often be a difficult task to enforce an expulsion order in respect of a foreign national who is determined to stay on a State's territory. Law enforcement officials may on occasion have to use force in order to effect such a removal. However, the force used should be no more than is reasonably necessary. It would, in particular, be entirely unacceptable for persons subject to an expulsion order to be physically assaulted as a form of persuasion to board a means of transport or as punishment for not having done so. Further, Committee must emphasise that to gag a person is a highly dangerous measure.

The CPT also wishes to stress that any provision of medication to persons subject to expulsion order must only be done on the basis of a medical decision and in accordance with medical ethics.

Appendix 8
CPT Document Citation

Country	Visit	Nature of Document	CPT Ref	Our Citation
Austria	20.05.90–27.05.90	Report	CPT/Inf (91) 10	Austria 1
		Comments	CPT/Inf (91) 11	Austria 1 R 1
	26.09.94–07.10.94	Report	CPT/Inf (96) 28	Austria 2
		Comments	CPT/Inf (96) 29	Austria 2 R 1
Belgium	14.11.93–23.11.93	Report	CPT/Inf (94) 15	Belgium 1
		Interim Report	CPT/Inf (95) 6	Belgium 1 R 1
		Follow-up Report	CPT/Inf (96) 7	Belgium 1 R 2
Bulgaria	26.03.95–07.04.95	Report	CPT/Inf (97) 1	Bulgaria 1
		Interim Report	CPT/Inf (97) 1	Bulgaria 1 R 1
		Follow-up Report	CPT/Inf (97) 1	Bulgaria 1 R 2
Cyprus	02.11.92–09.11.92	Report	CPT/Inf (97) 5	Cyprus 1
	12.15.96–221.05.96	Report	CPT/Inf (97) 5	Cyprus 2
Denmark	02.12.90–08.12.90	Report	CPT/Inf (91) 12	Denmark 1
		Interim Report	CPT/Inf (96) 14	Denmark 1 R 1
		Follow-up Report	CPT/Inf (96) 14	Denmark 1 R 2
	29.09.96–09.10.96	Report	CPT/Inf (97) 4	Denmark 2
Finland	10.05.92–20.05.92	Report	CPT/Inf (93) 8	Finland 1
		Interim Report	CPT/Inf (93) 16	Finland 1 R 1
		Follow-up Report	CPT/Inf (94) 3	Finland 1 R 2
France	27.10.91–08.11.91	Report	CPT/Inf (93) 2	France 1
		Interim Report	CPT/Inf (93) 2	France 1 R 1
		Follow-up Report	CPT/Inf (94) 1	France 1 R 2

Country	Visit	Nature of Document	CPT Ref	Our Citation
France (Martinique)	03.07.94– 07.07.94	Report	CPT/Inf (96) 24	France (Martinque) 1
		Interim Report	CPT/Inf (96) 24	France (Martinique) 1 R 1
		Follow-up Report	CPT/Inf (96) 24	France (Martinique) 1 R 2
France	20.07.94– 22.07.94	Report	CPT/Inf (96) 2	France 2
		Response	CPT/Inf (96) 2	France 2 R
Germany	08.12.91– 26.04.96	Report	CPT/Inf (93) 13	Germany 1
		Interim Report	CPT/Inf (93) 14	Germany 1 R 1
	14.04.96– 26.04.96	Report	CPT/Inf (97) 9	Germany 2
		Interim Report	CPT/Inf (97) 9	Germany 2 R 1
Greece	14.03.93– 26.03.93	Report	CPT/Inf (94) 20	Greece 1
		Interim Report	CPT/Inf (94) 21	Greece 1 R 1
		Follow-up Report	CPT/Inf (96) 8	Greece 1 R 2
Hungary	01.11.94– 14.11.94	Report	CPT/Inf (96) 5	Hungary 1
		Interim Report	CPT/Inf (96) 15	Hungary 1 R 1
Iceland	06.07.93– 12.07.93	Report	CPT/Inf (94) 8	Iceland 1
		Interim Report	CPT/Inf (94) 16	Iceland 1 R 1
		Follow-up Report	CPT/Inf (96) 6	Iceland 1 R 2
Ireland	26.09.93– 05.10.93	Report	CPT/Inf (95) 14	Ireland 1
		Interim Report	CPT/Inf (95) 15	Ireland 1 R 1
		Follow-up Report	CPT/Inf (96) 23	Ireland 1 R 2
Italy	15.03.92– 06.11.95	Report	CPT/Inf (95) 1	Italy 1
		Interim Report	CPT/Inf (95) 2	Italy 1 R 1
Liechtenstein	14.04.93– 16.04.93	Report	CPT/Inf (95) 7	Liechtenstein 1
		Interim Report	CPT/Inf (95) 8	Liechtenstein 1 R 1
Luxembourg	20.04.93– 25.01.93	Report	CPT/Inf (93) 19	Luxembourg 1
		Interim Report	CPT/Inf (94) 5	Luxembourg 1 R 1

Country	Visit	Nature of Document	CPT Ref	Our Citation
Malta	01.07.90–09.07.90	Report	CPT/Inf (92) 5	Malta 1
	16.07.95–21.07.95	Report	CPT/Inf (96) 25	Malta 2
		Interim Report	CPT/Inf (96) 26	Malta 2 R 1
		Follow-up Report	CPT/Inf (97) 8	Malta 2 R 2
Netherlands	30.08.92–08.09.92	Report	CPT/Inf (93) 15	Netherlands 1
		Interim Report	CPT/Inf (93) 20	Netherlands 1 R 1
Netherlands Antilles	26.06.94–30.06.94	Report	CPT/Inf (96) 1	Netherlands Antilles 1
Netherlands Aruba	30.06.94–02.07.94	Report	CPT/Inf (96) 27	Netherlands Aruba 1
		Interim Report	CPT/Inf (96) 27	Netherlands Aruba 1 R 1
		Follow-up Report	CPT/Inf (96) 27	Netherlands Aruba 1 R 2
Norway	27.06.93–06.07.93	Report	CPT/Inf (94) 11	Norway 1
		Interim Report	CPT/Inf (94) 12	Norway 1 R 1
		Follow-up Report	CPT/Inf (96) 16	Norway 1 R 2
	17.03.97–21.03.96	Report	CPT/Inf (97) 11	Norway 1
Portugal	19.01.92–27.01.92	Report	CPT/Inf (94) 9	Portugal 1
		Interim Report	CPT/Inf (9)	Portugal 1 R 1
	14.05.95–26.05.95	Report	CPT/Inf (96) 31	Portugal 2
		Interim Report	CPT.Inf (96) 32	Portugal 2 R 1
Slovakia	25.03.95–07.07.95	Report	CPT/Inf (97) 2	Slovakia 1
		Interim Report	CPT/Inf (97) 3	Slovakia 1 R 1
		Follow-up Report	CPT/Inf (97) 3	Slovakia 1 R 2
Slovenia	19.02.95–28.02.95	Report	CPT/Inf (96) 18	Slovenia 1
		Interim Report	CPT/Inf (96) 19	Slovenia 1 R 1
San Marino	25.03.92–27.03.92	Report	CPT/Inf (94) 13	San Marino 1
Spain	01.04.91–12.04.91	Report	CPT/Inf (96) 9	Spain 1
	10.04.94–22.04.94	Report	CPT/Inf (96) 9	Spain 2
		Interim Report	CPT/Inf (96) 10	Spain 2 R 1
	10.06.94–14.06.94	Report	CPT/Inf (96) 9	Spain 3
		Response	CPT/Inf (96) 10	Spain 3 R

Country	Visit	Nature of Document	CPT Ref	Our Citation
Sweden	05.05.91–14.05.91	Report	CPT/Inf (92) 4	Sweden 1
		Interim Report	CPT/Inf (92) 6	Sweden 1 R 1
		Follow-up	CPT/Inf (93) 7	Sweden 1 R 2
	23.08.94–26.08.94	Report	CPT/Inf (95) 5	Sweden 2
		Response	CPT/Inf (95) 6	Sweden 2 R
Switzerland	21.07.91–29.07.91	Report	CPT/Inf (93) 3	Switzerland 1
		Interim Report	CPT/Inf (93) 4	Switzerland 1 R 1
		Follow-up Report	CPT/Inf (94) 7	Switzerland 1 R 2
	11.01.96–23.02.96	Report	CPT/Inf (97) 7	Switzerland 2
		Follow-up Report	CPT/Inf (97) 7	Switzerland 2 R 1
United Kingdom	29.07.90–10.08.90	Report	CPT/Inf (91) 15	UK 1
		Interim Report	CPT/Inf (91) 16	UK 1 R 1
		Follow-up Report	CPT/Inf (93) 9	UK 1 R 2
	20.07.93–29.07.93	Report	CPT/Inf (94) 17	UK 2 R 1
	15.15.94–31.31.94	Report	CPT/Inf (96) 11	UK 3
		Response	CPT/Inf (96) 12	UK 3 R

B. CPT GENERAL REPORTS

General Report No	Calendar Year	CPT Ref	Our Citation
1	1990	CPT/Inf (91) 3	Gen Rep 1
2	1991	CPT/Inf (92) 3	Gen Rep 2
3	1992	CPT/Inf (93) 12	Gen Rep 3
4	1993	CPT/Inf (94) 10	Gen Rep 4
5	1994	CPT/Inf (95) 10	Gen Rep 5
6	1995	CPT/Inf (96) 21	Gen Rep 6
7	1996	CPT/Inf (97) 10	Gen Rep 7

Bibliography

Addo, M and Grief, N (1995) 'Is There a Policy Behind the Decisions and Judgments Relating to Article 3 of the ECHR?', 20 ELRev 178.

Alleg, H (1958) *La Question* (Paris: Editions de Minuit).

Alston, P (1992a) *The United Nations and Human Rights* (Oxford: Clarendon Press).

—— (1992b) 'The Commission on Human Rights' in Alston (1992a).

Amnesty International (1973) *Report on Torture* (London: Amnesty International, International Secretariat).

—— (1977), *Torture in Greece: The First Torturers' Trial* (London: Amnesty International, International Secretariat).

—— (1980) *Prison Conditions of Persons Suspected or Convicted of Politically Motivated Crimes in the Federal Republic of Germany: Isolation and Solitary Confinement.* EUR 23/01/80 (London: Amnesty International, International Secretariat).

—— (1984), 'Israel and the Occupied Territories' in *Torture in the Eighties* (London: Amnesty International, International Secretariat).

—— (1989) *Turkey: Torture and Deaths in Custody* (London: Amnesty International, International Secretariat).

—— (1990) *Austria: Torture and Ill-Treatment* (London: Amnesty International, International Secretariat).

—— (1991) *Statute of Amnesty International—as amended by the 20th International Council, Yokohama, Japan* (London: Amnesty International, International Secretariat).

—— (1994a) *'Disappearances' and Political Killings: Human Rights Crisis of the 1990s— A Manual for Action* (London: Amnesty International, International Secretariat).

—— (1994b) *Denmark: Police Ill-Treatment* (London: Amnesty International, International Secretariat).

—— (1995a) *Report 1995* (London: Amnesty International, International Secretariat).

—— (1995b) *Death by shaking: the case of 'Abd al-Samad Harizat* (London: Amnesty International, International Secretariat).

—— (1995c) *Denmark: Summary of Concerns*, EUR 18/01/95 (London: Amnesty International, International Secretariat).

—— (1996a) *Report 1996* (London: Amnesty International, International Secretariat).

—— (1996b) *Palestinian Authority: Prolonged Political Detention, Torture and Unfair Trials* (London: Amnesty International, International Secretariat).

—— (1996c) *Under constant medical supervision: torture, ill-treatment and the health professions in Israel and the Occupied Territories* (London: Amnesty International, International Secretariat).

—— (1996d) *Turkey: No Security Without Human Rights* (London: Amnesty International, International Secretariat).

—— (1997) *Amnesty International Report 1997* (London: Amnesty International, International Secretariat).

Anderson, DM (1992) 'Policing and Communal Conflict: the Cyprus Emergency, 1954–60' in Anderson and Killingray.

—— and Killingray, D (eds) (1992) *Policing and Decolonisation: Politics, Nationalism and the Police, 1917–65* (Manchester: Manchester University Press).

Anon (1989) 'In memoriam Jean-Jacques Gautier', 10 HRLJ 132.

Ashworth, A (1994) *The Criminal Process* (Oxford: Clarendon Press).

Association for the Prevention of Torture (1993a) *Rapport Sur Les Conditions De Detention En Belgique* (Geneva: APT).

—— (1993b) *Report on Detention Conditions in the Republic of Ireland* (Geneva: APT).

—— (1995) *The Implementation of the European Convention for the Prevention of Torture and Inhuman or Degrading Treatment or Punishment (ECPT): Assessment and Perspectives after Five Years of Activities of the European Committee for the Prevention of Torture and Inhuman or Degrading Treatment or Punishment—Acts of the Seminar of 5 to 7 December 1994, Strasbourg* (Geneva: APT).

—— (1996) *Working Group on the Draft Optional Protocol to the Convention against Torture and Other Cruel, Inhuman or Degrading Treatment or Punishment, Analytical Report of the Association for the Prevention of Torture* (Geneva: APT).

—— (1997) *20 Ans Consacrés à la réalisation d'une idée* (Geneva: APT).

Association for the Prevention of Torture/British Institute of Human Rights (forthcoming) *The European Convention for the Prevention of Torture: Issues and Mechanisms for Preventing Torture and Ill-Treatment*.

B'Tselem (1991) *The Interrogation of Palestinians During the Intifada: Ill-Treatment, 'Moderate Physical Pressure' or Torture?* (Jerusalem: B'Tselem).

—— (1992) *The Interrogation of Palestinians during the Intifada: Follow-up to March 1991 'Tselem Report* (Jerusalem: B'Tsalem).

Bank, R (1996) *Die internationale Bekämpfung von Folter und unmenschlicher Behandlung auf den Ebenen der Vereinten Nationen und des Europarates—Eine vergleichende Analyse von Implementation und Effektivität der neuen Kontrollmechanismen*, Doctoral Thesis (Max Planck Institute for Foreign and Inernational Penal Law, Freiburg).

—— (1997) 'Preventive Measures Against Torture: An Analysis of standards set by the CPT, CAT, HRC and Special Rapporteur' in APT.

—— (1998) 'International Efforts to Combat Torture and Inhuman Treatment: Have the New Mechanisms Improved Protection?', 9 EJIL (forthcoming).

Bellamy, R (ed) (1995) *Beccaria: On Crimes and Punishments and Other Writings* (Cambridge: Cambridge University Press).

Bennet Report (1979) *Report of The Committee of Inquiry into Police Interrogation Procedures In Northern Ireland* (Chairman, Bennet), Cmnd 749 (London: HMSO).

Bernhart, R (1995) 'Reform of the Control Machinery under the Eureopan Convention on Human Rights: Protocol No 11', 89 AJIL 145.

Bittner, E (1974) 'Florence Nightingale in Pursuit of Willie Sutton: A Theory of the Police' in Jacob, H (ed) *The Potential for Reform of Criminal Justice* (Beverly Hills, Calif: Sage).

duBois, P (1991) *Torture and Truth* (London: Routledge).

Bottoms, AE (1977) 'Reflections on the Renaissance of Dangerousness', 16, 2 *Howard Journal* 70.

Bottoms, AE (1987) 'Limiting Prison Use: Experience in England and Wales', 26, 3 *Howard Journal* 177.

Boyle, K (1995) 'Interview with Special Rapporteur on Torture Nigel Rodley', 13 *Neth Quart. HR* 435.

Bossuyt, MJ (1987) *Guide to the 'Travaux Préparatoires' of the International Covenant on Civil and Political Rights* (Dordrecht: Martinus Nijhoff).

British Medical Association (1992) *Medicine Betrayed: The Participation of Doctors in Human Rights Abuses* (London: BMA/Zed Books).

Burgers, JH and Danelius, H (1988) *The UN Convention Against Torture: A Handbook to the Convention Against Torture and Other Cruel, Inhuman or Degrading Treatment or Punishment* (Dordrecht: Martinus Nijhoff).

Cameron, I (1995) 'Protocol 11 to the ECHR: The Court of Human Rights as a Constitutional Court', 15 *YEL* 219.

Cameron Report (1969) *Disturbances in Northern Ireland: report of the commission: report of the commission appointed by the Governor of Northern Ireland* (Chairman, Lord Cameron), CMD 532 (Belfast: HMSO).

Casale, S (1995) 'Conclusions and Suggestions of the Seminar' in APT.

Cassese, A (1989) 'A New Approach to Human Rights: The European Convention for the Prevention of Torture', 83 *AJIL* 130 (French translation in (1989) *Revue génerale de droit international public*).

—— (ed) (1991) *The International Fight Against Torture* (Baden-Baden: Nomos).

—— (1993) 'Prohibition of Torture and Inhuamn or Degrading Treatment or Punishment' in MacDonald, R St J, Matscher, F and Petzold, H, *The European System for the Protection of Human Rights* (Dordrecht: Martinus Nijhoff).

—— (1994) 'The European Committee for the Prevention of Torture and Inhuman or Degrading Treatment or Punishment Comes of Age' in *Liber Amicorum HG Schermers*.

—— (1996) *Inhuman States: Imprisonment, Detention and Torture in Europe Today* (Cambridge: Polity Press), originally published in Italian (1994) *Umano– Disumano: Commissariati en prigioni nell'Europa di oggi* (Roma Bari: Laterza).

Compton Report (1971) *Report of the enquiry into allegations against the security forces of physical brutality in Northern Ireland arising out of events on the 9th August, 1971* (Chairman, Sir Edward Compton), Cmnd 4823 (London: HMSO).

Cook, H (1991) 'The Role of Amnesty International in the Fight Against Torture' in Cassese (ed).

—— (1992) 'Preventive Detention—International Standards and the Protection of the Individual' in Frankowski, SJ and Shelton, D (1992) *Preventive Detention: a comparative and international law perspective* (Dordrecht: Martinus Nijhoff).

Council of Europe (1977–84) *Collected Edition of the travaux préparatoires of the European Convention on Human Right*, 8 vols (Strasbourg: Council of Europe).

—— (1993) *European Committee for the Prevention of Torture and Inhuman or Degrading Teatment or Punishment (CPT): Some issues concerning the interpretation of the European Convention for the Prevention of Torture and Inhuman or Degrading Treatment or Punishment* CPT/Inf (93) 10 (Strasbourg: Council of Europe).

—— (1997) *SPACE: Council of Europe Annual Penal Statistics—1995 Survey* (Strasbourg: Council of Europe).

—— Parliamentary Assembly, Committee on Legal Affairs and Human Rights (1997) *Report on strengthening the machinery of the European Convention for the Prevention of Torture and Inhuman or Degrading Treament or Punishment,* Par Ass Doc 7784, 26 March.

Chaffee, Z, Pollak, WH and Stern, CS (1931) *The Third Degree: Report on Lawlessness in Law Enforcement* (National Commission on Law Observance and Enforcement, Vol IV, No 11, Washington).

Chomsky, N and Herman, ES (1979) *The Political Economy of Human Rights Vol I* (Montreal: The Washington Connection).

Clausewitz, C von (1982) *On War* (Harmondsworth: Penguin).

Cohen, S (1993) 'Human Rights and Crimes of the State: The Culture of Denial', 26 *Australian and New Zealand Journal of Criminology* 87.

—— (1995) 'State Crimes of Previous Regimes: Knowledge, Accountability and the Policing of the Past', 20 *Law and Social Inquiry* 7.

Comissió de Porteveus dels presos i encausats independentistes (1995) *Denúncies de Tortures Acció Popular i Particlar (annex 1 'Dossier Tortures'* (Barcelona).

Conquest, R (1990) *The Great Terror: A Reassessment* (London: Hutchinson).

Crawford, J (1994) 'The ILC Adopts a Draft Statute for an International Criminal Court', 88 AJIL 404.

Decaux, E (1988) 'La Convention européene pour la prévention de la torture et peines ou traitements inhumains ou dégradants', 34 *Annuaure francais de droit international* 618.

Dershowitz, A (1989) 'Is it Necessary to apply "physical pressure" to terrorists— and to lie about it?', 24 IsLR, 196–7.

Dinstein, Y (1981) 'The rights to Life, Physical Integrity, and Liberty' in Henkin, L (ed) *The International Bill of Rights—The Covenant on Civil and Political Rights* (New York, Columbia University Press).

Diplock Report (1972) *Report of the Commission to consider legal procedures to deal with terrorist activities in Northern Ireland* (Chairman, Lord Diplock), Cmnd 5185 (London: HMSO).

Downes, D and Morgan, R (1974) 'Dumping the 'Hostages to Fortune'? The Politics of Law and Order in Post-War Britain', in Maguire, M, Morgan, R and Reiner, R (eds) *The Oxford Handbook of Criminology* (Oxford: Clarendon Press).

Drzemczewski, A and Meyer-Ladevig, J (1994) 'Principal Characteristics of the new ECHR Control Mechanism', 15 HRLJ 81.

Duffy, P (1983) 'Article 3 of the ECHR', 32 ICLQ 316.

Euskadiko Amnistiaren Aldeko Atzordeak (1995) *Euskal Herrian, Tortura: Monografico 1994* (Hernani, Gipuzkoa, Spain: Gestoras Pro-Amnistia de Euskadi).

Evans, MD (1997) 'The Impact of the CPT: Lessons From Southern Europe', 1(3) *MJHR* 227.

—— (forthcoming) 'The CPT: Future Challenges' in Association for the Prevention of Torture/British Institute of Human Rights.

—— and Morgan, R (1992), 'The European Convention for the Prevention of Torture: Operational Practice', 41 ICLQ 590.

—— and Morgan, R (1994) 'The European Torture Committee: Membership Issues', 5 EJIL 249.

Evans, MD and Morgan, R (1997a) 'The Origins and Drafting of the ECPT: A Salutory Lesson? in APT.

—— and Morgan, R (1997b) 'The European Convention for the Prevention of Torture: 1992–1997', 46 ICLQ 633.

Facez, J-C (1988) *Une Mission Impossible? Le CICR, les déportations et les camps de concentration nazis* (Lausannes: Editions Payot).

Fawcett, JES (1987) *The Application of the European Convention on Human Rights* (Oxford: Clarendon Press).

Feest, J and Wolters, C (1994) *Verhutung von Folter und unmenschlicher Berhandlung oder Strafe—Ergebnisse einer Bestandsaufnahme und zugleich Enschätzung des Berichtes des CPT über seinen ersten Besuch in Deutschland und der dazu vorliegenden Stellungnahme der Bundesregierung* (Geneva: Asociation for the Prevention of Torture).

Fitzjames Stephen, Sir James (1883) *A History of the Criminal Law in England* (London: MacMillan).

Foucault, M (1977) *Discipline and Punish: The Birth of the Prison* (London: Allen Lane).

Foul, D and Murray, R (1978) *The Castlereagh File: Allegations of RUC Brutality 1976–1977* (No publisher or place of publication stated).

Gasser, H-P (1988) 'A Measure of Humanity in Internal Disturbances and Tensions: Proposals for a Code of Conduct', *International Review of the Red Cross*, Jan–Feb.

Gautier, J-J (1977) 'Le Proposition de Jean-Jacques Gautier' in *Contre La Torture: Une Arme Nouvelle* (Geneva: La Vie Protestante).

Gautier, J-J (1979) 'The Case for an Effective and Realistic Procedure' in ICJ/SCAT.

Gerson, LD (1976) *The Secret Police in Lenin's Russia* (Philadelphia: Temple University Press).

Gudjonsson, G (1996) 'Custodial Confinement, Interrogation and Coerced Confessions' in Forrest, D (ed) *A Glimpse of Hell: Reports on Torture Worldwide* (London: Amnesty International UK).

Hampson, F (1989) 'The United Kingdom and the European Court of Human Rights', 9 YEL 121.

Harris, DJ, O'Boyle, M and Warbrick, C (1995), *Law of the European Convention on Human Rights* (London: Butterworths).

Her Majesty's Chief Inspector of Prisons (1996) *Report: April 1995–March 1996* (London: HMSO).

—— (1997a) *Women in Prison* (London: Home Office).

—— (1997b) *Young Prisoners* (London: Home Office).

Heider, A and van Geuns, H (1976) *Professional Codes of Ethics* (London: Amnesty International, International Secretariat).

Higgins, R (1994), *Problems and Process: International Law and How We Use It* (Oxford: Clarendon Press).

Home Office (1991) *Custody, Care and Justice: The Way Ahead for the Prison Service in England and Wales*, Cm 1647 (London: HMSO).

Hopkins, EJ (1931) *Our Lawless Police: A Study of the Unlawful Enforcement of the Law* (New York).

Hood, R (1996) *The Death Penalty: A World-wide Perspective* (Oxford: Clarendon Press, rev edn).

Horne, A (1987) *A Savage War of Peace: Algeria 1954–62* (London: MacMillan, 2nd edn).

Huntington, SP (1968) *Political Order in Changing Societies* (New Haven: Yale University Press).

Human Rights Watch (1988) *Prison Conditions in Poland, June 1988* (New York: Human Rights Watch).

—— (1989) *Prison Conditions in Turkey, August 1989* (New York: Human Rights Watch).

—— (1991) *Prison Conditions in Poland, January 1991* (New York: Human Rights Watch).

—— (1992a) *Prison Conditions in the United Kingdom, June 1992* (New York: Human Rights Watch).

—— (1992b) *Prison Conditions in Spain, April 1992* (New York: Human Rights Watch).

—— (1992c) *Nothing Unusual: the Torture of Children in Turkey* (New York: Human Rights Watch).

—— (1993a) *16 Deaths in Detention in 1992* (New York: Human Rights Watch).

—— (1993b) *The Kurds of Turkey: Killings, Disappearances and Torture* (New York: Human Rights Watch).

—— (1994) *Torture and Ill-Treatment: Israel's Interrogation of Palestinians from the Occupied Territories* (New York: Human Rights Watch).

—— (1995a) *'Germany for Germans': Xenophobia and Racist Violence in Germany* (New York: Human Rights Watch).

—— (1995b) *Crime or Simply Punishment?: Racist Attacks by Moscow Law Enforcement* (New York: Human Rights Watch).

—— (1996) *Rights Denied: The Roma of Hungary* (New York: Human Rights Watch).

—— (1997a) *A Legacy of Abuse* (New York: Human Rights Watch).

—— (1997b) *Torture and Mistreatment in Pre-Trial Detention by Anti-Terror Police* (New York: Human Rights Watch).

Ignatieff, M (1978) *A Just Measure of Pain: the Penitentiary in the Industrial Revolution 1750–1850* (London: MacMillan).

International Committee of the Red Cross (1988) 'ICRC Protection and Assistance Activities in Situations not Covered by International Humanitarian Law', *International Review of the Red Cross*, Jan–Feb, 9.

—— (1992) *Visits by the International Committee of the Red Cross to Persons Deprived of their Freedom* (Geneva: ICRC).

International Commission of Jurists/Swiss Committee Against Torture (1979) *Torture: How to Make the International Convention Effective* (Geneva: International Commission of Jurists and Swiss Committee against Torture).

—— (1983) *The Draft European Convention Against Torture* (Geneva: International Commission of Jurists and Swiss Committee against Torture).

Jacobs, FG and White, RAC (1996) *The European Convention on Human Rights* (Oxford: Clarendon Press, 2nd edn).

Jenkinson, D (1993) *Torture? In Europe? A study of the European Convention for the Prevention of Torture and Inhuman or Degrading Treatment or Punishment* (Brussels: Quaker Council for Europen Affairs).

Kellberg, L (1991) 'The Case-Law of the European Commission of Human Rights' in Cassese (ed).

Kelly, M (1996) 'Preventing Ill-treatment: the Work of the European Committee for the Prevention of Torture', EHRLR, Issue 3, 287.

King, RD and Elliott, K (1977) *Albany: birth of a prison—end of an era* (London: Routledge and Kegan Paul).

King, R and Morgan, R (1980) *The Future of the Prison System* (Farnborough: Gower).

Koojimans, PH (1991) 'The Role and Action of the UN Special Rapportuer on Torture' in Cassese (1991).

Kremnitzer, M (1989) 'The Landau Commission Report: Was the Security Service Subordinated to the Law, or the Law to the 'Needs' of the Security Service?', 24 IsLR 237.

Landau Commission (1987) *Report of the Commission of Inquiry into the Methods of Investigation of the General Security Service Regarding Hostile Terrorist Activity, Part One* (Jerusalem).

Langbein, JH (1977) *Torture and the Law of Proof* (Chicago: Chicago University Press).

Lavine, EH (1933) *The Third Degree: American Police Methods* (New York).

Lea, HC (1866) *Superstition and Force* (Philadelphia: University of Pennsylvania Press).

Leo, RA (1992) 'From coercion to deception: the changing nature of police interrogation in America', in *Crime, Law and Social Change.*

MacDonald, R St John (1992) 'The European Convention for the Prevention of Torture and Inhuman or Degrading Treatment or Punishment' in Bello, E and Ajibola, B (eds) *Essays in Honour of Judge Taslim Olawale Elias* (Dordrecht: Martinus Nijhoff).

MacDowell, DM (1978) *The Law in Classical Athens* (London: Thames and Hudson).

Maguire, M, Vagg, J and Morgan, R (1985) *Accountability and Prisons: Opening Up a Closed World* (London: Tavistock).

Maran, R (1989) *Torture: the Role of Ideology in the French Algerian War* (New York: Praeger).

Marks, S (1997) 'Torture and the Jurisdiction al Immunity of Foreign States', 56 CLJ 8.

Massu, J (1971) *La Vrai Bataille d'Alger* (Paris).

Mavrogordatos, G Th (1983) 'The Emerging Party System' in Clogg, R (ed).

McConville, M, Leng, R and Sanders, A (1991) *The Case for the Prosecution: Police, Suspects and the Construction of Criminality* (London: Routledge).

McConville, S (1981) *A History of English Prison Administration, Vol 1 1750–1877* (London: Routledge).

McGoldrick, D (1991) *The Human Rights Committee* (Oxford: Clarendon Press).

Mellor, A (1966) *La Torture* (Paris).

Melossi, D and Pavarini, M (1981) *The Prison and the Factory* (Basingstoke: Macmillan).

Meron, T (1989) *Human Rights and Humanitarian Norms as Customary International Law* (Oxford: Clarendon Press).

Merrills, JG (1993) *The Development of International Law by the European Court of Human Rights* (Manchester: Manchester University Press, 2nd edn).

Millet, K (1994) *The Politics of Cruelty: an essay on the literature of political imprison-ment* (London: Viking).

Misra, S (1986) *Police Brutality: An Analysis of Police Behaviour* (New Delhi).

Morgan, R (1985) 'Her Majesty's Inspectorate of Prisons' in Maguire, M, Vagg, J and Morgan, R (eds) *Accountability and Prisons: Opening Up a Closed World* (London: Tavistock).

—— (1991) 'Woolf: in retrospect and prospect', 54 MLR 113.

—— (1993) 'Remand Prisoners: An awkward Anomaly' in Jenkins, M and Player, E (eds) *Prisons After Woolf* (London: Routledge).

—— (1996a) 'Tortures et Traitements Degradants ou Inhumains en Europe: Quelques Donnees, Quelques Questions' in Faugeron, C, Chauvenet and Combessie, P (eds) *Approches de la Prison* (Paris: DeBoeck Université, et Les Presses de L'Université de Montréal et d'Ottawa).

—— (1996b) 'The process is the rule and the punishment is the process', 59 MLR 306.

—— (1997) 'Imprisonment: Current Concerns and a Brief History since 1945' in Maguire, M, Morgan, R and Reiner, R (eds) *The Oxford Handbook of Criminology* (Oxford: Clarendon Press, 2nd edn).

—— (forthcoming) 'The CPT and the Academy' in APT/BIHR.

—— and Bronstein, A (1985) 'Prisoners and the courts: the US experience' in Maguire, M, Vagg, J and Morgan, R (eds) *Accountability and Prisons: Opening Up a Closed World* (London: Tavistock), 264.

—— and Evans, MD (1994) 'Inspecting Prisons: the View from Strasbourg', *BJC*, Spring, 145 (also published in King, R and Maguire, M (eds) *Prisons in Context* (Oxford: Clarendon Press)).

—— (1996) 'A European Committee for the Pevention of Torture' in *The Challenges of a Greater Europe (Les Enjeux De La Grande Europe)* (Strasbourg: Council of Europe).

—— and Smith, D (1989) *Coming To Terms With Policing* (Basingstoke: Macmillan).

Morris, N and Rothman, DJ (eds) (1995) *The Oxford History of the Prison: The Practice of Punishment in Western Society* (New York: Oxford University Press).

Mottet, C (1995) 'Preparatory Document', in APT, 187–92.

Murdoch, J (1994) 'The Work of the Council of Europe's Torture Committee', 3 EJIL 220.

—— (1995) 'Functioning of the CPT and Standard Setting' in APT.

Nicolay, C (1995) 'Five Years of Activities of the CPT: And Now?' in APT.

Nikken, P (1991) 'L'action contre la torture dans le système interaméricain des droits de l'homme' in Cassese.

Nowak, M (1993) *UN Covenant on Civil and Political Rights: CCPR Commentary* (Kehl am Rhein: NP Engel).

Nowak, M (1995) 'The Activities of the UN Human Rights Committee from 1 August 1992 through 31 July 1995', 16 HRLJ 377.

Observatoire international des prisons (1995) *Rapport 1995: les conditions de déten-tion des personnes incarcérées* (Lyon: Observatoire international des prisons).

Opsahl, T (1992) 'The Human Rights Committee' in Alston (1992a).

Oraá, J (1992) *Human Rights in States of Emergency in International Law* (Oxford: Clarendon Press).

Pakenham, T (1991) *The Scramble for Africa* (London: Weidenfeld and Nicolson).

Parker Report (1972) *Report of the Committee of Privy Counsellors appointed to consider authorised procedures for the interrogation of persons suspected of terrorism* (Chairman, Lord Parker), Cmnd 4981 (London: HMSO).

Pease, K (1994) 'Cross-National Imprisonment Rates: Limitations of Method and Possible Conclusions' in King, R and Maguire, M (eds) *Prisons in Context* (Oxford: Clarendon Press).

Peters, E (1995) 'Prison before the Prison' in Morris and Rothman.

—— (1996) *Torture* (Pennsylvania: University of Pennnsylvania, 2nd edn).

Phillips, B (1994) 'The Case for Corporal Punishment in the United Kingdom. Beaten into submission in Europe?', 43 ICLQ 153.

Physicians for Human Rights (1996) *Torture in Turkey and Its Unwilling Accomplices* (Boston, Mass: Physicians for Human Rights).

Ploski, H and Williams, J (1983) *The Negro Almanac: A Reference Work on the Afro-American* (New York: 4th edn).

Posner, TR (1996) 'Note: Kadic v. Karadzic' 90 AJIL 658.

Prison Reform International (1995) *Making Standards Work* (The Hague: PRI/UN).

Ragazzi, M (1997) *The Concept of International Obligations 'Erga Omnes'* (Oxford: Clarendon Press).

Rasmussen, OV and Skylv, G (1993) 'Signs of *falanga* torture', 3 *Torture* 16.

Raynor, M (1987) *Turning a Blind Eye?: Medical Accountability and the Prevention of Torture in South Africa* (Washington DC: Committee on Scientific Freedom and Responsibility).

Redgwell, C (1997) 'Reservations to Treaties and Human Rights Committee General Comment No 24(52)', 46 ICLQ 390.

Reiner, R (1981) 'The politics of police power' in *Politics and Power 4: Law, Politics and Justice* (London: Routledge).

—— (1992) *The Politics of the Police* (Hemel Hempstead: Wheatsheaf, 2nd edn).

—— (1997) 'Policing and the Police' in Maguire, M, Morgan, R and Reiner, R (eds) *The Oxford Handbook of Criminology* (Oxford: Clarendon Press, 2nd edn).

Rejali, DM (1994) *Torture and Modernity: Self, Society, and State in Modern Iran* (Boulder, Colo: Westview).

Robertson, AH and Merrills, JG (1993) *Human Rights in Europe* (Manchester: Manchester University Press, 3rd edn).

Robinson, P (1984) *Criminal Law Defences*, 2 vols (St Paul, Minn: West).

Rodley, N (1987) *The Treatment of Prisoners Under International Law* (Oxford: Clarendon Press).

Rouget, D (1995) *La Convention européenne pour la prévention de la torture et des peines ou traitements inhumains ou dégradants* (Univerisité de Lille).

—— (1997) 'Juges et Avocats, Acteurs Essentiels de la Prévention de la Torture' in APT.

Ruck, SK (1951) *Paterson on Prisons: Prisoners and Patients* (London: Hodder and Stoughton).

Ruedy, J (1992) *Modern Algeria: The Origins and Development of a Nation* (Bloomington, Ind: Indiana Univeristy Press).

Ruthven, M (1978) *Torture: The Grand Conspiracy* (London: Weidenfeld and Nicolson).

Ryan, M (1978) *The Acceptable Pressure Group: Inequality in the Penal Lobby—a case-study of the Howard League and RAP* (Farnborough: Saxon House).
—— (1983) *The Politics of Penal Reform* (London: Longman).
—— (1997) *Lobbying from Below* (London: UCL Publishing).
Sanders, A and Young, R (1994) *Criminal Justice* (London: Butterworths).
Scarry, E (1984) *The Body in Pain* (New York: Oxford University Press).
Schabas, W (1994) 'Soering's Legacy', 43 ICLQ 913.
Shaw, S (1995) 'The Role of NGOs in Assisting and Promoting the Work of the CPT' in APT.
Sim, J, Ruggiero, V and Ryan, M (1995) 'Punishment in Europe: Perceptions and Commonalities' in Ruggiero, V, Ryan, M and Sim, J (eds) *Western European Penal Systems: A Critical Anatomy* (London: Sage).
Sinclair, I (1984) *The Vienna Convention on the Law of Treaties* (Manchester: Manchester University Press, 2nd edn).
Smith, C (1992) 'Communal conflict and insurrection in Palestine 1936–48' in Anderson and Killingray.
Smith, D (1997) 'Ethnic Origins, Crime and Criminal Justice' in Maguire, M, Morgan, R and Reiner, R (eds) *The Oxford Handbook of Criminology* (Oxford: Clarendon Press, 2nd edn).
—— Gray, J and Small, S (1983) *Police and People in London*, Vol IV (London: Policy Studies Institute).
Sørenson, B (1995), 'Prevention of Torture and Inhuman or Degrading Treatment or Punishment: Medical Views', in APT.
Spierenburg, P (1995) 'The body and the state' in Morris and Rothman.
Stavros, S (1993) *The Guarantees for Accused Persons Under Article 6 of the ECHR* (Dordrecht: Martinus Nijhoff).
Swiss Committee Against Torture (1987) *Swiss Committee Against Torture* (Geneva: SCAT).
Sykes, G (1958) *The Society of Captives* (Princeton, NJ: Princeton Univeristy Press).
Taylor, P (1980) *Beating the Terrorists* (Harmondsworth: Penguin).
Tomashevski, K (1994) *Foreigners in Prison* (Helsinki: European Institute for Crime Prevention and Control).
Tonry, M (ed) (1997) *Ethnicity, Crime and Immigration: Comparative and Cross-National Perspectives* (Chicago: University of Chicago Press).
Torturaren Aukako Taldea (1995) *Informe Anual 1994* (Bilbao: TAT).
Trinquier, R (1961) *La Guerre Moderne* (Paris).
—— (1968) *Guerre, Subversion, Révolution* (Paris).
Twining, WL and Twining, PE (1973) 'Bentham on Torture', 24 Northern Ireland Legal Quarterly 305.
van Swaaningen, R and de Jonge, G (1995) 'The Dutch Prison System and Penal Policy in the 1990s: from Humanitarian Paternalism to Penal Business Management' in Ruggiero, V, Ryan, M and Sim, J (eds) *Western European Penal Systems: A Critical Anatomy* (London: Sage).
Vargas, F de (1979) 'History of a Campaign' in International Commission of Jurists/Swiss Committee Against Torture.
—— (1997) 'Bref Historique du CSCT-APT' in APT.

Vidal-Naquet, P (1962) *La Raison d'état* (Paris: Textes publiés par le Comité Maurice Audin).

Vigny, D (1987) 'La Convention européene de 1987 pour la prévention de la torture et peines ou traitements inhumains ou dégradants', 43 *Annuaire suisse de droit international* 62.

Walmesley, R, Howard, L and White, S (1992) *The National Prison Survey 1991: Main Findings*, Home Office Research Study No 128 (London: HMSO).

Wheatcroft, A (1995) *The Ottomans: Dissolving Images* (Harmondsworth: Penguin).

Wickersham Report (1931) *Report of the National Commission on Law Observance and Enforcement*, Vols I–VI (Washington).

Woolf Report (1991) *Prison Disturbances April 1990: Report of an Inquiry by the Rt Hon Lord Justice Woolf (parts I and II) and His Honour Judge Stephen Tumin (Part II)*, Cm 1456 (London: HMSO).

Zellick, G (1978) 'Corporal Punishment in the Isel of Man', 27 ICLQ 665.

Zuckerman, A (1989) 'Coercion and Judicial Ascertainment of Truth' , 24 IsLR 364.

Index